Court of Reason

It has frequently been remarked that it seems to have been reserved to the people of this country, by their conduct and example, to decide the important question, whether societies of men are really capable or not of establishing good government from reflection and choice, or whether they are forever destined to depend for their political constitutions on accident and force.

—The Federalist, *no. 1 (1787)*

The men he had reported in politics were all of them vessels of ideas. The armies, the navies, the budgets, the campaign organizations they commanded, flowed from the ideas that shaped them, or the ideas they could transmit and enforce.

Whether it was Mao and Chou, or Nixon and Haldeman, or Kennedy and McNamara, or de Gaulle and Monnet, their identities came from the ideas that had been pumped into them, the ideas they chose in turn to pump out.

—*Theodore H. White,* In Search of History

Court of Reason

*Robert Hutchins and
the Fund for the Republic*

FRANK K. KELLY

THE FREE PRESS
A Division of Macmillan Publishing Co., Inc.
NEW YORK

Collier Macmillan Publishers
LONDON

THE FREE PRESS
A Division of Macmillan Publishing Co., Inc.
866 Third Avenue, New York, N.Y.   10022

Collier Macmillan Canada, Ltd.

Library of Congress Catalog Card Number: 81-67165

Printed in the United States of America

printing number

1 2 3 4 5 6 7 8 9 10

Library of Congress Cataloging in Publication Data

Kelly, Frank K.
    Court of reason.

       1. Center for the Study of Democratic Institutions.
2. Fund for the Republic.   3. Hutchins, Robert Maynard,
1899–   I. Title.
H62.5.U5K38   061'.3   81-67165
ISBN 0-02-918030-9   AACR2

*To the fourteen directors who helped to establish
the Fund for the Republic:
James F. Brownlee, Charles W. Cole, Huntington Cairns,
Russell Dearmont, Richard Finnegan, Erwin N. Griswold,
William Joyce, Meyer Kestnbaum, Albert Linton,
Jubal R. Parten, Elmo Roper, George N. Shuster,
Eleanor B. Stevenson, and James D. Zellerbach*

CONTENTS

PART THREE   An Old Mansion Harbors a
Utopian Academy

ACKNOWLEDGMENTS

TWO PEOPLE ARE PRIMARILY responsible for encouraging me to write this book—Jubal R. Parten, a member of the original board of the Fund for the Republic, and my wife, Barbara Kelly.

The book was written under the auspices of Boston University with a financial grant from the Parten Foundation. Robert K. Straus of Santa Barbara provided additional aid at a crucial point.

The extensive files maintained by Mr. Parten from the time of his selection as a board member in 1952 until his resignation as chairman in 1975 gave me access to the documentation necessary for a full history. In addition to his files, Mr. Parten gave me many interviews, which supplied essential information.

Thomas C. Reeves, professor of history at the University of Wisconsin, turned over to me materials he had used in writing *Freedom and the Foundation*, an excellent book on the Fund's early years. My meetings with him were especially productive.

William V. Ballew of Houston, Texas, was helpful at every stage of this project. I am deeply grateful for his advice and his steady interest in the book.

John R. Silber, president of Boston University; Gerald J. Gross, vice president of that university; and Patrick Gregory, of the Boston University office for the arts, publications, and media, also aided me in many ways. Special thanks are due to Mr. Gross for bringing the book to the attention of the Free Press, and to Mr. Gregory for his editorial suggestions. I wish to express my appreciation to Claude Conyers and Edward Cripps of the Free Press for their excellent editorial assistance.

I also wish to express my gratitude to the late Robert M. Hutchins for all the things I learned from him; to Malcolm Moos, for his generous cooperation; to W. H. Ferry, for making available his papers at the Dartmouth College library; to Burns Roper, for access to the papers of Elmo Roper at Williams College; to Harry S. Ashmore and Peter Tagger, for access to the files of the Fund and the Center after I left the Center in 1975.

For interviews, I thank Gary Cadenhead, Harvey Wheeler, John Wilkinson, Milton Mayer, Joseph Schwab, James H. Douglas, Eulah Laucks, Irving F. Laucks, Francis J. Lally, Fagan Dickson, Stringfellow Barr, Raghavan Iyer, Hallock Hoffman, James A. Pike, Daniel Sisson, Bernard Rapoport, Harold Willens, John Cogley, Edward Engberg, and George Dell.

I thank Stuart Taylor and John Ball, of the Santa Barbara *News-Press*, for giving me permission to go through the files of that newspaper; Thomas M. Storke, who had an essential part in enabling the Center to make its headquarters in Santa Barbara; and Paul Veblen, former executive editor of the *News-Press*, for his understanding of the Center's work.

I am particularly grateful to Edward Engberg for critical suggestions; to Noel Young of the Capra Press for his encouragement; and to Hugh Downs, Norman Cousins, Ramsey Clark, Claiborne Pell, Henry Burnett, Richard Kipling, Larry Pidgeon, and Selmer O. Wake for their keen interest.

My nineteen years with the Fund and the Center gave me an unparalleled opportunity to meet and know hundreds of leaders from many fields and many countries. I am grateful to them all—and to all the staff members and directors of the Fund and the Center.

Finally, I want to express my appreciation to my sister, Catherine F. Kelly, who worked with me for so many years and whose devoted service is beyond any measurement. And I wish to add another word of thanks to my wife, Barbara, who transcribed many of the interviews I conducted in the course of my research.

Court of Reason

PROLOGUE

Pursuing Jefferson's vision

I N THE GENERATIONS since Thomas Jefferson and a few other revolutionaries proclaimed the independence of the American Republic, many men and women have tried to uphold his bold idea that we are all endowed by our Creator "with certain unalienable rights"—and among these rights are "life, liberty, and the pursuit of happiness." It is a vision that endures even in times of terror and despair. The story I present in this book—the stormy history of the Fund for the Republic—rises out of that vision: the dream of freedom and justice for all.

In 1976 we Americans hailed the 200th anniversary of Jefferson's great document, the Declaration of Independence. We celebrated with fireworks and frolics, with prayers and parades and pageants, with tall ships sailing up the Hudson River. That time of joy and confidence seems far behind us, but it reminded Americans and the world of the lofty dream on which this nation was founded.

To me, the best parts of the celebration were Jefferson's words, occasionally quoted in speeches, on radio stations, in television broadcasts. For me, they still vibrated with the promises that had stirred people for 200 years. I agreed with Robert Hutchins, the head of the Fund for the Republic, who once said: "Justice and freedom; discussion and criticism; intelligence and character—these are the indispensable ingredients of the democratic state. We can be rich and powerful without them. But not for long."

Enjoying that celebration, I was glad that I had served as an officer of the Fund for nineteen years in its struggle to keep Jefferson's vision before the people in an age of violence and revolutionary change—an age in which the survival of democratic institutions seemed very much in doubt. The Fund had never achieved what Hutchins and its directors hoped it would: a full public understanding of the vital necessity of maintaining the "unalien-

1

able rights" at the heart of American life. Yet it had fought a good fight, and the fight had to go on.

The Fund was launched in 1952, in a bitter time of division in America, when Senator Joseph McCarthy, the House Un-American Activities Committee, and other self-anointed patriots were hunting "spies" and people with "Communist connections." Blacklisters, bigots, censors, and right-wing organizations were active. The Jeffersonian tradition was overshadowed by another old American tradition—the tradition of witch burning.

In that year I had resigned from my job as staff director of the Senate Majority Policy Committee, disgusted by the fear and paralysis in the United States Senate. I was in New York when the Fund's creation was announced, working on a study of world news for the International Press Institute. I was impressed by the fact that the Ford Foundation's trustees had felt it necessary to establish an independent fund to preserve and advance the principles of the Declaration of Independence, the Constitution, and the Bill of Rights.

The directors of the Fund—whose names were disclosed by the Ford Foundation—were eminent in their fields. I knew that their eminence would not keep McCarthy and his cohorts from attacking them, but I believed they could withstand any attacks. With the $15 million provided to the Fund by the Ford Foundation, they could certainly help the civil liberties groups, the women's organizations, leaders in the churches, and others who were striving to support the Bill of Rights in the era of McCarthyism.

As an assistant to the Senate majority leader, I had witnessed McCarthy's rise to power. In the afternoon of February 20, 1950, I had been with Senator Scott Lucas of Illinois—then the majority leader—on the Senate floor when McCarthy shouted accusations that "Communists" known to the Secretary of State were shaping policies of the Truman administration. I had been a speech writer for President Truman in the campaign of 1948, and I knew and admired Secretary Acheson. I urged Lucas to challenge every statement McCarthy made. I could see reporters in the press gallery making notes, and I knew his charges would produce big headlines.

"I'm not going to get into a spraying contest with a skunk," Lucas muttered to me. Lucas was a tall, elegant man with an air of melancholy disillusionment. He was not ready to engage in a fight with any other Senator, but he did stir in his chair when McCarthy declared that he would cite 81 "cases" of people in the State Department with "Communist connections."

In Wheeling, McCarthy had spoken of 205 people. In Reno, a few days later, he had talked about "57" cases." How many "cases" did he claim to have?

Lucas rose reluctantly to his feet and asked McCarthy what relationship the 81 "cases" had with the 205 or the 57 previously mentioned by the senator. McCarthy shrugged.

"I do not believe I mentioned the figure 205," McCarthy said. "I believe I said over 200." He did not explain how that figure had dropped to 57 in Reno. He said that the 81 "cases" he had brought to the Senate included the 57 he had cited in Reno, plus 24 additional "cases."

Lucas asked him what he meant by "cases." Frowning impatiently, McCarthy said, "I am only giving the Senate cases in which it is clear there is a definite Communist connection." A few minutes later, he said that some of the "cases" did not refer to communists and "some of these individuals . . . are no longer with the State Department."

McCarthy searched through the piles of papers he had placed on his own desk and the desk of a senator who sat near him. He dropped some of the papers. When he came to what he called "case 72," he said, "I do not confuse this man as being a Communist. This individual was highly recommended by several witnesses as a high type of man."

McCarthy held the floor for nearly six hours, waving papers, contradicting himself, his voice rising and falling. Lucas interrupted him sixty-one times and was finally told by McCarthy that he would not respond to any more "silly questions" from the majority leader. Senator Herbert Lehman, of New York, asked McCarthy to clarify his language. McCarthy indicated that Lehman, who had been governor of New York for several terms, was not capable of understanding what he was talking about.

Senator Brien McMahon of Connecticut, who had been an assistant attorney general of the United States before he was elected to the Senate, made thirty-four efforts to pin McCarthy down. McCarthy brushed him off, waving and shouting.

Just before midnight, with a gesture of disgust, Lucas moved that the Senate should adjourn. The turbulent session was over. The fires of McCarthyism had proved beyond the power of the Senate to control.

Lucas and I were exhausted, but we clung to the hope that McCarthy's demagoguery would backfire against him. We did not realize then that McCarthy was on the verge of becoming one of the most powerful men in America.

In later years, after I had become an officer of the Fund for the Republic—which had really been created to combat the evils of McCarthyism—I realized that the clash between Lucas, McMahon, and McCarthy was a collision between two attitudes with roots in the early days of the American nation. There was a Jeffersonian heritage of reason and tolerance for radicals. And there was a heritage of conformity, of heresy hunting, of witch burning.

McCarthy had a deep undercurrent running for him—the undercurrent of distrust, the cynicism of many Americans. That current had been strong since the angry divisions of the American Revolution, when those who stayed loyal to the British king regarded the revolutionists as "traitors" and the revolutionaries denounced the royalists and drove many of them into

Canada. American politicians had exploited the suspicions of many people since the founding of the Republic.

McCarthy turned the "Communist issue" against the Democratic senators who ran for reelection in 1950. When Lucas and other senators defended Truman and Acheson, they were asked why they had not purged the government of people who had charges of "Communist connections" in the "loyalty files"—dossiers that had been established under Truman's own "loyalty program." They were accused of "coddling Communists."

As the majority leader of the Senate, Lucas was a prime target for the McCarthyites. Traveling with Lucas through Illinois that autumn, I heard people say, "Lucas is in with that crowd in Washington. He's not one of us any more. Maybe he's soft on the Reds." His role in the Marshall Plan, which had pushed back communism in Western Europe, was largely ignored. The Chicago *Tribune* attacked him day after day. Many people, including those who doubted McCarthy's charges, were swayed by McCarthy's diatribes.

At that time the United States was the most powerful nation on earth. But fears of a communist threat to American security had flared after the explosion of a Soviet atomic bomb in September 1949, three years ahead of the predictions of American scientists. People in Illinois asked Lucas why Truman had not kept the Russians from "stealing" the "secrets" of atomic bombs. They asked why Acheson had not denounced Alger Hiss, who was suspected of being a spy. They wanted "dangerous aliens" and "radicals" to be deported or jailed. They seemed to have little confidence in the democratic institutions established by Jefferson and the other founding fathers of the United States.

There was one man in Illinois who did speak boldly in the Jeffersonian style. That was Robert Hutchins, then the head of the University of Chicago, who had told an Illinois commission investigating "subversive activities" that "the policy of repression cannot be justly enforced." He had announced that he would not dismiss any teachers because of their ideas or associations, and the trustees of the university had stood by him. In the miasma of McCarthyism, Hutchins seemed to be a shining figure.

Lucas and other senators smeared by McCarthy were defeated. I found few exemplars of the Hutchins brand of Americanism in Washington when I returned there. The new Senate majority leader, Ernest McFarland, of Arizona, asked me to stay on as his research assistant, but I soon discovered that he was not willing to tangle with McCarthy under any circumstances.

The atmosphere in Washington and in the rest of the country deteriorated month after month. It seemed to me that the confident era of Roosevelt and Truman was being overwhelmed by an age of hate. I left the Senate staff in the spring of 1952, depressed and disturbed by the state of the country.

For a few weeks that summer I felt a surge of hope. Averell Harriman, encouraged by Truman, sought the Democratic nomination for president. I served as the Washington director of his campaign, because I knew that Harriman had many of the traits of leadership needed by the nation.

A man with an astonishing range of knowledge and experience, Harriman had been secretary of commerce, ambassador to Britain, ambassador to Russia, director of the Mutual Security Administration. With Paul Hoffman, he had administered the Marshall Plan with brilliance and enormous energy. He was cool, aloof, an aristocrat in many ways. Yet he believed in the Jeffersonian tradition. I thought he could become a president in the brave style of Franklin Roosevelt.

Harriman, of course, did not get the nomination. Soon after the Democratic convention opened in Chicago that July, Governor Adlai Stevenson of Illinois declared that he would accept a draft, although he had previously asserted that Harriman was the man best qualified to be president. Stevenson was nominated on the third ballot with Truman's backing. Stevenson offered me a place on his staff, but I had already accepted an appointment as the United States director of the International Press Institute study of world news.

After Harriman's withdrawal I took no part in the electoral battle of 1952. Eisenhower and Nixon, with the bruising participation of McCarthy and his friends, campaigned against "communism, corruption, and fumbling in Korea." Stevenson tried, as he put it, "to talk sense to the American people." His speeches were magnificent, but my experience in the Lucas disaster gave me a feeling that he was headed for defeat. Many Americans were not in a mood to listen to a man speaking in the Jeffersonian manner.

Stevenson's efforts were crushed in the Eisenhower-Nixon landslide in November 1952. McCarthy swaggered around the country like a military hero, claiming much of the credit. It seemed to me that the United States was sinking deeper into a quagmire of fear.

The Fund for the Republic gave me another surge of hope. Its directors seemed to know that they had to face controversy. When Robert Hutchins was chosen as the Fund's president in 1954 to succeed Clifford Case, who had resigned to run for the Senate in New Jersey, I was sure that the Fund would be a strong champion of civil liberties.

In 1954 and 1955 I watched with admiration while the Fund went into one battle zone after another. The Fund financed a report that showed the injustices in the government's loyalty program. It started an investigation of blacklisting in motion pictures, radio, and television, raising the hackles of the House Un-American Activities Committee. It financed a series of authoritative books on communism, provided money for an effort to strengthen the right of freedom of conscience, gave support for an exposure of the spreading fear among teachers, and aided many civil liberties groups. No other foundation in America had ever plunged so far into dangerous areas.

Attacks on the Fund increased, despite the prestige of its directors and the endorsement of the Ford Foundation. The national commander of the

American Legion excoriated it. Fulton Lewis, Jr., and other right-wing broadcasters and columnists slashed at it. Lewis predicted that it would feel the full fury of the Committee on Un-American Activities. I noted these attacks, but did not believe they would get anywhere. I thought the Fund was impregnable.

After the completion of the International Press Institute study, I took a job with the Stephen Fitzgerald Company, a public relations agency with headquarters in New York. I was astounded when Hutchins came to the agency's office in December 1955, asking for help.

Hutchins told Fitzgerald and me that the Fund's directors were worried about its future. He said he had been instructed to find an agency and a public information specialist who could make the public more aware of the Fund's value. He had received good reports on us, he said, from Martin Quigley of the Ford Foundation and Louis Lyons, curator of the Nieman Foundation at Harvard.

In March 1956, after I had been interviewed by several members of the Fund's board, I was elected a vice president of the Fund. The Fitzgerald agency was employed to give public relations advice. Before I moved to the Fund's headquarters, I was warned by friends in Washington that I had made a blunder. I was told that the Fund was marked for destruction.

Among the board members who had talked to me, only Jubal R. Parten, an independent oil producer who had served as chairman of the trustees of the University of Texas, seemed to have great confidence in the Fund's future. Parten had asked me what I thought of Hutchins. When I told him that I admired Hutchins for his record at the University of Chicago, Parten had said, "So do I. Of course, he shocks some people. He talks straight. That always shocks some people."

My conversations with other directors—who saw enemies closing in, and were sharply critical of Hutchins for "alienating possible supporters of the Fund"—made me wonder whether I had overestimated the Fund's strength. The possibility of its destruction no longer seemed utterly ridiculous to me.

Parten and Hutchins had reinforced my own conviction that the Fund was worth defending. I thought I had to do what I could. I believed that the Fund might still be able to rally many of the people who believed in the Jeffersonian tradition. The American Civil Liberties Union, the American Friends Service Committee, some noted lawyers, women's organizations, and church groups were valiantly defending civil liberties and civil rights—and the Fund could work with them.

So I entered the most exhilarating, exhausting, frustrating, rewarding, and wounding experience of my life. I stayed with the Fund and its creation, the Center for the Study of Democratic Institutions, for nineteen years, from the time of Eisenhower to the time of Jimmy Carter. The Fund proved to be much more durable than any of its foes had expected it to be—and more vulnerable to internal battles than its friends had envisioned.

When the Fund created the Center in Santa Barbara in 1959, it went through a sweeping transformation. It was no longer a grant-making foundation. Its remaining financial resources were devoted to the Center. The board's role diminished. The Center was run by Hutchins with the assistance and advice of the other officers of the Fund and the counsel of fellows picked by him.

Hutchins frequently referred to the importance of the directors and the significance of the Fellows, but nearly everyone knew that the Center was a monarchy. Hutchins was a king who wanted to save democracy. He was also a judge who reviewed the world's problems. He was intrigued by a proposal once made by a Center consultant, Gerald Gottlieb, for the formation of a Court of Man, a world tribunal with power to render judgments on those who misused authority. Hutchins would have relished being the Chief Justice of such a court.

Before he became president of the University of Chicago, Hutchins had been the dean of the Yale law school. President Roosevelt had once talked about appointing Hutchins to the Supreme Court of the United States. Hutchins studied that court and its opinions. He frequently led discussions of the court's rulings.

In the 1950s, Hutchins had described the Fund as "a small island of sanity in a McCarthyite world." He actually operated it as a court of reason, deciding what projects to undertake, what issues to examine, what organizations to aid. When he established the Center he called it "an intellectual community," yet his dedication to the law, his interest in the judicial process, made it a court of reason, too.

Sadly, Hutchins and his fellows—even after the drastic reorganization of the Center in 1969—were not able to devise a constitution for the Center that might have made it a truly democratic place. Hutchins and the directors of the Fund could not solve the problem of passing on his power to a successor while he lived.

In 1975, when the Center was split again by dissensions over its administration and its future, Hutchins wrote a rueful letter to my wife, who had proposed a continuous dialogue focused purely on the Center's internal problems. She had hoped that the Center could show what thinking could do to bring a solution. Hutchins said, "I'm afraid our experience shows that the achievement of an intellectual community can be thwarted by all kinds of apparently trivial factors and that it is possible only if luck is added to the basic requirements of character, commitment and intelligence."

Two months after he wrote that letter—and after Malcolm Moos, his temporary successor, had been removed and Hutchins had returned to the Center's helm—Hutchins decided to try again, perhaps hoping for better luck. Aware of his own faults and failings, aware of the limitations of his chosen colleagues, Hutchins kept on trying until he died in 1977.

I talked with Hutchins almost every day for nineteen years. I learned something in every encounter with him. He was challenging, astonishing, witty, ironic, sometimes very warm, sometimes cold, sometimes humble and exhausted, sometimes imperious, yet always searching, always learning. Sometimes he appeared to be Zeus on a mountain called Olympus. Sometimes he viewed his life as an avenue of ruined monuments.

That he managed to bring his vision of a community into being and to maintain it as an independent entity for twenty years is in itself a testament to his tenacity, resourcefulness, and intellectual vigor. His tragedy, and that of the institution, was that he could not keep it free of the insidious factionalism, the warring ambitions, the overbearing obsessions, and the backbiting that afflict all human communities, no matter how lofty their ideals. In a sense, Hutchins' Center belongs to that continuous tradition of Utopian ideas that have burst upon the American landscape throughout the history of this nation of pilgrims and immigrants.

A true community of minds, a court of reason, may be valid only as an idea to be cherished and reached for—not as a reality to be developed here on earth. To me, there were signs through all the years that Hutchins was seeking a heavenly city, a fellowship of kindred minds—like the fellowship of the saints in a hymn he loved, a hymn his father had taught him to sing: "Blest Be the Tie That Binds."

With the aid of many people who have opened their thoughts and their records for me, I have tried to describe in this book how the Fund and the Center developed and changed. No one will ever encompass the whole story and the connecting stories within the main tale. So many projects were conceived, so many ideas were offered and argued, so many meetings were held, so many publications were issued, so many conflicts occurred, so many notable people were involved—and the story expands and extends into the future.

The Fund started with the Jeffersonian idea. It made major contributions in the first phase of its existence, but it could not put an end to heresy hunting in America. McCarthy is dead, and the House Un-American Activities Committee has been abolished. Yet federal, state, and local agencies keep files on millions of Americans: the seeds of suspicion, the viruses of McCarthyism live on. In 1981, members of Congress began to talk of re-establishing committees to expose "subversive" people.

The Center lives on, too, although it is no longer the completely independent entity Hutchins and other founding fellows (including myself) established in 1959. It was taken over in 1979 by the University of California at Santa Barbara and its headquarters were transferred to the university campus. The dialogues on Eucalyptus Hill were ended—and new dialogues were begun. It now is called the Robert Maynard Hutchins Center for the Study of Democratic Institutions.

If this planet does not become a radioactive cinder in a nuclear war, this center may be a place of controversy and insights for a long time to come. It may excite many minds in the future, as Plato's academy has excited human minds in all the centuries since the Greeks tried to discover through illuminating dialogues what the potentials of human beings are, what ought to be done to foster freedom and justice and how to build a better world.

Let the readers of this book now judge.

PART ONE

Against the Tide
of McCarthyism

1

A father's voice, and $15 million for democracy

WHEN HE WAS FIVE YEARS OLD, his father woke him in the middle of the night to tell him that Theodore Roosevelt had been elected President. He never forgot the note of exultation in his father's voice. Roosevelt was a bold and brave man, his father said: a fighter for justice, a leader with strong moral fiber. That was what the country needed.

He never forgot the early mornings when he knelt beside his father on a bare floor, praying for God's guidance and the courage to do what was right. The evil in the world had to be opposed. True men had to stand up straight and speak out plainly against oppressors and exploiters, against persecutors, against those who were corrupt and spread corruption.

As he grew older, Robert Maynard Hutchins no longer believed that the answers to all the world's problems could be found in the Bible or in his father's wisdom. He felt the suffering men inflicted on men when he served as an ambulance driver at the front in Italy in the First World War. He encountered frustrations as a student at Yale, as a teacher in a boys' school, as dean of the Yale law school, as head of the University of Chicago. He grew more and more angry at the power and persistence of evil in the world, in others, and in himself.

On a day in February 1953, when he walked into the conference room of the Ford Foundation in Pasadena, California, Hutchins burned with rage against the spreading tide of McCarthyism. He was carrying on his father's work in his own way. As an associate director of the Ford Foundation, he had helped to spend $75 million on projects he considered to be for "the common good" of humanity; now he hoped that Henry Ford II and the other trustees could be persuaded to take another $15 million dollars from Ford's treasury to strengthen American democracy. He believed that the decision to be made that day might be a crucial factor in the battle to save the American Republic.

He was a tall, ruggedly handsome man whose features conveyed a rather awesome dignity. He was aware of the impression he made on other people, and he habitually kept in check the inner rage and deep depression that gnawed at him. He wanted to change the world, and he found that the world was hard to change. He had reformed the Yale law school, but he wasn't sure the reforms would last. He had remodeled the University of Chicago, but the university was already reverting to its old patterns.

That day in Pasadena, he was particularly disturbed because his friend and backer, Paul Hoffman, had been forced to resign from the presidency of the Ford Foundation. Hoffman had brought him into the foundation, telling him that the Ford organization had "the biggest blank check in history." His years with Hoffman had been years of great hopes and high visions. Without Hoffman, his own position in the foundation was precarious. He knew that Henry Ford II was perplexed by his wit and felt uneasy in his presence.

Paul Hoffman came into the conference room, shaking hands with the trustees who had driven him from the presidency. Hoffman had promised to come to the trustees' meeting as a representative of the Fund for the Republic, and Hoffman kept promises. Hutchins greeted him warmly.

Soon after the Fund had been created by the Ford trustees and announced to the press in December 1952, the directors of the Fund had invited Hoffman to serve as its first chairman. Hoffman had long advocated the creation of just such an organization to uphold essential freedoms. The Ford trustees had approved the election of Hoffman as the Fund's chairman. All of them liked and admired Hoffman as a person.

The question to be settled by the Ford trustees at the February meeting was whether the Fund would be given a large grant to enable it to operate in difficult and dangerous areas. Hutchins and Hoffman—and W. H. Ferry, Ford's public relations counselor—had urged Ford and the trustees to provide enough millions to enable the Fund to function effectively on a national scale. From the beginning, Ferry had played an important part in the development of the Fund idea.

Hutchins moved quietly around the conference room that day. He felt that the future of the Fund depended largely on three of the Fund's directors who were there to present the Fund's plans. These three men—like all of the Fund's board—had been chosen by Hutchins and Hoffman. Hutchins believed that the months he had spent with Hoffman in going over a list of 200 possible directors had been well used.

He had known each of the three men for a long time. Erwin Griswold, the dean of the Harvard Law School, had received a bachelor's degree and a master's degree from Oberlin College, where Hutchins' father had taught for many years. Jubal R. Parten and Hutchins had been friends for eighteen years, ever since they had worked together to establish an astronomical observatory. William H. Joyce, Jr., a successful manufacturer who had been brought up on the Bible and William Shakespeare, had been one of Hoffman's assistants in the Marshall Plan.

Griswold, who had served as chairman of the Fund's planning committee, was dedicated to the Bill of Rights and had been horrified by the behavior of Senator Joseph McCarthy. He had been on the faculty at Harvard for nineteen years and dean of the law school since 1946. Before going to Harvard, he had practiced law in Massachusetts and Washington and had been a special assistant to the attorney general of the United States under Presidents Hoover and Roosevelt.

Griswold was a solid, square-shouldered man with a Republican background and the sober manner of a legal expert, and he impressed Ford and the trustees as a man who would keep the Fund on a steady course. Behind Griswold sat Bethuel M. Webster, of the Wall Street law firm of Webster, Sheffield, & Chrystie, who had been retained as the Fund's counsel on Griswold's recommendation. Webster was dapper and confident, widely known and respected.

Griswold reviewed the first three meetings of the Fund's board. At the initial meeting on December 10 and 11 in New York, nine of the fifteen directors were present. They had elected the planning committee and had approved a grant of $50,000 to the American Bar Association's Special Committee on Individual Rights as Affected by National Security. At their second meeting, the directors had selected Paul Hoffman as their chairman and had decided that the Fund would need between $15 million and $25 million to finance its work over a period of five years. At their third gathering, they had approved a nine-page prospectus prepared by Griswold's planning committee.

While Griswold presented the prospectus in blunt terms, Hutchins watched the faces of the Ford trustees. He was not sure how much candor they could take. One of the most important trustees—Frank W. Abrams, chairman of the Standard Oil Company of New Jersey—had tried to get him to have the whole idea of the Fund reexamined by a panel of five notable people outside the Ford Foundation. In the summer of 1952, while Hutchins had been pushing the trustees toward a decision, Abrams had written to him: "Perhaps the most difficult of the programs to be certain about is the Fund for the Republic. I know of no topic that is of more fundamental importance—yet I know of none where the possibilities of inadvertently doing harm rather than good are more real." Hutchins had not accepted Abrams' suggestion. He felt that the Fund had to be launched as soon as possible.

The prospective program outlined by Griswold that day emphasized that the Fund would rely on research and educational methods, but the subjects to be explored would undoubtedly be hard to handle and might be hotly disputed. That was why the Fund's directors felt that they had to be completely independent—and why a large grant from the Ford Foundation was necessary, to assure the Fund's existence during years of controversy.

Under the prospectus, the Fund proposed to tackle "the extent to which information obtained by wiretapping, third degree interrogations, unlawful searches and seizures, had been gained by illegal police methods." This was a matter of particular concern to Dean Griswold and other legal defenders of the Constitution, who felt that the people's rights were being undermined by such violations of the Constitution's fundamental guarantees.

The Fund also planned to examine "the rights of witnesses in quasi-judicial proceedings, including availability of counsel, opportunity for cross-examination, etc.; the use and misuse of the Fifth Amendment privilege against self-incrimination; the availability of qualified counsel for indigent or unpopular defendants; and the extent to which the press influenced judicial or quasi-judicial decisions by giving unequal coverage to sensational accusations and subsequent denials."

These were all topics that had concerned Hutchins for years. He was enraged by wiretapping, unlawful searches and seizures, beatings of accused people, and the use of torture by the police. He was anguished by the obvious injustices in the federal loyalty procedures, which did not provide opportunities for cross-examination of accusers. He was troubled by wild stories in the press, which made it difficult for many people to be tried fairly in the courts.

In another section, the prospectus discussed by Griswold on that day in February referred to the possibility of "a study of the activities of the House Un-American Activities Committee, the Senate Internal Security Committee, and other Congressional investigating committees." The Fund was not going to flinch from examining some of the most powerful groups in American life.

Other thorny issues raised in the prospectus were the influence of communism in the United States—with a sharp sentence declaring that "communism will find in the Fund for the Republic no haven for its subversive activities"—blacklisting in the movies and in broadcasting; government secrecy provisions; immigration laws; equal voting privileges for minorities; released time for religious activities in the public schools; freedom of expression for teachers; discrimination in restaurants and transportation facilities.

In presenting that grim catalogue to the Ford trustees, Griswold showed no doubt that the trustees would be convinced of the absolute necessity of providing the Fund with money enough to become a resplendent champion of civil rights and civil liberties. He indicated that the Fund's directors were willing and able to take the heat that would certainly be generated by the projects he had outlined.

Jubal R. Parten of Madisonville, Texas, then spoke to the trustees. He was a tall, straight, slim man with a military bearing and had been called Major Parten by his friends since he had attained the rank of major as a young officer in World War I. In a letter to a friend, soon after Parten had agreed to be a director of the Fund, Hutchins had referred to him as "the best man on the Fund's board."

Parten had become an independent oil producer after he returned from his army service in 1919. He had earned a law degree from the University of Texas, and he had once thought of practicing law or entering the diplomatic service, but he had decided that seeking and finding oil offered more excitement and more opportunities to lead a productive life. He was a man of many interests, active in education and philanthropy. He had been chairman of the University of Texas regents and had served as chairman of the Federal Reserve Bank in Dallas for eight years.

Although he was a wealthy Texan, shrewd in business, persistent in pursuit of his aims, Parten did not conform to the pattern of hard-driving Texans who disdained ideas and intellectuals. He was a reader of history. His home town, where he had lived all his life, was named for James Madison, one of the founders of the American Republic. He shared the visions of Madison and Thomas Jefferson. He was alarmed by the reckless behavior of Joseph McCarthy and the House Un-American Activities Committee.

His first invitation to join the Fund board had come from Hoffman. He had told Hoffman that he was already on too many boards. Then Hutchins had called him. "This is going to be a rough ride," Hutchins had said. "We need battlers. You don't want to miss this." Parten hadn't been able to resist that challenge.

The light of battle was in his eyes when he addressed the Ford trustees. Like Griswold, he stressed the requirement for complete independence for the Fund. He foresaw that Ford dealers would put pressure on the foundation when the Fund got into trouble. If the Fund had complete independence, it could take full responsibility for its projects.

Parten supported Griswold's request for a grant of $15 million. With that much money available, Parten felt the Fund could make a substantial impact. A grant of that size would make it possible to find a first-rate man to serve as the full-time chief executive of the Fund, and Paul Hoffman had already indicated that he could not give much of his time to the actual operations.

William Joyce spoke as fervently for the Fund as Griswold and Parten had. Joyce had started a shoe manufacturing company with a small loan from his father, and his products were sold in many countries. He had been a speaker at conferences of businessmen, urging them to encourage their employees to participate in the development of their companies. He asserted that the advances of the American people were due to acceptance of "the idea of freedom and the idea of equality." He thought that the Fund could demonstrate to the world that Americans were really committed to those ideas—and the tide of McCarthyism would recede.

Bethuel Webster then offered a few comments to the Ford trustees. He did not speak for long. His presence in the room with Dean Griswold was evidence enough that he would be available to provide the advice of an experienced Wall Street lawyer whenever the Fund required it.

Ford and his trustees thanked the Fund directors and Webster for their statements. Watching them, Hutchins felt his confidence rise. He thought that the odds were in the Fund's favor, but he waited for the verdict of the Ford trustees with impatience. He believed that the Fund should have been started in 1951, when the spread of McCarthyism had first become shockingly evident.

Hutchins had been struggling to master his impatience since his years at the University of Chicago, when he had tried to reform the university at a breakneck pace and had aroused the implacable opposition of many faculty members. This time, his patience was not severely tested. The Fund directors were called back to the conference room after a brief interval, and Ford announced that the trustees—on a motion Ford had made himself—had authorized the transfer of $14.8 million to the Fund, with $2.8 million to be given at once and the balance to be provided when the Department of the Treasury certified the Fund as a tax-exempt foundation.

"I think we should turn you loose and let you do the job," Ford said.

Recalling the moment of decision later, Parten emphasized that there were two points the Fund directors had to accept. They were not to make any grants that would endanger the Fund's status as an educational foundation. They were not to hire a card-carrying communist as a staff member. Parten said, "Since we didn't regard the two conditions as tying our hands in any major way—because we didn't intend to do either of those things— we accepted."

It was a high moment for Hutchins. He had been pleased when the trustees had appropriated large amounts for two other projects he had pushed—the Fund for the Advancement of Education and the Fund for Adult Education. But it had been harder to get the Fund for the Republic through the foundation's labyrinth, so the taste of triumph that day in 1953 was sweeter.

Hutchins and Hoffman expressed their appreciation to Griswold, Parten, Joyce and Webster. The Fund had won the full backing of the Ford trustees at last. The struggle to win that approval went back to January 1951. At the urging of Hutchins and Ferry, Hoffman had first asked the trustees to consider a national commission to protect democratic principles in an era of international conflicts. Hutchins had talked with Hoffman several times before Hoffman had presented the proposal. It was discussed and put aside by the trustees.

In August 1951 Hutchins had tried to move the project forward with a two-page memorandum entitled "A Fund for Democratic Freedoms." In

September of that year, W. H. Ferry had sent a statement to Ford and his associates, calling for "bold experimentation." Admitting that such a policy might sometimes "prove irritating" to some of the Ford Motor Company officials and might "embarrass temporarily members of the Ford family," Ferry asserted: "In the long run it will bring more credit to the Ford name than the easy and innocuous course of making impressive contributions to established activities. . . . Here it should be remembered that the reputation of the Ford Motor Company largely centers around Henry Ford's lifelong preoccupation with experimentation and pioneering ventures." (Hutchins said later: "W. H. Ferry and I worked out the plan for the Fund for the Republic. . . .")

Henry Ford II and his trustees were willing to put money into "pioneering ventures" if they were sure that the men engaged in such ventures were solid men with excellent reputations. Griswold, Parten, Joyce, and the other directors of the Fund had been personally approved by every one of the Ford trustees. In the action the trustees took on that February day in 1953, they felt that they were placing approximately $15 million of the foundation's money in very safe hands.

Ford and the trustees had been pleased by the generally favorable response of newspaper editors to the announcement of the Fund's formation with an initial grant of $200,000 in December 1952. The *Christian Science Monitor* had declared: "Spokesmen for these philanthropic trusts have given a House committee and the American public some excellent lessons in the courage and intelligence necessary to sustain progress." Other newspapers had carried good headlines: "Foundation Will Seek to Protect Thought in U.S." and "Ford Foundation Fights for Freedom."

The list of the Fund's directors was reassuring. In addition to the three men who had spoken at the Pasadena meeting, the members were James F. Brownlee, legal partner in the J. H. Whitney firm; Charles W. Cole, president of Amherst College; Eleanor B. Stevenson, wife of the president of Oberlin College; George N. Shuster, a leading Catholic educator, president of Hunter College; Meyer Kestnbaum, president of Hart, Schaffner and Marx; Richard Finnegan, editor of the Chicago *Sun-Times*; Malcolm Bryan, president of the Federal Reserve Bank at Atlanta; Huntington Cairns, a noted lawyer in Washington, D.C.; Russell Dearmont of St. Louis, president of the Missouri Pacific Railroad; Elmo Roper, public opinion analyst; M. Albert Linton, president of the Provident Mutual Life Insurance Company, Philadelphia; James D. Zellerbach, president of the Crown Zellerbach Corporation of San Francisco; and Paul Hoffman. (Bryan, a man who sought to avoid controversies, had resigned after attending the Fund board meeting on December 10, 1952, where he had learned that the Fund planned to go vigorously into civil rights). But the other board members were apparently ready to face the strife ahead of them.

Hutchins hoped that the quick resignation of Bryan did not mean that the board would disintegrate under fire. He had examined the character of all the prospective directors. Hoffman and he had tried to find as many staunch conservatives as possible in order to show that civil liberties and civil rights had the support of intelligent conservatives as well as liberals. Yet he knew that every director could be shaken to some extent by the bludgeoning that might come from McCarthy and his allies. He had written to a friend: "It is a pretty good group, worried about civil liberties, and also worried about its respectability. I do not know which worry will win."

In the months following the Pasadena meeting, Hutchins began to show impatience. The Fund's board seemed to move very slowly. The Fund had received a "temporary" certificate of tax exemption on March 20, 1953, and the Ford Foundation promptly provided $2.8 million, with an assurance that the remaining $12 million would be given when the fund had a regular certificate. But the Fund directors were preoccupied with finding exactly the right man to serve as president.

The uproar that had followed the Fund's first allocation of money —$50,000 to be given to the American Bar Association's Special Committee on Individual Rights as Affected by National Security—had made the directors doubly determined to find a president acceptable to leaders in the Congress and the Eisenhower administration. Some members of Congress had labeled the Bar Association project "an investigation of investigations" and felt that it was an invasion into the prerogatives of Congress.

When the $15 million grant to the Fund and the election of Hoffman as its chairman were announced to the press, many newspapers commended the Fund and the Ford Foundation. The St. Louis *Post-Dispatch*, for example, praised Hoffman in an editorial on March 1, 1953: "Fortunately Paul Hoffman . . . is continuing as chairman of the board to administer the Fund for the Republic. This is fortunate because pressures of many sorts will be brought against a full inventory of our civil rights. It will take Paul Hoffman to stand up against these influences." But the Washington *Times-Herald* and the Chicago *Tribune* were skeptical and critical. The *Times-Herald* said: "All we have to say is that 15 million dollars would be a high price to pay to 'get' Senators McCarthy and Jenner and Representative Velde (of the Un-American Activities Committee)."

McCarthy seemed ready to pounce on the Fund. He wrote to Hoffman on March 31, demanding information on what the Fund planned to do and asking Hoffman when he could "appear in Washington" to explain the Fund's program. On May 1, after Hoffman had informed him that "both the executive staff and the program of the Fund are still in the process of organization," McCarthy asked for a complete list of the Fund's staff as soon as members were appointed.

Nixon, who had been elected vice president under Eisenhower, also kept an eye on the Fund. In response to an inquiry from Nixon, Hoffman assured him in a letter on March 24 that the Fund's initial research would be "directed toward as accurate a determination as possible of the extent and nature of the internal communist menace and its effect on our community and institutions."

Aware of the close scrutiny to which the Fund was being subjected, the directors had decided that a scholarly study of communism would be valuable in showing the facts about its impact and might reduce the hysteria induced by the McCarthyites who saw "communists" or "communist influence" everywhere. Hutchins doubted whether any number of studies would pacify McCarthy and Nixon, but he knew that the Fund had to sponsor such studies for its own protection.

Among the nominees for the Fund's presidency in March 1953 were Governor Earl Warren, of California; Justice Robert Jackson, of the United States Supreme Court; and Erwin Canham, editor of the *Christian Science Monitor*. Jackson did not wish to leave the Court. Warren was appointed chief justice of the United States. Canham was committed to his work as an editor.

While the search for a president continued, two committees on the board began to function. One, headed by Elmo Roper, tried to discover the best methods for conducting a broad study of domestic communism. The other, chaired by Huntington Cairns, delved into procedures for reviewing and publicizing "the legacy of American liberty."

In the middle of April 1953, Paul Hoffman found a Congressman who was willing to be considered for the Fund's chief executive position: Representative Clifford Case. Hoffman asked five of his fellow directors to talk with Case as soon as they could.

Case, described as "winsome but tough " by a colleague in Congress, was an energetic, affable man who had been in the House of Representatives for eight years. He had taken definite stands for civil rights, had vigorously supported Eisenhower in the presidential election campaign of 1952, and was respected by the Washington correspondents of the major newspapers. He had been endorsed in his congressional campaigns by the American Federation of Labor and the Americans for Democratic Action, a liberal group, but he was not a target for the right-wing organizations. He had the friendship of Nixon and the admiration of some Democrats.

Case impressed Charles Cole, and made an equally good impression on Huntington Cairns, Albert Linton, and George Shuster. John Lord O'Brian, a noted Washington attorney who had replaced Malcolm Bryan on the Fund's board, thought that Case might be just the right man. David Freeman, a lawyer who was serving as the acting president of the Fund during this interim, was also enthusiastic about Case.

At their meeting on May 18 in New York, the directors elected Case as a member of the board and as "president of the Fund for the Republic," subject to the negotiation of satisfactory terms of employment. Case accepted a few days later, saying that he would leave his seat in Congress early in August and would begin his duties as the chief officer of the Fund in September. Freeman agreed to become secretary of the corporation as soon as Case took over.

Hutchins was pleased by the selection of Case. He was known to be a congressman dedicated to the Bill of Rights. Case was quiet, discreet, patient, willing to listen to advice. He was ready to leave the public pronouncements on the Fund's policies to Chairman Hoffman and to carry forward the programs developed by the board's committees. He was a prudent man, who would not act in haste. He satisfied the board's desire for respectability, but he was likely to stand up to McCarthy.

At the May 18 meeting, the board appropriated $25,000 for "summer studies" on the legacy of American freedom, and $10,000 for Samuel A. Stouffer, a professor of sociology at Harvard, to compose a questionnaire and an outline of a survey on "popular attitudes on the extent of domestic communism and its impact." Another $10,000 was provided for studies of the records of congressional committees, trials of communists, and revelations of admitted communists, to be directed by Arthur E. Sutherland, of the Harvard law school.

When the board met again a month later, Case was welcomed as a director and as president-elect, but Paul Hoffman presided. The board granted $55,000 to the American Friends Service Committee for its extensive efforts in race relations, gave an additional $19,500 to Professor Stouffer for a "trial run sampling of his questionnaire," and another $2,500 to Dr. Sutherland. Hoffman proposed a "study of nonconformity," without any notable reactions from his fellow directors.

Although the directors were apparently satisfied with Case, a mood of caution still prevailed. The board members did not act on a suggestion that Case should have contingency funds to be "dispensed with the advice of a committee of the Board." Until Case had shown what he intended to do, his freedom as an executive would be limited.

Observing the Fund's first steps, Hutchins grew more restive. The House Un-American Activities Committee, headed by Harold H. Velde, of Illinois, was rampaging through the country, investigating teachers and spreading fear in schools. J. B. Matthews, a member of McCarthy's staff, claimed that 7000 Protestant clergymen were tainted with communism. McCarthy was branding people who invoked the Fifth Amendment protection against self-accusation as "Fifth Amendment communists." Hutchins hoped that the Fund would do more than just talk about "the legacy of liberty" and collect questionnaires on "popular attitudes."

In July the Fund established an office in New York. Requests for grants poured in from civil liberties organizations and educational institutions, but the board did not act on them at its August meeting, spending much of its time in discussing future policies. At the September session, the Fund board granted $40,000 to Columbia University's Bicentennial Committee for a film, radio broadcasts and pamphlets entitled *Man's Right to*

Knowledge and the Free Use Thereof, and $35,000 to the Voluntary Defenders Committee of Boston, a group formed to aid indigent defendants. Case was given authority to employ consultants and several assistants.

Hutchins wrote to Parten in November, chafing at the Fund's ponderous pace: "How about getting started at the local level? For example, we could organize a corporation with the same base as the Fund for the Republic, but limited to Southern California. We could raise money locally to match a grant from the Fund. . . . I am inclined to think that the Fund will eventually find that it will have to work through local and regional groups. I talked about this with Joyce and Hoffman. Bill was enthusiastic. Hoffman seemed primarily interested in other matters, such as getting your tax exemption and the balance of the money due from the Ford Foundation." Hoffman was eager to get the Fund under way, but he felt that it was essential to get a permanent certificate of tax exemption from the Treasury and the full Ford grant before the Fund began a large-scale program.

Hutchins also prodded Elmo Roper, asking him what he thought of the Fund's plodding course. Early in December 1953, as the Fund approached the end of its first year of existence, Roper wrote to Hutchins: "I think it is probably fair to state that progress is being made, but frankly, it is being made at what to me is a discouraging rate. But I think it is fair to add that no judgment ought to be passed for another three months' period."

That did not sit well with Hutchins, who saw the erosion of civil liberties in the United States proceeding at a rapid rate. He continued to be an associate director of the Ford Foundation, and he was frequently consulted by officials of the Fund for Adult Education and the Fund for the Advancement of Education as well as by directors of the Fund for the Republic. That was not enough for him. He yearned to be in the thick of the fight against McCarthyism.

The evil in the world seemed to be growing. The Fund for the Republic had a vital mission to fulfill. To Hutchins, there was no time to be lost.

2

Sound the alarm bells, alert the American people

IN HIS FAREWELL ADDRESS to the House of Representatives, Clifford Case had explained why he had agreed to become president of the Fund for the Republic. He depicted the Fund as a purely educational organization that would defend and advance the principles of the Constitution without engaging in political maneuvers. He asked his colleagues in the House for their understanding and support.

Case demonstrated in this speech, as he had shown in his four terms as a member of the House, that he was a conciliator, a bridge builder, a man who had a winning personality. He was one of them. He was obviously not a crusader. He understood the practical arts. He had his own personal code, but he could work comfortably with men who had very different standards.

His fellow congressmen listened politely and wished him well. Some of them were baffled by his decision to leave the House. Some of them were already critical of the Fund, believing it would certainly be controlled by Paul Hoffman and Robert Hutchins. Hutchins had been tagged as a liberal educator with "wild ideas," and Hoffman had been called a global spender when he had been running the Marshall Plan.

To many members of the House, an educational foundation upholding the Constitution was bound to be involved in politics—or totally ineffective. If it was political, it would invade territory belonging to the Congress and might have to be destroyed. If it wasn't political, it wouldn't have any clout and the Ford millions would be wasted. Some of the representatives did not think that Case would stay with the Fund very long.

"I am especially conscious of my personal responsibilities for the work of the Fund," Case said at the end of his speech. "I shall have to draw on all the resources which are available to me. The experience gained in this body will, I am sure, be invaluable. Especially, I shall look to you, my colleagues, for continued help and counsel."

When he delivered that address on August 1, 1953, he knew that some of his colleagues wanted to smash the Fund before it got any momentum. He knew that his fellow Republicans had voted almost three to one in favor of a resolution which had been approved by the House on July 27 authorizing a congressional inquiry into tax-exempt foundations.

The proposed investigation had been pushed by southern Democrats, who had heard that the Fund planned to spend much of its money on race relations. The inquiry had been placed in the hands of Representative B. Carroll Reece, of Tennessee, who was not expected to give Clifford Case any "help and counsel." Reece and Case were poles apart.

In an oration in the House on the need for such a probe, Reece had voiced his hostility toward the Ford Foundation, the Rockefeller Foundation, Americans for Democratic Action, the National Education Association, and many other groups and individuals, including Eric Sevareid of CBS. Calling the Fund "this king-sized Civil Rights Congress," Reece thundered: "There can be no question that Hutchins is behind this new Ford Foundation project, for he has consistently expressed his concern for the civil liberties of Communists." In Reece's mind, any man who contended that the Bill of Rights applied to all Americans was protecting communists.

Sevareid was subjected to Reece's scorn because he had told his audience on the CBS radio network that "a group of the most responsible, respectable and successful business and professional men in the country have banded together in a Herculean effort to roll back the creeping tide of what is called, for want of a better word, McCarthyism. . . . These are disturbed and alarmed individuals, these men who have taken over this Fund." Reece was angered by Sevareid, Elmer Davis, and other commentators who praised the Ford Foundation's projects.

Davis, in a broadcast on July 28 after the House had approved the inquiry headed by Reece, had declared on the ABC network: "This is an attack on liberalism disguised as an attack on communism. But it's the Ford Foundation that is Reece's chief target, and especially its Fund for the Republic, set up to work for the removal of restrictions on the freedom of thought, inquiry and expression, freedoms guaranteed by the Constitution but now obviously in considerable danger."

Paul Hoffman thought it was possible that Reece was out to get him because he had opposed Senator Robert Taft and had helped General Eisenhower gain the Republican nomination for president in 1952. Case had also campaigned for Eisenhower.

In response to a letter from Earl Hall, an editor in Iowa, Hoffman wrote: "What Mr. Reece's purpose is at the present time, I don't know. I haven't seen him in years but have been told that he holds me responsible for having busted up his 'procurement' of Southern delegates for Mr. Taft, and as a consequence, he proposes to teach me a good lesson. Ray Tucker, in a recent column, said Reece's real object is the smearing of the whole liberal wing of the Republican party as a preparation toward the Old Guard's taking over once Eisenhower steps out of the picture." In Hoffman's view, the survival of the Fund was tied in one sense to the liberal branch of the Republican party.

Westbrook Pegler, a vitriolic columnist whose syndicated articles appeared in many newspapers, had attacked Case as a member of "a mysterious group in President-Elect Eisenhower's headquarters last fall . . . who tried to win control of Congress for undisclosed eastern financial backers by sending money into states of small population to defeat anti-Communist candidates and all who stand against unrestricted immigration." Pegler's view of the men around Eisenhower as engaged in a conspiracy did not make sense to most newspaper editors, but it appealed to Reece and others in the Congress.

At the time of the vote in the House to authorize an inquiry into the tax-exempt foundations, a *New York Times* reporter observed: "A decision by the Ford Foundation to grant $15,000,000 to inquire into the methods of Congressional investigations into Communist infiltrations and civil rights appeared to rankle a large segment of the House." The very existence of the Fund apparently rankled Reece and other congressmen who feared that "liberals" were hatching secret plots to aid communists and admit hordes of aliens into the United States.

Confronted by Reece's threats and by McCarthy's demands for information on every step taken by the Fund, Hoffman and Case felt justified in moving slowly until the Fund got final approval from the Treasury Department. President Eisenhower had proclaimed his determination to work in close cooperation with the Congress. If many congressmen went after the Fund, it was not likely to get its permanent certificate as an approved educational organization.

In the atmosphere of 1953 the Fund was continually in peril. While struggles for power were going on between the two wings of the Republican party—and between the factions in the Democratic party, too—committees of the House and Senate made headlines by insinuating that Eleanor Roosevelt, former President Truman, former Secretary of State James Byrnes, and other Democratic leaders had "coddled communists" or had protected "spies." The anticommunist fever was running high.

Representative Harold Velde, of Illinois, the new chairman of the House Committee on Un-American Activities, demanded an investigation of "the influence of Eleanor Roosevelt in the promotion of communism, and of immorality and indecency among so-called minority groups in Washington." That was too much even for some members of his committee, and Velde turned again to the grilling of "controversial" teachers and clergymen. Educators who would not answer the committee's charges or who had associated with "leftists" were discharged or suspended in many cases.

Attorney General Herbert Brownell charged that Truman had known that Harry Dexter White was a "Russian spy" when Truman had appointed White to the International Monetary Fund. White was dead, so White could not reply to Brownell. Rushing to get in on the headlines, Velde subpoenaed Truman. Truman rejected the summons with a statement broadcast on radio and televsion: "I have been accused in effect of knowingly betraying the security of the United States. This charge is, of course, a falsehood." The attack on Truman backfired. The major newspapers denounced Velde's committee.

But the pillorying of Truman, Mrs. Roosevelt, and James Byrnes showed that the heresy hunters would go after anybody. The *New York Times* carried front-page headlines on the activities of McCarthy, McCarran, Nixon, Senator Everett Dirksen, and Velde. One such headline declared: "Professor Loses Fulbright Award After Wife Balks at Red Inquiry." Teachers and government employees were held responsible for the views and behavior of their wives, their cousins, and their friends.

Even the press came under fire. McCarthy sharply questioned James Wechsler of the New York *Post*, who had once belonged to the Young Communist League as a college student, and McCarthy demanded an investigation of the Washington *Post*, asserting that the owner of that paper had "prostituted and endangered freedom of the press by constant false, vicious, intemperate attacks upon anyone who dares expose any of the undercover Communists." McCarthy regarded his critics as "vicious."

The armed forces were next. As chairman of a subcommittee of the Senate Committee on Government Operations, McCarthy held hearings on "espionage" at the Army Signal Corps Radar Center in New Jersey. A few months later, McCarthy and Dirksen—who had defeated Scott Lucas in 1950 with McCarthy's help—suggested that labor camps be established for members of the armed services who were communists or who invoked the protection of the Fifth Amendment when asked about communist associations.

In that atmosphere, the Fund moved quietly. No press releases were issued on the first grants made after Case had been elected the Fund's president. In spite of that, enemies hit it with an occasional barrage. *Firing Line*, the American Legion's newsletter, denounced it as "a huge slush fund for a full-scale war on all organizations and individuals who have ever exposed and fought Communists." The Committee for McCarthyism of the right-wing Constitutional Education League asserted that "the master minds of the Communist conspiracy . . . have been able to enlist the support and cooperation of two supposedly super-intelligent, ultra-respectable and all powerful allies—the Ford Motor Company and the American Bar Association." That attack was sparked by the Fund's grant to the bar association for its committee on individual rights.

A turning point came in January 1954. The Treasury Department notified Case that the Fund had been awarded a full tax-exemption certificate. With that certificate as a legal recognition of the Fund's status, the directors could obtain the remaining $12 million from the Ford Foundation and finance a series of big projects.

In reporting this good news to the board, Case sent a memorandum to each director. He put the basic responsibility for opposing McCarthyism upon "the innate decency, sense of fair play and basic common sense of the American people." The Fund could sound alarm bells throughout the land, but the results would depend on the people's response.

Case asked, "Can we, by the means available to us as an 'educational' organization, alert the American people sufficiently to keep the balance on freedom's side?" Then he gave his own position: "The answer depends in great part on whether we are able to gain and hold public confidence. When we present facts, the public must believe we are giving it the true story and the whole story. When we present points of view, the public must believe we are fairly presenting both sides."

He realized that the heresy hunters had already cast shadows over the Fund. He wrote: "It would be unrealistic not to recognize that some suspicion exists that the primary concern of the Fund itself is not the preservation of our freedoms as such but the special interests of the liberal and intellectual groups whose freedoms are currently under particular attack." He felt that the Fund had to be continually concerned with its own public standing in order to be effective in defending the freedoms of all citizens.

With the board's approval, Case employed three temporary consultants to give him advice: Frank Loescher, former head of the American Friends Service Committee community relations staff, to advise him on intergroup relations; Harold C. Hunt, of Harvard's school of education, to give counsel on education; and Joseph Volpe, a Washington lawyer who had been on the staff of the Atomic Energy Commission, to suggest what the Fund might do about loyalty-security problems. Aware of the growing impact of television, Case also devoted much thought to how the Fund might reach millions of citizens through the mass media.

Case had to spend some of his time in answering letters from the Reece committee and inquiries from the committee's staff members. René Wormser, general counsel of the committee, informed Case in a letter dated January 18, 1954, that he wanted to know "the full story" of the Fund's birth. Wormser wrote: "If you cannot piece this together and would prefer me to address myself directly to the Ford Foundation, I shall do so; but it would seem wise for you, yourself, to know the generative, prenatal and obstetrical facts; they should be important as background atmosphere in your work. . . . I would like to know what persons suggested the Fund, and how; what discussions there were concerning its proposed field of operations and objectives; and whatever further material might bear directly on the accusation, frequently made, that the Fund was created to attack or weaken the Congressional investigations.''

Norman Dodd, the committee's research director, asked for additional information in another letter. At Case's request, the Ford Foundation prepared a comprehensive reply, covering the points raised by Wormser and Dodd.

Case sent Dodd a 31-page summary of the Fund's record since its incorporation in December 1952. It had done nothing radical or reprehensible. It had rejected forty-six applications for money from scholars and organizations such as the American Council of Learned Societies, the Tuskegee Institute, and the Scientists' Committee on Loyalty and Security. It had made four grants to tax-exempt bodies, totaling $174,500. Its studies of communism, for which it had allocated more than $250,000, were being done by notable scholars.

The Fund had certainly not begun to roll back the tide of McCarthyism. In fact, the boldest action the Fund had taken thus far was to come into existence. It had not started to live up to the expectations of Eric Sevareid, Elmer Davis, and other commentators who had expected it to enter the battle against McCarthy.

Still the Reece committee was not appeased. Wormser insisted on knowing exactly how grants were made. In a reply to him on March 10, Case said: ''The board of directors, which has the responsibility for approval, looks . . . not only to the substance of the proposal and its relation to our basic objectives, but to the standing and character of the applicant organization or group, the work it has done in the past, its sources of financial support, and the quality of its leadership. . . .

''By the terms of its grants, the Fund receives periodic program and financial reports as well as informal interim reports.

''The Board of Directors has authorized the staff to reject proposals which are deemed to fall outside the scope of the Fund's program and has directed that periodic reports of such action be made to the Board.''

At the time when he wrote that letter to Wormser, Case had decided to resign from the Fund. The very qualities that had made Case so acceptable to the Fund's directors—his friendships with many congressmen, his standing with Eisenhower and Nixon, his defense of civil liberties coupled with denunciations of communism—led to his departure from the Fund after a few months of service. He was asked by Eisenhower to run for the Senate from New Jersey, and he felt that he had to respond to his president's call.

President Eisenhower had told him that it was extremely important to get more ''moderate'' Republicans into the Senate. Eisenhower was having many difficulties with the right-wing Republicans who followed Senator Robert Taft, and he wanted senators who shared his own views on national and international affairs.

Case believed that he could serve the cause of civil liberties in the Senate as well as he could at the Fund. He was a political man with a sense of duty. He was not driven by a missionary fervor, as Hutchins was. He was sure that the Fund could find another chief executive to carry on its program.

Paul Hoffman, as a Republican close to Eisenhower, understood Case's decision. He called the executive committee of the board into session on March 16. The committee accepted the resignation of Case, named George Shuster, of Hunter College, as the acting president, and chose Griswold, Roper, and John Lord O'Brian as a special committee to find a successor to Case.

At the March 16 meeting, Case persuaded the directors to approve a grant to the Carrie Chapman Catt Memorial Fund for a program of community education in civil liberties. Case was also present at the meeting of the whole board on April 1, when the directors allocated $240,000 to the Southern Regional Council for education in intergroup relations in the southern states. The work of the council was later praised by many observers for its substantial contribution to the improvement of race relations in many places.

After he left the Fund, Case went through a grinding campaign for the Senate in New Jersey. He was accused of being "soft on communism" by the McCarthyites. Nixon defended Case. Nixon, who barnstormed over the United States in 1954 shouting that "thousands of Communists, fellow travelers and security risks" had been "thrown" from the government by the Eisenhower administration, endorsed Case in vigorous phrases. Nixon insisted that Case had proved himself to be "a bona fide, anti-Communist Republican" by helping to draft the Mundt-Nixon communist registration bill when Case was in the House of Representatives. Case was elected by only 3200 votes, and Nixon's backing was considered to be the decisive factor in putting Case into the Senate.

As a senator, Case served with distinction on the Appropriations Committee, the Armed Services Committee, and the Committee on Aeronautical and Space Sciences. His measure providing federal aid to the states to establish community colleges, passed in 1962, made possible the opening of hundreds of new colleges. He was frequently cited by Washington newspaper correspondents as one of the ten "ablest men" in the Senate.

In his few months as president of the Fund for the Republic, what did Case accomplish? His presence may have been useful in getting a permanent certificate of tax exemption from the Treasury Department, and in stimulating the Ford Foundation to provide the final $12 million of its grant to the Fund. He placated the Reece committee and may have staved off a full-scale attack on the Fund.

Dwight Macdonald, a writer for the *New Yorker* magazine, was sharply critical of Case in his book entitled *The Ford Foundation*. Macdonald referred to the Case administration of the Fund as a "fiasco" and quoted a

Ford Foundation trustee as saying that the Fund's directors had been "overcautious, overconservative—for understandable reasons."

Thomas C. Reeves, the historian who wrote the first comprehensive review of the Fund's development from 1952 to 1959, gave Case a higher rating and indicated that he understood why the Fund's board had been so circumspect. In his volume, *Freedom and the Foundation: The Fund for the Republic in the Era of McCarthyism*, Reeves wrote:

> Case has been criticized for timidity. . . . But the evidence suggests that once he had actually begun his presidential duties, he was a man of ideas and initiative. . . . By April, 1954, the directors had either explored or entered, if only slightly, most of the general areas in which the Fund was to work.
>
> The Stouffer study of public attitudes toward communism and civil liberties would be published in a year, and provide profound and valuable insights. . . . The projected studies of communist influences in major segments of United States society would produce many highly acclaimed volumes. Allocations to the American Friends Service Committee, the Southern Regional Council, and the Carrie C. Catt Memorial Fund would be increased in later years. . . .
>
> The papers delivered at the Columbia University Bicentennial celebration were published in the *Columbia Law Review*. The American Bar Association's Special Committee on Individual Rights as Affected by National Security used half of its grant to create an important 45-page report (plus a 166-page appendix) which was absorbed into a proposed code of investigative procedure. The Voluntary Defenders Committee used the Fund's money to provide legal assistance to a large number of defendants.

It was easy for the Fund's critics to point out that the Fund had not conducted the "Herculean effort" expected by Eric Sevareid and others. Yet the temper of the time, revealed in the snarling speeches of Vice President Nixon and Representative Velde, made it evident that the directors and officers had been compelled to move carefully.

The sudden departure of Case left the directors in a difficult position. They were now prepared to act in many fields, but they had no chief executive to carry the Fund's projects forward.

Erwin Griswold and William Joyce turned their attention quickly toward the man who had advocated such a Fund from his first days at the Ford Foundation—Robert Hutchins. Grenville Clark, noted author of a study entitled *World Peace Through World Law*, also had suggested Hutchins in a telephone call to John Lord O'Brian. O'Brian had favored the idea.

Joyce recalled later: "We sought a dynamic leader for a job badly in need of doing, and we turned to Hutchins, who had thought of the Fund.

Some exchange with trustees of the Ford Foundation was made in advance about a possible Hutchins appointment. They were not wild about the idea but there was no veto.''

Jubal Parten and Elmo Roper declared that they thought Hutchins should be invited to take the helm. It was known to these directors that relationships between Hutchins and Henry Ford II had become abrasive. Hutchins had no future in the Ford Foundation.

When Roper and Joyce asked him to become president of the Fund, Hutchins accepted with ''willingness and pleasure.'' He felt that the Fund might be the most important educational organization created by the Ford Foundation. He was ready to face any attacks that might be made on the Fund or on himself. He was eager to get into the fray.

3

Hutchins moves in— and the Fund gets going

His FATHER HAD TAUGHT HIM that a righteous man who held on to his own convictions in spite of all assaults could never be vanquished. When Robert Hutchins left the Ford Foundation to become president of the Fund, he brought with him a moral fervor that was never wholly concealed by an ironic style. His self-confidence had not been deeply shaken by his disagreement with Henry Ford II.

His challenging years as the dean of the Yale law school and as the head of the University of Chicago had made him known and admired by thousands of men and women who were active in many fields. He had many potential allies, many friends. His brilliance was unquestioned. The programs he had created at the Ford Foundation had produced repercussions around the world.

He felt that his own credentials and the credentials of the Fund's directors in American society were far better than those of Joe McCarthy, Westbrook Pegler, the House Committee on Un-American Activities, or any other possible foes of the Fund. He thought that the public would rapidly realize that the Fund could be trusted to help them defend their rights and liberties. With such beliefs, Hutchins got into more trouble than he had ever known before in his life.

Perhaps his excessive confidence was partly due to his swift climb to national recognition. He never failed at anything. He had been an illustrious student at Oberlin College and at Yale. He had served in the United States Army Ambulance Service as a private on the Italian front in World War I, and had been awarded a Croce di Guerra by the Italian government for his bravery. He had become secretary of Yale University at twenty-three and headed the law school there at twenty-six. In 1929, as he turned thirty, he had been elected president of the University of Chicago. He had run that university for twenty-two years before he joined the Ford Foundation. He had a continuing flow of ideas that seemed never to stop.

In college, he had wanted to study law. But when he got his bachelor's degree he had no money to pursue that interest. So he went immediately into teaching at a school for delinquent boys. He threw erasers at students who did not pay attention, and if they became obstreperous, he hit them over the head with books. He admitted later that he had carried his disciplinary methods a little too far.

Throughout his life, however, Hutchins felt that many people had to be jolted into learning what they ought to know for their own good. And though he soon ceased throwing erasers or hitting people with books, he did shock congressmen and other citizens by blunt statements on the corruption and hypocrisy of American society.

Long before McCarthyism had erupted in the United States, in a speech carried by the radio network of NBC in January 1941, Hutchins had questioned the devotion of many of his countrymen to the Bill of Rights. He said Americans had "barely begun to grasp the meaning" of "freedom of speech, freedom of worship, freedom from want, and freedom from fear." These were the "Four Freedoms" cited by President Franklin D. Roosevelt in his State of the Union message to Congress in that year.

"Have we freedom of speech and freedom of worship in this country?" Hutchins had asked. "We do have freedom to say what everybody else is saying and freedom of worship if we do not take our religion too seriously. But teachers who do not conform to the established canons of social thought lose their jobs. People who are called radicals have mysterious difficulties in renting halls. Labor organizers sometimes get beaten up and ridden out of town on a rail. . . .

"If we regard these exceptions as minor, reflecting the attitude of the more backward and illiterate parts of the country, what are we to say of freedom from want and freedom from fear? What of the moral order and justice and the supremacy of human rights? What of democracy in the United States?

"Words like these have no meaning unless we believe in human dignity. Human dignity means that every man is an end in himself. No man can be exploited by another. Think of these things and then think of the sharecroppers, the Okies, the Negroes, the slum-dwellers, downtrodden and oppressed for gain. They have neither freedom from want nor freedom from fear. They hardly know they are living in a moral order or in a democracy where justice and human rights are supreme."

These were the concerns Hutchins had felt when he was a boy in Brooklyn under the strict guidance of his father, a Presbyterian minister. These were the concerns he felt at Oberlin, where there was a very strong religious and moral tradition.

Speaking of his youth, Hutchins said once: "Oberlin was founded by missionaries who selected the most disagreeable part of Ohio they could find in order to make sure that they were not living in any kind of luxury that would be inappropriate to their aims in life. They began by admitting Negroes and women. They were the first college in the United States to do so."

Hutchins was proud of Oberlin's opposition to slavery. It had been a station on the Underground Railroad. He said: "A great episode in the history of the College is the Wellington raid. A fugitive slave was rescued in the village of Wellington (about eleven miles away) by the faculty and students of Oberlin."

When he was a student there, Henry Churchill King was the president of the college. Hutchins described King in these terms: "He had written several books on Rational Living (which is spelled with a capital 'R' and a capital 'L'). We were supposed to be dedicated to Rational Living. I remember once that King told us that he was very sorry that he had had a cold, and the reason was that he was not living rationally. . . . The pleasures of the mind were not considered irrational. But all other pleasures were. It was against the rules to dance; it was against the rules to smoke; and, of course, nobody ever *heard* of drinking."

He learned to smoke and swear in the army. His independent spirit caused him to spend a week under arrest: he had protested against the bad food provided to his ambulance unit and had been confined to his tent for a week by an officer's order; but the food improved.

Hutchins attributed his independence and his moral fervor to his ancestors. His father came from a long line of Connecticut doctors and ministers. His mother's people included a line of sea captains from Maine. His maternal grandfather went to sea in a sailing vessel at the age of eleven and was on a voyage for four years. Hutchins wrote once: "These ancestors of mine were all stubborn and some of them were vain. Their notion of success did not seem to involve material goods as much as it did holding onto their own convictions in the face of external pressure."

He admitted that stubbornness and vanity were visible in his own character. He believed that his father and mother had tried to keep him humble while encouraging him to stand on his own feet. He said of his mother: "She kept us in order." His father kept reminding him that the value of his own life depended largely on what he could do for his fellow creatures.

His successes at Yale, at the University of Chicago, and at the Ford Foundation had enabled Hutchins to obtain material goods without abandoning any of his own convictions. He saw no reason why he could not live as well as a Ford Motor Company executive and still be a servant of the people. In an autobiographical essay, he acknowledged that he was personally involved in a materialistic society, but he added: "I could not escape from Oberlin or from my family. . . . My missionary past pursued me and would give me no satisfaction in my work."

At the Fund, he could crusade openly for all the causes in which he believed. He saw the Fund as a university without limits, a university for the liberal education of the people. If the people did not get that kind of education, he did not think democracy could survive. The lack of that education had made it possible for McCarthy and many other demagogues to confuse and deceive millions of citizens. He believed that the recurrent emergence of such men in American history showed that American educational institutions were seriously defective.

In *The Great Conversation*, the first volume of a collection of writings he called Great Books of the Western World, Hutchins said: "Many claims can be made for the American people; but nobody would think of claiming that they can read, write, and figure. Still less would it be maintained that they understand the tradition of the West, the tradition in which they live. The products of American high schools are illiterate; and a degree from a famous college or university is no guarantee that the graduate is in any better case. One of the most remarkable features of American society is that the difference between the 'uneducated' and the 'educated' is so slight."

Such statements did not endear him to other educators or those who boasted of American cultural achievements. He had been accused of being an elitist, and he did have a tendency in that direction. But the tendency was kept in check by his realization that many people had never had opportunities for enough education to become fully self-governing citizens. He did not deny the potential intelligence of the people.

He had written those gloomy statements about the low level of American education in 1951, at the end of his twenty-two years as a university president. Yet he had not lost all hope. In the same book, Hutchins had insisted that the effort to educate all people to their highest capacities was an absolute necessity: "The democratic enterprise is imperiled if any one of us says, 'I do not have to try to think for myself, or make the most of myself, or become a citizen of the world republic of learning.' The death of democracy is not likely to be an assassination from ambush. It will be a slow extinction from apathy, indifference, and undernourishment."

In spite the failures he saw around him in America, in spite of his own frustrations as an educator, Hutchins took his stand with Thomas Jefferson. He quoted Jefferson: "I know of no safe depository of the ultimate powers of society but the people themselves; and if we think them not enlightened enough to exercise their control with a wholesome discretion, the remedy is not to take it from them, but to inform their discretion by education." By education Jefferson meant teaching people to think for themselves.

When Hutchins took over the Fund, he maintained his home in California during his first eighteen months as president. He asked W. H. Ferry, who had been close to him during his years with the Ford Foundation, to become vice president and manager of the New York office. The directors approved his action. Since Ferry had worked with Hutchins in developing the plan for the Fund, it seemed logical that Ferry would be the Fund's spokesman in New York.

Hutchins believed there would be advantages in having the Fund represented on both coasts of the United States. He saw California as a new frontier land, a place where new trends in American life developed most rapidly, an area where the radicals and the right-wingers were extremely active. Hutchins wanted to be there, because it was a crucible of change, and he had a private reason for wanting to keep his home in California: his wife's health was fragile and the California climate seemed beneficial for her. The board of directors accepted his views.

The man Hutchins had picked to manage the Fund's New York office had ideas about education similar to those of Hutchins, although he had a very different background. Ferry's father was chairman of the Packard Motor Company, and Ferry was accustomed to living well. He had been for nine years a partner of Earl Newsom & Company, a public relations agency that had several of the country's largest corporations as clients. But Ferry was not a Madison Avenue apologist for big business. He and Newsom had disagreed on many things, and Newsom had wanted him to move on.

After he had graduated from Dartmouth College, Ferry had taught briefly at the Choate School and then had been a newspaper reporter and editor in Michigan, Texas, New Hampshire, and Puerto Rico. In 1944 he had been director of public relations for the CIO Political Action Committee, which had played a significant part in the reelection of President Roosevelt. He had a direct, blunt style, which had won him many friends, but reporters and others seeking information about the Fund sometimes found him abrasive and short-tempered.

Ferry had not been eager to take the post with the Fund. He told an interviewer: "The main reason for my reluctance was fear of boredom. Most of the people I encountered who were advocates of civil liberties were bores—one-eyed fanatics; not nuts but unusual. . . . I decided to accept the position for only a year."

In the first months of the Hutchins administration, harmony prevailed between the officers and the directors. Hutchins flew regularly from California to New York and frequently sought the advice of board members. He appointed Hallock Hoffman (a son of Paul Hoffman) who had been executive secretary of the American Friends Service Committee, as his assistant in the California office. Ferry ran the New York office with brisk efficiency and forwarded all major grant applications to Hutchins for review.

All recommendations to the board were carefully prepared and heavily documented. Hutchins believed that directors who received extensive information about each proposed grant, well in advance of each meeting, would come to each board assembly with a favorable attitude toward the energy and thoroughness of the officers. He felt that too-frequent meetings caused the board to bog down in details. At his first session after his installation as president, he persuaded the board to change its schedule from monthly to quarterly meetings.

Hutchins, Ferry, and Hoffman did not expect any trouble with the Ford Foundation. Every member of the Fund's board had been personally approved by every trustee of the foundation. Henry Ford II had launched the Fund himself, in the presence of the other trustees, after being warned that controversies were sure to come.

The election of Hutchins as president of the Fund focused attention on his personality and on his record as a university administrator and a foundation executive. He was known to reporters and editors in New York and Chicago as "a newsmaker," a man who had fought Col. Robert McCormick of the Chicago *Tribune* and had incurred the wrath of William Randolph Hearst. He had been tagged a "boy wonder," a "boob-shocker," as the man who had taken the University of Chicago out of the frenzied competition of intercollegiate football, as the man who had been accused of harboring "communists" and "socialists" on his faculty. He had made hundreds of speeches on many topics; he had dozens of honorary degrees from colleges and universities; he had been considered for an appointment to the United States Supreme Court by President Roosevelt and had been talked about as a possible candidate for president of the United States.

When Hutchins had been elected by the Fund's directors, they placed the responsibility for any "public relations problems which might arise" on the shoulders of Chairman Hoffman. Hoffman was sure that Hutchins would consult him about any public statements, and Hutchins did. But the press soon began to identify the Fund with Hutchins.

In his first six months at the helm, Hutchins leaned over backward to convince the press and the public that the board was actually in control. Yet it was evident at his first session with the board that his influence was very powerful. He began to move the Fund away from its emphasis on studies of the "internal communist menace"—studies that were already approved— into other fields that needed exploration.

At the meeting of June 30, 1954, Hutchins obtained approval for the expenditure of $25,000 for the development of a commission on the federal security program. He knew how many lives were being ruined by the application of "guilt by association" and by procedures that were bringing the United States close to "a police state." He hoped that the proposed Citizens Commission on the Federal Security Program could check the excesses of the FBI and other investigative agencies.

Other actions taken at Hutchins' request at the June 30 meeting were the allocation of $25,000 for planning of a study of extremist groups; $86,500 for the American Friends Service Committee to support four projects in its community relations efforts; and $15,000 for the Common Council for American Unity, to extend its work in protecting and publicizing the legal rights of aliens. Hutchins also informed the board that he planned to move as quickly as possible to organize the study of blacklisting in the entertainment industry and other industries; a study of fear among faculty members and teachers under fire for "controversial ideas"; an examination of the mass media; and the development of awards, essay contests, and television programs to increase public awareness of civil rights and civil liberties.

The board members were reminded that the statement released to the press on February 26, 1953, announcing the grant of $15 million by the Ford Foundation to the Fund, had contained a declaration of policies: "We regard the sphere of operation of the Fund as including the entire field of freedom and civil rights in the United States and take as our basic charter the Declaration of Independence and the Constitution." Hutchins proposed to operate in that entire field.

Case had employed three consultants. Hutchins appointed twelve. He kept Frank Loescher, one of the three hired by Case, as a consultant on intergroup relations. In addition to Loescher, the consultants to Hutchins were Walter Millis, noted military historian and editorial writer for the New York *Herald-Tribune*, to analyze the federal loyalty-security programs; Paul Lazarsfeld, of Columbia University, consultant on the fear-in-education project; Robert E. Cushman, of Cornell University, who had edited several volumes on civil liberties, consultant on the preservation of liberties; Samuel Stouffer, of Harvard, consultant on the survey of public attitudes on communism and civil liberties; Howard Chernoff, television; John Cogley, former executive editor of the *Commonweal*, blacklisting; George Overton, legal assistance programs; Conrad Arensberg, extremist groups; Philip Woodyat, editorial competitions; and Elmer Davis, writer and broadcaster, general consultant.

Before each board meeting, Hutchins asked his consultants for reports on activities in their areas. He held day-long sessions in which all the consultants had an opportunity to exchange information and ideas. With these background briefings, Hutchins was prepared to answer all questions raised by the directors.

At the meeting on September 14, the board appropriated $100,000 for the study of blacklisting, which had been on Dean Griswold's original list of projects outlined to the Ford trustees, and granted $50,000 for the preliminary expenses of the study of fear in education. In addition, the board authorized the expenditure of $200,000 for "the production of three or four pilot films of a historical-fictional nature and for participation in the presentation of television programs of interest to the Fund where such support is indicated." Another $100,000 was committed for a national editorial competition to promote "the best discussion of the Bill of Rights in the United States today." This was related to the board's declaration that it would give much attention to "a clear statement in contemporary terms of the legacy of American liberty."

While a majority of the directors were delighted by the comprehensive projects placed before them by Hutchins, several of them became a little worried about the hazard of stepping beyond "education" into "propaganda" or what might be called attempts to "influence legislation." Hutchins had taken the precaution of having each project reviewed for its legality under the Internal Revenue Code by Bethuel Webster or members of Webster's law firm, Webster, Sheffield & Chrystie, which was getting sizable fees from the Fund. But these directors asked the lawyers how far the Fund could go.

In a memorandum to the board on October 1, 1954, Thomas W. Chrystie indicated that the Fund could go pretty far: "In spite of the obligation to operate with careful regard for the tax exemption requirements, it is believed that the tax limitations present no serious obstacle. The primary problem, we take it, is to convince large numbers of people that American concepts of freedom and democracy are as important in 1954 as they were in 1776. This they will believe not because the Fund or anyone else says so, but because they themselves see and understand that it is so, from their own comprehension of current events. And when people are awakened to the importance of applying these fundamental principles to the living problems of today, the detail of how the principles are to be implemented becomes relatively unimportant. The pressure of the tax law towards holding the Fund to fundamental principles, leaving it to the pupils (in this case the public) to work out the application of those principles in the myriads of complex situations in which they become involved, may very well be the course the Fund would wish to take even if there were no tax restrictions at all."

Hutchins shared Chrystie's view that the tax limitations presented "no serious obstacle." But he did not see the people simply as "pupils" to be tutored by the Fund so that they would know how to apply constitutional principles in "myriads of complex situations." He saw the Fund as a rescue operation, helping people to defend their rights and the rights of their neighbors. Describing his attitude and the attitude of his staff, Hutchins told an interviewer later: "We had several commitments left over from Case which we were willing to fulfill. But we were determined to see how far we could go to help people and at the same time maintain our tax exemption. That was the major difference.

In the last months of 1954 the atmosphere for civil liberties in the United States seemed to be improving. President Eisenhower and Vice President Nixon had turned against McCarthy after he had excoriated the secretary of the army and other high officials in the Eisenhower administration. McCarthy's wild behavior on television led to a steep drop in his popularity as measured by the Gallup poll, and he was condemned for his conduct by a vote in the Senate of 67 to 22. Nixon's charges of "treason" in the government had not brought a Republican victory in the 1954 elections; the Democrats regained control of Congress by taking twenty seats from Republicans in the House and two seats in the Senate. Under Chief Justice Earl Warren, the Supreme Court had made liberal rulings on constitutional issues.

The Reece committee floundered in a fog of confusion for five months and finally issued a 416-page report in December 1954, charging that the giant foundations—Ford, Rockefeller, Carnegie, Guggenheim, and others— were engaged in a "diabolical conspiracy" with radical research and educational organizations to enable "Marxists" and internationalists to dominate the United States. René Wormser, counsel to the committee, declared: "Over the past few decades the major foundation complex has operated almost as an informal but integral arm of government, acting, to a very considerable extent, as its collateral 'brain trust,' and determining policy. If a revolution has indeed been accomplished in the United States, we can look here for its motivation, its impetus, and its rationale."

Two Democratic representatives on the committee called the report "shocking" and "barbaric." Many newspapers and magazines denounced it as a foolish concoction. The executive director of the American Civil Liberties Union asserted: "The threat of governmental assault, punishment and control has been directed against ideas which happen to be disliked by certain Congressmen." It was evident to both the friends and critics of the Fund that the Reece committee had aimed many of its barbs at the Fund.

Although he was outraged by the Reece report, Hutchins had reasons for regarding his first six months in the president's chair as a period of achievement. His principal proposals had been approved or given favorable consideration. Action had been "deferred" on a few of them—including his long-nourished idea for a commission on the mass media—but the only projects flatly rejected had been the proposed studies of the police agencies and the FBI.

Three new directors were elected to the board when it gathered on November 18. Harry S. Ashmore, executive editor of the *Arkansas Gazette*, had written a report, *The Negro and the Schools*, based on the work of a group of scholars, and the two other new members also had fine records in civil liberties. Robert E. Sherwood was the author of many prize-winning plays. Chester Bowles had served as the American ambassador to India and had been governor of Connecticut and director of the Office of Price Administration. All three had been recomended by Hutchins with enthusiasm.

Hutchins was pleased by the steps taken by the board at the November session. The proposed Citizens Commission on the Federal Security Program (for which $25,000 had originally been requested) had been given a total of $100,000. The officers had received authority to spend $100,000 on studies of extremist groups, in cooperation with Columbia University's Bureau of Applied Social Research.

Other grants had included $115,000 for fellowships and financial aid to scholars, lawyers, and journalists on research projects; $10,000 to the National Council of Churches of Christ in America for counseling of teachers in race relations; $10,000 for a summary of existing laws and regulations of the federal personnel security system, to assist lawyers in handling loyalty-security cases; an additional $66,610 to continue the successful "freedom agenda" discussion programs sponsored by the Carrie Chapman Catt Fund; $15,000 to buy and distribute copies of a paperback edition of Erwin Griswold's book, *The Fifth Amendment Today*; $6000 for the American Library Association's *Newsletter on Intellectual Freedom*; and $2000 for distribution of four major books published as a result of the Cornell University studies in civil liberties.

One of the most significant grants was the allocation of $25,000 for the initiation of a nation-wide study of the housing problems of minority groups, particularly black people. The memorandum to the board showed what was happening: "About a million new dwelling units are being built every year. The pattern of segregation grows as Negroes are barred from new neighborhoods and communities."

Hutchins had hailed the school desegregation decision of the Supreme Court in May 1954 as a victory for all those who believed in the principles of liberty and equality. He knew that the decision would have far-reaching repercussions, not only in the South but in all parts of the nation. He felt that a thorough study of the patterns of segregation in housing—conducted under the auspices of people with high standing in the business and banking communities—would lead to substantial reforms that would benefit many communities.

The unanimous decision of the Supreme Court that "separate educational facilities" for children of different racial backgrounds were "inherently unequal" had stunned governors, Senators, mayors, and other political leaders who had believed that strict separation of whites and blacks had legal sanctions. Chief Justice Warren, speaking with the backing of the whole Court, had declared: "To separate (Negro children) from others of similar age and qualifications solely because of their race generates a feeling of inferiority as to their status in the community that may affect their hearts and minds in a way never to be undone. . . ." Local school districts and federal courts were instructed to evaluate their situations and then to make a "prompt and reasonable start" in obeying the Court's decision with "all deliberate speed."

In 1941 Hutchins had said that oppressed people living in slums "hardly know they are living in a moral order or in a democracy where justice and human rights are supreme." The Court had raised a banner of hope for people who had been ignored or kept in ignorance for generations. Hutchins knew—as other directors of the Fund did—that angry racists would try to nullify or destroy the effects of the Court's ruling. The Fund had to give as much aid as possible, as quickly as it could, to people in the South and elsewhere who would strive to prevent violence and build better relations between whites and blacks.

"Protection of the rights of minorities" had been the third of the five major areas cited for concentrated attention by Griswold, Hoffman, Joyce, Parten, and the other directors of the Fund when they had released a statement in February 1953 on what the Fund intended to do with the Ford Foundation money. The Supreme Court decision highlighted the wisdom of the grants that had been made to the Southern Regional Council, the National Council of Churches, and other organizations dedicated to equal rights for all.

In 1954 the Fund was the only large foundation active in the explosive area of race relations. Its work in this field began under Case and expanded under Hutchins. Its grants to help thousands of people make desegregation as peaceful as possible were later noted by Chief Justice Warren as a great contribution to American society at a critical moment.

There is much evidence to indicate, however, that the Fund's activity in this area stimulated a torrent of abusive letters to Henry Ford II and the Ford Foundation. These letters and the pressures of congressional criticisms led Ford eventually to a public blast at the Fund and a private assurance to the chairman of the House Committee on Un-American Activities that he would be willing to see the Fund dissolved.

There is no doubt that the Fund would have been assaulted by right-wing extremists and racists whether Hutchins had been its president or not. Yet the willingness of Hutchins to engage in hard-hitting exchanges with his critics—and his scathing remarks about opponents of the Fund—fanned the angry fires against him and against the Fund itself.

The condemnation of McCarthy and the ridicule heaped on Representative Reece did not diminish the strength of the well-financed extremist groups in the United States. Hundreds of foundations established by wealthy men—H. L. Hunt, of Texas, was a notable example—poured millions of dollars each year into these organizations. The National Foundation for Education in American Citizenship (NFEAC) received several hundred thousand dollars from J. K. Lilly, one of the owners of a very successful drug firm. H. L. Hunt put $219,000 into *Facts Forum*, a right-wing publication that assailed Democratic leaders, the Fund, and all groups considered "liberal" or "subversive." Fulton Lewis, Jr., had sponsors on radio stations throughout the United States. Westbrook Pegler's column appeared in many newspapers. While the amount of money given by the Ford Foundation to the Fund was regularly cited in Congress and in the press, the public generally did not know that the Fund's antagonists had more money than the Fund.

The vulnerability of the Fund was more evident in 1955 than it had been in 1954. The solidarity of the board gave way under barrages from open antagonists and hidden enemies. The obsession with "national security"—security founded on the power of the government, not on the liberties of a free people—was as prevalent in a Congress controlled by the Democrats as it had been when McCarthy had been rampant. Struggling to uphold the plain statements in the Bill of Rights, the Fund was painted with a red brush. The pressures brought to bear upon the very respectable directors of the Fund deeply affected their attitudes toward Hutchins, toward one another, and toward the large projects they had authorized in a surge of boldness.

What happened to Hutchins and the Fund revealed the anxieties and rigidities of American society in the 1950s. The idea that government existed to serve the citizen—not the citizen for the government—had almost vanished. The Fund was the foremost champion of individual rights. There were other groups fighting for the same principles—the Quakers, the American Civil Liberties Union, the American Veterans Committee, the League of Women Voters—but the Fund's board members were people of influence, and they managed to make their voices heard in Congress, in the courts, and in the White House.

So the aim of the heresy hunters became the dissolution of the Fund and the downfall of its president, Robert Hutchins.

4

In a gathering furor, Hutchins attacks the Fund's foes

Hutchins was forthright in his defense of the Fund. He had been infuriated by the report of the Reece committee. On the evening of January 26, 1955, he spoke at the National Press Club in Washington, with Representative Reece seated at the head table near him. Two Democratic representatives—Wayne Hays and Gracie Pfost, who had filed their dissent against the Reece report—were also in the audience, along with Supreme Court Justices William O. Douglas and Felix Frankfurter, friends of Hutchins.

Before he began his dissection of the Reece report, Hutchins insisted that he was speaking only for himself. He asserted that his remarks were not "on behalf of the Fund for the Republic, the directors of which I have not consulted; nor the Ford Foundation, of which the Fund for the Republic is completely independent; nor for other foundations." In fact, he was bitingly critical of some of the foundations.

Referring to his experiences at Yale, at the University of Chicago, and as a Ford Foundation executive, Hutchins said: "I have been dealing with the foundations in one way or another for more than thirty years. They have always been distinguished by their lack of fellow feeling. They have scorned a project if it required the cooperation of another foundation. It is therefore one of the more absurd charges of the Reece Committee that the foundations were an intellectual cartel. The Reece Committee forced them to huddle together in self-defense. One more investigation and they might become a cartel.

"The conduct of the majority, if it was the majority, of the Reece Committee was so scandalous that it outraged almost all of the press and apparently even one of its members. At any rate, Angier L. Goodwin of Massachusetts wrote a new kind of concurring opinion, one that disagreed with all the conclusions of the opinion with which it purported to concur."

Hutchins declared that Congressman Reece had "added some new wrinkles to the distortions that we have become accustomed to in congressional investigations." He pointed out: "The foundations were elaborately attacked by the staff and by some witnesses of dubious standing. Then, pleading that Mr. Hays of Ohio would not let him conduct the hearings as they should be conducted, Mr. Reece adjourned them and informed the foundations that they could file written statements. Perhaps the most depressing fact about the report of the so-called majority of the Reece Committee is that Mr. Reece takes credit for relieving the foundations of what he calls the 'embarrassment' of cross-examination. You might as well execute an innocent man without the embarrassment of a hearing."

Hutchins quoted the Reece committee majority as telling the foundations: " 'They should be very chary of promoting ideas, concepts and opinion-forming material which run counter to what the public currently wishes, approves and likes.' " Hutchins then emphasized: "Here the Committee throws overboard the principle accepted by the Cox Committee that the justification of the foundations is that they supply risk or venture capital in the field of philanthropy. That is what they are for, to take chances, the Cox Committee said. The Reece Committee would confine them to what a public relations man, presumably by a series of careful polls, found that the public currently wished, approved, and liked. The way to be safe would be to attract no attention, arouse no discussion, create no controversy."

To Hutchins, the way recommended by the Reece committee was the way of death for a free society. In his view, the Constitution was designed to foster discussion of every issue. The Constitution itself had been very "controversial" in 1787. Hamilton, Madison, Jay, and other American leaders had produced the Federalist papers to persuade their fellow citizens to adopt it—and the Constitution was approved by narrow margins after much opposition and debate.

Hutchins blasted the Reece report in scornful terms: "The Reece Committee achieved some of its gaudiest effects by the simple process of giving old words new definitions and then pinning the old words on the foundations. . . . Subversion now means, the Committee says, a promotion of tendencies that may lead to results that the Committee will not like. Hence support of the New Deal could be subversion. Social engineering, planning, world government, the United Nations, William James, John Dewey, the American Friends Service Committee, Dr. Kinsey and reform are all subversive in the bright new lexicon of the Reece Committee. And of course all these things are socialistic, if not communistic, too."

With scathing eloquence, Hutchins said: "The Reece investigation in its inception and execution was a fraud. Nobody in his right mind could suppose that the great accumulations of wealth left by our richest men were being intentionally used by their trustees to overthrow the institutions of this country. Hence the Reece Committee had to take another tack: the trustees were said to be so busy that they had to leave the foundations to officers who were often quite disreputable. Though this relieved the men of wealth and standing of the charge of being knaves, it did so only at the expense of charging them with being fools. Only fools could be so careless as to allow enormous sums entrusted to them for charitable purposes to be stolen away and lavished on the subversion of their country.''

The president of the Fund admitted that Congress could properly investigate the foundations and try to develop general legislative policy concerning them. Hutchins went on: ''But the most important question to ask about any given foundation is whether it is one. Is it actually using its money for religious, charitable, educational, or scientific purposes? The First Amendment suggests that tax exemption should not be denied or revoked because the particular views of religion, education, or science held or promoted by the foundation are unpopular.''

Hutchins concluded with a statement that was not well received by the trustees and executives of other foundations: ''Congressman Reece was scoffed at. It was agreed that his investigation was a farce. I think he had a good reason to be satisfied with himself. I think he won. Without firing a single serious shot, without saying a single intelligent word, he accomplished his purpose, which was to harass the foundations and to subdue such stirrings of courage, or even of imagination, as could be found in them. As I have said, there were not many there when he came on the scene. . . . If there ever was a foundation that was willing to be controversial, that was willing to take risks and to venture capital in areas about which people have strong prejudices, it learned its lesson by the time Cox and Reece got through. Who will venture now?''

He presented the Fund as an exception to the rule of timidity in foundations, describing it as ''a kind of anti-absurdity fund, a fund to remind us that we can't have things both ways. We can't brag about the Bill of Rights and talk about Fifth Amendment Communists. We can't say that every man has the right to face his accusers and go on using what the Denver *Post* has called 'faceless informers.' We can't proclaim our devotion to the process of law and then deny it to people we don't like.''

Hutchins had never been bolder than he was in that speech at the National Press Club. To the assembled Washington correspondents for many newspapers and broadcasting stations: ''The Fund for the Republic is a sort of Fund for the American Dream. I do not think the Fund can make the American dream come true; but perhaps it can keep it alive and clear. . .'' When Hutchins finished, he was loudly applauded and Reece came over to shake hands. Reece said he had learned not to be disturbed by what people said about him in his thirty-four years in politics.

The inner disturbance that Reece actually felt when Hutchins accused him of fraud and fakery became evident when Reece replied to Hutchins on February 23, 1955, at a Press Club luncheon. He lashed out at Hutchins

with fury: "As this man of wisdom spoke, I was somehow reminded of El-
bert Hubbard's definition of egotism. He defined egotism as 'the anesthetic
that nature gives to deaden the pain of being a damn fool.' . . .

"You know, these planners, of whom Dr. Hutchins is an outstanding
example, have clearly adopted a communist tactic. Communists charge that
the *rest* of the world is 'aggressive.' Similarly, these planners accuse the
Committee on Foundations of wishing to suppress freedom of thought."

After linking Hutchins to the communists and the would-be censors,
Reece criticized the Fund for distributing copies of the television film in
which Edward R. Murrow had interviewed J. Robert Oppenheimer, the
atomic scientist who had been labeled "a security risk." Reece said the film
simply gave Oppenheimer a chance to defend his behavior in associating
with people who had communist affiliations.

Then Reece tried to drive a wedge between Hutchins and the directors
of the Fund, declaring: "Despite Dr. Hutchins' fervent disclaimer in the title and first paragraph of his speech, Fund for the Republic is repeated four
times, once more than the number of times the sponsor's product needs to
be mentioned in a radio commercial.

"This disclaimer hardly balances the impression, and, by the way, if he
was speaking without even consulting his trustees, he reduces them to the
level of impotent window dressing.

"He avers, however, that the foundations have been doing 'a good deal
of talking lately.' Does he mean through their presidents and without consulting their trustees? Does this activity indicate the overt evidence of a hitherto covert condition?"

While many of the directors of the Fund admired the style and strength
of Hutchins' speech and agreed with what he had said about the Reece committee, some of them were regretful that he had increased the hostility of
Reece and other congressmen toward the Fund. It was evident, however,
that nothing could have placated Reece. Reece believed that Hutchins and
the other directors of the Fund were "planners," and "planners" were
linked to the communists directly or indirectly, because communists advocated "planning."

In an article published in June 1955, the *American Legion Magazine*
applauded Reece and contended that Wayne Hays had been planted in the
committee to disrupt it. The magazine reported: "Representative Hays had
told Norman Dodd, Committee Research Director, and General Counsel
René Wormser, that he was opposed to the investigation (he had voted
against the Reece Resolution in the House) and that he had been appointed
ranking Democrat on the Committee by Minority Leader Sam Rayburn
with the understanding that he would do everything in his power to prevent
the Committee from going too far in its inquiry." In a letter to a historian
some years later, Hays wrote: "May I say that I never made such a statement to Mr. Dodd, nor did I at any time say that Mr. Rayburn had put any

conditions on my appointment. As a matter of fact, any such statement is completely untrue.''

Hays was one of the members of Congress who saw the connection between the Reece committee and McCarthyism. He said: "I think the reason I was appointed, as I recall, was that I had talked with the Speaker some weeks before and expressed considerable disgust that no one was able to stand up to McCarthy, and I thought someone should. When the Speaker (actually Mr. Rayburn was minority leader at the time, when the Republicans controlled the House) called me in to tell me that he wanted to appoint me, he said: 'You have been complaining about the McCarthy tactics around here, and here is a chance to see what you can do about it.'

"I do not know whether you realize it or not, but the staff under Mr. Reece's direction brought in a verdict before the hearings were held, and the hearings were to substantiate the verdict, a sort of Alice in Wonderland operation. The fact that the principal witness had identified three unlabeled paragraphs from a papal encyclical as Communist literature broke up the hearings by pointing up how stupid and ridiculous it is to label an author Communist by taking part of something he says out of context.''

In addition to the article in the *American Legion Magazine*, the exchange between Hutchins and Reece had stimulated other reactions. Editors of the *New York Times*, the *Christian Science Monitor*, and other papers backed Hutchins and the Fund. John O'Donnell, Washington correspondent for the New York *Daily News*, expressed the hope that Congress would "reopen its once thwarted investigation into the operations of our multibillion-dollar tax-exempt foundations.''

O'Donnell referred to these statements by Reece: "Citizens with their own money may promote any cause, good or bad, not forbidden by law, but tax-exempt funds should not be used to propagandize for the theories of either Karl Marx or Mark Hanna. . . . The Fund for the Republic is now distributing a one-hour edition of Mr. Edward R. Murrow's teleshow with Dr. Robert Oppenheimer. This would be a perfectly legitimate thing for an individual to do with his own money, but it is not understandable how the tax-exempt foundation gets into it, since it is obvious that Mr. Murrow's program was not designed to be an objective study, but an opportunity for Dr. Oppenheimer to make a defense of his conduct.''

While the attacks on the Fund and on Hutchins continued to increase in intensity and frequency during the first nine months of 1955, progress was made steadily on dozens of projects authorized by the directors. In scope and variety, these projects ranged over all of the controversial areas in American society.

The Commission on Race and Housing, established in May on the basis of a preliminary study financed by the Fund, had work under way in many parts of the country. Earl B. Schwulst, president and chairman of the Bowery Savings Bank of New York, had agreed to serve as chairman of the commission. Other members included some of the most distinguished citizens of the United States: Gordon W. Allport, professor of psychology at Harvard; Elliott V. Bell, chairman of the executive committee of McGraw-Hill, Inc.; Laird Bell, a noted attorney and trustee of the University of Chicago; the Rev. John J. Cavanaugh, director of the University of Notre Dame Foundation; Charles S. Johnson, president of Fisk University; Charles Keller, Jr., president of the Keller Construction Corporation, New Orleans; Philip Klutznick, chairman of the American Community Builders, Park Forest, Illinois; Henry R. Luce, editor-in-chief of Time-Life-Fortune; Stanley Marcus, president of Neiman-Marcus, Dallas; Ward Melville, president of the Melville Shoe Corporation, New York City; and others.

While the commission worked in the bright light of public attention, another major project of the Fund went forward very quietly, although it was being watched by staff members of the House Un-American Activities Committee and others who were professionally employed in chasing or branding suspected "subversives." This was the study of blacklisting in the entertainment industry, which was directed by John Cogley, the former executive editor of the *Commonweal*, a Catholic weekly. Cogley was assisted by a staff of professional journalists and investigators, who interviewed more than 200 people in the broadcasting and film industries.

The Fund had made a grant of $150,000 to the American Friends Service Committee for a two-year program of support for court cases tending to strengthen rights to freedom of conscience. This freedom was defined as including rights to conscientious objection to military service, to refuse loyalty oaths, to reject demands to inform on the activities of one's friends; and to public or private employment without discrimination based on conscientious beliefs that did not conflict with job performance. The Friends Committee used parts of this grant to aid two groups who made headlines—a group of conscientious objectors in New York City who would not participate in an air raid drill, and people who had lost their jobs in the state of Illinois because they would not sign loyalty oaths.

With money from the Fund, Stanford University law school undertook to analyze testimony of the principal government witnesses in cases involving alleged communists. This project was criticized immediately by Fulton Lewis, Jr., and other commentators on the ground that it undermined the credibility of the government witnesses.

Five researchers at the Pennsylvania law school collected and examined all relevant statutes, regulations, and cases relating to the censorship practices of the United States Post Office. The Fund had provided support for this study after evidence had been presented that Post Office officials were barring Russian publications requested by scholars, were burning pacifist literature received from England, and were interfering with the right of privacy and freedom of expression by "mail covers" and by devising ways of reading private mail without opening letters.

Other projects financed by the Fund included a report by Ernesto Galarza of San José, California, on the civil and legal problems encountered by Mexican contract workers in the Southwest; a study by Benjamin Aaron of the Institute of Industrial Relations, University of California, of the impact of loyalty-security programs on unions; and the Rowland Watts report on the serious injustices in the army's military personnel security program.

Watts, a Baltimore attorney, produced a two-volume study entitled *The Draftee and Internal Security*, which revealed that the army had denied hearing to many men; had not given valid hearings to any of the men charged with "derogatory information"; had imprisoned men without trials; had inflicted punishment without convictions of crimes; had deprived men of their property rights; and had subjected them to attainder, causing them to lose their reputations and their dignity as citizens. Watts demanded a new system in which the army could make discharges only on the basis of behavior while soldiers were on active duty and would guarantee soldiers accused of being "security risks" or "almost subversive" the same rights to a full hearing granted to a soldier facing any other charge under the Uniform Code of Military Justice.

The Watts report was endorsed by the American Veterans Committee and received wide coverage in the press. To the right-wingers in Congress and the media, the Watts study and recommendations demonstrated a bias they found in other Fund studies—a bias in favor of protecting the rights of citizens who were "leftists" or associated with "leftists" and others whose loyalty seemed obviously doubtful.

When Adam Yarmolinsky's *Case Studies in Personnel Security*—on the handling of 50 federal security cases, sampled from a collection of more than 200—was published by the Bureau of National Affairs, Reece and others felt that this was another indication of what the Fund wanted to accomplish in discrediting the government's loyalty-security system. The cases edited by Yarmolinsky, a former law clerk of Supreme Court Justice Stanley Reed, disclosed that some of the basic concepts of American justice had been disregarded by government investigators and loyalty boards.

The Philadelphia *Bulletin* commented on the Yarmolinsky documents: "In security cases it is up to the accused to prove his innocence, not for accusers to prove their case. This may be necessary in rooting out the subversives who, of course, have no right to a government job, but it runs against the grain for Americans to be treated in this fashion. . . ." The *Bulletin* acknowledged the fact that Yarmolinsky and others who aided him in the study had proceeded carefully. Then the *Bulletin* said: "Americans have before them a situation they have never faced before—a tightly organized Communist conspiracy, supported by a powerful foreign government, to overthrow our institutions. The problem is to turn back this threat without abandoning the principles which gave this nation birth. The report indicates that a solution is being sought in compiling facts and not in a spirit of hysteria."

To the Brooklyn *Tablet*, a right-wing Catholic newspaper, the Yarmolinsky study was "detrimental to the conduct of loyalty investigations." In an editorial headed "Protecting the Communists," the *Tablet* asserted that the report had to be slanted because it was "financed by the Fund for the Republic, $15,000,000 spawn of the Ford Foundation."

"The Fund has already established the reputation of fostering, with dollars, movements that will impede or destroy efforts to expose agents of the Communist conspiracy in the United States," the editors said.

While the *Bulletin*, the *Tablet*, and other publications expressed deep concern about the "Communist conspiracy," most Americans did not seem to be alarmed. *Look* magazine published two articles by Samuel Stouffer, of Harvard, in March 1955 that disclosed the findings of what Stouffer called "one of the most searching public-opinion surveys ever conducted in the United States." According to Stouffer and his staff, only 1 percent of the American people were worried about communism or civil liberties.

Stouffer wrote: "Under a $125,000 grant from the Fund for the Republic, the study was planned by Frank Stanton, president of the Columbia Broadcasting System; Logan Wilson, president of the University of Texas; Roscoe Drummond, columnist for the New York *Herald Tribune*; Porter Chandler, attorney; Prof. Paul Lazarsfeld of Columbia University, and Prof. Alexander Leighton, Cornell University. I was privileged to serve as chairman. The interpretations here are entirely my own." Stouffer declared that the survey made it plain that "the internal Communist threat" was not felt by Americans as "a personal threat." The average American was not a person with "the jitters about Reds, or trembling lest he find a Communist under the bed."

Fortune magazine, in an article analyzing the Stouffer findings in its May 1955 issue, commented on data made available to the magazine on the attitudes of businessmen, showing that businessmen were more willing to keep "admitted Communists in certain jobs" than other groups in the general population. The survey disclosed that 64 percent of college-educated businessmen would keep a clerk employed in a store, even after the clerk had admitted being a communist. Only 42 percent of other college-educated Americans would permit the clerk to retain a job; among citizens with less than a college education, 21 percent would allow the person to keep working in the store. *Fortune* said: "Among Americans, businessmen are an outstanding group in the degree to which they will tolerate individuals who do not conform to dominant community opinion. . . . Tolerant does not mean approving . . . There is a clear distinction between endorsing a *political opinion* and, despite one's dissent from it, endorsing whatever *rights* the Constitution and the laws extend to the holder thereof. In short, tolerance is defined here as a recognition that the Communist danger should not be fought in such a manner as to mutilate the rights of all nonconformists and thus mutilate the U.S. Constitution itself.''

Representative Reece, the House Un-American Activities Committee, the Senate Internal Security Subcommittee, leaders of the American Legion, and others who denounced the Fund could not seem to make the distinction between protecting the constitutional rights of communists (as well as other nonconformists in American society) and approving of communism. Reece and his colleagues felt threatened by the Fund, because the Fund-financed reports seemed to be taking away the public support on which they depended for appropriations to sustain their investigations of ''the Communist conspiracy.''

A grant of $5000 by the Fund to the Plymouth Monthly Meeting in Plymouth Meeting, Pennsylvania, for the meeting's ''effective defense of democratic principles,'' set off a surge of rage in Reece and several senators. The Fund award had been given to the meeting because the Quakers had refused to dismiss Mary Knowles, a librarian, despite accusations against her. She had not taken a state of Pennsylvania loyalty oath, and she had invoked the protection of the Fifth Amendment when she had been questioned by a U.S. Senate committee in 1953 about ''an alleged Communist connection.'' The Library Committee of the Quaker Meeting had made a careful and thorough study of her background before employing her, and had concluded that she was a good librarian and a loyal American.

On July 6, 1955, a director of the Fund—Eleanor B. Stevenson—presented the $5000 award to the meeting, saying: ''I know that many millions of thoughtful Americans are deeply grateful that the Plymouth Monthly Meeting realizes that to deprive Mrs. Knowles of her rights would not only be undemocratic and un-American but also ungodly. In this instance the people of Plymouth Monthly Meeting are putting into practice what the people of our country believe to be the American way of life.''

Two weeks later Reece flayed the Fund in a speech in the House of Representatives. He hoped that the award to Mrs. Knowles would be regarded with indignation by many members of Congress.

Eight days after Reece's speech, Mrs. Knowles was subpoenaed to appear at an executive session of the Senate Internal Security Subcommittee. No reason was given to her or to her lawyer, Henry W. Sawyer III, of Philadelphia, who accompanied her to Washington. Senator James O. Eastland, of Mississippi, asked her a number of questions about her past associations. Sawyer told the press later: ''She was pretty candid in her replies. . . . I think Mrs. Knowles' statements at the executive hearing should set the question of her loyalty to her country completely at rest.'' Shortly afterward, a public session at which she had been scheduled to appear was canceled.

Undeterred by the maneuvers of Reece, Senator Eastland, and other critics of the Fund, Hutchins submitted proposals to the board in September 1955 calling for expenditures totaling $1,412,200. Most of the grants he recommended were in the area of segregation and minority rights—$700,000 all together, including $150,000 for the Southern Regional Council, $200,000 for a reporting service on legal problems of school desegregation, $100,000 for programs to assist American Indians, $135,000 for the Commission on Race and Housing, $50,000 for the Alianza HispanoAmericana, $40,000 for various church groups struggling to promote integration, and $25,000 for aid to Georgia teachers dismissed by school boards because of membership in the NAACP or for similar reasons.

But the most controversial recommendation offered by Hutchins in a series of suggestions dated September 1, 1955, was a proposal for a study of the American Legion and civil liberties to be conducted by Eric Goldman, professor of history at Princeton University and author of *Rendezvous with Destiny*, a history of modern American reforms, which had been awarded the Bancroft prize. Goldman was apparently willing to do a book on how the Legion began and how much of its "energies were shifted into a surveillance over thought, and what the exact nature and importance of the surveillance have been."

Fulton Lewis, Jr., learned of the proposal for a critical study of the legion and devoted several of his radio broadcasts to assailing the Fund for considering the idea. In response to these broadcasts and angry statements by other commentators, the Illinois state convention of the legion unanimously approved a resolution blistering Hutchins and the Fund, and asked for new congressional investigations of all foundations, which "have diverted sums of tax-exempt money to the propagandizing of alien philosophies, and to engage in left-wing political activities."

The national commander of the legion, Seaborn P. Collins, joined in the attack with a press release on September 11, declaring that he hoped "American Legion elements at the state and local levels will have no truck with Fund for the Republic enterprises."

Walter Winchell, who had one of the largest radio audiences in the world at that time, demanded: "Why in the world with hundreds of organizations on the U.S. government's list of subversive outfits—there's a lot more which should be—does this Fund for the Republic single out the American Legion for appraisal, for study, for even an inquiry? There is talk too that they plan to probe the FBI. . . .

"After a woman employed by a library took refuge behind the well-known Fifth Amendment before a Congressional committee, why did the Fund for the Republic give $5,000 of the money given to them by the Ford Foundation to the very same library which continues to employ her despite the great public protest? Ironically, ladies and gentlemen, there would be no Fifth Amendment to plead if the men of the American Legion hadn't been ready to bleed."

Hutchins sent a telegram to the national adjutant of the legion, Henry H. Dudley, describing Collins' statements as "misleading and libelous" and offering to send copies of the Fund's recently issued annual report to the commanders of the 17,000 legion posts in the nation. The Fund released the text of the Hutchins telegram.

Dudley telegraphed a reply, saying that the legion would be happy to distribute copies of the Fund's report but wanted to include a statement giving the legion's interpretation of what the Fund had done. The directors of the Fund then issued a public statement, asserting that Collins was misinformed about the purposes and program of the Fund. The directors reaffirmed the aims of the Fund, cited in a press release dated February 26, 1953, depicting the Fund as "an independent corporation established by the Ford Foundation . . . 'to support activities directed toward the elimination of restrictions on freedom of thought, inquiry, and expression in the United States, and the development of policies and procedures best adapted to protect these rights.' "

With the approval of the directors, the Fund's officers finally mailed copies of the annual report, which had been issued in August 1955, to the commanders of the 9000 largest legion posts with copies of the directors' statement. However, the report did not pacify some of the legion officers, because it contained a blunt description of the Fund's efforts that ran counter to the views of many legion members.

David Lawrence, in a column printed in dozens of newspapers on August 23, 1955, castigated the Fund: "Judging from its annual report just issued, the Fund for the Republic is primarily interested in investigating the investigators—the persons and institutions who recognize that a Communist conspiracy has existed in the United States and still exists."

George Sokolsky, a Hearst columnist with many readers, joined the attack on the Fund, concentrating some of his fire on W. H. Ferry: "Dr. Hutchins has long been one of those boy wonders who rushed across the American sky like meteors and do their damage most by the heat they engender, not by the light they cast. It is 'Ping' Ferry, the administrative vice president of the Ford Foundation's Fund for the Republic whom I want to discuss." Speaking on the ABC national radio network, Sokolsky recounted the well-known fact that Ferry had been the director of public relations for the CIO Political Action Committee in 1944, and then smeared Ferry: "In a book narrating the story of the CIO-PAC, Joseph Gaer included hundreds of photographs which tell a striking story of the Communist infiltration of the PAC. On page 280 of the book, which is entitled *The First Round*, Ping Ferry is shown at his desk at PAC headquarters."

Sokolsky tied Ferry in with the Stouffer survey, which had shown that few Americans were concerned about "the Communist menace" in the United States: "According to Professor Stouffer's book a Communist is really a non-conformist which creates a kind of sympathy for him. A Communist is not to be regarded as a spy, as an agent for a foreign country, as one who is actively engaged in the overthrow of government by force and violence. He is only a non-conformist who intellectually and spiritually does not accept the current patterns of American life.''

J. Edgar Hoover growled at the Fund in a speech to the annual meeting of the International Association of Chiefs of Police, at their gathering in Philadelphia on October 3, 1955: "It is through the 'pseudo liberals' that the Communists do some of their most destructive work. These fictitious liberals are the individuals who through insidiously slanted and sly propagandistic writings and reports oppose urgently needed internal security measures; conduct a one-sided campaign to discredit Government witnesses; present the menace of Communism as a myth of hysteria; urge that we tolerate the subversive acts of Communists because Communists are only 'non-conformists'; contend that the Communist Party is a 'political' movement and that it is improper to consider it a criminal conspiracy linked to a world conspiracy to overthrow our Government by force and violence.'' Hoover and others had been angered by Hutchins' statement in the Fund's 1955 annual report that "a political party in this country has been identified with the 'enemy.' " Legally, he was right: the Communist party had not been outlawed. In the eyes of Hoover, Congressman Reece, George Sokolsky, and all those who saw the communists as engaged in "a criminal conspiracy," Hutchins had given the communists standing as a legitimate political party.

In another address to the police chiefs, William F. Tomkins, the assistant attorney general, denounced Richard Rovere's article "The Kept Witnesses," which had been financed by the Fund. Tomkins said that the author "had the temerity to state that former Communists are hired by the Department of Justice to testify 'according to the wishes of its lawyers.' . . . Neither this author nor anyone else can cite any instance where the Department of Justice has 'purchased testimony.' " Tomkins acknowledged, however, that the government had used former communists as paid "confidential informants.''

During this uproar, several radio broadcasters tried to explain to their listeners what the Fund was striving to do. Among them were Edward P. Morgan on an ABC network, Chet Huntley on a regional NBC network, and Cecil Brown on the Mutual Broadcasting System. Brown sent words of encouragement to Hutchins: "As president of the University of Chicago, Dr. Hutchins tried to improve our higher education. That guaranteed him a career of controversy. And Dr. Hutchins, as head of the Fund for the Republic, the job he now holds, has become the sponsor of studies of just how American democracy is working—how secure are civil rights. That sort of concern is bound to arouse violent attack.''

Nathan Pusey, president of Harvard University, gave a salute to the Fund at the John Marshall Bicentennial Dinner sponsored by the Harvard law school. Several directors of the Fund, including Dean Erwin Griswold of the law school, heard Dr. Pusey deplore "an incredibly misguided attack on the Fund for the Republic and its much maligned president."

The Washington *Post* and *Times Herald*, expressing agreement with Dr. Pusey, carried an editorial strongly supporting the Fund: "The Fund for the Republic is explicitly devoted to the support of 'activities directed toward the elimination of restrictions on freedom of thought, inquiry and expression in the United States.' This means, of course, that it must devote itself, as it has indeed begun to do in recent months with some vigor, to a critical examination of such governmental activities as the security program and congressional investigations which undeniably impinge on traditional American liberties. It is indispensable to the American system that there be agencies outside the government—and wholly independent of government control—which are eternally vigilant against such threats to individual freedom."

Early in October 1955 the trustees of the Ford Foundation sent a confidential statement to the directors of the Fund, declaring unequivocally: "The Board of the Fund for the Republic has the authority and responsibility without reference to the Ford Foundation to undertake such projects and to take such positions as that Board in its best judgment may determine in carrying out the purposes of the grant. . . . The overall program of the Fund as it has thus far evolved appears to be within the general terms and purposes of the Ford Foundation's grant."

Yet the fusillade against the Fund continued. Hamilton Fish, a former member of Congress, wrote to Henry Ford II asking whether Ford really endorsed the findings of the Fund when "it tries to persuade the American people that Communism is harmless and that there's no Communist menace to America." Fish warned: "This deception is precisely what all Communists here and abroad are trying to put over on the American people." Earl Godwin, a radio commentator, told his listeners: "How on earth anyone in his right mind can escape censure, or hope to escape censure, when he claims that Communism is merely a political faith, is beyond me when you see the evidences of the sabotage and spy work that has opened American, Canadian, and British confidential government files and defense secrets to Russia."

The barrages were heavier when the press learned that Earl Browder, a former leader of the Communist party in the United States, was a paid consultant on the Fund's study of communism, and that Amos Landman, an ex-reporter who invoked the protection of the Fifth Amendment when he was asked whether he had been a communist, had been hired by the Fund for its publicity staff. The New York *Journal-American* and other Hearst papers assailed the appointment of Browder and the hiring of Landman.

The *Journal-American* criticized Ferry in an editorial: "W. H. Ferry, Fund vice president, made one of the most revealing statements of anti-anti-

Communist logic we have read: 'This fact (of taking the Fifth Amendment on questions of Communism) did not appear to officers (of the Fund) sufficient reason to bar him from temporary employment.' He said Landman is working on a per diem basis. It does not matter whether he is working on a daily, weekly, monthly or yearly basis. What does matter is that the Fund hired a man who crawled behind the Fifth on a matter of vital interest to this country."

Meanwhile, there were signs of internal dissension on the Fund's board. Arthur H. Dean, a Wall Street attorney who had been elected as a director on May 19, 1955, sent a letter to Chairman Hoffman resigning from the board. Erwin Griswold telephoned Hutchins and said he thought that Bethuel Webster could persuade Dean to reconsider the resignation. Griswold informed Hutchins that other members of the board were urging Dean not to resign, and he suggested that a board meeting might be called as soon as possible. Hutchins said he had already asked the executive committee to meet on October 6 and would invite other members of the board to attend that session.

.Hutchins wrote immediately to Dean, saying that his views about the employment of a person pleading the protection of the Fifth Amendment raised important questions of principle and policy, and that he would take them up with the executive committee. He urged Dean to attend the committee meeting.

Griswold expressed the feeling that it would be unfortunate to have any member of the Fund's board resign while the Fund was undergoing such a series of attacks. Hutchins discussed that matter with Elmo Roper and William Joyce. Both directors felt that if Dean's personal views were incompatible with those of the Fund, he should be asked to change his views and he should be allowed to resign if he wished to do so. Dean refused to withdraw his resignation.

In his letter to Hoffman, sent from his office at 48 Wall Street in New York City, Dean said: "For some time I have taken the position with the Trustees of Cornell University that Communists, fellow travelers or Communist sympathizers, whose thoughts are in effect directed by a foreign government and who are not free to make their own scholarly determination on the basis of all of the facts, have no place on the Cornell faculty. . . . I have further taken the position (as a trustee of Cornell) that we have no place on our faculty or staff for a person who pleads the Fifth Amendment. I do not take the position that the plea results in an inference of guilt or that you can infer the worst, but simply that society is entitled to investigate Communism and subversion, and that the individual citizen cannot himself determine whether or not the questions are relevant. I do not question the clear constitutional right of any individual to plead the Fifth Amendment, but I also think that others have the right to draw certain inferences in connection with that plea, the circumstances under which it is made, and the individuals' continued fitness for their jobs.

"The fact that the Fund for the Republic has made a grant to the Plymouth Meeting for their courage in retaining Mrs. Knowles after she had pleaded the Fifth Amendment and after she had persisted in refusing to answer certain questions at her second appearance has involved me in considerable difficulty because some of the members of the faculty believe that I have taken an inconsistent stand although this award was made after my election but before I attended my first meeting. I don't think I have any right to ask the Fund to review its prior action but under the circumstances I do not see how I can remain on the Board of Directors without seriously compromising the positions I have previously taken and in which I still believe. . . ."

It was clear that Dean placed the requirements of national security—as the government defined those requirements—above the right of employment for any person who sought the protection of the Bill of Rights against the investigatory procedures of congressional committees or other agencies. His position was not consistent with the aims of the Fund, as expressed by Erwin Griswold and other directors in their release to the press on February 26, 1953: "We regard the sphere of operation of the Fund as including the entire field of freedom and civil rights in the United States and take as our basic charter the Declaration of Independence and the Constitution. . . . *We propose to help restore respectability to individual freedom!*" (italics added).

When information about Dean's resignation reached the press, he did not speak frankly about his reasons for resigning. Through a spokesman he told reporters "he didn't have time to read all the documents" circulated by the Fund. The new national commander of the American Legion, J. Addington Wagner, who had renewed the legion's quarrel with the Fund, promptly said: "Evidently Mr. Dean recognized, as did the American Legion several months ago, that the Fund for the Republic is becoming increasingly identified with the sponsorship of projects contrary to the best interests of America."

At the October 6 session of the executive committee, several directors voiced their alarm at the rising fury of the storm over the Fund. Hutchins was asked to prepare an extensive memorandum, giving his views on "the present position of the Fund and of certain of its actions." He consulted Hoffman in the preparation of this document.

In the memorandum he drafted on October 19, 1955, Hutchins identified the Fund with the cause of justice and asserted that it was bound to incur the hosility of powerful persons or groups "profiting by injustice." He forcefully defended every project the Fund had launched, every major action taken with the approval of the board and the general counsel.

"We are trying to help save the Republic," Hutchins said. "We can expect few cheers from those we are saving it from. . . .

"If a large part of our task, as our chairman has said, is to make the Bill of Rights a living document today, we cannot hope to avoid hostility in high places. Recognition of this fact caused prolonged hesitation in the Ford Foundation about the establishment of the Fund and led me to warn the original members of this board when I invited them to join that they were sure to get into trouble. The trouble we have got into is exactly what we expected three years ago. We could have named then the columnists, commentators, politicians, and organizations who would attack the Fund if it had a program that meant anything."

Hutchins acknowledged that he did believe in using discretion. He was well aware of the fact that the Fund was a tax-exempt foundation and that Internal Revenue agents had already begun to audit the Fund's books. The enemies of the Fund sought to have its certificate from the Treasury Department revoked, contending that it engaged in "propaganda" and had gone beyond the boundaries of its charter.

"I do not believe that the Fund should go out of its way to find trouble or that it should get into trouble through negligence," Hutchins assured the board. "I know that there is a difference between bravery and recklessness, and that the Fund must be careful as well as brave."

He indicated his willingness to work with Bethuel Webster, the general counsel, who had the backing of Dean Griswold: "I believe that the way to keep the tax exemption of the Fund is to follow the opinion of Counsel. We cannot operate in this field if we have to ask ourselves before we act who will be sufficiently offended and sufficiently powerful to get the exemption taken away without color of law or justice. We must base our policies on the assumption that if what we do is clearly within the law we can successfully resist attempts to revoke the exemption."

Hutchins hoped that this memorandum, which was slightly revised before it was mailed to the board on November 3, would restore unity among the directors and renew their confidence in his administration.

The response was generally favorable. But a new tempest arose on November 7, when Hutchins underwent what a *New York Times* man described as "a two-hour cross-examination" by twenty journalists. He maintained his contention that membership in the Communist party or invoking the protection of the Fifth Amendment did not automatically make a person unemployable. He took essentially the same position as the one held by two-thirds of the businessmen in the Stouffer survey, who said that they would continue to employ a clerk who had admitted being a communist.

Under questioning, Hutchins was candid: "I wouldn't hesitate to hire a Communist for a job he was qualified to do provided I was in a position to see he did it." He rebuffed all criticisms of Fund projects: "If your object is to promote justice, you're likely to be attacked, because if people weren't profiting by injustice it wouldn't exist.''

His remarks made headlines in many places. Two days after his press conference, Adam Yarmolinsky learned that a review of the Fund's tax exemption had been ordered by Internal Revenue officials. On November 17, when the directors of the Fund gathered for their third annual meeting, the National Commander of the American Legion declared in a speech in Indianapolis: ''The American Legion formally charges that by its action under its current direction, the Fund for the Republic renders comfort to the enemies of America.''

The Fund board elected three new directors: Oscar Hammerstein II, composer of the lyrics for *South Pacific, Oklahoma!*, and many other outstanding theater productions; J. Howard Marshall, of Houston, an executive of the Signal Oil & Gas Company; and Roger Lapham, a corporation officer and the former mayor of San Francisco. Hutchins was reelected president without open opposition, although Erwin Griswold abstained from voting for president and did cast a ballot against the reelection of Vice President Ferry, who had originally hired Amos Landman and who had irritated several of the directors by his blunt style of dealing with people.

Hutchins had a difficult time at this meeting. His request for a grant to a scholar who had invoked the Fifth Amendment under questioning by the House Un-American Activities Committee was rejected. The board approved a few grants—$25,000 to the Committee on Internal Security of the Administrative Law Section of the Bar Association of the District of Columbia; $25,000 to Kenyon College, for a conference on the nature of liberty; $15,000 more for the Fund's television awards, named the Robert E. Sherwood awards in honor of the deceased playwright; $20,000 to the Association of the Bar of the City of New York Fund, Inc., to assist a study of methods of representing criminal defendants—but an argument occurred over the request for $115,000 for fellowships and grants-in-aid, which had been handled entirely by the officers. The board finally approved the request, despite the votes against it by Griswold and Joyce.

Restrictions were placed by the board on the powers that had been exercised by Hutchins and the other officers. Each publication to be distributed by the Fund had first to be cleared by counsel (Bethuel Webster) and approved by the board, both as to subject matter and as to recipients. The board also decided that each award to be given by the Fund had to receive unanimous approval at two consecutive meetings by the directors attending those meetings.

Hutchins had emphasized the importance of the opinions given by the Fund's counsel. At the November 17 meeting, it became evident that Webster's veto power over proposed actions by the officers was strongly supported by a number of the directors.

In letters and conversations, friends of the directors had indicated to them that the board had permitted the Fund to become almost completely the "Hutchins Fund." The steps taken in November were designed to reclaim the dominant position of the board.

Within a month, however, Griswold became convinced that these steps would not be sufficient to save the Fund from a catastrophe. He thought that Robert Hutchins—the man he had recommended to the board in the spring of 1954—would have to leave the presidency of the Fund. Griswold believed that the Fund—and the cause of civil liberties—had been severely damaged by Hutchins' head-on confrontations with the Fund's critics.

5

Henry Ford II turns against the Fund, and Hutchins is asked to resign

THERE WERE MORE THAN 18,000 tax-exempt foundations in the United States in 1955, with assets estimated at $10 billion to $15 billion. Only 107 of them issued reports to the public. The others conducted their affairs in secrecy and attracted little attention from reporters, congressmen, or other investigators. Under Hutchins' leadership, the Fund for the Republic—with the Ford Foundation, its parent body—was the subject of more newspaper and magazine articles, more broadcasts, more discussions and debates than all the others combined.

Thousands of people wrote to Henry Ford II about the operations of the Fund. Ford dealers in the southern states—particularly in Alabama and Mississippi—voiced fears of a boycott against Ford products, although Ford cars and trucks sold well in 1955. Listeners to Fulton Lewis, Jr., and other broadcasters wanted answers to the questions Lewis and Sokolsky and others raised about the patriotism of the Fund's directors and officers: "Was the Fund really coddling communists? Was the Fund hampering the efforts of the FBI to combat spies and saboteurs? Was the Fund spreading pro-communist propaganda?"

Roy M. Cohn, a former assistant to Senator Joseph McCarthy, lashed out at Ford in a speech at a dinner in Yonkers, accusing Ford of keeping "silence" on the Fund, which had "given unrivalled assistance to the cause of Communism in this country." William F. Buckley, Jr., gave a whole page of his *National Review* to the text of a letter he had sent to Ford: "What is your own judgment on those activities of the Fund for the Republic that are at public issue? Do you believe that the present management of the Fund is faithfully and effectively carrying out the intentions of the Foundation in establishing the Fund? . . . A statement from you on these matters is of crucial public importance."

Ford wrote to Paul Hoffman on October 27, indicating that he had been affected by "a great many letters . . . expressing disapproval of the Fund." He informed Hoffman: "Many of them have come from responsible people who seem to be sincere and constructive in their criticism." Hoffman asked Ford to refrain from any public statements until he could send a reply on behalf of the board.

On November 17 the directors approved the dispatch of a letter to Ford assuring him that the board was "engaged in a continuous audit, appraisal, and re-appraisal of the program and of the activities of the staff, to the end that mistakes may be avoided and that such changes as experience and judgment seem to require may be made." Hoffman hoped that the letter would calm Ford down, and that Ford would recognize the fact that some of the country's most influential newspapers—including the Boston *Herald*, the Atlanta *Constitution*, the Chicago *Sun-Times*, the Louisville *Courier-Journal*, the St. Louis *Post-Dispatch*, the *New York Times*, the San Francisco *Chronicle*, and the *Christian Science Monitor*—had lauded the Fund's work.

Three days later Hutchins appeared on a "Meet the Press" program carried by television and radio stations across the nation. Four hostile reporters—Frederick Woltman, of the New York *World-Telegram*; James McConaughy, Jr., of *Time*; May Craig, of the Portland (Maine) *Press Herald*; and Lawrence Spivak, initiator of the program—gave Hutchins only a brief time to describe the Fund's extensive projects and then cross-examined him on whether he would hire a communist and what he thought of the "communist conspiracy." Hutchins stood by the principles he had expressed in his previous statements.

At one point, Woltman asked, "Would you also hire a Nazi or a Fascist, or a Ku Klux Klanner?"

"This question is a real flying saucer," Hutchins answered. "So was the other one."

Woltman said, "Well, you didn't answer it."

Hutchins came back with, "I beg your pardon, I did."

"You would also hire a Nazi?" Woltman said.

Hutchins snapped, "No, I didn't say I would."

Under the hammering from the reporters, Hutchins did not display his usual brilliance. He had been advised to be evasive by public relations counselors who had talked with him before the program. He was obviously miserable during the entire broadcast.

Waves of antagonistic mail hit Henry Ford and directors of the Fund after Hutchins' appearance on that program. The *New York Times* disclosed on November 24 that inquiries into the Fund were scheduled by Representative Francis E. Walter of the House Committee on Un-American Activities and by the Senate Internal Security Subcommittee. Walter said he would hold public hearings early in 1956.

The heaviest blow to the Fund came on December 6, when Fulton Lewis read to his radio audience excerpts from a critical letter sent by Ford in reply to a complaint from the chairman of the Anti-Subversive Committee of an American Legion post. Ford's letter appeared in the New York *Herald Tribune* and many other papers. He said, in part: "Despite the fact that I have no legal right to intervene in the affairs of the Fund for the Republic, I have exercised my right as a private citizen to question the manner in which the Fund has attempted to achieve its stated objectives. Some of its actions, I feel, have been dubious in character and inevitably have led to charges of poor judgment."

Griswold, whose eloquence had helped to persuade Ford to support a $15 million grant to the Fund, met privately with Ford and was told that the "poor judgment" had been shown by Hutchins and Ferry. Griswold was encouraged by Ford to lead a movement within the board of directors to remove Hutchins, with the understanding that Ferry would have to go, too.

On December 19 Griswold wrote to Chairman Hoffman and sent a copy to every director of the Fund. Declaring that it was necessary to ask Hutchins "to step aside," Griswold said: "It has seemed to me that there are two elements in Mr. Hutchins' work for the Fund which have kept him from serving it effectively. I will try to summarize these briefly:

"1. His approach to the problems of civil liberties is too absolute. In his thinking and in his actions, he pushes things to their extremes. He feels that he must fight on all the frontiers. He has courage and boldness, which are fine qualities. But they are not, in my view, sufficiently tempered by careful judgment and sound discretion. He does not clearly enough—by my lights—see the problem as one of adjusting the competing claims of liberty and freedom on the one hand with those of security on the other. If he does see it this way, he does not adequately express himself in these terms.

"2. In the handling of these problems, his approach is too often not what I would regard as educational. He does not primarily seek to explain, to lead, to guide, to speak softly and persuasively, to inculcate wisdom and understanding. On the contrary, his approach tends to be combative, belligerent, provocative, dramatic. Rather than leading to better understanding, this approach evokes strong reactions, and often leads to increased opposition, and to misunderstanding. This, I think, is poor human relations. In my judgment the Fund for the Republic and the great cause to which it is dedicated are not well served by actions which alienate those who are genuinely seeking light on these important and difficult problems. . . .

"From the beginning it has been clear to me, and was generally understood by the Board, I thought, that the one unwise, fatal course of action for the Fund to take would be to create the impression that it underestimated the threat of communism to our civil liberties, that it was, in popular terms, 'soft on communism.' Yet it is quite clear, I think, that under Mr. Hutchins' leadership there is now misunderstanding about this among thoughtful people. For this I believe that Mr. Hutchins is largely responsible, both by his actions and by his failure to act as an effective spokesman for the Fund and its work. In my judgment, the actions which caused this misunderstanding were unnecessary, and the consequence was foreseeable. It is also my judgment that there is no reasonable chance that the impressions now created can be effectively rectified while Mr. Hutchins remains president of the Fund.''

Dean Griswold acknowledged the fact that "the Fund for the Republic has done many fine things under Mr. Hutchins' leadership," but he felt that "the executive management of the Fund has lost my confidence." He said he had been forced to spend "a great deal of time in trying to explain some of the Fund's activities, and on some points it has been far from easy.''

"I recognize, of course, that the Board must share responsibility for some of the errors that have been made," Griswold admitted. "Moreover, I was a member of the committee of the Board which recommended Mr. Hutchins for the presidency. We knew then that though we were getting great potentiality, we were also taking an appreciable risk. Now that that risk has turned out badly, as I see it, I feel an especial obligation to evaluate the situation and to recognize the facts as they have actually developed.''

Griswold was aware of the likelihood that "Mr. Hutchins' withdrawal at this time would doubtless be acclaimed by those opposed to a proper recognition of civil liberties." He said: "I recognize this, and I regret it exceedingly. Nevertheless, this is no reason for failing to recognize the facts." He went on: "It may be suggested that this is a novel field, and that Mr. Hutchins has now learned his lesson. But experience does not indicate that that will be the case. Despite the obvious objections to Mr. Hutchins' retirement now, the fact remains that I no longer have confidence in his leadership nor in the wisdom of his public actions and statements.''

James D. Zellerbach, in a letter to Chairman Hoffman (with copies to all board members), expressed full agreement with Griswold and assumed that Ferry would also be asked to resign. Zellerbach added: "Dean Griswold is not specific as to the time of retirement of Messrs. Hutchins and Ferry. My recommendation is that this retirement be made effective at the next meeting of the board on January 6 and 7. I feel it extremely important that this change be made prior to Congress convening and the commencement of the investigation or investigations of the Fund, which I am advised are now under active consideration." Zellerbach doubted whether he could attend the January meeting, but called for "a new management . . . which can have not only the confidence of all members of the board but of the public as well.''

William Joyce, who had been a member of the committee which had recommended the election of Hutchins as president, indicated in a letter to Griswold that the directors had "failed to provide our officers with the views of the Board in order that they might operate accordingly." He thought that the directors had to have a long meeting to "develop policies and guidelines to govern future activities."

Joyce raised the question of whether the officers or board members should "speak for themselves" in public statements on the Fund's policies or whether they should "simply express the position of the Fund as determined by the unanimous Board action." Joyce proposed restrictions on the officers: "As I understand it, in the November press conference held by Hutchins in New York, he repeatedly stated that he was expressing his own views. If it should be the will of the Board that the officers of the Fund express only the views of the Board—and the policies of the Fund as established by the Board—and refrain from discussing personal views, a great deal of confusion and misunderstanding conceivably might be eliminated in the future."

It was inconceivable to J. R. Parten, Elmo Roper, Eleanor B. Stevenson, and other board members that Hutchins and the other officers of the Fund would give up their right to speak freely on the fundamental questions with which the Fund was concerned. O'Brian wrote to Paul Hoffman, asking where the Chairman stood on the problems cited by Griswold. Hoffman replied: "We must take a long, hard look at our program and remedy whatever we find wrong." Hoffman was impressed, however, by the memorandum Hutchins had shown to him, answering all the points made by the Fund's critics.

Hoffman was personally loyal to Hutchins as a friend. But he was deeply disturbed, as he revealed in a reply to a letter from Mrs. Roger Lapham, wife of one of the new directors: "I share your disappointment that Mr. Hutchins did not give an unqualified 'no' to the question of whether he would employ a communist. If I had been asked that question, I would have so answered and would have explained that I believe that anyone who is a communist today is either a conspirator or a fool. I would have made this reply despite the fact that there are probably some intelligent people who are intellectually committed to communism and who conceivably might be employable. Whether this is what Mr. Hutchins had in mind, I do not know. I do know that he is a *totally* honest person and a purist. There are times that I wish he were a weak-kneed compromiser like myself."

The board met for a lengthy session on January 6 in New York, to decide what to do about Hutchins and Ferry and to discuss a memorandum from Hutchins containing proposals for a reorganization of the Fund. Before the formal meeting began, five of the directors battled over the points made in Griswold's letter to Hoffman. Roper, Parten, and Mrs. Stevenson staunchly defended Hutchins against Griswold and Joyce.

"Griswold and Joyce honestly believed that Hutchins was searching for people to aggravate, that he was using unnecessarily inflammatory methods to defend principles we all believed in," Roper recalled later. "If Parten or Stevenson or I had even wavered at any time in our belief in Hutchins, he would have been gone. We had no intention of wavering. You could say that he came that close to being removed as president."

Roper stood by Hutchins even though Henry Ford II had urged him to leave the Fund's board or to favor the removal of the Fund's president. Mrs. Stevenson did not accept Griswold's contentions that Hutchins had done great harm to the Fund. Parten, an independent citizen whose experiences in the Roosevelt and Truman administrations had made him aware of the dangers to the nation from right-wing extremists, admired the fighting spirit Hutchins had shown.

The three directors had read the supportive editorials in leading papers. One of the most effective statements had appeared in the Denver *Post*, headed "American Legion and American Rights." The *Post* said, in part:

> We have scanned the most recent annual report of the Fund for the Republic to discover any possible grounds for the charges and warnings issued by the American Legion Commander (Seaborn P. Collins).
>
> We do not know all the many men who are named as participating in the activities of the Fund but we know enough of them to give us confidence in the patriotism of the overall leadership.
>
> Chairman of the Fund is Paul G. Hoffman, chairman of the board of the Studebaker Packard Corporation. We know him as a strong supporter of President Eisenhower.
>
> Vice chairmen include Meyer Kestnbaum, president of Hart, Schaffner & Marx; M. Albert Linton, chairman of the board of the Provident Mutual Life Insurance Company; Chester Bowles, wartime director of the OPA and former ambassador to India; Jubal R. Parten, president of the Woodley Petroleum Company.

The *Post* put the record of the Fund in a favorable perspective:

> The annual report shows a large number of worthwhile projects. For example, the first grant made by the Fund went to a special committee of the American Bar Association which launched a study of how congressional investigations could be conducted without invading the rights of individuals.
>
> The special committee came up with recommendations: witnesses before congressional investigators should have the right to be represented by their lawyers, etc., etc. The recommendations were approved by the Bar Association as a whole last year and some have been put in effect by some congressional committees.
>
> Does Commander Collins seriously believe the American Bar Association can be hoodwinked into undermining American security?

The fund has financed the compilation of all official records, including court trials, relating to communism in the United States. Does Commander Collins object to that?

It has made possible a study of the program for testing the loyalty of government employees to determine if justice is being done. That such a study is more than justified has been indicated by Congress itself which recently has set up a special commission for the same purpose.

Racial discrimination, the inequities of immigration procedures, censorship by the post office department—many other matters are being examined under grants of money from the Fund for the Republic.

In general, the whole program looks to the preservation of our traditional rights and liberties.

Perhaps Commander Collins has so little faith in the ability of his country to resist communism that he believes any methods to expose communism are justified, regardless of the violence done by those methods to American freedom of speech, American due process of law, and other American rights.

If that is his view, his attack on those who believe we are entirely capable of resisting communism without sacrificing our fundamental liberties in the process becomes understandable even though we cannot agree with it.

If that is not his view, his attack becomes as unintelligible as it is unreasonable.

Why was Henry Ford unable to see the Fund's program as the editors of the Denver *Post* and other editors were able to see it? Why had he repudiated his own decision to give the directors $15 million and to "turn them loose to do the job"? He had been warned in advance that an onslaught would be brought against the Fund and that its principal enemies would be the Hearst press, the American Legion, Joe McCarthy, Westbrook Pegler, William Buckley, George Sokolsky, and others obsessed with "the communist menace." Why did he turn and strike such a damaging blow at Hutchins, Hoffman, and the other directors of the Fund?

He had clashed frequently with Hutchins and Hoffman during their years with the Ford Foundation. He felt that they wanted to move in too many directions and too rapidly. He thought that they appeared in too many headlines. Yet he had acquiesced in the election of Hoffman as chairman of the Fund and had not offered any objection to the selection of Hutchins as the second president. His conduct was baffling to many people, although Roper and Parten indicated that he had given them reason to believe that he felt overshadowed by the Fund and simply wanted to be rid of it.

Griswold had said: "It is clear that the Fund for the Republic has done many fine things under Mr. Hutchins' leadership.'' But Griswold insisted that Hutchins' abrasive behavior had alienated ''those who are genuinely seeking light on these important and difficult problems.'' He blamed Hutchins for compelling him to seek the president's removal; he had declared in his letter to Paul Hoffman: ''It is one of my chief disappointments with Mr. Hutchins' leadership that he has brought us, I think unnecessarily, to a point where such a choice is necessary.''

The tone of Griswold's statements to Roper and Parten showed that he felt Hutchins had seized too much of the limelight and had obscured the power and authority of the board. As one of the original directors, he made it plain that some of that power belonged to him.

With Paul Hoffman presiding, the board spent the entire day of January 6 discussing the criticisms of Hutchins and Ferry made by Griswold, Joyce, Linton, and other directors and examining the proposals for reorganization Hutchins had offered in his 22-page memorandum. At the end of that day a resolution was adopted, stating that ''it shall be and is the policy of the Fund that no member of the Communist Party will be employed for any purpose; and no former member of the Communist Party, and no person who has pleaded the Fifth Amendment in relevant circumstances, will be employed for any purpose, or receive a grant-in-aid, or be given a fellowship, except with the approval of the Board of Directors.'' Hutchins accepted the resolution, although he indicated that he thought it was inconsistent with the Fund's charter to limit the right of employment of any person who might be qualified for a job.

On the following day, January 7, the board authorized Hutchins to go ahead with his recommendations for a new organizational structure ''on a trial basis.'' Hutchins had declared that he would move his own office from Pasadena to New York; he would shift Ferry from general management of the New York headquarters to specific responsibilities for programs and planning; he would assign Freeman to run the New York office, talk with visitors, and deal with grantees and project supervisors; he would employ a third officer, to take charge of public information; and he would have all the officers report directly to him.

He stressed the importance of being able to maintain a united front against enemies, asserting: ''My experience and observation of organizations that have been attacked lead me to say that the most important aspect of their public relations is the face that those in control present to the world. The contrast between the attitude of the trustees of the University of Chicago in the Broyles investigation and that of the regents of the University of California in the loyalty-fight oath is instructive. Without a moment's hesitation the trustees of Chicago unanimously told the legislature that they would never permit it to influence the policies of the University. Broyles could not crack the solidarity of the University, and the result was that the press and the public got the impression of a strong and dedicated institution being insulted by a midget. The differences among the regents left the University of California defenseless. I know that the Board of Directors is united in its devotion to the principles of the Fund. If this can continue, and if it can be apparent on all occasions, the problem basic to any effective program of public relations is solved.''

Hutchins did not ask the board to unite behind him but to unite in their reaffirmation of the Fund's principles. He had tried hard to explain why his own dedication to these principles had led him to say that he would "hire a Communist." He had said in his long memorandum:

"There are at least three variables in these situations: the nature of the job, the qualifications of the man for it, and the man's relation to the Communist party. These variables are such that it seems stultifying to say that never under any conditions should any Communist be hired for any job.

"The problem is illustrated by the case of the Communist or near-Communist set designer engaged by a subcontractor on *Omnibus*. [A television program sponsored by the Ford Foundation.] His sets could not have possibly been regarded as propaganda. There was no doubt that he was the best qualified man available. The argument that he should not have been employed seems to me absurd.

"*It is also unchristian.* [Italics added] In the absence of a showing that a man is a conspirator or a spy it seems inhuman to deprive him of a chance to earn a living in a position that he is competent to fill and in which he can do no damage.''

The effects of the Christian education Hutchins had received from his father and mother were evident in his position. There were members of the board who agreed with him completely—including Chairman Hoffman—but they did not think the public could be rapidly educated to see why that position was morally right. They wanted to make the Fund invulnerable to the assaults of the communist hunters in Congress, in the American Legion, and in the mass media.

Hutchins knew that he had to follow the employment policy set by the board, but he didn't like it. He felt that the resolution barring any communist from any job showed that the board had been too disturbed by headlines and radio broadcasters. He thought that the board should be as scornful of sensational journalism as he was.

In the eyes of Griswold, Joyce, Linton, and other directors, Hutchins had been deliberately provocative in his meetings with journalists. Some of the directors who supported Hutchins conceded that there was an element of truth in Griswold's contention that Hutchins was eager to "fight on all the frontiers."

After the January 7, 1956, meeting, when he had been finally reelected as president after nearly thirteen hours of argument among the board members, Hutchins was somewhat subdued. But he did not think that his troubles were largely due to his own actions. He knew that he was a focal point for the continuing attacks on the Fund, because he was an unconditional supporter of the Bill of Rights: he had proclaimed in many places that the Bill of Rights extended to communists, crackpots, extremists, unsavory people, irritating people, people with bad ideas or obsessions.

When he talked with me about the possibility of becoming the public information officer for the Fund, Hutchins asked several questions: "Do you think the Fund should change its program with the hope of getting to be more respectable? Do you think we can really reach and educate the people on a wide scale, considering the state of the mass media? Do you believe we can get the Congress to understand what we are actually trying to do?" He sought specific suggestions, and he wanted to know how long it might take to make a national information program effective.

My first meeting with him had been in December 1955, when he had come to the offices of Stephen Fitzgerald & Company at 575 Madison Avenue in New York. He had outlined the Fund's problems frankly and had told Fitzgerald and me what he had planned to recommend to the board. He told us that he expected new assaults when the reports on blacklisting, the testimony of excommunist witnesses, postal censorship, and fear in education were made public.

Hutchins reiterated to Fitzgerald and me what he had said to members of the board: "If we operate in terms of tomorrow's headlines, we'll be permitting the Fund's enemies to manage it. They can write more headlines than we can." Fitzgerald and I agreed with that. We did not think there was any "Madison Avenue magic" that could keep the Fund from being involved in controversies. We did not promise instant results or guarantee popularity to any of our clients.

Fitzgerald was a former reporter for the Baltimore *Sun*, an admirer of the iconoclastic H. L. Mencken, and he had been a Nieman fellow at Harvard. I had been a Nieman fellow, too, after my service with the Kansas City *Star* and the Associated Press. I had kept in touch with Fitzgerald while I had worked in Washington for Truman and for two Senate majority leaders and had seen him frequently when I returned to New York as the American director of the International Press Institute's study of world news. I had joined his company in 1954 and had coordinated a national public information program for one of his clients. Fitzgerald was a calm, thoughtful man of integrity, who never dealt in slogans and was dedicated to freedom of expression.

When Hutchins telephoned me in January 1956 to tell me that he had recommended the use of the Fitzgerald Company as a consulting agency and my election as an officer of the Fund, I was filled with a mixture of joy and trepidation. I was pleased to be associated with Hutchins and the directors of the Fund, because I admired them. But I was concerned from the beginning about my relationship with W. H. Ferry. I knew that he was intelligent, hard-working, impatient with people who disagreed with him, and more experienced in public relations than I was. I realized that he was close to Hutchins and that I had been brought into the picture because there were some members of the board who wanted a public information officer who could keep Hutchins and Ferry from engaging in imprudent actions.

Hutchins assured me that Ferry realized the necessity for a reorganization of the Fund to restore harmony in the board. He also assured me that I would have direct access to him at all times and that he would not make public statements without giving me a chance to offer my advice. I said that my advice would be motivated not by any desire to "control" him but by a desire to be as helpful as possible in presenting the Fund's program.

On March 22 the board accepted the recommendation of Elmo Roper's Temporary Advisory Committee, which had endorsed the Hutchins proposals. I was elected a vice president with authority over the Fund's preparation and distribution of public information. David Freeman became a vice president and treasurer; Ferry was reelected a vice president, assigned to planning; and Adam Yarmolinsky became secretary of the corporation.

Paul Hoffman asked me to speak briefly to the board. I voiced my respect for the directors and staff of the Fund, declared that the Fund was performing an essential service to the American people, and said that I would do everything I could to get a better understanding of its work among the people and in the press. After the meeting several of the directors asked me to send frequent communications to the board. Griswold told me that he would expect to hear from me on all major issues that arose.

I promised the directors that I would keep in close contact with all of them. I did not agree to make private communications to any of them. I did not regard myself as an agent for members of the board who sought to remove Hutchins and Ferry.

At that meeting the board approved a letter to be sent to Henry Ford II by Paul Hoffman, inviting Ford to attend a special meeting of the directors in May and asking Ford to permit me to look at the letters Ford had received about the Fund. The idea of examining the letters came from me. It seemed to me that the directors should know the sources of the attacks on the Fund and why the letters had shaken Ford.

There was a heated discussion of the Cogley report on blacklisting at the March 22 session. A draft of the Cogley study had been sent to Earl Newsom, who was a public relations adviser to the Ford Foundation and the Ford Motor Company, by W. H. Ferry and Elmo Roper on January 23. Newsom had found the report "thorough, objective and perceptive in delineating a deplorable situation," but he did not think the Fund should publish it because it would "revive widespread public controversy and confusion about a complex problem to which no wise solution has yet been found." Cogley argued effectively that the blacklisting report could not be withheld from publication; its existence was already known to people in the mass media, and the Fund was deeply committed to it as a major project directly related to the Fund's charter.

Fitzgerald and I did not share Newsom's opposition to publication. It seemed to both of us that if the Fund held back the release of a report, which had cost $100,000, out of anxiety over "widespread public controversy," the Fund would be in an untenable position. Perhaps our backgrounds in journalism had inculcated in us a belief that controversy was vital for the health of a democratic society.

At the board's request Cogley had cut the length of the report from about 700 pages to less than 600. Copies had been sent to representatives of the entertainment industry and the professions "for the purpose (a) of catching possible inaccuracies and (b) of obtaining a statement or statements which might be published in or used in connection with the report." While expressing his willingness to cooperate with the board as far as possible, Cogley declared that he intended to see it published—if not by the Fund, then by a commercial publisher.

The directors finally appropriated $20,000 for the "final editing, printing and distribution" of 10,000 copies. Other actions taken at this session included the authorization of $105,000 for four church organizations for community education in civil rights; $15,000 for a six-month run of a cartoon feature for newspapers entitled "It's Your America"; $35,000 for an American Traditions project, to collect and publicize recent examples of how Americans had applied the Bill of Rights; $25,000 to finance the revision of a supplement to the "Bibliography on the Communist Problem in the United States"; $9300 for a preliminary presentation of James Real's program for a Popular Education Project; and $3500 to the University of Virginia for a research program on civil liberties issues in municipal laws. The board also voted for the distribution of three publications recommended by the officers, including a Department of Defense pamphlet entitled *Who Are Communists and Why*.

These actions—except for the appropriation of $20,000 for the blacklisting report—were relatively noncontroversial. But Representative Walter and members of the Un-American Activities Committee were not satisfied. Walter was angry because the Fund had refused to give him all the minutes of the board meetings and because the Fund had shown an interest in a handbook on immigration laws. (Walter considered himself an authority on immigration acts and resented any criticism of the McCarran-Walter Act restricting immigration.)

In my first two months as an officer of the Fund, I found it easy to communicate with Hutchins. I had heard that he was a demanding and temperamental executive, but he was calm and cooperative with me. Perhaps my obvious desire to help him and my confidence in the Fund's future relaxed him. I made it clear that I would not go around him to members of the board. When I had suggestions or criticisms to make, I made them directly to him.

When Paul Hoffman took me to lunch one day and told me that I had to get Hutchins to "recant" his statement that he would not hesitate to hire a communist properly qualified for a particular job, I promised Hoffman that I would discuss the matter immediately with Hutchins. I told Hoffman that I doubted whether Hutchins would do it. I went straight back to the Fund's headquarters and entered Hutchins' office.

"I've just been given a tough assignment," I said. I told him what it was.

"Do you think you can get me to recant?" Hutchins asked, grinning. He invited me to have dinner with him at the Yale Club and to exert my persuasive powers.

When we had finished dinner, I said, "At the request of our chairman, I ask you to recant your statement about hiring a communist."

"I won't recant," Hutchins said.

In spite of my determination to look frustrated, I was really happy. Hutchins knew it. If he had recanted, he wouldn't have been the man I admired so much.

"I'll try to explain your position to our chairman," I said. When I told Hoffman that Hutchins had refused to take back his statement, Hoffman looked relieved. If Hutchins had given way, Hoffman would have been disappointed too. I assured Hoffman that Hutchins' statement had not given a mortal wound to the Fund. I expressed my belief that a recanting statement, made under pressure, would have severely damaged both Hutchins and the Fund in the eyes of many people.

Since Hoffman considered me to be a public relations expert, he accepted my analysis of the situation. I realized that he had not really expected me to get Hutchins to back down.

At the May meeting, board members received a report on the 1200 letters I had found in the files of Henry Ford's New York office. I had asked Joseph Lyford of the Fund's staff to go through them. Most of the letters came from two southern states, Alabama and Mississippi; most of them had racist slurs. Many did not even refer to the Fund but expressed rage over the appearance of black people on the Ed Sullivan show, then sponsored by Ford. The letters did not provide any substantial reasons for Ford's turn against the Fund.

The directors at the May session also were given copies of the first issue of a Fund *Bulletin*, which I had initiated in cooperation with Lyford and Edward Reed. The four-page *Bulletin*, describing Fund projects and grants in a crisp style, went to 100,000 people across the United States, including business executives, American Legion post officers, Catholic clergymen, "opinion leaders," women's organizations, editors, publishers, broadcasters, educators, librarians.

It seemed to me that the Fund had to use some of its money to explain its projects in easily understood terms. The press and the broadcasting channels often focused on sensational "charges" and "replies." In order to break through that pattern, the Fund had to tell its own story with an array of facts. Hutchins and Ferry had previously discussed with the board—in 1954—the idea of a Fund magazine. The *Bulletin* was intended to be a possible forerunner of such a periodical.

In the spring of 1956 I learned from friends in Washington that the publication of the Cogley report on blacklisting was certain to lead to an all-out struggle between the House Committee on Un-American Activities and the Fund. People mentioned in the blacklisting report had close connections with several of the committee's staff members. The appearance of the Cogley report would be a signal for the committee and right-wing groups to join forces to crush the Fund.

When the struggle did become a confrontation, the *Bulletin* proved to be an effective instrument to alert the press and the public as to what was really going on. If the Fund had not had the resources to present its story—and if the directors had not supported Hutchins and Cogley—the Fund might have been destroyed in the fight over blacklisting.

6

The Fund exposes a ring of blacklisters—and comes under heavy fire

THE FUROR THAT DEVELOPED over the Fund's two-volume *Report on Blacklisting* can only be understood in the light of what had happened in Hollywood and in the broadcasting industry during the four years in the Second World War when the United States and the Soviet Union had been allies. In that period many film directors and actors and writers, as well as many people in broadcasting, developed a warm admiration for the courage and heroism of the Russians. Many Americans, headed by President Roosevelt, hoped that the United States and Russia could work together to build a better civilization after the war.

After Roosevelt's death in 1945, those hopes were dashed. President Truman was convinced that the Soviets wanted to rule all of Europe. People listened when Winston Churchill declared that the Russians had extended an "iron curtain" across Europe. Millions of Americans shuddered when Soviet Premier Stalin called for a "world revolution of the proletariat" in a rough speech at a huge rally of communist officials from many countries.

Truman was convinced by Secretary of State George Marshall and by George Kennan, former counselor of the American embassy in Moscow, that the Soviet Union had to be "contained" within the limits it had reached at the end of World War II. Early in 1947 the British government informed Truman that communist guerillas might conquer Greece and Turkey. The British did not have the resources to continue the aid they had been giving to those two countries. The fate of those nations—and perhaps of all the countries in Western Europe as well—seemed to depend on the United States.

Truman stepped forward as the protector of Greece and Turkey and unveiled the "Truman Doctrine" to the American Congress: "It must be the policy of the United States to support free peoples who are resisting attempted subjugation by armed minorities or by outside pressures. . . . This is no more than a frank recognition that totalitarian regimes imposed on free peoples, by direct or indirect aggression, undermine the foundations of international peace and hence the security of the United States."

Whether Truman misunderstood the Russians or not, he laid down a challenge to them. The era of American-Soviet cooperation—short and uneasy as it had been—was over. In such an atmosphere, blacklisting of hundreds of people involved in pro-Soviet groups was inevitable.

The development of organized blacklisting—with definite procedures for investigation, labeling, and "clearance"—had been made possible by the acceptance of conformity in the war years. As Robert Hutchins had predicted in 1941, the United States had taken on many of the trappings of a totalitarian society in its mobilization to defeat the Nazis and the Japanese militarists. Both Roosevelt and Truman, acting with popular support, had immensely expanded the power of the presidency and had successfully asserted the president's authority to define what Americanism meant.

When Truman enunciated his doctrine on March 12, 1947, there were some members of Congress who thought he had gone too far. Senator Robert Taft feared that the Truman policy would commit American power to too many struggles on too many fronts. General Albert C. Wedemeyer warned that "containment" could be exhausting to American resources. Walter Lippmann said the doctrine could plunge the United States into endless conflicts in Europe and in Asia.

Truman felt that there was no difference between totalitarian or police states—"call them what you will, Nazi, Fascist, Communist." He wrote to his daughter, Margaret, after he had placed his program before the Congress: "You know there was but one idealistic example of Communism. That is described in the Acts of the Apostles."

The House Committee on Un-American Activities was regarded with contempt by Truman. Under the chairmanship of Martin Dies, that committee had tried to prove that the whole of Roosevelt's New Deal had been put over on the country by the communists. Truman made a distinction between American liberals and radicals, and the "reds" who sought to subjugate "free peoples." The committee did not seem able or willing to make those distinctions in many cases.

The Committee on Un-American Activities, which had been sinking into disrepute for ten years, gained new life and power in 1947. Chairman J. Parnell Thomas and other members of the committee decided that Truman's doctrine gave the committee a chance to have an "open season" on any American who was then a communist or had ever been a communist or had known a communist or had associated with any group containing communists or persons believed to be communists. The committee saw no limits to what it might do. The time for blacklisting, for the elimination of all "subversive" persons, had come.

The committee realized that the biggest headlines could be obtained by exposing "reds" in the motion picture industry. Chairman Thomas announced in May 1947, a few weeks after Truman's speech to the Congress, that he would hold hearings on communist influence in Hollywood. The Truman program was moving slowly through the House and the Senate, but it seemed likely to be approved.

Chairman Thomas was jolted by the resistance he encountered at first. The Association of Motion Picture Producers blasted the Committee: "Hollywood is weary of being the national whipping boy for Congressional committees. We are tired of having irresponsible charges made again and again and again and not sustained. If we have committed a crime we want to know it. If not, we should not be badgered by Congressional committees."

Hollywood stars expressed their anger. "Who do you think they're really after?" Fredric March demanded, in a public statement. "Who's next? Is it your minister who will be told what he can say in his pulpit? Is it your children's school teacher who will be told what she can say in classrooms? Is it your children themselves? Is it you, who will have to look around nervously before you can say what's on your minds? Who are they after? They're after more than Hollywood. This reaches into every American city and town."

"Once they get the movies throttled, how long will it be before the Committee goes to work on freedom of the air?" Frank Sinatra asked. "How long will it be before we're told what we can say and cannot say into a radio microphone? If you make a pitch on a nationwide radio network for a square deal for the underdog, will they call you a Commie? . . . Are they going to scare us into silence? I wonder."

Judy Garland urged her fellow citizens to join the fight: "Before every free conscience in America is subpoenaed, please speak up! Say your piece. Write your Congressman a letter! Air mail special! Let the Congress know what you think of its Un-American Committee. Tell them how much you resent the way Mr. Thomas is kicking the daylights out of the Bill of Rights!"

Twenty-eight noted people in Hollywood joined many others in forming a Committee for the First Amendment. Among them were Larry Alder, Robert Ardrey, Lauren Bacall, Jules Block, Humphrey Bogart, Geraldine Brooks, Ira Gershwin, June Havoc, Sterling Hayden, Marsha Hunt, John Huston, Danny Kaye, Gene Kelly, Arthur Kober, Jane Wyatt, and others then known to millions of Americans.

The Hollywood group issued a statement describing the previous actions of the Committee on Un-American Activities that had brought that committee into disrepute:

I. The investigative function of the Committee on Un-American Activities has been perverted from fair and impartial procedures to un-fair, partial and prejudiced methods.

II. The reputations and characters of individuals have been smeared and besmirched in the following manner:

a. The Committee on Un-American Activities has been guilty of a violation of the long established Anglo-Saxon-American principles of individual accountability. They have accomplished this by adopting the "mass guilt" principle, i.e., guilt by association. Not only have the subpoenaed witnesses suffered by these methods, but mass lists have been publicized that contained many names of other people. These people were included in lists which have been designated by Committee members and counsel as "subversive," "pinko," "radical," "communistic," "disloyal," "un-American," etc. These people were neither subpoenaed nor given the opportunity to defend their characters.

b. The proceedings of the Committee have come to be regarded by the American people as a criminal trial. Nevertheless, American citizens have not been given the American privilege of ordinary self-defense statements and the right to cross-examine their accusers. The accused witnesses have become defendants in fact, have not been allowed the right of obtaining witnesses to testify on their behalf. Neither have they been allowed the full right of professional counsel in the defense of their characters.

c. Moreover, while theoretically the Committee is not supposed to apply punitive measures, because of its procedural abuses, it has punished individuals in a far more damaging way than the assessment of fines or personal imprisonment. They have done this by besmirching and damaging man's most precious possession, his reputation."

This statement was taken to Washington by a Hollywood delegation and presented to the Clerk of the House of Representatives as part of a petition for a redress of grievances. It was disregarded by Representative Thomas and other members of the Committee on Un-American Activities. In the cold war atmosphere, the committee felt that it could disdain such a description of its irresponsible behavior.

The Hollywood stars, directors, and producers who went to Washington believed they were behaving in accordance with the true principles of Americanism. Many of them shared the views of George Sokolsky, a columnist for the Hearst newspapers, who had made a slashing attack on the investigative methods of congressional committees and administrative boards.

"Civil liberties are always impaired by Congressional committees and by most administrative boards," Sokolsky had asserted in a column published on March 25, 1940. "The fundamental right of a trial by jury, the right of a day in court, the right to be represented by counsel and many other basic civil rights are impaired.

"You will say that Congressional committees only investigate; they do not try. That is, in fact, a false notion. These committees put a man on a spot, bring in the reporters, camera men, newsreelers and demand to know, yes or no, whether it isn't true that he did so and so. He says that he would like to read a statement proving that he is being maligned and his conduct misunderstood. Nothing doing! You can't read statements!"

Representative Thomas and his principal colleagues on the Un-American Activities Committee did not think that any American had a right to refuse to answer the questions of the committee. They contended that they were defending the liberties of Americans against conspirators, and they felt that they deserved the aid of every citizen.

During the two weeks of hearings on "communism in the film industry," it became evident that Thomas was determined to show that Hollywood was riddled with "reds." In the first week most of the witnesses were drawn from the Motion Picture Alliance for the Preservation of American Ideals, which had been created in 1944 to counteract "the growing impression that this industry is made up of, and dominated by, Communists, radicals and crackpots."

Rupert Hughes, a screen writer who had helped to organize the alliance, did not claim that there was direct communist propaganda in American films. He thought the problem was more subtle: "Where you see a little drop of cyanide in the picture, a small grain of arsenic, something that makes every Senator, every businessman, every employer a crook and which destroys our beliefs in American free enterprise and free institutions, that is communistic!"

Other witnesses who were friendly to the committee were Lela Rogers, mother of the actress Ginger Rogers, who insisted that "it has been a long time since you could get a good American story bought in the motion-picture industry"; Adolphe Menjou, who contended that the Alliance had kept "an enormous amount of sly, subtle, un-American class-struggle propaganda from going into pictures"; Robert Taylor, who said he had been reluctant to take the starring part in *Song of Russia*; and Ayn Rand, who called *Song of Russia* a false picture of what was going on in the Soviet Union.

In the Fund's *Report on Blacklisting*, John Cogley gave space to the views of these witnesses and those of others who testified that Hollywood communists had managed to keep anti-Soviet material from appearing in American films. Cogley wrote: "The Committee actually seemed more interested in films not made than in those written, directed or produced by the alleged Communists in the industry. Again and again, friendly witnesses were asked if they did not agree with the Committee that Hollywood should make more anti-Communist pictures patterned after the anti-Nazi pictures that appeared before and during World War II. The witnesses agreed readily that the field had been neglected. Other questioning led to the conclusion that movie producers had a patriotic duty to soft-pedal 'social' themes and make movies that would point up the benefits of free enterprise."

Cogley reported that the question of what to do about "Communist writers" or "Communist directors" arose frequently. Adolphe Menjou did not believe that a motion-picture worker suspected of communism should be blacklisted. "He could be very carefully watched," Menjou said. "We have many Communist writers who are splendid writers. They do not have to write communistically at all, but they have to be watched."

Menjou surprised some of the reporters at the hearings by saying that he did not object to communist propaganda on the screen if it was presented as such. Cogley wrote: "He agreed with Committee Member Richard M. Nixon, then a freshman Congressman, that 'if we refuse to allow a Communist picture to be made and advertised as such we would be falling into the same error that we criticize the Communists for in Russia.' "

Cogley described the testimony and treatment given to two of the most powerful men in Hollywood: "Jack L. Warner and Louis B. Mayer represented the top Hollywood executives at the hearings. Warner's testimony, while not overly coherent, was vehemently anti-Communist. He denied there was Communist propaganda in the films he produced but admitted readily that in all probability there had been Communists on his studio payroll who tried to get propaganda into the films they wrote. When he detected 'slanted' lines in scripts, Warner declared, he had the lines removed, bided his time, and then refused to rehire the offending writers when their contracts ran out. That way he had 'cleaned out' his studio.

" 'You have been doing exactly the same thing in your business that we have been attempting to do in ours,' the Chairman told the producer, and the latter agreed. But despite the chairman's prodding, Warner could not agree to an industry-wide ban on Communists. In his opinion, Warner testified, it would not be legal for any group of producers to band together to obstruct the employment of other men. He would continue to get rid of writers he suspected of 'un-Americanism,' but would not join any concerted attempt to blacklist them in the industry. . . .

"Louis B. Mayer, when his turn came, held that Communist writers could never succeed in influencing pictures made at M-G-M because in that studio scripts were read and reread by executives, producers and editors. On several occasions, Mayer recalled, writers on the M-G-M payroll had been charged with communism but no proof was ever offered. He personally studied the pictures written by these men and could find no slanting. . . ."

The hearings conducted by Thomas in 1947—like the hearings in 1951 under the chairmanship of representative John S. Wood of Georgia—disclosed the irreconcilable gap between Americans who believed that there were communists who could be employable (in the absence of any proof of their participation in spying or subversion) and those who contended that all communists were linked together in a criminal conspiracy. People who did not see that every communist had to be tied to this conspiracy were regarded as Rip Van Winkles, who had slept for years while the communists advanced in many places.

Ten well-known people in the film industry, later known as the Hollywood Ten, refused to answer any questions put to them in the 1947 investigation. Alvah Bessie, a screen writer who was one of the ten, took the position advocated in 1940 by George Sokolsky. So did all the others, who declared that the First Amendment protected them from unlawful inquiries.

"It is my understanding of the First Amendment to our Constitution that it expressly forbids Congress to pass any law which shall abridge freedom of speech or of opinion. And it is my understanding of the function of Congressional committees that they are set up by the Congress for the express purpose of inquiring into matters that may lead to the initiation of legislation in the Congress. . . . Since the only legislation this Committee could possibly initiate would automatically abridge freedom of speech and opinion, and would therefore be automatically unconstitutional, I have come to the conclusion . . . that this body is totally unconstitutional and without the power to inquire into anything I think, believe, uphold, and cherish, or anything I have ever written or said, or any organization I have ever joined or failed to join." This was Bessie's response to the questions asked by Thomas.

John Howard Lawson, a noted screen writer and also one of the defiant ten, showed his scorn of the committee: "It is absolutely beyond the power of this committee to inquire into my association in any organization. . . . It is unfortunate and tragic that I have to teach this committee the basic principles of American life."

The other defiant witnesses were Herbert Biberman, a writer and director; Lester Cole, who had written the screenplays for many famous films including *The President's Mystery*, based on a story conceived by Franklin Roosevelt; Edward Dmytryk, who had directed twenty-four popular movies; Ring Lardner, Jr., who had written screen plays for ten major productions, including *Forever Amber*, *Tomorrow the World*, and *Cloak and Dagger*; Albert Maltz, novelist and screen writer; Samuel Ornitz, who had worked on screenplays for many films, including *Little Orphan Annie* and *The Miracle on Main Street*; Adrian Scott, another writer with credits for many films; and Dalton Trumbo, whose work included the screenplay for *Thirty Seconds over Tokyo*.

Nine other Hollywood writers and directors indicated their determination to challenge the committee but were not called to the witness stand. No reasons were given by Thomas or other members of the committee.

The committee unanimously voted to charge each one of the Hollywood Ten with contempt of Congress, insisting that a committee of the Congress had the legal power to seek answers to any questions. By a vote of

346 to 17, the House upheld the charge of contempt. All ten of the Hollywood witnesses were sent to jail.

Cogley described what happened after the ten were convicted:

"It was generally agreed, if not in Hollywood then certainly in the financial circles which control the industry, that something had to be done. The industry acted promptly enough.

"On November 24, 1947, fifty members of the Motion Picture Association of America, the Association of Motion Picture Producers and the Society of Independent Motion Picture Producers, convened in Manhattan's Waldorf-Astoria. The gathering included such public figures as Paul V. McNutt and former Secretary of State James F. Byrnes, who served as industry Counsel.

"After two days of deliberation, Eric Johnston (president of the Motion Picture Association) announced the decision the industry spokesmen had reached:

> Members of the Association of Motion Picture Producers deplore the action of the ten Hollywood men who have been cited for contempt by the House of Representatives. We do not desire to pre-judge their legal rights, but their actions have been a disservice to their employers and have impaired their usefulness to the industry.
>
> We will forthwith discharge or suspend without compensation those in our employ and we will not re-employ any of the ten until such time as he is acquitted or has purged himself of contempt and declares under oath that he is not a Communist. . . .
>
> We will not knowingly employ a Communist or a member of any party or group which advocates the overthrow of the Government of the United States by force or by any illegal or unconstitutional methods.
>
> In pursuing this policy, we are not going to be swayed by hysteria or intimidation from any source. We are frank to recognize that such a policy involves dangers and risks. There is the danger of hurting innocent people. There is the risk of creating an atmosphere of fear. Creative work at its best cannot be carried on in an atmosphere of fear. We will guard against this danger, this risk, this fear.
>
> To this end we will invite the Hollywood talent guilds to work with us to eliminate any subversives; to protect the innocent; and to safeguard free speech and a free screen wherever threatened.
>
> The absence of a national policy, established by Congress with respect to the employment of Communists in private industry, makes our task difficult. Ours is a nation of laws. *We request*

Congress to enact legislation to assist American industry to rid it-self of subversive, disloyal elements [italics added].

Nothing subversive or un-American has appeared on the screen. Nor can any number of Hollywood investigations obscure the patriotic services of the 30,000 Americans employed in Hollywood who have given our government invaluable aid in war and peace."

Johnston's statement indicated that the film industry had made a complete surrender to the Committee on Un-American Activities. No mention was made of the First Amendment or the role of the Supreme Court in developing "a national policy." The film producers invited Congress "to enact legislation" to aid the industry in expelling all those who were considered to be "subversive" or "disloyal."

Cogley wrote: "The tone of the Waldorf Statement, as it came to be known, contrasted vividly with the defiant pronouncements that came out of Hollywood before the hearings, and with many of Johnston's own earlier statements. The switch did not pass unnoticed. The Los Angeles *Times*, for instance, commented:

A few weeks ago Mr. Johnston was chiding the Committee on Un-American Activities with smearing Hollywood. . . . Now, less than a month later, Mr. Johnston issues a statement in New York which will surprise the members of the Thomas Committee and quite a few Americans who are not in Congress. . . . First the Committee was wrong in questioning; then the witnesses were wrong in not answering the questions.

"Broadway columnist Ed Sullivan explained the apparent change of heart to readers of the New York *Daily News* on November 29: 'Reason that Hollywood big shots rushed to New York and barred the 10 cited by Congress was forecast in my November 1 column: "Hollywood has been dealt a body blow that won't please Wall Street financiers, who have not less than $60,000,000 in picture companies." Wall Street jiggled the strings, that's all.'

"In due time, the employed members of the Hollywood Ten were fired—Adrian Scott, producer (as well as writer); Edward Dmytryk, director; and writers Lester Cole, Ring Lardner, Jr., and Dalton Trumbo. Writers John Howard Larson, Albert Maltz, Alvah Bessie, Samuel Ornitz, and writer-director Herbert Biberman became unemployable.

"Such were the beginnings of blacklisting (on a wide scale) in the motion picture industry."

Cogley recognized the fact that communists and "fellow travelers" in the film industry had engaged in types of blacklisting during World War II. They helped their friends to get jobs as writers, directors, producers, and actors. They tried to keep Hollywood studio owners from hiring people who were suspected of being "reactionary" or "pro-fascist" or "against the cause of the workers."

"The blacklisting of anti-Communists was highly informal," Cogley reported. "It was a question of discrimination and mild treachery and was thoroughly despicable, but it did not involve the solid machinery, the institutionalization and formalization of the literal lists of 'unemployables' that have come to be taken for granted in Hollywood. The present blacklisting operation is a stable agreement in the industry that certain persons whose names are listed in the House Committee's reports are unemployable; the Communists' 'blacklist' was as elusive an undertaking as a rumor whispered over a luncheon table or a meaningful shrug in a conference room."

Confident that their case would win a victory for the First Amendment, the Hollywood Ten tried to get it before the Supreme Court. Hundreds of people in the film industry signed an amicus curiae brief submitted to the Court, indicating their support for the view of the First Amendment as a protective shield against legislative inquiries into opinions or associations. Most of them were confident that the Hollywood Ten would not be subjected to imprisonment.

When the case of the Hollywood Ten reached the federal court of appeals in the District of Columbia, the court held that Congress had the power to abridge First Amendment rights when it thought "the national welfare" required such an abridgment. The court of appeals also ruled that a witness who refused to say whether he was "a believer in Communism" could be punished.

Supreme Court Justice William O. Douglas, writing years later, commented: "Those ideas were appalling to me and to Justice Black. That decision was made in June, 1949. Frank Murphy, who had been appointed to the Supreme Court in 1940, died July 19, 1949. Wiley Rutledge, who took his seat in 1941, died September 10, 1949. The petition for certiorari (that is, the appeal of the Hollywood Ten) reached the Supreme Court in the spring of 1950. By that time Sherman Minton had taken Rutledge's place; and Tom Clark, Murphy's seat. It takes four votes to grant a petition. No one knows how Murphy and Rutledge would have voted. But they always held the First Amendment in high esteem. Justice Clark, who had been Attorney General when the convictions (of the Ten) were obtained, took no part. . . . The Hollywood Ten on April 10, 1950, got only two votes . . . Hugo Black's and mine."

Justice Douglas believed that if the composition of the Supreme Court had been different in 1950, the claims of the Hollywood writers and directors under the First Amendment would have been sustained by a majority of the justices. Their convictions would have been dismissed, and the House Un-American Activities Committee would have been rebuked. A few years later, under Chief Justice Earl Warren, the Supreme Court did rule that investigating committees of the Congress were restrained by the First Amendment.

But the Supreme Court in 1950 did not overturn the ruling of the District of Columbia court of appeals. The writers and directors had to serve their terms in prison, and the hundreds of prominent people who had gone on record against the proceedings of the Un-American Activities Committee found themselves caught in the spreading nets of the blacklisters, who had the power to destroy or to "rehabilitate" people who had been members of communist-front groups or had associated with suspected communists or had simply defended the First Amendment rights of the banished ten.

By 1954 it was evident to Cogley and those who assisted him in preparing the *Report of Blacklisting* that the practice of barring people from employment because of their past associations, beliefs, or activities had become "almost universally accepted."

Cogley wrote: "All the studios are now unanimous in their refusal to hire persons identified as Communist Party members who have not subsequently testified in full before the House Un-American Activities Committee. The studios are equally adamant about not hiring witnesses who have relied upon the Fifth Amendment before Congressional Committees." In effect, the Fifth Amendment had become "inoperative" for any one who wished to be employed in the motion picture industry.

The formal beginning of blacklisting in radio and television occurred in June 1950, a few days after the outbreak of the Korean War. The direct involvement of the United States in that conflict between the North and South Koreans intensified the feeling of many Americans that all communists were enemies of the United States and any person accused of being connected with communism or "leftism" had to be viewed with suspicion.

According to Cogley, the publication of a booklet entitled *Red Channels* was the principal instrument used by network executives, advertising agencies, radio-television program packagers, and sponsoring corporations to remove "subversive" people. The booklet was published by *Counterattack*, a weekly anticommunist newsletter that had been founded by three former FBI agents with some financial help from Alfred Kohlberg, a right-wing millionaire, founder of the China Policy Association, which supported the Nationalist Chinese government headed by Chiang Kai-shek. Kohlberg had made a fortune by importing Chinese textiles, and his source of profits had been cut off by the victory of Mao's communists in 1949.

The expulsion of Chiang Kai-shek's forces from the mainland of China and the triumph of the Maoists had sent a tidal wave of fear running through the United States. The "loss of China"—as though China had been part of the American sphere of control—had been blamed on the State Department and the Truman administration rather than on the corruption and failures of Chiang and his associates.

Members of the group known as the China Lobby had significant roles in the development of the blacklisting process in broadcasting as well as in the film industry. George Sokolsky and J. B. Matthews, two Hearst columnists, were particularly powerful members. Both of these men worked in collaboration with McCarthy and the House Committee on Un-American Activities.

Cogley declared: "J. B. Matthews provided the blacklisting movement with most of its root information with his 'Appendix IX,' but credit must surely go to Vincent Hartnett for showing how to put that information into tidy form, something like a job résumé." Appendix IX was compiled by investigators for the House Committee in 1944. It was printed in seven volumes, containing an index with 22,000 names, with information largely drawn from letterheads and programs of organizations suspected of being "subversive."

Robert K. Carr, in his book on the House Committee on Un-American Activities, described the appendix in these terms:

> It was prepared in the closing days of 1944 by the so-called Costello subcommittee of the Dies Committee, presumably to preserve the files of the latter committee which were thought to be threatened with destruction. Seven thousand sets were published at a cost of $20,000, and were delivered to the Committee. When the publication came to the attention of the full committee early in 1945, it was ordered restricted and the existing copies destroyed.
>
> However, a number of sets had already been sold by the Government Printing Office to private subscribers. Others had been distributed by the committee to the Government Service Commission, the FBI, the State Department, Army and Navy Intelligence, and the Legislative Reference Service of the Library of Congress.
>
> The volumes carry the title, *Communist Front Organizations* with Special Reference to the National Citizens Political Action Committee. There is no introduction to the volumes, and they carry no explanatory statement concerning their purposes or use. . . .
>
> An examination of this list immediately reveals that many of the persons named are neither Communists nor fellow travelers. Benjamin Mandel (of the Committee staff) admitted to the author that this was so, and said he regretted that the volumes did not carry an explanatory note warning users that the presence of a name in the index did not necessarily mean that the person was a subversive.

The most explosive parts of the Cogley *Report on Blacklisting* were his devastating descriptions of the "clearance" procedures through which many blacklisted persons had to pass in order to gain employment in their professions. His reference to Hartnett, who was one of those responsible for the blacklisting of John Henry Faulk and other noted broadcasters, was a telling example of how a "clearance man" worked.

"Without access to the chief 'clearance men' (who are often the same persons who make the damning indictment), the blacklisted artist can get nowhere," Cogley said. "These particular men are all-important. They have the power to wound and the power to heal the wound. They can hold off right-wing criticism, which in turn cuts off pressure on sponsors or networks when a 'controversial' artist is put back to work. If the performer is well-known he may need not only their passive sufferance but active support to re-establish himself with that section of the public given to telephoning networks and writing protest letters to sponsors. So it is fairly meaningless to say that no one can clear a blacklisted artist but the artist himself.

"What are the qualifications for a 'clearance man'? His own anti-Communist credentials should be recognized by the groups which stimulate blacklisting. He must be acceptable not only to other 'clearance men' but to the networks' and advertising agencies' 'security officers.' His word must mean something to persons like Laurence A. Johnson, the powerful Syracuse grocer, who hold the economic weapon which seemingly sends terror into the hearts of network and agency executives. His 'clearance' must stick with right-wing editors, columnists and public speakers. It is specially important that his 'clearance' stick with various Hearst columnists, the editors of *Counterattack*, and the officers in charge of the American Legion's anti-subversive committees. *In some cases the 'clearance men' have sold their services as public relations consultants and speech writers to the artist going through 'clearance.' In other cases 'clearance' activities are based on disinterested service*" [italics added].

In vivid terms, Cogley described the painful frustrations likely to be encountered by a person seeking "clearance." In one example, he quoted a New York public relations expert who had helped a dozen people become eligible for employment:

> "If a man is clean and finds his way to me, the first thing I do is examine his record [the expert said]. Once I am convinced that he is not a Communist, or if he has been a Communist, has had a change of heart, I ask him whether has has talked to the FBI. If he hasn't, I tell him the first thing he must do is go to the FBI and tell them everything he knows.
>
> "Then I find out where he is being blacklisted—where it is he can't get work, who in the industry is keeping him from working, and who outside the industry has made him controversial. If, for instance, I find it is the American Legion, I call one of the top Legion officials and tell him this man has come to me for help and says he is innocent. The official may say to me, 'Why this guy has 47 listings and I know people who say they don't believe him.' But

I say, I'm going to have him make a statement.' Then, when the Legion guy gets the statement and has read it, I call and ask him for a note saying he is satisfied by the statement. He will usually say, 'I won't put anything in writing but if anyone is interested have him call me.'

"Somewhere along the line I may find George Sokolsky is involved. I go to him and tell him that the Legion official thinks this boy is all right. If I can convince Sokolsky then I go to Victor Riesel (another columnist) or Fred Woltman (staff writer for the New York *World-Telegram and Sun*) or whoever else is involved. When I've gotten four 'affidavits' from key people like these, I go to Jack Wren at BBD&O (Batten, Barton, Durstine & Osborn, a large advertising agency) and to the 'security officer' at CBS.

"I wait a few days, then I telephone Wren. He may say to me, 'You're crazy. I know fifteen things this guy hasn't explained.' I ask him, 'What are they?' and he says, 'He didn't come clean.' So I send for the guy. He comes in here and he moans and wails and beats his head against the wall. 'I have searched my memory,' he will say. 'I have questioned my wife and my agent. There's not a thing they can remember.'

"I call Wren back and he says, 'When your boy is ready to come clean I'll talk to him.' In that case we've reached a dead end. My boy has been cleared but he can't get a job. I know cases where victims have sat around eight to ten months after 'clearance' before they got work.

"A second possibility is that Wren will say, 'I think you are right about this boy, but what do you want from me. I can't hire him.' In that case, the victim has to find a friend who is casting a television show and is willing to put him on the air to test his 'clearance.' If the attempt backfires and protests come in, the guy is through.

"Last of all, there is the possibility that Wren will pick up the phone and call a casting director or producer and say, 'Why don't you give Bill a part in the show'? Once the blacklisted performer appears on a CBS program, it is notice to the industry and to all the producers that he can be used.''

In case after case, Cogley disclosed the power of the blacklisters and the willingness of broadcasting companies, advertising agencies, and corporations to yield to the pressures exerted by legion posts, Hearst columnists, right-wing broadcasters, and supermarket operators such as Laurence A. Johnson of Syracuse, New York. Johnson was extremely effective in convincing sponsors that they would lose sales and anger their stockholders if they presented ''controversial'' actors or artists to the public.

Again and again Cogley revealed the pervasive fear in American society, the fear that made it possible for the blacklisters to operate, the fear of "invaders" or "infiltrators," the fear of the Red Chinese or the secret spies of the Russians, the fear that the people were not deeply committed to the "free enterprise system" and might be wooed into communism by communist broadcasters or communist programs filled with subtle propaganda that might poison the weak minds of millions of fickle citizens. Nobody wanted to take a chance. Freedom could only be permitted for those who had been certified as secure people, loyal Americans who did not question the danger of "the Communist conspiracy."

Edward Engberg, one of Cogley's principal assistants, was responsible for obtaining much of the information that led to the exposure of the blacklisters. From Philip Klutznick—a Chicago builder for whom Engberg had worked as a public relations director—Engberg obtained a letter of introduction to Arnold Forster, general counsel of the Anti-Defamation League. In a note to this writer, Engberg said: "Forster laid the whole thing out, including the system which had by then been instituted, as I wrote for the report, into a kind of jerry-built court procedure."

"It was apparent in many small ways that we were under surveillance, as they say, during work on the report and for years afterward," Engberg declared. "I was especially fond of the photographers . . . who would greet us from time to time as we walked out of the Shelton Hotel in New York, where we made our headquarters. Cogley once reported to me that the Internal Revenue Service had gone intensively through all of our expense accounts, and complimented me on the detail of mine, an art I had learned working for *Fortune.*"

The Cogley report proved to be particularly useful to John Henry Faulk, Louis Nizer, and Edward R. Murrow, who had the courage to challenge and defeat the blacklisters through legal battles. The title of Faulk's later book describing his long struggle for justice, *Fear on Trial*, summed up what these men did. With aid provided by the Cogley volumes, and their own work, they put fear on trial and won.

7

With the help of the press—and
a few friends in Washington—
the Fund defeats its foes

THE MONTH OF JUNE 1956 was a crucial month for the Fund for the Republic. In that month, the results of the blacklisting study made headlines in newspapers across the country. In the same period the Fund published a summary of its activities during its first three years and disclosed exactly how it had spent $5,414,201 of the Ford Foundation's grant. And in that month Chairman Walter of the Un-American Activities Committee asked the nation to consider whether "this foundation, with its vast reservoirs of funds and power" was "a friend or a foe in our national death struggle against the Communist conspiracy." And he subpoenaed John Cogley to appear at a closed session of his committee.

Chairman Walter had changed his tune. In January he had told reporters: "We're not going into the Fund for the Republic, we're going into Dr. Hutchins." But Hutchins had been reelected president of the Fund. And the Chairman of the Fund's Board, Paul Hoffman, had stated clearly in the Fund's summary of its work that "the policies and programs of the Fund have been determined by the Board of Directors." The board stood solidly with Hutchins in facing the committee's latest attack.

Early in June, Hutchins and I had heard that the committee was planning an onslaught. Thirty-five leading Washington correspondents were invited to have dinner with Hoffman in Washington to receive copies of the Fund's three-year report and to hear his answers to charges made by the Fund's critics. I went to Washington with Hoffman and participated in that dinner meeting.

Hutchins had informed J. R. Parten, a close friend of Speaker Sam Rayburn, that the committee intended to present adverse witnesses against the Fund and then close the hearings without giving the directors and officers of the Fund a chance to make replies. Parten communicated with Rayburn through the speaker's administrative assistant, and the speaker told Representative Walter that such proceedings should not be countenanced. Parten did not ask to have the hearings called off. On the contrary, he insisted that the Fund's directors wanted to be heard in public sessions covered by the press.

Walter's press release announced that hearings would start on June 27: "The Fund for the Republic is financing a number of activities which have aroused criticism and doubt on the part of members of Congress, prominent patriotic organizations, and individuals, including Henry Ford II himself, who has publicly described some of the activities of the Fund as 'dubious in character' . . . Are its extensive and diverse activities strengthening or weakening our security structure in the Communist cold war? Are the leaders of this force, who enjoy the benefits of tax immunity, serving an interest inimical to our basic American tradition?"

By questioning the patriotism of the Fund's directors—who had been elected to the Fund's board with the approval of the Ford Foundation—Walter stirred indignation among the foundation's trustees. H. Rowan Gaither, president and chairman of the board of the foundation, expressed for the trustees the foundation's "full confidence in the integrity and patriotism" of the Fund's board.

On June 15 Hutchins sent a letter to Walter, declaring that he and all the other directors of the Fund would attend the hearings and would expect to have "equal time, on each day of the hearings, to present witnesses of our selection, including members of our board and representatives of our grantees."

Five days later, the hearings on the Fund were abruptly postponed. Representative Walter told the *New York Times* that "preliminary staff work had gone slower than expected." He denied that any pressure had been brought upon him to drop the investigation. (Rayburn later indicated to J. R. Parten that he had strongly urged Walter to delay the hearings, to give the Fund time to assemble its own witnesses. Rayburn also arranged for Parten to talk with Walter, but the meeting was brief and unsatisfactory. After that, Rayburn again assured Parten that the Fund would have an opportunity to get its case into the record.)

The hearings on the whole program of the Fund were never held, although Representative Walter threatened to have them from time to time. He obviously had no intention of allowing the well-known members of the Fund's board to show the inaccuracy of his innuendoes about the Fund's purposes.

The committee and its right-wing allies concentrated their attention on the blacklisting report. A few days before the two volumes had reached the press, John Henry Faulk had filed suit for $1.5 million in a legal action against AWARE and other participants in the blacklisting process, declaring that they had engaged in a plot to deprive him of his livelihood. The black-listers felt that the Cogley study had to be discredited.

On June 25 Senator Karl E. Mundt, of South Dakota, denounced the report in a speech in the Senate, saying that it had given "aid and comfort to the Communists in this country and abroad," and he called upon the Commissioner of Internal Revenue to investigate the Fund. The New York *Journal American*, Hearst's New York outlet, slammed the study and asserted that it supplied "further conclusive evidence of the anti-anti-Communist slant" of the Fund. (The writer of this editorial later admitted that he had not read the Cogley report but had composed his comments after reading a news story about it and receiving "a note from Mr. Hearst, suggesting an editorial.")

Frederick Woltman of the New York *World Telegram and Sun*, who had been cited by Cogley as one of the "clearance men," acknowledged that the report was "not pro-Communist," but he claimed that it "cannot help but bring joy and comfort to the Reds." He said that Cogley "rubber-stamps the basic philosophy of the Fund's own president, Robert M. Hutchins" and "runs counter to the mainstream of American thought today."

J. Addington Wagner, the American Legion national commander, referred to the study as an "utterly ridiculous and highly melodramatic recital." He blamed it on Hutchins, although the Fund's directors had placed a study of blacklisting on their agenda long before Hutchins had become an officer of the Fund. Wagner deplored Hutchins' mental condition: "Dr. Hutchins is not only uninstructed on the subject of communism, but his mind seems to be impervious to any understanding of the Communist menace."

When Cogley received his subpoena from the Un-American Activities Committee on June 28, Hutchins declared: "While he accepts responsibility for this report as its director and author, the Board of the Fund for the Republic wishes to state its full confidence in the calm deliberation which he has given to its preparation." Cogley said: "The Committee's action involves freedom of the press. The question is: Should a man be summoned before his elected representatives to defend or explain a book he has written or divulge the confidential sources of his information? . . ."

Each volume of the *Report on Blacklisting* contained a careful foreword, which I had drafted for Paul Hoffman, explaining why the Fund had initiated the study. In this foreword Hoffman asserted that loyalty-security investigations of people working for the government "in sensitive positions" or seeking "key federal jobs" were necessary "to protect the government from the infiltration of persons who might try to destroy it."

"But when loyalty tests are applied by private groups to people in private industries—and people are barred from jobs because they are 'controversial'—many citizens become alarmed," Hoffman said.

"The present report embodies the results of a study initiated by the Fund for the Republic in September, 1954, when many Americans had become disturbed by the revelation of blacklisting practices in the radio, television, and motion picture industries.

"At the time this study was launched, such blacklisting was a subject of vigorous public controversy, involving civil liberties issues of a serious kind. . . . It was a controversy in which all participants commonly spoke in the name of the Constitution and civil liberty, but in violently conflicting terms.

"Those who advocated blacklisting practices did so on the ground that Communist and pro-Communist infiltration into the entertainment industries represented a serious peril to the American system of law and governance, and therefore to the freedoms which it enshrines. The peril might be direct, through giving Communists access to mass media into which they could introduce subversive propaganda, or which they might even sabotage given the proper circumstances. It might be only indirect, permitting Communist sympathizers to enjoy popular esteem, earning incomes which would help support Communist causes, operating their own blacklists against anti-Communists and promoting the interests of an international conspiracy directed toward the destruction of all liberties. In any case, it was contended, the extirpation from the entertainment industries of proven members of the Communist conspiracy and of all who were considered to have lent it their support or had been indifferent to its dangers (and remained impenitent) was essential as a protection to American institutions.

"Opponents of blacklisting contended that such a policy could only subvert the rights and liberties it sought to protect. Some held that it violated the Constitutional guarantees of freedom of speech and thought, since it destroyed an individual's livelihood on the sole ground of his political beliefs. This raised the issue whether a sympathy with Communism could properly be regarded as a 'political belief' or must be taken as a proof of complicity in a criminal conspiracy, even though no criminal charge could be brought. Beyond that, many who accepted the view that a convinced Communist should be barred from the cameras and microphones were disturbed by the methods being used to achieve this result. It was contended that blacklisting resulted in the ruin of many entirely loyal individuals without formal charges, hearings or other safeguards of due process, often on flimsy or mistaken charges and at the dictates of self-appointed censors or pressure groups."

Hoffman pointed out that the major arguments in the controversy did not appear to be on the same plane. He said: "It was not even clear whether a blacklisting system actually existed in the motion picture, radio and TV industries. If it existed, it was not known on what principles it worked, who controlled it, how accurate were the criteria it applied in screening Communists and pro-Communists out of the industries, what were the motives which might have contributed to its growth. Beyond the somewhat rough-and-ready disclosures of the various investigating committees, there was little useful data on the nature and extent of Communist influence in the industries; on the effect, if any, which it had exerted on the output; on the extent to which the Communists themselves had engaged in blacklisting practices, or on numerous other facts essential to formulating any answers for the issues of civil liberties here involved. The subject was being debated, in short, in a vacuum."

The Committee on Un-American Activities did not think that there was a vacuum, or that its disclosures had been "rough-and-ready." Chairman Walter insisted that the committee had done a thorough job of exposing "reds" in many fields but "blacklisting" did not exist. Driving "subversive" people from their jobs or opportunities for jobs could not be called "blacklisting," the committee contended.

Although he endorsed John Cogley's work as "thorough" and "scrupulous," Hoffman cautiously observed: "It was recognized that many in the industries are aware of the difficulties raised by blacklisting and have been wrestling earnestly with them. Mr. Cogley has tried to give a detailed picture of a situation as it exists. He has brought in no indictments, and has offered no recommendations. The Board of the Fund for the Republic offers none, believing that progress in resolving the conflicts of interest, viewpoint and principle involved must and will come in the first instance from the industries affected. But even this progress must ultimately turn upon public knowledge and understanding of the actual situation and its problems. This report seeks only to supply the data on which such knowledge and understanding may be established."

The House committee, executives in broadcasting and in the motion picture industry, American Legion leaders, and newspaper columnists who had served as "clearance men" in a blacklisting process that was not supposed to exist recognized immediately that the accumulation of facts Cogley and his staff had presented to the public actually added up to a series of indictments. It was clear that one strong recommendation emerged from the Cogley report: blacklisting should be abolished. Cogley did not say it directly, but the conclusion was inescapable.

Paul Hoffman had declared in his preface that "progress . . . must and will come in the first instance from the industries affected," but corporation sponsors and advertising executives who had yielded to pressures from McCarthyite groups were not likely to take steps to end blacklisting until they were compelled to do so by legal actions and signs of public disapproval. The Faulk suit for libel and the Cogley report sent tremors through the executive suites on Madison Avenue and in Hollywood, and the eyes of many people focused on the struggle between the Fund and the Un-American Activities Committee.

The committee decided to examine John Cogley in public rather than in a closed session. Fulton Lewis, Jr., who was frequently in contact with Chairman Walter, carried the news to millions of listeners on his 7 P.M. broadcast over 200 stations of the Mutual Broadcasting System on July 9. Lewis and the committee had been angered that day by the release of a report by a Special Committee on the Federal Loyalty-Security Program (sponsored by the Bar of the City of New York and financed by the Fund), recommending a drastic reduction in the number of people covered by the personnel security programs and the abolition—or complete revision—of the attorney general's list of "subversive" organizations. To Lewis and other right-wing activists, this was another example of the Fund's determination to limit governmental investigations, which they regarded as vital to "national security."

By putting Cogley on the stand before the Washington press corps, the committee hoped to show the Fund's bias and to question the loyalty of two of Cogley's staff members, Michael Harrington and Paul Jacobs.

Cogley entered the hearing room in Washington with an old friend at his side—Representative Eugene McCarthy, of Minnesota. McCarthy was widely known and highly respected in the House. He had one arm around Cogley's shoulders, as a visible sign to Chairman Walter and the other members of the committee that Cogley had friends who intended to defend him. When Cogley took the witness stand, McCarthy sat down in the first row of seats available for spectators.*

Bethuel Webster, the Fund's counsel, was in the front row. So were several of the Fund's staff members, including myself. Webster had offered to serve as Cogley's lawyer or to obtain special counsel for him. Cogley had declared that he did not need a lawyer or a spokesman of any kind. He did not plan to seek the protection of the Fifth Amendment or the First Amendment. He was there before the committee as an independent writer. With two of his assistants, Edward Engberg and Michael Harrington, he had gone over every page of his report. He was ready to defend it.

Cogley had been a Democratic candidate for Congress on Long Island, New York, in 1954. His articles in the *Commonweal* and other Catholic publications had shown his balanced judgment. He had never been affiliated with any Communist front organization. He had never been accused of being "pro-Communist" or "extremely radical." Conservative Catholics who disagreed with some of his views acknowledged his personal integrity. As a young man he had participated in the *Catholic Worker* movement headed by Dorothy Day, a movement composed of persons who tried to imitate Jesus of Nazareth by their aid to poor and suffering people.

Richard Arens—who had been an aide to Senator Joseph McCarthy and to Senator James Eastland of the Senate Internal Security Subcommittee, and had been the director of the antisubversive section of the American Legion's Americanism Commission—had been appointed staff director of the Un-American Activities Committee. Arens went after Cogley for four hours, casting doubts on his data, demanding to know why he had chosen certain words, why he had expressed certain ideas. Five of the representa-

*When Eugene McCarthy ran for President of the United States in 1968, John Cogley obtained a leave of absence from his position on the staff of the Fund and worked for McCarthy for several months.

tives on the committee were in the hearing room from time to time, but they left the questioning largely to Arens. With Arens was Karl Baarslag, who had written articles for *Facts Forum*, a right-wing publication financed by H. L. Hunt of Texas, and who had been on the staff of Joseph McCarthy's Senate Subcommittee on Government Operations.

Arens tried to insinuate that Cogley was "soft on Communism" by asking why he had given jobs to Paul Jacobs, who had once belonged to a communist club, and Michael Harrington, a socialist. Cogley reminded him that both Jacobs and Harrington were known to be anticommunists. Arens hinted that they were socialists, and remarked: "Socialists are only people who are conducting the transition from democracy to Communism." He could not deny that Harrington and Jacobs had vehemently voiced their opposition to communism.

Marie Jahoda—who had conducted an extensive study entitled "Anti-Communism and Employment Policies in Radio and Television," included as an appendix in the Cogley report—came under fire from Arens. She was a professor at New York University, at the Research Center for Human Relations there, and her study had disclosed that people in the broadcasting industry believed that the blacklisting "procedures, initiated and defended in the name of national security, have no bearing whatsoever on national security." The respondents in her survey said that "they were all aware of the watertight system of control over content before it goes on the air which excludes possibilities of direct subversion."

Arens and the committee could not accept the idea that the procedures for excluding "subversive" persons—which the committee had encouraged by its own investigations—had no bearing on national security. To have admitted that idea would have been to admit that much of the committee's work was a waste of time and energy.

Rather than confront such a possibility, Arens resorted to insinuations about Dr. Jahoda. He asked Cogley, "Did you know that she was admitted into the United States only in 1945?" Cogley replied, "She had a pronounced accent. I presumed it was not too long ago."

Arens asked, "Did you know that prior to her association with the study of which you were director that she had issued reports of studies of the loyalty programs of this government, published reports?"

"I had read nothing of Dr. Jahoda's before the grant was made to the Research Center of New York University," Cogley said.

Arens inquired, "Did you know anything about her connection with the Socialist Democratic Party in Austria prior to the time that she became identified with the Fund for the Republic?" Arens ignored the fact that she was connected with the Research Center for Human Relations at New York University and she was not "identified" with the Fund.

The committee members, Arens and Baarslag, were not willing to face the issues presented in the Cogley report. They did not regard the removal of suspected "Communists" or "Communist sympathizers" from jobs—or the denial of employment to such people until they had received "clearance" from the right sources—as "blacklisting" in a legal sense. They contended that any "good American" could get "clearance" by confessing past mistakes and naming other people who should be investigated.

When Cogley refused to reveal the names of people who had given him information on a confidential basis, the committee at this session did not try to force him to change his mind. Cogley did acknowledge that Frederick Woltman of the New York *World Telegram and Sun* had been the person mentioned by Arnold Forster, general counsel of the Anti-Defamation League, as a participant in the "clearance" procedures. Woltman had already released a letter from Forster, who said that some material in the Cogley report had come from him.

At the end of his testimony, Cogley was asked by Chairman Walter whether he wished to make a final statement. .

"I would like to know why I was called here," Cogley said.

Representative Walter, in the course of a rambling reply, made a declaration that brought many editorial denunciations upon him from newspapers: "We called you for the purpose of ascertaining what your sources were in order to determine whether or not your conclusions were the conclusions we would have reached had we embarked on this sort of project."

By that remark, Walter confirmed Cogley's contention that the committee's action in summoning him had challenged "freedom of the press." The Fund staff members who were present in the hearing room were jubilant. We felt then that we could persuade many editors and publishers to come to Cogley's defense. It seemed to me that this should be the basic strategy for the Fund.

The next day, in a release sent to all the channels of communication, Hutchins asserted that the subpoenaing of Cogley was "an unprecedented invasion of freedom of thought and expression in the United States." He released the text of a letter he had addressed to Walter calling for "a statement declaring that the Committee's study has convinced it of our patriotic purposes" or "a full and impartial hearing."

The committee brushed aside the issue of freedom of the press. Arnold Forster was placed on the witness stand. Forster did not repudiate the remarks attributed to him in the Cogley report. He said, however, that the quotations were "far from complete." He expressed his gratitude—and the gratitude of the Anti-Defamation League—to "men like George Sokolsky, men like Victor Riesel, and men like Jack Wren, and men like Fred Woltman, to whom we had gone innumerable times to solicit their opinions."

Chairman Walter thanked Forster for his testimony, and added, "You have confirmed the suspicion that this committee has had right along, namely, that this report isn't worth the paper it is printed on. I do not think there is a blacklist. I cannot find evidence of it."

Forster astonished him by answering: "I think there is, sir. I mean by blacklisting the denial of employment to a man on grounds other than merit without first giving him an opportunity to be heard. I know that in the cases that we attempted to help actors, actresses and others had been unable to get work and, according to them, had been told quietly, privately, and sometimes bluntly that they just could not get work because of past records; actors and actresses who had never had a hearing by a radio company or a television company or a motion-picture industry. . . . This is a dreadful thing, this is a problem that has plagued knowledgeable newspapermen, it is a problem which has plagued the Anti-Defamation League."

Then there occurred an exchange between Forster and Walter that illuminated the strange atmosphere of the hearings, in which the committee examined the "blacklisting" process although it denied the existence of "blacklisting" and in which the chairman approved the statement that "this kind of public hearing" was valuable and enabled the Fund to perform "a great public service—wittingly or otherwise, deliberately or otherwise." Forster disagreed completely with Walter and flattered him at the same time.

Forster declared: "If the Fund for the Republic Report results in this kind of public hearing and results in public discussion across this country about the problem to which I have pointed, if it does nothing else regardless of its accuracy or inaccuracy or anything on its pages, I think it will have performed a great public service—wittingly or otherwise, deliberately or otherwise."

"I think you are absolutely correct," Walter assured him.

After Forster came Frederick Woltman, who thought that he and the others who had tried to rehabilitate unemployed persons should be commended, and James F. O'Neil, publisher of the *American Legion Magazine* and a member of its National Americanism Commission. O'Neil had not examined the Cogley report as a whole, but he did say that "the American Legion has never been engaged in clearance activities, it has never been associated in any manner with so-called blacklisting." The legion had simply published and distributed the names of "suspects"—people who had not cooperated with congressional committees or had been listed in reports by these committees.

Arens asked: "Does the American Legion in its Indianapolis headquarters and its Washington headquarters keep abreast of the hearings of the House Committee on Un-American Activities and the Senate Internal Security subcommittee and of other congressional bodies dealing with the question of communism and subversion?"

O'Neil gave the answer Arens had certainly expected: "Yes, sir. I would say that most of the work of the Americanism division in this area is in implementing and supplementing the reports in the area of distribution of the House Un-American Activities Committee and the other committees of Congress and state organizations directly concerned with this problem."

Although he reiterated that the legion had not engaged in blacklisting O'Neil said: "The American Legion . . . feels very definitely that those identified with the Communist conspiracy, the Communist apparatus, should not be employed in the entertainment industry." He added that the legion did try to help people regain their jobs if they could be classed among "the innocent, the stupid, and the repentant guilty" who wanted to be rehabilitated.

As the hearings continued, it became clear that Walter and other members of the committee had not studied the Cogley report. Representative Scherer of Ohio said that he had "scanned it." Walter's questions indicated that he had not examined it carefully. The committee was simply interested in justifying its own behavior and in hearing witnesses who condemned Cogley and the Fund.

Vincent Hartnett—described by Cogley as one of the most active blacklisters and "clearance men," who made "a full-time occupation out of what for others is merely a sideline"—did not think that the term "blacklisting" should have been used for "honest, intelligent, reasonable and fair patriotic efforts to keep subversives out of radio and television." Urging the committee to increase its investigations, Hartnett snapped: "I would say that not more than 5 per cent, not more than 5 per cent of the past and present Communists in the entertainment industry have been uncovered."

Hartnett said that broadcasters were presenting American institutions in a bad light and felt that this must be due to hidden communists: "You will find script after script in which the policeman shoots an innocent teenager, not the bad teenager. It is always the innocent. The wrong man is identified and sent to jail. An honest official abroad is suspected of being a Communist agent and the man who points the fingers at him is always a fanatic, disgruntled. . . . We are being brainwashed."

No serious cross-examination of Hartnett or any of the other witnesses was conducted by Arens or permitted by the committee. When Hutchins asked again for an opportunity to enter rebuttals to the charges hurled against the Fund by Hartnett, O'Neil, and others, his request was not heeded.

Roy M. Brewer, a former union executive who had been involved in bitter labor disputes in Hollywood and who had been mentioned many times in the Cogley report as a blacklister, appeared before the committee to brand the Cogley study "a complete falsification." He then admitted that he had tried to drive "Communists" from Hollywood and had helped to "clear" those who repented. But he did not regard such activities as "blacklisting."

Paul R. Milton, a director of AWARE, INC., also testified that the Cogley report was full of "inaccuracies," but his testimony showed that Cogley's description of AWARE'S activities had been correct. Like Brewer, he expressed admiration for the Un-American Activities Committee, saying: "This committee provides a wonderful forum in which people may explain themselves."

Hutchins wrote again to Walter, asking for the right to have witnesses present to answer charges during the hearings. Walter replied: "When we are considering the Fund for the Republic—and we are not now—we are going to permit witnesses to be heard." Hutchins sent a letter to all the organizations and individuals receiving grants from the Fund, asking the grantees to file written statements with the committee "describing their experiences with the Fund" and to have such statements released to the press.

On July 13 President Eisenhower nominated Paul Hoffman, the Fund's chairman, as a member of the United States delegation to the United Nations. This set off new attacks on Hoffman and the Fund by Senator Joseph McCarthy, Fulton Lewis, Jr., and other right-wing critics. In spite of the fulminations of McCarthy and Lewis—and a letter-writing drive by subscribers of William Buckley's *National Review*—the nomination of Hoffman was confirmed a week later by a Senate vote of 64 to 22. That vote for Hoffman indicated that a large majority of the senators also rejected the attempt of the Un-American Activities Committee to smear the Fund.

Support for John Cogley came from religious publications, as he had expected, and also from the *New York Times*, the Washington *Post and Times-Herald*, and other leading newspapers.

"If the House Committee on Un-American Activities were really interested in examining all un-American activities it might long ago have used its great powers as an investigative arm of Congress to look into the thoroughly un-American art of blacklisting in the entertainment industry," the *Times* declared in an editorial. "Instead, it left that thankless job to the Fund for the Republic, but it has now suddenly raised its hackles because it didn't like what the Fund's independent inquiry produced."

The *Commonweal*—with which Cogley had been connected as an editor for some years—raised some important questions that disturbed many journalists: "Will a writer who upholds the Supreme Court decision on segregation . . . be subpoenaed and grilled by Senator Eastland? Will Keynesian economists be called to account by Congressional critics who are anti-New Deal?"

Patrick O'Donovan, who was writing about the hearings for the London *Observer*, was appalled by the committee's behavior: "At the risk of appearing John Bullish, I must say that such a quasi-legal chamber would not be tolerated for a day in a civilized European state." The *Christian Century*, a noted Protestant magazine, spoke up in an editorial: "We have the honor to count John Cogley as a friend, whose Christian integrity and ability as a journalist we greatly respect. If Mr. Walter compels us to choose between his brand of patriotism and that of John Cogley, we will choose that of John Cogley.''

Unabashed, Walter shifted the scene of his sniping at the Fund from Washington to Philadelphia, where he summoned two people who had been cited in the Cogley report—along with many others—as having been deprived of employment. Gale Sondergaard, an actress who had won an Academy Award, said she had been blacklisted since she had invoked the protection of the Fifth Amendment in 1951. Her appearance in a play in Philadelphia was being opposed by the American Legion there.

"For the Committee to recall me here at this specific time while I am deeply involved in a creative work, the first in five years, can only be construed as an act of harassment,'' Ms. Sondergaard said. She refused to testify about her former associations.

Jack Gilford, a well-known comedian, became angry on the witness stand, yelling at Walter and Scherer: "I would love to supply blacklist information. Everyone hates the blacklist—the whole TV industry.'' When he would not answer a question on whether he had been a communist, his testimony was cut off.

Walter then switched his attention to the $5000 grant made by the Fund to the Plymouth Monthly meeting to honor the meeting's defense of the civil rights of Mary Knowles, the Quaker group's librarian who had been retained in her job despite her use of the Fifth Amendment at a Senate subcommittee hearing.

"The Committee wishes to know more about the factors which prompted the Fund for the Republic to consider the retention of a Communist, a defense of 'democratic principles' worth $5,000 of its tax-exempt money,'' Walter said. "The Communists and their dupes will undoubtedly try to distort our inquiry into appearing as an interference with the great freedom of religion. . . . Our sole concern is with the seemingly dubious ventures of the Fund for the Republic, Inc.''

Walter would not allow any testimony by Eleanor B. Stevenson of the Fund's board, who had been a member of the group of directors that had recommended the award to the Plymouth Meeting. Mrs. Stevenson told the press that Walter had questioned "the patriotism of the Fund'' and had cast reflections "on the members of its board, on its staff, and on the many religious groups, educational institutions, civic organizations and individuals who have received grants from the Fund for work on civil liberty fields.'' She insisted that she had gone over the details of the award and regarded it as "a very, very American thing to do.''

Four witnesses hostile to the award were summoned before the committee and voiced their antagonisms toward Mrs. Knowles and her supporters. Maureen Black Ogden, a Fund researcher who had gathered information on which the Fund had based its award, was sharply questioned. Walter remarked at the end of the Philadelphia session: "The fact of the matter is neither you nor the Fund for the Republic was concerned with whether or not she had ever been a Communist.''

Walter's statement revealed again that he did not understand—and did not want to understand—the principles on which the Fund operated. He could not accept the fact that the Fund's award had not been made to Mrs. Knowles personally but to the Quakers, who had not succumbed to the pressures brought upon them in their community.

The bias shown by Walter and Scherer at the Philadelphia hearing led to a stinging statement by the Library Committee of the Quaker Meeting, issued on the day after the hearing was adjourned: ''A Committee of Congress has just spent virtually a whole day ventilating the unhappy internal affairs of a small religious group. . . . Not a single fact has been developed that was not known before. . . . It is hard to see what public service is rendered by dramatizing a difference over a matter of conscience. . . .

''The House Committee accepted reckless statements that many people 'in the community' wanted the Meeting's librarian removed; it gave no opportunity for evidence that there has been strong and enthusiastic support for the librarian's continued employment. The House Committee suggested that controversy in a community of itself is bad, ignoring the fact that only by controversy can there be tested that devotion to principle which is essential to democracy.''

The Plymouth Monthly Meeting retained Mrs. Knowles as a librarian and continued to back her when she was convicted later on a charge of contempt of Congress because she would not answer questions about people she had known in the 1940s. Her conviction was finally reversed by a United States Court of Appeals, and she was allowed to return to her library books.

Walter's rebuffs to the repeated demands of Hutchins and other Fund directors for an opportunity to be heard in public before the committee showed that he had no intention of giving the Fund a chance to place in the record its three-year report, which described hundreds of grants in many fields, with expenditures totaling nearly $5.5 million. Walter preferred to growl at a few actions taken by the Fund, involving a very small proportion of its grants.

My role in the fight in 1956 and 1957 was to keep editors and open-minded commentators informed of what was going on. I prepared and mailed 5000 copies of a booklet containing editorial comments on the blacklisting study, sending it to opinion leaders on a list I obtained from Elmo Roper. I included the unfavorable statements as well as the favorable ones, but the favorable comments actually outnumbered the negative statements by five to one. The June issue of the Fund *Bulletin*—which carried a digest of the Cogley findings—went to 100,000 people, including editors of 1800 daily newspapers and leaders of many organizations.

Copies of the Fund's massive three-year summary of its work, released on May 31, 1956, went to 140 editors on key publications. Five leaflets entitled *Facts*—four-page leaflets on major areas of the Fund's program—were mailed to 100,000 citizens. In addition, I urged grantees to make public statements of their views on the Fund's value, and distributed 10,000 reprints of an address made by Paul Hoffman to the Willard Straight Post of the American Legion.

The *Facts* leaflets were prepared by Joseph P. Lyford, who had been a public relations representative of the Fund before I was elected by the board as the Fund's information officer. At my suggestion Lyford went through each section of the three-year report and digested material of interest to the press and the public.

Walter did not summon Hutchins or Hoffman or any director of the Fund to explain or justify any of the hundreds of other projects mentioned in the Fund's three-year report. He was more interested in slipping material to Fulton Lewis, Jr., for radio broadcasts ridiculing the Fund or describing it in poisonous language. Lewis had painted the Fund's summary of its first three years as "a picture of planned attack and sabotage against the federal government's loyalty-security program, against Congressional investigations into communism and other subversive activities, and a general organized effort in the field of racial relations that follows the standard communist tactic of arousing racial strife and friction as a means of inflating trouble and disharmony on which to play for their own communist advantage."

When Lewis read to his radio audience on the evening of August 6, 1956, excerpts from documents that had been subpoenaed by Walter for use by his committee, he stirred the wrath of Bethuel Webster, the Fund's general counsel, who had supplied a number of documents to the committee with the reluctant consent of the Fund's board. Webster fired off an angry telegram to Walter on August 7:

"It is an inexcusable violation of the investigative process that you should have made available to a radio commentator documents obtained under subpoena from the Fund for the Republic that were never made a part of the record. The Fund cannot be harmed by your irresponsible use of this material, but the prestige of Congress cannot fail to be damaged by this abuse of the powers lodged in you. This is another example of the hit and run tactics pursued by you and Mr. Arens in your dealings with the Fund for the Republic."

In referring to "hit and run tactics," Webster was using a phrase that had appeared in an editorial in the *New York Times* on August 4. Ten days before, I had given John Oakes of the *Times* editorial board full information about Walter's treatment of the Fund. Oakes had written an editorial describing the hearings as "sorry sniping expeditions" and denouncing the "hit-and-run tactics employed by the Walter Committee and its counsel, Richard Arens."

Hutchins sent copies of Webster's telegram to each member of the committee, and wrote to Speaker Sam Rayburn: "We believe that you as the chief officer of the House will wish to be informed of this episode. We

venture to hope that in conformity with your long and distinguished record
of honorable dealings you will find it possible to check the excesses of the
Chairman of the House Un-American Activities Committee and its staff.''
Rayburn later told J. R. Parten that he had become indignant about the
treatment given to the Fund and had expressed his criticisms vehemently to
Walter.

Rayburn had been disturbed when Parten had given him copies of articles in *Facts Forum* written by Karl Baarslag, a committee staff member.
Baarslag had indicated in these articles that Democratic leaders in the nation had been "soft on Communism." Rayburn knew that *Facts Forum* had
been financed by H. L. Hunt, a Texas millionaire who had spent money lav-
ishly in attempts to defeat Democratic liberal congressmen when they
sought reelection. The speaker demanded that Baarslag be removed from
the committee staff, and Walter complied.

With the approval of Parten, Elmo Roper, and other members of the
Fund's board—and with the cooperation of Bethuel Webster—the September issue of the Fund *Bulletin* gave a step-by-step account of Walter's wild
blows at the Fund. The *Bulletin*—headed "Congressman Walter Investi-
gates"—was distributed to 100,000 prominent citizens, including many
newspaper editors and broadcasters. It contained the text of the *New York
Times* editorial and the text of Bethuel Webster's telegram.

Thomas Reeves, the historian, considering the Fund's action twelve
years later, commented in his book *Freedom and the Foundation*:

> The Fund was, of course, taking a great risk; there was no
> precedent for such a public attack on a Congressman by a tax-ex-
> empt foundation. But there was no precedent for the Fund for the
> Republic; its officers and directors knew that pressures from the
> Right had placed the corporation in serious jeopardy and that the
> possibility of its extinction remained very real. (On July 25, Beth-
> uel Webster had met with an officer of the Internal Revenue Serv-
> ice, who appeared puzzled and suspicious of the Fund's activities.
> Webster wrote to Hutchins: "Like others who seem to want to be
> friendly, he talks about bad public relations, saying that we have
> not 'sold' the Fund, that we are losing friends, etc., and that some
> of our officers and directors (and not just one or two) are contro-
> versial or provocative."). . . . The Fund's officers and directors
> knew that they could document a good case against HUAC; the
> facts surrounding and contained in the hearings condemned Wal-
> ter and his associates before any fair observer; the press had rallied
> to the Fund's support. This was as good a time and place as any to
> intensify the Fund's counterattack.

The *Bulletin* produced a new wave of friendly editorials for the Fund
and strong condemnations of Walter in the Hartford *Courant*, the St. Louis

Post-Dispatch, the Pittsburgh *Post-Gazette*, and the Louisville *Courier-Journal*. As a former Nieman fellow, I had urged ex-Nieman Fellows who were editors of papers to speak out on the Fund's combat with the Un-American Activities Committee. Many responded.

"Let Mr. Walter bring his charges in open hearings, and with a free flow of witnesses and information for defense as well as offense," the Hartford *Courant* said. "In the present circumstances Mr. Walter is discrediting the whole legislative investigative process. If he does not himself follow through, to allow a rebuttal to the attacks he makes, then Congress should act at the first opportunity. In the interests of its own reputation, it should remove Mr. Walter. For, strangely enough, the most un-American thing about this entire matter thus far has been the acts of the Committee itself."

Representative Walter reacted with rage, telling the press in Washington that the Fund had a "multi-million dollar propaganda machine." He declared that his hearings had disclosed the spending of tax-exempt money for "political subversion" and he announced: "The investigation by the Committee of the Fund for the Republic will continue in an orderly, objective manner."

What he called an "orderly, objective manner" did not seem so to the Fund's officers and directors. He demanded access to the Fund's files, but he showed little interest in the major projects. His staff members took up some of the time of Bethuel Webster and the Fund's staff but did not seem prepared to hold full-scale hearings at any time.

Paul Hoffman and Roger Lapham tried to win over William Randolph Hearst to a favorable view of the Fund by taking him to lunch and explaining what the Fund was doing. But Hearst would not be placated. He was suspicious of Hutchins and did not make a real effort to understand what the Fund was all about.

The Internal Revenue Service conducted an exhaustive examination of the Fund's records. The remarks made to Webster indicated that the Fund's involvement in "controversies" had jeopardized its tax exemption, even though no trace of "subversion" could be found. At one stage, Hutchins thought that the Fund might lose its certificate of tax-exemption despite all the supporting editorials and statements it had received. In the autumn of 1956 Hutchins said to me, "We may be done for, possibly by the end of this year." I insisted that Walter was being beaten, and I was sure that the Fund would survive.

I thought the Fund should demonstrate publicly in Washington that it did have friends in many places. At my suggestion the board authorized an American Traditions dinner, which was held in Washington on February 21, 1957. Invitations were sent to members of Congress, to businessmen and labor leaders, to clergymen of all faiths, and to the Washington offices of many national organizations. Five hundred correspondents from newspapers all over the country were included.

Elmo Roper, who had been elected chairman of the board as successor to Hoffman, presided at the dinner and introduced the many notable people who were there. Awards were presented to men and women who had acted in defense of the fundamental freedoms in the Bill of Rights. New members of the board—the former governor and former senator from New York, Herbert Lehman; Dr. Henry Pitney Van Dusen, president of Union Theological Seminary; and Monsignor Francis J. Lally, editor of the *Pilot*, the weekly newspaper of Cardinal Cushing's archdiocese of Boston—received applause from the audience.

Bruce Catton, Civil War historian and editor of *American Heritage* magazine, who had also been elected to the board, was the principal speaker. I had persuaded him to speak on "The American Tradition." Catton said, in part: "If any one word tells us what America really is, it is that one word—freedom. If any single thing gives us reason to have confidence in the infinite future of the American people it is the fact that this most basic of our traditions is capable of infinite expansion. It does not limit us. On the contrary, it forever invites us to grow. . . . The Fund for the Republic is founded upon this living concept of freedom—and that is why I am proud to be a director of the Fund."

Sixteen members of Congress—including Speaker Rayburn, who came as a guest of J. R. Parten—heard Roper describe the Fund's program that night. Representative Stewart Udall, of Arizona, placed the Catton speech into the *Congressional Record* the next day. In the same week Representative Morgan M. Moulder, of Missouri, informed reporters that he did not share Representative Walter's suspicions of the Fund. Through a friend in Congress, I had given Moulder information about the Fund. He was the second-ranking Democrat on the Un-American Activities Committee, had been at the dinner, and had noted the presence of Speaker Rayburn. Moulder said he had not sanctioned Mr. Walter's attempts to cast doubt on the loyalty of the Fund's officers and directors.

But opposition within his committee and criticism by the press did not deter Walter from renewing his demands on the Fund. On March 29, 1957, five weeks after Moulder's statement, Walter asked Bethuel Webster to get the Fund to provide office space for committee staff members "to review documents relating to the Fund's activities since December, 1952," and he wanted dozens of documents, including John Cogley's notes and other materials. The board refused to provide offices for the committee staff investigators, but Webster sent most of the documents requested by Walter for examination. Cogley would not make any of his materials available.

Early in May 1957 Cogley was subpoenaed for another appearance before the committee, scheduled for May 15, and he was ordered to bring all his papers and the confidential information given to his assistants in the course of his blacklisting study. He wrote to Walter on May 3, reminding him that a majority of the committee members present at his testimony on July 10, 1956, had not tried to force him to divulge his sources. He said that he felt "at the time that the Congressmen were upholding an American tradition according to which writers and journalists, as well as scholars, are not subject to harassment, are free to keep their sources confidential and in a very real sense enjoy the liberties guaranteed by the First Amendment."

After referring to editorials in newspapers endorsing his position, Cogley went on: "When members of my staff interviewed people or wrote to them—and hundreds were consulted—it was with the understanding on both sides that we were free journalists writing in a free country. No one we interviewed or corresponded with had any idea that what he said or wrote would be turned over to a governmental body. Were I to supply you with the materials you demand, I would feel that I had betrayed these people. . . . I do not believe that you want to investigate me personally. I have never belonged to any group that might be deemed subversive, even by the most elastic standards of the day. There is nothing in my record, nothing whatsoever, to justify suspicion."

Few men in American life in the 1950s could have made that claim, but Cogley's reputation was unassailable. Walter answered, in part: "The investigation that the Committee staff has made since your appearance before the Committee convinces me that you are not entitled to withhold the requested information from the Committee." Cogley had received a telephone call from a committee staff member, saying that if he supplied the information sought by the committee he would be treated favorably. After thinking it over, Cogley decided to burn his notes and other research papers.

Cogley had informed Walter that he would report to the committee on May 15 and would be willing to answer any questions "about my life, my actions or my affiliations." Then he added, "But I will answer no more questions about anything I have written and published. I will not supply you with the documents you demand. In stating this, I know I may be asking for a great deal of trouble. There may be a high price to pay. Please God, I will be ready to pay it."

In spite of Walter's bluster, the committee backed away from a confrontation with Cogley. Rayburn had made his disapproval of Walter's behavior known to members of the committee and other members of Congress. Representative Moulder, Representative Clyde Doyle, of California, and others did not want to try to force Cogley to disclose confidential information.

Shortly before the date for his testimony, Cogley was notified that his appearance in Washington had been postponed until June 5. He had telephoned a committee staff member, saying that he had destroyed the documents sought by the committee. It became evident that the committee could gain nothing by tackling Cogley again.

I had sent newspaper editors in many cities copies of Cogley's letter to Walter. The editors responded vigorously. The *Wall Street Journal*—which could not be labeled "subversive" even by the committee—saw the situation clearly: "Where the principle of freedom of the press is involved, we see scant difference between one Congressional committee demanding the names of people who buy books and another Congressional committee demanding the names of people who helped write books." *Editor and Publisher*, the trade journal for American journalism, said: "If authors, researchers, scholars, editors, reporters, or publishers cannot write and publish the facts as they see them, the opinions of others, or record their own opinions, without danger of inquisition, then we have no freedom of press or thought." In June, Cogley's testimony was postponed indefinitely. In a book he wrote later, Cogley declared, "Kelly's strategy had worked."

Walter had been defeated, but he never admitted it. He continued to try to destroy the Fund. He handed copies of a committee staff report—made to him but not signed by the committee members and not authorized for publication—to correspondents for the Scripps-Howard papers and the New York *Daily News*. A headline on the story based on this report appeared in the Washington *News*: "Report Urges Fund for Republic Be Stripped of Tax-Exempt Status."

Jack Steele, in an article for the Scripps-Howard chain, reported that the committee staff had learned that officials of the Internal Revenue Service on "the working level" had recommended the revocation of the Fund's tax-exemption certificate in 1956. The committee staff claimed that the IRS investigators had found that the Fund had disseminated "propaganda" rather than educational materials.

In a column that was printed in the New York *Mirror* three weeks later, Fulton Lewis, Jr., asserted that "the staff report" (obviously passed to him by Walter) had verified "everything that was ever charged against the Fund for the Republic—by me, the American Legion, or its hosts of other critics —was all true and a lot more." The headline in the *Mirror* said: "Report May Knock FFR Out of Business."

A month after the Lewis article, the Internal Revenue Service had not acted against the Fund. Walter struck again, sending a letter to the Secretary of the Treasury Robert Anderson with a copy of the staff report. He demanded the revocation of the Fund's tax exemption, insisting that the Fund had provided "aid and comfort" to the communist cause.

In April 1958—after the IRS had held a "hearing" at which no director or officer of the Fund had a chance to speak—the IRS ordered the Fund to "show cause" why it should not lose its tax-exempt status. Hoffman, Parten, and Webster went to Washington. Webster presented the Fund's case to Justin F. Winkler, assistant commissioner of internal revenue. Parten and Hoffman had a meeting with Secretary Anderson.

Parten said later: "I had known Bob Anderson for a long time. He was well aware of the excellent reputations of Paul Hoffman, Elmo Roper, and other members of the Fund's board. He knew we were trying to uphold the Constitution of the United States. He knew we weren't giving comfort to Communists or doing anything subversive."

The Fund retained its tax exemption, and it continued to hold its charter as an educational corporation through the 1950s and in the following decades. The foresight of Hutchins and Hoffman, in persuading well-established Americans to join its board of directors, was a major factor in its survival.

The Fund took its case openly to the press, to the people, and to the leaders in the Congress and the Eisenhower administration. On many occasions, in many ways, the Fund proclaimed that it was fighting for the fundamental liberties of all citizens. But it is doubtful that the strength of popular devotion to the Constitution or the Bill of Rights enabled the Fund to endure. The Fund's connections to powerful leaders were probably more important.

Several surveys in the 1950s showed that few Americans knew much about the Bill of Rights, and many were inclined to abrogate or abandon constitutional protections for "controversial" people. Fortunately the Fund had directors who could speak directly to the speaker of the House of Representatives, to the secretary of the Treasury, and to the president himself. Fortunately the speaker, the secretary, and the president did trust and admire Parten, Hoffman, Roper, and other directors of the Fund—and they did care about the Constitution and the Bill of Rights.

The struggle between the Fund and the Un-American Activities Committee in the 1950s—and the Fund's subsequent struggles in the 1960s and the 1970s—may have demonstrated that the United States has a government of men, not of laws. The laws are interpreted by leaders, and the continuation of freedom and justice depends on the quality of the leaders and their dedication to fundamental principles.

Hutchins interpreted the Fund's experience to indicate the necessity of getting the leaders and the people to understand how democracy could possibly work in a bureaucratic, technological society in an age of rapid change. The second phase of the Fund's development—the "basic issues" program—was a plunge into a thorough examination of the forces that were reshaping modern society and threatening to make democracy obsolete.

PART TWO

Diving into the Waves of Change

8

Seeking to clarify the world's thinking, Hutchins swings the Fund in a new direction

WHEN THE FUND BEGAN, its mission was described in terms of the evils it was supposed to combat: the evils of communism, the evils of violations of the rights of minorities, the evils of witch hunting, the evils of censorship and boycotting and blacklisting, the evils of restrictions on the freedoms of teachers and writers, the evils of injustices in the application of laws. It was given $15 million at the request of a group of thoughtful and widely experienced directors, but nobody knew whether that was too much money or too little. Nobody knew how far the Fund could go or how long it should be in existence.

At a special meeting of the board in New York on January 29, 1953, the eleven directors who were present—James Brownlee, Huntington Cairns, Russell Dearmont, Richard Finnegan, Erwin Griswold, William Joyce, Meyer Kestnbaum, Elmo Roper, Jubal Parten, M. Albert Linton, and George Shuster—had signed a statement of "ultimate objectives" and sent it to Paul Hoffman, then the president of the Ford Foundation.

These directors said that the "sources of strength" in American society should be thoroughly explored in deciding how to foster and maintain "a climate favorable to the full development and expression of the individual." They expressed the belief that such a climate had made possible the development of the United States. They envisioned constructive actions in the future.

Then they went further: "Once our sources of strength are determined and the responsibilities that go with freedom are reappraised, we should be in position to examine the more recent effect on our society of the rise of big government, big labor, and big business." And they said, "We believe that we can intelligently and effectively spend somewhere between $3,000,000 and $5,000,000 a year over a period of five years. It may well be that a much larger sum would be needed to make the contribution which the Ford Foundation and the Fund for the Republic desire. We do feel that it is important that the Fund be guaranteed a minimum existence of five years.''

In April 1956, at a time when the Fund's existence was precarious and its critics were howling for its termination, President Hutchins circulated a memorandum to the directors suggesting the formation of an Institute for the Study of the Theory and Practice of Freedom, which would carry the Fund's work into "a different, and perhaps more significant, context." He saw in this project the possibility of crossing the gaps between the Fund and its enemies.

Referring to the Declaration of Independence and the Constitution, Hutchins wrote: "A remarkable characteristic of these documents is that they have been able to appeal to persons of different religious faiths, different philosophical positions, and different races and traditions. Everybody says that he is for these documents. The critics of the Fund say so. We reply that the Fund is misunderstood. It seems more likely that the Declaration and the Constitution are misunderstood, or are differently understood, sometimes so seriously that grave clashes can occur between proponents of different interpretations."

He stated a proposition that showed his willingness to undertake what might seem to be an impossible task: "It is vital to demonstrate, if it can be done, that *no matter what the ideas or background of the citizen*, he can and must be dedicated to the principles of the Declaration and the Constitution." Did he really believe that Representative Walter and Fulton Lewis, Jr., and the commanders of the American Legion and the editors of the Hearst papers could be dedicated to the same principles as the directors of the Fund? As a clergyman, his father had been unwilling to abandon hope for anybody. Hutchins seemed to have that hope—or to believe that such hope had to be kept in view as a possibility.

"The Fund has not done much to clarify these principles," Hutchins said. "It has for the most part assumed that everybody understood civil liberties and was in favor of them. It has supposed that the disclosure of failures in this field would result in efforts to remedy them. It has not sufficiently reckoned with the proposition that in the present disorder one man's failure can be another man's success."

He asserted that "the present disorder" might be overcome by more creative thinking. He quoted A. J. M. van Dal of the Hague, the secretary general of the International Commission of Jurists, who had called for "a simple set of fundamental principles expressing in a readily understandable way the common denominator of our legal-political beliefs." Hutchins reported that Dr. van Dal felt that "leaders of the democracies lacked definite purpose and clear conceptions of what they stood for." The confusion of leaders increased the skepticism of the masses, Dr. van Dal said, and this produced "too much improvising, too much taking a stand on incidental issues, too much changing of ground, too much confusion, disagreement, and disappointment.''

Hutchins appealed to the directors, who felt that the United States had to offer leadership to other relatively free nations: "Now that we stand at the head of what is called the 'free world,' we are called upon to explain ourselves. This is an indispensable step in holding the free world together and in attracting adherents to it.''

In 1941, in a speech opposing American participation in World War II, Hutchins had stressed the duty of the United States: "It is our task in this country to realize the true ideals of human life, the true organization of human society, the true democracy." He drew these "true ideals" from the Great Books that he later urged Americans to read and discuss: "It is our task to work out a new order in America . . . based on the premise that society exists to promote the happiness of its members and that happiness consists in the development of the highest powers of men. The good life and the just society—not the luxurious life or the powerful state—these are the goals toward which America must strive.''

As the president of the Fund in 1956, he asked the directors to move the Fund to a different plane of activity. He acknowledged the fact that the first three years of the Fund's work had been valuable: "The Fund has stirred up interest in civil liberties; it has produced some changes in the public attitude toward them and has contributed to improvements in public policy. In the light of what it was supposed to do and of the circumstances of the time, the Fund probably had to start as it did. Perhaps we could be led to examine the issue this memorandum raises only by experience. Both the Board and the staff now realize that there is no more difficult or complex field than civil liberties.''

Then he told the directors that he did not think they would be able to set aside the time for a "prolonged discussion of principles." They were too busy with other things. In their first meeting, in December 1952, the directors had talked about having such discussions. Hutchins had tried to get them to hold meetings for several days at a time, but they had had too many other obligations to make it possible for them to gather for such sessions.

William Joyce and Meyer Kestnbaum also had tried to get the board to have a series of seminars, but most of the members were not ready to give such philosophical gatherings a high place in their schedules. Their energies flowed in other directions. They wanted to deal with immediate problems as efficiently and effectively as possible.

Kestnbaum, who had been an enthusiastic advocate of the Great Books discussion programs developed by Hutchins and Mortimer Adler at the University of Chicago, had suggested at a Fund board meeting on September 14, 1954, that the Fund had reached a point at which it might "engage in a different kind of discussion." The minutes recorded Kestnbaum as saying: "The basic problems, the two or three central issues, should be defined, within which broad areas the Fund could work. Fear and resultant hysteria might then be attacked at the base rather than through various symptoms.'' Chairman Hoffman observed that the results of a previous study by the Planning Committee had "given the Fund its present sense of direction." Hoffman added: "Possibly a review of this might be made at the end of the second year of operation."

Hutchins had conducted the review and had developed recommendations that required a transfer of the planning functions of the Fund from the board to a group of thinkers who would attempt to "work out the concepts basic to freedom" in a modern technological society. He presented this fundamental proposal in words designed to reassure the directors that their ideas would always be considered and their decisionmaking power would be retained.

"The object would be to promote coherence and intelligibility in the program of the Fund, to relate every study to every other," Hutchins said. The aim would also be "to enable the Board to function with confidence even though it could not afford the time for protracted philosophical discussion, to permit the officers to proceed with confidence in the absence of clear agreement on fundamental principles in the Board, to give the studies sponsored by the Fund permanence and universality, to develop a basis of common conviction in the West, and to show a pluralistic society how it can reach unanimous devotion to justice and freedom."

These breathtaking objectives seemed impossible to some of the directors, but others were excited by his vision and were willing to give him a full opportunity to develop his ideas. They shared his view that the Fund's charter could be stretched to cover such an effort.

"It is suggested that these objects might be achieved through an institute for the study of the theory and practice of freedom," Hutchins said. "This would be an educational, not a philanthropic, activity. . . . Since the aim would be to arrive at common convictions in spite of profound philosophical differences, the members of the Institute should represent different points of view and different backgrounds."

Although the institute would be an innovative educational organization, it would not be composed entirely of professional scholars. Men and women with extensive knowledge and experience would be welcomed.

"The Institute would be something like a university, except that it would be limited to the study of freedom, it would do no classroom teaching, it would not confer degrees, and it would not require them of its members," Hutchins said. The members of the institute would do some research but they would be primarily involved in seminars, conferences, discussions, and debates. Hutchins continued: "They might give public lectures. They would publish factual reports made by them or made at their request; they would publish the results of their individual and collective labors. Young men, analogous to students, drawn from all over the world, would assist them."

The institute would resemble the Center for the Behavioral Sciences at Palo Alto and the Institute of Advanced Studies at Princeton. But the Institute for the Study of the Theory and Practice of Freedom would differ from the Palo Alto Center and the Princeton organization in one respect, Hutchins indicated: "They are principally devoted to providing the best conditions for the *solitary* work of distinguished or promising scholars. The (proposed) Institute . . . would not be composed exclusively of scholars; it would have a corporate intellectual purpose, and cooperation in the achievement of that purpose would be expected of every person who worked under its auspices."

Although Hutchins said that he had been stimulated to make this proposal because of the painful experience which the Fund had endured, several directors and staff members recognized that Hutchins was really advocating a Platonic academy in a new guise. He had not been very happy as a philanthropist, dispensing money to worthy groups on the basis of their applications and the recommendations of staff investigators. He was an educator, and he wanted to get into the deep kind of education that he found exciting and believed to be necessary for the future of humanity.

While at the Ford Foundation, he had helped Mortimer Adler establish the Institute for Philosophical Research. Through the Fund for the Advancement of Education—an offshoot of the Ford Foundation, created largely at his urging—he had participated in two conferences in London that had generated ideas for a "world academy" in the spring of 1953. But the Ford trustees had not pursued those ideas after Hutchins and Hoffman had left the Foundation.

In drafting his proposal for an Institute for the Study of the Theory and Practice of Freedom, Hutchins had been aided by John Cogley and Hallock Hoffman. After Cogley had finished the blacklisting study, he had been appointed to the Fund's staff in New York. Cogley soon grew tired of reading the papers submitted by people seeking money. "After about three months I went to Hutchins to resign," Cogley said later. "Foundation life just wasn't cut out for me—reading long requests for money and so on. Hutchins said: 'If you're bored there must be a reason. I'm bored too. If we're both bored we must do something about it. Facts are boresome.' " Then Hutchins outlined the idea for the institute and asked for Cogley's comments. After Hutchins returned to Pasadena, he invited Cogley to come there for a meeting with Hallock Hoffman and himself to develop a memorandum for submission to the directors.

Hutchins circulated the memorandum of April 18, 1956, to some of the directors for comments. Encouraged by their responses, he sent a slightly revised version of the proposal to the entire board on May 4. At the suggestion of George Shuster and Elmo Roper, he attached a covering statement in which he recommended the appointment by the board of a committee "to advise the Board of Directors on the desirability, feasibility, program, organization, financing, location, and personnel of an institute or council for the study of the theory and practice of freedom."

He said bluntly: "The proposed organization cannot be discussed in detail until a report is presented. At that time the Board would have the opportunity to accept, reject, or modify the plan. The Board should not authorize the committee, however, unless it thinks well enough of the idea to believe that the organization suggested might become a major effort of the Fund." This was characteristic of Hutchins' method of operation. He presented a proposal that would require a sweeping reorganization of the Fund, then asked the board to take one immediate step that was hard to refuse—simply the formation of a committee to examine the proposal—but made it clear that such a step might commit the board to an organization that "might become a major effort."

Roger Lapham, John Lord O'Brian, James D. Zellerbach, and Erwin Griswold had reservations about the Hutchins proposal. But the board had already reaffirmed its support for Hutchins' leadership at the January 1956 meeting, and a large majority of the directors voted to establish the committee Hutchins had requested.

In his first draft of the proposal—the one dated April 18—Hutchins had said: "The Institute could doubtless be carried on as a project of the Fund. It might be better, if it is feasible, to establish a separate educational corporation and to make a grant to it. In either case the Directors of the Fund could be the Trustees of the Institute and the administrative functions of the Institute could be conducted by Officers of the Fund." The comments of several directors had persuaded him to drop this paragraph from the memorandum given to the whole board.

Hutchins told the directors in the May 4 memorandum: "Looking back over the activities of the Fund since its establishment, we see that most of the investigations that have been carried on would have been made by the proposed organization if it had been in existence. The difference is that they would have been made in another, and perhaps more significant, context. They would have been related to one another and to the clarification and resolution of some important intellectual and practical issue."

As a specific example of what the institute might do, Hutchins said: "One approach to the work of the institute or council might be to ask whether the Bill of Rights meets the needs of the citizens of a huge, industrial, 20th Century democracy as well as it served those of the citizens of thirteen small agricultural states 165 years ago.

"If the aim of the Fund is to make the Bill of Rights a living document today, what is needed to make it live? The tremendous growth of governmental activity and power suggests the possibility that new life might be injected into the Bill of Rights by a thorough examination of its adequacy to protect the citizen today. Nor is the change in scope of governmental intervention in the life of the citizen the only new phenomenon affecting the Bill of Rights.

"Maintaining the freedom of the press, for example, in an age of electronics, films, and enormous costs is a different and more complex matter than it was when the press was made up of newspapers that could be run off by anybody who had access to a printing shop. If we turn to the kind of economic and social pressure that can now be put upon the dissenter, the problem of protecting the citizen becomes still more complicated. This kind of pressure undoubtedly bore down on the inhabitants of the thirteen original states. But the history of the internal migrations of the period shows that nonconformists had an escape that is not readily available today: they could go from one atmosphere to another by the simple expedient of moving away."

Hutchins repeated that he had not proposed that the institute should be "the only effort of the Fund." He explained: "1. If the plans that James Real* is preparing for popular education through the mass media come up to expectations, they should be carried through. 2. The search for sound programs of adult education in civil liberties should be carried on. 3. The effort to assist bar associations and law schools should be continued. 4. The work on race relations, particularly in the South, should be maintained and developed."

The Fund had approximately $11 million at the time of the Hutchins proposal. He assured the board: "Reserving sums adequate to deal with the items listed above and with possible opportunitites now unforeseen, the Fund has the money to establish the proposed Institute or Council on any scale that is likely to be immediately feasible."

After some discussion at the directors' meeting on May 15, 1956, the board provided funds for an advisory committee to study the proposal and make recommendations. The members included three directors—George Shuster, Meyer Kestnbaum, and J. Howard Marshall, all friendly to Hutchins—and five scholars: Eric Goldman, Princeton historian; Robert Redfield, anthropologist, and Richard McKeon, philosopher, both from the University of Chicago; Clinton Rossiter of Cornell; and John Courtney Murray, a Catholic theologian and a professor at a Jesuit institution, Woodstock College.

The advisory committee on the Hutchins proposal met three times during the summer of 1956 under the chairmanship of Hutchins. He made a brief oral report on the progress of the group at the June 22 gathering of the board and promised a full report at the September session.

In the months between the June session of the board and its special

---

*James Real was a writer and an adverising consultant.

meeting on September 12, Hutchins met with scholars in Chicago, Princeton, and New York. In addition to the five men he had mentioned to the board in May, he conferred with Mortimer Adler, of the Institute of Philosophical Research; Eugene Burdick, a political scientist, University of California; Jacques Maritain, a noted French scholar in residence at Princeton; George F. Kennan, diplomat and author of the article on "containment of Communism" that had been one of the initiating factors in the "cold war"; Robert F. McNamara, vice president of the Ford Motor Company (and later Secretary of Defense under Presidents Kennedy and Johnson); Gerard Piel, the publisher of *Scientific American*; Samuel Lubell, a polling expert; Joseph N. Welch, the Boston lawyer who had helped to bring about the downfall of Joseph McCarthy; Arthur Cohen, editor of the Noonday Press; Joseph Klein, of St. John's College in Maryland; Richard Rovere, Washington correspondent; Gilbert White, of the University of Chicago, and Robert McAfee Brown of Union Theological Seminary.

On September 6, 1956, Hutchins transmitted to the Fund board what he described as a "Report of the Committee to Advise the Fund for the Republic on Basic Issues in Civil Liberties." The report was signed by Eric Goldman, Richard McKeon, John Courtney Murray, Robert Redfield, and Clinton Rossiter, but its ideas were completely consistent with those expressed by Hutchins in his April proposal. But the five scholars went much further than Hutchins had done in advocating that responsibility for the Fund's program should be transferred from the board of directors to a new group of men who could devote their "full time over a period of years to examining the state of the free man in the United States, and ideas and institutions associated with the terms 'liberty' and 'justice.' "

"We propose that the Fund for the Republic organize and support a major effort to deal with the basic issues involved in civil liberties questions," the scholars said. "The effort should be directed and conducted by a group of men of the highest distinction, aided by assistants and consultants, who will devote full time (to the work) over a period of years. . . . This group should carry on the work that the Fund has been doing in providing the nation with reports on the operations of American institutions connected with freedom and justice.

"But the primary function of the group should be to interpret and analyze the meaning of these reports, to relate one to the other, to re-examine (and reformulate, if that seems necessary) the framework of principle which will give meaning and coherence to the discussion of such reports.

"The group should represent different, and differing, points of view. It should be established on a long-term basis with guarantees of professional security and independence."

When the directors read this report, many of them became aware that the "major effort" recommended by the scholars might require most of the Fund's remaining resources.

"Normally we agree with the wisdom in 'starting small'," the scholars asserted. "But in this case the wisdom does not fit the need. The organization we have outlined is absolutely dependent on men of experience and achievement. Such persons must be convinced that the kind of work the Fund does is of the utmost significance and worthy of their full-time attention and devotion. If they are to be had, the Fund must convince them that an enterprise of this kind is important enough for them to leave what they are now doing. The Fund will have to assure them of financial independence and professional employment for years to come. They will require the same assurances that a good university gives to a sought-after professor, and comparable facilities. All this will require large and long-range commitments."

The Fund had originally been created as an emergency operation to counteract the hysteria generated by McCarthyism. The directors had believed that it might function for five years, expending $3 million to $5 million a year. The scholars envisioned a much longer period of life:

"There are many opportunities open to the Fund for the Republic. We are aware of several ourselves, and the Board of Directors must be acutely conscious of many avenues of action unknown to us. As we survey the present scene, however, and ask ourselves what a foundation might best do to advance the cause of freedom and justice in the world, we are bound to say that the kind of concentrated effort we have recommended deserves priority. Such an undertaking could contribute something truly fundamental. As it did its work, the struggle for freedom and justice would take on a new dimension. Perhaps the best word for that new dimension is 'intelligibility.' "

Goldman, McKeon, Murray, Redfield, and Rossiter went on: "Something has been lacking in all the heated public discussion about civil liberties during recent years. We believe the ingredients needed more than any others are coherence and perspective. Abuses of civil liberties have generally been regarded as isolated phenomena; they have been treated in a vacuum. Basic questions and large considerations have either been neglected or avoided altogether. Reports and studies are issued regularly but are left to stand alone without interpretation or analysis. The journalists and commentators who undertake to explain their meaning are rarely equipped for the task. The result is that such reports sometimes sow more public confusion than enlightenment. *The real issues get lost in a hopeless tangle of conflicting claims.*"[Italics added.]

The scholars made an eloquent plea to the board in their conclusion: "We believe that the Fund, as the only educational foundation specifically dedicated to strengthening the basic fabric of the nation, can make an outstanding contribution to America and the world by correcting this. We believe the Fund should support the kind of work we have described."

Hutchins asked the board for authority to prepare a plan for carrying out the proposals—with the advice of the three board members assigned to the project—"so that the Board at the November meeting may judge their practicability and their effect on the total activities, present and potential, of the Fund." Several of the board members had reservations about the whole idea—notably Dean Griswold, who had voted against Hutchins' request for the appointment of a committee—but the board agreed to consider such a plan.

One month before the annual meeting scheduled by the board for November 15 in New York, Hutchins sent all the directors a long memorandum endorsing the principal recommendations of the group of scholars. He urged the board, in terms considerably stronger than those he had used in April and May, to shift the program of the Fund toward "the study and discussion of basic issues in civil liberties."

"My reconsideration of the program of the Fund began with the three-year report," he reminded the board in his October 15 memorandum. "It did not lead me to conclude that what the Fund had been doing was wrong. On the contrary, it confirmed the view that the program was inevitable and desirable. It did, however, suggest that we had reached a stage at which we should look around, take stock, and decide whether the methods we had used in the past were necessarily the best for the future.

"I did not come to this conclusion for public relations reasons, because of a wish to avoid controversy, to propitiate the Treasury and the House Un-American Activities Committee, or to evade the responsibility of making some contribution to education on current, practical problems. I was impressed by the tremendous range of the Fund's work, and I was compelled to admit that the criteria used to arrive at the recommendation or rejection of grants and projects were not altogether clear and consistent. It seemed to me to follow that if more intelligible standards of action could be developed the Fund would be better understood, but any advantage that might arise from this I regarded as incidental and secondary. My object was to work out a program that *we* understood and in which we believed."

Hutchins did not refer to his own interest in developing a council of scholars who might at last develop into a Platonic academy. He did indicate, however, that his effort at systematic thinking "should have been made even if the work of the Fund had been obviously perfect in every way." As he saw it, the Fund was an educational institution, and educational institutions had to be dedicated to thinking in a clear, coherent style.

He cited the repercussions of the Fund's report on blacklisting as a primary example of why hard thinking was needed: "The reason why a factual report on a current problem, like blacklisting, might not have the educational effect intended was that the prejudices, preconceptions, or ideas of those who read it were such that they could draw widely varying inferences from the facts. If ideological tests for private employment are good, the fact that such tests are applied in the entertainment industry is not alarming. If the employer may properly determine whom he may employ, the fact that he, with others, decides that he will not employ persons with an ideology that he dislikes, is natural enough. The educational task would seem to be to promote some intelligent discussion of the question whether ideological tests for employment *should* be applied. In the present state of the media of mass communications it is naive to suppose that the mere presentation of the facts will automatically lead to such discussion."

Hutchins did not deal with a question that had been crucial in the dispute between the Un-American Activities Committee and the Fund: the question of whether all communists or communist sympathizers had to be regarded as aiding a conspiracy to destroy the United States, wittingly or unwittingly—or whether some communists seeking jobs were simply people with nonconformist ideas or ideology. It was extremely difficult to see how that question could be resolved.

"Whether ideological tests for employment should be applied is a practical question," Hutchins insisted. "Any question that asks what ought to be done is practical. The answer to such questions as blacklisting and to all others in the field of civil liberties depends on the actual situation of the country at the moment and on the kind of country we are trying to have. Data, current and historical, are indispensable, but they are insufficient. What is needed in addition is hard, practical thinking."

Striving to convince the board that the scholars were not advocating a retreat into an ivory tower, Hutchins continued: "We have to grant that eighteenth-century principles and practices may not apply today. We face dangers as a nation that our forefathers could not have dreamed of, and the individual confronts an economic, social, and governmental order quite different from that of 1790. Some hard, practical thinking ought to be done about the limitations on freedom that the security of the nation requires and the methods of protecting the individual against the social pressure and governmental interference that now, on a scale that would have been thought fantastic 150 years ago, affect every citizen every day of his life."

Over and over again, he used the phrase "hard, practical thinking" or the word "practical." He cited two examples to show what he meant: the growing conflicts between "church and state" and the bitter differences over the desegregation of the schools.

On the first issue, Hutchins said: "For the Fund to compile the legal enactments with regard to the use of public money for parochial schools or to report on the cases in which the legal enactments on the separation of church and state are disregarded might not be wholly useless; but it certainly would not be as useful from the educational point of view as the presentation of these facts as part of a more general attempt to understand what the relationship of church and state, as a practical matter, ought to be. The point is that *the facts would continue to be presented*, but in such a way that they might be better understood, and, *in addition*, an effort to comprehend and explain the basic issue would be made. The effect of this should be to promote discussion that would be less heated and more enlightening than what we would be likely to get otherwise." [Italics added.]

Several of the directors did not think that the Fund should tackle the thorny question of the relation between the churches and the government but thought that the Fund should stick to the areas in which it was already working.

The second issue—the argument over the abolition of segregation in the schools—was described by Hutchins as "the most serious issue in civil liberties today." He asked, "What can thinking in the practical order accomplish here? Can the Fund do anything more than to collect and present facts and promote friendly discussion among sincere and 'moderate' people?"

He answered these questions with a hopeful statement: "I believe that a group of men trained in thinking about practical problems, eminent, disinterested, and public-spirited, could take the whole problem of race relations and put it outside the realm of acrimonious controversy among reasonable people by tackling the question of what ought to be done and *at the same time* presenting one factual study after another, on housing, on the intellectual potential of the Negro, on the effects of desegregation on intermarriage, on the progress of integration, on the organization and financing of the White Councils, etc. . . . This is what the Advisory Committee called 'raising the level of public debate.' The group would make clear what the place of the Negro in our society should be in the light of the American tradition and of a defensible conception of freedom and justice, and it would deal one by one with the principal sub-issues involved. The reason why I believe that this is the most useful thing an educational corporation dedicated to civil liberties could do about the race question is that this procedure would be more likely than anything else to accomplish the prime desideratum in this field, which is to reduce the heat in the controversy and advance rational discussion. Such an effort would have important effects abroad as well as at home."

His words seemed highly idealistic in the atmosphere of the nation in October 1956, when violence was flaring in the South and the White Citizens Councils were vowing to resist the Supreme Court's order for desegregation with every means at their command. When Hutchins asserted that the whole problem could be taken "outside the realm of acrimonious controversy," the directors noted that he had added that this could be done "among reasonable people." But millions of people who had lived in a segregated society were not likely to regard the removal of barriers between whites and blacks in schools as "reasonable." Some journalists who traveled through the South reported that the majority of white citizens would "never" accept desegregation.

In his pursuit of a comprehensive vision, Hutchins said: "I may be wrong, but it seems to me that there is one set of underlying issues, and then many issues dependent upon it. The underlying issue is that of the meaning today of the American tradition of freedom and justice, an issue that can be framed in more general terms by asking how much diversity a pluralistic society can stand and how much unity it requires. The dependent issues are the meaning and condition of the various civil liberties that we have enjoyed and the question whether there are others that ought to be added. There are, of course, numerous sub-issues under each of these heads.

"If it is true that there is one underlying set of issues and that the others are dependent on it, then it would seem to follow that one group is needed to work on the underlying issues and that their inspiration and supervision of study of the dependent issues is desirable. Then it would be possible to relate every study to every other and to have an intelligible body of work at the end."

'Was it possible to gather a group of "practical thinkers" whose discussions would produce a God-like view of the whole American society? Hutchins believed it was. But these thinkers had to be willing to give their "continuous attention" to the program.

"We can see this clearly if we ask why the Fund could not now, without the aid of additional full-time personnel, undertake the kind of program I am proposing," Hutchins declared. "The reason is that the Board has not the time to do the job. If the Board could devote its full time to the work of the Fund, the organization I suggest would not be necessary. Neither basic issues nor the program of the Fund should be entrusted to part-time people."

If the "practical thinkers" were not available at first on a full-time basis, Hutchins still wanted to get the new program under way. He said: "We should have to do the best we could with part-time arrangements at the outset, hoping to turn them into full-time as we went along."

What would be the role of the board? Hutchins emphasized that the board "in addition to making appointments, approving the program, and passing on the budget, would be expected, under the plan proposed, to take an active part in the private and semi-private discussion groups that would be organized for the criticism of the work in progress." He added: "If this system had been in effect, the directors together with interested persons outside the Fund could have had the chance to scrutinize the Cogley report as it was being prepared instead of doing so after it was completed, when all they could do was to accept or reject it as a whole."

Hutchins suggested that the group of full-time thinkers—or part-time thinkers who might be persuaded to become full-time participants—could be named "The Council on Rights and Liberties." The council would develop ideas for studies, which would be submitted for approval by the board with budget allocations. As the studies proceeded, they would be reviewed and revised in accordance with criticisms coming from various experts and board members, who would meet together in discussion groups. The final products would be publications shedding light on "the basic issues" and pointing out possible actions by policymakers.

He left no doubt in the minds of board members that he wished to have the Fund put nearly all of its money into the council. He did not think that many of the projects previously approved by the directors would need additional grants. He suggested that the awards program and the television news-clip service could be terminated.

It was also evident that Hutchins believed that the Fund should become a permanent organization. He encouraged the board members to consider the possibility of finding more money. He felt that the new council should be generously supported.

Among the Fund's officers and staff, the Hutchins plan was enthusiastically backed by John Cogley and Hallock Hoffman. Ferry had some doubts about it, but he saw its possibilities. I was for it, because it seemed to me that the plan was a logical extension of what the Fund had been trying to do. I did not know whether the program could be carried out, but I admired its daring and its scope. In some ways, it appeared to be a Utopian dream—but such dreams made American life exciting.

James D. Zellerbach, who had sought to have Hutchins removed as president of the Fund, was against the proposal. So were Chester Bowles and John Lord O'Brian, who planned to leave the board at the November meeting. Roger Lapham was not happy about it.

"Perhaps I'm not educated enough to deal in the abstract along the lines Bob seems to enjoy," Lapham wrote to Paul Hoffman. "When I consider this proposal to study the theory and practice of freedom I'm reminded of what I believe Thomas Huxley said about philosophy: 'Philosophy is a hunt in a dark room of an empty house at midnight for a black cat that isn't there.' "

David Freeman, the vice president for administration, and Adam Yarmolinsky, who had been elected secretary of the Fund in March 1956, were actively opposed to the council idea. They wrote a 17-page memorandum, urging the Fund to distribute a large number of grants to many groups and to terminate its functions by 1961.

Freeman and Yarmolinsky were skeptical about counting on a single group of thinkers to direct the Fund's program and to develop a new public philosophy for the people of the United States. They said: "Particularly in the civil rights area, we suggest that a program of grants assumes what we believe to be the case—that no individual or group of individuals can find *the* answer to the problem, but that many groups, with different approaches, will help to work out common-sense solutions. We believe that the Fund, for practical as well as public-relations reasons, should eschew the position that it knows best how to solve the major problem in its field."

These two officers wanted the Fund to continue to be a grant-giving philanthropic foundation. Hutchins was bored by the process of reviewing applications and dispensing money to groups engaged in "common-sense solutions." He wanted to gather great thinkers around him and break new ground. He believed that the United States faced a dangerous situation in which its institutions were decaying or breaking down, a situation in which radical thinking was required.

Adam Yarmolinsky said later: "Freeman and I felt it our obligation to our employers—the directors—to disagree with Hutchins' proposal. We were not challenging his authority, but Hutchins was outraged by what he considered insubordination." Hutchins indicated to me that he felt that all the officers of the Fund had an obligation to speak freely to the President, and it was the President's obligation to inform the board of differences among the officers. He did not think that subordinate officers should take their differences directly to the board members.

In any case, the Freeman-Yarmolinsky proposal was not formally considered at the gathering of the board for two days of sessions on November 14 and 15. The board had many matters to discuss at these sessions. Paul Hoffman had asked to be relieved as chairman, because of his involvement in other activities. Elmo Roper was elected to succeed Hoffman. The resignations of O'Brian and Zellerbach were accepted, and Chester Bowles asked that he not be nominated for reelection as a director. Bruce Catton and Alicia Patterson, publisher of *Newsday*, were elected to the board by unanimous votes.

The board appropriated $130,000 in addition to the $325,000 previously authorized to complete the eleven-volume study of communist influence in American life; $100,000 was allocated for a program to recruit and train personnel in intergroup relations, with the cooperation of other foundations; $10,000 went to the National Planning Association for a study of the effects of racial tensions on the location of industrial plants; $19,250 to the National Council of the Protestant Episcopal Church to help meet the costs of its "Church and Freedom" program; another $50,000 for the distribution of books and articles; and $30,000 for miscellaneous grants, including $4,850 to the Association for Education in Journalism and $15,000 for experiments in radio and television.

Hours of argument were devoted to the Hutchins proposal for a council to explore "the basic issues." Hutchins said the group could be in operation by July 1, 1957, if the board approved his plan. He estimated the maximum possible cost of the group in its first year would be $270,000. He said, "Meanwhile, the Fund would stop making new commitments under its present program, and old commitments under that program would be in the process of liquidation."

In the detailed memorandum he had sent to the board on October 15, he had tried to anticipate every possible objection. He was especially forceful in rejecting any suggestion that the board might give the plan a trial run, perhaps for a period of one year. Hutchins wrote: "The argument might be that the amount involved is large; we do not know whether we can get the kind of men who are wanted; we cannot be sure that the organization will work." Then he declared: "I think it would be better to give up the idea than to try it on a one-year basis." He gave seven reasons: "The experience of one year would shed no light on the value of the organization. A group of this kind would have to spend almost the whole of the year in establishing communication among themselves and in planning. . . . The kind of men who might be obtained for one year may not be the kind who could be obtained for a longer period. Experience with one kind would not be proof that we would have the same experience with another. . . . If they were simply taking a year off, they might view the enterprise as a paid vacation. . . . If the group knew that it had only a year to go, it could not start anything that would not be completed in that period. . . . If the group had a year to go, the most that could be hoped for would be a critique of the work of the Fund, which we are able to make ourselves, and a recommendation that the group here proposed should be set up, which we have already received from the advisory committee. . . . Appointing a trial group could have no beneficial effects on the public position of the Fund, and might have some harmful ones, such as giving the impression that we had called in the doctor. . . . During the period of trial, what would be done about new commitments under the present program of the Fund? We would not want to stop them, because we could not tell whether the trial would be successful. On the other hand, we might not want to make new commitments, because we might believe that the trial would be successful."

But Hutchins' eloquence did not prevail at the November 1956 assembly of the board. Every board member was asked to voice his or her opinion. Most of the members seemed to be convinced that it would be a good idea to focus the Fund's attention on "the basic issues," but they were not ready to launch the council in the form recommended by Hutchins. They finally decided to appropriate $20,000 for use by the president in employing temporary consultants to identify the most significant areas that might be studied. Negative votes against even that step were cast by Griswold and Lapham.

Hutchins was disappointed; yet had known from the beginning that it might take many months to persuade the board to authorize such drastic changes in the Fund's operations. He said, "This approach could be a first step which, if successful, might lead to the establishment of the kind of council recommended in my memorandum." He was determined to win the board over to his viewpoint. He looked ahead to the meeting scheduled to be held in Washington on February 20, 1957.

At that meeting, his eventual triumph was assured. Three new directors who were sympathetic to his ideas were added to the board: Msgr. Francis Lally, editor of the *Pilot*; Henry P. Van Dusen; and Herbert H. Lehman.

Hutchins requested and received a $100,000 appropriation to retain full-time consultants, who would try "to work out and clarify the meaning and significance of civil liberties in the United States today."

These consultants were to examine the country's "principal institutions": government, the corporation, the church, the union, the voluntary association, the educational establishments, and the mass media. Each project would have advisers and two or more board members as "liaison directors." Three studies were outlined: "The Corporation and the Freedom of the Individual," "The Common Defense and Individual Freedom," and "The Church in a Democratic Society." At the suggestion of board members, a fourth project was added: "The Labor Union and the Freedom of the Individual."

When the board met again on May 15, 1957, Hutchins again tried to get approval for his proposal in its full scope, but the directors were not quite prepared to go that far. Despite Hutchins' previous statement that "it would be better to give up the idea than to try it on a one-year basis," he was persuaded by Roper and other directors to accept a resolution stating that the Fund would concentrate its activities for a year "on the basic issues, on the support of the group of consultants authorized at the February meeting of the board, and on the projects, publications, and popular education growing out of or related to its work."

At the May 1957 meeting the board also appropriated a terminal grant of $200,000 to the Southern Regional Council to support that group's program in race relations, and instructed the officers to develop a preliminary plan for "implementation" of the findings of the four "basic issues studies" that the board had authorized in February. Joyce, Roper, Parten, and other directors were much concerned about implementing the results of these studies. They did not wish to have any critics claim that the Fund had retreated from the firing line of direct involvement in the conflicts over civil liberties and civil rights.

All the directors recognized that the conditions of American life had changed tremendously since the founding of the United States. They all knew that the impact of a gigantic military establishment and expansion of government in every field affected the life of every citizen. All of them were aware of the influence of huge corporations and of the power of giant labor unions. The role of the churches in race relations and in defending freedom of conscience had become increasingly significant.

If the "basic issues studies" did not produce notable results within a year, the directors were prepared to explore these problems through other avenues. Hutchins was not sure that a single year would be enough to demonstrate the value of his plan—in fact, he was afraid that the consultants would not be able to show what they could do in less than three years—but he took the gamble.

9

The new program gets off to a stumbling start and then stirs strong reactions

Hutchins moved as rapidly as he could during the last six months of 1957 to get the new program of the Fund organized effectively and to stimulate results that would be satisfactory to the Fund's board. Although these efforts did not generate any publications or produce any headlines in the press until the end of November, he gained the participation of fifteen Fund directors in the first projects. These directors saw for themselves that the program had exciting possibilities, and their gradually increasing interest in the projects was not severely damaged by the inability of the newly appointed Consultants to communicate clearly with one another or with the board.

Hutchins assembled what he called "a group of distinguished Americans" to serve as the guiding brains for the "basic issues" projects. Called Consultants (with a capital "C" to differentiate them from other consultants), they included people with experience in government, education, science, publishing, and labor relations, as well as two theologians, a professional philosopher, a historian, a novelist and political scientist, and an anthropologist. They were so eminent in their various fields—and so full of their own ideas—that they found it extremely difficult to listen to one another.

The Consultants were Adolf A. Berle, Jr., attorney, author, and former assistant secretary of state (who said in one session: "It fell to my hand to hold the pen that wrote the Atlantic Charter, the Four Freedoms" advocated by President Roosevelt in World War II); Scott Buchanan, philosopher, author of *Poetry and Mathematics*, (and former dean of St. John's College in Annapolis); Eugene Burdick, political scientist at the University of California in Berkeley, author of a best-selling novel, *The Ninth Wave*, and later coauthor of *Fail-Safe*; Clark Kerr, a former labor economist, chancellor of the University of California at Berkeley, and later president of the university; Henry R. Luce, editor and publisher of *Time, Life,* and *Fortune*; Reinhold Niebuhr, vice president and graduate professor at Union Theological Seminary and author of *Moral Man and Immoral Society* and many other books; John Courtney Murray, S.J., internationally known as a brilliant Catholic theologian; Isidor I. Rabi, Nobel prize winner in physics, Columbia University; Robert Redfield, professor of anthropology, University of Chicago; and Eric Goldman, professor of history at Princeton University.

The purpose of this group, Hutchins declared, was "to try to discover what a free society is and how it may be maintained."

In addition to the four projects originally approved by the board, two others had been authorized—one on the mass media (which Hutchins had sought for a long time) and one on organizations exercising unofficial or semiofficial power, such as pressure groups, political parties, and professional associations. One Consultant was designated as "specially responsible" for each project—with the exception of the study of "Religion in a Democratic Society," which had two Consultants—and there were two or three Fund directors and a staff administrator for each one.

A. A. Berle had the principal responsibility for the study of "The Corporation." M. Albert Linton and J. Howard Marshall were the "liaison directors." W. H. Ferry was the staff executive.

Clark Kerr took responsibility for the project on "The Individual and the Trade Union." The Fund directors involved in this project were Paul Hoffman, Meyer Kestnbaum, and Oscar Hammerstein II; the staff man was Paul Jacobs, the former labor organizer who had aided Cogley on the Fund's study of blacklisting.

Charles Cole and J. R. Parten were the directors concerned with "The Individual and the Common Defense." Isidor Rabi, who had been chairman of the advisory committee of the Atomic Energy Commission, was the Consultant. Walter Millis, military historian and author of *The Road to War* and other books, was the staff administrator.

Reinhold Niebuhr and John Courtney Murray were the Consultants on the examination of religion in a free society. Msgr. Francis J. Lally, Henry Van Dusen, and Eleanor Stevenson were the directors particularly interested in this project, which was administered by Cogley.

The study of the mass media was a special responsibility of Eric Goldman, with my assistance as the staff administrator. The directors involved in this study were Bruce Catton, Alicia Patterson, and Harry S. Ashmore.

Eugene Burdick was the Consultant on the exploration of political parties, pressure groups, and professional associations. Herbert Lehman and William Joyce, who had been active in politics in California, were the liaison directors. Hallock Hoffman served as the administrator.

Each of the outside Consultants associated with a project was expected to make regular reports to the entire group of Fund consultants on the progress of their projects. The Fund directors on each project were expected to inform the whole board of their impressions and to make any suggestions or recommendations which might be helpful.

In the first phase of their work as a group, the Consultants struggled with definitions of freedom and justice that might be applicable in twentieth-century society. In several of their meetings they were troubled by their evident failure to define these terms adequately or in ways that could be accepted by all of them. They began from different starting points and often did not make contact with one another.

At the invitation of Cyrus Eaton, a Cleveland industrialist, the Consultants met at the Greenbrier hotel in White Sulphur Springs from September 8 to 13, 1957. They spent much of their time on the topics of "Religion in a Democratic Society" and "Individual Freedom in Relation to the Common Defense," and then discussed the impact of the mass media (particularly television) and the functions of voluntary or semivoluntary associations (political parties, political pressure groups, and professional societies).

They reached agreement that freedom was impossible in Western society without the coexistence of four factors: (1) a continuing dialectic between religion and secularism; (2) an economic situation that made a considerable degree of independence for individuals possible; (3) a free middle class; and (4) a self-limited government permitting any needed changes.

One Consultant advocated a "noninstitutional approach" to modern society—an examination of the modern American person, who appeared to be a much different individual from the kind of person who founded the United States or the type of person who existed in America in the nineteenth century. This Consultant suggested that the definition of freedom in the past had been created by a consensus "based on the values of a white, Protestant Anglo-Saxon society." This consensus had been broken by "the rise of new and different racial, national and ethnic groups."

This Consultant contended that "the increase in the percentage of the elderly within the population serves to enhance the value placed on security rather than freedom." He cited the increasingly migratory nature of the work force, compelling "the abandonment of old roots and a shift from rural to urban living, with an accompanying craving for conformity and stability." He asserted that "the economic security provided by today's abundance and the domination of economic frontiers by big business and industry have influenced the young and their sense of ambition." He suggested that the old shibboleths of "liberalism and freedom" might be outworn.

"The goals then were economic and social," this Consultant said. "Today the underlying mission is free expression, free thought, and independence of mind. The search is for a higher dimension of freedom, transcending social utility."

Another member of the group phrased it in a different way: "No matter how satisfactory a social situation is, there is an individual freedom that transcends the social or political processes and is not immediately relevant to society's purposes. It is this essense of individual freedom which is threatened by a technical society."

Many of the ideas that motivated student leaders in the campus rebellions of the 1960s were brought up as possibilities in this six-day meeting of the Fund's Consultants in September 1957. Many of these possibilities were brought to the attention of the public in later years through Fund pamphlets and periodicals and through the Fund's study of the American character, which was one of the products of the "basic issues" program.

At the Greenbrier conference the Consultants gave much attention to a paper prepared for them by Walter Millis. The Millis paper dealt with three aspects of national defense that seemed to present "a challenge to freedom greater than at any time in the nation's history." These were: the military manpower system, the measures taken against "sedition" and "subversive beliefs," and the increasingly stringent measures for controlling espionage, protecting government secrets, gathering intelligence, and developing counterintelligence systems.

In a summary of the discussions prepared later for the Consultants, these points were made:

"The military manpower system is militarily unsound and to that degree unjust. It has failed to produce anything approaching combat-ready formations by part-time peacetime training of the reserve and national guard types.

"The introduction of nuclear weapons in tactical as well as strategic warfare has changed the concept of war and the requirements of a modern peacetime military establishment. The national need actually will be for smaller numbers of long-experienced, highly trained soldiers, naval technicians and airmen, with larger reserves of scientists, engineers and specialists. . . .

"Universal military training in peacetime is ill-suited to these specifications and doubtless would have been discarded but for the conviction of some of those in charge that the manpower needs would still be greater even under the new requirements than could be met without the compulsion of the draft.

"Military service has caused significant distortion in the educational process, restricting individual liberty, interrupting schooling (notably professional training) and interfering with the proper development of new scientists."

The summary analyzed the efforts to combat sedition: "The Constitutional mandate to provide for the common defense requires defense against military attack from without and violent sedition from within.

"The defense that has been built has included investigations, executive orders, regulations, statutes and court decisions on un-American and subversive activities—all justified as essential to defend us against acts of treason, espionage, sabotage, revolution and treacherous influences on policy. The method of defense has been to suppress the faiths, political beliefs and utterances from which acts were believed to result. The defense developed out of a theory that since communist political faith appears to be the root of evil the faith itself must be eliminated.

"The defense was found to have developed almost consistently in violation of the spirit if not the letter of the Constitution. The basic issue was found to revolve around the estimate of the dangers. In 1951, for example, the Supreme Court established the doctrine of 'clear and present danger' in its decision on the Smith Act (which led to the trials of American communists). It declared, in effect, that although danger of violent overthrow of the government seemed remote, the evil would be so grave if it ever happened and its likelihood was probable enough in view of the success of communist infiltration in other countries, that a ban against conspiracy to teach and advocate violent overthrow of the government was justified."

The Millis paper indicated to the Consultants that it would be "impossible to decide the true requirements of common defense" until "the debate on the real nature and magnitude of the dangers from subversion and sedition can be demonstrated in more meaningful terms."

Millis depicted the growth of secrecy in government agencies under the cloak of national security "into a vast, spreading structure of restrictions." He feared that one result might be that "all operations may pass beyond normal controls—outside the debate which free societies are accustomed to apply to their major institutions." Deeply impressed by his paper, the Consultants urged the Fund to publish it as soon as possible.

(Nearly twenty years later, the report of the Senate Select Committee on Intelligence Activities revealed the scope of that "vast, spreading structure of restrictions." The Committee also found that "the breadth of the FBI's investigations of 'subversive activities' led to massive collection of information on law abiding citizens." By 1960, the report disclosed, the FBI had opened approximately 432,000 files at its headquarters on individuals and groups, and an even larger number of investigative files were maintained at FBI field offices. The number of files far exceeded the FBI's own estimate of the "all time high" in Communist party membership—80,000 members in 1944, with the number steadily declining thereafter. (William C. Sullivan, a former head of the FBI Intelligence Division, testified before the Senate committee that the FBI deliberately exaggerated the threat of communist influence in order to justify its files on many thousands of active citizens.)

The summary of the Consultants' meeting at the Greenbrier was sent to all members of the Fund's board. It offered evidence that the Consultants were not climbing into an ivory tower but were grappling with the hardest problems facing the people of the United States in the 1950s. The clashes between the Consultants—and their apparently irreconcilable conflicts on some issues—did not discourage Hutchins or other directors who saw the magnitude of the task the Consultants were attempting to perform.

In November the whole group of Consultants gathered again for two days of exasperating and exhaustive sessions. Mortimer Adler, who attended, sent Hutchins a 31-page memorandum filled with sharp criticisms of the Consultants and their methods. Adler declared that they had bogged down completely on four fundamental questions because they weren't listening intelligently to one another or explaining their positions intelligibly. He proposed and illustrated a method for improving future sessions and aiding the Consultants to communicate sensibly. If better meetings could not be held, he thought that it would be useless to have other conferences involving such an oddly mixed and incompatible group.

Several of the Consultants—notably Scott Buchanan, who said there was "no meeting of minds"; John Courtney Murray, who felt frustrated; and Eric Goldman, who seemed to doubt the value of the enterprise—wondered whether it was worthwhile to go on with the rambling conversations of the Consultants as a group. But the six specific projects turned up interesting results, and the Consultants involved in these projects admitted that these studies should be continued.

Hutchins, who presided at the general sessions and kept in touch with all the projects, had apparently unending patience with the Consultants, the Fund directors, and the staff administrators. His objective was to see the world as a whole, to develop a picture of what was really happening to people enmeshed in technology and gigantic institutions, to get at the roots of the forces that were overwhelming humanity, and to present ideas that might shock people into constructive actions.

Although he had reluctantly accepted a one-year trial period for the program, he kept reminding the directors that a year might not be enough to test the mettle of the Consultants. The Consultants were strong-minded people, with long records of achievement as individuals. It might take at least a year for them to realize that they had much to learn from one another, from the Fund's directors, and from the peculiar process of multifaceted dialogue.

The directors were keenly aware of the Fund's position in the limelight. The friends—and the enemies—of the Fund expected it to be relevant, to have a stream of effects on the events occurring in the age of McCarthy and Eisenhower. The directors were still concerned about other projects of the Fund, about the requests for grants that continued to pour into the Fund's headquarters, about the Commission on the Rights, Liberties and Responsibilities of the American Indian, which had been established by the Fund, about the Sherwood Awards for the best plays on television with civil liberties themes.

Staff administrators of the "basic issues" projects, including myself, were not as confident of the extension of the program as Hutchins seemed to be. Those who attended the Consultants' meetings—and heard the famous men wrangle over whether philosophy as well as history was necessary, or whether American society should be regarded as pluralistic or unitary, or whether there was any sense in talking about "justice," or how much "consensus" was needed to enable a society to function—sometimes were depressed and skeptical about the entire endeavor.

Yet the Consultants did show many flashes of brilliance and came to grips with issues that were not being systematically examined anywhere else. And they were quick to recognize that the Millis paper should be widely circulated as a service to a nation that had not begun to comprehend the damage done to democratic government by the hidden growth of "the secret police and intelligence operations."

The paper by Walter Millis, entitled "Individual Freedom and the Common Defense," was published as a pamphlet by the Fund on November 26, 1957, with an announcement by Hutchins that it was the first in a series of pamphlets generated by the Fund's study of the impact on a free society of the development of "ideas and practices" not contemplated by the founders of the United States.

"From the beginning of our government it has been recognized that while the true requirements of defense are absolute and must be met, this does not authorize any or every demand which the government may make in the name of defense," Millis declared. "If the free society is to remain a free society, it must set limits upon what its government can ask of it for defense; otherwise security will, as has happened in the totalitarian states, swallow liberty altogether."

After reviewing the steps taken to control "subversion" and "sedition" in the United States, Millis asked: "Were these defenses against subversion and sedition compatible with the requirements of freedom and justice under contemporary world conditions? . . . Can a free society enforce a proscription of a belief, as such, without peril to its freedom? . . . A tentative conclusion is that, where the perils are real, the free society is warranted in proceeding against subversion as such. . . . But if this principle is accepted, it must at the same time be recognized as one peculiarly open to abuse. It cannot be applied in the suppression of any or every dissentient or 'disloyal' political faith; it can safely be invoked only where the dangers to be apprehended from the sedition appear, under as calm, unbiased and realistic analysis as possible, to be real, grave, and 'present' dangers."

Millis' description of the spread of secrecy in government indicated that the American people had no way of knowing whether the government was conducting its police work calmly and realistically or not. Millis did not know—and neither did the Consultants—that the FBI and CIA were engaging in illegal actions in many cases and that high officials of these agencies regarded themselves as "above the law." That was revealed later.

Millis called for a stringent reexamination of the uses and effects of both secrecy and intelligence agencies in the relations of modern nations: "The true problem here is not one of catching and punishing spies; it is a problem of the proper formulation and protection of over-all national policy. The entire secrecy system needs clearer definition as to its aims, purposes, and uses; it needs greater flexibility in practice. It should be purged, if possible, of extreme concepts of an impossible total security."

In October and November of 1957, the Soviet Union fired two rocket-launched satellites into orbits around the earth. Both of them were much larger than the satellites being developed by American scientists, and the second one weighed half a ton and carried a dog, proving that living creatures could be orbited beyond the planet. President Eisenhower and other officials undertook an "agonizing reappraisal" of the military and defense policies of the United States. Much emphasis was suddenly placed on training more American scientists and catching up with the Russians.

Millis took note of these occurrences in his pamphlet, saying: "The military problems presented by the Russians' advance in rocketry are quite obviously not to be solved by half-training all young Americans to become the raw material for infantry divisions. The cry is suddenly for manpower policies which will produce, not conventional soldiers, however good, but men trained to the scientific and technical skills requisite for progress in missile warfare.

"It is rather suddenly discovered by responsible officials, many in the armed services themselves, that our excessive preoccupation with secrecy and 'security' is an important reason for the relative backwardness of our missile program."

Thirty-five thousand copies of the Millis pamphlet were distributed to "opinion leaders" across the country. Advertisements were placed in the *New York Times*, the Washington *Post*, and *Editor & Publisher* announcing that free copies would be sent to citizens who requested them, with a limit of ten copies available for each person making such a request. Requests came in to the Fund from all parts of the nation.

While many newspapers hailed the Millis pamphlet as an outstanding example of constructive thinking, Millis and the Fund were attacked by a columnist for the New York *Mirror*—Ruth Alexander—who claimed that "the net effect of the pamphlet is to downgrade our great investigative bodies and the FBI." She went on: "Millis considers the cost of secrecy too high in terms of individual liberty and refuses to relate secrecy significantly to security. But J. Edgar Hoover pays tribute at year's end to those brave and inquisitive patriots by stating that confidential informants have enabled the FBI to 'penetrate vast subversive conspiracies against the entire country.' Does the exposure of these 'vast conspiracies' mean nothing to the Ford Fund which selected Millis as a 'distinguished American' to mould public opinion on the delicate and crucial balance between survival security and hog-wild freedom?''

Dr. Alexander and other right-wing critics of the Fund—as well as some of the left-wing critics, including Sidney Hook and other members of the American Committee for Cultural Freedom—regarded Millis and other scholars associated with the Fund as ''ritualistic liberals'' who placed too much emphasis on civil liberties and stubbornly refused to see the ''vast conspiracies'' against which J. Edgar Hoover fought so valiantly. Hook and others continued to advocate revocation of the Fund's certificate of tax exemption.

Encouraged by the response to the Millis pamphlet and eager to enter the national debate generated by the Russian space satellites, the Consultants decided to try to draft a statement on what American foreign policy should be in an age of missiles and satellites. The Consultants spent months on this effort, wrestling with the questions of what controls the people in a free society could or should have over the management of foreign and military policy, the character and effects of popular influences on these policies, and the theory advanced by Walter Lippman and George F. Kennan that such policies with their complexities should be in the hands of ''a wise elite.''

Meanwhile, other publications emerged from the projects. Two pamphlets were released together early in 1958: *Economic Power and the Free Society* by A. A. Berle, Jr., a study of corporate influence; and *Unions and Union Leaders of Their Own Choosing*, by Clark Kerr, a study of the state of democracy within the large trade unions. Special mailings were made to business and labor editors, calling their attention to the two booklets, with a note reminding editors that the Fund was examining both the labor union and the corporation, to make certain that editors did not feel that a one-sided project was under way.

These pamphlets were launched at a luncheon in New York for a dozen leading correspondents from the Associated Press, United Press, the *New York Times*, the Chicago *Daily News*, the Baltimore *Sun*, CBS and NBC news departments, and others in the media. Front page headlines based on the statements by Berle and Kerr appeared in many papers.

The wire service agencies and the *New York Times* gave equal space to both pamphlets. The *Times* quoted six specific suggestions made by Kerr for increasing democracy in the unions and focused attention on Berle's ''pivotal finding'' that the rise of giant corporations and the concentration of economic power in pension funds ''can enslave us beyond present belief or perhaps set us free beyond present imagination.''

The New York *Daily News*, which had denounced the Fund on other occasions, recommended the Berle pamphlet in an editorial headed ''Will Pension Funds Rule Us?'' The *News* referred to Berle's suggestion that ''lawmakers and the general public begin thinking now about possible fair and firm (not demagogic) laws to head off the economic slavery which un-wise use of the pension funds' corporate power might clamp on a lot of peo-ple.'' The *News* concluded: ''Unlike many of the Fund for the Republic's fuzzy-minded and/or subtly pro-Red publications, this booklet of Berle's strikes us as a constructive contribution to economic thinking.''

The *AFL-CIO News* carried an article summarizing Kerr's ideas: ''The author is inclined to favor four types of legislation: secret election of of-ficers, under some circumstances; appeals to the courts or to private bodies for the protection of dissenting members; lifting of barriers to joining a union; and the prohibition of 'compulsory political contributions.' '' The labor paper then commented: ''Some of Professor Kerr's viewpoints may be regarded as extreme. Certainly they suggest new paths for union action and legislation, which are sure to raise many objections. But they reflect the thinking of a tested 'friend of labor'—and so they deserve serious contem-plation by the labor movement.''

Scott Buchanan's *The Corporation and the Republic* was the fourth pamphlet issued by the Fund in the ''basic issues'' program. It also had a good reception in the press. The New York *Post* published an article about it bearing the headline: ''The Organization Man—That's You, Fund for the Republic Says Sadly.'' The article said, in part: ''It seems we've become a nation of joiners. So the Fund for the Republic has found. 'We are develop-ing a passion for indiscriminate togetherness,' writes Scott Buchanan, former dean of St. John's College. Man the individual is lost, says Buchan-an, in the labyrinth of these corporate affiliations. 'We distribute ourselves in parts,' he says. 'Inside we are hollow men, zero members of the ''lonely crowd,'' shadowy participants in the American way of life.' ''

The first publication that came from the study of the mass media was called an occasional paper rather than a pamphlet. It was the initial one in a series of such papers, which were generally shorter and more journalistic than the pamphlets. Entitled *Freedom to See*, it dealt with the controversy over Soviet Premier Khrushchev's appearance on the CBS television pro-gram ''Face the Nation.'' That broadcast had evoked a storm of protests in Congress and brought a remark from President Eisenhower that he was ''not willing to give an opinion'' on whether CBS ''was remiss in its news judgment in seeking to get Mr. Khrushchev to appear on the program.''

Herbert Mitgang, an editor in the Sunday department of the *New York Times*, prepared the paper at my request. He examined the question of whether American television ''in its role as a news gatherer and broad-caster'' had the ''same freedom as the American newspaper.''

''If a newspaper had published an interview with Khrushchev, no responsible person in any communications field would have thought of questioning the propriety of the publication,'' Mitgang said. ''But when a television network, after great precautions to protect the integrity of the performance and after making its intentions known to the highest level of the Government, telecast an interview with the Kremlin leader, the propriety was very seriously questioned. The President of the United States made a statement which at least implied criticism. Important members of Congress openly challenged the wisdom of the presentation. The press was ambivalent. Under the circumstances it is reasonable to assume that the networks will bear the criticism in mind when they are considering future 'controversial' telecasts of this nature.''

Although the report was prepared by Mitgang and he took full responsibility for it, the United Press and many newspapers attributed its findings to the Fund. The United Press declared: "The Fund for the Republic said today response to the Columbia Broadcasting System's televised interview with Soviet leader Nikita S. Khrushchev indicated that American television is not as free to gather news as is the press.''

Mitgang's paper was released at a luncheon that Joseph Lyford and I arranged in New York. Editors from the *New York Times*, the New York *Herald Tribune, Broadcasting-Telecasting Magazine, Radio-TV Daily*, the Chicago *Daily News* Syndicate, the *Saturday Review, Harper's, Newsday*, and other publications were present. The attendance of these editors confirmed our feeling that the Fund's plunge into "the basic issues" was closely followed by the mass media.

With the approval of Hutchins and the Public Information Committee of the Fund's board, I sent Lyford on trips to twenty-five cities—Cleveland, Pittsburgh, Toledo, Lincoln, Detroit, Chicago, Milwaukee, Minneapolis, Omaha, Kansas City, Dallas, Houston, San Antonio, Phoenix, Indianapolis, Baltimore, Hartford, Richmond, Atlanta, Birmingham, Tampa, Miami, El Paso, Tucson, and Albuquerque—to give information about the Fund and to get the reactions of people outside the Fund to what the Fund was doing.

In each city Lyford had meetings with editorial writers and columnists, university professors, magazine writers, television and radio commentators, and others interested in the Fund's studies. As an outgrowth of his visits to the Universities of Wisconsin and Nebraska, arrangements were made for discussions to be held by faculty members and students on the major projects of the Fund.

His reports were perceptive and extensive. I circulated copies to members of the board and to the Consultants. The results of his talks with editors became evident in better-informed editorial comments and in generally better coverage of the Fund's products. Through his contacts with people in many communities, information flowed out to those communities and information about the thinking of people in those areas became available to the Fund.

From the beginning of the basic issues program, the board had been concerned about maintaining connections between the Consultants and the public. Implementation of the ideas generated in the scholarly discussions depended on "widening the circles of discussion" to reach as many thoughtful people as the Fund could stimulate through its own publications and the mass media.

In each area of interest, there were particular periodicals aimed at particular readers. In each case, the editors of those magazines were invited to luncheons and meetings to hear about what was happening on each Fund project. For example, the Fund's religion study was announced at a gathering of twenty-one editors from religious and secular publications. Special stories were written for the Religious News Service, which reached hundreds of publications issued by Protestant, Catholic, and Jewish groups.

The response from the educational world was especially encouraging. The pamphlets and occasional papers were used in discussion groups, adult education courses, graduate seminars, and high school and college classes in all parts of the country. Many labor unions bought copies of all the Fund's publications for use by their educational departments.

Hutchins had entered the new program because he had believed that it was time for a complete analysis of modern society and for the offering of ideas to support freedom and justice in an age of anxiety and turmoil. He did not know whether the program would strike a response from many people or not. He had expressed the hope that the Fund's new program would move American concern about liberty and justice from the wings—where eccentric and obstreperous people had to be protected—to the center of the stage, where millions of people could see what was at stake. He was not sure that his hope would be sustained.

When he had asked me for a statement on what could be done, I voiced my views in a memorandum: "My theory of communication calls for a large-scale drive to make people throughout the country aware of what the Consultants and their associates are up to. This theory is based upon the belief that the leaders of our society are interested in the same things as the people around them are interested in. If we want to convince the leaders that it is good public relations to take the deliberations of the Consultants seriously, we should get sizable numbers of people thinking and talking about the things which are engrossing the Consultants.

"Under this theory, the primary targets for our informational efforts would be the 200,000 active citizens who read 'highbrow' magazines, go to civic meetings, write letters to editors, communicate with their Congressmen, speak at political party meetings, etc.

"But we would also try to reach far beyond this group—to the millions who got excited about Adlai Stevenson (as a man of principle, as a thinker, as a non-conformist, rather than as a politician or a partisan candidate); to the millions of students and teachers who may find things in this program to release them from the frustration and helplessness which breed apathy and withdrawal; the millions who regard themselves as 'responsible liberals' or 'forward-looking conservatives.' "

It seemed to me that the Fund should pay much attention to the women's magazines with national circulations: "Many of these readers include the wives of 'highbrow' husbands, who are movers and shakers—executives, board members, powerful in the economic and political life of the nation. These wives communicate with their husbands; and their ideas often have more impact than the husbands realize."

Hutchins and all the members of the Fund's board cooperated in the Fund's communications efforts. Letters went to editors of newspapers and professional journals, asking for their comments and suggestions. Editors from Oregon to Virginia, from Minnesota to Alabama, replied with warm notes and a variety of advice that showed their sense of being invited to participate in the Fund's program. The editor of a small paper in Virginia wrote a three-page letter, concluding with these words: "Thanks for the invitation to stop and think."

The most important development in the broadcasting field was an arrangement reached by the Fund with the American Broadcasting Company for a series of thirteen interviews to be conducted by Mike Wallace on "Survival and Freedom." Hutchins and I made the arrangement, and I was responsible for obtaining many of the speakers and preparing material for Wallace to use on the wide-ranging discussions.

Wallace had been doing a fairly sensational program called "Night Beat," in which he cross-examined and sometimes humiliated the people who appeared with him. Hutchins and Elmo Roper, the Fund's new chairman, were a little reluctant to enter an agreement with Wallace. I felt confident that Wallace had the intelligence, the capacity to study issues, and the oral skill necessary for such dialogues. Finally Wallace and the American Broadcasting Company agreed to stipulate that the questions Wallace would ask participants would be relevant to the topics under examination by the Fund. Wallace lived up to this agreement scrupulously. He managed to be a vigorous interrogator without using the harsh tone he had shown occasionally on "Night Beat."

In these broadcasts, the Fund had an opportunity to place many aspects of its new studies before an audience of millions. The reactions were much stronger than Hutchins and other directors had anticipated.

10

*The Fund takes to the air
to promote freedom—and
old enemies threaten it*

IN THE SERIES OF BROADCASTS on "Survival and Freedom," the Fund and
the American Broadcasting Company presented the first series carried by a
national network on serious subjects in what the broadcasters called "prime
time"—the show was aired from 10 to 10:30 P.M. on Sunday nights. Nearly
all broadcasts on significant topics—aside from news and special "docu-
mentaries"—had been confined to Sunday afternoons, described by the
broadcasters as "the Sunday ghetto."

The "Survival and Freedom" broadcasts attracted an astonishing
amount of attention, perhaps because of the controversial issues discussed
and the quality of the participants, who included Reinhold Niebuhr, Cyrus
Eaton, Supreme Court Justice Douglas, Aldous Huxley, Erich Fromm,
Adlai Stevenson, Henry Kissinger, and others from various fields. The
broadcasts revealed that important people connected with the Fund were
not simply intellectuals or philosophers. Reporters for the *New York Times*
and other major newspapers wrote articles based on these broadcasts that
produced headlines in Washington, New York, and other cities across the
country.

Reinhold Niebuhr was the first guest on a program broadcast in the
spring of 1958, when some people were already beginning to notice that
Senator John F. Kennedy might be a candidate for President. Wallace
asked Niebuhr, who was one of the leading Protestant theologians, about
the relationship between Catholicism and a man's political freedom.

Wallace said: "Obviously you feel that a man can be a devout Catholic
without in any sense owing his first allegiance as an American to the Pope.
. . ." Niebuhr replied sharply: "That is one of the flagrant misconceptions
about Catholicism in America; that if a man is a Catholic he owes allegiance
to what they say is a foreign sovereign, or something like that. In our study
in the Fund for the Republic on religion in a pluralistic society we're dealing

with both policies and attitudes. . . . Now the ordinary Protestant, Jew or secularist has a stereotype about Catholicism. The stereotype doesn't do justice to the genuine relation that Catholicism has had to democratic society, not only in our country but in France since the war, in Germany after the first world war, in the Germany of Adenauer. . . ."

Niebuhr and Wallace explored the causes of Christian anti-Semitism in the United States, the question of whether freedom was required for a prosperous society, the role of religion in the confrontation with communism, and the fundamental sources of human dignity.

Wallace revealed his deep respect for Niebuhr and the Fund on this initial broadcast. He concluded by saying: "Reinhold Niebuhr is a man of God, but a man of the world as well. Dr. Niebuhr would seem to be saying that if a nation would survive and remain free, its citizens must use religion as a source of self-criticism, not as a source of self-righteousness."

The second person to appear in the "Survival and Freedom" series was Cyrus Eaton, who had been the host to the Consultants at the Greenbrier Hotel. Eaton headed a $2 billion empire in coal, iron, and railroads. He had organized the Republic Steel Company, was a member of the banking house of Otis & Company, served as chairman of the board of the Chesapeake and Ohio Railway, the Steep Rock Iron Mines, Ltd., and the West Kentucky Coal Comapny. He was also the owner of large farms in the United States and in Canada, and a breeder of prize bulls.

Wallace began by referring to the international conferences of scientists that Eaton had sponsored at his home in Pugwash, Nova Scotia: "You've financed conferences among scientists of the free world and from Communist countries like Russia and Red China. What do you think you accomplish when scientists who are devoted to communism meet and talk with British and American scientists?"

"We demonstrated that men of different languages and different philosophies can get together and discuss crucial questions, come to a common understanding, and part great friends," Eaton declared. "One of the most important things we agreed on was that an all-out war between Russia and the United States would be a catastrophe of the first magnitude."

Eaton said that the conferences were held in Canada rather than in his Cleveland home because it would probably be impossible to hold such meetings in the United States: "The Chinese would not be permitted to come in; if the Russians got in, it would be with very great difficulty." He asserted that the Americans were more cautious about what they said in these meetings than men from other countries because "if they said anything that offended the political forces of this country they would be aware that they might be called on the carpet and subjected to serious examination. I think most of our American participants, when they got back home, were probably visited by the FBI and asked what went on and what they said."

"And as far as you know, they told what went on?" Wallace inquired.

"Oh, very completely," Eaton said. "Because there were no secrets. The discussions were completely above board."

Eaton acknowledged the fact that he had been investigated by the FBI on three occasions, because he was an officer of corporations engaged in defense production. He described such investigations as humiliating and useless: "They keep alive the spirit of suspicion which is one of the evils that plague us. But there are no secrets in the industrial or scientific world. Any idea that anything we can do in America is a profound secret if it is done industrially, with workmen and all other sorts of people engaged in it, is just a hallucination and an emphasis on the importance of the police side of our government."

Eaton asserted that the FBI had enjoyed "a tremendous build-up." He added: "It has enjoyed wonderful propaganda and sold itself in a marvelous way. But I always worry when I see a nation feel that it is coming to greatness through the activities of its policemen. And the FBI is just one of the scores of agencies in the United States engaged in investigating, in snooping, in informing, in creeping up on people. This has gone on to an extent that is very alarming."

Wallace defended the FBI: "From the time that J. Edgar Hoover was appointed its director in 1924 until now, more than 200,000-odd convictions have been recorded in cases investigated by the FBI. That includes the cases of Alger Hiss, atom spies Julius and Ethel Rosenberg, Harry Gold and David Greenglass, as well as Russian spy Rudolf Abel, who was captured last year. Are you in any sense suggesting that this work is unnecessary and that the FBI should go out of business? In these areas?"

"I don't think necessarily that it should go out of business but it should confine itself to legitimate police work," Eaton said. "I think its importance is enormously exaggerated and that it makes no such contribution to the upbuilding of this country or to our respect abroad as its literature and those who support its publicity suggest."

Wallace came back: "The fact remains that the FBI has served to the satisfaction of five Presidents. It recently had the overwhelming support of Congress when it asked for protection of its secret files. And as J. Edgar Hoover himself has said, the FBI is 'zealously watched by the executive, the judicial, and the legislative branches' of the government. What more can you want?"

"If we want a police state that is all right," Eaton said. "But add to the FBI the scores of other agencies that are engaged in the same thing; for instance, the Central Intelligence Agency. One of its jobs is to check the FBI to see whether it is doing its duty. You get one organization checking another and you get to a state of affairs that I think this nation is not going to be proud of.

"I am just as sure as I am alive," Eaton went on, "that one of these days there will be an enormous reaction against this in the United States because every department of government now has its own investigators and, in many cases, its own police force, to creep up on the citizens."

Then Eaton startled Wallace and the millions of viewers in the television audience by saying: "If you were to take the police forces of the cities and of the counties and of the state and the governmental agencies and add them up, Hitler in his prime, through the Gestapo, never had any such extensive spy organizations as we have in this country today."

"We must be a very insecure people if we feel the need for this kind of police supervision," Wallace said.

Eaton agreed: "Yes, I think we have less confidence in our people maybe than any nation that I know of on earth. We're certainly worse in that respect than the Russians."

"How did we get this way?" Wallace demanded. "Here was an America that was free and independent, and suddenly we have turned into, if we are to believe what you say, a frightened and insecure people."

Eaton responded: "Two world wars and the prospect of a third have created these conditions. We are always afraid we will be accused of doing something for our enemy. Recently our enemy was Germany and Japan, and everyone was suspected of being pro-German or pro-Japanese. Now we are suspected of being maybe not friendly enough with Germany and Japan. Also, we are under suspicion if we are friendly to Russia and Red China. It's a spirit of suspicion that is unworthy of this nation; it must be abandoned."

The *New York Times* put excerpts from Eaton's statements on its front page under a headline: "Eaton Sees Liberty Periled by Snooping." The New York *Herald Tribune* carried a story that began: "Cyrus Eaton, Cleveland financier, last night charged that the United States is being turned into a police state with a spy organization surpassing that of Adolf Hitler." The headline read: "Cyrus Eaton Sees U.S. Becoming Police State."

Chairman Walter of the Un-American Activities Committee held a closed meeting of the committee and authorized Richard Arens, the committee's staff director, to ask for equal time to answer Eaton's criticism of the FBI. ABC gave Arens a half hour in which he lauded the FBI and attacked Eaton. Arens announced that a subpoena had been prepared to compel Eaton to appear before the committee.

Drew Pearson, who had just returned from a visit to the Soviet Union, compared the issuance of a subpoena for Eaton with the actions of police agencies in Russia. He said that the Un-American Activities Committee had been put "in the same light as Communist governments behind the Iron Curtain" and "it put the FBI in the same light as the security police behind the Iron Curtain."

Eaton took the position that the committee's movement against him had confirmed the truth of what he had said on the program with Wallace. He telegraphed Representative Ayres of Ohio, asking Ayres to call for an investigation by the House into the arbitrary issuance of a subpoena. He asserted that such action destroyed the respect of citizens for the Congress.

Two leading Senators—Hubert Humphrey of Minnesota and Paul Douglas of Illinois—chided the committee. Douglas said that Eaton was "a free-wheeling capitalist" and should not have been brought under suspicion. Humphrey declared that government officials should use "restraint" in exercising their powers.

Pearson reported that two members of the committee—Representatives Moulder of Missouri and Doyle of California—were disturbed by what Walter and Arens had done. "I have the impression that Cyrus Eaton is under subpoena solely because certain members of this committee may disagree with his views," Doyle said. "If that is so, then we are engaged in personal recriminations and we are abusing the authority Congress has granted to the Committee."

"There is nothing personal involved here," Representative Scherer contended. "I think all members of the committee will agree that if the FBI engages in Gestapo tactics, as Eaton claims, then that is un-American and something we should look into." Doyle returned: "I still do not like the way this matter has been handled, including our staff director's television attack on Cyrus Eaton."

The committee came under heavy fire from newspapers and many commentators. The New York *Herald Tribune* said: "Go right ahead and speak your mind, Cyrus. Representative Walter is making a fool of nobody but himself." The New York *Post* commented: "Ultimately we may all be indebted to the House Committee. It has finally drawn the issue as to whether Americans may criticize their secret police without fear of reprisal."

Although J. Edgar Hoover did not make a direct response to Eaton's statements, Hoover participated in a filmed interview with Representative Kenneth Keating of New York two weeks after the Eaton broadcast. He took the opportunity to tell the nation that the FBI was operating ninety telephone wiretaps on "internal security cases" and that the FBI would continue to crack down on subversive activities "despite the carpings of the professional do-gooders, the pseudo-liberals and the out-and-out Communists."

Hoover's conversation with Keating, which was broadcast on television stations, outraged the Washington *Post*. In an editorial headed "The Law and the FBI," the *Post* said on May 24, 1958:

> When FBI Director J. Edgar Hoover acknowledged in a filmed television interview on Sunday that his bureau was operating 90 telephone wiretaps across the country, he in effect pleaded guilty to 90 violations of federal law. The tapping of telephone wires is a crime. It is a crime whether done by private detectives for purposes of blackmail or by the FBI for purposes, as Mr. Hoover put it, of

keeping tabs on "internal security cases." Congress, in 1934, adopted the Federal Communications Act with a section, 605, providing that ". . . no person not being authorized by the sender shall intercept any communication and divulge or publish the existence, contents, substance, purport, effect, or meaning of such intercepted communication to any person." . . . And when the Department of Justice argued that this statute applied only to private persons, not to Government officers, the Supreme Court ruled unequivocally in 1937 that "the plain words of 605 forbid anyone, unless authorized by the sender, to intercept a telephone message, and direct in equally clear language that *no person* shall divulge or publish the message or its substance to *any person.*"

The pretext on which the FBI has violated the Federal Communications Act ever since its adoption is that President Franklin Roosevelt, in 1941, when the country was on the brink of war, advocated legislation which would authorize wiretapping in cases involving espionage or sabotage against the United States. Such legislation has been advocated in session after session of Congress. But Congress has never adopted it. Unless or until Congress in its wisdom decides to change the clear stipulations of the Federal Communications Act, every wiretap will be a federal crime; and it will remain a crime whether authorized by the Director of the FBI, by the Attorney General of the United States or even by the President of the United States. This is a government of laws; and laws can be made only by legislatures.

The *Post* editorial did not generate a public demand for the removal of Hoover or of any attorney general or presidnet who authorized the illegal actions of the FBI. No one sought Hoover's indictment or the indictment of the attorney general or the president at that time, who happened to be Eisenhower. Members of Congress, the president, officials in all federal departments, correspondents of the Associated Press and the United Press, columnists for the *New York Times* and the Chicago *Tribune* and hundreds of other newspapers knew that the FBI engaged in wiretapping. It was not considered to be a scandal. The *New York Times* had only a few paragraphs about Hoover's frank admission.

Cyrus Eaton's clash with the Un-American Activities Committee attracted much more attention. Senator Thomas Hennings, chairman of a Senate Committee on Constitutional Rights, invited both Eaton and Hoover to testify before his group. Eaton said he would be "delighted to appear before any Congressional committee for a serious discussion of the federal secret police and intelligence agencies, and the effects, as I see them, of their sub rosa activities on the freedoms guaranteed to the citizens by the Constitution and the Bill of Rights." Hoover did not accept.

Arens had charged that the communist propaganda machine was using Eaton's statements all over the world "against the United States and our internal security system." Eaton replied: "The charge that anyone who challenges them is 'giving aid and comfort to the enemy' is the familiar but threadbare line that is constantly employed to throttle the traditional American freedoms."

"I shall be proud to match records with any member of the Un-American Activities Committee, as well as any secret police or intelligence agent," Eaton said. "For nearly three-quarters of a century I have been dedicated to the development of the capitalistic system and the democratic form of government under which it flourishes."

The New York *World-Telegram*, which had often carried favorable comments about the Committee, supported Eaton's right of free speech: "if what Eaton has said makes us look bad abroad, that is unfortunate. But his words couldn't make us look any worse than the action of the House Committee." The New York *Post* applauded Representative James Roosevelt for declaring that Congress should take "a hard look at the Un-American Activities Committee with a view toward overhauling or abolishing it."

It was at this time—in May 1958—that Chairman Walter was still trying to get the Internal Revenue Service and the Secretary of the Treasury to revoke the Fund's tax exemption. The controversy over Eaton's television appearance divided the Un-American Activities Committee and weakened its influence. Eaton wrote to Hutchins, saying that he was getting many letters from people who thought the committee should be terminated.

On June 28 Representative Scherer told a reporter for the Scripps-Howard newspapers that a majority of the committee would not support any attempt to bring Eaton before the group. Two days later Walter announced to the press that the committee had abandoned plans to summon Eaton, because Eaton's charges against the government's police agencies were "without foundation." Walter said: "It is believed that no useful purpose can be served by permitting Mr. Eaton to repeat the groundless accusations that Iron Curtain countries have used for propaganda purposes."

Supreme Court Justice William O. Douglas was the next participant in the Fund's series on "Survival and Freedom." Douglas made additional headlines when he told Mike Wallace that he believed that many Americans were afraid to speak freely or act freely and that the United States had "lost ground in science" because of restrictions on freedom of speech and expression.

"You feel that our scientists should have the right to talk freely about science with Russian or Red Chinese scientists?" Wallace asked.

"With everyone," Douglas said. "Espionage, of course, is one thing. All of these things involve a certain amount of risk. England turned up with a Fuchs who was a traitor, and so on. But those are risks that must be taken. Being alive is itself quite a risk. But keeping the avenues open between scholars is very important. When I was in Russia, I was amazed at the extent to which the Russian libraries are filled with American scientific magazines. Everything is there that we publish, and so little of the Russian is here.''

Douglas chided his fellow citizens: ''I think that we're all in default in not being alive to the encroachments that have been going on, in not being alive to the dangers of continuing encroachment, and in not being willing to stand up in the school-hall or in the auditorium or in the courtroom and saying: 'This should not be done.' ''

Aldous Huxley, the English author who had predicted in his book *Brave New World* that the whole earth might fall under a frightful dictatorship, came after Justice Douglas in the television series. He joined Douglas in urging every person to work for freedom.

Huxley said there were two very powerful impersonal forces ''pushing in the direction of less and less freedom.'' One was the explosive expansion of human births: ''The mounting pressure of population upon existing resources is an extraordinary thing. It's something that has never happened in the world's history before.'' The other dangerous force was what he called ''over-organization:''

''As technology becomes more and more complicated, it becomes necessary to have more and more elaborate and hierarchical organizations—and, incidentally, the advance of technology has been accompanied by an advance in the science of organization. It's now possible to make organizations on a larger scale than was ever possible before. You have more and more people living their lives out as subordinates in these hierarchical systems controlled by bureaucracies—either the bureaucracies of big business or the bureaucracies of the government.''

Huxley also pointed to the danger of damaging the environment: ''The whole essence of biological life on earth is a question of balance. What we have done is to practice death control in a most intensive manner without balancing it with birth control at the other end.''

To prevent the arrival of the technological dictatorship that he saw on the horizon, Huxley stressed the urgent need to have an educational system designed ''to insist on individual values'' and to recognize that ''every human being is unique.'' He also stressed the necessity for decentralization, for the use of ''smaller units'' and the realization that huge organizations did not necessarily bring efficiency.

''That was all very well in Jefferson's day,'' Wallace said. ''But how can we revamp our economic system and decentralize, and at the same time meet militarily and economically the tough challenge of a country like Soviet Russia?''

Huxley said: ''The answer to that is that production—industrial production—is of two kinds. There are some kinds of industrial production which obviously need the most tremendously high centralization—like the making of automobiles, for example. But there are many other kinds where you could decentralize quite easily, and probably quite economically. You begin to see it now if you travel through the South and observe the decentralized textile industry that is springing up there."

Other participants in these unprecedented broadcasts included Erich Fromm, author of *The Sane Society*, an internationally known psychoanalyst; Adlai Stevenson; Henry Kissinger; Charles Percy; Sylvester L. Weaver, Jr.; Msgr. Francis J. Lally; Mortimer Adler; Henry M. Wriston; Harry S. Ashmore; and Robert Hutchins. The ideas discussed in these programs ranged over all the complex issues that were to become crucial in the life of the United States and other nations in the following decades.

Henry Kissinger, who was then the director of the special studies project of the Rockefeller Brothers Fund, outlined to Mike Wallace his ideas for American foreign policy, which were later adopted by Presidents Kennedy and Nixon. Kissinger said the "massive retaliation" policy of President Eisenhower was "too risky" and "too expensive." He proposed that the United States be prepared to fight "limited wars" and to avoid direct confrontation with the Soviet Union, because such a policy might "involve the destruction of all mankind."

Erich Fromm said that "there has never been a better society than in the United States in 1958" but he feared that "if the United States goes on in the direction it is now taking, it is in serious danger of destroying itself."

"We have seen many societies that have devloped in one direction and then are so proud of the problems they have solved that they don't see the defects and dangers which have arisen," Fromm declared. "We are so eager now to make things that we are in the process of transforming ourselves into things. . . . What people really mean by happiness is unlimited consumption. We are a society of consumers, we and the whole Western world, more and more. We try to make men who act like machines."

Former Governor Stevenson, twice the Democratic candidate for the presidency, said he was disturbed by the increasing tendency to hold politicians and politics in contempt.

"It is well to remember that behind every corrupt politician is someone who corrupted him," Stevenson said. He declared that the low state of politics was often due to the apathy of the citizens or their desires for favors. He added: "If we want democracy as badly as I think we do, we are going to have to pay a heavier and heavier price for it, and the most important price that we can pay for it is participation in it. . . . I would like to see more people who are willing to pay the sacrifice, who are willing to risk ingratitude and abuse for service to their fellow-man."

Stevenson attacked the merchandising methods used in modern elections: "The basic condition of classical, successful democracy is an informed electorate. We have to be able to make choices. This is what is meant by self-government. We have to know what the choices are and we have to understand the alternatives that are before us. How can you do that

unless you are willing to listen to the issues, unless they are actively presented by the candidates, unless they are elaborated and honestly presented
by the press? Now, insofar as advertising does this, well and good; insofar
as it tends to obscure the issues and create merely emotional responses, then
I think it does us an injustice and I think there's been too much of that.''

The man who followed Stevenson in the "Survival and Freedom"
series was Sylvester L. Weaver, Jr., former president of NBC, who had created the "Today" and "Tonight" programs for that network. Weaver declared that television was failing to fulfill its educational role in a democratic society.

"You can't really have in your hands the power that television has in
this country in this time of crisis and be agreeable to solving the problems by
letting it become the jukebox in the corner of the room to keep the kids
quiet," Weaver said. "You can't just pile on one crime or western show or
game show after another . . . gradually abdicating any responsible role on a
whole series of assumptions about the public.''

Weaver offered specific suggestions on what should be done: "We
should have a great important report to the nation at least once a month by
each of the networks, at night, in premium time. . . . I think we should have
a news service that really spends a lot of money in developing a coverage of
this country and everything that happens in it, live and with tape. That is far
beyond what we are presently doing. I think that beyond the information
programs—and there should be all sorts of informational telementaries—
we should be going into the cultural field and showing all the good things
that we know people, when they have a chance to learn about them, will become interested in . . . their tastes upgraded and their standards elevated.''

"'Do you feel there is sufficient editorial comment on television currently?'' Mike Wallace asked.

"No," Weaver said. "I think that we should use television to bring in
the opinions of men who have done enough and said enough to have stature
and the respect of most thinking people, regardless of the shift of their opinions from left to right. . . . Frankly, I would rather hear what Walter Lippmann has to say than most television commentators. . . . We should use
television to bring into every home in the country the product of the best
minds on the situation as they see it.''

Weaver asserted that there was a division in the United States between
those who believed in the open society, in a free marketplace for ideas, and
those who advocated censorship and management of the flow of information. He said that network executives, advertising agencies, and corporate
sponsors engaged too often in censorship or yielded to those who put limits
on what the people could see or hear.

Weaver's candid commetns on the Fund program gave millions of
viewers a glimpse of how tightly controlled many television programs were.
He advocated pay television and other outlets for programs that could not

be presented on the major networks. He predicted that the networks would become more receptive to a wide variety of programs under the pressures of competition.

The decisionmaking processes in American broadcasting were almost never discussed on radio or television. The Weaver statements opened up issues that had not been considered before by millions of citizens. Some of his specific suggestions were later adopted by the networks in response to demands by viewers and listeners.

Monsignor Francis J. Lally, editor of the *Pilot*, the weekly newspaper of the Roman Catholic diocese of Boston, one of the most influential Catholic papers in the United States, faced the probing of Mike Wallace in the next broadcast, which dealt with the relationship between the growing power of the Catholic church and the future of democracy.

Wallace quoted John Cogley, who had acknowledged that "there is a conviction or a hazy feeling that the Roman Catholic Church represents a threat to democracy and the American way of life." Then he asked: "What does separation of church and state mean to you? Where should the church, any church, say to itself 'Hands off'?"

"General Catholic teaching, Catholic theology, that is, tells us there are two separate societies," Father Lally answered. "One is the Church, the spiritual society—its concern is spiritual realities. The other is the civil society—the state—and its concern, of course, is the good order of the community. The Church restricts itself to the spiritual life, the state restricts itself to the civil order; but they meet—they must meet—in the individual citizen who is both citizen and believer. . . . There is where the area of conflict comes in."

Wallace referred to an article in the *New York Times* that reported Pope Pius XII as insisting that "the belief that the Church's authority is limited to purely religious matters is in error." "Social problems," said the *Times*, "whether merely social or socio-political, were singled out by the Pope as being not outside the authority and care of the Church."

"What does that mean?" Wallace inquired.

"This means simply that the Church cannot be restricted to the sanctuary," Lally said. "The Church can speak on social questions. It speaks on the relationship between management and labor, for example. It speaks on unemployment. It can speak on child labor—all the things which have moral aspects and which touch the soul of man as well as upon his physical person."

Wallace raised another question: "When the Catholic Church speaks in these areas, does it speak only for Catholics or does it not occasionally try to speak for non-Catholics too?"

Lally declared that the Church addressed itself to the whole world: "But the authority of the Church is restricted to those who are baptized—those who are part of it."

"We protect, we even encourage dissent and diversity in a democracy," Wallace said. "Is this compatible with Catholicism, Father Lally?"

Lally assured him that it was: "I think the general disposition of our non-Catholic neighbors suggests that Catholics are not interested in the open mind, the open discussion, the free forum. That's a grave mistake. Catholics believe in an open mind but not, in Chesterton's phrase, 'a mind open at both ends,' where everything flows in and flows out. The mind is a discerning thing. It reaches out and grasps new facts, new ideas, brings them to mind to be judged, to be analyzed, to be sifted. This is a distinctly human process. The Church encourages this and for centuries, of course, the Church has been the upholder of the rational position in the Western world."

"You will agree, though, that certain pressures are brought to bear by Catholic organizations, publications, etc., to prevent the spread of, specifically, birth control information or prevent loosening of divorce laws?" Wallace asked.

"Catholics are not trying to legislate for their neighbors," Lally insisted. "Acting in accordance with their consciences, they themselves work by persuasion, not by pressure but by persuasion, to influence people to feel the same way. . . . The Church moves by persuasion. To persuade the world, to convince the world, I think, is the apostolic word."

Such a frank discussion of the authority and influence of the Catholic church had never been presented before on a national television network. Lally agreed with Wallace that religious tensions were usually covered up or ignored by newspapers and broadcasting stations.

Henry Wriston, former president of Brown University, who was then the executive director of the American Assembly and president of the Council on Foreign Relations, declared when he appeared on the Fund's television series that the United States would eventually recognize Communist China.

"I think if the Chinese Communists stay in power, as they appear likely to do, sooner or later we will do business with them, as best we can," Wriston said. "Not happily—but we're not happy about our relations with Russia either."

Wriston was one of the few leaders in American public life who was willing to discuss relations with Mao's China in 1958, when there seemed to be no practical possibility that the United States would change its policy in the Far East. He was criticized for his statements, as were many of the other participants in the "Survival and Freedom" series, but the reactions of most viewers were extremely favorable.

Wallace summed up the programs in the last broadcast, before he examined the views of Robert Hutchins, who was the final participant: "We have interviewed two religious leaders, one a Protestant, one a Catholic; a millionaire industrialist who feared that we were endangered by police activities; a Supreme Court Justice who defended the rights of free expression even for dangerous ideas; a noted writer haunted by a vision of over-population and impersonal forces eating away our freedom; a former Presidential candidate who talked frankly about the hazards and frustrations of politics; a television executive who criticized the quality of TV today; a psychoanalyst who declared that we worship machines and care too little about our fellow men; a Pulitzer Prize-winning editor who asserted that our press could stand considerable improvement; a leading businessman who deplored government incursions into the free enterprise system; and a military analyst [Henry Kissinger] who said we must be ready and willing to fight limited nuclear wars if necessary. One thing, I think, came through in most of those interviews: that somehow, as a nation, we are unprepared, that our response to the challenges we face is inadequate.''

Then Wallace asked Hutchins: ''What do you think are the enemies of our freedom?''

''I think the principal enemy of freedom is illusion,'' Hutchins said. ''I think this series in effect shows that. Whether the items in our life described by these gentlemen are really illusions or not, that's what they were actually calling attention to.''

Hutchins cited four illusions that affected Americans: ''The great pervasive illusion is the illusion of the importance of size or quantity. I would say that there is the illusion of technical superiority. There is the illusion that we don't have to think. And there is the illusion which is related to all these illusions—the illusion of progress.''

Requested by Wallace to explain what he meant by each one, Hutchins went on: ''The illusion of size or quantity is that the bigger a thing is, the better it is. I don't think that this is materialism because I don't believe that Americans are as materialistic as Europeans are. The idea that you count things or measure things and in that way tell how good they are is a result of laziness. It is also a result of the fact that we're trying to keep the peace in a pluralistic society. We don't want to argue about anything important.''

''The second illusion was that of our technical superiority?'' Wallace intervened.

''You really don't need to discuss that because it has been so obviously exploded,'' Hutchins said. ''We first thought that the Russians couldn't produce an atomic bomb. We then thought that they couldn't produce a hydrogen bomb. We then thought that they couldn't send up a satellite. They've done all three.''

Wallace continued: ''The third illusion was that we don't have to think.''

''Yes, this is the real basis of the anti-intellectualism in the country,'' Hutchins asserted. ''We're a group of practical people hacking out the continent, you know. We're going to develop all these material goods which we're going to count and measure, and if you can count you don't have to think.''

"The fourth illusion was that of progress?" Wallace said.

"The illusion of progress is perhaps best illustrated by the remark of a Burmese who attended an international conference," Hutchins said. "He said that since his country was rather backward he had no sex crimes to report, but they were making rapid progress and he hoped that at the next meeting he might be able to do better. Here, again, the question is: What is the total effect of the social organization on the total society and can you delude yourself into pointing to your material accomplishments as a measure of that society?"

"How did we get that way?" Wallace demanded. "Where did these illusions come from?"

Hutchins answered: "You get some light on that if you think about what Thomas Jefferson's prescriptions for the successful republic were. He said that there were four reasons why the American republic was going to succeed in spite of the fact that he thought such a form of government could not succeed in Europe. He said, first, we weren't going to live in cities; second, we were all going to be self-employed; third, we were all going to participate in local government; and, fourth, we were all going to be so well educated that we could cope with any problems that confronted us.

"As it happens, the first three of these have not been fulfilled. We know that most of us are employed by others. Most of us live in cities. Nobody would suggest that local government is a training ground for civic virtue. And I certainly would not suggest that we were so well educated that we could cope with any problems that confronted us.

"Jefferson's ideals are valid. But how do they maintain their validity when the facts to which they were applied have been entirely altered? What happens is that we hide behind a cliché curtain, a veil of slogans and illusions that separates us from reality. We go right on talking as though we were still in the eighteenth century. But the facts are quite different.''

"What do you suggest that we do about it?" Wallace asked. "Are you suggesting that we rewrite the Constitution set up by our Founding Fathers—that they did not understand the conditions that prevail today and that we've got to do something about it?"

Hutchins expressed his admiration for the Founding Fathers and for the Constitution. Then he added: "But I think that conditions have drastically altered. The world has not only been industrialized but polarized. Conditions have altered in such a dangerous way that we must be prepared to recognize, as the other men in this series have tried to suggest in the fields with which they have dealt, the difference between illusion and reality—the difference between a slogan and a principle, and the difference between the eighteenth century and the second half of the twentieth.''

"Why is it that I and so many of my fellow-citizens are willing to buy illusion instead of reality?" Wallace wondered.

Hutchins looked at him closely. "I am sure, Mr. Wallace, that you are not the victim of any such sales talk, but I think that the reason for these illusions is that they are comfortable. Why did we say, for example, when we were able to drop an atomic bomb that the Russians would never be able to make one? A moment's reflection on the state of Russian science, on the state of secrecy affecting the processes underlying this bomb, would have assured us—as all the scientists did assure us—that the atom bomb would be produced by the Russians within five years. But if we had accepted that idea, it would have been extremely disagreeable."

Hutchins had been aware for years before the atomic weapon had been successfully tested that a nuclear explosion could be produced. Much of the research on atomic energy had been conducted at the University of Chicago while he was president of that university.

"What is the way back?" Wallace asked, leaning toward him. "I'm probably searching for oversimplified answers here."

Hutchins gave an answer that had a mixture of confidence and anguish: "Anybody who said he knew the way back would be presumptuous, but I think the way back may be, first, to recognize that the situation has changed—something that we usually refuse to do. Second, to try to identify the issues that these changes produce. Third, to try to clarify these issues and proceed by the method of democratic discussion to see if we can invent a program of action."

Wallace then asked: "Have you worked out for yourself a logical, effective philosophy of what kind of world we should be striving for—what kind of world you would like to live in—a specific political, social, economic system that you believe would bring about the kind of world you would like to live in?"

"Certainly not," Hutchins said.

Wallace returned: "Why not?"

"I would think that if I did finally map out a blueprint I'd better throw it away and see whether I could improve it immediately," Hutchins told him. "Because to me life is learning and the life of a democracy is a common educational life in process."

Wallace was dissatisfied. "There's nothing wrong with discussion and study but we're challenged right here and now for our existence by a force—communism—which has a very clear and definite purpose and philosophy and we here in America seem to be floundering. . . . What the American people are looking for, I imagine, is answers—how to cope directly and effectively with our most pressing problems. Your answer is to keep thinking?"

Hutchins responded: "My answer is a little bit more than that. It is to identify the problems, to try to clarify the issues, and to promote the most active discussion. . . . It is only in these things that we can have faith, and we must have it.''

Edited transcripts of the most notable programs were distributed in pamphlets to many thousands of leaders. The Fund received more than 18,000 letters as a result of the interviews. Ninety-nine percent were favorable. Some of the letters contained financial contributions.

In a report sent to the board on May 6, 1958, Hutchins said: "The public interest in the basic issues program has been surprisingly great. I attribute this in part to the reputations of the Consultants. But I think the principal reason for it is that they are wrestling with questions that have been bothering (perhaps subconsciously) a good many people, who are glad to know that somebody is at work on them."

Hutchins recalled the fact that ''members of the Board of Directors at one time feared that the studies of the Consultants might be esoteric: hence the Board's insistence on 'implementation.' The public demand for information about and participation in the basic issues program has overwhelmed us and has at times threatened to overwhelm the program."

Then he acknowledged: "We have a good deal yet to learn about the methods of making the most of the intellectual resources at our command. The procedures for the conduct of meetings, of relating the work of the projects to that of the central group, and of using outside experts can—and I hope will—be improved.

"The casualty rate has been high. Mr. Rabi first had a heart attack and then became scientific adviser to NATO. Mr. Luce has been ill. Mr. Redfield and Mr. Niebuhr are not well. Mr. Kerr has become a university president."

Hutchins was not willing to let go of any of them, however: "Since they are all interested in the work and attend meetings when they are not incapacitated by illness or official duties, I am happy to have them continue. It may be desirable to add two or three members so that the representative character of the group may be maintained if any of the present Consultants are ultimately compelled to withdraw."

The public response to the television series and the Fund's pamphlets gave Hutchins an opportunity to urge the board again to make a long-range commitment to the work. This time he got the approval he had tried to obtain for two years. The board gave him the resources and the authority he desired.

11

*A $4 million plunge:
the Fund's board assigns most
of its remaining money
to the basic issues program*

THE VIEW FROM THE FUND'S LOFTY HEADQUARTERS on the 55th floor of the
Lincoln Building in Manhattan was magnificent on the evening of May 21,
1958, when the directors assembled for a special meeting. The skyscrapers
of New York glittered all around the great building named for Abraham
Lincoln, and the streets of the giant city pulsed with life far below the quiet
room where the directors shook hands and smiled at one another. The atmosphere in the conference room was good. The directors felt that the
Fund's standing was high and going higher.

Paul Hoffman and Jubal Parten reported the results of their friendly
meeting with the secretary of the treasury, Robert Anderson. The board
briefly discussed the recurrent demands of Representative Walter and the
Internal Revenue Service. Then Hoffman presented a recommendation
from the nominating committee, urging the election of Arthur J. Goldberg,
a noted attorney, as a member and director. Goldberg—who later became
Secretary of Labor and served for a time on the United States Supreme
Court and as delegate to the United Nations—was unanimously elected.
After the recess for dinner, the directors reconvened at the Yale Club.

Bethuel Webster, the Fund's counsel, and John Lindsay, then a member of Webster's law firm and later a congressman and mayor of New York,
were present for the discussion of the board's policy in preparing for any
hearing to be held by the Revenue Service. Webster assured the board that
he would request a public hearing and an opportunity to present expert witnesses on the Fund's program and "the difference between education and
propaganda."

M. Albert Linton, a board member who had been appointed as controller of the corporation at the suggestion of other members, was reap-

pointed controller. President Hutchins had circulated a report from Linton to the board; Linton had written: "I am able to keep in close touch with the way the money is being spent. However, the chances of anything going wrong are rather remote." Hutchins had recommended Linton's reappointment: "He reassures us as to the procedures of our accounting, and his presence enables us to discuss regularly with him the management of the Fund investments."

The major decision before the board was, of course, the proposal by Hutchins and the other officers that most of the Fund's remaining resources should be allocated to the "basic issues" program. The board went into a recess overnight to think about it. But no one had raised any strong objections. Erwin Griswold and Roger Lapham, who had been doubtful about the program, were not present at these sessions.

At 9:30 the following morning, the directors gathered again on the top floor of the Lincoln Building. Elmo Roper, the chairman, asked for a discussion of projects and grants outside the "basic issues" projects. The board decided to continue the Sherwood Awards for television productions for another year and allocated $22,500 for that purpose. A small grant of $1250 was made to the Southern Regional Council. The Investment Committee was authorized to invest up to $1.5 million in stocks.

Then the attention of the directors focused on the president's recommendations. Hutchins had declared that the effectiveness of the Consultants would be enhanced if the members knew that the board of directors was committed to the program for more than one year.

"I think we are now entitled to say that the program, in spite of the imperfections and uncertainties in it, is soundly conceived and will be successfully carried out," Hutchins had said in his memorandum before the meeting. "Even if it succeeds beyond our hopes, it will not solve all the problems—or even clarify all the issues—that plague our society. But it is already an important educational force, and there is every sign that it will continue to be so. I therefore suggest that the board make a three-year commitment to it."

After a discussion that went on for an hour and a half—with assurances from Hutchins that the board "would be required to approve purposes, projects and personnel as in the past"—the directors voted unanimously to provide $4 million to finance the basic issues program for a period of three years. That left a little more than $1 million for other projects.

In addition to Chairman Roper, the directors who took this action included Bruce Catton, Charles Cole, Paul Hoffman, Robert Hutchins, Herbert Lehman, Oscar Hammerstein II, Alicia Patterson, Eleanor Stevenson, Henry Van Dusen, and Jubal Parten. The board adjourned shortly before noon. Hutchins was jubilant.

"You got what you wanted," I said to him.

Hutchins nodded. "I thought it would take longer. Now we can really get going."

Hutchins made it clear to me and other officers of the Fund that he still had in his mind the idea of establishing a center where the Consultants—or others of their caliber—could give their whole time to the program for the years ahead. With the board's support, he hoped that such a center could be formed on a lasting basis. He hoped that the center would be located in Santa Barbara, where he had bought a home.

Hutchins canceled the June meeting of the Consultants. He asked them to rearrange their plans and participate in a five-day meeting to be held in Santa Barbara from July 30 through August 3. He wrote to each one: "I hope very much that you can come. Santa Barbara is beautiful in the summer.

"I think it is very important that we should try to figure out where we are going and how to get there," Hutchins told them. "I also think that we must give serious consideration to enlarging the group so that we can count on a fairly substantial attendance at all the meetings. . . . I do not want to add members without the approval of our present Consultants. I have therefore arranged for the exposure at Santa Barbara of three men whom we have thought about from time to time."

The possible candidates invited to the Santa Barbara conclave were B. F. Skinner, professor at Harvard, described by Hutchins as "the leading experimental psychologist in the country"; Harvey Wheeler, professor of political science at Washington and Lee University; and Mortimer Adler, Hutchins' old friend. Hutchins told the consultants that Adler had "just completed an enormous work on freedom that is to be published in the fall."

Skinner, Wheeler, and Adler were asked to write papers on problems relevant to the "basic issues." These were circulated in advance of the Santa Barbara sessions and were used for cross-examination of the three men at the gathering. Wheeler made such an impression that he was later invited to join the Fund's staff.

In the middle of July, two weeks before the Santa Barbara sessions, the Fund published a booklet based on four meetings of the Consultants devoted to an examination of "the consequences for liberty of the foreign and military policies of the United States." All the Consultants participated in these discussions and all were represented by statements in the booklet except Dr. Rabi, who felt that his position as a member of the President's Science Advisory Committee would not permit him to place his views on the public record.

The booklet, issued by Oceana Publications for the Fund, was entitled *Foreign Policy and the Free Society.* It produced headlines in many newspapers, and was read by members of the President's staff in the White House and by many members of Congress, including Senator John F. Kennedy. It contained two statements of possible foreign policy developments

—one by Walter Millis and one by John Courtney Murray, the Jesuit theologian whose views had an impact on the Kennedys and on Henry Luce.

Millis urged the United States to find an alternative to "courses of military and foreign policy which now appear to tend only toward eventual catastrophe." "Competitive coexistence" with Russia was the alternative to "competitive coextinction," he warned.

- In terms that proved to be prophetic of the development of relations between the United States and the Soviet Union in the 1960s and 1970s, Millis wrote: "There seems to have emerged a kind of tacit agreement between the two superpowers more significant than the issues which divide them. They are in agreement that neither wants war. They are agreed in that neither wants nor intends to force issues to the ultimate. Each realizes that the missile-megaton arms race, now only in its early stages, must break them both if carried to its logical conclusions. Working from such a foundation as this, it should be possible to arrive at a *detente* in those areas—primarily Germany, the Middle East, and perhaps Southeast Asia—where interests of the two come most directly and significantly into contact. . . .

"For the time being, at least, the "balance of terror" appears to be operating," Millis said. "It has thereby created an opportunity for creative good as tremendous as its potentialities for the ultimate destruction of civilization." He added that both sides must be willing "to take at least the same risks for peace that we normally take for guaranteeing victory in war, and that we use the chance which the great deterrents have provided to bring international relations into some framework in which the race toward total catastrophe can first be slowed and ultimately be ended."

John Courtney Murray declared that the United States should continue to fight a "cold war" and should pursue a "policy of continuous engagement at all levels of action." He asserted that the Soviet Union "cannot be provoked into taking risks that exceed the minimum, for it does not act under external provocation but under an internal dynamism."

"Our policy should envisage a minimum of security and a maximum of risk," Father Murray said. "Only by such a policy can we seize and retain the initiative in world affairs. And it is highly dangerous not to have the initiative. On the premise of this balance we did, in fact, enter the Korean war, which was right. But then we retreated from the premise to a policy of minimum risk, which was a mistake."

The priest-philosopher expressed the view that the major problem put to American policy "at the moment is the problem that the Soviet Union has already solved in terms of policy, namely, how to be prepared to use force on all necessary or useful occasions, and at the same time to withdraw 'survival' from the issues at stake in the use of force. 'The children of this world are shrewder than the children of light in their dealings with their own kind' [Luke 16:8]. The children of this world understand better the uses, and the uselessness, of the world's darkest thing, force. They are shrewd enough to know that the institutions of this world can be advanced by force; but that their survival should not be put to the test of force."

Murray's advocacy of a policy of "maximum risk" and "minimum security" to stop Soviet expansionism had a deep effect on the thinking of John F. Kennedy. Murray's ideas were reflected in the rhetoric of Kennedy's inaugural address when the Massachusetts senator became President of the United States, and in the actions Kennedy took in Cuba and in Asia.

The Consultants as a group were concerned about "just principles of government" but could not agree on how those principles could be applied in a modern technological society. The situation of the United States and other countries involved in conflicts of ideology and propaganda was too complicated for the immediate application of such principles.

Thousands of Americans bought the booklet at a price of $1 a copy. When they read the foreword by Hutchins, they were warned that they could not expect to find in its pages "definitive answers to the extremely complicated questions involved in the foreign and military policies of this country." It was simply "a contribution to public understanding."

While some readers of the foreign policy booklet were disappointed by the disagreements of the Consultants on certain points, the booklet may have helped to relieve the anxieties of those who had feared a Soviet nuclear attack. Perhaps it was a factor in making Americans more realistic about the nature of the struggle with the Soviets. It may have aided in paving the way for the invitation sent by President Eisenhower a few months later to the Soviet premier—an invitation that led to a tour of the United States by Premier Khrushchev and a joint declaration by Eisenhower and Khruschev that general disarmament was the most important problem facing humanity. The Luce magazines gave strong support to Eisenhower's efforts to lower the tensions of the cold war. While the atmosphere of hope generated by the Eisenhower-Khrushchev declaration quickly disappeared, it became understandable to many Americans that the Russians did want a form of "peaceful coexistence" with the United States.

"Understanding" was the key word in the development of the Fund's basic issues program. To Hutchins, "understanding" was the object of true education. To understand meant to perceive the meaning of what was going on, and to grasp it clearly. The pursuit of understanding was as essential to him as the pursuit of happiness. In fact, he did not believe that the people in a democratic nation could be happy if they did not really understand what they had to face and what they had to do.

The five-day conference of the Consultants from July 30 through August 3, 1958, did not produce the clarification of principles that Hutchins sought. The principal results seemed to be enthusiasm for the beauty of Santa Barbara and encouragement for Hutchins to establish the Fund's headquarters there.

Just before the Consultants met in the California city, the Fund set off new arguments by publishing a five-part examination of the role of religion. The booklet entitled *Religion in a Free Society* included articles by William Lee Miller, professor at Yale Divinity School; William Clancy, education director of the Church Peace Union; Arthur Cohen, publisher of Meridian Books; Mark de Wolfe Howe, professor at the Harvard Law School, and Maximilian Kempner, an attorney, member of the New York law firm of Webster, Sheffield & Chrystie.

In the Eisenhower years, Professor Miller noted "a widely prevalent and intellectually debilitating relativism" in American life: "There is an inclination to believe that almost all positions are equally valuable and true. . . . Believers are often sublimely vague about just what it is they believe in." He found a widespread attitude of "belief in believing, faith in faith itself . . . in the religiosity of Americans from the President on down."

"The 'wall' of separation between Church and State, as it is conceived by most 'absolute separationists' in America, is not really a constitutional concept," Clancy said. "It is rather a private doctrine (of militant secularism in some cases, of one version of Christian theology in others) which a minority of Americans seem intent on imposing on all."

Cohen declared that the demand by organized religious groups for positive governmental support and encouragement had placed on government a burden that only the courts seemed competent to bear: "Where once it was assumed that the role of government was to grant full independence to religion but not positively to advance its course, it is now widely assumed that government has an obligation to 'encourage' religion by assisting it in tangible ways." He did not think that the truly significant problems could be solved by the courts: "There can be no lasting resolution of the Church-State problem until the people, not the courts, reflect upon just what it is that aggrieves them, what vagueness torments them, what fears aggravate their suspicions and compel them to reject the conciliations of reason and appeal to the 'paternalism' of the law."

"In our present scheme of things religious liberty has no higher constitutional sanctity than other substantive rights," Professor Howe said. "We are compelled by our respect for the intention of the framers [of the Constitution] to read the non-establishment clause of the First Amendment as a barrier not only to federal action which infringes religious and other liberties of individuals, but as a prohibition of even those federal aids to religion which do not appreciably affect individual liberties."

Kempner's study of major Supreme Court cases bearing on the free exercise of religious belief led him to conclude that "the religious freedom of individuals and groups has been restrained only in those rare cases where the needs of society would have been seriously prejudiced by unbridled freedom." He pointed out, however, that "many issues remain unresolved by the Supreme Court" and cited the granting of tax exemption for properties owned by church organizations as "a governmental action that might not be constitutional."

In November 1958 national attention was focused on one of the principal organizations financed by the Fund during its initial stage, the Commission on Race and Housing, which issued a report calling for an end to "the evil of housing discrimination" in the United States.

The 80-page report, entitled *Where Shall We Live?* and published by the University of California Press, urged the federal, state, and local governments; the housing industry; and voluntary associations of citizens to "take certain definite steps to purge our national life of the evil of housing discrimination."

The commission asked President Eisenhower to "establish a committee on the elimination of discrimination in Federal housing and urban renewal programs." Realization of the goals of national housing policy as declared by the Congress, the report stated, "is seriously hampered by racial segregation and discrimination in the distribution of housing facilities and benefits provided under federal laws."

In addition to the general report, thirty special studies and research memoranda were prepared for the commission by social scientists at a dozen universities, including Atlanta, California, Chicago, Columbia, Fisk, Howard, New York, North Carolina, Pennsylvania, Texas, and Wayne. These studies had lasting repercussions on policy decisions made by local, state, and federal governments in housing during the next eighteen years. Legislators, bankers, realtors, municipal officials, members of citizens' planning groups, and thousands of other people concerned with housing policies consulted these studies and acted upon the results.

With the *Report on Blacklisting* and the reports on federal loyalty and security programs—and the thirteen-volume study of communism in the United States—the report of the Commission on Race and Housing was one of the notable achievements that could be traced to the grants made in the 1950s by the Fund for the Republic. The housing report and subsidiary studies had a long-range impact on the living conditions and opportunities of millions of people who had been cut off from full participation in American life.

Ten days after the release of the report on race and housing, the Fund announced that it would sponsor an examination of the state of public information. A television series called "The Press and the People"—which I had planned with the cooperation of Louis Lyons, curator of the Nieman fellowships at Harvard, and Hartford Gunn, general manager of the Boston educational station WGBH—went into production.

The coverage of major events by newspapers, magazines, radio and television was explored in thirteen broadcasts. Lyons served as moderator. Joseph Lyford of the Fund staff went to Boston at my request and aided Lyons in preparing the series. Lyons, a veteran newspaperman and daily commentator on radio and television at WGBH, had been curator of the Nieman fellowships for eighteen years. He had been a reporter and editor for the Boston *Globe* and had won the George Foster Peabody Award for local television and radio news in 1957.

Participants in these programs included Clifton Daniel of the *New York Times* and James P. Warburg, commentator on European affairs, discussing the clash between the United States and the Soviet Union over the future of Berlin; Earl Ubell and Stanley Livingston, science writers, on "The Bomb and the Press"; John Kenneth Galbraith and J. A. Livingston, noted economists, on "The Economic Facts of Life"; Barry Bingham, publisher of the Louisville *Courier-Journal*, and Walter Millis, on "Foreign Policy and the Press"; Sam Romer and Gordon Cole, journalists in the labor relations field, on "Labor and the Press"; Theodore H. White and John K. Fairbank, on "The News from China"; W. Eugene Smith and Dan Weiner, on "The Photo Journalist"; Elmo Roper and Palmer Hoyt of the Denver *Post*, on "The Public and the Publisher"; Edward R. Murrow, of the Columbia Broadcasting System on "The Responsibilities of Television"; Clark Mollenhoff and Edwin Lahey, two prize-winning Washington correspondents, on "Secrecy in Government"; Adlai E. Stevenson and Barbara Ward, on "The Soviet Challenge"; Eric Sevareid and Martin Agronsky, on "The Television News Commentator"; and James Reston of the *New York Times*, on "Washington and the Press."

Forty educational and commercial television stations in the United States and Puerto Rico, as well as dozens of radio stations, carried the programs, which were also broadcast by the Voice of America around the world. More than 640 kinescopes were distributed to television outlets, and 850 audiotapes were made available to radio stations. Such a series of critical examinations of the mass media had never been done on television or radio before. The Fund received hundreds of commendatory letters from viewers and listeners.

At the annual meeting of the board on November 19, 1958, Hutchins accentuated the positive aspects of the basic issues program. He indicated to a number of directors that he would soon propose again the establishment of a center where the exchange of ideas could occur day after day, week after week, all the year round.

The resignations of Russell L. Dearmont and Erwin N. Griswold—two of the original directors—were accepted with regret. Only eight of the fifteen directors who had founded the Fund in 1952 remained on the board. Paul Hoffman, who had been the first chairman, was elected honorary chairman at this meeting. Hoffman stayed on the board, but he did not give the Fund as much of his attention as he had in the early years.

With the departure of Griswold and other directors who had occasionally challenged Hutchins, the shaping of the Fund's future was almost entirely in the hands of Hutchins. He was ready for the next stage: the forming of what he called the Center for the Study of Democratic Institutions.

In preparation for the May 1959 board meeting, Hutchins dispatched a memorandum to the directors on May 7, referring to the many broadcasting stations carrying the Mike Wallace "Survival and Freedom" programs, and the extended circulation of "The Press and the People" kinescopes and audiotapes. He announced that 1.2 million copies of fifty-four Fund publications had been issued.

"Apparently many people have become aware of the crisis through which democratic institutions are passing and hope that some sustained attempt can be made to promote understanding of it," Hutchins said. "The Fund is the only organization dedicated to this task. How well it is performing its task is another matter. In the present state of the public mind, any effort seems to be welcome. The Fund is working on problems that are causing increasing anxiety. The basic issues are becoming burning issues."

Then he recommended the next step: "We should look forward to a residential center, composed of men who will devote their whole time to the program for considerable periods. Men who are interested and qualified, but who cannot look upon their connection with the program as a primary obligation, should be regarded as critics and should not be expected to initiate or direct the work." He indicated that some of the Consultants could give enough time to join in initiation and direction of projects; others could not. He added: "If the Board does not object, I propose to effect a differentiation in the roles of the two groups.

"The full-time group should move out of New York City at the earliest opportunity. Our present location is not adapted to the kind of work we are trying to do. Freedom from distraction—at a low rent—is now more important than easy availability to applicants for funds. Our lease expires next April and could not be renewed at any price. I think that well before that date we should establish a residential center elsewhere."

Hutchins had a place in mind, although he did not specify it in his statement. He had a small house and 26 acres of land in the hills above Santa Barbara, California. He planned to build a home there for his final years of life. He though that Santa Barbara would be the ideal location for the Fund's residential center.

"It would be useful to change the name of the basic issues program to something less vague and more descriptive," Hutchins said. "I suggest that it be called 'Center for the Study of Democratic Institutions.' "

The name seemed very long and hard to remember when it was first mentioned to the officers and staff members of the Fund. It was not greeted with much enthusiasm by several directors who received the May 7 memorandum from Hutchins.

Hutchins reminded the board: "At the present rate of income and expenditure the money the Fund has will last about three years more. It is unlikely that the need for the work the Fund is doing will have disappeared by 1963. Nor is it probable that some other agency will take over the Fund's responsibilities if it goes out of business. I suggest that the Board begin to plan now to obtain funds to maintain a Center for the Study of Democratic Institutions for an indefinite period."

A week before the board meeting scheduled for May 20, Hutchins and I flew to Cleveland to ask Cyrus Eaton for a large pledge. Hutchins knew it would take an unusual offer to get the board to approve the shift from New York to California. He had obtained promises of gifts totaling $100,000 from friends in Los Angeles to pay some of the costs of moving twenty staff members across the continent and providing severance pay for others. But he expected much more from Eaton.

When we went into Eaton's elegant suite in the Terminal Tower overlooking the south shore of Lake Erie, the old entrepreneur greeted us cordially. Tall, sharp-featured, radiating an aura of command, Eaton resembled a Roman emperor. He had enjoyed his victory over the Un-American Activities Committee; he wanted to know what he could do for us..

Through the deaths of Mr. and Mrs. Girard Hale, a 42-acre estate on Eucalyptus Hill in Santa Barbara had become available for educational use. Mrs. Horace Gray, a civic leader in the California city, had called the estate to Hutchins' attention. It could be purchased for $250,000. Hutchins suggested that Eaton might buy it and permit the Fund to use it for the proposed Center.

Eaton clapped his hands together. Staff members appeared. Eaton asked for atlases and reports on Santa Barbara and the whole area around the city. When his staff assistants brought them in, Eaton studied them for a while, and then he gave a wintry smile: "I think I'll take a flier with you boys." He promised that he would give a definite decision within a few days.

Hutchins and I returned to the airport and boarded a Lockheed Electra plane for the flight back to New York. As we were flying over Pennsylvania, about a hundred miles from Manhattan, one of the engines began to belch black smoke. I remembered that another Electra had crashed not long before. My body began to shake.

Hutchins noticed my trembling. He seemed absolutely calm. "Don't worry about it," he said. "They've stopped that engine. We'll make it on the other three."

"It's easy for you to keep cool," I said. "You're not concerned about an afterlife. But I believe that if this plane goes down now, I may have to face an immediate judgment by God on what I've done and haven't done."

Hutchins regarded me. "What makes you think I'm not concerned about that?" His face revealed nothing. "But we're not going down until we land at LaGuardia airport. So I see no need to worry about it now."

We landed safely, of course. Hutchins and I did not talk any more about the possibility of a final judgment on the worth of our lives. But I knew he thought about it. Any man who had lived in a deeply religious family, as he had in his youth, would always be conscious of that possibility.

At the age of sixty, he was driving himself to establish an institution that would make endless demands on him. He was committing himself to another risky venture, subjecting himself again to those who would accuse him of building a tower to his own ambition, those who would scorn him and try to defeat him as he had sometimes been scorned and defeated at the University of Chicago and the Ford Foundation.

Was he primarily moved by a missionary purpose, or did he have an insatiable desire to learn and to get other people to realize that the meaning of life was learning? On his sixtieth birthday, my friend Hal Boyle of the Associated Press had interviewed him and asked him at the end of the conversation to put the significance of life into a single word. Hutchins shrugged and answered: "Learning." Boyle told me later that most people, when asked that question, replied: "Love."

In all the years I knew him, he spoke of the hunger to know. Frequently he referred to Aristotle's saying that learning was accompanied by pain. So learning and pain were to him the fundamental elements of life. He did not separate learning, love, and pain: he though those things went together. His first marriage had been a mixture of love and pain; his second marriage was more joyful. He had a deep affection for children—for his own daughters, for my two sons, for the children of all those associated with him—but his passion for education had kept him from becoming as close to them as he wanted to be.

"The only overwhelming feeling that I have is a feeling of pressure," Hutchins said to me once. "I always have a tendency to commit myself to do things about which I ought to hesitate and ask myself whether there's any possibility that I can ever perform them."

His sense of pressure drove the Fund from one project to another and changed the lives of many people.

Two days after Hutchins and I made that trip to Cleveland, Eaton's administrative assistant telephoned me: "The old man will buy the Santa Barbara place and let the Center have it as long as you need it." And the assistant chuckled: "He says that when your board hears what Cyrus Eaton is willing to do, they'll buy it themselves."

When Hutchins told Albert Linton of Eaton's offer, Linton snapped: "If it's such a good investment, why don't we buy it ourselves?" When the board convened on May 20 in New York, Hutchins presented the case for the movement to Santa Barbara.

The board minutes for that meeting at the Biltmore Hotel tell what happened: "The President stated that Clark Kerr, president of the University of California, and Sam Gould, who is assuming the office of Chancellor of the

University of California in Santa Barbara on June 1, 1959, had encouraged the Fund to pursue its studies on the basic issues in Santa Barbara, working with the University of California there and other academic institutions on the Pacific coast.

"Mr. Hutchins also reported that donors in California had offered to contribute $100,000 to make a move possible. The Hale Estate, a property of 41.5 acres, which includes a residence that could be readily converted to accommodate the study programs of the Fund, was available at a price of $250,000. Mr. Hutchins reported the judgment of competent persons, including Board member William H. Joyce, Jr., a resident of Santa Barbara, that at a purchase price of $250,000 the land not required for the Fund could be sold at a profit.

"After discussion, it was unanimously (with more than two-thirds of the Directors present and voting) resolved that the basic issues program and the study activities of the Fund be removed from New York to Santa Barbara, Californai; that the purchase by the Corporation of the Hale estate at a price of $250,000 be and hereby is approved."

Hutchins then informed the board that a small New York office would be retained for the few staff members who might continue to be situated in New York. Hutchins formally proposed that the name of the Fund's activities be changed to "The Center for the Study of Democratic Institutions," and the directors agreed with the provision that the executive committee would have the power to amend the title before it was announced publicly if they believed it wise to do so.

George Shuster, who was retiring from the presidency of Hunter College, had been approached by Hutchins before the meeting and asked to accept an appointment as a consultant in charge of the Fund's New York office. Shuster had indicated his willingness to do it. Shuster was one of the most enthusiastic supporters of the Center. In fact, Hutchins attributed the idea of the residential Center to him.

On June 4, 1959, Hutchins announced that the directors of the Fund had voted to establish a Center for the Study of Democratic Institutions in Santa Barbara. He said that the headquarters of the Fund would be transferred from New York to the new Center by September 1, and that the Center would continue and develop the basic issues program. He also disclosed the addition of George Shuster and Harrison Brown, a professor at the California Institute of Technology, to the committee of consultants.

"Two of our major projects have been centered in California," Hutchins said. "The labor project has been directed by Clark Kerr and the political parties project by Eugene Burdick. We have been much impressed by the plans for the University of California at Santa Barbara that have been put forward by Clark Kerr and by Samuel Gould, the new Chancellor at the Santa Barbara campus. The city of Santa Barbara is destined to become an intellectual center of the first importance."

Hutchins knew that some of the conservative residents of Santa Barbara would not welcome the Center. But he had been assured of support by Tom Storke, the fiery editor and publisher of the Santa Barbara *News-Press*, who had been a dominant figure in the city for sixty years. With Storke's backing, he thought the Center could gain a permanent place in Santa Barbara.

PART THREE

An Old Mansion Harbors a Utopian Academy

12

*In an old mansion in a golden
city, the Fund gathers thinkers
to renew a free society*

Hutchins called the old mansion on Eucalyptus Hill "El Parthenon" because it combined some aspects of Greek and Spanish architecture. The house formed a large rectangle, with enough room for twenty-two offices on the main floor, and a row of cubicles on a lower level. The front wall was made of white plaster and extended in two wings on each side of a tall entrance with glass doors protected by iron grilles. Wide curved marble steps led up to this entrance. On each side of these steps stood gigantic cactus plants as big as trees.

A pair of pillars partly covered with ivy, standing a few feet back from Eucalyptus Hill Road, stood at the beginning of a long drive which wound through a grove of trees for half a mile up to the broad parking lot. There was enough parking space for dozens of cars.

When you approached the front of the house, its size was not immediately apparent. Inside there was a marble lobby where a receptionist sat at a walnut desk. Beyond the lobby you could see a courtyard with thick pillars on two of its sides. Corridors on each side of the courtyard led to the conference room, which had tall French doors. In this room, tables had been placed together in an oblong shape. Comfortable chairs for participants in dialogues were arranged around the rim of the oblong. Against one wall there were a few chairs for observers.

Through these doors the softly contoured mountains behind Santa Barbara were visible. Beyond the conference chamber was a wide curving terrace. Just below the terrace lay a vast swimming pool never used by the Center scholars. It was covered with a mesh of wire and flowers. The view from the terrace on a bright day—and Santa Barbara had many such days—was dazzling. The blue Pacific glittered far below, and birds rose into the sky from a little lake near the ocean.

It was a place for soaring visions, for young men to try their wings, for old men to feel immortal. It seemed far away from the racking problems of humanity. But the people who worked at the Center never escaped those problems, which were brought into the conference room day after day.

With the help of real estate agents recommended by Hutchins, Center staff members bought homes or rented apartments in Santa Barbara. In 1959 there were many houses for sale and many apartments available. The city was just beginning to change under the impact of the development of the University of California campus there. The leaders of Santa Barbara, headed by Storke, thought that the city could absorb the influx of students and professors without too many dislocations.

At that time, Santa Barbara was largely controlled by the wealthy residents of the suburb called Montecito. Quite a few of these rich people had made fortunes in the harsh climates of Chicago, Boston, and New York and had moved to Santa Barbara to enjoy a relaxed life in their remaining years. Some of them were interested in the university and a few of them were intrigued by the idea of the Center, but most of them had no desire to encounter "radical" professors or to mingle socially with the "big thinkers" at the Center. Some of them were actually hostile, especially the members of the John Birch Society, which had a thriving chapter in Santa Barbara.

During the first months of the Center's establishment in the city, many of the people in the community seemed to be baffled by what was going on there. It was not regarded as an organization closely connected to Santa Barbara. Hutchins and his associates were considered to be aloof, remote, occupied with questions of national and international significance, not concerned about the mundane affairs with which ordinary citizens wrestled.

Kenneth Boulding, a British economist who came to one of the Center's early meetings, later described it in a song to be sung to the tune of "Men of Horlech":

> In a time Apocalyptic
> on the mountain Eucalyptic
> Full of thought Acropolyptic
> Stands the Hutchins Hutch.

> In this intellectual Attic
> Institutions Democratic
> Are studied by the Mode Socratic
> With the Midas Touch.

In October an articulate, clever, and ambitious man who eventually became second in power to Hutchins—Harry Ashmore, a Fund board member who had been a lieutenant colonel in the army in World War II and was referred to by Hutchins as Colonel Ashmore—arrived in Santa Barbara with his family. Ashmore had been first elected to the Fund's board in 1954 and had resigned late in 1955, when he had become an aide to Adlai Stevenson in Stevenson's second campaign for the presidency. After Stevenson's defeat in 1956, Ashmore had returned to his job as executive editor of the *Arkansas Gazette* and rejoined the Fund's board. He had always voiced approval for projects suggested by Hutchins.

Not long after the Center had begun to operate, Hutchins told me, "Colonel Ashmore would like to be with us here. What do you think of it? I'd expect you to work closely together." Like Hutchins, I admired the courage Ashmore had shown during the struggle over school desegregation in Little Rock in 1957. He was deeply interested in the mass media study, and I had consulted him frequently on its development. "I think it's a fine idea," I said. "Good," Hutchins said. "I believe Bill Benton will put up the money to pay Ashmore's salary."

William Benton, the publisher of the Encyclopaedia Britannica and an old friend of Hutchins, was interested in the possible establishment of a commission on the mass media and had given the Fund $8,250 through the Benton Foundation. Hutchins found that Benton was willing to provide another $25,000 to have this project carried forward. Hutchins appointed Ashmore as a special consultant to the Center with Benton's grant.

In a statement describing his reasons for making the $25,000 gift, former Senator Benton said: "For better or worse, the mass media of communication in the United States are instruments of education. . . . In their role as leaders of public opinion and as channels of education, the media today suffer grievously from a lack of systematic outside appraisal. They do not enjoy a fraction of the constructive review, audit and criticism their importance warrants. I hope the Center will direct my contribution to a study of this problem." Ashmore agreed that both the press and the broadcasting industries needed what he called "informed criticism—criticism they provide only peripherally for each other, and hardly at all for themselves."

Although Ashmore spent much of his time during his first year on the mass media project, he also participated in the daily discussions on all the topics with which the Center was concerned. He sat next to Hutchins at the head of the table, and it was soon obvious that Hutchins sought his advice on many matters. Ashmore was a voluble man with a quick laugh and a fund of ribald stories, a man who liked martinis and parties, and he had a hearty vitality and a decisive manner that appealed to Hutchins.

On October 26, 1959, the Center published the first pamphlet issued after its initial meetings in Santa Barbara. The 122-page publication, *The Corporation and the Economy*, was divided into two sections: an opening part devoted to extensive "Notes" by W. H. Ferry, then the administrator of the Center's study of the corporation, and a second section containing excerpts from discussions by the committee of consultants and staff members of the Center. The report included a preface stating that "contributors to publications issued under the auspices of the Center are responsible for their statements of fact and expressions of opinions. The Center is responsible only for determining that the material should be presented to the public as a contribution to the discussion of the free society."

Ferry declared in his "Notes" that the large industrial corporation, although it had become one of the most powerful and pervasive institutions in American life and had attained the status of "a private government," did not have a clear understanding of its own goals. Most of the consultants shared Ferry's view on this point.

The report showed agreement that the corporation and the economy in general should be "subsidiary" to society, that the economy had to serve "the general welfare," and that there was a need for continuous critical appraisal of the performance of the corporation. There was general assent to the proposal that a new critical agency, financed by foundations and universities, should be created for this purpose.

The participants in the discussion did not agree on how the public should attempt to influence the role of the corporation. The discussion reflected different viewpoints on suggestions for various types of social and governmental control. Some of the participants objected strongly to Ferry's contention that the corporation should restrict itself to "profit-making."

"The corporation's essential genius, that of organizing collective effort to make money, is being diluted in ways that have questionable worth," Ferry said. "I regard the corporation as an instrument that is sprawling over too much of society now and imposing its own goals, which it cannot clearly comprehend, on the rest of the community. I recognize, of course, the variety of corporations, large and small, with differing outlooks. When I say I have a bias in favor of profit-making as the standard or the rationale for corporate activity, I mean to say that I cannot see anything else that is as reasonable."

Hutchins raised the question of whether corporations should be free to make donations to educational institutions, since "education and support of higher learning are aims of the American people."

Isidor Rabi, the Nobel prize-winning physicist, who took part in this discussion, asserted, "I see no particular quality of a corporation which makes it a judge of education. It is a fundamental mistake to ask corporations to do this."

"What we are trying to do always is to effect a balance, to link the flexibility of a free society and the spontaneity of centers of power with the over-all purposes," Reinhold Niebuhr said. "We still have the problem of guaranteeing the rights of the individual against centers of power. Perhaps we have two great problems—how to guarantee the rights of the individual against the centers of power, and, on the other hand, how to guarantee the vitalities of the centers of power, influence, creativity against bureaucracy, if you will."

"I suggest that the American ideal is 'bumps and grinds,' " Hutchins said, referring to Clark Kerr's description of conflicting forces in a free society. "Every time it is necessary for the government to intervene to ease the effects of bumps and grinds, there have to be the deepest apologies to everybody, and the greatest possible concealment of what is going on."

"Aren't you glad about what is going on?" Rabi inquired. "If you had complete government control in a country like the United States without a system of selection as in a country like Russia, we would be run by incompetents."

Several of the consultants indicated their awareness of the dangers of too much government planning. They found it difficult to reconcile planning with freedom and creativity.

"I am not myself at all sure that plans for economic growth or plans for economic decrease really fall within the political function," John Courtney Murray said. "I start with the premise that the stability of the country's economy must inevitably be in some sense a concern of the government. How the concern manifests itself and the value of the mechanism would depend on whether it was duplicating a lot of other things that were going on. The government might say, leave it to the Rockefeller Brothers."

Hutchins asked the consultants to comment on the advisability of a national resources planning board, which could "actually allocate resources of one kind or another instead of having only the right to advise."

"What would they be empowered to do?" Murray wondered.

"If they were more than an advisory body, they might have to begin with natural resources," Hutchins said. "They might be required to consider what could be done to get more schools and fewer lipsticks produced. This might carry over into allocation of labor. The thing that everybody always talks about is the control of wages and prices, both said to be indispensable to any kind of public planning. I would give them any powers that you think are necessary."

Scott Buchanan declared that "the disturbances and miscarriages of private enterprise at present are so frequent and general and systematic that it looks as if we ought to have more legal understanding. The law might consist in setting up institutions which would have a chartered or constitutionalized framework within which they would operate."

Murray was wary: "You defend these interventions on the ground that there is malfunction, that there is some manner of injustice in equity that has to be corrected. Indeed, it often happens that in correcting this malfunction here and getting it functioning something goes wrong somewhere else, and you tinker. This is a kind of sloppy way to do things. . . . This is where the word 'planning' is bad. It is not enough to say that it is all right for government to intervene in the mode of law. What I am against is some dream or image of the world or the country as it ought to be which we will now fulfill by appropriate steps."

"Suppose your technological system is what is creating all these problems?" Buchanan speculated. "The innovations bring on crises. I don't mean necessarily the big depressions but a crisis of operation and understanding between the people involved. Shouldn't the government take cognizance and find some regular way of dealing with innovations in technology?''

Murray nodded. "I do think now you are getting very close to the heart of the problem. Technology is at the root of a great deal of disorder, the disorder being systematic in itself and being created systematically."

The exchange between Buchanan and Murray dealt with two of the major themes with which the Center concerned itself during its first years of operation—the question of relationships between "private governments" such as corporations and labor unions and that of the functions of law and planning in attempting to bring technology into a constitutional structure for the benefit of the people. Concern about the effects of technology had been expressed by many thinkers since the Industrial Revolution had begun in England. But the basic problems were unsolved.

Buchanan advocated federal charters for corporations and a congress of corporations that would deal with political-economic matters through legal means: "There are two possibilities. One is to give the corporation a constitution and a rule of law within its own body; the second is to change the federal Constitution or state constitutions in such a way that they regulate and take their full responsibility with relation to corporations."

Niebuhr intervened: "Why couldn't you say that the corporation is a quasi-sovereignty and the public charters it on the old principle that you have to harness it for the public good? . . . What you are dealing with is a quasi-sovereignty, as with a labor union."

"We treat the corporation to some extent as having the rights or responsibilities of an individual," Rabi said. "I don't understand in theory how a corporation which does not have a soul or conscience can be said to have certain responsibilities, and how you attach responsibilities to such a zombie."

Hutchins observed: "Lord Thurlow said that the corporation had no backside to be kicked."

Adolf Berle, an authority on corporate legal practices, said it appeared that "we are coming to a point in which the corporation is to submit itself to and become an active and assisting member of some planning mechanism of some kind.

"We are coming into the national planning mechanism now. At the same time come some negative aspects. The corporation must not steal from its stockholders; it is not to exploit its customers; it is not to exploit its labor. It is supposed not to discriminate in buying or selling. It must not monopolize. It must not grow too big, although the anti-trust cases are shifting. It must not contribute too much to political campaigns, and the length and breadth of campaigns becomes pretty indefinite, too."

Berle, who had been a member of President Roosevelt's "brains trust" and had helped to shape the New Deal, was skeptical about the benefits of planning: "When people say planning is the answer to anything, they obviously have not thought it through. It only sets up machinery for settling conflicts which otherwise can be determined only by the open market or by the rule of power or something of that kind, with results you wish to avoid."

"When you talk about planning, you are really talking about structuring a society," Kerr commented. "The really planned society is one that is structured to minimize the individual decisions. The great struggle in the world at the present time is about which is the better way to structure society."

Berle favored "a critical agency" to keep corporations under scrutiny and to inform the public of its findings: "It would be an accessory to a planning agency, if we formulated one, to the extent that it is needed."

Hutchins reminded the group that the relationship of planning to technological development was a crucial issue: "Ferry's paper recommends guiding and directing technological development in the public interest."

"We are all terribly conscious of what technology has done to us," Walter Millis said. "But how are you going to control it?"

Ferry answered: "At first we found some difficulty in controlling patent medicines. We have them under control now. We have done the same thing with food. I suggest that it is not difficult to control technology, as soon as one says, 'Yes, the public has an immediate interest in this.' But when we say we ought to have some method of appraising technology and keeping it under control, it does not mean to march into the laboratories and say, 'Don't investigate; don't get into research.' Our concern would be with the social effects of things turned up by research."

"When you say that, you should stop," Kerr responded. "Technology and science and thought are all tied together. When you say you want to control technology, you are saying you want to control new ideas. This is one of the greatest potential attacks on freedom of thought I have ever heard about."

Hutchins spoke: "Suppose we said we were for the orderly introduction of the application of new ideas."

Kerr objected. "I don't know that they have ever been introduced in an orderly way. If we start to introduce them in an orderly way, somebody would introduce them in a disorderly way and get a long way ahead of us."

"There is a tendency on our part to be solving all problems by setting up a commission to serve as a kind of watch-dog," Goldman pointed out. "We will have one to watch the corporation and one to watch technology. This could tend to be a fairly superficial solution of these problems."

Hutchins was sensitive to Goldman's criticism: "When you get into almost any public question, the issue is, shall this social phenomenon be allowed to run wild? Is the best answer essentially that of 'bumps and grinds'? Or shall you control it, which has to be by governmental action? The reason why commissions are recommended often is not because they are easy, but because the only alternative between letting things run wild and controlling them through government action is criticism of some sort. This is one of the things that is grossly lacking in the United States as compared with England, where the tradition of the Royal Commission is established and under which many useful services have been performed."

In a sense, the Center's committee of consultants constituted an American equivalent of the English royal commissions. The consultants were expected to review and give their findings on the conditions of all of the major institutions in American life. But the consultants, while they were illustrious and highly respected in governmental circles as well as in the press, had no official standing.

If the "bumps and grinds"—that is, the collision of random forces—really determined what happened in modern society, then the impact of the intellectual community formed by the consultants, staff, and advisers of the Center would be relatively limited. Hutchins was very much concerned about that. As an educator, of course, he knew that the effect and the eventual influence of an educational institution could not be measured in precise terms, and he was sure that the exchange of ideas was valuable in itself, but he realized that the Fund's board members and the financial supporters of the Center expected "practical results."

Father Murray had said: "What I am against is some dream or image of the world or the country as it ought to be which we will now fulfill by appropriate steps." Hutchins did not wish to impose his dream on others through governmental power but he did have a vision of an orderly world in which learning would have a higher priority than the production of lipsticks.

Hutchins' ideas were frequently opposed in Center meetings by his fellow educator, Clark Kerr. In the discussion of technology, Kerr said: "As individual things come along, as the automobile came along, you do start certain rules for their use. . . . But to talk about some kind of a commission to study technology over-all or some government commission to control technology over-all is absolutely impossible. This thing was unleashed on the world. It is going to keep growing. We have no idea what the ultimate consequences are going to be. I don't know how you would ever tackle it."

Hutchins would not abandon the idea that "this thing" unleashed on the world had to be tackled. In the 1950s and the early 1960s, long before the Club of Rome issued its report *The Limits of Growth*, before Ralph Nader had become a popular crusader, the Fund and the Center grappled repeatedly with the giant thing called technology, trying to find ways of keeping democracy alive while technology took over many human activities.

A 15-page press release was sent from the Center's office in New York to editors and broadcasters throughout the United States, containing extensive excerpts from the statements made by the consultants in *The Corpora-*

tion and the Economy. The use of direct quotations from the participants in the Center sessions enabled readers to see the variety of viewpoints expressed in the dialogue. No one expected that editors or broadcasters would use all the material made available to them, but it was hoped that the sampling of many ideas would show what the Center was trying to do.

On November 23, 1959, the Fund and the Center released another report bearing on another significant and difficult problem: the lack of citizen participation in the political life of a major American city. This 125-page document prepared by James Reichley, a Pennsylvania newspaperman, dealt with the frustrations of the reform movement in Philadelphia, a city where the founders of the United States met to draft the original American Constitution.

In the booklet *The Art of Government*—one of several studies of local, state, and national government sponsored by the Center—Reichley declared that efforts for reform led by Mayor Richardson Dilworth in Philadelphia had "failed to change in any way the practice of politics in the city." He cited evidence that voting fraud and a corrupt alliance between politicians and organized racketeers continued to exist.

Noting that the Philadelphia reformers had accomplished some gains through the installation of civil service by Joseph Clark—Dilworth's predecessor in the mayor's office—Reichley deplored the lack of citizen support for Dilworth's defense of these gains. He declared: "The maintenance of good government in Philadelphia is almost entirely dependent on the continuance of enlightened leadership in the mayor's office."

The Reichley pamphlet produced some angry reactions from political leaders in Philadelphia, who denied that corruption was as widespread as Reichley had indicated. But there could be no doubt about the apathy of the voters or the willingness of many citizens to abandon participation in the political process. Recognizing the seriousness of this problem, the Center made many efforts through its publications in subsequent years to circulate ideas for the encouragement of more activity by citizens.

In 1959 and 1960 a stream of controversial publications demonstrated that Hutchins and his colleagues had not retreated into a sanctuary in Santa Barbara. The Center managed to disturb almost as many people as the Fund had done. To members of the Birch Society and other right-wing citizens it became known as "little Moscow on Eucalyptus Hill" because it issued so many criticisms of what was happening in American life. In the eyes of these people, criticisms of American institutions helped the communists.

Several publications emerged from the study of the mass media, which I directed. In *Broadcasting and Government Regulation in a Free Society*, two former FCC commissioners and a former general counsel to the FCC asserted that it had failed to ensure that commercial broadcasters would run their stations in the public interest. One former commissioner, Clifford

Durr, said that the FCC had not effectively checked the performance of stations against promises made by owners and operators when they aplied for their licenses. Lawrence Fly, the other former FCC chairman, charged that the FCC considered itself to be merely an "electronic traffic cop," and he advocated more controls over the "coercive power" of the major networks.

Fly reported that attempts to revise legislation affecting broadcasting were subjected to "an amount of political heat" that was "indescribable." He described what occurred: "Every station affiliated with a network or that owned a local newspaper would get in touch with its Congressman; these people have a real voice with their Congressmen and Senators. Right down to the grass roots they have tremendous political influence."

The blocking of pay-television experiments by the television networks and the motion picture industry was explained in another booklet published by the Center in March 1960, *To Pay or Not to Pay*. Robert W. Horton, author of the pamphlet, was a former information director for the National Defense Advisory Commission and the Office of Emergency Management. Horton said that the networks and the proponents of pay TV had so misrepresented and obscured issues in the controversy that "an intelligent decision (about Pay TV) has been made almost impossible for millions of set owners and for the FCC itself."

Four months later the Center released another report in which a group of leading television writers declared that domination of television by advertising agencies and sponsors had deprived many creative writers of the freedom to write "in terms of their own truth" and had driven them out of the medium. Participating in this discussion were Robert A. Aurthur, Rod Serling, and Irve Tunick, dramatists; Marya Mannes, a television critic; Evelyn Burkey, executive director of the Writers' Guild of America; and Eric Goldman, Robert Horton, and myself.

Horton showed how all the people involved in broadcasting could evade responsibilities: "The agency has no function except to sell, so it obviously assumes no public responsibility, which is quite right. The FCC has no control over it, and so they can say, 'We are out.' The networks say—well, they don't say it frankly, but we know they are not controlled by the FCC—they say in effect that they don't have any responsibility, either. The sponsor, who is the furthest removed of all, obviously has no responsibility. So we come down to the local station licensee who does have the responsibility (under the federal communications law). But it is not enforced by the FCC. And since the local station is under network influence and control, it cannot in effect discharge the responsibility which it has under its license."

"What you have is an interplay of pressure groups, an interplay of various forces, which results in a chaotic condition, rather than any broad pattern of providing service and programming to people," Miss Burkey concluded.

As the persvasive influence of the mass media—and especially television—became increasingly notable in the political, economic, social, and cultural life of the United States and of other countries rapidly developing a technological civilization, the Center returned again and again to the question of what could be done to make the media instruments of education rather than channels of entertainment, sensationalism, and propaganda. No satisfactory answers were found, but the publications of the Center were read by thousands of young people who later moved into positions of influence in the press and broadcasting fields. The demand for self-criticism by journalists, which led to the launching of journals to review the media in major cities, was encouraged by the Center, and this encouragement aided in the establishment of the *Chicage Journalism Review*, one of the first of these publications.

While the publications generated by the basic issues projects poured into circulation in the United States and other countries, the Center held meetings on a variety of topics. In November 1959 two assistants to President Eisenhower—Karl Harr and Malcolm Moos—came to Santa Barbara for discussions of the administrative responsibilities of the President. In December 1959 Hutchins gave his first public address in Santa Barbara at a gathering sponsored by the United World Federalists, who recalled that Hutchins had been instrumental in organizing the Committee to Frame a World Constitution in 1946. Hutchins speech was titled "Pre-Conditions of World Organization."

In April, 1960, Hutchins announced the appointment of Rabbi Robert Gordis as a special consultant, declaring: "Dr. Gordis has been participating in the examination of the relationship between church and state conducted by the Fund in the last three years. Now he is coming to the Center to take part in our continuing discussions of the problems underlying the maintenance of democratic institutions."

Dr. Gordis spent nine months in residence at the Center and was an active participant in many seminars. A professor at the Jewish Theological Seminary of America and the author of several books, Gordis had been a president of the Synagogue Council of America and a president of the Rabbinical Assembly of America. While he was at the Center he was appointed a member of the Central Committee of Consultants; he represented the third of the three major faiths in the United States to have a spokesman among the Center's consultants.

Reinhold Neibuhr came to the Center in July 1960 and took part in the daily dialogues until October of that year. John Courtney Murray was present with all of the other Consultants (except for Kerr and Luce) during the month of August. The Consultants reviewed the work of all the projects during that month and explored new avenues for future studies.

In the last week of July 1960 the Center held a seminar called "The Crisis in Collective Bargaining Practices." Participants included, in addition to visiting Consultants and the staff, Leon Keyserling, who had been chairman of the President's Council of Economic Advisers under Truman; Fred Whitman, president of the Western Pacific Railroad company; Arthur

Goldberg, who was then general counsel for the United Steel Workers; and
Monsignor George Higgins, director of the National Catholic Welfare Conference, who had commended the Center in a column distributed to Catholic newspapers. On September 25, 1960, leaders and regional directors of
the National Conference of Christians and Jews met with the staff and some
of the Consultants at the Center to develop wasys of creating better understanding among the religious groups in the United States. Bertrand de Jouvenel, a noted French economist and author, came to the Center for a meeting on economic problems on October 8. Afterward, he told a reporter:
"This Center is probably a unique institution in the world today, and I hope
similar Centers will be set up in Europe."

In the autumn of 1960, the Center seemed to be well established in Santa Barbara. It was still referred to as the Fund for the Republic, but its identity as an intellectual organization concerned about humanity was beginning
to be accepted by the press and the public. It embodied the principles of the
Fund, but it went beyond the issues of civil rights and civil liberties to the
problems that worried people everywhere.

The rumblings of the Birch Society, the angry letters that appeared in
the daily paper, the signs of hostility still encountered by staff members did
not seem likely to do the Center any substantial damage. Then a fire threatened its headquarters.

13

*The Center is tested by a fire—
and signs a contract
that keeps it alive*

ON A HOT OCTOBER NIGHT IN 1960, people stood in the streets of Santa Barbara and saw flames leaping from the Center's main building on the high hill above the city. For a few hours it seemed likely that the Center would be destroyed. But firemen from Santa Barbara and Montecito kept the blaze from spreading from the north wing, where it had erupted, to the other side of the structure, which contained Hutchins' office and most of the records of the Fund. Hutchins and other staff members, who arrived at the scene soon after the fire trucks, carried many papers and books from the building.

The fire was first described as one "of undetermined origin." After an investigation, the fire marshal, D. W. May, blamed "faulty wiring" in the old mansion. May said the blaze started in Scott Buchanan's office. Defective wires apparently ignited a gas heater directly beneath Buchanan's desk, and the heater caused papers in a waste basket to blaze up against the office wall.

Buchanan lost hundreds of books on philosophy and other subjects collected during his lifetime. Stanley Sheinbaum, an economist from Michigan State University who had joined the Center staff shortly before the fire, lost the Ph.D. dissertation on which he had been working for three years. These materials were irreplaceable, but other damage to the Center building and offices had been covered by insurance.

Hutchins was disturbed but undaunted by the fire. He told the press: "We can use our conference room and we are going ahead with our meetings." The daily dialogues resumed a few days later.

Remodeling of the large guest cottage on the estate had begun before the conflagration occurred, with money supplied by the Encyclopaedia Britannica. Eleven offices in the cottage became available three weeks after the fire. The Britannica had also agreed to pay the salaries and expenses of a group of scholars called "Fellows in Residence," including Buchanan, Gordis, Gorman, Sheinbaum, and several others appointed by Hutchins.

In addition to being president of the Fund and head of the Center, Hutchins was chairman of the board of editors of the Britannica. He had long advocated a complete revision of the Britannica, and had finally received the approval of the editors and of William Benton for "a re-examination of its major classifications, looking toward its bicentennial in 1968." Under the agreement, the Center was to receive more than $425,000 a year for two years.

On a recommendation by Hutchins, Harry Ashmore was designated editor-in-chief of the Britannica on October 1, 1960, with the understanding that Ashmore would make his headquarters in Santa Barbara. In a report sent to the Fund's directors on November 7, Hutchins said: "The officers of the Fund agreed, subject to the approval of the board, to look at the fields of the Center's interests from the standpoint of the Britannica. They felt justified in doing so because it appeared that Britannica would endeavor in 1968 to clarify the basic issues in much the same way in which the Center is trying to do so."

Hutchins had been assured by legal counsel that the Britannica work could be done without endangering the Fund's tax exemption. He told the board: "At the moment we see no conflict between what we would be doing anyway and what we shall undertake to do for Britannica. . . . The new residents at the Center, many of whom were brought in under the Britannica agreement, strengthen our work on the economic, legal, political, and moral orders. As reported at the last meeting of the board, we have long intended to take up the question of the control of technology in the free society. The Britannica arrangement will make it possible."

Keenly aware of the financial needs of the Center, Hutchins said: "The Britannica arrangement will prolong the life of the organization by a year, or possibly two. Although it is not inconceivable that some form of cooperation with Britannica might go on indefinitely, this possibility is now slight and cannot be counted on."

Through the fund-raising efforts of George Shuster and Joseph Lyford in New York and of Christopher Janus in Chicago, financial pledges totaling $164,400 had been received in the period from November 9, 1959, to September 30, 1960. Cash contributions had totaled $40,518 and real property worth $25,000 had been assigned to the Center. Hutchins felt that the results were inconclusive.

Trying to stimulate the board members to make contributions themselves and to get other people to contribute, Hutchins warned: "At present, therefore, we must expect that the Center and the Fund will go out of business in three or four years." He added: "I believe, however, that we are finding out how to do our work. . . . The Britannica arrangement enables us to commission writing by men anywhere in the world, and to bring them to

Santa Barbara if we wish. . . . I am confident that with time and patience the Center will justify the hopes that the board has had for it.''

At the board meeting on November 19, 1960, reports were submitted on all the projects then in progress. Two of them—the study of religious institutions, and the trade union study—had reached their final stages. Another project—an examination of the American character, which had grown out of the religion study—was brought into being with financing from the Britannica agreement.

At the gathering of the board in Santa Barbara, the staff director of the trade union project, Paul Jacobs, described the seminar "The Crisis in Collective Bargaining,'' which had been held at the Center from July 18 to July 25, 1960. Twenty-six men from industry, unions, government, and arbitration panels had argued freely in off-the-record discussions unique in their candor and scope. Minutes of the sessions, after being revised by the participants, were circulated to people engaged in collective bargaining throughout the United States.

Jacobs said that the union study had covered all of the basic issues in labor-management relations and in the problems of democracy faced within the unions. No additional researches were contemplated. He listed dozens of magazine articles and books expected to emerge from the study, including a 10-volume analysis of national union administrations, a comparison of American and British laws governing unions, and a book on democracy in European unions and the relevance of the European experience to the United States.

John Cogley's report on the study of religious institutions was very brief and did not mention the fact that the Fund's work in this field had helped to make possible the election of John F. Kennedy, a Roman Catholic, as president of the United States in November 1960. Cogley simply declared: "The 'dialogue' initiated at the Fund seminar on religion and the free society in May, 1958, now involves hundreds of persons of all faiths. It is caried on in the religious press, via books and publications, and through radio and television.''

Cogley had received a leave of absence to work on Kennedy's 1960 campaign. He had been a principal composer of the address given by Kennedy to a group of Protestant church leaders in Houston, Texas, on the night of September 12, 1960. Kennedy had said: "I believe in an America where separation of church and state is absolute,'' and had received a standing ovation. In that speech—and in others on which he was advised by Cogley and by John Courtney Murray, a Center Consultant—Kennedy dispelled many of the suspicions that had made Protestants reluctant to vote for him.

No one connected with the staff or Consultants of the Center then claimed that the Fund's religion project had produced powerful political effects in the 1960 presidential campaign. But Monsignor Francis J. Lally, a member of the Fund's board, did write later in a book that the Fund's study had been a vital element in Kennedy's election. And Garry Wills, in a volume published twelve years later, asserted that Cogley and Murray had a deep impact upon the political atmosphere of the United States in 1960 and upon the policies of President Kennedy during the three years before his assassination.

At the time of the Fund's board gathering in November 1960, however, Cogley was most concerned about the study of the American character, which had three parts: a general analysis of the behavior and distinguishing qualities of Americans; a series of case histories of contemporary Americans involved in significant ethical dilemmas; and a study of juvenile delinquency in urban, suburban, and rural areas. In developing this study, Cogley had the aid of William Lee Miller of the Yale Divinity School, who was doing a book on the role of ethics in American life, and of Eugene Burdick, a Center consultant, as well as Paul Jacobs and Philip Selznick, a sociology professor at the University of California at Berkeley.

At its November assembly, the board was informed by Hallock Hoffman, staff director of the study of the political process, that he and all the others on the study wrestled with a fundamental question: "Is self-government possible in an urban, industrial society of large population, large-scale organization, and representative institutions of government, in an era of rapid and accelerating change, in the presence of a ramifying technology that is only partially intelligible—and then only to specialists?"

"The work in prospect with the Encyclopaedia Britannica project appears likely to be of great advantage to the study of the political process," Hoffman said. He referred to the fact that Carl Stover, formerly of the Brookings Institution and the Department of Agriculture, would be added to the group of advisers. Stover had been responsible for major inquiries into the administrative process in the federal government, and had been named as assistant to the chairman of the board of editors of the Britannica.

Hoffman told the Fund's directors that the intention of the Britannica project to produce material on what "the intelligent, curious layman ought to know about modern politics" coincided "precisely with the intention of the Center's Study to determine how the aspiration for self-government should be understood under modern conditions." In addition to Stover, the advisers to the political process study included Stephen Bailey, Buchanan, Richardson Dilworth, Walter Millis, the Harvard psychologist B. F. Skinner, Donald Rivkin, and Harvey Wheeler.

While the directors were delighted by the Britannica arrangement and impressed by the increasing response to the Center's efforts in many fields, they were reminded by Hutchins that the Center was far from the financial stability necessary for future plans. In the autumn of 1959, soon after its establishment in Santa Barbara, a drive had been started to find 1000 people who would contribute $1000 a year. Only 49 such persons—called founding members—had signed up in the twelve months after the call for support had been issued.

Elmo Roper and several other directors expressed the hope that the Ford foundation might be willing to be generous again. Roper declared that the Center's reputation was high, and he believed that the trustees of the Ford money might listen to an appeal from the directors of the Fund. After much discussion, the Fund's board decided to consider the formation of a continuation committee, which could approach the Ford Foundation and other large philanthropic organizations.

Up to that point, the Fund directors had placed the burden of fund raising almost entirely on the shoulders of Hutchins, George Shuster, and Joseph Lyford. Shuster and Lyford had not been able to obtain any substantial grants, although they had tried energetically to do so. The largest gifts thus far had come from John Elliott of Los Angeles—who had pledged $75,000 and deeded property worth $25,000 to the Center—and from William Benton, who had made contributions totaling $41,500 to the study of the mass media. These gifts had come through Hutchins.

There were many wealthy people in Santa Barbara, but the one founding member in the Center's home community—aside from W. H. Ferry and Hutchins himself—was an intellectual doctor, William F. Kiely, who had attended several sessions on Eucalyptus Hill and was fascinated by the interaction of the minds there. The Birch Society continued to grow in some areas of the city, and the Center was attacked in leaflets and in letters in the Santa Barbara *News-Press*.

The *New-Press*, at the direction of T. M. Storke (who was not a flaming liberal but admired the Center's courage in tackling "hot questions"), had welcomed the Center with a statement that its presence would be "an asset of inestimable value to the community" and had given extensive coverage to the Center's activities, including a reception at the Coral Casino to enable the officers and staff to meet prominent Santa Barbarans. Some of the Santa Barbarans had been friendly—and one of them, Alvin C. Weingand of the San Ysidro Ranch—had written an enthusiastic letter to the editor, describing the Center's work as "exciting and tremendously important."

But a month after the Fund's directors had finished their November meeting, signs of antagonism toward the Center in the community became evident when the trustees of the public library voted against a proposal to cosponsor a series of talks scheduled to be given by Center staff members and consultants at the Lobero Theatre. The talks were to be presented under the auspices of the Adult Education Division of Santa Barbara City College and the Lobero Foundation, and the library trustees had simply been asked to add their endorsement.

"The request was decisively turned down without any preliminary discussion by the trustees," the *News-Press* reported on December 16, 1960. "So swiftly did they act that Herbert V. Shepard, chairman of the Counter-subversive Activities Committee of American Legion Post 49, decided not to make a speech condemning the request. Instead, he congratulated the trustees.

"John Smith, librarian, said that the library had received twenty-nine letters opposing library sponsorship and none in favor. . . . Sam Wake, director of the Adult Education division, said today that despite the decision of the library trustees, the talks would be given."

The letter writers were swayed by old accusations against the Fund, particularly the charges made by American Legion commanders and the House Un-American Activities Committee. The library trustees yielded to pressures despite a *News-Press* editorial strongly recommending the Center series and asserting: "The library should take an active part, and be a living force, in the life of the community."

W. H. Ferry stirred up the antagonists of the Center again in December 1960, when his letter advocating unilateral disarmament by the United States was published in the *New-Press*. He said he would rather risk the presence of Russian soldiers in Santa Barbara and other American cities than take the risk of a nuclear war. At the urging of John Cogley and other Center staff members, I issued a statement on behalf of the Center, declaring that Ferry's ideas were his personal convictions and were not declarations of policy by the Center.

Letters and phone calls received at the Center indicated that some Santa Barbarans were outraged by Ferry's statement. At the invitation of the Santa Barbara chapter of the American Association for the United Nations, Ferry presented "The Case for Unilateral Disarmament" to a large audience at the Unitarian Church auditorium. Two weeks later, I offered "The Case Against Unilateral Disarmament" to a crowd in the same hall. John Wilkinson, then an associate professor of philosophy at the University of California at Santa Barbara and an occasional participant in Center meetings, served as chairman at both meetings.

The differences of opinion expressed by Ferry and myself made it clear to many members of the community that the Center had room for two vice presidents with conflicting ideas. But the exchange between Ferry and Kelly did not diminish the hostility of the Birch Society and other right-wing groups, which regarded the Center as a haven for radicals and a hatching place for revolutionary plots.

The clash over unilateral disarmament gave Santa Barbara a glimpse of the disagreements that occurred in the daily discussions at the Center. Members of the community were invited to observe the meetings from time to time, and the Center announced repeatedly that single free copies of its publications were available to any citizen who wished to know what was really going on in the mansion on Eucalyptus Hill. Very few people took advantage of these opportunities.

Although events at the Center were covered frequently by newspapers, magazines, radio, and television, many people preferred to think that there was something mysterious occurring at the Center. Because of Hutchins' reputation as a reformer and because the Center's directors were known to be powerful people involved in economics and politics, the Center was believed to be a conduit for drastic changes in American institutions and a fostering agent for the development of a world government.

When the agreement with the Britannica became known, some critics thought that the Britannica would be used as a vehicle for ideas on world order, which Hutchins had been advocating since he had helped to establish the Committee to Draft a World Constitution at the University of Chicago. Hutchins was persistent: he returned to his ideas year after year and he had an influence on all the scholars who came to the Center.

Over and over, Hutchins said to reporters and to visitors from many places: "We are just trying to understand what is going on in the world and to put ideas into circulation." The reporters did write what he said, but they always linked the Center to what he had tried to do in Chicago and at the Ford Foundation. The Center was labeled as the Hutchins Center, as the Fund for the Republic had become known as the Hutchins Fund.

With the implementation of the Britannica agreement, an influx of scholars from universities and experts from other countries brought profound changes to the Center. Hutchins had a decisive voice in what the Center did, but he was open to suggestions from staff membes and all the visitors who came to Eucalyptus Hill. He spent much of his time listening and taking notes.

The emphasis on such institutions as the trade union, the corporation, the churches, and the mass media gradually declined, although publications resulting from these studies continued to appear. Groups of scholars were assigned to consider the future of law, economics, philosophy, and politics. The Center dialogues ranged over a dozen topics related to the birth of a new encyclopedia.

Through the Britannica, the Center was able to have an influence on the understanding of the contemporary world received by the thousands of teachers and students in many countries who used the collection of knowledge in its many volumes. The effects of the thinking done at the Center would be felt on many levels and disseminated through the generations to come.

As the year 1960 came to a close, Hutchins and the staff of the Center were in consultation with the editors of the Britannica to plan meetings on science and world affairs, on the systematic study of technology, on the prospects for democracy in the new nations that had arisen after the collapse of the European colonial empires, on the possible changes in the

American character in an apparently affluent society, and other issues far beyond those on which the Fund had spent its money and its attention.

The inescapable connections between American problems and world problems, the pervasive repercussions of technology, and the importance of law in a developing world order were given a notable priority at the Center in the 1960s, when the United States moved into the Kennedy era—a nation conscious of its immense power and confident of its ability to solve all problems with American brains and American economic and military strength.

14

John Kennedy sounds a trumpet, and the Center digs into the American character

WHEN JOHN FITZGERALD KENNEDY TOOK the oath of office as President of the United States with the sun blazing across the snow on the Capitol Plaza, he declaimed: "Let the word go forth from this time and place, to friend and foe alike, that the torch has passed to a new generation of Americans . . . tempered by war, disciplined by a hard and bitter peace, proud of our ancient heritage." His inaugural address won great acclaim. His popularity soared.

The volatility of the American people was shown by their willingness to shift from Eisenhower to Kennedy. Americans had given Eisenhower the trust he had earned as a leader in World War II. The old general was a symbol of stability. Kennedy appeared as a symbol of change. The admiration for Kennedy—which rose to new heights after he admitted his bad judgment in the Cuban episode—was apparently due to his dashing style, his beautiful wife, and his energy as a president who worked 16 hours a day and took a personal interest in every problem, large and small.

What were the distinctive qualities of the American character? Had that character undergone fundamental alterations in the course of American history? Did Americans have any permanent values, or did they take on new views with new trends and new leaders? These were the questions that concerned the Center while John Kennedy was floundering around in the White House during the painful year of 1961.

Hutchins declared that the Center's inquiry into the values and behavior of Americans would focus on two broad questions: "What, in the view of modern Americans, constituted the good life? How are our new institutions, or radically changed old ones, affecting the moral and ethical standards of the nation?

197

The scholars and thoughtful citizens who participated in this study recognized at once that it had both philosophic and empirical aspects. Hutchins reminded them: "We are dealing not only with changes in thought, but also with changes in the structure of democratic institutions. Anyone studying the American character has to consider the interaction between the two. For example, it might be argued that the TV screen reflects the dominance of certain values, or lack of values, in American life—but how much influence does television have in creating the very values it later reflects? In one way or another, the same question might be asked about publishing, the corporate enterprise, labor relations, education, the military establishment, the political process, and even the administration of legal justice."

Indicating that the United States might be going through a spiritual crisis, Hutchins observed: "The tattered copy-book maxims that served our fathers appear to be hopelessly inadequate for solving our present problems. We need more than maxims. . . . The crisis is such that what is needed is an intellectual grasp of our moral responsibilities."

He referred to the postwar scandals in television, sports, academic life, politics, and municipal governments: "In the view of many, the major shock was that so many clever quiz-show experts, basketball fixers, classroom cheaters, political grafters, and corrupt policemen allowed themselves to get caught. The true scandal was not that a few Americans behaved badly but that so many, especially among the young, could see nothing particularly wrong in what was done. . . . A prominent anthropologist said not long ago that ours may soon have to be classified as a 'shame culture,' where loss of face, rather than betrayal of standards, is the ultimate dishonor."

The Center shared one intention with John F. Kennedy: its president believed that something had to be done. Hutchins said: "The Center does not believe we should be content to drift aimlessly. Consequently, we are interested not only in examining modern institutions and moral dilemmas arising from them but also in initiating a dialogue between spokesmen for various viewpoints on the standards proper for public life in the second half of the twentieth century."

The Center approached the American character from many directions—through dialogues at the Center itself; through interviews—later published in pamphlets—with leaders of various institutions, conducted by Donald McDonald, then the dean of the College of Journalism at Marquette University; through other booklets and reports prepared by Center staff members and consultants; and through the remarks of twenty-eight speakers at a Center conference in Washington. One hundred leaders in American life—theologians, scientists, educators, physicians, journalists, business people, labor leaders, philosophers, political officeholders, and college students—took part in the four-day assembly, which ended with a dinner attended by members of the Supreme Court and members of President Kennedy's staff and cabinet.

Speaking at the Modern Forum at a Beverly Hills high school on May 20, Hutchins referred to the shock felt by many Americans when people in other countries rejected government by the people and of the people.

"How is it possible to reject democracy as an ideal?" Hutchins asked. "It is the most just form of government. It is the most compatible with the rational, political, social nature of man.

"But it is now said in Europe that the world is too precarious for its inhabitants to be trusted with it. Scholars call for a Utopian elite group to take on the responsibilities of government. The people are to have civil liberties but no political discussion."

The president of the Center, who had gathered some noted scholars to do some long-range thinking for the benefit of the people, appeared to be shocked by such political elitism. In publishing the comments and proposals of scholars, jurists, journalists, and others who met at the Center, the Center was sending forth sparks from an anvil. If the sparks blazed into spreading fires of illumination, the glow might lead people in all communities to see what could be done.

"We have individualistic, liberal ideals—and a bureaucratic culture," Hutchins said to the audience of a thousand in the high school. (Through an audiotape recording, his voice would reach many more thousands in radio broadcasts.) "We think all technology is good—even if it means that we shall be blown up, poisoned by chemicals, suffocated by smog, or trampled to death. We constantly exalt the active, independent, creative individual—and yet we function as consumers, as job-holders, as objects of propaganda, as statistical units.

"We need an educational system that develops intellectual power and encourages independent thought—but we have fostered one that produces good consumers, job-holders, objects of propaganda, statistical units to keep our industrial machine going. We have emphasized accommodation and life-adjustment at the expense of thought and the creative spirit."

Too many Americans thought of politics in terms of power or simply as the clash of powers, Hutchins asserted with anger: "The result is that we think of law as coercion or command. We regard law as a fabrication of political deals. We say that government is best which governs least. Actually it is clear that government is best which governs best—and that government governs best which best promotes learning. Only through government, law and politics can we learn the true significance of human beings in relation to one another."

In proclaiming that "the true significance of human beings in relation to one another" could be learned "only through government, law and politics," Hutchins revealed that he was still occupied with the ideas that had motivated him at the University of Chicago in the 1930s. Some writers questioned his emphasis on government, law, and politics as the channels for learning "the true significance of human beings in relation to one another."

Gertrude Stein had erupted against him and against Adler at a dinner party in Hutchins' house in the 1930s, shouting: "Government is the least interesting thing in human life. . . . Teaching is your occupation and naturally what they call ideas are very easy to teach and so you are convinced that they are the only ideas, but the real ideas are not the relation of human beings as groups but a human being to himself inside him." And later she had said to him, "To me when a thing is really interesting it is when there is no question and no answer. . . . That is the reason that anything for which there is a solution is not interesting, that is the trouble with governments and Utopias and teaching, the things not that can be learnt but that can be taught are not interesting."

To Hutchins in the 1960s, as in the 1930s, teaching and learning were vitally interesting. He believed that learning was the most important thing—and learning often went on inside a human being, without immediate effects visible to other people—but he continued to believe that government, law, and politics were crucial in enabling people to develop their hidden potentialities and to begin to understand one another.

He urged his audience in Beverly Hills in May of 1961 to prepare for a world that would be very different from the world that had shaped the American character: "We face a world without work, without want, without disease, without war. Unless we blow our selves to pieces with nuclear weapons or destroy ourselves in some other way, such a world is inevitable. What will we do with our material goods? What will we do with ourselves? Perhaps the alternatives are that we will all be killed or all bored to death."

Pointing to the American commitment to the highest possible rate of technological change, regardless of the consequences, Hutchins feared that such a commitment might mean a steadily increasing number of unemployed workers.

He depicted the devouring advance of technology: "We have a shrinking world and a shrinking universe, in which astronauts roam at will. Technology is uniting the world, despite the paradox of multiplication of sovereignties and the development of dozens of new 'nations.' This is a temporary stage on the march to a situation in which all nations will be parts of a federal system." He asked: "Can we learn to guide technology? It can only be done by law. It will have to be done by law. Since it is a world phenomenon, it will be dealt with by world law."

Hutchins regarded the development of a world community as an imperative necessity for the future of humanity: "We have the beginnings now, in the United Nations and in the various forms of international law described by Justice Douglas in a pamphlet published by the Center. We have accepted the idea that foreigners cannot be abolished."

He chided the Kennedy administration for sanctioning the raid by Cuban exiles against Castro's government: "Most of us have recognized that the recent intervention in Cuba was a backward step—contrary to our laws and to international law. Much as we dislike Castroism and some other revolutionary movements, we cannot dispose of them through military force. Our policy must be to unite with other peoples in support of international law.''

As a desirable step in that direction, Hutchins called for repeal of the Connally Amendment—a measure sponsored by Senator Tom Connally, of Texas, which had been approved by the United States Senate; it restricted the jurisdiction of the International Court of Justice in cases involving the United States. Hutchins said: ''At a time when a political community does not exist in the United States, we must begin to work for a world political community. This is a strange paradox, but we must face it.''

In terms as sweeping as those used by President Kennedy in his inaugural address—but without the overtones of military combat—Hutchins said: ''The propositions of liberty and justice for all, to which the Declaration of Independence dedicated us, now must be extended to the whole world. The world ought to be a decent place for all men to live in. We must learn together within the framework of law, to make it such a place.''

Michael Harrington, a young journalist who had helped in the production of the *Report on Blacklisting*, had been asked by John Cogley to participate in the Center's study of the American character. Harrington had become increasingly aware of the plight of millions of people who had been submerged or largely ignored in American society—the millions of poor people of all colors and creeds and ethnic backgrounds, who could not get jobs or obtained only menial jobs with low pay, who were often ''workless'' or on welfare, who were often disregarded by labor unions as well as employers. In his eyes, these people had become virtually a separate nation.

Harrington wrote a book based on his findings—entitled *The Other America* at Cogley's suggestion—which caught the attention of President Kennedy and led to the planning of the ''war on poverty,'' which was waged by Lyndon Johnson after Kennedy's assassination. Thus the Center study convinced these presidents that the nation's economic policies were not bringing benefits to millions of Americans.

Harrington aided Cogley in the organization of the conference on the moral and ethical standards of the American people, held in Washington in June 1961. In the four days of meetings there, leaders from all the professions and all sections of the United States participated. In addition to these leaders, five hundred others attended the closing dinner, where addresses were given by Justice Hugo Black, Reinhold Niebuhr, and Hutchins. Senator Eugene McCarthy placed these statements in the *Congressional Record* and urged his colleagues in the Congress to consider the ideas presented at the Center gathering.

Just before the Washington conference, leaders of the National Conference of Christians and Jews met at the Center to continue their discussion of interfaith issues and their impact on American life. This was the third of a series of such special seminars. Participants included Lewis Webster Jones, president of the NCCJ; Franklin Littell, professor of church history at Southern Methodist University, Dallas; Walter Ong, S.J., of St. Louis University; Irving Lehrman, rabbi of the Temple Emanu-El, Miami Beach; Dean Leonidas Contos, of St. Sophia Cathedral, Los Angeles; and others from New York, Washington, San Francisco, Omaha, Milwaukee, Houston, South Bend, San Antonio, Seattle, and Cleveland.

The extensive range of the Center's activities was displayed again in four press releases emanating from the Santa Barbara headquarters in September, 1961. The small size of its staff and the dwindling amount of its financial resources could not have been guessed from the global scope of the information sent that month to broadcasting stations and newspapers in the United States and other countries.

On September 21 Hutchins announced that in October the Center would hold a conference in Greece on world order and freedom with the cooperation of the American Department of State and at the invitation of the Royal Greek Government. The sessions were scheduled to be held in the Greek parliament buildings in Athens, with Hutchins presiding.

On September 24 the world was informed that the Center had devoted two days to an encyclical by Pope John XXIII that dealt with many of the problems on which the Center had spent much time and thought. "The Pope calls upon thinking people everywhere to face the urgent questions," Hutchins said. "These are the questions raised by the expansion of automation, the increasing interdependence of all nations, the growth of a worldwide communications system, and the network of supranational organizations dedicated to economic, social, cultural and political ends."

On September 25 Hutchins disclosed that American and Soviet scientists who had taken part in a discussion of science and world affairs at Stowe, Vermont, had come to the Center to talk about what scientists could do to improve the prospects for world peace. Their visit to Santa Barbara was approved by the State Department. It was arranged by Harrison Brown, a professor at the California Institute of Technology, who had become an outside consultant to the Center.

At the end of September, plans for meetings on the American character were announced by the Center and Joseph Shane, head of the Modern Forum of Los Angeles. All the meetings were scheduled to be held in the Beverly Hills high school. A thousand people from the Los Angeles area paid registration fees to attend these sessions, and the fees were given by the Modern Forum to the Center.

The series got under way on October 13 with an address by John Cogley on the cultural and historical factors that had shaped the American character. Louis Lyons, curator of the Nieman fellowships for Journalism at Harvard University, spoke on the media of communication at the second meeting a month later. In subsequent months the speakers included Senator Eugene McCarthy, on politics and American traits; James A. Pike, then the Episcopal Bishop of California, on the churches and American attitudes; Justice Douglas, on law and the American character; Harrison Brown, on science in American life; Erich Fromm, on American expectations and attitudes toward love; and Robert Hutchins, on democratic institutions and the American character. I organized these meetings.

In October 1961 William V. Shannon, a Washington correspondent for the *New York Post*, arrived at the Center for a year's stay as a fellow in residence. Shannon had collaborated with Robert S. Allen on a critical book about the Truman administration—*The Truman Merry-Go-Round*—and had won the Page One Award of the New York Newspaper Guild for his articles on the late Senator Joseph McCarthy and the effects of McCarthyism.

On October 30, 1961, the Center published a pamphlet by Fred Warner Neal, a professor at the Claremont Graduate School and a former member of the Office of Strategic Services and the U.S. State Department, entitled *United States Foreign Policy and the Soviet Union*. Neal pointed to what he considered the "dangerous inadequacies" of American policies and made specific recommendations for changes that might diminish the danger of war with the Soviet Union. The publication of this pamphlet marked the beginning of Neal's long association with the Center as an adviser on studies and conferences on international issues.

In that month of October, Harry Ashmore and I went to Ecuador to participate in the second annual conference sponsored by the International Center for Advanced Studies in the Field of Journalism for Latin America. Our trips to Ecuador were financed by the Albert Parvin Foundation, established by a Los Angeles businessman who supplied furniture and other equipment for hotels. The International Center for studies in journalism had been formed in Ecuador by a group of Latin American editors headed by Jorge Fernandez, editor of *El Commercio*, a daily paper in Quito, the capital of Ecuador. It was supported by grants from UNESCO and the government of Ecuador.

In a release to the press on November 13, 1961, Hutchins announced that the Parvin Foundation had agreed to provide $25,000 annually to the Center to bring leaders from Latin America to meetings at the Center. He also indicated that James T. Brady, a Santa Barbara real estate agent who had become his executive assistant, would serve as executive director of the Parvin Foundation.

A close relationship between the Parvin Foundation and the Center existed for several years, with the foundation making gifts to the Center that eventually totaled more than $260,000. Directors of this foundation, besides Albert Parvin, included Robert Goheen, president of Princeton University; William O. Campbell, a United States judge in Chicago; Jaime Benitez, chancellor of the University of Puerto Rico; Justice William O.

Douglas; and Hutchins. Parvin had created the foundation in 1959, in the year when the Center had begun to operate in Santa Barbara, and he was particularly interested in educating Latin American leaders who opposed communism and supported democratic ideas.

At a meeting of the Fund's board on June 1, 1961, Hutchins had informed the directors of the arrangements he had proposed to make with the Parvin Foundation and had received the board's approval. Four new directors had been elected at that meeting—William Baggs, editor of the *Miami News*; James H. Douglas, Jr., a noted Chicago attorney who had served as deputy secretary of defense under President Eisenhower; Crane Haussamen, a New York advertising executive; and Seniel Ostrow, president of the Sealy Mattress Company of Los Angeles. These directors had taken part in the discussion of the Center's financial needs, and Haussamen had been appointed to the Continuation Committee along with Alicia Patterson, Herbert Lehman, Elmo Roper, and Jubal Parten.

When the board gathered in Santa Barbara on November 18, much time was given to a proposed letter requesting additional money from the Ford Foundation, which had been prepared by Haussamen and myself. Amendments were suggested, and Hutchins was asked to write the final draft of this application to the Ford trustees. Members of the board agreed to talk to several of the trustees with the hope of gaining their support.

In December 1961 two of the interviews conducted by Donald McDonald with leaders in various fields on the relationships between major institutions and the American character were published by the Center. One was an interview with Jack Gould, then the television critic for the *New York Times*, with a comment by Harry Ashmore. The other was a conversation with A. Whitney Griswold, president of Yale university, accompanied by comments from Robert Hutchins.

Gould wondered whether the American people cared much about the quality of most television programs. The largest audiences went for Western programs with hard-riding cowboys and much shooting. The television producers insisted that they had to appeal to the majority of viewers in order to survive and make money.

"Everybody in the television industry argues that they have 'a democratic obligation' to 'give the most people what they want most of the time,' " Gould said. "I say that that is true only to a limited extent because the public, the disorganized public, really has no way of articulating its demands and its desires." He added: "As trustees of the air waves, the broadcasters have an obligation to furnish leadership in all fields. The way in which the public expresses its wishes, its likes and dislikes, is—to a great extent—the way in which it responds to the leadership that is offered."

"Mr Gould is pleading for greater diversity in television," Ashmore commented. "Far from being an assault on the sacred precepts of free enterprise, this could be a blueprint of salvation for private broadcasting; diversity means competition, and competition is the life of trade."

Gould and Ashmore agreed that the best possibilities for television lay in the expansion of financial support for educational television stations and programs of cultural value, and in the development of subscription TV as a means of serving minority viewers at their own expense.

In the pamphlet entitled *The University*, containing the views of Whitney Griswold of Yale and Robert Hutchins, both educators voiced severe criticisms of the American educational system. Griswold declared that educational values had been "desperately corrupted" by inadequate teacher training programs on the secondary school level. Hutchins said that a "fanatical zeal for money" had "seized the universities, with government and business participating more and more in university affairs."

Griswold deplored the fact that the teacher training program had become a "political problem," with the training curriculum "frozen into law in many states." Behind these laws stood the Naitonal Education Association, which he described as "a militant organization with branches in every state and an elaborate headquarters in Washington." Teachers had to go through a certification process filled with "icicles of the old system of pedagogy."

"I believe we've got all the necessary talent in this country to produce a proper ration of trained, competent teachers to the number of students," Griswold said. "What is lacking is the sense of purpose. . . . I think that if the curriculum of the teacher training programs for secondary education could be made more liberal this would be the greatest single thing that could be done to increase the flow of competent and properly trained people throughout the whole system of education."

Hutchins was pessimistic about the likelihood of progressive change in the universities: "A man who has given any public indication that he has thought about the purpose of the university and that he wants to do something about it is almost certain to be unwelcome to the vested interests."

The statements of Griswold and Hutchins were printed on the front page of the *New York Times* and appeared in newspapers and magazines across the country. But the National Education Association and other powerful organizations in American education resisted the reforms advocated by Griswold and Hutchins. The high schools and universities continued to be rigid structures, increasingly bureaucratic and mechanistic, boring and frustrating to teachers and students, until the explosions of the 1960s turned schools and campuses into places of combat.

The ideas and criticisms flowing from the Center through its publications were ignored or opposed by leaders in many institutions in American society, but the Center continued to release a bombardment of booklets and pamphlets year after year—not campaigning for the adoption of any specific recommendations, simply striving for more thinking and more realistic consideration of problems that had to be faced.

While the Center attracted almost as much attention as the Fund had gained, the publicity did not generate the money that the Center needed.

The controversial reports and suggestions its associates produced probably alienated some people who might have given it substantial financial backing. The number of contributors donating $1000 a year or more actually declined in 1961, droping from 49 to 45. Aside from the Britannica and the Parvin Foundation, there were no large-scale donors in that year.

On November 27 Hutchins sent the members of the Continuation Committee a draft of a suggested memorandum to the Ford Foundation, requesting a grant of $16.4 million. He estimated that such a grant—with contributions from other sources, income from publications, interest from bank accounts, and dividents—would keep the Center going for another ten years.

In his memorandum Hutchins reminded the Ford trustees that the Fund had encountered the risks anticipated by the foundation, but it had not lost its tax exemption. It had successfully resisted attacks from the House Un-American Activities Committee and other enemies. It had earned the right to be considered for additional support.

"The Center has no alumni, and it is not engaged in the kind of work on which a national money-raising campaign can easily be based," he said. "It must appeal to those wise enough to understand the importance to the maintenance of democracy of maintaining a promising center of independent thought and criticism."

He referred to the impact that the Center had already had on "the educational system, on the relations among religious denominations, and on the understanding of the political, economic, social and technological phenomena" of the modern world. He declared: "It has already aroused the interest of foreign countries interested in making democracy work. So Justice Douglas, speaking in Washington at the seminar on the American character, repeatedly asserted that the hope for democracy was the establishment in as many countries as possible of Centers for the study of democratic institutions."

He gave the Ford trustees credit for what they had done in making the Fund and the Center possible: "We take this opportunity to express our gratitude to the trustees of the Ford Foundation for having had the courage to establish the Fund for the Republic. We hope they will share our vision of the future of the Center."

The Continuation Committee thought the memorandum was excellent. They decided to approach the Ford trustees, hoping that Henry Ford II and the other trustees would share their enthusiasm for the Center.

15

The Center hunts for money while tackling hard questions

W<small>HILE SOME OF THE TRUSTEES</small> of the Ford Foundation were personally sympathetic to what the Center was trying to do, Elmo Roper and the other members of the Continuation Committee learned in January 1962 that the foundation was not willing to give the Center any money. The $16.4 million grant sought by Hutchins was beyond the realm of possibility, the Ford trustees told Roper, Parten, and other directors of the Fund. The Center would have to look elsewhere for the large gifts it needed for survival.

While Hutchins and Roper pondered over the next step to be taken, the Center maintained its schedule of meetings and conferences, using money supplied by the Britannica and Albert Parvin. If the Center could keep on showing that it could do significant things that other educational institutions were not able to do, Hutchins believed that it could find enough donors to meet its requirements.

On January 8, 1962, the Center convened a three-week assembly called "Democracy in the New Nations," attended by scholars and administrators from Australia, Africa, Southeast Asia, Israel, and American universities. Hutchins greeted the group with a resounding declaration: "No problem in the world now is more important for the future of civilization than the development of democracy in the emerging nations."

Zelman Cowen, dean of the Law School of the University of Melbourne, Australia, and Stanley Sheinbaum of the Center staff served as coleaders of the conference. As a faculty member at Michigan State University, Sheinbaum had studied the political and economic development of Vietnam.

"The questions to be probed at this conference will range widely over the major economic and political problems affecting hundreds of millions of people," Sheinbaum said. "We hear much said that the peoples in the underdeveloped countries are not prepared for democracy. What does this mean? What conditions can be identified as being necessary in any culture if the people are to be prepared?

"What do we really know and what can we say about the level of economic advancement required before we can talk seriously about democracy in a given country? Is authoritarianism really necessary in the early stages of development?

"Almost everyone agrees that planning is an essential thing for economic development in the countries we have in mind. Oddly enough, in the least advanced countries it seems more difficult to get agreement to implement planning than in the capitalistic West. What stands in the way? How would democratic processes help to remove the impediments? How compatible is democracy in these areas with planning?

"How does the receipt of foreign aid, either from the Western bloc or from the Eastern—or even from China—affect political goals? There is evidence that U.S. economic aid may have affected both economic and political institutions in a disadvantageous way. What should be done about the administration of economic aid? What kinds of strings that are attached should be removed? What kinds of conditions, if any, should be required?

"The existence of aspirations in the emerging countries and the demands made by them in Africa, Asia and Latin America are imposing changes on the world today that we little understand. We hope that from the dialogue at the conference we will obtain better insights both empirically and normatively."

In the lineup of speakers and in the variety of topics, this was one of the most ambitious conferences ever held at the Center.

American intervention in Vietnam—which had begun under President Truman and had deepened under Eisenhower and Kennedy—was analyzed by Robet Scigliano, a Michigan State University political scientist who had been in a United States mission in Vietnam for three years.

A socialist view of the new nations was presented by Paul Baran, of the economics department at Stanford University. Economic developments in Latin America and other areas were reviewed by Rexford G. Tugwell, former adviser to President Franklin Roosevelt and former Governor of Puerto Rico.

Dialogues on democracy and world order were led by Scott Buchanan and Stringfellow Barr, former president of St. John's College. Economic progress in Israel was described by David Horowitz, governor of the Bank of Israel.

Robert Theobald, a consulting economist for the Foreign Policy Association and the United Nations, expressed his ideas on economics and international relations. Chinese culture and the impact of economic development on that culture were analyzed by Franz Schurmann, sociologist and historian at the University of California.

Guy Pauker, a political scientist who divided his time between the Rand Corporation and the University of California, examined the roles of the military forces and the bureaucracies in new nations. He had had much experience in Indonesia. Democracy in the new African countries was discussed by David Apter, African specialist at the University of California. James Coleman, director of African studies at the University of California, presented another view of Africa.

Emile Despres, former director of the Economic Development Institute at Williams College, described his experience in Pakistan. Others participating in the three weeks of meetings included Frank Child, Stanford University economist; Arthur Wina of the National Independence Party of Northern Rhodesia; George Wise, chairman of the board of the Hebrew University in Jerusalem; and Joseph Lapalombara, of the Center for Advanced Study in the Behavioral Sciences at Stanford.

On January 29, 1962, the Center in Santa Barbara published a booklet entitled *Cybernation: The Silent Conquest*, written by Donald Michael, formerly of the Brookings Institution and later the director of planning and programs for the Peace Research Institute in Washington. "Cybernation" was the term used by Michael and others to describe the linking of computers to automated processes.

The capabilities and potentialities of computers were "unlimited," Michael wrote: "They contain extraordinary implications for the emancipation and enslavement of mankind."

Michael predicted that cybernation would create immense areas of unemployment, with machines eliminating entire job categories ranging from factory and farm workers to bank tellers and "middle management" executives. The millions of unemployed people would compel the government "to support part of the population through public works for the indefinite future."

One dangerous effect of cybernation might be the lack of employment for "untrained adolescents," Michael warned. Twenty-six million of these young workers would be seeking jobs in the 1960s, and many of them would not be able to get on payrolls. He wrote: "Almost inevitably, they are going to become delinquent. Thus, without adequate occupational outlets for these youths, cybernation may contribute substantially to further social disruption."

The enormous increases in crime rates among unemployed young people in the 1960s and the 1970s bore out Michael's predictions. The efforts of the federal government under Kennedy, Johnson, Nixon, and Ford to create more jobs were extremely expensive and expanded the government's bureaucracy without providing enough jobs.

Perhaps the most serious problem for democracy described in the *Cybernation* report was the indication that governments would be forced to turn to computers to handle major dilemmas, including defense and military decisions, because "the data involved are so massive and the factors so complex that only machines can handle the material fast enough to allow timely action."

Michael felt that "there may not be any easy way to insure that decisions based on computers could not become a threat to democratic government." Public ignorance of key government issues might be "inevitable" in a "cybernated society." Even if political parties and private organizations could gain access to the government's computer programs, Michael said, "most people will be incapable of judging the validity of one contending computer program compared to another, or whether the policies based on them are appropriate."

"Significant public opinion may come only from a relatively small portion of the public," Michael said. "Those who are able to follow the battles of the computers and to understand the implications of their programs; and those who are concerned with government policy but who are outside of or unfamiliar with the computer environment."

A computerized government might require a new type of personnel in its policy and planning divisions, the report indicated. Emphasis would be shifted toward engineering and laboratory backgrounds, and there might be a trend "toward the recruitment of authoritarian personalities."

The role of computers in American involvement in the Vietnam War under President Johnson in the 1960s was obvious in the reliance of the Pentagon "experts," under Secretary of Defense Robert McNamara, on computer projections and computer-based recommendations for strategic policies. The American public was repeatedly informed by President Johnson that he had the information necessary to make wise decisions. The Congress and the people followed Johnson (and later, Richard Nixon) until it became overwhelmingly clear that the nation had plunged into a disaster.

In the Center booklet issued in 1962, Donald Michael glimpsed the possibility of a catastrophe ahead but he saw no chance to limit the computers: "As long as we choose to live in a world guided by science and technology, we have no choice but to encourage the development of cybernation. . . .

"Education must cope with the transitional period when the disruption among different socio-economic and occupational groups will be the greatest; and the later, relatively stable period, if it ever comes to exist, when most people would have adequate income and shorter working hours.

"The problem involves looking ahead five, ten, twenty years to see what are likely to be the occupational and social needs, and attitudes of those future periods; planning the intellectual and social education of each age group in the numbers needed; motivating young people to seek certain types of jobs and to adopt the desirable and necessary attitudes; providing enough suitable teachers; being able to alter all of these as the actualities in society and technology indicate; and directing the pattern of cybernation so that it fits with the expected kinds and distribution of abilities and attitudes produced by home and school. . . .

"If we do not find the answers to these questions soon, we will have a population in the next ten to twenty years more and more out of touch with national and international realities, ever more the victims of insecurity on the one hand and ennui on the other, and more and more mismatched to the occupational needs of the day."

But what would become of individual freedoms in a world controlled by computers? How could such freedoms be maintained, if young people had to be allocated to certain types of jobs and motivated to have "desirable attitudes"? Could freedom and scientific planning really be reconciled—or would skillful planning by leaders who understood how to use computers give people the illusion of freedom while managing their lives?

These were questions Donald Michael and all the other scholars who came to Center meetings and wrote Center pamphlets could not satisfactorily answer. The Center went on month after month, year by year, approaching these questions from a thousand avenues. Hutchins and his colleagues knew that the quest could never end unless freedom came to an end, unless the restless probing of the human mind could be stilled. No one at the Center wanted that to happen. No one thought it could happen.

The problems of the modern world were extremely difficult to comprehend and handle. Hutchins and his associates hoped that every intelligent person could grasp the fundamental issues, but they had never taken the position that one man's opinion was as good as any other. Jefferson had said: "There is a natural aristocracy among men. The grounds of this are virtue and talents." Hutchins and others at the Center were Jeffersonians, believing that the abilities and "virtue" of the most talented people should be recognized by the people as a whole. In a democratic society there had to be leaders, and the leaders should come from the "natural aristocracy"—not from what Jefferson called "an artificial aristocracy, founded on wealth and birth, without either virtue or talents."

But should only those who understood how to put programs into computers be considered the "natural aristocracy" of the future? Would other talented people, not gifted with the ability to manage computers, be reduced to living in an incomprehensible world? These were questions that cast a cloud over the dialogues at the Center.

With these questions hanging in the air, the Center hurried on to other topics. Two weeks after the *Cybernation* pamphlet had appeared, the Center printed and circulated the views of a leading Israeli financier who sought a "projection of the Welfare State onto the international scene" in order to bring about a "world community" of nations for the preservation of peace.

David Horowitz, governor of the Bank of Israel, declared in this pamphlet, entitled *The Haves and the Have Nots*, that the economically advanced countries were not investing sufficient capital in the underdeveloped nations, and that more joint government planning and action for aid was badly needed. His views were in direct opposition to those expressed in a Center pamphlet issued five months earlier—*Government and Business in International Trade,* by Heinrich Kronstein, a West German economist who had recommended that the U.S. government withdraw from economic assistance and let private investors take over.

Horowitz saw world economic problems in terms of "haves" and "have nots" rather than in terms of the East-West cold war. He wrote: "The growing reliance on market forces in the Soviet bloc and the growing consciousness of the need for direction and planning in the Western world are leading to some degree of assimilation of the different economic systems. Some day it may seem absurd to fight wars or to hurl nuclear weapons around because there happen to be technical differences in the methods of economic control in one group of countries and another."

Pointing to the need of the underdeveloped nations for capital, Horowitz said that "help from outside sources is the only possible substitute for forced formation of capital. The alternative to both is economic stagnation. . . . The worldwide shortage of capital is becoming one of the most decisive and influential factors in the economic pattern of the world." He asserted that the funneling by Western countries of their capital into automated production and military equipment was a major hindrance to the flow of private investment into the underdeveloped nations.

A few days after the release of the Horowitz pamphlet, the Center issued another in the series of booklets on the American character, containing interviews with George Gallup and Elmo Roper on opinion polls, their effects, and their value in a democracy.

Gallup declared that "the judgment of the people has often been wiser" than that of congressmen "or even of the experts" on many important issues, despite the fact that many citizens were not well informed and did not know much about the functioning of their own government. As an example, he cited attitudes of Americans toward Hitler.

"One of the earliest issues on which we polled came at the time when Hitler was beginning to raise his ugly head and menace world peace—that was in 1935," Gallup said. "The public was overwhelmingly in favor of building up our defenses; and 90 per cent of the people wanted to build up our Air Force.

"But in 1935 and for the next few years, Congress was not willing to increase appropriations for defense, and the expert heads of the Navy and the Army were telling us that air power would never be important in the next war. That is why this country entered World War II so badly prepared.

"I believe that if the will of the people had been followed, if we had gone as far and as fast as they wanted to go, there is even a chance there might not have been a World War II. I cite this as one of many examples of the superior judgment of the people."

Roper told Donald McDonald, the Center interviewer, that only 10 percent of the people were "politically active" and blamed the situation on widespread apathy and huge "areas of ignorance." He said that 56 percent of the voters could not name either of the senators from their home states and knew very little about economic issues.

Roper shared Gallup's view that the main purpose of opinion polls should be to educated citizens: "I think the mass of the American people are passionately indifferent to polling. But I think it has had an effect, nevertheless, on the American character in that it has called to the attention of various molders of public opinion certain great flaws in the American educational system." Neither Roper nor Gallup knew how to remedy these flaws.

Two other publications drawn from interviews with notable Americans were published by the Center in the spring of 1962. In a pamphlet entitled *Science*, Hans Bethe—a nuclear physicist who was a member of President Kennedy's advisory committee on nuclear testing—and James H. Douglas, who was deputy secretary of defense under President Eisenhower, joined in warning against the consequences of an unlimited arms race. In *Stage and Screen*, Walter Kerr—the drama critic for the New York *Herald Tribune* —and Stanley Kramer, the film producer, discussed the despair shown by many dramatists and the low state of the American film industry.

Bethe and Douglas voiced concern at the powerful influence of the military establishment. Bethe doubted whether the debate on scientific and military policy in Washington was conducted through "a democratic process." Douglas declared, "The defense process still suffers from the enthusiasm of Army, Navy, and Air Force to meet, each by itself, all military requirements for security against any enemy."

"Scientists who advocate development of weapons without restraint find a very ready public," Bethe said. "Those who warn against the dangers of an unlimited arms race find a very hostile reception from members of the Washington community."

Douglas pointed out: "In the world of today, with nuclear weapons and with each service possessing missile power and reaching for more, the need for unified planning and qualified objective review is of a new magnitude. It certainly calls for more planning by the Joint Chiefs of Staff and less by the services."

Walter Kerr asserted that many Americans were impatient with playwrights who treated man as if he had no will or dignity or "spiritual importance in the universe." He thought that more revivals of classical drama would help to rekindle public interest in the theater. He recommended a subsidy for a national repertory theater to produce the classics, although he did not favor any subsidy for the commercial theater.

While all these publications were being distributed in the United States and other countries, the Center had to face a decision involving its integrity and its freedom to operate without strings. Contributions were not arriving fast enough to keep the Center running. The Center had to decide whether to shift its low-keyed fund-raising efforts into an all-out campaign, or to prepare to close its doors.

In May 1962 Hutchins put the finishing touches on a summary of the Center's achievements in its first two and a half years, which he planned to offer to the public with a statement that the board of directors were determined to take the lead "in raising the money needed to maintain the Center for another ten years." At a meeting of the Center's officers in that month, he asked each one whether he would be willing to participate in the search for money on a long-term basis, or whether anyone felt that the Center might severely damage its program in a strenuous attempt to get funds.

The independence of the Fund for the Republic and the Center—obtained by the Fund's directors when the Ford Foundation gave its $15 million in 1953—had made it possible to go into extremely controversial topics without worrying about the possible loss of donations. But the necessity of pleading for money might restrict what the Center could do in the future. Programs might have to be planned with particular donors in mind.

W. H. Ferry and Hallock Hoffman had misgivings about what a fund-raising drive might do to the atmosphere of the Center. Ferry raised the possibility that the Center could decide to use its remaining resources on a few hard-hitting reports showing the drastic reforms needed in American society—and then close its record with blunt recommendations that might have an impact for years to come.

Harry Ashmore and I thought that the Center could carry on a financial drive without losing its freedom. The Center was too valuable an institution to close down. Hutchins indicated that he was confident of the Center's ability to do much more than it had been able to accomplish thus far, and he felt that the officers and directors were strong enough to preserve its independence while seeking gifts to meet its budget of $1.2 million a year. Ferry and Hoffman declared that they would do everything they could to bring in money, if a decision was made to engage in such a campaign.

Soon after this meeting Hutchins, Ashmore, Ferry and I talked with Harold L. Oram, a New York fund raiser recommended by Joseph Lyford and Elmo Roper, and with Irving Warner, a Los Angeles money raiser who had the endorsement of Seniel Ostrow, another Fund board member. Oram and Warner outlined a program based on a celebration of the tenth anniversary of the establishment of the Fund. Hutchins agreed to submit the program to the Fund's directors at their June meeting.

On June 6—the day before the directors met in New York—Hutchins released a report describing the Center's growth and development since it had been formed in Santa Barbara in 1959. Although he did not claim large achievements, he said: "The Center is trying to do what has never been done before and is not being done anywhere else in the world. If democratic countries are to remain democratic, and developing countries are to become democratic, they require centers of independent thought and criticism about the problems that democracy faces today.''

Acknowledging that the universities should have been performing such functions, Hutchins asserted: ''In the United States, because of the obligations that have been forced on them in specialized research and professional training, the universities have some difficulty in bringing criticism, in any concerted way, to bear on contemporary issues. There is tremendous proliferation of knowledge; there is inadequate comprehension of what it signifies. There is a need for general principles. The Center does not claim that it is as effective as it should be in meeting this need and filling this gap. What is important is that it is making the effort.''

Hutchins referred to the work being done for the Britannica; the grant of $25,000 a year from the Parvin Foundation, which paid for trips to South America by Ashmore and me and had covered the expenses of Latin American leaders who had attended Center meetings; the seminar in Athens conducted with the cooperation of the Greek government; the visit of Center scholars to Israel; and the invitations received by the Center to hold meetings in Australia, Germany, France, and England. His report showed that the Center was recognized in many countries.

''The principal source of the Center's financial support up to the present has been the Fund for the Republic, which was originally established by the Ford Foundation,'' Hutchins said. ''This grant is being gradually exhausted, and the Center is now inviting contributions from other sources. . . . The Center has never conducted a financial campaign, and yet it has received for general purposes $166,000 and for special purposes $203,000 in the last three years.''

While expressing gratitude for the gifts received in the first stage of the Center's existence, Hutchins went on: ''At the present level of income and expense, the funds supporting the Center will be gone in the first half of 1964. It is necessary to raise the question of financing now in order to make planning possible.'' He disclosed the existence of the Continuation Committee created by the Fund's board, and said that ''the Center is confident that it will be successful in finding the necessay support from individuals and organizations that believe its work is woth sustaining.''

''The Board and officers are aware of the difficulties of such an undertaking,'' Hutchins said calmly.

One of the difficulties arose from the fact that nearly all the board members had been elected at a time when their principal responsibility was to spend the Ford Foundation's money wisely. During the first eight years of the Fund's activity, each of the directors received $3000 in fees annually for services. The token fee had been reduced to $1000 a year in 1960, and it was later eliminated. But some of the directors were slow to realize that their duties included giving money and raising it; others were willing to give but did not wish to ask their friends and others for money.

Oram had sent a memorandum to Hutchins on June 1, 1962, saying plainly that the outcome of a fund-raising drive would depend largely on the directors. If the current directors were not enthusiastic about the Center, other directors should be added to the board—directors who could give substantial contributions and could persuade other people to do so. A forceful, emphatic man, Oram made his views known to several members of the board in frank conversations. The directors were equally frank with him.

Oram's program was approved by the Fund's board at the special meeting in New York on June 7. His agency was designated to coordinate the fund raising on a national scale, and Warner was employed as the West Coast representative. At this meeting the directors also elected Mrs. Marshall Field to the board, replacing Eleanor B. Stevenson, who resigned to accompany her husband, William E. Stevenson, on a diplomatic mission to the Philippines. Stevenson had been appointed ambassador to that country by President Kennedy.

On July 16 Oram dispatched a six-page description to Hutchins of what he intended to do and what he wanted the directors and staff members of the Center to do. He reiterated his recommendation that the theme for the tenth anniversary celebration should be "The Crisis of Democracy in the Second Half of the 20th Century," and the Fund should announce that it sought contributions totaling $10 million for its work in the coming decade.

Oram did not hesitate to define the topics and name the speakers he wished to have at the Tenth Anniversary Convocation. He thought it should be held in New York or Washington in December 1962, it should deal with topics of interest to "thoughtful people across the entire country," and it should have "authoritative speakers whose addresses will receive national and international attention." He said it should be followed by a dinner in Los Angeles in February 1963, at which each person in attendance should be expected to contribute $1000.

"Board and Founding Members will be called upon to extend personal invitations to persons whom they know and to others who know of them," Oram said. By mid-October, he expected to have a list of "two thousand support prospects, as well as members of the national and international press for invitations to the Convocation." Preliminary luncheon and dinner meetings—and visits to prospective donors—were to be done by Fund directors and Founding Members before the two principal events.

"Mr. Warner reports that the western campaign office is exploring the feasibility of an event to revive support prospects in San Francisco; to begin Los Angeles work with an auspicious dinner party, and a special gifts effort in the San Diego area," Oram said.

In the course of the fund-raising campaign for the Center, Hutchins and his famous friends were called upon many times to participate in luncheons, cocktail parties, and dinners where wealthy people gathered to learn what the Center was "all about" and why the noted minds on Eucalyptus Hill deserved to be supported by their dollars. Stevenson, Douglas, Aldous Huxley, Senator J. William Fulbright, Hyman Rickover, Arthur F. Burns, Pierre Mendes-France, Lewis Mumford, and many others who appreciated the Center helped immensely.

While the Center geared up for a large-scale money drive in the spring and summer months of 1962, its dialogues went on with the participation of speakers on many subjects and its publications came from printing presses month after month. Its meetings were recorded for regular broadcasts by the Pacifica Foundation, which had educational radio stations in Los Angeles, San Francisco, and New York. Florence Mischel, who had arrived in Santa Barbara in November 1961 to do the audiotapings for the Pacifica organization, later joined the Center staff and edited hundreds of tapes, which were used in many schools and colleges. This project was supported and encouraged by Seniel Ostrow.

The meetings in these months ranged from discussions of the future of law—in a conference jointly sponsored by the Center and the Britannica—to sessions with a Cuban jurist who denounced Castro's government as an instrument of a global "Communist conspiracy"; to a dialogue with Denis Healey, a Labor party leader in the British parliament; to an exchange of ideas with Dallas Smythe, a communications research professor at the University of Illinois, who called the launching of the Telstar satellite "the biggest giveaway of all time"; to a session with Malcolm Moos, a former assistant to President Eisenhower, on the future of the Republican party in the United States.

Enemies of the Center in Santa Barbara intermittently bombarded the *News-Press* with angry letters, accusing the Center of promoting attacks on American institutions. When Hutchins spoke at a public meeting in the Santa Barbara high school, a man ran into the auditorium and passed out leaflets containing reprints of Congressman Francis Walter's verbal assaults on the Fund.

Without regard to their effects on prospective donors, the Center issued three highly critical publications in July 1962. One pamphlet, containing statements made at the Washington symposium "The American Character," gave the views of leaders who claimed that the average American shirked political responsibilities, had allowed the educational system to go downhill, lacked understanding of people in other countries, and had become hopelessly separated from black fellow citizens.

In this booklet Edward Cushman, vice president of American Motors Corporation, agreed with Professor Perry Miller of Harvard that business had never sought to reform itself, but he declared that other American institutions—the church, government, the labor union, the school, and the family—were also failing in many of their functions. Several contributors said the sad condition of American democracy was due to political misgovernment, not to the American character.

Irving Kristol, a New York writer and editor, contended: "I don't think the mass media are bad because of the American character. I think that the mass media are bad because the political authorities have not seen to it that they are better. I resent the decline of our educational system, and I think this is bad, again, because the political authorities have not taken adequate action."

"I am tired of seeing so many issues being put on the shoulders of psychiatrists," declared Leonard Duhl, director of the professional services branch of the National Institute of Mental Health. "There are psychiatrists who have accepted this burden. They have, for example, accepted delinquency as a mental health problem, whereas it is basically a social problem. Delinquency has to be dealt with socially at all levels—urban renewal, job opportunities, education, and many other things."

Rabbi Eugene Lipman, of Washington's Temple Sinai, did not think that political leaders of government should be made scapegoats: "I have to face the fact that if the American educational system has failed, I have failed. If our civil rights system is failing, then I as a citizen have failed. We all must bear a part of the guilt."

Michael Harrington felt that one of the mistakes frequently made in assessing the American character was to assume that it was essentially shaped by affluence. He said that between 32 million and 50 million people in the United States were living in poverty and had a character structure very different from that of most middle-class Americans.

William Worthy, a black journalist, declared that Americans tended to leave out of their considerations the behavior and attitudes of black citizens: "It seems to me there has been a corrosive effect on white America's mental health as a result of evading the problem of race discrimination for three hundred years." Dr. Duhl answered: "Almost all people avoid issues outside the social system they know well. I would guess that if we really looked searchingly into the Negro social system we would find that Negroes have the same kind of stereotypes about other communities that the whites may have about them. . . . How do we break out of our own system so that we can start taking cognizance of things outside of it? If we don't realize that every human social system and system of values is interrelated with every other one, we are not going to survive at all."

The glaring evils existing in the United States might make it necessary for many Americans, especially young people, to start "going to jail for their beliefs," Scott Buchannan declared in the next pamphlet issued by the

Center on July 30, 1962. He applauded the young "freedom riders" who had risked their lives by breaking the segregation rules established in the South.

Buchanan thought that the world might be on the verge of nonviolent revolutions and said that "academic people more than other people in this country" were thinking about "civil disobedience" and "doing things about it." He asked every citizen to try to understand the John Birch Society, which had frequently attacked the Center: "They are making us stand to our colors a bit, making us ask ourselves whether we really believe in free speech among other things, and whether we want them to be allowed to talk. This is a pretty good test of how closely we hold to our principles."

Commending the college students who were suffering blows and imprisonment for their principles, Buchanan said: "This is a technique that is worthy of consideration, and I'm considering it myself. . . . In some cases they are saying, I am willing to die for this. This is another point beyond jail-going which has something to do with revolution."

Representative Charles M. Teague, a Republican member of Congress whose district included Santa Barbara, reacted angrily in August 1962 to some of the statements coming from the Center. In particular, he was disturbed by the words of W. H. Ferry, who had referred scornfully to J. Edgar Hoover in a speech Ferry had given at a conference of Western Democrats in Seattle.

Ferry was, of course, speaking for himself and not for the Center. In a note to the *News-Press*, I tried to make it clear that only the directors could speak for the Center as an organization. Many citizens, however, continued to believe that the views of Ferry, Buchanan, Wheeler, Hoffman, Hutchins, and others published by the Center represented the official policies of the Center. In all its publications, the Center explained that writers and scholars were personally responsible for "their statements of fact and expressions of opinion." The Center took responsibility "only for determining that the material should be presented to the public." The directors of the Fund— who actually had a controlling power over the Center—included a broad range of views. But many people—including some congressmen and some journalists—felt that the Center itself had a "liberal" or "left-wing" leaning, which was manifested in the employment of Ferry and other staff members as well as in the "tone" of many of its publications.

The appointment of Richard Lichtman, a neo-Marxist philosopher from the University of Kansas City, for a year beginning in August 1962— an appointment subsequently continued for several years—confirmed these suspicions in some of the Center's critics. Hutchins said that the appointment had been made because Lichtman had written "some excellent papers on philosophical questions related to freedom and justice." Lichtman became one of the most vocal participants in the Center dialogues during his time at the Center. His ideas were heard without being endorsed by Hutchins or others there.

Changes in the staff occurred fairly often in this phase of the Center's development. In the summer of 1962 Yosal Rogat—the young law professor who had produced the Center pamphelt on the Eichmann trial—left to join the faculty at the University of Chicago. Carl Stover, a director of studies in science and technology, accepted an offer to become a staff member at the Stanford Research Institute in Palo Alto. James Brady, a Santa Barbara business executive who had served as an assistant to Hutchins, returned to the real estate business.

To give the directors of the Fund opportunities to review what was happening in Santa Barbara and to sustain their determination to raise money, Hutchins scheduled two meetings of the board in the autumn of that year. Both were held in New York, and considerable time was spent on what had to be done to keep the Center in existence.

Justice Douglas was elected as a director and as cochairman of the board with Elmo Roper at the session on September 6. In accordance with the recommendation of Harold Oram, the bylaws were changed to increase the number of directors from twenty-one to twenty-seven. It was hoped that the added directors would bring in generous gifts. At the meeting, all the board members agreed that they would serve without fees and all promised to help in the hunt for contributions.

Announcing the election of Douglas to the press, Roper said: "Since the Fund was established to preserve and extend the principles of our Constitution, I think it is particularly fitting to have a member of the Supreme Court as Co-Chairman." It was also helpful to the fund-raising campaign, although Roper did not mention that. Roper noted that Paul G. Hoffman continued to be honorary chairman; George N. Shuster was vice chairman; and Robert Hutchins had been reelected president.

On October 10, 1962, a few days before the development of the Cuban missile crisis, John Cogley was asked by President Kennedy to serve for six weeks on the Foreign Service Selection Board at the State Department in Washington. Kennedy had kept in communication with Cogley, who had been so helpful to him in the presidential campaign of 1960.

When the installation of Soviet missiles in Cuba was discovered and photographed by American air force officers in high-flying U-2 planes on October 14, the United States and the Soviet Union moved within a few days to the brink of nuclear war. On October 22 Kennedy announced the formation of an American naval blockade around Cuba, with all Russian ships to be boarded and inspected before being allowed to enter Cuban ports. After Kennedy had mobilized 250,000 troops and 90,000 marines and paratroopers for a possible invasion of Cuba, he exchanged messages with Soviet Premier Khrushchev on terms for a settlement of the crisis. On October 28 Radio Moscow disclosed that Khrushchev had ordered the dismantling of the Soviet missiles and their return to Russia. Kennedy canceled the American plan for a landing in Cuba, and the confrontation between the United States and the Soviets ended.

During those days of agony, Kennedy's staff members gave John Cogley messages for transmission to the Vatican. Cogley, who was then the leading Catholic journalist in the United States, had opened channels of communication to the men around Pope John XXIII. Kennedy, the Pope, and Khrushchev had communicated with one another during the crisis. The Pope, horrified by the abyss of destruction that had appeared so near, began the preparation of his encyclical *Pacem in Terris*, in which he pleaded for all men of good will to work together for peace.

The Center later took the *Pacem in Terris* document as the basis for a series of international convocations, which helped to bring about at least a temporary relaxation of tensions between the Soviet bloc and the Western nations headed by the United States.

A novel by Eugene Burdick and Harvey Wheeler, turning on the possibility of a nuclear disaster in a confrontation between the U.S. and Russia was published on October 17, 1962, and soon became a bestseller in the atmosphere of the Cuban confrontation. Entitled *Fail-Safe*, it disturbed millions of people who were reminded again of the precarious situation in which every human being lived while nuclear arsenals were expanding rapidly.

The wide distribution of *Fail-Safe*, through its serialization in the *Saturday Evening Post*, its selection by book clubs, and its large sale in a paperback edition, aroused intense interest in Burdick and Wheeler, who collaborated on the Center's studies of political parties and other projects. The two men were in demand as speakers on radio and television, and were admired by the well-to-do people who aided the Center financially. Hutchins was impressed by their ideas and their impact on the public, and these two men had much influence on the Center's later programs.

While the American naval blockade was in force and the obliteration of civilization seemed to be on the horizon that October, the Center continued to hold its dialogues. On October 25, eight members of the Council for International Progress in Management—sponsored by the West German government—met with the Center staff to consider its aims, activities, and methods. These planners sought ideas that could be applied to European and German problems. If the world managed to survive, some of them hoped that institutions similar to the Center could be established in the European countries.

Hutchins and all of us were always excited by visitors who talked of forming branches of the Center—or creating organizations modeled on the Center—in other countries. Hutchins didn't see how any country could build a truly democratic society without having a free group of thinkers acting as gadflies. He was increasingly troubled by the fact that it was difficult to get enough funds to nourish the Center in Santa Barbara, and he knew that it was not likely that Centers in Europe, Asia, or Africa would materialize if the one in California had to shut down.

On October 29 the Center released a report by Charles A. Reich, a professor of law at Yale and a specialist in conservation research, declaring that the American people had "lost control" over federal policies on the use of 200 million acres of public lands. In *Bureaucracy and the Forests*, Reich said that "an overwhelmed Congress has been forced to delegate a large measure of legislative power to specialized executive and administrative agencies, the officials of which are not elected or directly controlled by the people."

Reich, who later wrote a provocative book called *The Greening of America*, asserted that Congress had put such vague standards into laws governing the forests that it had virtually turned over all its authority to the bureaucrats. He had five specific recommendations: "adequate public notice of most major plans and decisions."; "an opportunity by citizens to submit written views" challenging these plans and actions; "outside groups or viewpoints" to be given "permanent representation within the agency"; "those supporting a decision should be required to give reasons for it"; and "one final right—the right to initiate . . . a procedure is needed to ensure serious consideration and review of public proposals about the forests." Long before Ralph Nader became a well-known public crusader, Reich was advocating citizen action.

Early in December, the Center sponsored the first in a series of educational-social conferences, which the professional fund raisers called "events." A weekend symposium, with some sessions at the old mansion on Eucalyptus Hill and some at the luxurious Santa Barbara Biltmore, was attended by eighty or ninety wealthy people rounded up by Seniel Ostrow and Irving Warner. It was designed to celebrate the tenth anniversary of the Fund, and its theme was "Prospects for Democracy"—a theme that was to be covered again at a more massive assembly in New York six weeks later.

The Santa Barbara gathering began with a reception and dinner at the Biltmore, where the rich people from Los Angeles and Beverly Hills and San Diego rubbed shoulders with Justice Douglas, Paul Hoffman, Aldous Huxley, Jonas Salk, Harrison Brown, Walter Millis, Eugene Burdick, Sir Robert Watson-Watt, Hutchins, and other celebrities who were listed as the speakers at the seminars on subsequent days. The speakers had been chosen for "box office appeal" as well as their expertness in various fields.

Hutchins and Douglas assured the possible donors that they would be expected to ask questions and to participate vigorously in every session.

At the first session Harrison Brown, Huxley, and Salk dissected the impact of science and technology on democratic institutions. What was boiling up on the international scene was analyzed at the second seminar by Hoffman, who was then the director of the United Nations Special Fund, and Kenneth Boulding, economist and director of the Center for Conflict Resolution.

Sensational statements were made on the second day, principally by Eugene Burdick, coauthor of *Fail-Safe*. Burdick declared that he believed the decisionmakers in Washington and Moscow were often under the influence of drugs. He made his affluent audience feel that they were living under a shadow of imminent doom.

Burdick was one of four speakers at this session. Walter Millis felt that the pressures of the cold war were robbing American citizens of their rights through governmental secrecy, a "legacy of McCarthyism," and the "indoctrination rather than instruction" of schoolchildren. Wheeler said the United States must alter its fundamental institutions to protect the rights of the people in a modern society that had become "war-oriented." Sir Robert Watson-Watt said the world must "rehumanize itself" and divert technology and science from the development of engines of death to the improvement of the quality of life for mankind.

Indicting the United States for its failure to secure equal rights for its black citizens, Ashmore declared: "This is the greatest constitutional crisis since the Civil War."

Ashmore and other speakers indicated that the work being done by the Center to get the American people to face the problems that were being evaded by many politicians and educational institutions had earned the support of all thinking citizens. At the end of the symposium, the invited guests gave or pledged $338,000 in contributions to the Center.

The array of notable speakers and their sharp statements about the severity of the crises facing the United States caused many of the guests to announce that they would try to persuade their friends to give money to the Center. The first fund-raising "event" was an unmistakable success.

Democracy and revolution were brought under scrutiny by Scott Buchanan and Justice Douglas at the third session. Buchanan thought that many revolutions were just around the corner, and Douglas declared that Americans should not be afraid of revolutions if the revolutions led to more freedom and more justice for the oppressed peoples of the earth.

The background, the purposes, and the needs of the Center were presented by Harry Ashmore, then the editor-in-chief and a vice president of the Britannica, in a talk entitled "The Past, Present, and Future of the Center for the Study of Democratic Institutions" at the fourth session. As he put it, he was there to "rattle a tambourine" and get the guests to open their checkbooks.

At the fifth and final session, Burdick, Harvey Wheeler, Millis, and Watson-Watt—a British physicist who was credited with the development of radar and who was now aiding the Center in its study of science and technology—looked at the impact of the cold war on democratic institutions. They were all opposed to the cold war and felt it had severely damaged the essential institutions of a free society.

As the Fund for the Republic and its offspring reached the last month of its first decade, Hutchins and his colleagues continued to be provoking, but with enough signs of support to keep right on talking and shaking people up in many places.

16

In a year of strife, the Center struggles to raise funds and plans a peace convocation

FOR MILLIONS OF AMERICANS 1962 had been a year of exultation and depression, a time of rejoicing when John Glenn went around the earth in an American spacecraft, a time of fear when the clouds of nuclear annihilation seemed to hover over every city, a time of subdued joy when Khrushchev and Kennedy agreed to hold the rockets back. As 1963 opened, people hoped that it would be a calmer time, a better year. But it was a year of violence, a year of shock and suffering, a year when people sat stunned before their television screens and many wept when they heard the bitter news pouring from their radios.

There was blood in the streets of Birmingham and Dallas, blood spilled in Saigon. It was the year of a peaceful uprising met by violence, when blacks in Alabama demanding civil rights were beaten with bullwhips and attacked by police dogs. It was the year when the president of South Vietnam, Ngo Diem, and members of his family were murdered. It was the year when John F. Kennedy was shot to death and the man accused of killing Kennedy was mortally wounded by a gunman three days later in the presence of seventy Dallas policemen and the television cameras.

It was a rough year for thinking people, for all those who clung to the notion that disputes could be settled reasonably, for all those who tried to understand what was going on. As one thing happened after another, people began to believe that nothing made sense, that nobody could figure anything out. It didn't pay to try to think.

The Center continued to try. For the Center the year began in a full ballroom at the Americana Hotel in New York, with 1500 people assembled for two announced purposes: "To bring together world and American leaders to consider how democratic man can meet problems affecting the survival of freedom with justice in the world. To call upon concerned Americans to assume leadership in marshalling financial support to carry forward the work of the Center for the Study of Democratic Institutions over the next decade.'' It was the second in the series of convocations celebrating the tenth anniversary of the Fund for the Republic and examining the prospects for democracy.

President Kennedy wasn't there, but his brother Robert Kennedy— then the attorney general of the United States—delivered an address entitled ''The Bill of Rights and the Cold War,'' proclaiming: ''All great questions must be raised by great voices, and the greatest voice is the voice of the people. We think with Jefferson that our government is 'the world's best hope; the only one where every man at the call of the law would fly to the standard of the law and would meet invasions of the public order as his own personal concern.' . . . It is clear that the standard of law in America flies to protect the civil liberty of all American citizens from private as well as public invasions.'' These were noble words, and yet the investigations that followed the Watergate scandal in the 1970s revealed that the Kennedys themselves had sanctioned invasions of the civil liberties of some Americans.

Other speakers at the Center convocation included Admiral Hyman Rickover; Justice Douglas; Adlai Stevenson; Paul Hoffman; Elmo Roper; Secretary of Labor W. Willard Wirtz; Arthur F. Burns; FCC Chairman Newton Minow; United States Senators Clifford P. Case, Joseph S. Clark, and J. William Fulbright; Lord Hailsham, minister for science and technology in the British government; Lord Francis-Williams, critic and journalist from London; Pierre Mendes-France, former premier of France; Jose Figueres, former president of Costa Rica; Lord James of Rusholme, vice chancellor of the University of York; and Gunnar Myrdal, the noted economist from Sweden.

In a statement to the press, Hutchins described this gathering as ''the greatest intellectual outburst since the Constitutional convention'' in Philadelphia in 1787. He urged the speakers to take long leaps into the future, trying to see how democracy would fare in the decade ahead. ''The road to wisdom is candid and intrepid thinking about fundamental issues,'' Hutchins affirmed again.

All of the speakers tried to be ''candid'' and ''intrepid.'' Myrdal, the internationally known author of *An American Dilemma*, warned the leaders of the Kennedy administration that America had ''lapsed into stagnation'' and ''even America's *low* rate of economic growth is dependent upon very heavy armament expenditures.'' He declared that ''the affluent society is largely a myth, except for a privileged upper stratum.''

Asserting that ''unemployment in America is increasingly becoming a structural and not a cyclical matter,'' Myrdal said: ''The present relative stagnation in the American economy is dangerous for the successful pursuance of America's foreign policy. Internally, it is apt to create rigid class chasms and, in particular, to cause the growth of an underprivileged class not sharing in the nation's opportunities, which would be a development contrary to American ideals. To get America out of the rut of relative stagnation with mild recessions, weak and hesitant recoveries, and a rising trend of unemployment will require very much more of long-range planning and of government intervention.

He doubted whether American leaders would do what he thought should be done. He didn't think Americans understood economic planning or long-range forecasting, which he considered absolutely essential. He asked for a wider recognition of what rational planning with popular participation could really do.

"As a result of this planning and coordination, it would certainly be possible to scrap a lot of specific controls, which have spuriously grown up ad hoc," Myrdal contended. "Instead, successful planning should free the citizen from a lot of nuisance public intervention, of which there is astonishingly much in America."

Lewis Mumford, president of the American Academy of Arts and Letters, told the convocation that many people had surrendered easily "to the controllers, the manipulators, the conditioners," because the technological system offered every citizen "a magnificent bribe." While many citizens were not affluent, the possibilities of affluence were offered to all, Mumford insisted: "Under the democratic-authoritarian social contract, each member of the community may claim every material advantage, every emotional and intellectual stimulus he may desire. . . . But on the one condition that one must not merely ask for nothing the system does not provide, but likewise agree to take everything offered, duly processed and fabricated. . . . Once one opts for the system, no further choice remains."

In terms that were later used by leaders of the youth movement in the last half of the decade, Mumford favored a revival of the "do-it-yourself" idea, saying that the "seat of authority" had to be shifted from "the mechanical collective" to "the human personality and the autonomous group."

Admiral Rickover, who had been battling bureaucracies in the armed services, declared: "It is important for us to see clearly that what diminishes the individual is bureaucracy turned rigid." In corporate bureaucracies, he said, Americans confronted one another under conditions of extreme inequality and with the weaker guaranteed no "inalienable rights."

"Corporations have long striven to obtain full citizenship rights as 'persons' in the sight of the law. They have largely attained that objective. The courts for all practical purposes treat them as state or federal citizens. Does the achievement of citizenship status then not entail on the part of corporations the obligations to assume as well the civic duties of natural citizens? . . . It seems to me a clear obligation for all bureaucratic organizations—private as well as public—to do nothing that will diminish individual autonomy. Public bureaucracies need constant watching, but they *can* be restrained. With private bureaucracies, the obligation cannot be imposed or enforced.''

Harrison Brown, of the California Institute of Technology, shared Admiral Rickover's alarm at the expansion of bureaucracies: ''The tribal councils in which each individual could make his voice heard have all but disappeared. We are governed by a system of technology, and the technologists themselves do not know that they are governing us. Let us return to the human values of our forefathers.''

Senator Fulbright, then the chairman of the Senate Committee on Foreign Relations, joined several of the other speakers in asserting that the vitality of a democracy depended on the character and quality of public education. He deplored the immense spending by the Kennedy administration on rockets and space vehicles designed to beat the Russians in the ''space race.''

''It seems to me an astonishing distortion of priorities that the American people and their government gladly spend billions of dollars for space exploration while denying desperately needed funds to their public schools,'' Fulbright protested. ''I do not believe that a society that has shamefully starved and neglected its public education can claim to have exploited its fullest possibilities and found them wanting.''

Fulbright proved to be accurate in foreseeing that ''we must contemplate the further enhancement of Presidential authority in foreign affairs.'' Congress was not effectively organized to deal with foreign policy decisions; the people were not well educated enough to make wise decisions in such difficult areas. He felt that the power to act in foreign policy had to be placed in the president: ''The prospect is a disagreeable and perhaps a dangerous one, but the alternative is immobility and the paralysis of national policy in a revolutionary world, which can only lead to consequences immeasurably more disagreeable and dangerous.''

Senator Clark of Pennsylvania, another speaker at the Center convocation, was equally sure that the decisionmaking authority had to be placed in the president: ''The executive should be strengthened at the expense of the legislature. Perhaps De Gaulle has shown the way. . . . We need not fear executive tyranny in this country merely because the legislature is more responsive to executive recommendations.''

Neither Senator Fulbright nor Senator Clark anticipated that President Kennedy's authorization of the sending of 16,000 men to Vietnam—and President Johnson's subsequent commitment of more than 500,000 men there—would eventually cost the United States $150 billion, bring on a runaway inflation, set off a series of student rebellions, divide the nation, and finally end in a severe military defeat. Some of Kennedy's advisers—Chester Bowles, George Ball, and others—saw the dangers of American involvement in a Far Eastern war, but Kennedy and Johnson followed the advice of other ''experts.''

Charles Frankel, a professor of philosophy at Columbia University, another participant in the Center conference in January 1963, issued a note of caution on the perils of relying on "experts." Frankel commented wryly: "One of the questions, for example, that is often raised is why the people with their passion and their foolishness should be allowed to rule and to get in the way of those who know better. An assumption here is that technical experts agree. This is just not so. Technical experts do not agree. Perhaps the range of disagreement is a little narrower than it is for the rest of us, but it is not the case that those who occupy 'elite' positions in modern society— these technical experts—can be held to some one position. . . .

"A second assumption is that the decision made in the political field by so-called 'experts' are technical decisions. They are, but within extremely narrow limits. I can think of very few important political decisions that do not involve the weighing and assessing of evidence from a wide variety of different specialists. *This means that even those who are experts in one field quickly become laymen the moment they move into another field. . . .* [Italics added.]

"What is called for in making public decisions, accordingly, is not omniscience or omnicompetent knowledge but something closer to wisdom, and common sense, and an understanding of when and where and for what reasons to rely on the advice of experts."

Participants in the Center convocation also grappled with the problems created by concentrations of private power, the responsibilities of the mass media, and the relationships between education and democracy in the coming decade.

Citing the fact that the Constitution of the United States represented an attempt by the founders of the nation to deal with the distribution of governmental powers, Walter Reuther said: "The new forms of private power had not yet been created. These new private-power centers are not the product of evil men. They are the product of a technological revolution. General Motors is the product of the gasoline engine, of automation, of the electronic computer; and the United Auto Workers is the product of General Motors.

"We cannot displace or dismantle these new power-concentration centers, except as we are prepared to expand greatly the power of the central government. We must learn to live with bigness; we must meet the problems of the growing concentration of private power by developing new concepts, new procedures, and new democratic mechanisms. . . .

"I believe we will eventually have to create some mechanism to bring a rational sense of direction into private decisions. It seems to me that only a national planning agency can provide this direction. Somehow we must get over the notion in America that private planning for profit is good but public planning for people is subversive. The Common Market nations, the Scandinavian countries, and England are all proving that democratic planning is compatible with a free society."

Reuther also advocated a "public pricing agency" to "function in those limited areas of our national economy where powerful corporations and powerful unions dominate an industry and essentially have repealed the market forces in the economy and adopted a system of administered prices."

Adolf Berle, another speaker concerned about the enormous powers of giant organizations, declared that the Bill of Rights should be extended to people involved in such organizations: "The American state is not merely a political democracy. It is also an economic republic. It has been so declared and recognized as a matter of law."

Arthur Burns, then the president of the National Bureau of Economic Research and later the head of the Federal Reserve Board, supported Berle's proposal for an economic Bill of Rights. But he was highly critical of Reuther's recommendation for a governmental price board: "If Mr. Reuther's board really accomplished his purpose of restraining price increases through public review and criticism, it would in effect become a price-fixing board. . . . In all probability, the ultimate result would therefore be a vast network of price-fixing by the government, and—sooner or later—of wage-fixing as well."

Secretary of Labor Willard Wirtz, taking part in this discussion, applauded Reuther's statement that both unions and management had responsibilities to the total community: "I am frank to say, however, that I see comparatively little sense of this public responsibility in connection with any of the particular disputes that develop. . . . I think we fool ourselves when we seem to count on any effective expression of the public interest in a particular crisis."

Another participant, Robert Heilbroner, said there had been a drastic change in the way in which a person in modern society thought of himself: "There was a time when an average person thought of himself, first and foremost, as a citizen. Today I believe that an average person thinks of himself, first and foremost, as a consumer." Connected with this change was a rise in cynicism among young people: "My children, looking at the great silver television screen, already mock that stentorian and phony seriousness with which products are sold to them and measure their disbelief in what a man says against the so-called 'sincerity' with which he says it."

Acknowledging that there seemed to be a consensus at the Center convocation that "we will 'muddle through,' " Heilbroner questioned that idea. "The revolutionary world presents us with problems of adaptation which will strain to the hilt our ability to formulate new methods of international operation," he warned. "A great deal of our capacity to make progress . . . depends on the ability of men in power—business power, private power, government power—to think in new terms of reference."

"Are we rising to the profound influences that television presents?" Newton Minow asked, in his address at the session of the convocation devoted to the responsibilities of the mass media. "Is our free society keeping what the Supreme Court called 'a grip on the dynamic aspects' of this new communications medium? Where is television going these next ten years? How should it get there?"

"We believe that broadcasting in the 1960s should be encouraged to become even more interested in controversy, to help feed and shape public opinion," Minow said.

Minow endorsed Senator William Benton's proposal for a national citizens' advisory board for radio and television, originally offered to the nation by Benton in a 1951 speech. The board then suggested by Benton would have issued an annual report, reviewing the year's progress and failures in the public service supplied by the broadcasting industry. Hutchins had supported the idea, and Harry Ashmore and I had tried to get it into operation eight years later.

Insisting that broadcasting needed "outside criticism" and an independent review of its policies year after year, Minow said: "The board was never created. It should have been. It is not too late."

Lord Francis-Williams, who also analyzed the role of the media at the Center conference, was one of the founders of a cooperative enterprise, Television Reporters International, which was striving to make television reporting in depth "on issues of current international importance simultaneously available to many countries." He mentioned this to indicate that he regarded radio and television as extremely important in communicating ideas and information. But he focused attention on the impermanence of broadcasting.

"There is nothing as transient as a radio or television report, especially a report on current affairs." the British journalist said. "This impermanence in the means of communication is particularly important in the realm of ideas—without which civilization, particularly democratic civilization, cannot survive. The most potent ideas, like the most enduring expressions of the creative spirit, are rarely capable of being grasped in all their implications at one hearing. They need to be read and reread. And I toss out, in passing, the sobering thought that in television and radio—these masters of space and enemies of time—the only element that commands the durability denied to all else is advertising, for it alone is permitted the gift of constant repetition."

Francis-Williams spoke before the widespread use of audiotapes and videotapes made it possible to preserve and repeat many radio and television programs. But public affairs programs dealing with major problems were rarely recorded and rarely repeated, even when the tape machines became generally available. The entertainment programs were the ones that were run again and again by the broadcasting stations.

At the Center convocation Francis-Williams insisted: "The democratic need for a press that stands aside from all established forms of authority, holding an independent position as a reporter of and commentator on the news, is likely to grow not less but greater in the next decade. . . . It is the function of the press to look at the face of authority from below, from among the governed not the governing: its role is to be dangerous to those who rule even when they rule with the best of intentions. *Its business is to establish a minefield through which all authority, at whatever level, must walk with care."* [Italics added.]

Francis-Williams did not predict the Watergate scandal, which brought down President Nixon, but he did foresee the growing role of the press in checking the excesses of people in power. The courage of the *New York Times* in publishing "the Pentagon papers" and the relentless investigations of two young reporters for the Washington *Post*—and the exposures of corruption in high places by Jack Anderson and other columnists—were vital elements in keeping the American democratic system alive in the decade between 1963 and 1973. This watchdog function of the press was saluted at the Center conference.

Perhaps the most sweeping suggestions offered to the mass media came from Sylvester L. (Pat) Weaver, former president of the National Broadcasting Company: "The mass media can make people work miracles if the rewards that are pictured are realistically attainable. The management of the mass media should mount a major offensive against poverty and against the other great crimes of ignorance and stupidity and bigotry and fear. The mass media should focus their reporting and exhorting powers on the potential of each individual across all the quintiles of our society. We are moving up. It can be seen in book sales, in record sales. . . . We should want all people to join the literate and civilized world of the elite, to become involved in our common future, and we can do this only by exposing all of them to all the cultures and the knowledge and the adventures of man."

To Weaver, the media had virtually no limits: "The big changes that are taking place [today] really come not from basic industry, not from technology, but from the massive effect on people of our incentive system as demonstrated by the mass media. Let the people of Japan and Australia, of Brazil and Mexico, see in programming and editorial matter and advertising what can be theirs if they will work for it, and you get a quantum jump in their attitude and their condition overnight."

In the decade between 1963 and 1973 the world did become Americanized. The mass media led people everywhere to demand more and more things faster and faster. The results were revolutionary—much more revolutionary than Weaver had expected. The generation brought up on television had a smattering of information about many cultures, a desire to experience every possible sensation, a willingness to throw old habits overboard and smash old institutions, a short attention span, and a restlessness often degenerating into disgust and despair.

Whether education could cope with the speed of change was the focal point for statements by three thoughtful men and a perceptive woman at the Center convocation session on "Education: For What and For Whom?" All four were aware of the "quantum jump" to which Weaver had happily referred.

Lord James of Rusholme, vice chancellor of York University, said: "Whatever experiments we try in the fields of general education, one task is of supreme importance. Our education must aim at strengthening their critical faculties so that our pupils may have some hope of withstanding those mass suggestions and imposed and unexamined assumptions that today assail them with such force . . . "

Admiral Hyman Rickover, who spoke at this session as well as in the panel on technology, asserted: "We must have better teachers. We must get the best people in this country into the profession. In order to do that, since we are essentially a commercial society, we will have to increase the salaries of teachers. I, for one, think that any teacher worth his salt should get more than a Senator—or even an admiral. And if there is not enough money to pay for education, I would take it out of the military funds *because education is more important than the military*." [Italics added.]

Rickover also recommended the establishment of national standards for proficiency in teaching, as other countries did: "We have some 40,000 school boards in the United States, each trying to set its own standard of education. The argument is that the Constitution did not give any right for education to the federal government. And yet the federal government, ever since the Northwest Ordinance of 1787, has been granting funds and other property to education. It now amounts to 2 billion dollars a year. . . .

"I do not advocate a *mandatory* national standard. I advocate a *permissive* standard, which every community could adapt as it wished. Educational standards are set abroad by the central government, but the local communities decide how much of it they want to carry out and what teachers they want to hire."

In his ironic style, Hutchins said that "education" had been put into the Center's program because so many speakers, after describing problems without solutions, would claim that such problems could only be handled by "education."

"Education in the United States can be defined as 'what goes on in institutions that are called educational,' " Hutchins explained. "In California, for example, there are three magic words: water, highways, and education. Mention any one of the three and you will get all the money you want. The water is undrinkable, the highways are impassable, and the education is unintelligible."

Becoming a little more solemn, Hutchins expressed agreement with the ideas of Lord James of Rusholme: "I believe that the great job of all countries in the near future, by which I mean the next ten years with which this convocation is concerned, is to promote the intellectual development of all the people to the maximum of which they are capable. . . . I believe that the scientific and technological revolution makes any other conception of our education archaic. . . .

"I therefore reject the suggestion advanced from very high quarters that the object of education is to produce marketable skills. There may be no market for these skills, or they may be taught the wrong skills for the markets that are available."

Hutchins also rejected the idea that the aim of education should be adjustment to the environment: "We need to improve the environment, not to adjust to it. The rate of change means that we have no idea of what the environment will be."

The saddest statement at the Center convocation came from a thoughtful woman, Rosemary Park, president of Barnard College. Like Robert Heilbroner, she felt that many Americans had lost the sense of citizenship that had been founded on an ethical discipline.

"This kind of citizenship has slipped through our fingers," she said. "We no longer, any of us, I think, honestly believe that because we are members of a democracy we have submitted to certain ethical disciplines in order to carry out the mandates of that society. This is the innermost part of the human being, the area in which he decides not to do certain things even though he would be able to do them. This is the area with which education has to be most vitally concerned, and it is the area in which up to date, I am afraid, we have been totally remiss."

She saw a society in which hope had vanished: "Our society today is one that has very largely lost hope. It has lost hope in the sense that it does not adhere to any accepted, basic thought about reality into which hope is built. It does not accept the Marxist hope, for instance, that the lapse of time and history will produce the classless society after we get over the dictatorship of the proletariat. It does not adhere—except with undue sentimentality—to the Christian insight that the Kingdom of God may and will come. It has failed to hold on to the basic insight of science, or at least of nineteenth century science, that reason will produce progress and that continued control over nature will also produce progress."

As the head of a college attended by many gifted young women, she had learned that this generation wished for a revival of hope: "They wish that they could fight with us, the older generation, because they disapprove of what little we do hope. But it *is* so little that there is small opportunity to fight with us. We have, then, an educational system that can produce specialists but that is rather short on producing the kind of disciplined citizen the Greek state aimed to produce."

From this generation without hope, without ethical discipline, emerged many of the people involved in the deceptions and the "dirty tricks" of the years when Lyndon Johnson and Richard Nixon ruled in Washington. The grim words of Rosemary Park vividly depicted what had happened in American society. She did not say what the consequences would be, but her forebodings were impressive to all who heard her.

Yet the convocation did not close on a bleak note. Adlai Stevenson, speaking on the prospects for democracy, gave one of the most moving addresses of his career. His voice rang through the hotel ballroom with passionate conviction.

"Whether democracy can prevail in the great upheaval of our time is a valid question," Stevenson said. "Certainly, after 150 years of uninterrupted expansion of the idea of government by consent of the governed, it has recently met with mounting and formidable challenges all over the world from Fascist, Nazi, Communist authoritarians, and a variety of dictatorships. And we have good reason to know how clumsy, slow, inefficient, and costly it is compared to the celerity, certainty, and secrecy of absolutism.

"But the important thing is that it *has* survived. The important thing is that even the absolutists masquerade as democrats; even the military and quasi-military dictatorships strive in the name of democracy to manage the public business. And all of them say that authoritarianism is only a necessary transition to democracy.

"Why? Because it is the most popular form of government yet devised; because it is, as it always has been, not only the prize of the steadfast and the courageous but the privilege of those who are better off; because, in short, as Jefferson said, it is 'the only form of government which is not eternally at open or secret war with the rights of the people.'

"I have, therefore, no doubt that, distant as it may be for many people, it will ultimately prevail, that it will rewin lost ground, that it will expand its dominion—that it can withstand the winds that are blowing through the world—*if*, and I repeat *if*, we who are its custodians continually re-examine and adapt its principles to the changing needs of our changing times. . . .

"Democracy is perhaps mankind's most audacious experiment. There is precious little dignity, precious little equality, in our natural state. Most human beings have to spend their lives in utter vulnerability; all are murderable, all are torturable, and survive only through the restraint shown by more powerful neighbors. . . .

"For nearly 3,000 years, the political and social genius of what we can permissibly call 'Western man' has struggled with these brute facts. . . . The effort has been made, with setbacks and defeats, with dark ages and interregnums, to create a social order in which weak, fallible, obstinate, silly, magnificent man can maintain his dignity and exercise his free and responsible choice."

In New York, despite the spectacular array of speakers and their excellent performances, the financial results were a bit disappointing, although gifts and pledges totaling more than $400,000 were made. Hutchins and Ashmore had expected a larger total, but a number of new donors had been found and the fund raisers felt that these donors would lead to others.

On April 11, 1963, the Center distributed thousands of copies of a pamphlet featuring statements by Stevenson, Hoffman, Roper, and Hutchins on the value of the Center's work and asking the public to aid the Center as generously as possible. The Center no longer had any inhibitions about seeking contributions of all sizes.

People who wanted to help the Center were invited to make gifts in categories ranging from associate memberships ($10 to $25 a year) to the founding memberships ($1000 or more a year). "We shall need the support of every interested person, from every community, and in every contributing category," Hutchins said.

The Center's president reported that the Fund and the Center had already received more than 5000 contributions from people in more than 1500 communities across the nation. He indicated that the total in cash and pledges had risen to nearly $1 million. But the fund goal was now $20 million—to pay operating expenses for the next ten years and to give the Center an endowment fund to preserve its independence for future studies.

The response to the plea for donations was moderately encouraging, but many of the gifts were small. At the Fund board meeting on May 15, Oram asked for more activity by the directors. All of them promised to do more, and they extended the employment of Oram's firm through September 30, 1964. The board allocated additional money for the Center's projects and elected four new members, who were ready to make contributions and obtain gifts from others.

All four of the new directors were successful in business. Edward Eichler, a Los Angeles home builder, was chairman of the California Governor's Commission on Housing. Ralph Ablon of New York was president and chairman of the Ogden Corporation, a huge conglomerate organization. Morris L. Levinson, president of Associated Products, Inc., of New York, was a trustee of the Federation of Jewish Philanthropies of Greater New York and director of the executive committee of the United Jewish Appeal in the New York area. Patrick Crowley, a noted Chicago lawyer and head of a paint company, was president of the Catholic Council on Working Life and treasurer of the Foundation for International Cooperation.

Crowley presided at one session of the third convocation celebrating the Fund's tenth anniversary, a convocation held in Chicago and featuring an address by J. Robert Oppenheimer, the atomic scientist, called "The Scientific Revolution and Its Impact on Democratic Institutions." Other speakers at that convocation included Senator Eugene McCarthy, the economist Robert Theobald, and the Rev. Paul P. Harbrecht, a Jesuit scholar.

The new directors, as well as the other members of the board, were informed by Hutchins of the Center's plans for a series of dialogues in the summer and fall on topics with high public interest—including a session on June 22 with twenty-one diplomats from the United Nations; a session in July with the governor of California, Edmund G. Brown, Sr., and his staff on "the ten most important problems facing the people of California"; and a private conference in September on the collective bargaining controversies in the newspaper industry.

Before the United Nations delegates arrived on June 22, telephone calls were received at the Center, threatening demonstrations against the UN as "a hotbed of communism" and against the Center for its involvement in such a gathering. The mayor of Santa Barbara, Don MacGillivray, alerted by these calls, had police on hand at the airport and greeted the UN diplomats himself when they left their plane. More than 150 citizens of Santa Barbara were there with welcoming signs. No hostile demonstrators appeared, and the conference at the Center was held without any disruptions.

When Governor Brown came to the Center on July 10 with his staff, a line of pickets marched in a circle around the Center's front gates, waving placards with inscriptions saying: "Fun for Whose Republic—Brown?" "Is Hutchins in a Brown Study?" "Who Is Studying Whom?" "What Is Left of the Center?" Some of the pickets were young men who told reporters they were students; others were middle-aged housewives. One of the group photographed each car entering the Center's grounds before and after the governor's car, and another wrote down the license numbers of the automobiles.

Governor Brown descended from his car and attempted to shake hands with the pickets, but he was rebuffed. Seniel Ostrow, a Fund director from Los Angeles, asked a picket what he had against the Center. "I would rather not talk about it," the young man said. Another claimed that the group did not have affiliations with the John Birch Society or any other group, asserting, "We just got together because we wonder what the Center is up to."

At a dinner in the Santa Barbara Biltmore that evening—attended by publishers, editors, industrialists, Fund directors, and prospective donors to the Center—Governor Brown presented his list of major problems and said he had come to the Center to get the best thinking he could find to aid him in dealing with them. The problems included a review of the most efficient and effective ways of spending the $12 billion he expected the state of California to expend during his remaining three years as governor; solving the human rights problems of California citizens, with particular attention to blacks and other minorities; deciding on the trusteeship and leasing of the tidelands oil resources of California, worth billions of dollars; proper conservation and development of agricultural lands; development of California's huge educational system, then taking more than half of the state's annual budget; crime and punishment; traffic safety and highways; completion of the gigantic state water project; protection and development of natural resources; handling the difficulties caused by unemployment due to automation and cybernation.

While the meetings with Governor Brown and other sessions were being held, the officers and staff at the Center were beginning to consider the idea of having an international convocation to be called "The Requirements of Peace," taking Pope John's encyclical *Pacem in Terris* as a starting point. The idea was first suggested in a telephone call to me by Fred Warner Neal.

Neal had called me in June of 1963, when Pope John was dying in Rome. He said he thought that the Pope's statement on the necessity for world peace—issued in April—might open a path that could lead to more sensible relations between the United States and the Soviet Union. He believed that the Center could persuade intellectual leaders from both sides to begin a thaw in the cold war.

When I went in to tell Hutchins about the suggestion and to express my enthusiasm for it, Hutchins looked at me with an ironic smile. He said, "You want me, a descendant of a long line of Presbyterians, to put on a convocation based on a Pope's encyclical?"

"You know what nuclear war could do to everybody, Catholics and Presbyterians included," I said.

"But where would we get the money?" Hutchins asked. "You know we don't have the money. An international conference, with the people we'd want to have there, might cost a quarter of a million dollars."

"We could raise it."

"We have to raise enough to make sure the Center survives," Hutchins said. "That comes first."

"This might lead to enough money to endow the Center," I said. "It's worth doing in itself, but I believe it would bring in a lot of money. Since the Cuban crisis, everybody's been worrying about a nuclear war. Let me try the idea on a couple of our directors."

Hutchins nodded. "You might try Seniel Ostrow. He's always worrying about war. But I'm not making any commitments."

I called Neal and asked him to send me a memorandum on the themes and possible participants in a *Pacem in Terris* convocation. He sent the memorandum a few days later. I sent copies to Ostrow and to other directors who had a particular interest in international relations.

Ostrow came to Santa Barbara, full of excitement. He saw tremendous possibilities in the idea. He assured Hutchins that the money could be raised to pay the costs of such a convocation, and he knew the costs would be large. Hutchins asked Ashmore, Ferry, Hallock Hoffman, and me to come into his office. Ashmore, Ferry, and Hoffman were generally favorable to the project, although they foresaw that it would be extremely difficult to carry it through.

At the end of June, I went to Rome at the invitation of John Cogley, who had been covering the Vatican Council as a correspondent for the Religious News Service and a number of publications. He was on a leave of absence from the Center but very much interested in the Center's future. He introduced me to Monsignor Luigi Ligutti, who had an office in the Vatican. Ligutti immediately endorsed the *Pacem in Terris* project.

From Patrick Crowley, one of the Center's new directors, I had learned that a Monsignor Pietro Pavan had done most of the writing of the *Pacem* encyclical, as an assistant to Pope John. Pavan was also reported to be close to Paul VI, who had been elected Pope after John's death. When I met Pavan, he told me that he was traveling to the United States in August. I invited him to visit the Center.

When I returned to Santa Barbara in July, I wrote a memorandum to Hutchins, with copies to Ashmore, Cogley, Ferry, and William Gorman, who had led a discussion of a previous papal encyclical at the Center in 1961. In that memorandum, I said: "Pavan told me that the Cuban crisis last October stirred Pope John very deeply. It appeared that the world was actually facing a conflict which could develop into a nuclear war. A suggestion came from the United States that the Pope should issue an appeal for negotiations to prevent such a catastrophe. (I have reason to believe that the suggestions came from John Cogley.)" The Pope had played a role in preventing the Cuban confrontation from becoming an actual war.

Pavan made it clear to me that the Pope wished to appeal to the Russians as well as the Americans. Pope John thought it could be done by emphasizing the necessity of using human reason to give mankind a chance to survive. The Soviets glorified reason; therefore they might respond to a papal statement that described the nuclear arms race as a form of madness contrary to the aspirations of all reasonable men.

In giving me these impressions of Pope John's thinking, Monsignor Pavan also conveyed his own feeling that the Pope knew he was running the risk of being misunderstood by Catholics around the world, of giving comfort to the communists and disheartening some staunch supporters of the Church who were fighting communism. But John XXIII felt that most men in most nations, whether in the communist bloc or the noncommunist areas, would share his belief that his obligation to humanity required him to issue such an encyclical and to foster actions based on its principles.

The discussion of possible topics and preparation for a Center convocation on world peace went on all through the summer of 1963, while sessions on other subjects were proceeding. With the aid of Patrick Crowley and his wife Patricia Crowley, Monsignor Pavan was persuaded to come to the Center during the last week in August for intensive conversations on the whole project. (Mr. and Mrs. Crowley had received the Pro Ecclesia Medal from Pope Pius XII, and their support for the project carried weight in the Vatican.)

Monsignor Pavan, who stayed in my home while he was in Santa Barbara, was filled with admiration for the Center and its staff members. He was convinced that the conference would be conducted with high seriousness, and he was sure that it would have the blessing of Pope Paul.

Pavan left Santa Barbara on September 3 to return to Rome. A few days after his departure, the Center published a pamphlet entitled *Science, Scientists, and Politics*, which led to the addition of Linus Pauling to the Center staff and eventually to gifts from a wealthy inventor—gifts that finally totaled $10 million and enabled the Center to launch a membership campaign that brought the Center into contact with 100,000 supporting citizens.

In the pamphlet on science and scientists, Hutchins said: "A scientist has a limited education. He labors on the topic of his dissertation, wins the Nobel prize by the time he is thirty-five, and suddenly has nothing to do. . . . He has no alternative but to spend the rest of his life making a nuisance of himself.

When Linus Pauling, the noted chemist at the California Institute of Technology, won a Nobel prize as a peacemaker for his role in the promotion of a treaty banning nuclear test explosions in the air—a treaty signed by the United States and the Soviet Union and ratified by the U.S. Senate in September 1963—he was criticized in a Los Angeles *Times* editorial as a scientist who had often made a nuisance of himself. The statement by Hutchins was quoted in the editorial.

On the day when that editorial appeared, I called it to Hutchins' attention. Hutchins immediately wrote a letter to the editor of the *Times*, saying that the quotation had been misused, and expressing admiration for Pauling. He sent a copy of his letter to Dr. Pauling.

Shortly after Pauling received the letter from Hutchins, he telephoned the Center. Hutchins came into my office. "Pauling would like to join the Center staff," Hutchins said. "He thinks he'd have more freedom here than he has at Cal Tech. He was disappointed because Lee DuBridge didn't write a letter to the *Times*, backing him. Of course, we'd like to have him here, but how could we pay him? We don't have the money to match the salary he's getting at Cal Tech."

"He knows a lot of people," I said. "Maybe he could get some of them to make contributions to the Center to cover his salary."

Hutchins grinned. "I thought of that, too. He does have a former student, a man named Chester Carlson, who has a lot of money suddenly. I think Carlson is the one who invented the Xerox process."

Carlson agreed to give the Center enough to pay Pauling. On October 18 Pauling called a press conference in Pasadena and announced that he was resigning from Cal Tech, where he had taught and conducted research for forty-one years. His discoveries in chemistry had brought him a previous Nobel prize in that field of science.

Pauling disclosed that he was moving to Santa Barbara. He told reporters that he expected to have "more freedom of action" at the Center, especially to do some writing on aspects of medicine and molecular biology. He said he would divide his time between science and the study of "peace, world affairs, and democratic institutions." He declared that the Center was concerned with issues that were very important to him.

On September 30 the Center returned to the problems of minority groups in a booklet entitled *The Negro as an American*, which contained an eloquent statement by Vice President Lyndon Johnson on the demands of blacks for simple justice. It also contained a grim warning from Robert C. Weaver, administrator of the United States Housing and Home Finance Agency, who declared that the employment opportunities for black Americans—half of whom lived in extreme poverty—were growing narrower because unskilled and semiskilled jobs were disappearing at a "frightening rate" as a result of automation.

Weaver recommended a national job-training program for millions of black Americans—and millions of other Americans condemned to poverty —with recognition of the fact that "many of them are functionally illiterate and require basic education prior to any specialized preparation for a job."

In his final days as President, Johnson said to Doris Kearns, a biographer: "God knows how little we've really moved on this issue, despite all the fanfare. As I see it, I've moved the Negro from D + to C − . He's still nowhere. He knows it. And that's why he's out in the streets. Hell, I'd be there, too."

The Center tried repeatedly to awaken the social conscience of the upper two-thirds of the American population. The Fund for the Republic had been dedicated to civil rights as well as civil liberties. The directors and officers of the Center did not forget that fact. Changes did occur in the South and in many other areas of the country: talented black people did break through in sports, in radio and television in some places, in the universities, and in some of the professions. But most of the black people—like millions of poor whites—remained on the subsistence level, and many were on the welfare rolls.

In all the years of its existence the Center wrestled with the stubborn problem of getting people to change, to open their eyes, to consider new ways of making government serviceable. Frequently the friends of the Center insisted that the Center had to reach the millions who read newspapers but not pamphlets or books. In response to my urging, Hutchins began to write a weekly column for the Los Angeles *Times* syndicate in the autumn of 1963. The column had been proposed to him by Richard Buffum, owner of a weekly paper in Santa Barbara, who was a nephew of Mrs. Norman

Chandler, one of the owners of the *Times*. In this column—headed "What Kind of World?"—he dealt crisply with the basic issues always under examination at the Center. The column soon appeared in thirty-five papers, some of them with large circulations.

At the Center in November 1963 the dialogues had focused several times on the topic "Science and Disarmament." Helmut Krauch, director of a systems research group at Heidelberg University in West Germany, had come to the Center to talk about planning for the economic effects of disarmament.

On the morning of November 22 Hutchins and his colleagues gathered in the conference room. Krauch, Linus Pauling, and others were engaged in a wide-ranging discussion. Word came that the President of the United States had been shot. Hutchins announced that terrible event, and then he went on with the meeting. In a violent world, he believed that the voices of thoughtful people had to go on speaking.

The murder of Kennedy and the murders on November 2 of the President of South Vietnam and his brother in Saigon had demonstrated again the power of hatred to alter the course of history. The funeral of Kennedy, displayed on television screens around the world, created a somber mood verging on despair in the minds of millions of people in many nations.

In that nightmare time, some of the Fellows of the Center wondered whether the voices of reason could ever prevail. Was not the Center engaged in a futile enterprise that would have to be abandoned? How could people be continuously persuaded to give the money needed to maintain it? The Center could not promise a cure for cancer, or relief for the millions suffering from physical ills. It could not stir a heartwarming wave of hope for crippled children or for the blind or for other causes that were supported by millions of citizens. Many people doubted its value.

The Center's appeal to the public, made by Adlai Stevenson, Paul Hoffman, Elmo Roper, and Hutchins, had produced some contributions but not the big gifts that were still needed. The situation was critical—and growing worse because the Fund's last reserves were being used.

Hutchins had asked Harold Willens, a Los Angeles businessman who had become a founding member at the Santa Barbara symposium in December 1962, to take on the chairmanship of a founding members committee and to try to raise a million dollars a year through that committee. Willens had told Hutchins that he had never tried to raise a large amount of money, and he didn't believe he could do it. He agreed to think about it, because Hutchins had convinced him that the Center might be forced to close its doors. He thought that would be a sad day for humanity.

While he was thinking about the request from Hutchins, Willens took a trip to Washington. He talked with Hubert Humphrey and other political leaders who informed him that they leaned heavily on the Center's reports for information on long-term trends and ideas for the future. He also learned that his son, who was a freshman at the University of California in Berkeley, used Center materials in classes and encountered professors who respected what the Center was doing.

When he returned to California he told Hutchins he would give much of his time to the search for founding members. "I still think I'll be awful, but I'm willing to try," Willens said. He did not know whether he could get many businesspeople to become as enthusiastic as he was.

On December 6, 1963, the Fund's directors met in Beverly Hills and regretfully accepted the retirement of Elmo Roper as cochairman and the resignations of Mrs. Marshall Field and Henry Van Dusen. Roper agreed to stay on the board but indicated that he could not be active. The death of another director—Herbert Lehman—was mournfully noted.

The fourth convocation marking the tenth anniversary of the Fund was held at the Beverly Hilton hotel on December 7 and 8. The speakers included Supreme Court Justice Thurgood Marshall, Senator Humphrey, and others who had participated in the previous convocations, including Admiral Rickover and Newton Minow. The audience was large, and some of them became supporting members of the Center.

As the terrible year receded into its last days, the nation was still in shock from the murder of President Kennedy. The Center was active although its financial condition was shaky. Yet the new members of the board who had been elected in May—Ablon, Eichler, Levinson, and Crowley—were keenly interested, and the plan to hold an international conference based on the encyclical *Pacem in Terris* was vehemently advocated by Seniel Ostrow and Edward Lamb.

While Hutchins continued to proclaim that the Fund did not have the money in sight to endure beyond the middle of 1964, he clung to his belief that the necessary donors could be found. With the recruitment of Willens, he had enlisted a man who had almost unlimited energy and determination. He was ready to go anywhere with Willens to get the money the Center had to have.

17

*The Center attacks racism,
pleads for human rights, plans
an international meeting based
on a pope's letter to the world*

THE VULNERABILITIY OF A DEMOCRATIC SOCIETY to a demogogic leader became increasingly noticeable month after month in 1964, when President Lyndon Johnson turned the government of the United States into his personal instrument. He cajoled and persuaded the Congress to give him vast powers, he controlled every utterance by his cabinet and staff, he dominated the press and the broadcasting networks, and he edged the nation into a major war in Vietnam by a process of deception. He knew the weaknesses of the American constitutional system, and he took advantage of every one.

In the Johnson era, the Center's ideas were seldom heeded by the president or his immediate advisers, although the "war on poverty" had stemmed from a book by a Center staff member, Michael Harrington. But the Center continued to generate a stream of reports on the hard problems that the president and the Congress had to face sooner or later. And the Center moved ahead with its plans for an international conference on peace, based on Pope John's plea for dialogues between East and West.

In January 1964 the Center published a booklet entitled *Race and Housing*, designed to contribute to domestic peace by relieving the fears of many Americans who thought that the entrance of blacks and other minorities into their neighborhoods would destroy the value of their houses. The booklet was based on an interview with a new Fund director, Edward Eichler, head of a company that had become the leading builder of medium-priced homes.

Eichler declared that his policy of selling to all racial groups had not reduced the financial success of his developments, and houses in his integrated subdivisions had risen by 50 percent in their market prices in some instances. He admitted that there were"some risks in selling on an open occupancy basis" but he added: "I believe that builders really don't have any choice. They are in a position that they have denied for too long; that is, when they build a lot of houses or apartments, they create communities. . . . The government must use all its strength to improve the situation even where the operators don't want it."

While Eichler was urging businessmen to back a fair housing law, Harold Willens was asking other business executives to "make an investment" in the Center. At a luncheon at the Beverly Hills Tennis Club at about the time when the Eichler pamphlet was released, Willens plunged into fund raising. He was nervous. Before the prospective givers arrived, Hutchins calmed him: "Think of this as a fishing trip. Relax and enjoy it. We're going to spend some time with some pleasant people. We'll have a fine time whether we'll catch any fish or not." When the potential donors appeared, Hutchins described the Center's large projects and Willens gave them a chance to "invest" in the Center's "preventive social medicine to keep democracy alive." Four of them promptly became founding members. Willens found that he could win converts more easily than he had expected.

A wealthy chemist who had long been concerned about the dangers of nuclear war—Irving F. Laucks, who had developed the adhesives that made possible the establishment and expansion of the plywood industry—joined the Center as a consultant in the spring of 1964 and agreed to provide $100,000 a year to help finance the Center's efforts in the promotion of world order, attacking poverty, and encouraging better race relations. He moved his residence from Honolulu to Santa Barbara and took a vigorous part in the Center's dialogues for the next five years.

Irving Laucks and his wife, Eulah, made a special contribution to the Center to aid it in financing the proposed convocation based on the papal encyclical *Pacem in Terris*. The Johnson Foundation offered its headquarters at Wingspread in Racine, Wisconsin, as a meeting place for the Center to gather a group of leaders from various nations, ideologies, and religions to form a plan for the convocation. (The Johnson Foundation, headed by Leslie Paffrath, had no connection with President Lyndon Johnson.)

In May 1964 the Center announced two actions taken as a result of the establishment of the Laucks Fund. Michael Harrington, author of *The Other America: Poverty in the United States*, was appointed to the Center staff to work on the studies of race relations and the possible emergence of a world order based on human rights. And the Center disclosed its sponsorship of a study of the civil rights movement in San Francisco to be conducted by a research staff headed by Louis S. Levine, professor of psychology at San Francisco State College and past president of the California State Psychological Association.

The San Francisco study, to be done during the period from May through December 1964, was expected to uncover what was happening to the democratic processes in a large city as it attempted to secure increased opportunities for minority groups in employment, education, and housing. The study was designed to include an evaluation of the activities of various partisan groups with different objectives.

On May 16, 1964, the directors of the Fund went to a special meeting at the Wingspread Conference house in Racine to act on several proposals presented by Hutchins and to participate in three days of discussions with twenty-two leaders on the topics of the *Pacem in Terris* convocation. The directors voted to change the bylaws to permit the expansion of the board from twenty-seven to twenty-eight members, and then elected five new directors: Percy L. Julian, Stanley Marcus, Lyle M. Spencer, Bernard Weissbourd, and Harold Willens. The appointment of Irving Laucks as a consultant was approved, and the board appropriated $5000 to the Central Methodist Church of Detroit for a World Peace Study Mission.

The countryside around the Johnson Foundation headquarters at Wingspread was in full bloom that spring, and there was a euphoric atmosphere around the Fund's directors and the leaders who had come to plan for giant steps toward peace on earth. The cold war between the United States and the Soviet Union was in a frigid stage, but no large military clashes were occurring that May. The situation in Vietnam was extremely dangerous, but few Americans realized it. Opinion surveys indicated that two-thirds of the American people gave little attention to what was developing in the Vietnamese struggle.

At the end of three days of dialogues, the Center informed the press in a formal statement that the participants had agreed that the subjects of the *Pacem in Terris* conference—scheduled to be held in New York in February, 1965—would include: "(1) How to obtain universal acceptance of the idea of coexistence of nations of differing ideological and social systems; (2) How to achieve sufficient flexibility so that all international conflicts can be settled by negotiation, and how to devise mechanisms for peaceful social and political change; (3) How to obtain recognition of the urgent need for rapid progress toward nuclear and conventional disarmament; (4) How to take actions and develop understanding to create mutual trust among the nations; (5) How to achieve the elimination of racism in all countries; (6) How to achieve international cooperation in assisting the developing countries in the interests of the prosperity of the world, and how to make full use of science and technology for developing cooperation among nations; (7) How to encourage further development of the United Nations so that its means and structure may become equal to the magnitude of its tasks."

The Center declared that "statesmen and scholars from all over the world, representative of the major religious and political communities," would be invited to explore these topics in the light of "the wisdom and spirit of the Encyclical" and of several statements on "coexistence" made by Premier Khrushchev of the Soviet Union and other political and religious leaders. It was an enormously ambitious undertaking for a small educational organization whose reserve funds were almost exhausted.

Participants in the Wingspread gathering included Senator George McGovern, later the nominee for president of the Democratic party in 1972; Senator Gaylord Nelson of Wisconsin; Brooks Hays, a former member of Congress who was serving as a consultant to President Johnson; Joseph E. Johnson, president of the Carnegie Endowment for International Peace; Eugene Rabinowitch, editor of the *Bulletin of the Atomic Scientists*; Andrew Shonfield, director of studies, the Royal Institute of International Affairs, England; John Tomlinson, director of mission and world service liaison for the National Council of Churches in the United States; Sir Muhammad Zafrulla Khan, a judge of the International Court of Justice; C. V. Narasimhan, representing the Secretary General of the United Nations, U Thant; Nelson Glueck, president of the Hebrew Union College Jewish Institute of Religion; Ambassador S. O. Adebo of the Nigerian mission to the United Nations; Ahmad Al-Nakib, deputy to the Ambassador to the United Nations from Kuwait; Xavier Deniau, rapporteur of the Foreign Affairs Committee of the French National Assembly; the Rev. John Cronin, S.S., assistant director of the social action department of the National Catholic Welfare Conference; Hudson Hoagland, director of the Worcester Foundation for Experimental Biology; Monsignor Luigi Ligutti, permanent observer of the Holy See to the Food and Agriculture Organization, Rome; Hans J. Morgenthau, of the Center for the Study of American Foreign Policy, the University of Chicago; and Livingston Biddle, representing Senator Claiborne Pell of Rhode Island.

Several officials from communist countries also participated. Georgi Kornienko, minister counselor of the Soviet embassy to the United States, came from Washington to give his views. So did Marian Dobrosielski, minister counselor of the Polish embassy, and Josip Presburger, counselor of the Yugoslav embassy. All of them expressed the hope that leaders from their countries could attend the Center convocation in New York.

The trustees of the Johnson Foundation aided the Center by making Leslie Paffrath, the foundation's president, available to serve as secretary general of the convocation, and agreeing to handle many of the administrative costs of the assembly. The Western Publishing Company Foundation, based in Racine, donated a substantial financial amount—$33,333—to assist the project.

Harold Willens, one of the five men elected to the Fund's board at the Racine meeting, used the announcement of the *Pacem in Terris* conference to persuade dozens of wealthy citizens to contribute $1000 a year or more to the Center. The other new directors—Percy Julian, head of the Julian Laboratories in Chicago; Stanley Marcus, president of the internationally known Neiman-Marcus department store in Dallas; Lyle Spencer, president of Science Research Associations; and Bernard Weissbourd, president of

Metropolitan Structure, in Chicago—were willing to contribute and to get other people to write checks or pledge future contributions.

In a note to all founding members, with which he enclosed a copy of the Center's press release on the Wingspread meeting, Willens termed the proposed convocation "an epochal event . . . an event that might well become the turning point on the road to a peaceful world and a better life for all mankind." Then he said: "Tickets for this history-making convocation in February 1965 will be in great demand, and in very limited supply. Founding Members of the Center will naturally be given first consideration. If you can arrange to attend, please let us know." Responses came in rapidly. People who could afford to contribute to the Center were eager to take part in the making of history.

A week after the Wingspread gathering, Hutchins appointed Marjory Collins, a woman active in Women Strike for Peace and other antiwar groups, as a Center staff member in New York, working on projects financed by the Laucks Fund. Eleanor Garst, a cofounder of Women Strike for Peace, had been added to the Santa Barbara staff on the recommendation of Irving Laucks.

On June 8 Hutchins announced the appointment of Tom E. Shearer, president of the College of Idaho, as director of development for the Center. He said that Shearer would coordinate the Center's campaign to raise $20 million to maintain and continue its operations. A former lawyer and political scientist, Shearer had been a sales manager for the Prentice-Hall publishing company before he became a college administrator.

The Center calendar was crowded in July 1964 with seventeen dialogues in Santa Barbara and a public dinner in honor of Seniel Ostrow in Los Angeles. Fifteen of the sessions in Santa Barbara were devoted to the First Amendment of the American Constitution, with Scott Buchanan arguing that the amendment required the government to promote free speech positively and other scholars saying that the government simply had to refrain from passing any laws or taking any actions that might interfere with such speech. Topics included "Public vs. Private Law," "Free Speech and Its Relation to Self-Government," "Government of the Mind," "The First Amendment and the Loyalty Program," "Seditious Libel and the First Amendment," and "The First Amendment and Congressional Investigations." Principal speakers in these dialogues, in addition to Buchanan, were Harry Kalven, Jr., professor of law, University of Chicago; Joseph Tussman, professor of philosophy, University of California at Berkeley; Alexander Meiklejohn, former president of Amherst College; and William Gorman, Richard Lichtman, and Harvey Wheeler of the Center staff.

At the testimonial dinner for Ostrow on July 25, attended by 700 civic leaders, Justice Douglas lauded Ostrow as a staunch defender of the Bill of Rights. Ostrow was a founder and director of the Constitutional Rights Foundation, a sponsor of the Committee for an Effective Congress, a member of the advisory board of the American Civil Liberties Union, and honorary chairman of the Community Service Organization, which had been formed to obtain recognition for Mexican Americans. The people who came to honor Ostrow were asked to support the Center—and many of them did.

Justice Douglas had been deeply disturbed by the nomination of Senator Barry Goldwater as the presidential candidate of the Republican party in San Francisco ten days before the Ostrow dinner. Douglas knew the arrogance of President Lyndon Johnson and the belligerence of Senator Goldwater. He saw a hazardous time ahead for the world.

"We have had recurring eras of arrogance in our history and we seem to be on the verge of another," Douglas said. "America seen from abroad is rich and arrogant. She is great in military prowess but often weak in principle."

He warned his fellow Americans: "In the planetary scene we the whites are a small minority. The browns, yellows, and blacks vastly outnumber us. Our present arsenal gives us temporary leverage; but in the long view our security lies in devising durable arrangements whereby military force will not subjugate anyone—whereby each nation, irrespective of ideology, will be given a place in the society of nations—whereby law rather than troops or bombs will settle disputes."

Two weeks after Justice Douglas spoke these noble words, on the night of August 4, American warplanes from two aircraft carriers bombed torpedo-boat bases and an oil depot in North Vietnam. President Johnson went on television to tell the American people that the raids were his response to attacks by North Vietnamese torpedo boats on two United States destroyers in the Gulf of Tonkin. Eight-column headlines in the *New York Times* declared: "U.S. Planes Attack North Vietnam Bases; President Orders 'Limited' Retaliation After Communists' PT Boats Renew Raids."

Many well-known senators, including several who had participated in Center conferences on the future of democracy, rushed to give the President unfettered power in foreign relations. Among them were George McGovern, Eugene McCarthy, Frank Church, John Sherman Cooper, Birch Bayh, Albert Gore, Jacob Javits, George D. Aiken, and others who later branded the Vietnam war as a frightful disaster.

Fulbright rejected Morse's plea for hearings on the resolution to give senators time to consider its implications. President Johnson was in a hurry, and he had convinced Fulbright that the Senate had to back him with an immediate vote of confidence.

Walter Lippmann approved of the bombing. The Washington *Post* said: "President Johnson has earned the gratitude of the free world." The *New York Times* trumpeted: "The nation's united confidence in the Chief Executive is vital."

"I believe that history will record that we have made a great mistake in subverting and circumventing the Constitution of the United States,'' Wayne Morse shouted in the Senate. But the House of Representatives passed the resolution after 40 minutes of discussion by a vote of 414 to 0.

The people apparently approved of the president's course, believing that aggression had to be stopped, not knowing that the American destroyers had been on an aggressive mission against North Vietnam and that no torpedos had come near those vessels. A Harris poll soon showed that Johnson had the endorsement of 72 percent of those surveyed; in July, 58 percent had been critical of his handling of the Vietnamese situation.

While the United States plunged on into a war that led to internal disruptions and enormous costs in lives and supplies—and released an inflation that was devastating to millions of people—the Center turned its attention in August to the economic system and the possibilities of planning.

Stanley Sheinbaum led off the series of meetings with two days of examination of the economic issues related to freedom and a ''positive program for *laissez-faire.*'' Paul M. Sweezy, publisher and editor of a Marxist publication, *Monthly Review*, followed with a discussion called ''Consumer Sovereignty: Freedom of Choice in the Market-Place.''

Sometimes the Center had two dialogues a day, one in the morning on the theme of the month and one in the afternoon with a visiting speaker who had a different topic. On August 5, after the morning discussion with Sweezy, there was an afternoon session with Wallace Brode of the American Association for the Advancement of Science, who was concerned about the supply of scientists.

On August 6, while Senator Morse was striving futilely to keep the United States Congress from transferring its warmaking powers into the hands of the president, a British member of Parliament—Anthony Crosland, later a cabinet member under Prime Minister Harold Wilson—spoke at the Center on the topic ''Four Reasons for Government Intervention in the Economy.'' In the afternoon the Center staff met with Mayor Houlihan of Oakland to discuss the churches and the city.

The next day, when Lyndon Johnson gleefully accepted the Tonkin Gulf Resolution, the topic at the Center was ''Mismanagement of Monetary Policy as the Explanation of Recessions,'' and the discussion leader was Karl Brunner, professor of economics, University of California at Los Angeles.

Governor Edmund G. Brown, Sr., and his staff returned to the Center on August 8 and 9 for another weekend conference. This one focused on the roles of free enterprise and government in handling the impact of technological change, with particular emphasis on California's unemployment problems, its industrial dependence on military contracts, the thorny aspects of minority rights, and the damaging effects of urban sprawl. California's state government was attempting to develop a coordinated plan to master problems that threatened to overwhelm its agencies.

On August 10 and 11, there were two dialogues on the topic "The Social Costs of the Private Market," with Armen Alchian, professor of economics, University of California at Los Angeles, as the visiting speaker. The next day, Rexford G. Tugwell—one of the original members of Franklin Roosevelt's "brains trust"—described what had happened to the National Recovery Administration when it tried to get business enterprises to operate under codes and guidelines in the 1930s.

Repercussions of the ideas of the famous British economist John Maynard Keynes were discussed by Professor Brunner on August 13 under the heading "Laissez-Faire Revisited: Keynes and After." There was an afternoon meeting with Franco Perna of the International Fellowship of Reconciliation on "The Peace Movement in European Countries."

Topic followed topic with dizzying rapidity that month—and in many other months at the Center. The dialogues usually lasted an hour and a half (and occasionally two hours), but staff members were expected to have read the papers and articles circulated in advance of the meetings. Hutchins felt that everything was related to everything else, and he expected his associates to read quickly and speak cogently on many subjects. But he was often aware that too many meetings were being held, and he tried repeatedly to limit the number of sessions to three or four a week.

It struck me during that summer of 1964 that the activities of the Center were marked by the ceaseless energy and determination to understand everything that seemed to be characteristic of the Texan in the White House. One of President Johnson's favorite phrases was: "Come, let us reason together." That was the unofficial motto of the Center, of course. Hutchins declared again and again that the Center was concerned with practical reason, not theological or metaphysical speculation.

Yet the dialogues of the Center led it into an expanding field of questions—and on to possible actions but not final conclusions. The Center was open to an infinite number of variations on what could be done and what should be done. Johnson told his staff members, senators and representatives, visitors of all kinds, newspapermen, advisers, that he was always ready to take new options. Still he had an overriding obsession: he had to be in control.

How could reason prevail in the political and economic life of the United States in the Johnson era, when the man at the top did not want the people to know what he knew or thought he knew? Johnson did not want the people or the Congress to know about the concealed Pentagon plan 34A for attacks on North Vietnam. In his eyes, the communist regime in North Vietnam was a hideous danger to the free world, and it had to be blocked and defeated by one means or another.

The Center's plans for an international convocation based on the papal encyclical *Pacem in Terris* included the hope that the president would make the opening address at the conference. Justice Douglas had informed President Kennedy about the *Pacem in Terris* convocation before Kennedy's assassination. Kennedy had indicated that he would make the first statement at the convocation if it were convened after the presidential election of 1964. As the first Roman Catholic president, he had not wished to speak at a conference founded on a papal encyclical until he had won reelection to the White House.

After Kennedy's murder, the invitation to speak at the *Pacem in Terris* gathering had been given to Johnson. Johnson had promised to give it thorough consideration. Kennedy staff members who had been retained by Johnson indicated that Johnson would certainly send a message to the convocation if he did not appear in person.

In September, while plans for the *Pacem in Terris* assembly continued to be expanded, the Center had thirteen dialogues. In the first fifteen days of the month, the topics ranged from "The Legal Status of Planning," with Scott Buchanan, to "Further Reflections on the Triple Revolution," with W. H. Ferry as the discussion leader.

"The Triple Revolution," which Ferry discussed on September 15, was a memorandum that had been sent to the president and released to the press some months earlier. It had been prepared by an Ad Hoc Committee of thirty-two economists, scholars, and public figures, including Ferry, and he had circulated preliminary drafts of it to the Center staff. It consisted of an analysis of three concurrent "revolutions"—the revolutions in weaponry, race relations, and cybernation—and among its recommendations was a suggestion for a guaranteed annual income for the workers who would be displaced from jobs by modern technology.

The statement on the triple revolution was not a Center publication but became identified with the Center because Ferry discussed it on a number of public occasions and sent copies of it to many people. Irving Laucks was one of the signers of it, and Laucks also distributed it to people across the country. (Two years later, a commission of industrialists, economists and others appointed by President Johnson issued a report that included a recommendation for a guaranteed yearly income.)

On September 22 a raging fire in the dry brush above Santa Barbara roared around the city for three days and nights. The elegant home Hutchins had built on his small ranch in Romero Canyon was destroyed. Hallock Hoffman's newly finished house and a hundred others were consumed by the fire, which covered the city with smoke and ashes. The Center closed down temporarily, while thousands of men fought the flames.

Four days after the fire had been brought under control, Hutchins insisted that the Center should resume its meetings. While smoke still hung in the sky, the staff members gathered to participate in a discussion of a paper by Robert K. Woetzel, former faculty member at Fordham University and New York University, on the topic "Two Pillars: Toward a Political Philosophy for Our Time."

Rexford Tugwell presented his views on what he called "The Emerging Constitution" on September 30. Hutchins had long been interested in the changes in the American Constitution brought about by amendments and by Supreme Court decisions. In 1964 Tugwell began one of the most significant studies undertaken by the Center, a study that eventually led to the publication of a proposed new Constitution, which involved the Center in another wave of controversy.

While the meetings continued at the Center, publications also were distributed as usual to the press and the public. On September 8 the Center published an extraordinarily hopeful paper by Walter Millis entitled *The Demilitarized World* in which he contended that the nuclear stalemate had made large military organizations "irrelevant" in deciding major power struggles between nations, with the result that gradual demilitarization was "inevitable."

"Military establishments will progressively decline into forces policing, through their defensive roles, a more or less established world order," Millis predicted. "A general and complete disarmament . . . will come increasingly to seem possible and practicable."

Aware of the growing danger of large-scale American intervention in Vietnam, the Center offered ideas for the creation of a "third force" of neutral nations to provide mediation services in international conflicts. In a pamphlet entitled *Peace Requires Peacemakers*, William B. Lloyd, Jr.—an editor and author specializing in the study of international conciliation and the development of new nations—asserted that the mediation machinery inside and outside the UN was inadequate and suggested that "in cases where UN procedure becomes stalled through legal technicalities, a quick recourse to the good offices of a few mutually acceptable nations might, in some future crisis, divert humanity from catastrophe."

Lloyd said that the "third force" group should be prepared to give its services without waiting to be summoned, it should be financed by an unaligned cluster of countries, and it should offer solutions of its own to the problems being disputed. He recommended that Switzerland be granted a special UN status to take a leading role in peacemaking.

If the suggestions emanating from the Center in 1964 had been adopted —or if the advice of the wisest advisers around President Johnson had been followed—the deep American involvement in the Vietnam War might have been avoided. The scholars at the Center were not the only people alarmed by Johnson's course in 1964, but the Center went further than any other educational organization in presenting possibilities for alternative policies that they thought might avert the disaster.

During the six months since Harold Willens had become the chairman of the founding members, the number of such members had grown to more than 200 and the number of sustaining members—those who gave substantial amounts, but less than $1000 a year—had increased to more than 250.

"We have proved that there does exist, in sufficient numbers, that rather special kind of American who can appreciate the vital importance of the Center's work and who is financially capable of membership contributions," Willens said. "These are the Americans who realize that in the fanatical extremism at both ends of the political spectrum lie the seeds of freedom's destruction. These are the Americans who understand that freedom and justice can be preserved only by the effective use of man's reason. They recognize in the Center a unique medium for applying human reason to the complex problems of our brand-new world."

The strenuous efforts of Willens, Ostrow, Hutchins, Ashmore, and other directors of the Fund, with the assistance of the professional fund raisers, produced a stream of money and new pledges for additional gifts in the last five months of 1964. Hutchins no longer spoke of a possible termination point for the Center. More than 2000 new members were added in these months, and their pledges totaled $439,977. Contributions actually paid in the same period amounted to $398,033.

Yet Hutchins, Willens, and all others concerned with money raising— and that included all of the officers and staff members—knew that the campaign had to go on month after month without relaxation. The $20 million endowment fund had not been achieved, and no one was sure that it could be reached.

Justice Douglas presided at the Fund's board meeting in Chicago on November 11. Leslie Paffrath of the Johnson Foundation gave a glowing report on the prospects for the *Pacem in Terris* convocation. Time, Inc., had made a contribution of $75,000, and other contributions were arriving. Hutchins informed the board that Chester Carlson had offered to give up to $200,000 to the Center between November 1, 1964, and October 30, 1965, to match new contributions in excess of $1000 received during that period.

It was evident, however, that the contributions for the *Pacem in Terris* assembly were not going to cover the costs of that convocation. The eminent speakers who had agreed to participate had been promised generous fees and travel expenses. Arrangements were being made to record all the sessions on videotape. The printing and distribution of pamphlets expected to be drawn from the proceedings also would be expensive.

Morris Levinson, one of the new directors, had an idea. He thought that a large amount of money, perhaps $1 million, might be obtained by having a banquet in honor of Robert Hutchins at the end of the *Pacem in Terris* conference. Hutchins was asked to withdraw from the board meeting, and the remaining directors discussed the proposal. All favored it.

When Hutchins returned to the meeting, he was told that the directors had decided to sponsor a fund-raising dinner for him. He objected strenuously, saying that he had never permitted such an event at the University of Chicago and he did not want the directors of the Fund for the Republic to call on his friends to donate money out of personal affection or respect for him. Finally he yielded, after Levinson and others had convinced him that he had to accept the project as a major factor in keeping the Center alive.

While the plans for the international convocation to strengthen "peace on earth" went forward, the Center continued to be concerned about peace in the United States. In 1964 there had been explosive riots in New York, Philadelphia, Chicago, and other cities as well as bursts of hostility between blacks and whites in many places. The crumbling ghettos had become battlegrounds of violence and fear.

On December 14, 1964, the Center published a daring proposal for the formation of new interracial towns on the edges of suburbia and the clearance of industrial slums from the decaying central sections of the cities. Bernard Weissbourd, another relatively new director of the Fund, was the author of these suggestions, which were based on intensive studies of metropolitan areas. Weissbourd's corporation—Metropolitan Structures, Inc.— had planned and constructed hotels, apartments, and office buildings in eastern and midwestern cities.

In a Center pamphlet entitled *Segregation, Subsidies, and Megalopolis,* Weissbourd said: "If America is not prepared to accept interracial communities, there is little hope of arresting the decline of the city." He asked for a reversal in the use of federal subsidies, declaring that FHA-insured and VA-guaranteed mortgages had accelerated the flight of the white middle classes from the cities by encouraging home ownership in the suburbs.

Weissbourd also pointed out that federal subsidy power had contributed to the decline of the cities by supporting public housing programs that were racially segregated and concentrated low-income and welfare families in the central sections, damaging the tax bases on which cities depended.

"The federal subsidies that have encouraged highway construction instead of mass commuter transportation—and thus drawn industry out of the city—have reduced the city's tax base," Weissbourd said. "A lower tax base means less money for education and for the adjustment of rural migrants to urban life. Poor schools and changing neighborhoods encourage middle-class white families to move to the suburbs. Higher welfare costs increase the tax rate and thus encourage industry to relocate in outlying areas.

"All these factors are interrelated. If they can be altered, it might be possible to reverse the cycle of urban decay and deterioration, and move the forces of the market-place toward renewal and reconstruction."

On the last day of 1964 the Center and the Johnson Foundation released to the press an impressive list of speakers scheduled to address the *Pacem in Terris* convocation. Among them were Hubert H. Humphrey, the newly elected vice president of the United States; Chief Justice Earl Warren of the United States Supreme Court; U Thant, the Secretary General of the United Nations; and other world leaders.

President Lyndon Johnson was unable to participate. His letter to Justice Douglas, then the chairman of the Center's board, was quoted in the press release. The President said he had "no doubt that such discussion, under private auspices, of the problems of peace will provide a major contribution to the greatest single problem of our time."

Hubert Humphrey was eager to speak at the Center's convocation. He was trying to keep the president from hurling American bombers at North Vietnam. He wanted to raise his voice once more for a policy of restraint and for another attempt to strengthen the United Nations.

18

*Operation Rolling Thunder
rumbles over the Center's
Assembly for Peace—but the
assembly has an impact*

In February 1965, theologians and scientists, politicians and diplomats, jurists and economists, from the United States and Europe, from Asia and Africa, from Latin America met under the Center's sponsorship in New York to discuss opportunities humanity might have to escape nuclear annihilation. Three days before the *Pacem in Terris* convocation began, President Johnson approved Operation Rolling Thunder—a plan for continuous bombing of North Vietnam—accompanied by the issuance of a State Department "white paper" that asserted that it was "beyond question that North Vietnam is carrying out a carefully conceived plan of aggression against the South." The American bombers had been ordered into action to teach the North Vietnamese that aggression did not pay.

The thunder of the bombers in the Far East alarmed leaders in many places, including Vatican City. Pope Paul VI, who had sent a mild letter of greetings to Robert Hutchins on February 5, sent a telegram on February 17 to Francis Cardinal Spellman in New York, urging him to tell Dr. Hutchins —the chairman of the convocation—of the Pope's "prayerful desire that these deliberations lead to positive action for world peace."

"Particularly during the present grave international crisis is it necessary to invoke higher principles of the moral order and to recall the collective responsibility of all nations for the preservation of friendly relationships and the avoidance of armed conflict, which in Our day would have incalculable and frightful results for all mankind," the Pope said in his telegram to the Cardinal. "Increasingly more important, then, is the irreplaceable mission of the United Nations in promoting mediation of disputes and restoration of peace."

At the *Pacem in Terris* convocation Hutchins made it clear that he did not think bombers were the proper instruments for bringing peace.

"This is not an ecumenical council assembled to debate religious topics," Hutchins said. "This is a political meeting. The question is: How can we make peace, not peace through the medium of war, not peace through the dreadful mechanisms of terror, but peace pure, simple and durable. If the principles of *Pacem in Terris* are sound, how can they be carried out in the world as it is? If they are unsound, what principles are sound, and how can they be realized today? What does it mean to 'coexist,' and how can we do it?

"It may turn out during these sessions that the reason why *Pacem in Terris* was applauded throughout the world was that it was so general as to be meaningless or so vague that any partisan could put his own meaning into it. Surely we should all agree that this is no time for pious platitudes. Few aspects of modern life are more repellent than the spectacle of governments proclaiming peace while they are armed to the teeth, while they are busily trying to get into the nuclear arms race or forge ahead in it, and while they are assuring their peoples that others cannot be trusted."

Hutchins declared that the late Pope John had consigned nuclear arms, nationalism, colonialism, racism, and nonconstitutional regimes to the wastebasket of history: "He rejects the devil theory of politics. He asserts the unfashionable doctrine that 'the same moral law which governs relations between individual human beings serves also to regulate the relations of political communities with each other.' "

"He is equally unfashionable in refusing to see power as the object of politics," Hutchins pointed out. "The object is the common good, that good which accrues to every person because he is a member of the community and which he would not have if the community did not exist. And finally the Pope maintains that no nation is any longer capable of serving the common good. We are all members of one community, we share one common destiny, the common good we seek is the good of the human community. We must now supply the political fabric of an existing world community, and the place to begin, the Pope says, is the United Nations."

Hutchins expressed the hope that participants in the convocation would refrain from saying that nothing could be done without a "consensus."

"Human beings are not insects caught on the flywheel of history," Hutchins said. "They make history. *Pacem in Terris* has already given an historic turn to international affairs. The Pope did not wait for a consensus. He decided to take the lead in forming one. His example deserves emulation."

Vice President Humphrey, who had opposed the decision to bomb North Vietnam so persistently that he had been excluded from National Security Council meetings by President Johnson, delivered a speech that had been tailored to fit Johnson's policy. Humphrey hewed to the president's line.

"Clearly, one of the requirements of a workable peace system is to supplement and complement and improve the peace-keeping machinery of the United Nations," Humphrey said. "Eventually we would hope that this machinery would be in a position to seek the peaceful resolution of disputes and incipient conflicts, ideally by quiet conciliation but if need be by verbal confrontation before the bar of world opinion, and *in extremis* by placing whatever kind of peace-keeping force is needed in a position between antagonists so that no sovereignty is without potential international protection—and no nation need call upon other nations to help protect them from predatory neighbors.

"Today we recognize that this is not possible. The case of Vietnam is an example. In 1954 the Geneva Accords were ratified, guaranteeing the independent status of South Vietnam. Today in Vietnam that freedom is endangered by the systematic attempt of foreign-backed subversives to win control of the country. Today peace in Southeast Asia can be obtained if the violators will cease their aggression.

"Our policy is clear. We will continue to seek a return to the essentials of the Geneva Accords of 1954. We will resist aggression. We will be faithful to a friend. We seek no wider war. We seek no dominion. Our goal in Southeast Asia is today what it was in 1954—what it was in 1962. Our goal is peace and freedom for the people of Vietnam."

Many participants in the *Pacem in Terris* convocation did not believe that "peace and freedom" for Vietnam could be obtained by raining bombs upon the North Vietnamese. H. Stuart Hughes, professor of history at Harvard, challenged the Johnson policy in a round-table discussion at the end of the convocation's first day.

"Let us give our government the benefit of the doubt," Hughes said. "It started off by defending a government and a people that were defending their liberties. That was the official line, let us say. A few years back, it was correct. But somewhere in the past year or two we crossed the line, and we are no longer defending liberty in any meaningful sense of the term. We are exporting counter-revolution. This is the great distinction between the Korean war and the Vietnamese war. We should recognize it and, in the terms of traditional theology, realize that what may have been originally a just war is no longer a just war."

Stanley Sheinbaum, a former economic consultant to the government of South Vietnam, declared: "We have opted for the vigilante role because there is no alternative in the minds of our policy makers. As a result, we undertake steps that are not only disastrous for a country such as Vietnam but, as we now recognize, disastrous from the point of view of our own self-interest. . . . What I am calling for, of course, is an international police force. The most important thing is that the decisions about what is aggression and what is not aggression should not be made by any one country unilaterally."

Most of the speakers at the convocation did not refer to Vietnam directly. They dealt with the larger issues of human survival and the measures necessary to create a world community.

Former Governor Adlai Stevenson, then the United States representative to the United Nations, saw the central question as "whether the wonderfully diverse and gifted assemblage of human beings on this earth really knows how to run a civilization."

"And day by day the problem grows more complex," Stevenson said ruefully. "It was recognized clearly and with compassion by Pope John; to him, the human race was not a cold abstraction. Underlying his messages and encyclicals was this simple thought: that the human race is a family, that men are brothers, all wars are civil wars, and all killing is fratricidal.

"Peace is the one condition for survival in the atomic age. Our human family must be organized for peace. This entails building at the world level the civil authority, the peace-keeping functions, the effective social institutions, without which human communities cease to be peaceful."

Paul Tillich, professor of theology at the University of Chicago, speaking as a Protestant theologian and as an existentialist philosopher, gave one of the most penetrating addresses at the conference. Acknowledging that a world police force might work in minor conflicts not directly involving the interests of the great powers, Tillich said: "But a conflict between those who give power and authority to such a police force could not be solved in this way. The problem is neither power nor coercion, but the use of coercion with or without justice in the necessary exercise of power."

Tillich thought that Pope John's appeal to "all men of good will" in the encyclical had not been realistic. He felt that human beings were perpetually torn between "good will" and "bad will." He asserted: "One should appeal to all men knowing that in the best will there is an element of bad will and that in the worst will there is an element of good will. This view of the ambiguity of man's moral nature has direct consequences for the way a peace conference should look at the chance for a future state of peace."

He emphasized the importance of distinguishing genuine hope from Utopian expectations. People who believed in a universal law of progress, based partly on confidence in "man's growing reasonableness," had been bitterly disappointed, over and over.

"We cannot close our eyes any longer to the fact that every gain produced—for example, by scientific and technical progress—implies a loss; and that every good achieved in history is accompanied by a shadow, an evil which uses the good and distorts it," Tillich told the 2000 people in the ballroom of the New York Hilton. "It is understandable that hopelessness has grasped large masses in the Western nations, especially in the younger generation. And it is understandable that a conference like this meets a widespread skepticism, perhaps by some in the conference itself.''

In spite of the nuclear arms race, in spite of the events in Vietnam, in spite of the weakness of the United Nations and the hypocrisy of national leaders, Tillich glimpsed four significant bases for ''genuine hope.''

''The first basis for genuine hope is something negative, which, however, can have and partly has had positive effects: the atomic threat and the fear of mutual destruction,'' Tillich said. ''The limited peace forced upon us by the threat is in itself merely negative. But it does something which is somehow positive: it makes the conflicting groups of mankind feel that there is mankind with a common destiny. This experience of a 'community of fear' is still weak and easily overwhelmed by a stronger feeling of national and ideological conflict. But it does exist as a small seed.''

He found a second basis for real hope in ''the technical union of mankind by the conquest of space,'' which compelled men to recognize the essential unity of the earth and ''the technical oneness of our world.''

''A third basis of genuine hope for peace is the increasing number of cross-national and cross-ideological fields of cooperation.'' Tillich said. ''Some of them are desirable, as, for example, exchange in the humanities and religion; some of them essential, as, for example, collaboration in the sciences; some of them necessary for the future of mankind, as, for example, the problems of food, medicine, overpopulation, conservation of nature.''

Tillich found a fourth basis for ''genuine hope'' in the existence and the effectiveness—within certain limits—of ''a legal roof for all these types of limited groups.'' He aded: ''But man can extend the realm of peace which nature cannot. He can establish a legal structure which guarantees peace among those who are subject to it, not absolutely but to a certain degree, for everyone subjected to the legal structure can break through it for his own interest or his conviction.''

A lasting peace depended upon ''something more than the legal structure.'' Tillich hoped for the development of what he termed ''a communal *eros*, that kind of love which is not directed to an individual but to a group.'' He referred to the saying that ''one cannot love another nation'' and commented: ''This may be true in relation to a national state; but it is not true with respect to the people of the other nation. One can have *eros* toward them in their uniqueness, their virtues, their contributions, in spite of their shortcomings and vices. It seems that no world community is possible without this *eros* which transcends interest as well as law.''

''There is no hope for a final stage of history in which peace and justice rule,'' Tillich concluded. ''History is not fulfilled at its empirical end; but history is fulfilled in the great moments in which something new is created, or, as one could express it religiously, in which the Kingdom of God breaks into history conquering destructive structures of existence, one of the greatest of which is war. This means that we cannot hope for a final stage of justice and peace within history; but we can hope for partial victories over the forces of evil in a particular moment of time."

Linus Pauling, winner of a Nobel peace prize and a Center staff member, was more hopeful than Tillich. Pauling evoked a wave of warmth and applause from the conference audience when he cried in a ringing voice: "I believe that we have now reached the time in the course of the evolution of civilization when war will be abolished from the world and will be replaced by a system of world law based upon the principles of justice and morality."

Pauling attacked American policy in Southeast Asia with hot indignation, denying that the United States was upholding the Geneva Accords of 1954 which had been cited by Vice President Humphrey in his speech.

"I must say that one great country, my own country, the United States of America, although present at the Geneva Conference of 1954, refused to sign the final agreement to bring an end to war in Vietnam," Pauling said. "And then, in 1956, together with the new government which had been imposed upon South Vietnam, refused to allow the people of South Vietnam to select their own government by ballot, as required by the Geneva Accords. . . . These facts are omitted in most recent official statements."

In angry tones, Pauling declared: "This repudiation of the principles of arbitration and negotiation and of the principles of democracy had led to ten years of savage guerrilla warfare and to retaliation with helicopters, fire bombs, chemical defoliation and destruction of crops, the uprooting of hundreds of thousands of peasants from their homes and their forced concentration into strategic hamlets, great air raids with modern fighter-bombers, and the threat of nuclear destruction through attack from Polaris submarines lying offshore. And now there impends the horrible danger of escalation to the catastrophe of a civilization-destroying nuclear war. Now the time has come to obey the exhortation of Pope John: the exhortation to cease military aggression, to bring this evil war to an end, to meet and negotiate and make a great practical application of the principles of morality and justice."

The two Russian leaders who were among the principal speakers at the convocation referred briefly to Vietnam but were not as harsh in criticizing American actions there as Pauling and other Americans were. They devoted most of their statements to "peaceful coexistence" and the meaning of such "coexistence."

N. N. Inozemtsev, deputy chief editor of *Pravda* and an influential Communist party theoretician, cited five "concrete tasks" as urgent: "elimination of the hotbeds of danger such as Vietnam, the Caribbean basin, the Congo, which have developed as a result of the military intervention of certain powers and their attempts to interfere in the internal affairs of peoples; the solution through negotiation . . . of outstanding issues associated with the consequences of World War II . . . ; the reduction of the danger of nuclear conflict through the prevention of further proliferation of nuclear weapons and the barring of the so-called NATO 'multilateral nuclear forces,' which would open up access to nuclear weapons to the West German revenge-seeker; the banning of underground tests; and the creation of atom-free zones in different regions of the globe; the slowing down of the arms race, particularly through the reduction of military budgets . . . ; the futher relaxation of international tensions, the strengthening of trust between states, the establishment of international relations based not on dictate and threat, not on violence and arbitrariness, but on the equality and self-determination of all nations and on respect for their sovereignty.''

"The Soviet Union has not concealed its intention to win the economic competition with the capitalist world, but this does not at all mean abandoning economic cooperation,'' Inozemtsev stated. "The principle of peaceful coexistence provides for the development of normal economic and political relations between states of different social systems and the development of various forms of international cooperation.''

Yevgenyi Zhukov, director of the institute of history in the Soviet Academy of Sciences, stressed the Russian devotion to "peaceful coexistence" with the understanding that it meant "general competition in the sphere of economics and culture, competition in bringing happiness to mankind and in meeting its material and spiritual needs.'' Then Zhukov said: "There can be no peaceful coexistence between oppressor and oppressed. . . . From this point of view the struggles for national liberation waged against colonial domination have enjoyed and will in the future enjoy support from the progressive forces everywhere.''

Adam Schaff, a Polish philosopher and a member of the central committee of the Communist party of Poland, bluntly observed: "Coexistence is a fight, a competition, a noble competition for the hearts and minds of people. This will continue, but let us hope that our conduct will be rational. On your side you will go further and further in expanding your economy, increasing social security, and so on, not only because you recognize that this is the normal course of development but because there is pressure from the socialist countries. On our side we are rapidly changing our political situation—bringing in more and more democracy, liberalizing the internal life of our society. This is also the normal course of our development, but it is also the result of competition from you. We are coming closer and closer, and this is the great hope.''

George F. Kennan, former United States ambassador to the Soviet Union and to Yugoslavia, whose views had been very influential in shaping American policies in the cold war, pleaded for "a basic revision of assumptions concerning Soviet intentions, both hypothetical and actual.''

"Western policy is apparently based on an assessment of these intentions which has not changed appreciably from the days of the Berlin blockade and the Korean war, and which, even then, probably embraced serious elements of misinterpretation," Kennan said. He described the European policy of the "Western coalition" as marked by four characteristics: an assumption of a "strong Soviet desire to attack, or at least to intimidate by military force, the western half of the continent . . ."; a belief that "the Soviet government could be deterred from acting on this desire only by a Western defense policy relying heavily on nuclear weapons and including, as a primary component, the military power of a heavily re-armed West Germany"; "pressure for German unification, by procedures which apparently envisage a unilateral retirement of Soviet forces from East Germany . . ."; and "the cultivation, not everywhere but in some instances, of a species of "little Europism," in the form of efforts to organize the European community for peaceful purposes within the framework of the western half of the continent alone."

Referring to the "present sad and dangerous moment" in international relations, Kennan went on to advocate drastic changes in the policies of the "Western coalition."

"I see no reason why a primary reliance on nuclear weapons should be considered permanently essential to the defense of my own country or of Western Europe," Kennan said. "I fail to see why we could not at least explore and discuss seriously the various proposals that have been brought forward over the years by the Polish government, looking to a restriction of the place of nuclear weapons in Europe's defenses.

"I think we could usefully re-examine our acceptance of the principle of 'first use' in the employment of any and all weapons of mass destruction, and thus place ourselves in a position where we could proceed more effectively towards the eventual elimination of these weapons and, above all, their delivery systems from national arsenals. Without such a change I can see no possibility of halting the present trend towards the proliferation of control over such weapons to a point where all hope of preventing their eventual use, somewhere and at some time, would have to be abandoned."

Kennan continued: "We should not, I think, leave the rearmament of Western Germany effectively open-ended, as it must today appear to be in the eyes of people in the East. . . . And if, as it appears, there is to be no military disengagement in Germany in this present historical period, then one must learn to accept with better grace at least the provisional existence of a separate East German political entity."

The veteran diplomat, known for his sophistication as an ambassador, surprised many members of the convocation audience by ending his remarks with "a plea for something resembling a new act of faith in the ultimate humanity and sobriety of the people on the other side; and I would like to address this plea to our Communist contemporaries as well as ourselves."

"History reveals that the penalties for over-cynicism in the estimation of the motives of others can be no smaller, on occasions, than the penalties for naivete,'' Kennan concluded. "Our sole hope lies in the possibility that the adversary, too, has learned something from the sterility of past conflict; that he, too, sees—if only through the dim lens of ideological prejudice, suspicion, and accumulated resentment—the identity of fate that binds us all."

Henry R. Luce, a Center consultant and editorial chairman of Time, Inc., who had been responsible for a $75,000 donation to help pay the costs of the *Pacem in Terris* convocation, presided at a round-table discussion with some of the participating speakers on the third and last day. Luce listed the subjects that seemed to him to have been most emphasized in the conference.

"First, there is the matter of national sovereignty," Luce said. "The question is whether the nation state is obsolete, or whether and how nation states can develop their own individualities within a world-wide frame of order. Second, there is the matter of advancing the rule of law. This, I believe, is the creative answer to the first question.

"Third, there was frequent reference to the obligation of rich nations to help poor nations. Fourth, there was, of course, the pervasive theme of disarmament. The demand was frequently made for the complete elimination of nuclear weapons, and this sentiment almost invariably received loud applause. I, for one, am not sure that anything was said about disarmament that would be of practical use to the statesmen of the world in their wrestling with this horrendous problem."

Participants in the round table included three United States senators— George McGovern of South Dakota, Eugene McCarthy of Minnesota, and Claiborne Pell of Rhode Island—in addition to Grenville Clark, attorney and coauthor of *World Peace Through World Law*; Jerome Frank, professor of psychiatry at Johns Hopkins University medical school; Steve Allen, author and television personality; Eugene Burdick, novelist and professor of political science; Gerard Piel, editor and publisher of *Scientific American*; George Shuster, assistant to the president, University of Notre Dame; and Carl F. Stover, executive director of the National Institute of Public Affairs.

Senator Pell said that the most important matters on the agenda were revision of the United Nations Charter, establishing relations with Communist China, and settling the question of Germany and the status of Berlin. He was disturbed by a statement made by the foreign minister of China, who had indicated that "peaceful coexistence" with the United States was out of the question. That statement did not seem consistent with the declarations of the Marxist leaders at the convocation.

Pell offered several suggestions for the future of Germany: "Perhaps we could get an international corridor to Berlin, recognize the Oder-Neisse frontier as permanent, accept the reality of the East German government and strive for a detente . . . It is only with the relaxation of tensions that the reunification of Germany can be hoped for. If it should come about, I think it would be acceptable if it is not a militarized Germany.''

Dr. Shuster, who had been United States Commissioner in Bavaria in 1950 and 1951, favored the Pell proposal if it could be developed with ''the concurrence of the Germans, desirably both East and West,'' but he felt that ''the likelihood of our being able to get such an agreement seems to me relatively remote.''

''I think this is a good time to talk about the possibilities of a settlement,'' Eugene McCarthy intervened. ''Unless we are willing to accept that Berlin and East Germany will remain as a kind of hostage to both the East and the West for the next thirty or forty years, we ought to begin to talk about the problem. . . . It used to be that one could put off decisions of many kinds in international relations and not have to answer for it; but the fact is that in the movement of politics today the postponement of decisions becomes almost a matter of guilt and responsibility; and non-decisions are almost as important as decisions. This is true in Africa, certainly true in Latin America.''

Grenville Clark declared that ''there is only one way in which we can obtain genuine peace as distinguished from a precarious balance of terror, and that is through a supranational body equipped with powers that can honestly be described only as those of government.''

''But no action will take place toward the establishment of the necessary world organization until two things happen,'' Clark said. ''One is a world-wide program of education whereby people will come to understand in detail what needs to be done. . . . The other is real governmental leadership.''

In a sorrowful voice, Clark asserted that ''not a single government in all the world in the last twenty years has brought forward a really adequate plan for disarmament and enforceable world law.'' He thought such leadership was indispensable, and he did not place much hope in Lyndon Johnson: ''President Kennedy in his second term would probably have furnished it; the great tragedy of his assassination is that the greatest potential leader for world peace was cut off.''

Carl Stover asked Clark not to underestimate the force of the thinking reflected in Pope John's encyclical and in the Center's convocation. He also urged that more attention be given to the points made by Abba Eban, deputy prime minister of Israel, in an address that had brought the 2000 members of the convocation audience to their feet with shouts of applause. Eban had suggested that the heads of all sovereign governments, within and outside the United Nations, should devote a week each year to an assembly on the problems of mankind—world population, the use of the world's resource pollution of the environment, the expansion of education, and the conquest of hunger.

Eugene Burdick thrust a cutting question at his colleagues: ''No one at the Convocation has directed himself to the problem of whether the human animal is pacific. Does he want peace rather than war? . . . In the opinion of many anthropologists, war is instinctive in men. I hate to say it but Africa and Southeast Asia are good examples: the people win their freedom, and at once they are at one another's throats."

"I agree that man is the most vicious creature, the most destructive creature, on earth," Dr. Frank said. "We have to face this. We are the only creature that destroys its own kind in the wholesale fashion that we do. But it is very important to distinguish that fact from war. War is a social institution, and it has to be learned fresh by every generation. There have been societies without it. . . . This seems to me to create an area of hope."

Piel asserted that the "viciousness" of man was "an invention of agricultural civilization. It is a curse laid upon mankind arising out of original sin, which historically is the crime of slavery." To him, the record of history showed "that man's ugliness was the creation and expression of his social institutions, institutions that were set up to provide for inequity in the distribution of goods which, until the industrial revolution came, had been chronically in scarce supply throughout the world."

"We now live in an era in the life of mankind in which human slavery has been made forever obsolete through the genius of technology," Piel said. "Now the institutions of the world must be reorganized to provide for abundance. We must eradicate from the world and from the moral code of our societies the sanctions that were given to inequity and injustice in the past."

Senator McGovern declared that "the great appeal Pope John had for the entire world, and the great significance of *Pacem in Terris*, is that both the man and his message touch on forces that are moving in the world which I believe are more powerful than any commitment man might have to war. I think they are more powerful than armaments, more powerful than the machinations of power politics."

McGovern brought the attention of the group back to the situation in Vietnam: "Almost eleven years ago, when John Kennedy was the junior Senator from Massachusetts, he took the floor of the United States Senate to discuss the war then in progress in Indochina and tried to point out why the methods that were then being used by the French would not work. He said there are some problems in the world that do not lend themselves to military solution. He went on to say, in effect, that until the people of that area could enlist behind a government that had their confidence, until they could develop a leadership of their own, no amount of military aid from the outside would reverse the trends in progress there. It is interesting that eleven years later history has swung full circle, and now the French are giving the United States the same advice that we were giving them in April, 1954."

McGovern and the other senators who participated in the Center's conference had deep misgivings about Operation Rolling Thunder. The thunder of the warplanes, which Lyndon Johnson called "my bombers," made every participant in the conference keenly aware of the dangers of Johnson's pursuit of peace through bombardment. The senators who had given Johnson a blank check in the Tonkin Bay Resolution in 1964 were beginning to believe that they should have heeded Wayne Morse.

Fred Neal, who had originated the idea of the *Pacem in Terris* convocation, took part in the round-table "summary session." Neal referred to "two of the most profound things" that were uttered at the conference.

"The first was from George Kennan, who said, and I think illustrated his opinion, that we do not face a threat of Soviet military aggression, despite the fact that most of our policy is based on it," Neal recalled. "And most revolution is not imported, despite the fact that the other part of our foreign policy is based on that. The second statement was from the Deputy Chief Editor of *Pravda*, who can be assumed to have been speaking with some official support, that in the opinion of the Soviet government there is no problem—and he repeated "no problem"—that cannot be solved by negotiation.

"If all this is true, I believe we must start thinking about what coexistence means in specific terms, because only then can we acquire the kind of minimal mutual trust that Pope John was talking about and reach a position where we can negotiate specific things. . . . The great thing about the encyclical, in my opinion, is that it helps to make this kind of discussion respectable, and therefore possible."

In the closing hour of the convocation U Thant spoke of the strange paradox in the human situation: "We have, at last, both the means and the general desire to secure peace and justice for all. We know all too well the price we shall surely pay for failing to secure that peace and justice. We are not basically disagreed, whatever our ideological differences, about the kind of world we wish to have. The United Nations Charter, already accepted by 115 nations, describes it; the encyclical describes it; and it is also described in many great works of literature, scholarship and prophecy which are the common heritage of all mankind.

"What element, then, is lacking, so that, with all our skill and all our knowledge, we still find ourselves in the dark valley of discord and enmity? What is it that inhibits us from going forward together to enjoy the fruits of human endeavor and to reap the harvest of human experience? Why is it that, for all our professed ideals, our hopes, and our skill, peace on earth is still a distant objective, seen only dimly through the storms and turmoils of our present difficulties?

"All great moves forward in the history of mankind have required changes of existing attitudes and states of mind, so that real life can catch up with the creative ideas that underlie our evolution. We are now trying to make the step forward from a world of antagonism, domination, and discord to a world of cooperation, equity, and harmony. This is a large step and an important break with the past. It is not to be expected, therefore, that men will easily and immediately accept it—and adapt themselves to it.

In the preamble to the UNESCO Constitution it is said: "Since wars begin in the minds of men, it is in the minds of men that the defenses of peace must be constructed." This sentence may well provide one key to our present difficulties. It is an aspect of our problems to which the encyclical *Pacem in Terris* is especially relevant.

"Thus, although we have abjured war as an instrument of policy, all nations have not yet abjured the state of mind which has so often led to war —the nationalistic urge to dominate and extend, by various means, their own particular traditions, forms, and ways of life. Nor has it been possible effectively to eliminate the use of force, whether openly or covertly, as a means of furthering political or other ends. Such attitudes inevitably breed in other nations the fears, resentments, and suspicions which historically have also created the atmosphere of tension in which wars break out.

"Again, although we speak loudly for equal rights and against discrimination, there are still many nations and groups throughout the world which are not prepared to accept the practical consequences of these ideals, while an even greater number still suffer from discrimination or lack of equal opportunity. It is this failure of everyday, practical behavior to keep pace with professed ideals and aims which makes the promise of our infinitely promising world a mockery for so many of its inhabitants. . . .

"We now have the means to achieve a great objective, an enlightened world public opinion. One of the revolutions of our age, the revolution in communications of all kinds, has made a well-informed world public opinion technically possible for the first time in history. Our problem is to ensure a beneficial use of these means of communications. This is a challenge to leaders both temporal and spiritual, to intelligent and creative men and women everywhere."

In disseminating the proceedings of the *Pacem in Terris* convocation, the Center made use of every possible means of communications—audiotapes for radio stations and discussion groups; videotapes for television broadcasts and classroom use; 16-millimeter films edited from the videotapes for adult education courses; articles in magazines and newspapers; and a paperback book, *Pacem in Terris: Peace on Earth*, edited by Edward Reed, published and distributed in the United States and other countries by Pocket Books.

On March 5, 1965, a summary of the conference prepared by John K. Jessup, chief editorial writer for *Life* magazine, appeared in *Life* with several pictures of what Jessup called "an extraordinary assemblage of the world's movers and shakers."

"The speeches and seminars, recorded for distribution to 90 U.S. educational TV and 125 radio stations, are only a beginning," Jessup wrote. "But it is a beginning that holds promise for new departures in world statecraft."

Jessup said the guest list would have done credit to a UN Charter gathering or a funeral for a head of state: "If the dramatis personae were impressive, the subject matter of the three-day *Pacem in Terris* Convocation was even more so. The participants aimed to explore the requirements of a durable world peace through panels covering the rule of law, peace-keeping institutions, a solution to Europe's territorial dilemmas, the problems of neutralist and non-nuclear nations, the terms of co-existence, and the implications of the papal encyclical for U.S. policy. The approach to these great issues was a series of panel discussions conducted by the most prestigious delegates.''

While the *Pacem in Terris* convocation received remarkable coverage in *Life, Time, Newsweek*, the *New York Times*, and other secular publications with millions of readers, its repercussions were particularly notable in the Catholic press. While the conference was primarily a political and educational meeting, as Hutchins had said at its opening, it was based on a papal encyclical. It was the first time in history that such a conference of leaders from many nations had been initiated on such a basis. Consequently it aroused much interest in the editors of Catholic publications.

Three national Catholic leaders joined in hailing the conference. Auxiliary Bishop John J. Dougherty of Newark, assistant for United Nations affairs to the chairman of the administrative board of the National Catholic Welfare Conference, called it ''a giant stride toward the goal of peace on earth.'' Other expressions of praise came from the Rev. John F. Cronin, assistant director of the National Catholic Welfare Social Action Department, who had taken part in the preliminary planning, and William E. Moran, Jr., dean of the Georgetown University foreign service school and president of the Catholic Association for International Peace.

Hundreds of Catholic papers in all sections of the United States printed articles from the Religious News Service, the Catholic news services, or their own correspondents on various aspects of the conference. Headlines ranged from ''Vice President Hails Peace Legacy of Pope'' to ''Global Solutions to Problems Needed'' and ''Amid Threats of War, Men Talk of Peace.'' A few of the articles reflected the deep antagonism among Catholics toward communism, but most of them emphasized the relatively conciliatory statements made by the Soviet participants in the conference.

On February 21, the day after the convocation ended in New York, Pope Paul VI expressed his joy that it had been held. In a talk from his balcony to 20,000 visitors from all over the world who had gathered in St. Peter's Square in Rome, the Pope said that it had given an extension to ''the teaching of peace.''

''It is to this that we must educate ourselves and the new generations, not to make them timid but to give them confidence in the might of right—and not in the right of might,'' the pope declared.

The Center's first *Pacem in Terris* convocation brought the Center to the attention of people around the earth. But the conference appeared to have little effect upon one powerful leader—President Johnson. General

William Westmoreland, head of the American Military Assistance Command, Vietnam, had asked for two Marine Corps battalions to defend the Da Nang air base, from which American bombers were attacking North Vietnam in Operation Rolling Thunder. Johnson had approved. On March 8, 1965, the Marines landed in Vietnam, ready for combat.

Hutchins was heartened by the financial results of the banquet given in his honor at the New York Hilton on the closing night of the conference. Thanks to the indefatigable efforts of Harold Willens, the assistance of the professional fund raisers, the generosity of Fund board members—particularly Morris Levinson, Jubal Parten, Edward Lamb, and Seniel Ostrow—and the munificence of Chester Carlson (who told Willens "if you raise a million, I'll give $200,000 more"), and the contributions of dozens of other donors, the total in gifts and pledges had amounted to $1.4 million. Moved by that outpouring of affection and the substantial evidence of support for his intellectual enterprise, Hutchins found it difficult to speak that night. He was on the verge of weeping.

Elmo Roper, the man who had first recommended the election of Hutchins as president of the Fund, was the chairman of the dinner. The co-chairmen were Senator William Benton, publisher of the Britannica; Norman Cousins, editor of the *Saturday Review*; Morris Levinson; and Henry Luce. The honorary chairmen were Ralph J. Bunche, Paul Hoffman, and Adlai Stevenson. The speakers included Senator Eugene McCarthy, Mortimer Adler, Abba Eban, Harry Ashmore, and Jubal Parten.

The dinner sponsors' list showed the broad range of the Center's supporters, including business executives, lawyers, clergymen, educators, labor leaders, philosophers, government officials, historians, poets, novelists, ambassadors, legislators, film producers and actors, foundation officers, scientists, and leaders from other fields. The reporters and broadcasters who were present that night realized the extent of Hutchins' influence in American life and the expanding outreach of the Center.

The Center did not rest on the prestige it had gained from the *Pacem in Terris* conference. On February 26 its attention shifted to a crucial issue in American public life—the power of money in politics. This issue was examined for three days in Santa Barbara, with participants including Senator Albert Gore of Tennessee, Governor Brown of California, Justice Stanley Mosk of the California Supreme Court, and Herbert Alexander of the Citizens Research Foundation at Princeton.

In March 1965 Chester Carlson spent several days at the Center. At the end of his visit, he told a Santa Barbara *News-Press* reporter: "I am tremendously impressed with the Center. It is a necessity. I don't see how the country can do without it." He indicated to Hutchins that he would continue to increase his contributions to the Center.

In the summer of 1965, tens of thousands of American troops poured into Vietnam, while Lyndon Johnson concealed his decisions from the public and hid the costs of the war in secret items in the enormous Pentagon budget. The warnings of Clark Clifford, former counsel to President Truman, Senator Mike Mansfield of the Foreign Relations Committee, Senator Frank Church, and others who opposed the president's actions were not heeded. Although the Joint Chiefs of Staff indicated that a million men would be required to win a "victory," Secretary of Defense Robert McNamara assured the president it would be over long before any such commitment would be required.

A comprehensive picture of this state of affairs, entitled *How the United States Got Involved in Vietnam*, was presented to the American people in a Center booklet released on August 18, 1965. It was written by Robert Scheer, a correspondent for *Ramparts* magazine who had recently returned from a trip to Southeast Asia. The foreword said: "The path of America's slow, gradual, and then steadily mounting involvement in Vietnam has never been fully explored. This report reveals some important sources of that involvement. . . . The facts he cites and opinions he expresses in this report are his responsibility; the Center is responsible for the decision that the material in the report should be published in the interest of public discussion."

Scheer disclosed that Justice Douglas—then the chairman of the Fund's board—had been one of a group of American leaders who had championed Ngo Dinh Diem, the man who had become premier of South Vietnam in 1954 with American backing. Others who helped to propel Diem into power were Francis Cardinal Spellman, the Roman Catholic archbishop of New York, a CIA agent named Edward Lansdale, Joseph Buttinger (an ex-Austrian socialist who had become an aide to Leo Cherne, head of the Research Institute of America), and Joseph P. Kennedy, father of John F. Kennedy.

Douglas had believed that Diem could lead an independent nationalist movement in South Vietnam and could keep it from falling under communist domination. He had introduced Diem to Senators Mike Mansfield and John Kennedy. Mansfield and Kennedy became severe critics of the French role in Vietnam and advocated "an independent nationalist alternative." Diem, who was described by Douglas as "honest and independent," was supported by Allen Dulles, director of the CIA, and Dulles persuaded President Eisenhower to give Diem's government almost $2 billion in economic and military assistance.

"From the spring of 1955 on, the U.S. commitment to Diem was complete," Scheer wrote. "This meant that the United States would ignore any French protestations and the Geneva Accords—including the provisions calling for reunification [of Vietnam] through free elections, which, as even Diem's most ardent supporters conceded, would bring the Communist-oriented Viet Minh to power."

The American advocates for Diem believed that the people of Vietnam would gradually realize the evils of communist rule and that the time would come when Diem's "democratic" government would be able to win a free election. Until that time arrived, they felt that Diem had to be maintained as a leader who would teach the Vietnamese how to govern themselves.

Referring to the Michigan State University Group, which had been paid by the United States government to advise Diem in many fields, Scheer said: "Among their 'advisory' duties was the formation of what is now referred to by 'foreign adventurers' and the foreign press as 'the secret police of Mr. Ngo Dinh Nhu' (Dinh Nhu was Ngo Dinh Diem's brother.). . . . The M.S.U. group proceeded with 'training' for several years. . . . Not only did they 'train' but they also 'controlled' in large measure the now famous 'secret police.' "

When John Kennedy became president of the United States in 1961, the Diem regime was slowly disintegrating. After the military coup in Saigon in 1963, Kennedy had begun to shift away from full support of the South Vietnamese regime. When Johnson entered the White House after Kennedy's murder, Johnson reversed that shift and gradually made the United States a complete participant in the conflict between North and South Vietnam.

In the Center booklet, Scheer asserted that Americans had been misled and deceived by the mass media as well as by their government in every stage of American involvement in Vietnam.

"It is sometimes claimed that ours is a commitment to peaceful change and theirs a commitment to violent revolution," Scheer wrote. "But it should be obvious by now that ideologies that are in power will always be concerned for peace and respect for the rules they have created, while ideologies out of power must stress the opposite. This was the case in Vietnam: first the French were dominant, and the Communists out of power were interested in violating the rules that assured French domination. By 1954, the Communists had won, and at Geneva they were able to write a new set of rules. But the United States, interested in reasserting its ideology, broke those rules and succeeded in establishing Diem in power. At that point the rebel reappeared, this time in the form of the Viet Cong."

Scheer said that he had not found a single instance in the American mass media in which a "Communist" had been described as "altruistic" or "genuinely committed to the well-being of his fellow man."

"If individual Communists appeared to be so, it was because they were being deceptive or were themselves deceived by higher-ups who better fitted our image of the Communist," Scheer commented. "The idea that Communist or Viet Minh rule under Ho Chi Minh might be better for the Vietnamese than any alternative political system has never really been examined in the United States because it is unthinkable.

"And although it was often admitted that a good portion of the Vietnamese population seemed to have this idea (Eisenhower thought it might be 80 per cent), it has never been seriously suggested that this view is worthy of any respect by Americans. Rather, it has been attributed to the ignorance

of the peasants and the effectiveness of Viet Cong propaganda or their terror tactics or to the thesis that the Vietnamese do not understand the true
and inevitable nature of communism and that Americans, who do, have the
responsibility of containing communism wherever it might spread.''

Scheer thought that American ideology had tended to become flabby
or meaningless to many people: "The consensus that obtained in the United
States during the cold war years, aided by the systematic purging from
American life of all those suspected of harboring sympathies toward communism, has suffered from not being seriously challenged internally. Big
ideas, as well as little ones, lose their vitality when they are not systematically challenged—a truth acknowledged by Mao Tse-tung as well as by John
Stuart Mill.''

Scheer then emphasized the importance of what the Center was attempting to do: "Serious dialogue alone can keep alive the basic nerves of a
democratic society—in fact, of any healthy society—for in the modern
world, where masses of people are inevitably involved with, and affected
by, public policies, a society cannot remain healthy if the important policies
are solely the business of various elites. This is not merely a matter of ideology, but rather of the mechanics of power and the tone of a society.''

Publication of the Scheer pamphlet on Vietnam won the admiration
and support of many citizens for the Center. It also increased the suspicion
and hostility of right-wing groups, such as the John Birch Society. On the
night of September 14, vandals hung a hand-printed paper sign on the Center's front gate. The sign said: "Mr. Hutchins should be shot. Oh, yes, the
Commies will shoot you after you have done their dirty work." The Santa
Barbara *News-Press*, in an article describing the sign, reported that police
had "no clues" to discover the identity of the vandals.

On a burning night in August, the smoldering violence in a large city
ghetto—which had been cited by several Center scholars as a possible starting point for a revolt that might tear the fabric of American society—
erupted in the Watts area of Los Angeles. Anger sparked by the arrest of a
young black man and his mother set off riots that spread over 46 square
miles in the next six days. Ten thousand black people poured into the
streets, burning buildings, attacking policemen and firemen, looting stores.
Fourteen thousand National Guardsmen, armed with rifles and bayonets,
eventually imposed order.

The national government had no solutions for the problems of unemployment and poverty in Watts and other black sections in American cities.
The "war on poverty" launched with fanfare by President Johnson was not
conducted with the massive spending that Congress authorized for the war
in Vietnam. The President and the Congress were not able or willing to undertake large-scale programs for job training and the building of new towns
or the reconstruction of the central cities.

Whether President Johnson's dream of a "Great Society"—which he had outlined in the spring of 1964 as a society in which all the needs of human beings would be met by the wise use of America's wealth and wisdom —could have been fulfilled if he had not committed so much to Vietnam can never be determined. His aspirations for the United States were greater than the nation could attain for its own citizens or for its allies abroad.

In September, the Center published a paper by Harvey Wheeler recommending drastic constitutional reforms to protect individual rights against the expanding federal government of Johnson's "Great Society," and Stanley Sheinbaum of the Center staff suggested that the Unites States might have to consider an international monetary system that did not have gold as its base. Sheinbaum warned Americans that United States gold stocks were being rapidly depleted by shipment of gold abroad to pay for imported products. He foresaw a growing gap in the balance of trade.

At the Fund's board meeting in November, Chester Carlson was pleased by the amount of money that had been given or pledged to match his own gifts. Hutchins had hoped that he would establish an irrevocable trust fund of $10 million for the Center, but he did not do so. He said, however, that he would match all new money received by the Center through September 30, 1966, up to a total of $750,000.

Carlson was particularly interested in the effects of technology on human institutions. On December 15, Hutchins announced that the Center would sponsor a five-day international symposium on the future of human values in a technological society. Carlson had agreed to pay the costs of the meeting.

"The prospects of humanity turn upon its ability to find the law that will direct technology to human uses," Hutchins said, declaring that the symposium would concentrate on the ideas presented in a long book by a French philosopher, Jacques Ellul, entitled *The Technological Society*, translated into English by John Wilkinson of the Center staff.

Participants in the symposium came from England, Greece, Canada, Israel, Belgium, Poland, Germany, and other countries, as well as from leading universities in the United States. While the technological might of the United States hammered the Viet Cong, the scholars at the Center tried again to discover how technology could be brought under control.

19

*The Center decides to rewrite
the American Constitution,
examines the university, and gets
more than $1 million in stock*

WHILE THE EXPANSION of the American presidency under Johnson and the derelictions of Congress intensified the interest of the Center staff in possible reforms of the Constitution, the conditions in American universities came under renewed scrutiny in the first five months of 1966. Student demonstrations and revolts by young militants—who disdained vocational training, conventional clothing, and the "old politics" of bargains and compromises—had rocked the Berkeley campus of the University of California in 1964, spread to other colleges and universities in 1965, and burst into new uproars in many places in the spring of 1966.

Hutchins, who had ripped into the universities for years as institutions that had lost sight of their purposes, decided that the time had come for "a distillation of the best thought on the condition of higher education. . . ." He asked Donald McDonald, who had served temporarily as the Center's acting director of development after the death of Tom Shearer in October 1965, to aid him in organizing a conference to be called "The University in America."

While the plans for this meeting of minds were being outlined, the Center returned to the examination of the Constitution that had initially begun in 1964 with a series of papers prepared by former Governor Rexford G. Tugwell. In the *Center Diary*—a newsletter sent to the increasing numbers of Center members—Tugwell explained: "The proposal to undertake the exploration arose because, in spite of its being deeply venerated, the Constitution had so obviously been evolving into something with new meanings.

. . . We have been looking into all the branches with equal curiosity, but the presidency has seemed to have a peculiar need for definition. It is no exaggeration to say that our lives and fortunes as individuals and our security as a nation depend on the judgment and decision of this one man. . . . It is with a sense of urgency that we have understaken this study."

On Februay 4 civic leaders and Founding Members of the Center attended a dinner meeting in Santa Barbara to hear a statement by James MacGregor Burns, professor of political science at Williams College and author of several books on American politics. Burns gave his views in a statement called "The Presidency," and a far-ranging discussion followed.

It seemed to me that Tugwell, Burns, and others were right in trying to clarify the functions of the presidency. I recalled a speech given in the Senate on March 9, 1949, by Lyndon Johnson when Johnson had been a senator for about two months. Johnson had predicted that the final fighters for freedom against a dictatorial president might be a few members of the Senate.

"A man elevated to the office of the President has virtually unlimited powers of influence over his countrymen," Johnson had said then. "His own personality is a force of great impact upon all the people of the nation and, in fact, upon the people of the world. Add to those powers directly his, all the less conspicuous powers of his aides, his administrative agencies, and the multitude of channels which feel his influence, and you have a force no other representative government has ever entrusted for long to one man.

"If on occasion you grant to the titular head of government the further intoxicant of an overwhelming majority of loyal supporters in the legislative branch, then you have a force well-nigh irresistible. The distinctions between executive and legislative are difficult to preserve under such circumstances; mere memoranda become laws, and laws become mere memoranda."

Since 1933, when Franklin Roosevelt had been given enormous powers by a frightened Congress to deal with an economic emergency, the constitutional relationships between the executive and legislative branches had been distorted. Truman had won a national election in 1948 by lambasting a "do-nothing Congress," and the institution of the presidency had gained additional stature in the administrations of Eisenhower and Kennedy.

In 1966, when the Center had the temerity to tackle the radical question of revising the Constitution in a series of dialogues, President Johnson had "an overwhelming majority of loyal supporters" in Congress, but his critics were becoming vocal as the effects of the Vietnam war began to hit millions of American homes. His deceptive methods of attempting to conceal the scope and the price of the war became more and more visible. In the universities, professors and students were demonstrating that the American freedom of expression could not be smothered even by "a force well-nigh irresistible."

Chester Carlson, the Xerox inventor who had already become the Fund for the Republic's largest financial supporter since the Ford Foundation, sent the Fund a very large gift in February 1966. He was alarmed by Johnson's policy in Vietnam, and he was certain that the Center was trying to awaken the people to the right issues. He decided to give the Center enough money to extend its influence.

In a letter to Hutchins, Carlson said he was transferring 7000 shares of Xerox stock—then worth more than $1 million—to the Fund with the hope that this gift would "increase the effectiveness of the Center in these very critical times." He declared that this contribution was entirely separate from his willingness to match gifts from other donors. He noted that he had been stirred by one of Hutchins' syndicated columns, which had been printed in a newspaper in Rochester, where he lived.

"I liked very much your column in this morning's paper entitled 'Why Not Withdraw From Vietnam?' " Carlson said. "This certainly makes very good sense. It should have been done a year and a half ago when we were presumably merely military advisors. We had an excellent excuse for withdrawing on the basis that there was no viable government to support."

With the Carlson gift enabling him to look ahead for at least a year—and the rising flow of other contributions indicating that thousands of citizens appreciated what the Center was doing—Hutchins increased the Center's promotional staff. On the recommendation of Harry Ashmore, he appointed John L. Perry as the director of development, freeing Donald McDonald to devote his energies to the Center dialogues and to the projected conference on the problems and possibilities of the universities.

Perry came to the Center from the Department of Commerce in Washington, where he had been a principal deputy to Under Secretary LeRoy Collins, with responsibilities in the Commerce Department's personnel, budgeting, and administrative functions. Before that, Perry had been a reporter on the Buffalo *Evening News*, the Tampa *Tribune*, and the St. Petersburg *Times*, and had been a speech writer on Kennedy's campaign staff in 1960 and Johnson's in 1964.

With Perry's approval, Peter Tagger of Los Angeles, a direct-mail marketing specialist, was employed by the Center as a consultant to help produce plans to add many thousands of people to the Center's lists of supporters. Tagger later became the director of the Center's membership services, and had a significant part in the growth of the membership.

The Center's convocation on "The University in America" was announced to the press and the public in a statement released on March 13, 1966. Hutchins said that the convocation would be addressed to the "main issues" affecting university life, including "organization and control of the university," "the question of whether university education can simultaneously be massive, specialized and liberal"; the "relation of the university to society"; and the "quality and quantity of teaching."

The changes that concerned Hutchins particularly were the explosive growth of universities, huge government subsidies for research in fields of interest to the government, heavy emphasis on publication of research results, student demands for voices in university policies, the decline of liberal arts education, the splintering of knowledge into "ever-narrower specializations," and the pressures on university presidents to provide new programs for special interest groups.

"The Center is under no illusion that any one convocation can wholly carry off so formidable an undertaking," Hutchins admitted. "Such an undertaking is a process; a convocation is an event. But we think it is worth starting the process with such an event."

Invitations to attend the convocation at the Beverly Hilton Hotel in Los Angeles were sent to university and college presidents all over the United States, to business and government leaders personally and professionally interested in "the condition of university education," and to other leaders in "the intellectual community of the nation." Editors and writers specializing in educational matters for newspapers and magazines, as well as representatives of radio and television, were also invited.

Hundreds of university administrators, faculty members, trustees, educators, and students in many fields attended the convocation. At the opening dinner on May 8, Justice Douglas welcomed all the participants, Hutchins defined the issues, and Walter Lippmann spoke on the topic "The University and the Human Condition."

Eleanor B. Stevenson of the Fund's board presided at the first formal session on the morning of Monday, May 9, introducing Clark Kerr, president of the University of California, who presented his ideas on the subject "Towards a More Perfect University," and Rosemary Park, president of Barnard College, who had spoken with such mournful eloquence at the Center's 1963 conference on the prospects for democracy, offered her views on the idea of "community" in the university.

Three critics were given an opportunity to shoot at the views offered by Kerr and Park. J. Douglas Brown, a dean of the faculty at Princeton; John Weiss, associate professor of history at Wayne State University; and W. H. Ferry of the Center staff made some cogent comments and sharp observations. Ferry aimed most of his shafts at Kerr, who continued to advocate what he called "the multiversity" to meet the needs of a society with many requirements for education.

Monsignor Francis J. Lally, another Fund board member, chaired the luncheon session. The only speaker was Sir Eric Ashby, master of Clare College, Cambridge University, who spoke with English elegance on the subject "The Future of the University Ideal."

The afternoon session was divided between a discussion of the roles of regents and trustees—with the speakers including J. R. Parten, former chairman of the University of Texas board of regents; Lyle M. Spencer, chairman of the board of trustees of Roosevelt University in Chicago; Arnold Grant, a trustee of Syracuse University; and Terry Sanford, former governor of North Carolina—and the rights and responsibilities of students, with the speakers ranging from Saul Landau, a graduate student at the University of California, to Martin Kenner, a student at the New School for Social Research, and Margaret Levi, a sophomore at Bryn Mawr College. John Seeley, professor of sociology at Brandeis University, delivered a statement that was critical of the trustees and sympathetic to the students.

Chester Carlson presided at the morning session on May 10, the final day of the convocation, with attention at this session pointed at the place of science in the university and the possible effects of federal research expenditures on the university's independence. The main speakers were Detlev Bronk, president of the Rockefeller Institute, and Harrison Brown, professor of geochemistry at the California Institute of Technology. Stringfellow Barr, former president of St. John's College; I. I. Rabi, Nobel prize-winning physics professor at Columbia University; and Linus Pauling, Nobel laureate and Center staff member, formed the critics' panel.

The largest headlines and the widest news coverage of the conference came at the luncheon gathering on May 10, when Senator J. William Fulbright—former Rhodes scholar and chairman of the Senate Foreign Relations Committee—discussed the topic "The University and the Requirements of Democracy."

Fulbright attacked what he described as slavish adherence to government policy by the universities. He said that both the universities and the government, closely linked in developing technology, "seem . . . to have accepted the idea that the avoidance of nuclear war is merely a matter of skillful crisis management."

If that attitude persisted, Fulbright regarded an "all-out nuclear war" as almost inevitable: "Sooner or later, the law of averages will turn against us. An extremist or incompetent will come to power in one major country or another, or a misjudgment will be made by some perfectly competent official, or things will just get out of hand without anyone being precisely responsible, as happened in 1914."

Fulbright was fully aware by then that he had been misled by Lyndon Johnson in 1964. He urged the universities to be intelligently critical of such issues as the war in Vietnam. Referring to a statement by Secretary of State Dean Rusk that there was "something wrong, not with the United States but with the other side," Fulbright declared: "The universities must not fail to ask as well what is wrong with our side—remembering that the highest devotion we can give is not to our country as it is, but to a concept of what we would like it to be."

The university convocation concluded with an address by Jacques Barzun, provost of Columbia, entitled "The University as the Beloved Republic," and observations and reflections by Robert Hutchins. Comments were made by Jacob Bronowski, of the Salk Institute for Biological Studies;

Clarence Faust, vice president of the Ford Foundation; Philip Selznick, professor of sociology at the University of California at Berkeley, and Scott Buchanan, consultant to the Center.

Newspapers in all parts of the country carried articles on the ideas offered by the notable speakers. ABC had an hour-long discussion program on the topic "The University in America," using participants from the convocation. The California educational television network had broadcasts on the proceedings each day, and excerpts were transmitted to millions of viewers by educational stations in many cities.

The Los Angeles *Times* summarized the conference in a column published on May 15:

> For three days last week in Beverly Hills, prominent educators and a few prominent non-educators spoke before 1,400 other educators in a convention of the nation's academic elite called to consider "The University in America." The Center for the Study of Democratic Institutions in Santa Barbara sponsored the meeting and its president, Dr. Robert M. Hutchins, hoped it would start this argument: Should a university be "a real intellectual community" and nothing else, or should it be a "vocational training center," providing skills ranging from harvesting of crops to making more deadly nuclear bombs?
>
> Dr. Hutchins himself touched off the argument. He proposed that universities junk their freshman and sophomore classes and their vocational training, and concentrate on supplying intellectual leadership.
>
> Somewhat supporting this stand was columnist Walter Lippmann, who said that because modern man—in his search for truth —has turned away from kings, clergymen, commissars and bureaucrats, "he is left, for better or worse, with the professors."
>
> Said Hutchins: "The university could fashion the mind of the age. Now it is the other way around: the demands of the age are fashioning the mind of the university."
>
> Noted historian Jacques Barzun, provost at Columbia, said the university is too entangled with the world around it. In the name of "public service," he said, the worldly university practices "genteel prostitution." Professors profit in money and prestige in sponsored research; and, said Barzun, they are busy with "conference trips, project writing, and budget making," not with scholarly work. (This criticism had been voiced nearly two years ago by students and others during the Free Speech Movement at Berkeley).
>
> Harrison Brown, noted geochemist at Cal Tech, said that government pressure for "results" in its multi-billion-dollar re-

search programs has produced a "massive pursuit of the obvious in American science today." Brown urged that a greater share of research money be spent on basic research—research undertaken without thought of specific applicability.

In another section of the Los Angeles *Times*, a columnist named Art Seidenbaum had taken the occasion of the university convocation to salute the Center under a headline reading: "Knowledge—Making It Pay." In his article, Seidenbaum recalled that he had once feigned outrage at the Center's gall in trying to make people think about so many problems. He had written: "In this suspicious world, what could be more suspect than a collection of scholars thinking free on somebody else's money about everybody's problems?"

"Some people misread my sentiments as sarcasm," Seidenbaum said. "One friendly columnist called to congratulate me for exposing the menace of the men from Santa Barbara. On the contrary, I said, I found them creatures of excellence, doing the talking that had to be done so the rest of us might have a clear notion of the survival questions. Somewhere up my cheek, my tongue had obviously twisted, ambiguously."

Seidenbaum declared that in those days—in 1963, when the Center had held a symposium in Beverly Hills on the "Prospects for Democracy"—most citizens "had only the wooliest notions of what the Center was about, and uncertainty may breed hostility. . . ."

Two weeks after the completion of the university conference, Hutchins and Ashmore flew to Geneva for a gathering at the Palais des Nations to continue the exploration of possibilities for a second *Pacem in Terris* conclave. They met there with Alastair Buchan, director of the Institute for Strategic Studies, England; Jean Chauvel, diplomatic Counselor to the government of France, who had been in Peking and Hanoi; Mrs. Kiyoko Cho, professor, International Christian University, Tokyo; Xavier Deniau, ranking Gaullist member of the Foreign Affairs Committee of the French National Assembly; Justice Douglas, chairman of the Fund's board; Mohamed El-Zayyat, undersecretary for foreign affairs, United Arab Republic; Albert Gore, United States senator from Tennessee; N. N. Inozemtsev, a Russian editor who had become the director of the Institute of World Economics and International Relations, Soviet Academy of Sciences, Moscow; Manfred Lachs, professor of international relations, Warsaw University; George S. McGovern, United States senator from South Dakota; Pierre Mendes-France; Dmitri D. Murayyev, secretary-general of the Institute of Soviet-American Relations, Moscow; C. V. Narasimhan, chef de cabinet, United Nations; Luis Quintanilla, a Mexican diplomat and professor of international relations, University of Mexico; Edgar Snow, author of *Red*

Star over China, who knew Mao Tse-tung and other leaders of Communist China; and Sonn Voeunsai, ambassador of Cambodia to France.

Ashmore reported later: "Hutchins put two questions to them: How could we persuade Peking to participate in *Pacem in Terris II?* If we could not, was there any point in going ahead? The first question drew a variety of suggestions, all admittedly doubtful. The answer to the second was yes. And the participants of their own motion added an item to the agenda that was to determine the character of the second convocation. . . .

"The senior Russian at Geneva, N. N. Inotzemtsev, observed that while those present might agree among themselves that Vietnam was only one among urgent issues of coexistence, the world no longer thought so; the fighting in Southeast Asia was bound to dominate any program we might devise for *Pacem in Terris II.* This suggested a concentrated effort to bring Hanoi into the convocation, and thereby to initiate a direct American contact that conceivably could open the way for diplomats to make a formal move toward peace negotiations.

"The three Frenchmen responded with enthusiasm, and they bore impressive credentials. Pierre Mendes-France headed the French government at the time of the [French] defeat at Dien Bien Phu and the subsequent Geneva Accords; Ambassador Chauvel was an old China hand who had recently returned from Peking via Hanoi; and Xavier Deniau had served in then-French Indochina as a foreign service officer. They agreed to arrange with the North Vietnamese legation in Paris to transmit to Hanoi a letter suggesting a meeting with representatives of the Center."

Several months later, Hutchins received a letter from Ho Chi Minh, saying that a meeting was not possible at that time but indicating that it might be arranged at a later date. Luis Quintanilla, the Mexican diplomat, who was on good terms with the Chinese government in Peking and Ho Chi Minh's government in Hanoi, then took invitations to both governments.

When he reached Peking, he did not find the Chinese foreign minister, Chen Yi, receptive to the idea of Chinese participation in a peace conference. Chen Yi informed him that a third world war was bound to occur and that China would be a victor in such a conflict. He did, however, give Quintanilla permission to go to Hanoi from Peking. In Hanoi, Ho Chi Minh told him that a visit to North Vietnam by Center representatives could be considered.

The Center designated two members of its board of directors—Ashmore and William Baggs, editor of the Miami *News*—to go to Hanoi. Their prospective journey was approved by the State Department, which seemed to welcome an opportunity to open another channel of communication with the Hanoi government. They were asked to make inquiries on several questions in Hanoi on behalf of "high officials" in the American government.

When Hutchins and Ashmore returned from Geneva in the summer of

1966, they talked with a number of the directors of the Fund and the Center (the same board had the corporate responsibility for the Center), and the plans for the second *Pacem in Terris* convocation began to develop rapidly. John Perry was assigned to aid Ashmore in handling the administrative organization of the conference.

In July and August a dozen meetings of the Center staff were devoted to discussions of chapters of a projected book on the possible contributions of the behavior sciences to the avoidance of war and the maintenance of peace. These chapters were written by a visiting scholar, Jerome Frank, who was at the Center on leave from the Johns Hopkins Medical School, where he had been chief of the department of psychiatry. The book was later published under the title of *Survival and Sanity.*

Participating vigorously in the August dialogues was a new Center staff member who stimulated and sometimes irritated his colleagues and attracted more publicity than any of the others. James A. Pike, the controversial clergyman who had been the dean of the Cathedral of St. John the Divine in New York before his election as the Bishop of the Episcopal diocese of California, had resigned from his position in San Francisco to become a resident scholar in Santa Barbara. He had arrived on August 1.

Pike, who was an uncompromising advocate of civil rights and civil liberties, had been one of the vocal defenders of the Fund for the Republic when it had been under the onslaught of the House Un-American Activities Committee, the American Legion, and Senator Josephy McCarthy. He had been keenly interested in the Center from the time of its establishment in Santa Barbara in 1959, and had encouraged wealthy people in San Francisco to donate money to the Center.

Pike was a restless man with an unconventional style of life. He had been buffeted by opposition to his policies and his activities in San Francisco and deeply shaken by the suicide of his son. He had informed Hutchins that he was frustrated and fatigued by his administrative battles, and that he would welcome a chance to take part in the relatively calm and scholarly life at the Center. In the spring of 1966, after consulting members of the staff, Hutchins had invited him to join the group on Eucalyptus Hill.

In a release to the press in the middle of July 1966 the Center announced that Pike had been appointed to "the Center's permanent staff" along with John R. Seeley, who had left a tenured position as chairman of the sociology department at Brandeis University to take a place at the Center's table. The Center announcement also disclosed that two other notable scholars were at the Center for the summer months—Dr. Frank and Stringfellow Barr, former president of St. John's college and author of authoritative books on Greece and Rome, who had been a speaker at the Center's convocation on the university.

Pike told the reporters who interviewed him that he would continue to be "a bishop of the Episcopal church" and that he would be "an assisting bishop in the Diocese of California and an honorary canon of Grace Cathedral in San Francisco.''

Pike was a graduate in arts and law from the University of Southern California. He had been an attorney for four years for the U.S. Securities Exchange Commission and had been on the faculty of the George Washington University law school. While in the navy in World War II, he had decided to become a priest. He had been ordained in 1944 and had served as chaplain at Columbia University and as head of that university's department of religion before he became dean of the Cathedral of St. John the Divine.

While he had been dean of the cathedral in New York, Pike had been featured on a national television program carried by ABC. He was in demand as a lectureer on college campuses. He had produced articles and books on federal, judicial, and administrative procedures and on the principles of the Christian religion. His background of wide experience made Hutchins and his associates hopeful that Pike would bring valuable perspectives to many of the Center's sessions.

Stringfellow Barr, who stayed on at the Center for several years after the summer of 1966, had a powerful and penetrating mind. He had gained international attention at St. John's College for his work in collaboration with Scott Buchanan, abolishing ''elective courses'' and making the Great Books the core of the college's studies. Barr had been a Rhodes Scholar at Oxford, a faculty member at the University of Virginia, and an editor of the *Virginia Quarterly Review.* He had originated the CBS radio program *''Invitation to Learning.''*

Seeley was born in Canada, and he had obtained his basic education in England and Germany and his undergraduate and graduate studies in sociology at the University of Chicago. He had taught at the College of the University of Chicago and in the departments of psychiatry and political economy at the University of Toronto, at York University, and at Brandeis. He was a Fellow of the American Association for the Advancement of Science, the American Sociological Association, the Center for Advanced Study in Behavioral-Sciences, and the American Association for Humanistic Psychology. He had been an associate editor of the *American Sociological Review* and was the author or coauthor of several books, including *Crestwood Heights, The Alcohol Language,* and *The Americanization of the Unconscious.*

In the summer and autumn of 1966, Hutchins relied on Harry Ashmore to carry forward the plans for the second *Pacem in Terris* convocation. While these plans were maturing—and while Ashmore and Bill Baggs were preparing for a trip to Hanoi—Hutchins presided at a series of dialogues at the Center on a wide variety of topics. Visiting scholars came and departed during these weeks.

Donald McDonald of the Center staff presented several papers on public affairs reporting. Bishop Pike initiated a discussion of the possible "discorrelation" between people's involvement in the church and their social and ethical attitudes. Yitzhak Ben Aron of the Israeli parliament talked about planned and private economies in a democracy.

Rexford Tugwell had two meetings on "The Emerging Constitution." There were two discussions of a paper by Stringfellow Barr on the topic "Consulting the Romans," exploring an analogy between the imperial Romans and Americans under the Johnson administration. Joseph Tussman gave a report on the Experimental College that Tussman and other faculty members of the University of California had started in Berkeley.

While these and other meetings were being held, the Center's staff economist—Stanley Sheinbaum—was worried about inflation. In two dialogues, Sheinbaum examined the economic effects of the Vietnam War. The monetary stability that had existed in the United States for six years had been destroyed by huge federal expenditures for the Vietnam conflict. President Johnson had told his Council of Economic Advisers that he could not get Congress to approve a tax increase, which might have checked inflation; actually, he had given the congressional leaders inaccurate figures on the costs of the war, and they had a surge of inflation: prices rose twice as fast in 1966 as they did in 1965, and no end seemed to be in sight.

The Center was one of the first educational institutions in the United States to become concerned about the economic and political dangers of an inflationary spiral. The fact that government officials did not act in time to stem the inflation—or to mitigate the economic consequences of the Vietnam War—was disturbing to the scholars at the Center and added weight to the arguments of Tugwell and others who felt that the whole constitutional system had to be revised or replaced.

In September 1966 the attendance of many wealthy and powerful people at at testimonial dinner for Paul G. Hoffman demonstrated again that members of the Center's board were widely known and respected. Former Presidents Eisenhower and Truman were on the honorary committee for the Hoffman dinner. Speakers included U Thant; Averell Harriman, United States ambassador-at-large; John Cowles, publisher of the Minneapolis *Star* and *Tribune*; Hutchins; and Elmo Roper, who served as general chairman.

Among the sponsors were Chief S. O. Adebo, Nigeria's representative at the United Nations; Mr. and Mrs. David Astor; Eugene Black, of the World Bank; McGeorge Bundy, President Johnson's national security assistant; Senator Clifford Case; Erwin Canham, editor of the *Christian Science Monitor*; Alfred W. Friendly of the Washington *Post*; General Alfred M. Gruenther; Roscoe Drummond, columnist for the New York *Herald Tribune*; Chet Huntley of NBC; Sir Robert and Lady Jackson of Britain; Senator Jacob Javits; Douglas Fairbanks, Jr.; John Jessup of *Life* magazine; Walter Lippmann; Ralph McGill, editor of the Atlanta *Constitution*;

James Reston, of the *New York Times*; Earl Warren, chief justice of the United States Supreme Court; Eric Sevareid of CBS; and others with notable influence in American life.

In 1966 the Center grew in many ways—in the number of its members, in the attention paid to its publications and convocations, in the quality and size of its staff, and in its plans for new projects. With the beneficent generosity of Chester Carlson—an "angel" who gave large amounts without telling the Center to do what he wanted—the fear of financial exhaustion had been removed.

The total receipts of the Center in its fiscal year 1966—the period from October 1, 1965, to September 30, 1966—were $3,305,057, including Carlson's gift of Xerox stock worth more than $1 million. For the first time since the Center had begun its operations in 1959, there was an excess of receipts over expenses. Its expenses in the 1966 fiscal year were $1,455,153, so the surplus of income for that year totaled $1,849,904.

The number of contributing members in the 1966 fiscal period was 7,441, an increase of 1,721 over the number in the preceding year. With the advent of a Center magazine—which was planned for publication in 1967—and a direct-mail campaign for new members financed by the Carlson gift, it was anticipated that the number of new Center supporters would rise rapidly in future years.

In this atmosphere of affluence—or anticipated affluence—it is not surprising that the Center released a pamphlet in December 1966 entitled *Looking Forward: The Abundant Society*. The pamphlet was based on papers prepared for a conference in which the participants assumed that the United States was capable of providing reasonable subsistence for all its people, that serious consideration would be given to a "guaranteed annual income" in some form, and that there would be increasing concern about "the quality and direction of American institutions."

The questions put to the participants were: What new rules might people adopt to govern themselves and their ingenuity? What changes might occur in values and customs? What were likely to be the new functions of education? What political, economic, and cultural effects might replacement of scarcity by abundance and the elimination of poverty produce? How much planning might be needed for such a society?

The opening statements in the pamphlet were written by Walter A. Weisskopf, chairman of the department of economics at Roosevelt University in Chicago, and Raghavan Iyer, a political philosopher from India who had become a visiting consultant to the Center and was a faculty member of the University of California in Santa Barbara. W. H. Ferry, who had written a paper entitled *Caught on the Horn of Plenty* organized the conference.

Sharply varying comments on the promises and perils of "the abundant society" were made by the participants, who included Michael Davis of the Students for a Democratic Society, a radical student group; Irving

Kaplan, program director of the U.S. Naval Personnel Research Activity, San Diego; David W. Kean, of the IBM Company office in Sunnyvale, California; Samuel W. Allen, general counsel of the Community Relations Service, U.S. Department of Justice, Washington D.C.; Linus Pauling; Harry Ashmore; Hallock Hoffman; Harvey Wheeler, and other members of the Center's staff.

While it seemed quixotic to some critics—who deprecated the issuance of a report on such a conference while the United States was wasting much of its economic strength in Southeast Asia—the *Looking Forward* pamphlet did strike a positive response from many people who thought the Vietnam War would be terminated in a few months and who believed that the United States would then resume its economic growth with more and more goods available for everybody.

Three weeks after the release of this pamphlet Harry Ashmore and Bill Baggs flew to Vietnam, carrying the Center's quest for peace into the complexities of the struggle there. Their primary mission was to invite North Vietnam to send representatives to the second *Pacem in Terris* convocation, but they also hoped to have a part in ending the war.

20

*The Center's peace efforts are
blocked, and angry voices
are raised against it*

WHEN TWO DIRECTORS OF THE CENTER flew 10,000 miles to North Vietnam in January 1967, it was hard for some members of the Center staff to understand why that trip was necessary. The Center had already proved that dialogue between people with different ideologies was possible. The two directors who made the journey were well-known journalists, and their trip added much information to the world's knowledge of what American bombing was doing to North Vietnam, but they were not professional diplomats and they were not scholars who had devoted years to Vietnam's problems.

Ashmore and Baggs were ebullient men, enormously self-confident, full of good will, aware of the traps into which they might fall yet hopeful that they might accomplish something that the diplomats and the experts had been unable to do. They had been impressed by the response to the *Pacem in Terris* convocation, and they were sure that a second convocation had to deal with the growing war in Vietnam. And they were willing to believe that their direct contact with Ho Chi Minh and his ministers might open a new path that would lead to formal negotiations by the diplomats on both sides.

Both men were Southerners, both were lifelong members of the Democratic party, both were sympathetic to the aims of President Lyndon Johnson, both felt personal obligations to do what they could to help the president shift the struggle in Vietnam from military conflict to the bargaining table. Both had been informed by leaders of the United Nations that the war in Vietnam might break down the East-West detente and bring the world again to the brink of nuclear destruction.

Under the leadership of Hutchins—and with the approval of the board of directors—the Center had moved a long way from the original programs of the Fund for the Republic. Hutchins had acknowledged that the search for peace was incidental to the Center's main purpose, which he had defined as "clarifying the basic issues," but the Center had been called upon to help humanity and that call could not be ignored.

There were hundreds of private organizations dedicated to the fostering of better international relations, but none of them had created the repercussions on many levels that had followed the *Pacem in Terris* meeting in New York. The bringing together of religious and political leaders, the encounter of Soviet spokesmen and American senators, the exchanges of ideas between representatives of many viewpoints with utter candor had started new currents of thought flowing warmly through the ice of the cold war. Those currents had reached Vietnam as well as other countries.

In Hanoi, Ho Chi Minh and his colleagues gave Ashmore and Baggs a courteous welcome. Ho indicated that his government would probably send representatives to the second *Pacem in Terris* conference, scheduled to be held at the end of May 1967 at the United Nations European headquarters in Geneva. He reiterated what he had said previously in public statements and in private communications to UN Secretary General U Thant and to a Canadian diplomat, Chester Ronning: "If the United States wants to begin talks with the Democratic Republic of Vietnam your government knows what to do—stop the bombing."

The Hanoi government had repeatedly listed four conditions for negotiations with the United States: withdrawal of American troops; acceptance of the military provisions of the Geneva accords; settlement of internal affairs in South Vietnam "in accordance with the program of the National Liberation Front (Vietcong)"; and "peaceful reunification of North and South without foreign interference."

In his conversation with Ashmore and Baggs, Ho Chi Minh gave them the impression that all four of these points were not absolute requirements for the beginning of negotiations. He told them that the one essential step was the cessation of the American bombing. Ho declared that he sought friendly relationships with the American people and that he would be happy to greet Johnson in Hanoi "if he came in peace."

Ashmore and Baggs hurried to Washington and gave Ho's messages to Undersecretary of State Nicholas Katzenbach, McGeorge Bundy of Johnson's staff, and Averell Harriman, former ambassador and former governor of New York, who had been assigned by Johnson to give all his time to possible arrangements for peace in Vietnam.

In their book entitled *Mission to Hanoi*, Ashmore and Baggs recorded:

> We had brought back nothing that could be described as a hard proposition from Hanoi, but in context it appeared that Ho had met all the stated American conditions for opening negotiations except a guarantee to close the border between North and South Vietnam in return for a cessation of the bombing. Privately,

most Washington insiders conceded that the so-called "infiltration" guarantee was an unrealistic demand under the circumstances. The North Vietnamese could hardly agree to halt the maintenance and supply of fighting forces dependent upon them unless they were prepared to leave them wholly at the mercy of the massive American expeditionary force roaring through the countryside on its "search and destroy" mission. . . . In any case, the way was wide open for a further probe—either through us, or directly through diplomatic channels—without any risk of compromising the official U.S. position. . . .

We had an attentive audience, and in the beginning no reason to doubt that what we said was being taken seriously. The Department's Vietnamese experts manfully swallowed their irritation at having persons they regarded as diplomatic amateurs instruct them in their own specialties, and if any of the professional hardliners entertained the notion that we were innocent dupes who had been taken in by a wily old Red he did not voice it in our presence.

However, there were passing indications that our report was being received with something less than acclaim in precincts beyond those where we were immediately engaged. We did not expect to be greeted as returning heroes, but we thought we would arouse some simple curiosity as the only Americans who had talked politics privately with Ho Chi Minh since the attack on his country was launched more than two years before. We were, it is true, functioning at the highest level in the State Department, but it also began to be evident that we were limited to a narrowly proscribed circuit. Secretary of State Rusk, although we passed him in the corridor outside the Under Secretary's office, never stopped in to ask a single question of his own. . . .

We began to suspect that Katzenbach might be telling us something by indirection with his constant reminders that we must not be impatient, that it took time to get a reading on such delicate matters, that we really didn't appreciate the kind of problems the government would have with its Asian allies if it began to move toward negotiations, and that, after all, the Department had other channels available to it and was constantly checking other sources. He even resorted to the hoary cliché with which foreign service officers traditionally brush off unwelcome views—a man can't possibly have a valid opinion on a diplomatic matter unless he enjoys the privilege of reading the secret cables. This was doubtless true, we replied, unless he had been out talking to the people the men who sent the secret cables ought to be talking to, but can't reach.

The pressures brought upon Johnson by generals and admirals were cited by Harriman. The president had ordered pauses in the bombing several times. Every time, the American military chiefs had brought the president evidence of the troops and supplies moving into South Vietnam from the north. Harriman said it was obvious that no president could "leave his own boys at the mercy of the enemy." If Ho's government would stop the stream of men and supplies pouring down the Ho Chi Minh trail into the south, then the peacemakers would be able to counter the arguments made to the president by the American generals.

Harriman told Ashmore and Baggs that the plight of the president was made more difficult by the barrages of criticisms laid down by intellectuals connected with the Center and other educational institutions. Harriman thought that such critics should stop talking about "getting out of the war" and support "those who were trying to keep the war from getting any bigger."

Ashmore and Baggs had agreed to be cautious in their public statements and to refrain from any indication that they were attempting to participate in negotiations with Ho's government on the terms of a Vietnam settlement. When they were asked to testify at a closed session of the Senate Foreign Relations Committee by Senator Fulbright, the chairman, and by a group of members of the House of Representatives, they were requested by Undersecretary Katzenbach not to testify. They turned down the invitation believing that diplomatic conversations with other governments or the North Vietnamese might be under way.

On January 25, when they had heard nothing more from the State Department, Baggs dispatched a personal and confidential letter to Harriman, asking for action:

> It is our thinking, from the experience and conversations we had in Hanoi, that a response of some nature should be sent in order to keep this channel open. Perhaps it should be so informal that we could simply pass along our impressions and maintain for both parties this rather flexible and uncommitting position which is possible with unofficial persons.
>
> In any event, we are confident that the appropriate persons in Hanoi do expect some kind of word, private or otherwise, to what we regarded as the next possible thing to a hard and formal proposal. We do not believe we can overemphasize our conviction that a response, in some form, would be most useful in many ways at this time.

Senator Fulbright, who was a personal friend of Ashmore and Baggs, learned from Baggs that the two Center directors had not received an opportunity to see Johnson after their return from Hanoi. Fulbright urged Johnson to get a "first-hand account on such a vital matter from a couple of supposedly competent reporters." Johnson replied: "I'd like to see them, Bill, but you know I can't talk with everybody who's been over there talking with Ho Chi Minh.'' When this conversation became known to journalists later, David Brinkley, of NBC, commented that Johnson was evidently referring to ''a multitude of two.''

Fulbright's words to the President did, however, soon produce a request from the State Department for another visit to Washington by Ashmore and Baggs. Johnson telephoned Fulbright and declared that he didn't want Fulbright to ''get the idea that Ashmore and Baggs weren't being taken seriously, and that his administration wasn't prepared to follow up any opening that might lead to negotiations.'' The president said he had issued instructions to all officials to be available, but he thought they would get along best with Undersecretary Katzenbach—''who, he noted, was likely to be disposed toward peace since he once had been a prisoner of war himself.''

At the president's request, Fulbright attended the next meeting between the two Center directors and the officials representing the president. The session was held in Katzenbach's office, with Harriman and Bundy present. Fulbright declared that he didn't think the meeting would accomplish anything.

''The trouble is that I believe we ought to negotiate a settlement of this war in Vietnam, and you don't,'' Fulbright said. ''You're all committed to a military victory, and all this talk about being willing to go to the table doesn't mean a damned thing and you know it.''

According to Ashmore and Baggs, Fulbright then expressed his feeling of frustration and disgust:

> The State Department goes right on with the same old bankrupt foreign policy, making the same mistakes over and over. All you people over here think of is power, and so you have this country throwing its weight around all over the world, and if anybody points out that this is not only immoral but it isn't even working you say they're isolationist, or unpatriotic, or maybe both. I say you're caught in a trap and you can't get out because you won't do the one thing you've got to do—admit you're wrong and start off in a new direction.

Fulbright made a pessimistic prediction:

> I'm prepared to bet that you're going to prove me right by hanging so many conditions on whatever reply you send to Ho Chi Minh you'll make sure he'll turn you down, and then you'll use that as an excuse to step up the bombing even more.

Katzenbach, Harriman, and Bundy insisted that they favored peace in Vietnam just as much as Senator Fulbright did. Katzenbach said the senator seemed to feel there was only one side to the question of negotiations. Harriman reminded him that there were hard problems that couldn't be swept aside.

Bundy offered a draft of a letter that his assistants had prepared as a possible communication to Ho Chi Minh. Ashmore and Baggs thought it was "unduly turgid," and Bundy agreed that it could be revised. The two Center directors had an appointment with Secretary of Defense McNamara and promised to work on a revision after they returned from the Pentagon.

Ashmore and Baggs left the State Department with Fulbright, who was still blazing with indignation. He told them:

> I've been up against these fellows, one way or another, for the past 26 years, and the one lesson I have learned is that you can't trust them. It's mutual, of course—they don't trust you, either, and they'll tell you that's the first rule of diplomacy.
>
> We talk about the Russians acting on the principle that the end justifies the means, but let me tell you that you have just been in the ultimate citadel of that policy. These State Department people figure they're entitled to use you, in any way they see fit, to further what they call the national interest, but the national interest is whatever they decide it is and can sell the President.
>
> Their big weapon is secrecy; they let you have just as much of the pertinent information as serves their purpose and hold back the rest. And you'll find the classification system gets some rapid revision when you cross them and they begin leaking out whatever they've got that can serve to discredit you.

It became evident that Johnson's use of Fulbright to put over the Tonkin Gulf Resolution in the Senate in 1964 had distressed Fulbright severely:

> As chairman of the Foreign Relations Committee I took the lead in putting that Resolution through the Senate, and they've been using it ever since to justify escalating the war. I never would have endorsed it if I had been given the facts, nor would a majority of the Senators have supported it. You can call that dissembling, or you can call it lying—but it comes out the same way. It's a hell of a way to run a foreign policy.

When Ashmore and Baggs returned to the State Department, they worked with Bundy on a careful revision of the proposed letter to Ho Chi Minh. After the second draft had been approved by Bundy, they gave him an opportunity to clear it with Secretary Rusk and the White House. On the following day, they received a final draft with a few small changes. This draft—which they believed to have been approved at the highest levels in the American government—was delivered to them at Senator Fulbright's house, and a copy was given to Fulbright.

Ashmore mailed the letter to Ho Chi Minh at Dulles International Airport in Washington on February 5. Ashmore and Baggs did not know at the time that President Johnson was sending another letter to the Hanoi government through Moscow, laying down stiff conditions for negotiations in terms that Ho Chi Minh would not accept.

The State Department has expressed itself as most grateful for your thoughtful approach to the possibility of an ultimate settlement of the hostilities between the United States and the Democratic Republic of Vietnam [Ashmore said in his letter to Ho].

In our several discussions with senior officials of the State Department they took occasion to reiterate points we believe are already known to you. They emphasized that the U.S. remains prepared for secret discussions at any time, without conditions, and that such discussions might cover the whole range of topics relevant to a peaceful settlement. They reiterated that the Geneva Accords might be the framework for a peaceful solution.

They expressed particular interest in your suggestion to us that private talks could begin provided the U.S. stopped bombing your country, and ceased introducing additional U.S. troops into Vietnam. They expressed the opinion that some reciprocal restraint to indicate that neither side intended to use the occasion of the talks for military advantage would provide tangible evidence of the good faith of all parties in the prospects for a negotiated settlement.

In the light of these concerns, they expressed great interest in any clarification of this point that you might wish to provide through a communication to us. . . .

. . . There is no doubt in our minds that the American government genuinely seeks peace. As private citizens our sole concern is in facilitating a discussion that will bring all matters at issue to official consideration. It is in this sense that we convey these comments, and invite any reply you may wish to make, which of course we would report to our government in complete discretion.

When no reply had been received from the Hanoi government by February 27, Ashmore and Baggs prepared to make another trip to Hanoi. They asked Luis Quintanilla to send a cabled message to the North Vietnamese government, saying that Ashmore and Baggs were planning to leave on March 10. On March 2 a North Vietnamese official answered by cable: "U.S.A. undertaking new serious steps of war escalation against D.R.V. Visit to Hanoi as requested by Ashmore and Baggs not opportune."

Ashmore and Baggs thought at first that the reference to "new serious steps of war escalation" meant the resumption of bombing by the United States, which had begun on February 14 after a lull of six days during the Tet lunar new year holiday. On March 21, however, Ho Chi Minh released the text of a stern letter he had received from President Johnson, which had been transmitted through Moscow and had reached Hanoi five days before the Ashmore-Baggs communication.

In this letter, Johnson said: "I am prepared to order a cessation of bombing against your country and the stopping of further augmentation of U.S. forces in South Vietnam as soon as I am assured that infiltration into South Vietnam by land and sea has stopped." Such acts of restraint on "both sides" would make it possible, Johnson asserted, "to conduct serious and private discussions leading toward an early peace."

Ho Chi Minh replied with a statement reminding Johnson that the United States had initiated the aerial attacks on North Vietnam and had sent large numbers of soldiers thousands of miles to participate in the fighting in South Vietnam. Ho said: "The United States government is entirely responsible for the critical situation in Vietnam. . . . Only after the unconditional stopping of the bombing and all other American acts of war against the Democratic Republic of Vietnam can the D.R.V. and the United States enter into conversations and discuss the questions in which both parties are interested. The Vietnamese people will never yield to force nor agree to talks under the menace of bombs."

Ashmore and Baggs regarded the dispatch of the Johnson letter at approximately the same time as the letter mailed by Ashmore to Ho Chi Minh as evidence of the same kind of duplicity by the State Department and White House officials that had angered Senator Fulbright. The two Center directors had interpreted Ho's statements to them in Hanoi as meaning that private conversations could begin when the United States stopped its bombing and refrained from sending more American troops into Vietnam. In his reply to President Johnson, Ho made it clear that this was his position.

But the Johnson letter sent on February 8—drafted after the sessions Ashmore and Baggs had with McGeorge Bundy on the preparation of the letter mailed by Ashmore on February 5—contained conditions that Ho had repeatedly rejected. In President Johnson's book *The Vantage Point*, published after he had left the White House, the Ashmore-Baggs episode was summarized in two paragraphs:

"Harry S. Ashmore and William C. Baggs, both U.S. journalists, met with Ho Chi Minh on January 12. On February 5 Baggs and Ashmore returned to Hanoi with a message similar to the official messages being exchanged in Moscow.

"Ho Chi Minh insisted that there could be no talks unless the United States stopped the bombing and stopped all reinforcements during the talks. He was adamant against any reciprocal military restraint by the D.R.V."

In 1967 Johnson was trapped by his own commitment of thousands of American troops in South Vietnam. His military advisers told him that if he halted the American bombing for a long period without a cessation of the movement of Hanoi's troops he would expose the American soldiers to the possibility of heavy casualties if the North Vietnamese launched a sudden onslaught.

In the spring of 1967, while Ashmore and Hutchins were shaping the program for the Center's second *Pacem in Terris* convocation, Ashmore and Baggs let it be known in Washington that they felt they had been badly used and deceived by the State Department and by Johnson's aides, possibly with the president's knowledge. They did not regard the letter mailed by Ashmore on February 5 as "similar to the official messages being exchanged in Moscow." They had not returned to Hanoi on February 5. When they had not received a response from Ho Chi Minh to the letter of February 5, they had planned to go back to North Vietnam, but their plans had been wrecked by Johnson's actions.

Despite the collapse of their peace efforts, Ashmore and Baggs hoped that the North Vietnamese would send representatives to the Center assembly in Geneva. The North Vietnamese had accepted—in principle—their invitation to participate in a discussion of the possible neutralization of Southeast Asia. The Saigon government headed by Marshal Nguyen Cao Ky, chief of the South Vietnamese air force, had also been invited to send spokesmen, along with Thailand, Cambodia, Laos, Indonesia, and Malaya.

The Center's invitations specified that neither side in the Vietnam War would be allowed to speak at the convocation if the other side was not represented. This stipulation, which was designed to keep the discussion from becoming a forum for propaganda by one side or the other, was criticized by the American ambassador in Bern, Switzerland, who informed Ashmore that by giving the first invitation to Ho the Center's directors had enabled the Hanoi government to keep the Saigon regime from participating in the Geneva conference simply by refusing to send a representative. Ashmore pointed out that Saigon could checkmate Hanoi in the same way.

In the weeks before the convocation was scheduled to open, State Department representatives in Geneva and elsewhere made negative remarks about the gathering. The cooperation that the White House and the State Department had given to *Pacem in Terris I* in 1965 was no longer available. That made it extremely difficult for the Center to get representatives of the Johnson administration to have anything to do with the Geneva meeting.

"We had not sought any formal blessing for the convocation from the State Department," Ashmore and Baggs wrote later. But they knew that "any open and reasonably balanced foreign policy dialogue was bound to include much criticism of the American position," so they sought participation by Johnson, Humphrey, Secretary of State Rusk, and the Secretary of Defense, Robert McNamara.

McNamara had been invited to make a major statement at the Geneva conference on the urgency of nuclear arms control and had indicated that he would like to do so. Humphrey was interested and apparently willing to go to Geneva, but he could not accept without President Johnson's approval. By April it was evident that the president did not want to have any high officials of his administration present at the *Pacem in Terris II* convocation. Humphrey and McNamara sent regrets.

George Ball, the former undersecretary of state who had been deeply troubled about American policies in Vietnam, had tentatively agreed to speak in Geneva and then decided that he could not be there. Finally Arthur Goldberg, President Johnson's representative at the United Nations, who had been a Fund board member, agreed to present the Johnson administration's case in Geneva.

On May 19, nine days before the convocation was to begin, the Hanoi government announced that it could not participate. A new American bombing offensive had started at the end of April, with explosives falling on Hanoi and Haiphong. In a cablegram, Hoang Tung of the North Vietnamese government declared: "The U.S.A. talks 'peace and negotiations' only to camouflage new extremely serious escalation steps."

When the word of Hanoi's withdrawal was received, Ashmore cabled the foreign minister of South Vietnam to tell him that there would be no Vietnamese participation in the panel on the Vietnam war in Geneva, since the North Vietnamese had dropped out. But the minister, Tran Van Do, had left for Geneva. At the conference, he asked for permission to speak to the participants from the floor. The permission was denied, on the ground that he could give only one side of the Vietnamese conflict.

While Hutchins, Ashmore, and other Center directors involved in the *Pacem in Terris II* conference were having problems with the American government and the Vietnamese, the Russians created other problems. The Soviets objected to the presence of Tran Van Do in Geneva, and announced their withdrawal at the last minute.

Ashmore ascribed the withdrawal of the Russians—who had urged that the conference be held in Geneva and had encouraged the Center to try to get Vietnamese participation—to the deterioration of American-Soviet relations due to the bombings of North Vietnam and to the Arab-Israeli crisis, which was on the verge of exploding into another war in the Middle East.

"A dialogue requires at least two sides, as Mr. Johnson's former press secretary, Bill Moyers, was to observe publicly in writing off *Pacem in Terris II* because of the last-minute shortage of Russians," Ashmore said later. "Actually, we came out pretty well on the East-West score. Able Communist-bloc participants from Poland, Czechoslovakia, East Germany, Hungary and Rumania stayed on at Geneva despite the defection of their Soviet peers, and Peking's view was set forth by Professor Paul T. K. Lin of McGill University, a Chinese-Canadian citizen sympathetic to Mao's revolution."

The difficulty that could not be overcome actually was the refusal of high officials of the Johnson administration to present the American government's position on Vietnam and other issues. Because of an emergency session of the United Nations on the Arab-Israeli confrontation, Arthur Goldberg was not able to fly to Geneva. The American senators who participated in the convocation—Joseph Clark, of Pennsylvania; Fulbright; Pell, of Rhode Island; and others—were regarded "as doves," not supporting President Johnson's policies.

Yet there were quite a few delegates at the convocation who spoke vigorously for the American government. Among them were Senator Edward Brooke of Massachusetts, Porter McKeever, executive vice president of the United Nations Association of the United States; Edmund G. Brown, Sr., the former governor of California; and others. Thanat Khoman, the foreign minister of Thailand, strongly defended American actions in Southeast Asia.

More than 300 people from seventy nations were present when the conference opened on May 28 at the Palais des Nations. Those who spoke that evening included Secretary General U Thant—by way of Telstar, the television satellite, which carried his image and voice from New York—who was unable to attend the convocation because of the special United Nations Security Council meeting on the Middle East crisis.

Solemnly admitting that humanity might be on "the brink of a third world war," U Thant refused to abandon hope: "For the participants in this important conference, this situation is in itself an opportunity and a challenge. It is a challenge not only to seek specific ways out of the present impasse, but also to consider the overall international situation. It is an opportunity to restore international morality to the high level of the United Nations Charter, so that, even on the brink, we may pause, reflect and retreat."

At the first panel discussion, "Threats to Coexistence," participants included Senator Brooke, Galo Plaza Lasso, the former president of Ecuador; Arsene Usher Assouan, the foreign minister of the Ivory Coast government; Roger Garaudy, a professor of philosophy at the University of Poitiers and staff member of the Center for Marxist Studies and Research, Paris; and Brigadier General Said Uddin Khan of Pakistan, a former officer of the United Nations Security Forces, who presided.

"Peaceful coexistence cannot be a futile attempt to immobilize the world," Garaudy said. "Peaceful coexistence does not exclude social revolutions, nor movements of national liberation by colonialized or dependent people. Coexistence implies only that revolutions and counterrevolutions shall not be exported. Each country must find that the laws of its own internal development are respected."

The panel discussion "Intervention: The Case of Vietnam" was chaired by Chester A. Ronning, a diplomat who had served as Canada's ambassador in India. Ronning explained that no Vietnamese faction would be heard, since North Vietnam and the National Liberation Front (Viet Cong) had refused invitations.

Panel members included Princess Tiao Moune Souvanna Phouma, of Laos; Sonn Voeunsai, of Cambodia, ambassador to France; Thanat Khoman, the foreign minister of Thailand; Nugroho, of Indonesia, ambassador to North Vietnam; Jean Chavel, ambassador-at-large of France; Marian Dobrosielski, counselor to the foreign minister of Poland; and M. J. Desai, of India, who had been chairman of the first International Commission for Vietnam.

Princess Phouma called for a settlement based on the Geneva Accords of 1954. Sonn Voeunsai asserted that the United States had made it impossible for the Geneva agreements to become effective. He said that peace could be attained by "immediate, final and unconditional cessation of active war by the United States and their allies against the entire territory of Vietnam and by the return to the Geneva agreements."

"Why should it be impossible for the non-Communist world to coexist with a Communist Vietnam?" Ambassador Nugroho demanded. "After all, we have been able to coexist and even cooperate with a Communist Yugoslavia and a Communist Eastern Europe for a long time."

When other participants in the convocation were given a chance to voice their ideas on Vietnam, two United States senators and the Rev. Martin Luther King, Jr., stood up at once.

"I criticize America because I love her and because I want to see her stand as the moral example of the world," Dr. King said. "Since the United States is the most powerful nation in the world and superbly equipped to take the risk for peace, I hope that this conference will call upon her to take the initiative to end this onerous war in Vietnam."

Senator Claiborne Pell, of Rhode Island, a member of the Foreign Relations Committee, reminded the members of the convocation that although many harsh things had been said about the United States, its record for peacekeeping since World War II had been a generally good one.

"Until man is more perfect, or until we live under a world system of enforcible law, frictions will exist between nations and between men," Senator Pell said. "Our job here is to turn the torrent of words that will come out of this Convocation into a sluice that will turn a little bit the wheel of progress towards peace."

Senator Joseph Clark, of Pennsylvania, cried out from the floor: "Ladies and gentlemen, do not despair of the United States of America. . . . There are seven of us from the Congress of the United States in this convocation—two members of the House of Representatives and five members of the Senate. Most, but not all of us, are members of the Congress for Peace Through Law—an organization formed in October, 1966, to coordinate congressional concern for world peace through international cooperation, a strengthened United Nations and other steps necessary for the achievement of the United States foreign policy objective: general and complete disarmament under enforcible world law."

Many of the leaders from other countries at Geneva were not convinced that Senator Pell and Senator Clark represented the government of the United States under President Johnson. The continued bombing of

North Vietnam—on the greatest scale since World War II—seemed to these leaders from Europe, Asia, Africa, and Latin America an example of "lawlessness," a ferocious example of an attempt by a superpower to impose its will on a small nation.

In a panel devoted to a consideration of the future, "Beyond Coexistence," the chairman was Vladimir Bakaric, a member of the federal assembly of Yugoslavia. Participants included Senator Fulbright; Prince Jean de Broglie, a member of the French national assembly; Doudou Thiam, minister of state for foreign affairs, Senegal; and Professor Paul Lin from McGill University, Montreal, Canada, a Chinese-Canadian friend of Mao Tse-tung.

Bakaric said that Yugoslavia had "adopted the principle of active, peaceful coexistence as the basis of its foreign policy in 1948, a time when it was possible for Stalin to exert pressure on us. The question before us then was whether under those circumstances a socialist country could survive without any support, and even with a hostile attitude, from the remaining socialist countries. The general view then was that this was not possible. We were told we would not escape becoming an American colony. Later, people insisted we were trying to sit on two chairs at the same time."

"None of these things came true," Bakaric declared. "Our decision was an historic one. It proved that a country could have an independent existence, not supported by any big power. This has encouraged all those who disapprove of foreign tutelage."

Senator Fulbright said that the first step toward the concept of a community "beyond coexistence" was the development of understanding of why men fought. Citing the enormous destructive powers available to human beings, Fulbright stated: "Only on the basis of such self understanding can we hope to go beyond coexistence, creating step by step, a state of mind which will breathe life and spirit into the United Nations, turning an organization into a community. Our chance of success is probably not really great. But we have no choice except to try."

The American economist John Kenneth Galbraith, of Harvard, who had once served as the United States ambassador to India, presided at the opening session of the last day of the convocation. The subject was "Interdependence," and the panelists were Masamichi Inoki of Kyoto University, Japan; J. L. Hromadka, of the Ecumenical Institute of Prague, Czechoslovakia; Terence Nsanze, Burundi's permanent representative to the United Nations; and Silviu Brucan of Romania, the former Romanian ambassador to the United States.

Galbraith said the question was not whether the interdependence of nations was growing, because everybody agreed that it was, but whether the interdependent relations between nations was "damaging" or "benign." He felt that the motives in these relations were more often benign than malignant. Using the steel industry as an example, he said: "A man finds himself a member of essentially the same broad industrial structure, given not by the basic characteristics of capitalism or the basic characteristics of socialism, but by the even larger imperative of needing to make steel."

Pierre Rinfret, president of an economic consulting company in the United States, raised a question from the floor: "To what extent is the continued prosperity of the United States dependent on the pursuit of war?"

Galbraith answered: "In the present enormous size of the American economy, the Vietnam war takes less than 10 per cent of the production, between 6 and 8 per cent. . . . Were the economic effects of this miserable conflict in Vietnam removed tomorrow there would be no reason whatsoever for economic despair and there would be, parenthetically, many reasons for rejoicing." Galbraith did not deal fully with the effects of the huge Department of Defense budget on the economy.

"Development"—a topic that had entered into almost all of the panel discussions—was the focal point for the final session of the Geneva convocation. Chester Carlson presided, and the panel included Chief S. O. Adebo, permanent representative of Nigeria at the United Nations; Paul Hoffman; Archbishop Dom Helder Camara, of Brazil; and E. R. Richardson, Jamaica's ambassador to the United Nations.

"The developed countries are not making a contribution to world economic development proportionate to their share of the world's economic resources because too much of their income is consumed by military expenditures," Chief Adebo said bluntly. "Such aid as is given is given to the wrong people or for the wrong purpose, or on the wrong terms. In some cases the aid doled out is more than taken back by means of unfair terms of trade."

Paul Hoffman—who was then the head of the UN Development Fund —quoted a statement by Secretary of Defense Robert McNamara, who had found that since 1958 only one country whose per capita average annual income totaled $750 or more had experienced a violent internal upheaval, while 87 percent of the countries with a per capita income of $100 per year or less suffered an average of two major violent upheavals per country in the same period of time.

Hoffman said that the most encouraging fact about the work of development was that it was underutilization rather than lack of natural resources that was responsible for poverty in 90 percent of the countries where the UN had projects. His surveys showed that approximately 80 percent of the physical resources and 90 percent of the human capabilities were not being used in the developing countries.

"Development is one of the many names of peace," Archbishop Camara said. He thought that a major effort was required to help "the masses turn into people" and a great challenge to religion was to help raise the status of all men as creators.

The Brazilian archbishop, noted for his devotion to the poor and oppressed people in Latin American countries, suggested that it might be necessary to establish "anti-trust laws on a world-wide scale" to bring international corporations under control.

"They are the true masters of the world, cold calculators of high finance, impassive manipulators of peace and mainly war," Dom Helder Camara passionately proclaimed.

Human rights and economic development had to be considered together, Ambassador Richardson indicated: "It is absolutely essential that we recognize the peculiar dependence of civil and political rights on the protection and advancement of the economic development of a country or a people."

Before the convocation closed, all the participants and invited guests heard a performance of *El Pessebre*, an oratorio for peace composed by the renowned cellist Pablo Casals. He had hoped to be present, but illness had kept him at his home in Puerto Rico. He had sent a message, which was read to the audience:

"Dear friends, dear lovers of beauty, dear lovers of peace!" Casals said. "We live in an age in which men have accomplished magnificent things and made miraculous advances, an age in which man embarks upon the exploration of the stars. Yet on our own planet we continue to act as barbarians. Like barbarians we fear our neighbors on this earth; we arm against them and they arm against us. The time has come when this must be halted if man is to survive. We must become accustomed to the fact that we are human beings.

"The love of one's country is a splendid thing. But why should love stop at the border? There is a brotherhood among all men. This must be recognized if life is to remain. We must learn the love of man."

In his summary of the work of the Geneva convocation, Hutchins listed eleven points on which he believed the participants had reached an agreement:

"The first is that the United Nations must be strengthened and made more independent.

"The second is that the membership of the UN must be universal.

"The third is that the war in Vietnam is, at best, a mistake.

"The fourth is that Southeast Asia must be neutralized.

"The fifth is that the Cold War must be ended.

"The sixth point of general agreement is that racial discrimination is intolerable.

"The seventh is that aid to the developing countries must be given by those which are better off, and this must be, or ought to be, multilateral.

"The eighth point is that terms of trade are intolerable for developing countries and that the ratio of the prices of industrial products to the prices of primary products must receive the most earnest, explicit and immediate attention.

"The ninth point is that no military solutions are adequate for the present day.

"The tenth is that no national solutions are adequate for the present day. Hence, we are brought back to the necessity of the first point—the United Nations must be strengthened and made more independent, and steps to the development of that organization into a new plane of international government must be taken.

"Finally, it seems to me, that we have agreed that coexistence is a necessary but not sufficient condition of human life. Survival is not, perhaps, an ignoble aim, but it is not a noble one either. We must move onward and upward from coexistence to what Pope John XXIII called 'the universal common good.' This is an aim worthy of humanity, and it will require the organization of the world for continuous peaceful change and a revision of the status quo without war.

". . . The problem is that the world consists of structures of power. The question is how to reform and redirect these structures. This is the task that *Pacem in Terris II* set for all men of good will.

"Let us, therefore, each in his own country, in his own sphere, press forward in the spirit of *Pacem in Terris.*"

James Roosevelt, a son of President Franklin Roosevelt and a former United States ambassador to UNESCO, served as secretary general of the convocation. As president of the Investors Overseas Services Management Company, based in Geneva, he had been largely responsible for persuading Bernard Cornfeld, president of the IOS group of companies, to provide nearly all the funds to meet the costs of the conference. The IOS Foundation, established in 1963, had previously given support to 155 humanitarian projects in fifty-five countries.*

"It was logical for us, an international business organization whose viability depends on peace on earth, to support the Center in their effort to build a private initiative toward peace," Cornfeld told interviewers in Geneva. "If the cause of peace has been advanced at all, the convocation has been worth the effort. If it hasn't, the effort still had to be made."

Hundreds of reporters, commentators, and observers from newspapers, magazines, and broadcasting units from Europe, Asia, Latin America, and Africa, as well as correspondents from the United States, attended the Geneva gathering. Daily briefings were given in several languages, and participants were made available for interviews.

*Cornfeld's financial empire later collapsed, and he was found guilty of illegal manipulations of funds. But the Center, like other nonprofit groups aided by Cornfeld and his associates, had no connection with his business affairs.

Coverage of the second *Pacem in Terris* convocation in the United States was not as extensive or as friendly as the coverage of the first convocation in New York. Apparently the disparaging remarks about the "anti-American tone" of some of the statements at the meeting—remarks circulated by State Department staff members and White House officials—had a chilling effect on the mass media.

The New York *Daily News* described it as a "hate-the-U.S.-on-account-of-the-Viet-war talkathon," and the Chicago *Tribune* tagged it as "Dumb and Disgraceful" in an editorial. William F. Buckley, Jr., assailed it as the "Hutchins International Conference to Hate America," and the Indianapolis *Star* urged that the convocation's sponsors be fined and jailed for violating the Logan Act, which barred American citizens from engaging in negotiations with foreign powers.

One correspondent who was deeply impressed by the Geneva assembly, however, was Robert Lasch, editor of the St. Louis *Post-Dispatch*, who chided his fellow journalists: "Deprived of headline-making government participants who would have provided fodder for their typewriters, correspondents looked down very long noses at the whole affair. . . . Less jaded observers, however, found it stimulating that a company of great intellectual diversity could short-circuit their governments and find large areas of agreement on key issues of war and peace. If governments and their spokesmen didn't like it, that was only to be expected."

The convocation was overshadowed by the eruption of the Six-Day War in the Middle East—the savage clash between Israel and several Arab countries, which ended with an overwhelming victory for the Israelis. To Hutchins, Ashmore, Baggs, Fred Neal, John Perry, and others who had put the conference together in spite of all obstacles, there was a terrible irony in the bloody fighting that occurred so soon after the conclusion of the second *Pacem in Terris* convocation. Yet it was evident that there were people in many countries who saw the urgent necessity of continuing to work for peace.

The critical repercussions of the Geneva meeting died away slowly in the press. On June 19 an article on the comprehensive program of the Center was distributed by the *New York Times* news service. "Hutchins Center Examines the Nature of Democracy," the Santa Barbara *New-Press* said in a headline on this article, which was written by Richard Reeves. The *Times* correspondent asked Hutchins why he had ten staff members at the Center who had been in journalism. Hutchins answered: "Journalists are the only people who are really awake in the areas we're interested in. They are the last generalists in an age of specialization."

On July 8 the Center announced that a bimonthly *Center Magazine* would be published, beginning in September and absorbing and replacing the *Center Diary*, which had been distributed monthly to members. John Cogley was appointed editor; Edward Reed, the Center's director of publication, who had edited the *Diary*, was designated as executive editor of the new periodical; and Edward Engberg, formerly an associate editor of *Fortune* and editor of the *Insider's Newsletter*, was named as the managing editor.

The announcement stated that the magazine would be provided to persons who were members of the Center by virtue of annual contributions of $10 or more. The price per copy for nonmembers had not been determined, but the era of free copies of Center publications for inquiring citizens was over.

Harry Ashmore's appointment as executive vice president of the Center was disclosed in another release to the press on July 14. Hutchins was sixty-eight and was suffering from age and fatigue. Ashmore, who continued to serve as chairman of the executive committee of the board of directors, took over a steadily increasing range of responsibilities at Hutchins' request. At the same time, John Perry's election as secretary and treasurer was made public. Perry succeeded Hallock Hoffman, who was asked to devote his full time to the Center's academic program.

John R. Seeley, who had joined the staff in 1966, was named to the newly created post of dean and director of academic studies. In addition to my functions as a vice president, I was given additional duties as director of continuing education.

Richard Gilbert, who had been a magazine marketing executive in Los Angeles, was appointed to handle some aspects of the Center's public relations. Peter Tagger, who had been a consultant, became director of membership services and manager of the West Coast office in Beverly Hills.

Crane Haussamen, a New York advertising specialist and a former United States minister to UNESCO, who had been elected to the Center's board, was placed in charge of the Center's New York office and asked to arrange a series of meetings for Founding Members, opinion makers in the press and broadcasting media, and scholars involved in the Center's work.

21

Radical student leaders advocate disruption of American society at Center conference, bringing new wrath upon the Center

I N AUGUST 1967 the Center sponsored a gathering of student leaders at its headquarters in Santa Barbara to get at the causes of the demonstrations and revolts on many campuses. The oral assaults on American institutions by some of the students, reported in the press, stirred more anger against the Center than the Geneva convocation had produced and led to demands for a congressional investigation and a revocation of the Fund's tax exemption.

Tom O'Brien declared in a front-page article in the *News-Press* on August 24:

> A master plan of how best to destroy the American university system as it is today seemed to be the goal as a conference of militant student leaders and ex-students opened yesterday at the Center for the Study of Democratic Institutions.
>
> The participants were described by the Center as all having been prominent in demonstrations and movements within their own colleges and universities.
>
> "Until now there has been no opportunity for student leaders in America to assemble and discuss among themselves the issues confronting students as students," a preconference statement said. "The Center felt that such a meeting would be of great value, and so has sponsored this convention."
>
> The opening day suggestions ran the gamut from out-and-out revolution to the massive boycott of university classes across the nation. Several student speakers stressed that since a university

simply reflects society, it is basic that you must change society it-self if you wish to make things right within the university.

Deveraux Kennedy, student body president at Washington University, St. Louis, called for outright revolution and the over-throw of the United States government. He advocated terrorism on such a scale that it would "demoralize and castrate America."

Kennedy's main objection to universities, repeated several times, is that they produce scientists and engineers for "Monsanto to make napalm, and McDonnell Aircraft to produce Phantom jets for Vietnam."

Not all the participants (in the conference) will return to a campus. Some are ex-students, like Stan Wise (Howard Universi-ty, 1960–64), now secretary of the Student Nonviolent Coordinat-ing Committee (SNCC), who represents Ralph Featherstone, SNCC program director, Atlanta, Ga., who was invited but un-able to attend.

Wise, who repeatedly announced that the "institutions of this country must be destroyed," boasted that his organization (SNCC) was "absolutely without doubt responsible for the racial riots throughout the country" this summer. Wise said he is com-mitted to the destruction of the present set-up of the United States government. He said he is also dedicated to getting Negro soldiers in U.S. bases around the world to quit their jobs.

"They will, when we tell them enough about what's happen-ing to their folks here at home," Wise said. "This country is racist from top to bottom, from left to right. The atmosphere must be created to bring about the necessary changes."

When the discussion actually revolved around changing the university itself, the ideas were more moderate.

Jeff Alexander, from Harvard College, said a boycott of classes was the students' No. 1 weapon and should be used nation-ally to bring the universities to a halt. Only then would student de-mands be met.

Ewart F. Brown, student body president at Howard Universi-ty, called for "student infiltration" of the university system. "You have the power to make the university what you want. You must infiltrate the system and destroy the parts of it that upset you."

Delegates to the unique convention also engaged in some po-litical arguments. Frank Bardacke, from the University of Califor-nia at San Diego, spoke for saving "the life of the mind" in uni-versities, and claimed that the New Left called for an immediate halt to the Vietnam war and when it didn't come "they became hippies." Kennedy objected, saying that the New Left had not become hippy but revolutionary.

David Seeley, of the University of California at Santa Barbara, said "the revolution is coming. We're bound to destroy the university—not pull it apart, brick by brick, but bring it to a complete stall." Seeley is a son of John Seeley, a Center staffer.

Seeley defended the hippies. "Hippies just want to change how people feel, change their outlook on life. They love one another. They give away clothing and food."

Rick Richman, a June graduate of Harvard, who has spent the summer as a Junior Fellow at the Center, is chairman of the conference. He helped to organize it with three other Junior Fellows, Jeff Elman, Stephen Saltonstall, and Dan Sisson.

Robert Maynard Hutchins, president of the Center, was there, making notes. . . .

O'Brien's story in the *News-Press*—which was accurate in its quotations but did play up the wildest statements made by the students—sent a shock wave through the Santa Barbara community and aroused the anger of Representative Charles Teague and other members of Congress. Tom Storke, who had sold the *News-Press* to Robert McLean of Philadelphia, was still active in the community. He asked me to come to his home and told me that many leaders in Santa Barbara and elsewhere were enraged by the Center's provision of a forum for revolutionary radicals. He had received telephone calls, asking him why he had helped the Center to establish itself in Santa Barbara.

The headline in the *News-Press* on the second day of the conference was less frightening: "Ways to Get Student Power Are Debated." But the story was not very reassuring to disturbed citizens.

> Young activists disagreed here yesterday on whether "student power" should be persuasion to reform or such "disruption" as nonviolent university sabotage or putting LSD in government workers' coffee [Barney Brantingham wrote in his report for the paper].
>
> Stephen Saltonstall said: "We have the power to bring the American Juggernaut to a halt. Let us paralyze the United States; let us ball up the economy. One day soon, Congressmen and Presidents may petition us, not we them."
>
> Both dialogue and "arming ourselves" are impractical, he said. He proposed immobilizing the ROTC by packing classes, breaking up drills and harassing instructors; stopping defense research by blocking government advisers from their offices and harassing them at home; hampering the efficiency of office staffs

—"the introduction of a small quantity of LSD in only 5 or 6 government coffee urns might be a highly effective tactic."

Government apologists such as Hubert H. Humphrey and Robert McNamara (Secretary of Defense) should be kept from using universities as forums for "intimidation and humiliation."

Saltonstall, 23, a cousin of Leverett Saltonstall, a late United States Senator, and a Phi Beta Kappa at Harvard, plans to go to Yale for graduate study. He told newsmen that although he is a Quaker he advocated disruption tactics because he thinks students can help end the Vietnam war.

The third story on the conference was headlined: "Accusations Traded at Student Parley." The student activists and Center staff members were depicted in a lurid light, supposedly engaged in "accusing one another of not being radical enough." The reporter, Barney Brantingham, wrote:

Some of the 19 young militants at a three day student conference that ended yesterday sneered at the Center as a haven for "quaint" aging liberals.

"You don't know what's going on in the world," charged Deveraux Kennedy. "There is going to be a revolution. You may not be here to see it. I hope you won't because you're not ready for it."

A Center consultant, Scott Buchanan, expressed "anger at you students playing house with the idea of power. You act like children."

Another staff member, John Wilkinson, challenged those around the table with "schoolboy Marxism" ideas to come up with some relevant theories.

Harvey Wheeler, who had previously disassociated himself from criticisms of the students made by Robert Hutchins and others, returned with Wilkinson and Buchanan in the afternoon to exchange criticisms.

"What passed for radicalism here was very conservative," Wheeler chided.

"We've been trying to get beyond the conservatism of the right and the left, and work out at the Center the problems of law, government, corporations, and the impact of technology," Buchanan said. "This is much more radical than anything you're doing. You're old hat."

Dr. Hutchins led off the critique by saying that the student radicals sounded like Tammany Hall in their quest for power. "I can't see that the new Tammany Hall would be any better than the old."

Goldfield said the conference was not productive. He said the Center was a "friendly place" that accepted radicals, but its need to raise funds caused a "bias" that made it difficult to be objective.

To Goldfield, being "objective" obviously meant being sympathetic to himself and the other radical students. Like many of the conservative citizens in Santa Barbara who denounced the Center for having the conference, he did not understand what the Center was intending to do. The conference was financed by a wealthy New Yorker who wanted to know what student leaders were thinking. The donor did not participate in the assembly or make any suggestions to have the dialogue slanted one way or another.

It was a painful experience for the Center fellows, and it showed the severe difficulties in communication between the older scholars and the militant students. Its value in revealing the strategy and tactics of student movements became apparent later to an editor of the *Wall Street Journal* and commentators on other newspapers, when these editors realized that the Center had provided an early warning of what was going to happen to many universities and other institutions if the students did not get creative responses to their grievances.

At the time it occurred, many important points in the dialogue were not covered by the reporters who attended some of the sessions. A transcript of the remarks made in the three-day gathering—plus the formal papers written by students—ran to 75,000 words. Out of all these statements, the reporters picked a few phrases that made eye-catching headlines.

The first paper, circulated to all participants in advance of the first session, was prepared by Frederick Richman, a graduate in the Harvard class of 1967.

"The end of a college education ought not to be to create eggheads but to create people who can contribute actively to the achievement of a humane society," Richman said. "The reform I propose is that the university become a political institution. As time goes by Congress will be of decreasing utility as a democratic institution. The country is too large, too complex, and too diverse to be managed adequately by the Congress. It possesses neither the time nor the expertise nor, apparently, the willingness to lead the country towards the social progress that invigorates a nation and keeps it alive.

"The university might serve this function. People after 30 tend to retire into personal interests and private concerns. Students, however, have fewer private responsibilities and fewer commitments to established ways of living. The time when they are in college is the time they can make their most idealistic and constructive contribution to society—provided they have an institution which encourages social and political participation.

"In the university of the future, political activism, which the Greeks called citizenship, would be the central educational experience. The really important political developments would be taking place among youth. If someone wanted to see what was really going on politically in the country, he would look to the university to see what students were doing; there would be vastly increased numbers of them out working in society for various forms of social change or social progress.

"Such an institution would invigorate society as a whole, as the formative experience for American youth becomes four years not of abstract or irrelevant knowledge, but of awareness of social problems and participation in social action."

"What is relevant?" Hutchins asked, after he had welcomed the students to the Center. "Is it possible that the best practical education is the most theoretical one? Is it possible in a world that is changing every day that the object might be to find out what is not changing? Or how to judge the changes that are taking place?

"Another thing I'd like to get some illumination on is commitment. What should not merely a young person, but what should a university be committed to? If the university is committed to a certain political view, what happens to those who have different political views?

"The name of the new anti-university or Gegen-Universitat in Berlin is the Critical University. . . . The program of the Critical University is political and social activism and suggests that this is to take place concurrently with or after attempts to formulate economic, social, political standards of action. Is a university sufficiently committed if it is a 'critical' university in this sense?

"My final question is one that is implicit in many of the papers that have been circulated. I can state it very simply and then turn the meeting over to Mr. Richman. And that is: How do you keep from growing old?"

Richman brushed Hutchins' questions away without deigning to deal with them. He said: "The main contention in my paper is that youth is now in a position to exert considerable power. . . . However, if we are going to achieve a revolution consciously carried forth by American youth, that youth will have to be organized as youth and given a new position in American society. . . .

"The characteristic of the student experience today is its desire to turn education from being abstract or merely educational into something profoundly politicized. I hope that at last American students are becoming like students in other countries, who have traditionally been fulfilling a definite political role. . . ."

Michael Lerner, one of the leaders of the Free Speech Movement at Berkeley, disagreed strongly with some of Richman's statements.

"Specifically, the reforms you mention would help to focus the growing energy of the students into the mainstream of society instead of aligning that energy with substantial alienation from society,'' Lerner said. "Well, that is just what I don't want to see happening. I don't want that alienation transformed into alignment with a lousy, corrupt society. Furthermore, I am not even sure that after the revolution it would not be a good idea for people to have some wide realm of alienation, because alienation may well be a creative and positive force in history.''

"It makes a big difference what kind of demands you place on the university through the student power movement,'' Deveraux Kennedy interjected. "If the demand is only for a little more control of curriculum or control over dorm hours, I agree with you. But if the student power movement were to demand control over how the university spends its money—to get university investments out of places like South America and out of industry and into the ghetto—then you are making a positive connection between the university, the student power movement, and the problems of the rest of society.

"There are two kinds of reforms you can ask for. You can ask for revolutionary reforms, reforms that really can't be met within the logic of the system. Or you can ask for reforms that can be met, reformists' reforms that can be met. If you ask for reformists' reforms then I agree the student power movement could be a real reactionary force. If you ask for the other kind, the positive connection can be made.''

"Your distinction is not helpful,'' Jeffrey Elman of Harvard said. "Both types of reforms are part and parcel of the same basic change. Students should have the ability to determine how the university is going to be run. This is just as important as the decision as to where the university is going to invest its money, or whether it will undertake government research. It's just not helpful to distinguish the two.''

Mary Quinn of Mount Mercy College didn't see why all students had to be activists: "I want the girl in the dormitory to scream her head off and shoot off her mouth like I do. But what makes her wrong and me right? Just because I'm that way? Or are they right, the 98 percent that just sit there? Is it right for us to impose this activism on everybody? I think it's right; you think it's right; we all think it's right. But what about them?''

Richman questioned the positions taken by Kennedy and Lerner. "How strong is your student movement going to be if you require that all students joining it will have to believe that the United States is an imperialist society conducting imperialist wars and that the society itself is totally bad and that any form of cooperation with it is reactionary? It seems to me that it would be better to try to set up an institution in which all students would have the experience of exerting power and could have some reforming effect without having to drop out.''

Peter Lyman, the student body president from Stanford, showed his awareness of what Hutchins had been driving at: "If we are going to talk about student consciousness I think we can start talking about education. I think in the university there is no more radical reform than beginning to orient the university toward education. This also is at the center of defining student consciousness, since students' primary interest or sole interest in the university is their own education.''

"Why can't we take politics out of the university completely?'' asked John Blood, president of the student body of Indiana University. "I think politics is what has subverted its purpose to begin with. If students do take power I wonder how you are going to stop the power-seekers from taking over.''

"You can't take politics out of the university,'' Kennedy snapped. "It's implicit in the way the the university is structured. You can't change, for instance, the fact that boards of regents or boards of trustees run the universities and that they are all businessmen. As far as I am concerned, they have no business at all to do with the universities. And you can't change the fact that universities invest their endowments in various areas.''

Frank Bardacke of the University of California at Berkeley scoffed at the idea that university students were members of an "oppressed social class.'' He reminded all of the participants that youth was glorified in America.

Bardacke tried to bring the discussion back to the significance of restoring respect for the mind in American universities, where (he believed) hatred for books and ideas had been fostered.

"There's a dysfunctional aspect of a university, and that is that it has to deal with books, and books have ideas in them,'' Bardacke said. "Ideas have a tendency to make people rambunctious, and make them feel that the way they live is not the only possible way to live, and that they might do something collectively to change it. If books are taken seriously, they have to lead to trouble.

"So, in most large universities you have, in effect, to destroy books. One result of college education today is that students end up hating books. It's done systematically. You can't learn to like reading if you have to pull something out of every book you pick up, if you have to produce a paper out of it, if you have to do well in a seminar out of it. . . .

"The vision of a university dedicated to the life of the mind is being destroyed by comtemporary universities. . . . If you tried to make the kind of university I'm talking about, it would involve you in incredible struggle. It would involve changing the society ultimately, because I don't think the society at this point can afford to have its young people educated.''

David Seeley pointed out: "There are two kinds of revolution. One is a destructive kind where you tear down things; the other kind is where you build up a parallel institution. What we have to decide first is whether the university and the society it serves are so rotten that they ought to be destroyed. Secondly, we ought to decide whether we can do that, or if we should simply build a parallel institution.''

"Seeley implies that we've been using the word revolution loosely and sort of mumbling it under our breath, and I think that's true," Kennedy broke in. "I'm going to say loudly and explicitly what I mean by revolution. What I mean by revolution is overthrowing the American government and American imperialism and installing some sort of decentralized power in this country.

"I'll tell you the steps that I think will be needed. First of all, starting up fifty Vietnams in Third World countries. This is going to come about by black rebellions in our cities joined by some white people. People in universities can do a number of things to help it. They have access to money and they can give these people guns, which I think they should do. They can engage in acts of terrorism and sabotage outside the ghetto. Negro people have trouble getting out because they cordon those areas off, but white activists can go outside, and they can blow things up, and I think they should.

"But that's just a minor part of it. The major thing student activists can do while this is going on—I mean completely demoralizing and castrating America—is to give people a vision of something other than what they have now. They can give them a vision of people living as whole men, not as engineers for Monsanto or McDonnell Aircraft, but as people who have some real say over the whole productive apparatus, who relate to one another as human beings. . . . They can be given this alternative vision right now."

"How do you do that when you're engaged in activism?" Bardacke demanded.

"That's easy," Kennedy responded. "Terrorism isn't a full-time job."

Mary Quinn protested vehemently: "We can't talk any more; we have to go around and take on guns. This is really the saddest thing in this society, that we can't really be like men. We've sort of reverted to the animal stage. . . .

"Where has the mind gone? It's gone, you know, and it seems that as university students we should be saying, 'Yes, great God, what do we do?' But we don't. Instead we're going to give the hemlock to everybody. . . .

"Nobody really knows what education is. You can't change something that isn't there. We have to define what education is. . . .

"Your college president says, 'We want you to think.' But that's the very thing he doesn't want you to do, because once you start, you're running in and out of jails, and in and out of offices, and in and out of rotten eggs and tomatoes. This is what we have to deal with: the lack of any ideal of education or any ideal of the mind."

"I'd like to hear more about Bardacke's life of the mind," Saltonstall said. "It sounds exciting. I'd like to know how he intends to bring this new university or old university about."

Bardacke sighed. "Something can happen in conversations like this that is really destructive. We can, that is, use words like revolution and the new university and changing society and all that with a kind of apocalyptic tone in our voices. You talk like that and you talk about terrorism, but it's not going to come, it's not going to come overnight, you're not going to be putting barricades around the Center for the Study of Democratic Institutions tomorrow afternoon.

"Probably the only people who have the right to talk in such terms in this country at this moment are the black people. For all the white middle-class students who talk about terrorism—and it's a favorite topic of conversation—the one in 5000 that actually does something about it ends up like those kids who were in the federal penitentiary for ten years because they had a casual conversation about the Statue of Liberty. . . .

"I would like to hear less talk about revolution and more thought about what at the moment we can actually achieve. And this is quite limited. If we don't recognize this, what will happen is what has already happened to the New Left, which talked in apocalyptic terms about ending the war in Vietnam right now. They wanted changes in society right now, and when the war didn't end immediately, and the society didn't change right away, they all became hippies.

"Sure, you want a revolution; sure, you want to change this country fundamentally—absolutely agreed. You have to have that long-range goal, but you also have to think about what actually can be achieved in our own lifetimes."

"Your statement about the New Left is historically inaccurate," Kennedy came back. "Students for a Democratic Society started out with three or four thousand members. Now it's got about 30,000, and so the New Left is growing. When they found out they couldn't end the war in Vietnam right away they found out that the war in Vietnam was related to a lot of other social problems. Then you've got a thing called the Radical Education Project, and you got the New Left Notes, which are probably the most sophisticated sociology coming out of the United States today. So, I don't think that the New Left has become hippie. It's become revolutionary."

Former Governor Rexford Tugwell, one of the architects of the New Deal, declared: "I have some news for my younger colleagues here—there isn't going to be any revolution. . . . I think you should realize that you've got to work with or in the existing institutions and with the materials you have at hand. Not that the institutions don't need changing. All of us here recognize that they need changing very fundamentally, but while they are being changed things have to go on; and it's been possible in our lifetime to have changed things very greatly. Perhaps you don't realize that; it seems to me as I have listened here that you people can't have studied American history, because our history has changed fundamentally in my lifetime, and I expect it'll change even more fundamentally in the next two decades. The technology that at the moment seems to have got the best of us I think we will get the mastery of, and turn it to the benefit of more human institutions."

Rick Richman maintained that the Center staff members did not understand why the students talked so much about power and why they wanted power without being required to indicate their goals.

"Power is the first requirement for any type of change," Richman said. "We don't, in a democracy, say that people can't have elections or any type of power unless they specify what they are going to use it for."

"I thought we insisted on party platforms and campaign speeches, even though we didn't believe them," Hutchins answered.

Richman asked, "Suppose there were no platforms, only the candidates running?"

"Then it would be a television beauty contest," Hutchins contended.

"Our concern for power is essentially a moral concern," Richman insisted. "It's immoral when people are in a powerless position, whether they are students, or poor people, or any type of citizen, in a democracy. Therefore, power seems to me something of a natural right."

"You may have misunderstood some of our strictures," Stringfellow Barr intervened. "I accept your statement that people want to have something to say about where they live. On the other hand, if a university was healthy and I matriculated into it, I would expect to delegate a good many choices to the people under whom I was trying to study. I am haunted by the medical metaphor, because the last thing I want is a doctor who asks me which pill I prefer."

"What has just been said is terribly revealing," Michael Lerner asserted. "The medicine analogy is perfect for the kind of things that we've been saying. It shows that the education that you received was as corrupt as the kind of education we are receiving now.

"The point we've been trying to make in our various critiques of the university, and which we haven't been making here because we had gotten beyond that stage, is that acquiring an education of the kind that we wish is not like learning a technique. It's not like knowing what medicine to prescribe under various circumstances. That's precisely the model of the university that we are rebelling against. That is not what the light of the mind is about. Throwing the right plug into the right hole is the notion that has taken over the university and made it a service station to a corrupt society."

Barr wondered whether the students had any reason to think that if they seized power over the university they would be able to produce "a better university."

"The question about power is not a question about me getting power instead of you; that's precisely the radical critique," Lerner instructed Barr. "The radical critique is that it's not a question of better men having power than the bad man who had it before. It's a question of redistributing power. This does not mean allowing our good guys to have the power to run the society over your bad guys. This means rather distributing power throughout the society to each member of it in such a way that it becomes impossible for any given individual to dominate other people, in the way that present people dominate others. In a way, this means we want to use power to destroy power. We are not saying an elite has to have power; we are not saying that we want the dictatorship of a party over the masses.

"We are calling for power for people; that means black power, that means student power, because those are the people who are there. When we say student power, we are not talking about power for a group of student leaders; we are asking for power to be distributed throughout the student body. When people call for black power, they are not calling for more black congressmen; they are talking about real power to be distributed throughout the people who live in the ghetto. So, any criticism of us which says, 'Well, wait until you get to be president and you'll see how difficult it is,' totally misunderstands what we want and what we are interested in."

W. H. Ferry, who had obtained the financial contribution which had made the conference possible, declared at the final session that he agreed with "most of the analyses of the current situation." Ferry urged the students to do a "radical critique" of the high schools and grammar schools of the United States, which he regarded as a "source of much of our malaise," and to get out of the ghettos and into the suburbs.

"There's no Negro problem; but there is an enormous white problem," Ferry said. "There is no city problem, there is a suburb problem. It has been tiresomely predicted often that because you are all middle-class, you are all going to be absorbed into present institutions. I don't think that's going to happen at all. Yet I think you might keep in mind that the suburbs, full of the familiar middle class, are a place where, with your background, you might be able to do a good deal more than you can in ghettos or other places where things are already popping like hell."

In the closing minutes Stanley Wise, executive secretary of the Student Nonviolent Coordinating Committee, spoke fiercely: "Perhaps what we are talking about will not be a revolution. But the great experiment that we are engaged in is based on realities that are evident even in our own distorted history. One of these realities is that America is on a collision course with herself. . . . There's no doubt that America is heading for a collision with the black community. I have no doubt, further, that America is on a collision course with three-fourths of the world. And if you doubt it, you are fooling yourself. . . .

"One other thing I want to say is that one of the faults of this kind of gathering is that you sit here and say, 'Oh, gee, listen to the young people. Or, boom! That is a radical idea.' Once it's established that we have a radical idea, you ask, how did you come to it? Then you want to know, how will it work? Then we attempt to tell how it works, and after that, you will say, but what will the results be?

"But we have no models to go by, so we just suggest what we hope it will look like. If it does not, you say it is impractical and won't work. That is the way the profit system in this country operates, on the same reasoning —how does it work?—how does it fit? So, you conclude it won't work because people won't make enough money.

"Next, I agree with Mr. Ferry that it's a white problem, and I think that most of the world agrees with that. It seems to me that the last possible hope rests with the young white people if there's going to be a feasible solution. None of us wants to be on a collision course, but none of us has the power to change it. It's that simple, and I think you do a tremendous disservice to young people here when you aren't more constructive. People are, after all, grappling with a thing that has never, ever been experienced in history. It's not practical to ask what it will look like, or how it will go. Obviously, existing institutions will decide to a large extent how it is to be shaped.

"The only value I see in the hippie movement is that here is one attempt —and I think it's a total failure—but here is one attempt on the part of the white community to love itself. But I don't think they are trying to love Johnson, or to love the Fords or Rockefellers—they are just trying to love themselves."

Acknowledging that the hippies might "well be ground to bits between the two mass armies of reaction and the revolution," John Seeley asked the radical students not to turn away from the warm and extensive affection offered by the hippies. Reviving a suggestion he had made several years before, he recommended the creation of a university "in which activism—at every level that people are willing to commit themselves to—will be a requirement and a core of the university, apart from its own self-government."

Seeley thought that all education could "be organized around the activism in terms of two possibilities: first, trying to bring to bear the reason, the intellectual heritage, that would help you to pursue and develop and win in 'doing your thing,' and second, drawing your attention to what might make you review your 'thing' in the light of competing factors that you might discover to be more inclusive and more radical. If we had such a university, the things we now have to choose between could be united in a form that would release the full moral force and full energy of students at the same time that they were acquiring an education relevant to what they were doing."

The students listened restively to the suggestions of Seeley, Hutchins, Barr, and others—and went their separate ways, still burning with fury against their education and their society. Some of them had come to the Center with strong prejudices against it, and they retained their biases after several days of dialogue.

Sheila Langdon of Marlboro College expressed appreciation for the concern shown by Hutchins and others, and she felt that they had touched "our most profound problem." Then she added: "But I don't think it's going to be solved by denying activism or the desire for power."

"I think it's really true that after the age of 50 you are lost," Deveraux Kennedy told the Center's senior staff. "You people really are far, far out of it. . . . I don't think you'll ever understand. I didn't come here to talk to you. . . . I came here to talk to the other students, because that's where it's at.''

The Center may not have had much of an impact on the students, but the students shocked and depressed some of the Center's scholars. Scott Buchanan's voice broke when he said to them: "The thing that makes me weep, almost literally, is the impression I get that you, as a generation, have never had any good teaching. . . . And you are talking about power in ways that make me want to spank you.''

The coverage of the student conference in the Santa Barbara *News-Press* generated attacks on the Center that could not be ignored. On August 30, 1967, after the students had left Santa Barbara, the *News-Press* printed a letter from Harry Ashmore, who took issue with the news stories and an editorial in which the paper had chided the students and the Center.

"Your reporter, Tom O'Brien, seized upon the radical pronouncements of the most militant 'student power' advocates and presented them as typical of the wide range of opinions actually presented at a conference that had hardly begun,'' Ashmore wrote. "A comparison with the excellent, balanced reporting of the conference by Dorothy Townsend of the Los Angeles *Times* would have set the record straight. In your second and third day reports by Barney Brantingham you did in fact manage to get the conference somewhat more in perspective. However, your editorial writer had already compounded Mr. O'Brien's error with his own prejudgment.''

The *News-Press* defended its editorial decisions in a statement published two days later, headed "Comments on Mr. Ashmore's Comments":

He complains about a story reporting what was said "at a conference that had hardly begun.'' Of course, the conference had hardly begun at that point. But subsequently the News-Press published more than 2,500 words reporting the discussions day by day.

. . . He praises the Los Angeles *Times*, whose story the next morning was based on papers issued before the conference started, not on attendance at the discussions themselves. Nevertheless, compare the *News-Press* lead with the *Times* lead: "A blueprint for mobilization of student power to disrupt the university structure, alter political institutions and the economy, and conceivably to affect the war in Vietnam was presented Thursday to national student leaders.'' Pretty much the same! (The News-Press lead had been: "A master plan of how best to destroy the American university system as it is today seemed to be the goal as a conference of militant student leaders and ex-students opened yesterday at the Center.'')

"He criticizes a *News-Press* editorial that took exception to the "shocking and destructive viewpoints . . . expressed by students and ex-students . . . in a conference of 'protest' leaders still in session." He does not mention the statement in the editorial that "not all of the participants expressed their views at the opening session—so it can be assumed that among them are some who feel there is something worth saving in both the academic world and American society."

Some expressions of moderate views were made during the second and third days of the conference, and reported in the *News-Press*. But the *News-Press*, to quote its editorial again, "deplores and despises the voices of hate, racism, anarchy and violence that were raised by several of the student participants."

Harry Ashmore, Hutchins, and others at the Center did not feel that reporters had a constitutional right to cover all meetings. After several discussions with Hutchins, John Perry, Richard Gilbert, and me, Ashmore decided to bar reporters from the next conference. It seemed to me that barring reporters would cause many difficulties for the Center. Hutchins supported Ashmore, and a policy of closing some meetings—and limiting reporters to "briefing sessions"—was established.

The next conference held at the Center happened to be a two-day seminar, "Public Affairs Journalism." Participants included editors from the St. Louis *Post-Dispatch*, the Washington *Post*, and the Los Angeles *Times* and others in broadcasting and education. They accepted the Ashmore policy. A *News-Press* reporter, who came to cover the conference, was not permitted to enter the conference room.

On September 8 the *News-Press* carried an indignant editorial headed "Public Affairs Confab—In Secret."

A two-day seminar on "public affairs journalism" opened yesterday at the Center, with a distinguished list of participants billed [the editorial said]. There was an editor of the St. Louis *Post-Dispatch*, bearing the resplendent name of Pulitzer; the editor of the Los Angeles *Times*, the dean of the Columbia University journalism school, and other notable men in newspaper, broadcasting and educational fields.

Not present was a reporter from the *News-Press*, assigned to get a story for Santa Barbara residents on any new, interesting and challenging ideas about the job of keeping the people informed.

The reporter was turned away at the door. Center spokesmen said the press was invited to cover conferences only in "exceptional cases," and this was not one of them (in the Center's opinion). They also said there was no room for a reporter in the conference room. . . .

We hope that some among the distinguished editors and writers and teachers of journalism may have felt a twinge of embarrassment at participating in a secret conference on the problems of keeping the public informed—while an assigned working reporter waited outside.

On the same day, Representative Charles M. Teague—who had clashed with W. H. Ferry on the value of J. Edgar Hoover—told the members of the Thousand Oaks Republican Women's Club that he regarded the Center as a "noneducational facility" and he had asked the Internal Revenue Service to investigate the Center.

Teague said he had acted after he had read articles in the *News-Press* about the Center-sponsored conference with student leaders. He asserted that the student activists at the conference "appeared to be advocating two things: overthrow of the government by force and inciting to riot."

According to the *News-Press*—which gave his speech coverage in a prominent position—Teague also said that he had requested an investigation of the students by the United States attorney general, declaring: "If the conference was a forum where all sides were called, I feel this is educational; but when it is simply 'far left' only, I question its educational role." He called the Center's leaders "far-out left-field intellectuals" and said the Center was a "think factory with only one side."

It apparently did not occur to Representative Teague that the Center had brought together a group of militant student leaders in order to show the people of the United States what such leaders were thinking and planning to do. In his view, these leaders had to be investigated by the attorney general for possible indictments and should not have been given a chance to express their ideas openly in the atmosphere of the Center. He had never been at a Center meeting, and he had no conception of the critical cross-fire to which ideas were subjected at the Center.

Three days later, under a headline stating "End to Center Tax Exemptions Asked," the *News-Press* reported that the directors of the California Republican Assembly—an organization predominantly controlled by directors as conservative as Representative Teague—endorsed Teague's effort to flatten the Center. The directors adopted a resolution asserting that the Center "has endorsed and sponsored political action organizations such as the Students for a Democratic Society, the Vietnam Day Committee, and others. Such actions constitute a violation of the tax-exempt statute for non-profit organizations."

Reached by a reporter, John L. Perry, of the Center staff, said simply: "The Center doesn't endorse or sponsor any organization, politically or otherwise."

The deterioration of relations between the Center and Santa Barbara's only daily newspaper became evident in a chilly editorial on September 11. The new owners of the paper did not wholeheartedly support the Center, as Tom Storke had done on several occasions.

> Representative Charles M. Teague touched a most sensitive nerve of the Center for the Study of Democratic Institutions when he said the Center is a non-educational facility and should be removed from tax-exempt contributions to survive. . . .
>
> The congressman said he is disturbed by a fact that has disturbed many others—an apparent left-wing orientation of almost all of the Center's leaders. The Center professes to be a forum where a variety of points of view are discussed and disseminated, and to some extent that is true. But through a process of selection or intellectual inbreeding the Center's staff has become representative of one limited point of view on many issues. It would be interesting, for example, to see the results of a survey on the Vietnam war issue among the men who lead the discussions day in and day out atop Eucalyptus Hill.
>
> The Center, as an institution, scrupulously avoids taking a position on issues. It must do so to keep its tax-exempt status. But the material that pours out of the Center, representing the viewpoints of many participants, seems to have a predictable, built-in bias. The concern of Congressman Teague and many other taxpayers about having their tax dollars used, in effect, for this sort of education is understandable.

In many public statements, Center officers had made it plain that the Center was not a debating society, taking up issues on a "pro" and "con" basis. The Center was attempting to "clarify" fundamental questions, and this often led to meetings with persons who challenged or criticized the institutions of society. Efforts had been made to get "thoughtful" conservatives—such as William F. Buckley, Jr., and Barry Goldwater—to participate in some of the dialogues. Buckley had come to one meeting; Goldwater had informed Hutchins that he would like to visit the Center, but he had never managed to fit such a visit into his schedule.

Robert Hutchins and Harry Ashmore, the two top officers of the Center, were usually surprised to find themselves described as men with "an apparent left-wing orientation." W. H. Ferry was a gadfly, a stinging critic in many areas, but he was not easy to label. Other officers and fellows of the Center regarded "left-wing" and "right-wing" as meaningless terms. I thought of myself as a "liberal" in the Jeffersonian tradition.

It was true, of course, that there were few defenders of the Vietnam War at the Center in September 1967—and the Center had published a pamphlet on the origins of American involvement in Vietnam in 1965—but there were critics of the war in many places by the autumn of 1967. Secretary of Defense Robert McNamara was reported to be turning against it at that time. If the Vietnam war was to be taken as a criterion for defining "bias," it was notable that "bias" against the war had spread widely through the nation.

At the University of Chicago, Hutchins had not inquired into the political views of prospective members of the faculty. Teachers and scholars were supposed to be judged only on their erudition in various fields and their willingness to learn from others. When the Illinois legislature had investigated the university, Hutchins had defended teachers who had views very different from his own.

Yet the Center was not a university in the conventional sense. It was dealing with controversial questions, with political, economic, and social issues, and it did have an obligation to bring a long spectrum of viewpoints into its discussions. It was responsible to a board of directors of the Fund for the Republic as well as to the citizens it was trying to serve.

Most of the directors of the Fund—admirers of Hutchins and confident of his integrity as an educator—felt that the Center was continuously trying to get many viewpoints into the dialogues. Most of them were businessmen, committed to the "free enterprise system," but they were willing to have that system—and all other systems—brought under a radical analysis at the Center. They believed that the very existence of such a Center contributed to the health and vitality of a society that claimed to be dedicated to freedom and justice.

The action of Representative Teague in asking the attorney general to investigate the students who participated in the Center conference was repugnant to the Fund's directors and to many citizens who were critical of the Center. The *News-Press*, after chiding the Center, dissociated itself from Teague's action: "Considering the seditious nature of the remarks some of them made, this request by the Congressman is understandable, too. But there is another danger here—the danger that an investigation of alleged seditious talk will become a weapon of thought control and be considered an effort to impose conformity.

"In the United States, no one must ever be afraid to voice his thoughts, radical though they be. But when he voices those thoughts he must be prepared to bear the heat of public indignation and denunciation from those who disagree."

A few days after its criticism of the Center, the *News-Press* reprinted a scornful article written by Joan Didion and John Gregory Dunne, which had appeared in the *Saturday Evening Post*. Didion and Dunne had spent a small amount of time at the Center, and gave it a roasting:

> The place is in fact avidly anti-intellectual, the deprecatory use of words like "egghead" and "ivory tower" reaching heights only matched in a country club locker room. Hutchins takes pains to explain that by "an intellectual community" he does not mean a community whose members regard themselves as "intellectuals." Harry Ashmore frets particularly that "men of affairs" may fail to perceive the Center's "practical utility"...

It helps, too, to present the donor with a fairly broad-stroke picture of how the Center is besieged by the forces of darkness and in this effort the Center has had an invaluable, if unintentional, ally in the Santa Barbara John Birch Society. . . .

Actually, even without the Birch Society as a foil, Hutchins has evolved the $E = MC^2$ of all fund-raising formulae. The Center is supported on the same principle as a vanity press. People who are in a position to contribute large sums of money are encouraged to participate in clarifying the basic issues. Dinah Shore, a Founding Member, is invited up to discuss civil rights with Bayard Rustin. Steve Allen talks over "Ideology and Intervention" with Senator Fulbright and Arnold Toynbee. Kirk Douglas, a Founding Member, speaks his piece on "The Arts in a Democratic Society." Paul Newman, in the role of "concerned citizen," is on hand to discuss the "University in America" with Dr. Hutchins, Supreme Court Justice Douglas, Arnold Grant, Rosemary Park, and another "concerned citizen," Jack Lemmon. . . .

Everyone goes home flattered, and the Center prevails. Well, why not?

Didion and Dunne asked a question that Hutchins often asked. Why not invite Dinah Shore, Steve Allen, Kirk Douglas, Paul Newman, Jack Lemmon, and other well-known, intelligent, and wealthy persons to discuss topics of concern to the Center? These people did not attempt to dictate what the Center's program should be, and they often offered ideas that were worth considering. Their participation in meetings as well as their gifts brought benefits to the Center.

It was true that Hutchins and Ashmore and others at the Center—including me—took pains to emphasize the fact that the Center was not simply a collection of "intellectuals" talking to other "intellectuals." That did not mean that the Center was "anti-intellectual." Scholars were always present, and the scholars were close to the heart of the Center's work, but the Center was not designed simply for scholars.

Writers like Didion and Dunne often came to the Center with ready-made pictures in their heads—pictures of "intellectuals" strolling through marble halls, far above the pressures and problems of people who had to struggle for their bread and butter. The very location of the place, high on a hill above beautiful Santa Barbara, reinforced the notion that the Center was a remote "think tank," an aquarium full of strange fish swimming in filtered water.

So Hutchins and Ashmore—and all of us who talked frequently with journalists and skeptical visitors—sometimes gave the impression of being overly committed to "practical utility." Such comments were often reactions to questions hurled by busy people from the big cities, who said,

"How did you get so lucky, to spend your days sitting around thinking in a place like this? What did you ever do to deserve it? How can you justify your existence?"

The conference with the militant students, which brought the Center a flash flood of publicity, should have made many people realize finally that the Center wasn't just a retreat for "eggheads" or a haven for scholars who couldn't face realities. But the label of "think tank" could not be removed. The Center was regarded after that conference as a place where "dangerous thoughts" were encouraged—"seditious ideas" that shouldn't have been uttered.

That confrontation revealed again the difficulties that had to be endured year after year by a unique educational organization—scorned by the radicals who were charging the barricades, denigrated by sophisticated columnists like Didion and Dunne, deprecated or ignored by many professors in colleges and universities, viewed with alarm by newspaper editorial writers, attacked by members of Congress, examined by the Internal Revenue Service.

In December 1967 the Center published a 64-page booklet entitled *Students and Society*, which contained two-thirds of the 75,000 words in the transcript of the conference. In a foreword, Ferry said: "Riots in black ghettos have led Americans to wonder why they were not informed of such tragic possibilities. There was always the chance, they say, that healing and preventive steps might have been taken if only an effective early warning system had been in operation, if they had realized the depth and strength of the feelings running through resentful hearts and along neglected streets.

"The proceedings of the conference on Students and Society should be viewed as signals from another early warning system. The discussion that follows might have been called The Worried Citizen's Guide to Tumult on the Campus. It is easy to disagree with these young people, but they should not be ignored. . . ."

The signals were not heeded. The frank statements by the militants on what they planned to do were not taken seriously in many places. The Center's objective in having the conference was misunderstood and misrepresented. The "healing and preventive steps" were not taken.

In response to a demand by Congressman Teague, who did not take the trouble to read the full text of the booklet, an Internal Revenue agent was sent to Santa Barbara to go over the Center's records. People in the city were still irritated by the Center's temerity in bringing that "pack of students" together on Eucalyptus Hill.

And the United States plunged toward a year of dynamitings, riots, attacks on college presidents and policemen, threats against the Congress and the White House, a year in which President Johnson traveled with a phalanx of guards around him, a year of obscenities and the marching of troops in American cities, the fractious and fearful year of 1968.

22

In a year of turmoil, the Center undergoes an agonizing reappraisal

I~N 1968 THE DIVISIONS~ in the country increased day by day. The warnings from the Center in its first nine years—warnings of the eroding effects of the Vietnam War, of the smoldering fires in the ghettos, of the rebellion among students, of the spread of inflation and the deepening of distrust, of the apparent inability of the American system to cope with these problems—proved to be depressingly accurate in that year when the United States seemed to be on the verge of breaking into pieces. The Center's foresight justified its existence in the minds of many thinking people and yet raised the question of whether its results could stir enough citizens to seek constructive changes in time to revive and reinvigorate democracy.

While the Vietnam situation was getting worse and the tensions in the country tightened, the Center dialogues continued on many topics. The dialogues were audiotaped for distribution throughout the country and often produced material for the *Center Magazine*, which had become the Center's principal channel of communication. The first issue which had attracted national attention through Harry Ashmore's article ''The Public Relations of Peace,'' had been well received. Thousands of new Center members had been enrolled.

In addition to Ashmore's long article, that issue had presented excerpts from a conversation with Arnold Toynbee (by Scott Buchanan, John Seeley, and Raghavan Iyer, an Indian scholar) in which Toynbee had expressed doubt about the survival of the human race; an interview with Gunnar Myrdal, in which Myrdal declared that the United States was being isolated ''morally and politically'' by its behavior in the Vietnam War; a proposal for building new cities offered by Edgardo Contini; articles by Donald McDonald, Elisabeth Mann Borgese, Edward Engberg, William Gorman,

327

Rexford G. Tugwell, and W. H. Ferry; and my suggestion for an annual report on the state of mankind, to be delivered by the secretary-general of the United Nations.

My proposal was taken up by eight United States Senators, who introduced a resolution in the Senate in January 1968 urging Congress to direct the President to ask the United Nations to adopt the idea. The resolution—cosponsored by William Proxmire, Gaylord Nelson, Claiborne Pell, Joseph Tydings, George McGovern, Joseph Clark, Ralph Yarborough, and Hirman Fong—was opposed by officials in the State Department and did not get through Congress. (The idea of an annual review of where humanity was heading evidently intrigued Richard Nixon, who issued annual reports on the state of the world after he entered the White House.)

The second issue of the *Center Magazine*—released in January, while the Vietcong offensive was stunning many Americans—contained a letter from Ashmore, reacting to private comments by President Johnson and Secretary of State Rusk, who had told friends that there were lots of people "running around the world trying to win a Nobel Peace Prize." Ashmore accused the Washington *Post* of arrogance in suggesting in an editorial that Ashmore regarded the Center as "a sovereign power" and that Ashmore imperiously sent what sounded like "a communiqué from a greater to a lesser, and infinitely more stupid and worse governed, minor state."

Acknowledging that "a good many columnists and editorial writers, and a few diplomatic correspondents" had "used the occasion to point out that amateurs have no business fooling around with diplomacy," Ashmore said: "This, of course, is an unassailable proposition. However, when it is applied to transmittal of a letter actually written in the State Department, it is irrelevant and patently diversionary.

"Neither William Baggs, the editor of the Miami *News*, nor I ever presumed that we were acting as diplomatic representatives when we went to Hanoi, or that we might be in the position of negotiating terms of settlement of the Vietnam conflict. The purpose of our trip was to present an invitation to the Center's 'Pacem in Terris' convocation, which was to be held in Geneva in May. The trip was of course cleared by the State Department and they asked us to pass on our impressions. We did so."

In March 1968, deeply disturbed by a *New York Times* report that President Johnson had decided to send another 206,000 troops to Vietnam on the recommendation of General Westmoreland, Ashmore and Baggs decided to make another trip to Hanoi. They were in touch with Senators Kennedy, Fulbright, McCarthy, and McGovern, and these senators feared that another escalation of the war was likely.

Ashmore cabled Hoang Tung, a North Vietnamese official, on March 11: CONTINUING EFFORT CENTER STUDY DEMOCRATIC INSTITUTIONS TO CLARIFY ISSUES PROLONGING WAR MAKE IT IMPERATIVE WILLIAM BAGGS AND I RETURN HANOI FOR FURTHER CONVERSATION WITH YOU. After receiving a reply from Hoang

Tung, indicating that entry visas would be available, the two Center directors informed the State Department that they were ready to depart. Baggs was invited to stop in Washington for a meeting with Assistant Secretary of State William Bundy and his assistants—Heywood Isham and Frank Sieverts.

Sieverts handed Baggs a summary of United States views on the question of American prisoners in North Vietnam, and asked Baggs to see whether the Hanoi government would be willing to enlarge the exchange of prisoners captured by both sides. Bundy informed Baggs that such an exchange might lead to cooperation in other matters.

Bundy asked Baggs—and Ashmore, through Baggs—to remind the Hanoi government that the United States was prepared to "de-escalate" the war in South Vietnam if the Hanoi government was willing to "match the deescalation."

Since 1968 was an election year, Bundy anticipated that Baggs and Ashmore would be led into a discussion of the possible impact of American politics on the war. Bundy said that the Hanoi government should understand that not a single candidate for the presidency had publicly favored a "unilateral withdrawal of U.S. troops from South Vietnam," and that some of the candidates, "if elected to the presidency, might inaugurate a more harsh war policy than the present one of Mr. Johnson."

Baggs and Ashmore felt that a further intensification of the war might involve an increasing risk of a conflict on a global scale. They felt that they had to do whatever they could to diminish the risk of a third world war.

"Thus, despite all the public and private recriminations of the past, we were recast in our ambivalent role as demi-unofficial emissaries—too important a contact with Hanoi to be dismissed, and too demonstrably independent and recalcitrant to be entrusted with any mission that required absolute fealty to State Department policy," Ashmore and Baggs wrote later.

Ashmore and Baggs were in Hanoi when Johnson announced that he would not be a candidate for the presidency in 1968 and disclosed that he was restricting the American bombing of North Vietnam to "the area north of the demilitarized zone where the continuing enemy build-up directly threatens allied forward positions."

"We are prepared to move immediately toward peace through negotiations," Johnson said. "I am taking the first step to de-escalate the conflict . . . Now, as in the past, the United States is ready to send its representatives to any forum, at any time, to discuss the means of bringing this ugly war to an end."

The two Center directors had met twice with Hoang Tung, the editor of the Hanoi government's newspaper *Nhan Dan*, who served as official spokesman for the government. After Johnson's speech on March 31, Hoang Tung asked for their reactions. They assured him that Johnson had certified the sincerity of his step toward peace by removing himself as a possible presidential candidate in 1968. They urged Ho Chi Minh and his associates to take the offer seriously.

Then Ashmore and Baggs went to the Indonesian embassy in Hanoi and asked Ambassador Nugroho—who had attended the Center's Geneva conference—to transmit a message to the American embassy at Vientiane, the capital city of Laos, for relay to Bundy in Washington. They told Bundy that their discussion in Hanoi of proposals previously reviewed with him had produced a "tentative agreement on procedure" for a meeting between representatives of the Hanoi government and the United States.

On April 3 the Hanoi government sent a message to the American government saying that it would participate in talks with American officials. On April 5 Ashmore and Baggs were given an official *aide-mémoire* outlining Hanoi's position and suggesting that "Phnom Penh or another place to be mutually agreed upon" could be the place of contact. They were asked to deliver this document to the American ambassador in Vientiane.

Before they boarded the plane for Laos, the two Americans were told by the North Vietnamese editor that Martin Luther King, Jr., had been murdered in Memphis and that riots were occurring in American cities. Ashmore and Baggs wrote later: "We had both known King well, from the days when he came out of the obscurity of his Alabama pastorate to lead the Negro Protest against discrimination on Montgomery's buses. . . . We could remember the young preacher's fatalistic, imperturbable courage on occasions when mobs howled outside. And we could hear him again at the *Pacem in Terris* meeting in Geneva, proclaiming in his measured, prophetic tones: 'I criticize America because I love her, and because I want to see her stand as the moral example of the world.' "

They delivered the *aide-mémoire* to Ambassador Sullivan in Vientiane and flew to Washington, where they were astounded to see troops patrolling the streets. Johnson had ordered 4000 regular army and National Guard soldiers into the city to try to end the looting, burglarizing, and burning that had erupted after the slaying of Dr. King.

In Washington, they received the confused treatment which indicated again that the State Department officials did not know how to handle them. The American government refused to treat the *aide-mémoire* they had handed to Ambassador Sullivan as a direct response from the Hanoi government. Assistant Secretary of State William Bundy complained that they had exceeded their "understanding" of what the State Department had authorized them to do in Hanoi.

While they were in a meeting with Bundy, Katzenbach, Averell Harriman, and others, Katzenbach disclosed that Ambassador Sullivan had met with the North Vietnamese chargé d'affaires in Vientiane and that the North Vietnamese had confirmed the fact that they had suggested Phnom Penh in Cambodia as a possible conference site for the negotiations. Harriman then requested that they give all the relevant details of their sessions with Hoang Tung.

In his memoirs, Johnson described the crucial events leading to peace negotiations in these terms:

> Several Americans were in Hanoi at that time, among them William Baggs of the *Miami News*, Harry Ashmore of the Center for the Study of Democratic Institutions, and Charles Collingwood of CBS. Baggs and Ashmore had gone to North Vietnam with our knowledge but with no authority to speak for the U.S. government. They hoped to open a channel of communication that might pave the way for peace talks. Collingwood was in Hanoi gathering news and film for the CBS television network. The day after our acceptance was delivered to the North Vietnamese, these three Americans arrived in Vientiane. Baggs and Ashmore gave William Sullivan, our Ambassador to Laos, a message they had received from the editor of North Vietnam's principal Communist newspaper. They believed that it represented the official position of the Hanoi regime. The message suggested our contact be at the ambassadorial level in Phnomh Penh, Cambodia, "or another place to be mutually agreed upon." Collingwood had received the same message during an interview with North Vietnamese Foreign Minister Nguyen Duy Trinh.
>
> I was interested in these messages, for it appeared the logjam might be breaking. I wanted to move ahead, but I felt we had to show reasonable caution. Apparently the North Vietnamese had given their views to the Americans in Hanoi before Ho Chi Minh and his colleagues had received, or had had a chance to study, our proposal. Hanoi was not replying to our offer on either time or place in these messages. Also there is always some doubt that messages passed through private channels are legitimate reflections of official policy. Hanoi could always disavow as a "misunderstanding" anything sent through newsmen or private citizens. We wanted to have this matter in the hands of official representatives as soon as possible.

There was no doubt, from Johnson's statement, that the two Center directors had opened "a channel of communication" that helped to "pave the way for peace talks." Ambassador Nugroho of Indonesia made it clear to Ashmore and Baggs, in several conversations they had with him, that the Hanoi government had been deeply impressed by the Center's *Pacem in Terris* convocation in Geneva and had been convinced that the two Center directors were trying to aid in ending the war through negotiations acceptable to both sides. The two trips to Hanoi by these two men had helped to "clarify the issues."

The negotiations that began in the spring of 1968 went on for nearly five years under the administrations of Johnson and Nixon. But the escalation of the American involvement stopped in April 1968, after Johnson had withdrawn from the presidential race. The danger of a global war developing from the fighting in the far east then diminished.

Rioting in the ghettos subsided soon after the outbursts following the shooting of Martin Luther King. Tormented by anxiety, Johnson had said in April: "We will have a bad summer. We will have several bad summers before the deficiencies are erased." Nixon, running for the White House, shouted to the voters that a Democratic president could not keep order in America: "There will be war in the streets."

But the worst eruptions came on college campuses. Between January 1 and June 15 there were 221 major upheavals on 101 campuses, involving almost 39,000 students. The demonstrations occurred at small colleges and large universities, from coast to coast. Deans and college presidents were shoved around and their offices were occupied. Foul phrases appeared on walls and epithets were hurled at policemen, sometimes accompanied by rocks and bottles. Buildings were damaged or destroyed by dynamite.

At the Center in Santa Barbara, an agonizing reappraisal of its work and its future was undertaken. Hutchins was in his sixty-ninth year, and he invited the staff members to tell him how the Center could be converted from a relatively benevolent monarchy into a really democratic organization. Week after week, the staff gathered in the conference room to grapple with the difficulties of "constitutionalizing the Center."

In April 1968 Hutchins had released a president's report covering the Center's operations in the three preceding years. The opening pages contained excerpts from a lecture Hutchins had given under the auspices of the Encyclopaedia Britannica at the University of Chicago—*The Truth About the Center.*

"I used to say of the University of Chicago that it was not a very good university; it was just the best there was," Hutchins said in his report. "The truth about the Center for the Study of Democratic Institutions is that it is not a very good center, but it is the only one there is."

After describing the dialogue sessions—which usually occurred five days a week—Hutchins noted that "about a sixth of the papers presented and the tapes of the meetings are made available to the public." Some 7 million copies of Center pamphlets and other documents were in circulation around the world.

"The Center has an annual budget of around $1,500,000 currently supplied by some 40,000 members who contribute annually sums ranging from ten to several hundred thousand dollars," Hutchins said. "The Center receives no money from government and none from large foundations or corporations.

"It is not a think tank hired to do the planning that public agencies or private businesses cannot do for themselves. Neither is it a refuge for scholars who want to get away from it all to do their research and write their books. It is an organized group, rather than a collection of individuals. It is an organization of men who are free of any obligation except to join in the effort to understand the subjects they have selected to study. It is a community, and, since its members are trying to think together, it may be called, at least in potentiality, an intellectual community."

Hutchins immediately added: "This description may be a little high-flown. An eminent philosopher was asked what people would do with themselves when automation had thrown them all out of work. Mortimer Adler replied, 'They could talk with one another.'

"The Center may be regarded as a happy augury of this bright future, as a prefiguring of those activities in which human beings may engage when the curse of Adam is at last repealed. In this light the staff of the Center, having received prematurely, as it were, the gift of leisure, may be seen as proposing a model for the behavior of all of us when we have, as we surely shall, a guaranteed annual income and nothing to do."

Hutchins hastened to say: "But the Center is still hypnotized by the Protestant Ethic, however anachronistic that may be. It could not think of justifying itself by a program so imprecise or so suspiciously egocentric. Its talk is oriented to action. It talks about what ought to be done. The Center Fellows come to the conference table in their capacity as citizens. The talk is about the common good."

Hutchins denied that the Center engaged in political activity but pointed out that the Center Fellows were free to take any public positions they wished to take as individuals. He said wryly: "They all avail themselves of this privilege, sometimes in violent opposition to one another. When the staff is unanimous on any subject, as it is, with varying degrees of warmth, on the war in Vietnam, it earnestly tries to lure into its meetings representatives of a different point of view."

The Center had encountered many difficulties in trying to "lure" supporters of the Vietnam War and other policies into its sessions. With some bitterness, Hutchins observed: "Those who disagree with you will not join in discussion with you because, they say, you are not impartial. This is a self-fulfilling prophecy, for if all those who disagree with you will not join in your discussions, their point of view will not be represented—the charge of partiality will be proved. The prophecy is not merely self-fulfilling; it is self-perpetuating.

"Yet it is evident that at all times in all countries questions have to be raised, if only because change is always occurring everywhere. In a country that aspires to be democratic, the questions have to be discussed by as many of the citizens as possible. When change is going on at the present rate, discussion is a matter of life and death. We are now in the position of the little boy who asked Santa Claus for a volcano—and got it."

Returning to a theme that had dominated his thinking for many years, Hutchins pleaded again for an understanding of the necessity of intellectual communities. He declared that any society without "centers of independent thought and criticism" was bound "to make some sad mistakes."

"A country with great knowledge factories, but without independent thought, systematic criticism, understanding, and wisdom, may be the richest and most powerful, but it will disintegrate, for justice is the cement that holds a political community together."

Hutchins then expressed his deep concern about the future of the Center and his frank recognition that he and his associates might have attempted to do something that was impossible: "Uniqueness does not necessarily imply excellence; it may signify nothing but foolhardiness. Other people may simply have too much sense to attempt similar efforts. This may well be the verdict of history on the Center."

He saw many obstacles to the Center's success: "When philosophy is in disrepute, the Center is committed to it. When standards of moral and political conduct are thought of as personal idiosyncrasies, the Center is struggling to find those which may be universal norms. When the pursuit of knowledge is in the ascendant, the Center has no more interest in it than is necessary to the pursuit of understanding.

"When the dialogue is a joke, the Center takes it seriously. When questions about American policies and American culture are regarded as disruptive, if not unpatriotic, the Center insists on asking them."

There was another difficulty that was extremely hard to overcome, a difficulty that troubled me through all the years of my participation in the Center's work. Hutchins was aware of it: "All this has to be done through men who are themselves products of American culture, who are themselves trained in the pursuit of knowledge, who have trouble, therefore, even in formulating a common vocabulary, who have to turn themselves from full-time specialists into full-time citizens."

Beyond that, there was the question of how men who were steeped in a culture could get "outside" that culture to criticize it from a different perspective. The Center never quite managed to separate itself from the culture in which it existed. Perhaps no educational organization—or any group of people born and educated in a certain culture—could ever do so.

The character of the Center was shaped, in part, by the attacks made on the Fund for the Republic, its parent body. Hutchins noted: "The Fund maintained itself as a small island of sanity in a McCarthyite world and may perhaps take some small credit for the gradual decline of the hysteria the Senator had evoked. . . . The fight was successful, but even success was depressing. For the question was, after the McCarthy period was over, why we had had to suffer from it. What was going to save us from another like it? *Nothing in the American character seemed to guarantee the protection of American ideals.*" [Italics added.]

Actually the fears and suspicions of the late Senator Joseph McCarthy and other cold warriors had affected the policies of Presidents Kennedy and Johnson. Men in the State Department, who knew what had happened to experts on Asia in the 1950s, hesitated to express opposition or raise questions about the expansion of the war in Vietnam. In the 1960s (and the 1970s), men in the American government took every precaution against being accused of being "soft on communism." McCarthyism had penetrated the whole structure of the government.

In his statement *The Truth About the Center*, Hutchins faced the fact that some people were suspicious of the Center because they were suspicious of all institutions. And he took notice of the accusations thrown at the Center by Senator Everett Dirksen of Illinois, the Republican leader in the Senate and an ally of Lyndon Johnson.

"The senior senator from Illinois, according to that newspaper which admits it is the greatest [The Chicago *Tribune*], recently blamed the 'strange mood' of the country on 'such organizations as the Center,' " Hutchins remarked. "The Center, he said, had given instruction to "revolutionaries such as Stokely Carmichael and financial support to movements such as the recent New Politics convention.' "

Hutchins regarded the statement by Senator Dirksen as "hilariously absurd." He was not acquainted with Carmichael—a self-styled black revolutionary leader—and Carmichael had not been at the Center. He said: "Anybody familiar with the balance sheet of the Center would allow himself a rueful smile at the thought of its financing New Politics or anything else."

Hutchins recognized the fact that it was hard for many people to believe that the Center did not have a hidden agenda: "When something is like nothing else, it is hard to comprehend it. The Center is not a school, college, university, or research institute. What is it? Can it be that it is actually trying to understand democratic institutions? Far more likely that something so mysterious is up to no good."

"On the whole, however, the Center cannot complain of its reception," Hutchins said. "In my view we have fared better than we deserve. I regarded our publication program when it started as a worthwhile but probably vain experiment. I opposed the distribution of the tape recordings of our discussions. I fought off for ten years the proposal that we should have a magazine. I was skeptical of the results of any mass appeal for financial support. I have been proved wrong on all counts."

Hutchins exaggerated his pessimism about the Center's publications, its sale of audiotapes, its magazine, and its mass mailings to get contributing members. He had been afraid that there were only a very few citizens who would consider the Center important. But it was true that other members of the Center staff—Edward Reed, John Cogley, W. H. Ferry, Hallock Hoffman, Harry Ashmore, and I—had persuaded him that the Center's publications and tapes would find a wide response.

"I underestimated the number of people in this country who share the concern of the staff of the Center," Hutchins said. "I underestimated the depth of their concern. They are certainly a tiny minority of the population

—but in absolute terms there are a great many of them. The Center expects to have 50,000 members by June, 1968. They are aware of the gap between American ideals and American policy and performance. They want to narrow it. They want to join the search for justice and understanding, and they do not believe they can look for much light from traditional sources, such as the church, the press, and the university. Inadequate as they must feel the Center is, they nevertheless appear grateful for the illumination that issues from it."

Illumination was not enough for several members of the Center staff and several Center consultants who plunged into the political struggles of 1968. John Cogley took a leave of absence to aid the presidential candidacy of Senator Eugene McCarthy, and Harry Ashmore campaigned for McCarthy in California and supported his candidacy with advice and counsel. Harold Willens, who had helped to form a committee of businessmen against the Vietnam War, raised money for McCarthy and other antiwar candidates.

Stanley K. Sheinbaum became a candidate for Congress, and so did Paul Jacobs and Fred Warner Neal. John Seeley and Bishops Edward Crowther and James A. Pike spoke passionately against the war and showed their sympathy for the students who rallied to McCarthy's banner. Only Rexford Tugwell, who still had some respect for Lyndon Johnson, and a few others at the Center did not participate actively in the antiwar movement.

The nation was shaken by two violent deaths in 1968—the murder of Martin Luther King in Memphis and the shooting of Senator Robert Kennedy in Los Angeles. Death struck hard at the Center too. At the meeting of the board of directors in Santa Barbara on May 10, 1968, Hutchins mourned the passing of Walter Millis and Scott Buchanan, two of the most fertile contributors to the Center's program.

For seven weeks in April and May of 1968, the Center participated in a Centennial Lecture Series presented as a tribute to the people of California on the 100th anniversary of the founding of the University of California. The sessions in this series were held in Campbell Hall at the Santa Barbara campus of the university and were organized by Raghavan Iyer and me.

"Powerful and impersonal forces of change are impinging upon our lives in America today," the University of California said in announcing the series. "The coming decades hold the prospect of a radical transformation of our society and the emergence of a world community. In confronting and meeting these changes, what are our creative capabilities and potentials, our individual and collective responsibilities?"

Participants in this series, which was entitled "Man in the Age of Revolutionary Change," included Stringfellow Barr, Hutchins, James Pike, John Wilkinson, John Seeley, and me. Iyer, who was a professor in political philosophy at the university as well as a consultant to the Center, served as moderator and was the final speaker on the topic, "The Unfinished Revolution: Elitism and Equality."

Each session provided speakers from the university faculty and two students as commentators. Faculty participants were Vernon I. Cheadle, chancellor; Stanley V. Anderson, from the department of political science; Edward S. Casey, from the department of philosophy; Richard W. Comstock, from the department of religious studies; and Robert L. Kelley and Leonard Marsak, from the department of history. The sessions were open to the public and to students seeking credits in the social sciences.

The possibilities of various kinds of revolution were in the air all through the summer and fall of 1968. The students who participated in the University of California–Center series were moderate and peaceful compared with the militants who had taken over Columbia University that spring, occupying buildings and camping in the president's office until they were evicted with bloody force by a thousand policemen, who clubbed their heads and arrested 698 of them, including Mark Rudd, who had mobilized the militants. The police brutality at Columbia had horrified John Seeley, Bishop Pike, Stringfellow Barr, and others at the Center, who had hoped that such confrontations could be avoided.

In August thousands of young people gathered in Chicago's Lincoln Park to demonstrate against the Vietnam War and to try to get the Democratic national convention there to nominate Eugene McCarthy or George McGovern, the peace candidates for president. Mayor Richard Daley ordered the police to clear the park each night, refusing to allow the young demonstrators to sleep in its meadows. Clashes occurred between the police and the young people. Priests, ministers, and other concerned citizens tried to form a line between the two groups but were swept aside. The police, angered by taunts and insults, pelted by beer cans and rocks, gave a final warning and then attacked the young people, spectators, reporters, and clergymen, beating them with clubs and pistols and hurling tear gas.

Among the people who went to Chicago with the hope of averting violence were the Center's dean, John Seeley, and another Center fellow, Bishop C. Edward Crowther. Both returned to the Center in a state of burning indignation at what had happened. Both spoke out vigorously, urging their fellow citizens to oppose the injustices in American society.

Richard Nixon made the maintenance of "law and order" a principal issue in his drive for the presidency in 1968. But what did "law and order" mean in a society as divided as the United States was in that year? How could laws and liberties be reconciled in such an atmosphere?

The Center devoted some of its attention to these hard problems, facing the issues in statements drafted by consultants and staff members. These statements were published in the *Center Magazine* in its November issue, just before the national election.

"Violence is antilaw, but nonviolent civil disobedience should be recognized by the courts as a legal method of dissent," declared Harrop Freeman, a Center outside consultant and a professor at Cornell law school. "The young are telling us that the revolution (or 'radical restructuring,' to use a milder term) to bring all men—poor, Negro, young—into full society is *now*."

"Freedom of dissent is predicated on the loyalty of dissenters," Rexford Tugwell insisted. "Men who are free to object are still not privileged to disrupt. . . . If they refuse the expected loyalty, they will risk suppression. It may be worth it; they will certainly make that claim if they rebel and win. But the landscape of revolution, after it is over, is often as barren as a valley after the dam at its head has given way."

Expressing sympathy for the young people protesting against some American policies, John Cogley wrote: "Our salvationist policies have led us into one irony after another. The desire for peace, for instance, has led to militarism; the preoccupation with security has led to the development of weapons whose very existence is enough to keep the nation jittery; the wish to save other peoples from themselves has led to their determination to be protected from us. . . . The older generation by and large still looks on America through eyes that only two decades ago saw nothing but idealistic motivation and good will. The protesting young, though, have their eyes on the present and they brand our idealism as hollow rhetoric."

Harry Ashmore contended that the young rebels had also produced a peculiar rhetoric: "The activists are few, but from them emanates an idealized version of the dream in which the great, corrupt American establishment comes tumbling down before the onslaught of the innocent. . . . But these are not all or even most of the young." He had been in Chicago at the Democratic convention, and he had noted that the National Guardsmen called into the city to preserve order in August were also young: "These were boys from Skokie and Peoria and East St. Louis, largely bypassed by the affluence that underwrites the middle-class protest movement." He thought such guardsmen would not hesitate to shoot the rebels if ordered to do so: "This would be the ultimate tragedy, and the ultimate irony, for if reality ever overtakes the rhetoric, the old and corrupt will be somewhere else when the young provide their own executioners."

"The limits of dissent cannot be the limits set by law, because nobody knows what the law is, and while the Supreme Court sits nobody will," Robert Hutchins said. "What was illegal yesterday is lawful today, because the Court changes its composition or its mind. The only way to find out whether an ordinance, regulation or statute is Constitutional is to violate it and see what happens. . . . Where the object of the infraction is to test the constitutionality of the law in question, and no illegal violence is done by the defendants, they should not be held to have passed the limits of dissent."

In the same issue of the magazine, the difficulties confronting the American legal system in a time of crisis were raked over by two judges, a sociologist, a former district attorney, and Center staff members. Federal Judge Warren E. Burger—later appointed by President Nixon to be the Chief Justice of the United States—said that his observations of courts in the Netherlands and Denmark, during five summers of study, had convinced him that the American system needed major improvements.

"The professional criminal prefers the American adversary system because it has many things built into it that he can exploit," Judge Burger said. "In Europe, instead of a jury, there are three professional judges who try every type of case. At some lower levels and in the case of minor violations, one professional judge may try. These judges have made this their life work. They started as magistrates and as junior judges and moved on up. They are not drawn from the practice of law as judges are in the United States.

"Some might argue that such professional judges will become hardened, calloused, insensitive. My observation has been to the contrary. I believe that they are sensitive, responsive, compassionate, and much more tolerant of human frailties than American judges. They will never send a man to prison on a first offense. For a second offense, more often than not, a man gets probation, with the threat of confinement hanging over him. In the view of European judges, the threat of confinement is a greater deterrent than confinement itself."

Judge Burger asserted that European courts did not have the "restrictive rules of evidence" used in the United States. He added: "In northern European countries, the system is one of inquiry instead of an accusatory-adversary method. I do not mean there is no contention. The defense lawyer works to put his client's best foot forward. But the European court is concerned to find out from everyone who has any possible connection with the case everything it can through questioning, and this includes questioning defendants. In our system we cannot ask the defendant questions unless he takes the stand voluntarily."

Doubts about the value of juries were voiced by Judge Burger, although he recognized that two amendments in the American Bill of Rights were designed to guarantee trials by juries. He indicated that juries were being used less and less often in England, and had almost disappeared on the continent of Europe. But more and more defendants were demanding jury proceedings in criminal cases in America.

Judge Burger favored a reconsideration of the Fifth Amendment, another important part of the Bill of Rights. He stated: "I heard one Supreme Court justice say in a seminar that the presumption of innocence is 'rooted in the Constitution.' Well, it may be rooted there, but you cannot find it there. . . . Certainly you have heard—and judges have said—that one should not convict a man out of his own mouth. The fact is that we establish responsibility and liability and we convict in all the areas of civil litigation out of the mouth of the defendant."

At the Center, the reappraisal of its programs and personnel had gone on through the year. The gentle, soothing dean of the academic program, John Seeley, who tried to understand everybody and spoke in soft ecclesiastical tones, seemed to feel that much progress had been made. But the fellows still sparred with one another and still leaned heavily on Hutchins for ultimate decisions on important matters.

When the directors flew into Santa Barbara for a meeting on November 22, they had in their briefcases copies of an optimistic report from Dean Seeley sent to them with other materials by Chairman Hutchins.

"The transaction of business, in a now-regular weekly meeting of the Senior Fellows (and Consultants in Residence, and Administration and Publications people with responsibilities closely related to the academic program), has ordered and routinized and settled a great many matters in a manner more satisfactory than heretofore," Dean Seeley said in his report.

"It has also served to draw together and strengthen the Fellowship, while at the same time better, more readily and more surely coordinating the Center as a whole. It marks a true, good and important advance into Collegiality—something upon which the Center will have to come more and more to rely. (By 'Collegiality' I mean nothing more or less than is meant by the term in the renewal of the Church: the effective and mutually enhancing interdependence of Head and Members.)"

But Dean Seeley felt that the most notable result of the months of talking and maneuvering had been the adoption of a Center program for several years ahead, "subject only to alteration upon sufficiently weighty new considerations."

The Center Program of Studies and Projects—a "study" was defined as a topic deserving long and deep examination; a project was defined as a matter requiring "brief attention"—had been adopted by the fellows at their session on October 23, Seeley reported.

In Seeley's outline, the studies fully defined and under way were listed as constitutionalization of the world, with Elisabeth Mann Borgese chiefly responsible for this study; constitutionalization of the United States, with Rexford G. Tugwell in charge; constitutionalization of science and technology, with Harvey Wheeler responsible; constitutionalization of criminal justice administration with Robert Hutchins chiefly responsible; organization theory, with Harvey Wheeler and John Wilkinson sharing responsibility; and the civilization of the dialogue, with Wilkinson generally responsible.

Studies "preliminarily or well defined and in development" included federalism, with Wheeler as the anchor man; development, with William Gorman responsible; policing and policy (closely related to the study of criminal justice), with Hallock Hoffman as coordinator; national service, a topic for which Dean Seeley took responsibility; corporate development, coordinated by Donald McDonald; the professions, with Edward Engberg responsible; potentials of the United States Constitution, with Gerald Gottlieb; the school (and education), with Peter Marin, Hallock Hoffman, and John Seeley.

Other studies described by Seeley as "not yet adequately defined but definitely to be explored" were the church and religious institutions, with Donald McDonald, and the city, with Harry Ashmore. To be "further defined and adopted only if definition is adequate and resources permit" were a number of studies including one on youth, the family, and conservation. Major projects listed by the Dean were "The Deep Seas," with Mrs. Borgese responsible; "Africa," with Bishop C. Edward Crowther to develop it; and "The Law of Disruption and Dissent," with Robert Hutchins chiefly responsible.

No study of the mass media or of continuing education—my own principal interests—was included in this agenda. My major responsibility at this time was administrative: to "extend the dialogue" by arranging meetings and programs in cooperation with the University of California, educational broadcasting and television, community colleges, and other educational institutions. I took part in most of the dialogues at the Center, but I was not expected to be responsible for any of the academic studies.

W. H. Ferry, another officer of the Center, was not mentioned in the outline of the Center program, which was given to the board of directors as an appendix to Seeley's report. Ferry had been a vociferous participant in dialogues on nearly all the topics Seeley had listed, and it was surprising to see that he was not cited as a person chiefly responsible for one or more of them.

Seeley did say, however, "The list is firmly adopted, but not frozen, so that experience may lead us to amend it by addition, subtraction or transformation; but we will not now entertain such changes lightly.

"We have failed so far to develop a unifying view and statement as to what holds together each of the studies adopted severally, even though they were adopted on good grounds after lengthy reflection," he said. "We trust to coming experience to reveal the unity, and permit a statement of its nature.

"I look to this next year for some fruition from all this labor, and a happy issue out of some of our afflictions," Seeley concluded. He attached to his report the names of dozens of subjects and more than 100 papers presented at the Center in the period from April 17 to October 31. He had been an active and imaginative Dean, and the scope of the program was impressive to the board members, who congratulated Dr. Seeley.

It seemed evident that Robert Hutchins had placed much confidence in John Seeley. Hutchins usually took the lead in discussions of the academic program of the Center. At the November 1968 meeting of the directors, however, attention was focused on Dean Seeley.

Members of the board were saddened by the absence of Chester Carlson, who had died of a heart attack in New York two months before the Santa Barbara meeting. Carlson had remembered the Center in his will, leaving a bequest of approximately $5 million. The money had not yet been received, but it was expected to reach the Center within a year.

John Perry, the secretary and treasurer, reported that the Center was in better financial condition than it had been for a long time, with assets totaling more than $4 million. With this rosy picture before them, the directors quickly appropriated more than half a million dollars to eliminate deficits in various accounts, transferring money from the general fund.

Perry told the board that the Internal Revenue Service had finished its audit of the Center's books, but there had been no indication of its findings. The audit had been undertaken, of course, at the instigation of Representative Teague. The revenue agents had shown no signs of hostility toward the Center, and it was not anticipated that the Center's charter as a tax-exempt educational institution would be revoked.

The board was informed that the number of Center members had increased to 68,000 and continued to rise at a satisfactory rate. The Center's total income during the 1967–68 fiscal year was $2,546,414, including a large donation from Carlson. The Center seemed to have the momentum necessary to carry it forward for several years.

William Baggs, who died from a sudden illness a few weeks after this gathering of the board, thought that the moment had come to free the Center from its continual pleading for funds. He proposed a resolution—which was adopted after some discussion—declaring that board members should contribute substantially to the Center and persuade other donors to do so as soon as possible to get the Center permanently endowed. The resolution asked the vice chairman—J. R. Parten—to appoint a Committee on Funding to handle this task.

An endowment committee already existed. But it had not been able to obtain any large amounts for the Center. Baggs and the other directors who supported his resolution hoped that a new effort would be more successful. Parten had tried hard to get action from the endowment committee, and Parten was willing to try again.

Two wealthy men were elected to the board at the November 1968 meeting to fill the vacancies caused by the deaths of Chester Carlson and Lyle Spencer. Stewart Rawlings Mott, who owned many shares of General Motors stock, was a New York investor and philanthropist who had been a major financial contributor and active supporter in the 1968 presidential nomination campaigns of Nelson Rockefeller, Republican governor of New York, and of Eugene McCarthy, Democratic senator from Minnesota. Howard Stein, president of the Dreyfus Fund and the Dreyfus Corporation, had raised millions of dollars for Senator McCarthy's campaign.

With the addition of these two men, the directors were hopeful that the money to put the Center on an enduring basis could be obtained. The board members seemed to be well pleased by the academic program, the publications, the distribution of audiotapes, the continuing education projects, the magazine and other elements in the communications program, and the expansion of the Center's influence. Relations between the directors and the staff seemed to be harmonious.

There was one jarring note in the meeting, however, that made some of the fellows and staff members wonder how long the harmony would last. Hutchins was asked by Levinson whether there was a possibility that the Center had a "frozen" staff. Hutchins said that every effort was made to get the best possible staff and "to keep them as long as they are useful." He did not define what he meant by "useful" or who would decide which staff members were "useful" or not useful.

Then Hutchins added that there was "a policy against permanent appointments." He went over the composition of the staff—in the presence of most of the staff members, who were in the room with the directors—and described his plans to "improve the balance" to "cover the studies planned for the next few years." This disturbed staff members who had been with the Center for long periods of service and who had been described in the report issued to the press and the public in the spring of 1968 as "the permanent members of the Center, now designated as Fellows."

While there may have been "a policy against permanent appointments," the staff members who had been "designated as Fellows" had come to believe that they were "permanent members" of the intellectual community called the Center. In the Hutchins statement *The Truth About the Center*, incorporated in the report that covered the years 1965, 1966, and 1967, he had asserted: "The Center consists of twenty-five men who meet every day. . . . It is an organization of men who are free of any obligation except to join in the effort to understand the subjects they have selected to study. It is a community. . . . "

The Hutchins statement sent a shiver through some of the staff members who were there that day. It did not appear to bother Seeley, who had given up an appointment as a tenured professor at Brandeis University to join the Center community, or others who felt that Hutchins had made commitments to them that would prevent their removal from the staff in any reorganization. I thought I understood what Hutchins meant by a "policy against permanent appointments." Since the Center did not have the money to guarantee its own permanence, such a policy had to be taken for granted.

If Chester Carlson had not left the Center $5 million in his will, the Fellowship might have continued indefinitely along the lines indicated by Dean Seeley in his report. But the prospect of receiving that $5 million revived an old vision in the mind of Robert Hutchins—a vision of establishing a "world academy" with great thinkers drawn from a number of countries.

The Center's table was already crowded. If the thinkers from other countries were to have places there, some of those who regarded themselves as fellows—and had been recognized as "permanent" members of the staff —would have to be removed through persuasion or compulsion. The Center would have to be "refounded."

But how could it be done? After months of arguments, held week after week, the fellows had adopted a program on October 23. By accepting Seeley's report, the board had endorsed that program. Could the Center be turned in a new direction without severely disrupting the "intellectual community" and the board?

Those of us who saw Hutchins almost daily in the closing days of 1968 knew that he was a troubled man. His face had a gray color. He was approaching the age of seventy, and he made it plain to me and to others that the Center was still far from what he had hoped it would become.

While Dean Seeley apparently believed that the fellows had made "a true, good and important advance into Collegiality"—by which he meant "the effective and mutually enhancing interdependence of Head and Members"—the head of the Center appeared to be suffering from frustrations and disappointments. Some of the fellows were not revealing the brilliance or the ability to contribute to the dialogues that he had expected from them. Others seemed to irritate him by being immediately critical of most of the proposals offered by their colleagues.

The members who seemed to be in the closest rapport with Hutchins in these weeks were Harry Ashmore, Harvey Wheeler, John Cogley, and John Seeley. He was frequently closeted with Ashmore, who was ready to carry out his every wish. A noticeable distance had developed between Hutchins and Ferry, who seemed to feel that his most effective service was to be a perpetual critic.

As the year ended, there was an air of uncertainty at the Center. No one seemed quite sure about what Hutchins was going to do.

PART FOUR

Struggles in the Nixon Era

23

In the era of "a new Nixon," Hutchins goes back to an old dream

AFTER THE RIOTS AND RAGES of 1968, the next year began bleakly for many Americans. When Richard Nixon swore to uphold the Constitution at his inauguration in January 1969, most of the fellows at the Center feared that the Constitution was in grave danger. Nixon was a cold warrior; he had attacked liberals and intellectuals; he had smeared the Democrats with accusations of coddling traitors. He seemed capable of anything.

But when he became president on January 29, Nixon appeared as a man of reason. He tried to calm the country down. He had gained a very narrow victory over Hubert Humphrey, and his shrewd sense prompted him to present "a new Nixon." In his inaugural address, he reached heights of noble rhetoric. He might have been reading Center pamphlets.

"We are torn by division," Nixon said. "To a crisis of the spirit, we need an answer of the spirit. And to find that answer, we need only look within ourselves. . . . We cannot learn from one another until we stop shouting at one another—until we speak quietly enough so that our words can be heard as well as our voices. . . ."

When Nixon took office, the state of the American union was bad. The state of the Center, in terms of its rising membership and its growing prestige, seemed to be good. Yet there was a crisis of the spirit at the Center—a crisis that dialogue did not seem able to dissolve.

Three days after Nixon's inauguration, the international recognition of the Center's value was demonstrated in a conference of Japanese and American leaders who gathered there to consider new approaches to Mao's China and other possible changes in Japanese and American policies. The Japanese participants were leaders from the Japanese parliament and successful businessmen. The American participants—besides Hutchins, Ashmore, and other Center fellows—included Senator Fulbright; Senator John Sherman

Cooper, former American ambassador to India; Senator Mark Hatfield; Senator Alan Cranston; Arthur Goldberg, former American ambassador to the United Nations; and others with knowledge of Asia and influence in Washington. President Nixon had not sent a representative, as he had been invited to do, but members of his staff had expressed interest in the meeting's results.

The Japanese-American conference received extensive coverage in American and Japanese newspapers, and some attention on the broadcasting networks in the United States and Asia. The Center was hailed for its role in bringing the leaders together for frank and productive conversations. The Japanese hoped that another such meeting could be held in Tokyo, or perhaps in China.

The admiration generated for the Center by such activities, by the success of the *Center Magazine,* and by the steadily increasing demand for the Center's audiotapes in schools and colleges did not seem to satisfy Robert Hutchins. It was a famous and apparently valuable Center, but it was not the kind of Center he wanted it to be.

Tension was evident in words and glances at the weekly staff meetings. There were moments of humor and relaxation, but the atmosphere was frequently clouded. Various fellows had lists of those regarded as effective in the dialogues and those whose status seemed to be dropping. Dean Seeley was supposed to have a list. Ashmore reportedly had a list. Rumors flowed from office to office.

In February 1969 I was taken to a hospital for an emergency operation. My despair at the divisions in the Center made it difficult to recover. Perhaps I had been too idealistic about it. I had hoped that it could be free of the factions and animosities that caused so much havoc in human relations.

What hope could there be for the world if the Center staff members, dedicated to the use of reason, could not find a way of reorganizing without expelling some of the members? What future would there be for those who might be forced to leave? If such a breakup occurred, could friendships be maintained? Or was friendship a meaningless idea in an intellectual community? How could such a breakup be explained to the Center members, to the people in many countries who regarded the Center as a rare place, a place of peace, a light upon a high hill—a peak in man's evolution?

While these thoughts went mournfully through my mind, many of my colleagues came to see me. Hutchins, John Cogley, Irving Laucks, and Ping Ferry came frequently. Ferry brought more books than I could manage to read. Bishop Pike anointed me with oils from Jerusalem. Bishop Crowther, who had just returned from a trip to Nigeria, where he had tried to help the starving Biafrans in the civil war there, also visited me and held eucharistic services in my room.

Buoyed by these signs of affection, I began to recover. But I learned that there was no healing at the Center. Cogley and Laucks told me that the bickering and backbiting among the fellows deeply disturbed them. In the staff meetings, the same arguments were repeated, the same ground was covered again and again.

One night in the hospital, Hutchins struck the railing at the end of my bed with his fist. He'd had enough. He didn't think the fellows could ever agree on what kind of constitutional structure they could accept. There were few references to the common good, to the future of the community as a whole. He was going to resign.

I couldn't believe that he would resign, but he seemed serious about it. He paced up and down the room. He told me he had thought about turning the Center over to Harry Ashmore. "Ashmore should be my successor. He's earned it."

"Could he hold the place together, if you left?" I asked him.

Hutchins shrugged. "Maybe nobody can hold it together, the way it is now."

A few days later he came in again, looking more frustrated and despondent than ever. "I'm going to quit," he said. "I can't see any way of making the place what it should be." I told him again that I thought his resignation might mean the end of the Center.

It seemed to me later that he talked about resigning because he hated to face the surgical pain of a reorganization. He did not like to inflict pain, or to confront it personally, although he did make sharp and cutting remarks occasionally in the dialogues and in his public speeches. When he had been a director of the Ford Foundation he had refused to go on a trip to India because he could not bear the prospect of the poverty and suffering he was sure to encounter there.

When I returned to the Center after my convalescence, I found that the fellows were still bogged down. Proposals were made and discussed, but no consensus developed. Dean Seeley apparently did not wish to bring the arguments to a conclusion. Seeley also was reluctant to inflict pain on anyone.

At the staff meeting on April 30, Hutchins passed Seeley a handwritten note: "I am gradually coming to the conclusion that, much to my regret, self-government of this group as it is at present is impossible. 1. Members of the present group are not by mere membership—in many cases accidental—qualified to 'be' the Center. 2. Members are not actuated (in all cases) by a desire to achieve the common good. They are expressing their 'individuality' or individual prejudices often without regard to the topic under discussion."

Seeley scribbled a comment: "But I do not know how this is remediable. . . ." Hutchins wrote back: "Fire some or start over." Seeley replied: "But I count upon (half faith, half dogma) that a long slow process will turn all further to the common good. Patience and guidance and strength." Hutchins then wrote: "You are a young man. . . ." Seeley was intensely aware of Hutchins' sense of his age and the shortness of time. But he did not seem to realize then that Hutchins was about to take some decisive action.

Ferry had not realized it either. Ferry had left on a vacation trip to Britain, apparently believing that the talking about the Center's future would go on indefinitely.

On April 30 Hutchins spoke with Ashmore, Cogley, Seeley, Wheeler, and Neil Jacoby—a professor from the University of California in whom he had confidence—about naming them to a special committee to advise him on a reorganization procedure. Cogley did not like this idea. He felt that some of the fellows might believe that the group on the committee might not be impartial enough in choosing new fellows. He did not want to take that responsibility.

As an alternative, Cogley suggested that Hutchins might appoint himself as the first of a new group of senior fellows. He could then appoint a second new fellow. These two could appoint a third, if they agreed on a choice. A majority of the three could appoint a fourth, and the process would continue as long as they could agree on other selections. The idea appealed to Hutchins. He wanted a new Center, but he did not want the sole responsibility for picking all the new fellows.

At the afternoon meeting on May 7, Hutchins began by referring to the approach of the fifteenth anniversary of his service as president of the Fund and to the fact that the Center was nearly ten years old.

"I think we ought to refound the place," Hutchins said. He did not explain what he meant by "we." He had the powers of a constitutional monarch. Perhaps he was using a royal "we."

He declared that the time had come to form the "academy" or the "true university" to which he had been dedicated for many years. He had tried to make the idea a reality at Yale, he recalled, and he had tried again at the University of Chicago.

"When I got to the Ford Foundation, I tried it there," Hutchins said. The foundation had sponsored gatherings of brilliant people in 1952 and 1953 to consider the formation of a "world academy," but the project had died when Paul Hoffman and Hutchins left the foundation.

"I thought we came fairly close when we started the Center in 1959 with the Consultants we had then," Hutchins said. But the consultants had not been willing to be full-time participants in the Center, and the Center had moved from project to project without becoming the place he had envisioned.

"It is probably more difficult to do now than ever before," Hutchins admitted. "But it is more necessary to try it."

He had decided to revive that dream again, that dream he had treasured before the formation of the Fund for the Republic, the dream of bringing together in the right place in the right atmosphere the finest minds in the world with absolute freedom—so that streams of wisdom might flow for the benefit of humanity now and for the generations to come.

He wanted the Center to be released from any limitations implied in the study of democratic institutions or in the American past. He said: "Until the Ford money was gone, it might have been argued that we had to confine ourselves to civil liberties and civil rights.'' But the Ford money had been spent. The Center had new sources of income, and it could develop in a new direction.

In a soft, low voice Hutchins told the group at the green table in the Center's conference room that the reorganization would involve ''a reconstitution, a reconsideration of who constitutes the senior fellows.'' He said, quietly, ''We were all brought together on a different basis for a different purpose.'' He did not say who had brought them together.

''The method would be for me to appoint myself a senior fellow, then a second,'' Hutchins said. Then others would be selected ''from the present members and from outside.''

He indicated that he hoped ''to move very rapidly'' and that consideration might even be given to changing the name of the Center. He hoped it would be possible to achieve the reorganization ''with a minimum dislocation'' for the existing staff.

After he finished his brief outline of what he proposed to do, there was a silence. Harvey Wheeler later described it as ''a tomblike silence.'' Hutchins invited questions. The questions came haltingly. No one challenged the basic idea.

Several questions focused on whether the Center needed a new name. Elisabeth Borgese strongly favored keeping the old name because of ''its international prestige.'' Cogley said, ''What's in a name? I'm in favor of keeping what we have.''

There were questions about whether the ''true university'' would have students. Hutchins said that could be settled by the new senior fellows. He gave a similar answer to a question about whether the Center or the Fund would need a new charter.

Then Peter Marin, a visiting fellow, said, ''If I do understand what's going on, I'm surprised at the public equanimity shown by people here in accepting the dissolution of the old Center.'' He expressed his disturbance at what he regarded as a lack of bravery on the part of the ''older men'' on the staff. Bishop Pike, Dean Seeley, Hallock Hoffman, and others voiced warm approval of the plan. Perhaps all of them thought they would be among the chosen ones.

In public statements Hutchins had depicted the Center as ''an organized group'' of ''twenty-five men who meet every day . . . '', but on that afternoon of May 7, 1969, the men at the table did not behave as ''an organized group'' with any real authority—except the authority to place their lives in the hands of Robert Hutchins. And that was what they did.

Responding to Marin, Dean Seeley said that if he had thought the procedure was wrong he would not have hesitated to oppose Hutchins. Donald McDonald was torn by his commitment to the Center as a community and his deference to Hutchins, the founder. He admitted that the unwillingness of the men there to speak for the existing community might appear as ''a lack of bravery," but he added that everyone deferred to Hutchins as "a wise man, a good man."

That was my feeling, too. Hutchins had brought the existing Center into being, and Hutchins could change it or dissolve it. Hutchins had persuaded the Fund's board to change the Fund from a grant-making foundation into a place for studies conducted by a professional staff. All our years of working with him had not given us the right to tell him he could not do what he seemed to be determined to do. For me—and perhaps for McDonald and others—Hutchins had a kind of papal authority.

"If members of the group would like to argue me out of this position, I'm open to it," Hutchins said. No one tried to do that. No one offered a counterproposal.

Two days later, on May 9, at an executive session of the Fund's board in the Santa Barbara Biltmore hotel, Hutchins described again what he had in mind. He mentioned his age, and indicated that he felt "actuarial considerations" required new arrangements. He referred to his previous attempts to engage the best minds available in dialogues at Yale, at the University of Chicago, and in the Ford Foundation.

With the Carlson bequest, he thought there was enough money in sight to make another effort to scale the mountain, to reach the heights of wisdom. A tenth anniversary endowment campaign was being designed, with a goal of $15 million. So he felt that the resources were in hand or in view to bring together "a small group of distinguished intellectuals who would assume full-time responsibility for the academic program of the Center, and for its academic governance."

Hutchins reminded the board that it had endorsed such a concept when the Center was formed. But the Fund's finances at that time had not permitted him to give the guarantee of permanence necessary to attract fellows of the highest quality.

Many of the fellows and staff during the first ten years of the Center had been appointed for purposes unrelated to the projected program, Hutchins said. The fellows who were qualified did not provide a proper balance among the academic disciplines. Some of those serving as fellows were not really interested in the program the majority had approved, and contributed little to it.

The directors were told that the proposal for reorganization had been "unanimously approved" at a meeting of the fellows on May 7 "with all qualified members present except W. H. Ferry, who was on vacation. . . . John R. Seeley, who had let the movement for constitutionalization, and Hallock Hoffman, who had been his principal supporter, informed the fellows that they endorsed the proposal 'enthusiastically.' "

Seniel Ostrow asked how many of the existing fellows would qualify for appointment as new senior fellows. Hutchins estimated that "six or seven, at the most, would be named senior fellows under any objective procedure based on demonstrated qualifications or past performance." He added that "another four or five probably could be continued on a full-time basis to carry out editorial or administrative duties in which they were already engaged, since there would be no lessening of the publication, development, and public relations requirements under the new program."

Hutchins requested that the board should permit him to make "very generous severance arrangements," saying that among those who might be discharged under the plan were persons whose service went back to "the very earliest days of the Fund for the Republic." (Ferry and Hoffman, who were severed, had been with the Fund for fifteen years.) He suggested that the maximum arrangement might provide a terminated person protection against loss of income for a period as long as two years. Adjustments for others would be made on the basis of longevity and special circumstances, he said.

The board of directors spent about an hour on the proposal for a drastic reorganization of the Center. If Hutchins was for it, they welcomed it. The meeting convened for the executive session at 11 A.M., and ended at 12:15. About 15 minutes were spent on a proposal for a conference of Arab and Israeli scholars, and the directors authorized Hutchins to explore the possibilities of such a gathering.

When the time came for a vote on the reorganization plan, several of the directors spoke ardently for it. No one opposed it. On a motion by Morris Levinson, seconded by Joseph Drown, the chairman—J. R. Parten—declared that the board "had unanimously approved the reorganization procedure proposed by the president, and authorized him to initiate the plan forthwith."

At the special meeting of the directors in the afternoon of May 9 at the headquarters of Eucalyptus Hill, the members took note of the resignation of John L. Perry as secretary and treasurer, and expressed sorrow at the death of William Baggs. Hutchins reported that Linus Pauling, who had taken a leave of absence to serve as a professor of chemistry at the University of California in San Diego, had been given another year's leave to take an appointment as a professor at Stanford University.

The directors had before them another optimistic report on the academic program from Dean Seeley, who said that the strength of the fellowship was growing—"though more slowly than I had hoped"—and asserted that the fellowship was attempting to define "the role it believes it should play and be able to play, as the Center moves more and more, as it must, from a loose and uncertainly enduring association gathered around one extraordinary and charismatic figure, to an institution hoping of indefinite duration, and capable of surviving such changes of personnel and circumstance as are implied in that new status."

No director commented on Seeley's report, according to the minutes. No director said to Seeley that the "extraordinary and charismatic figure" to whom he referred—quite evidently, Robert Hutchins—had already received approval for proceeding to form a new academy. Seeley was aware that there were "changes of personnel," which were bound to come. He thought he had an assurance from Hutchins that he would be one of the survivors.

In this open session Ashmore summarized the results of the Japanese-American conference held at the Center in January. Arrangements for another international conference sponsored by the Center were moving along, Ashmore told the board. A seminar of Latin American economic and social changes had been developed by Raul Prebisch, an Argentine economist, and Justice William O. Douglas, who had long been concerned about poverty and oppression in Latin America. The seminar had been designed to assemble Latin American experts for candid talks, with limited participation by North American leaders.

The conference, which would be held in Mexico City, would be financed by the Parvin Foundation with a grant of $25,000 to the Center. Fred Warner Neal and Luis Quintanilla had aided in its organization, Ashmore said.

At the prodding of Elisabeth Mann Borgese, the Center had become deeply involved in studies of proposals for peaceful development of the resources of the oceans. Ashmore said the Fellows had approved a recommendation by Mrs. Borgese for an international conclave to be called *Pacem in Maribus*, to be held in June of 1970 on the island of Malta, with the Republic of Malta serving as host and sharing in the cost.

Ashmore informed the board that John Perry, who had formed a new public relations agency, had been employed by the Fund as a consultant for promotion and fund raising. With Perry's help, the Center had begun to hunt for $712,000, its estimated share of the expenses of the Malta conference.

The desirability of obtaining a $15 million endowment fund for the Center came up again. Ashmore said Perry had been retained to prepare and carry out a program for getting that endowment. Again the board members expressed their willingness to cooperate in this effort.

Ashmore said that the direct mail program launched in September 1967 had brought the total number of paid Center memberships to 92,897 in April 1969. He declared: "It appears that by the end of the second year we will have absorbed the entire cost of the publications program, which had been running at a deficit of $320,000 a year. After paying for all editorial overhead, production, promotion, distribution and membership servicing the two-year program should return a net profit of $1.26 for each member, or a total of $126,000 (annually, with 100,000 members) to the Center's general fund. The net profit should increase as the proportion of renewals to new memberships increases."

The directors generally were pleased by results of the direct mail drive. Some of them seemed to be confused by the complexities of the operation. Ostrow suggested that the basic price of Center memberships be increased from $10 to $15. Ashmore promised that a test of the feasibility of such an increase would be conducted.

In a report on the development of the *Center Magazine*, John Cogley said: "With more than 100,000 copies in circulation, it reaches a significant number of the opinion-makers of the United States and abroad. Subscribers are found in every one of the 50 states and on every continent." He noted that articles from the magazine were being reprinted in textbooks, in business publications, in professional journals, in newspapers, and in religious periodicals and were used by teachers and students in many colleges and universities.

Hutchins commended Cogley, Donald McDonald, who had become the managing editor, and all others connected with the magazine. He was sure that it had exceeded the expectations of the board and the staff in its quality and its growth.

At the May board meeting the directors voted for the budget proposed for the 1969-70 fiscal year, with only one director—Ostrow—in opposition. There appeared to be little uneasiness about the financial situation, although the report of Richard L. Gilbert, the assistant secretary and treasurer, stated plainly that the prospective deficit would be $862,155 and only nine new founding members—contributors of $1000 a year or more—had been added in the first six months of the current fiscal year. The total number of founding members had reached 485, far short of the thousand large contributors necessary to close the financial gap.

Gilbert declared blithely that the income picture would be greatly improved when the large bequest from Carlson's estate reached the Center. He referred to another asset possessed by the Center—thousands of shares of stock in the Presidio Savings and Loan Corporation, whose founders had given the Center an opportunity to invest in its initial shares. Presidio Savings was being taken over by Imperial Corporation of America, and the value of the Center's holdings had been estimated at $600,000.

"We have not attempted to estimate here the possible additional income that may be derived from investment of the reserve funds that will accrue from the Carlson bequest and liquidation of the Presidio holdings," Gilbert said. In any case, the Center was assured of enough money for at least five years—enough for Hutchins to provide "very generous" severance payments to the fellows who would have to be removed in the reorganization plan and to enable him to offer substantial salaries to new fellows who were to form the faculty of his "world academy."

After the directors departed from Santa Barbara, Hutchins acted swiftly. The old Center was, in effect, dissolved. A new Center, dominated by a few senior fellows, rose in its place. Under the new plan, however, there was one continuing element: Hutchins was still the king, although he insisted that he had divided his powers among those chosen to be in the ruling group.

Harry Ashmore had been the one closest to Hutchins in the 1960s. Communications to Hutchins—except in the dialogue sessions and in general staff meetings—were expected to be sent through Ashmore, who then explained what Hutchins had decided. Ashmore told his colleagues that he had not sought the mantle of authority: it had been draped upon his shoulders by Hutchins.

All the fellows expected that Ashmore would have a major role in the new academy, but some of them felt that he did not have the academic background to be one of the new senior fellows. Those at the old Center, who had notable academic achievements were Stringfellow Barr, John Seeley, William Gorman, Rexford Tugwell, Bishop James Pike, John Wilkinson, and Harvey Wheeler.

When the fellows had agreed to the Cogley reorganization plan, Wilkinson had reminded everyone that the second person to become a senior fellow would have a strong voice in determining the choice of the others. Some of the fellows then in residence thought that Hutchins would pick Barr or Tugwell. But Barr and Tugwell were in their seventies, and others felt that Hutchins would pick one of the younger scholars.

The man Hutchins called to join him on Olympus was Harvey Wheeler, a slim sardonic man with fast-moving eyes and a persuasive style of speaking, an energetic and ambitious man, a scholar with a keen sense of the value of publicity, a man who was convinced that the world was going to explode before very long but until the explosion it was necessary to advance visions of "a new and better and different world." Hutchins enjoyed Wheeler's ironic manner and his worldly wisdom. Hutchins and Wheeler had similar ideas on many subjects and had become close personal friends.

Wheeler was a little more than fifty years old. He was vigorous, provocative, productive. He pursued ideas relentlessly, he was sharp in the dialogues but usually polite and often ready with compliments. He was almost as urbane as Hutchins.

In choosing Wheeler, Hutchins indicated the kind of scholar he wanted to have in his world academy. Wheeler had been a faculty member at prestigious universities—Harvard and Johns Hopkins—and had obtained his Ph.D. at Harvard. He knew scholars in many other countries, and he had participated in academic meetings in the United States and in Europe. Yet he had gone beyond the academic mould; he was widely known as the co-author of a novel about a possible nuclear war, *Fail-Safe*.

Wheeler had been brought to the Center as a result of the omnivorous reading habits of Ferry, who had been impressed by an article Wheeler had published in a small magazine called *Dissent* in 1958. Ferry had involved

Wheeler in the Fund's study of the corporation, with the approval of Hutchins, and Hallock Hoffman had drawn him into the study of political parties and constitutional politics. He had moved to Santa Barbara to join the Center staff in 1961.

A contributor to many professional and polemical journals, Wheeler was the author of *Democracy in a Revolutionary Era*, a book generated by the Center's work for the Encyclopaedia Britannica, and of several Center pamphlets, including *The Restoration of Politics, The Rise and Fall of Liberal Democracy,* and *The Politics of Revolution.* He also spoke at colleges and universities and participated in radio and television broadcasts.

During the months when the fellows had wrangled about the future of the Center, Wheeler had spent many hours in private conversations with Hutchins. He had impressed Hutchins as a man who was genuinely sympathetic to Hutchins' long-cherished dreams for "the academy"—a man who could be "useful."

After Wheeler had been chosen, there was a curious interlude at the Center. No additional fellows were added to the original two for several days. Wheeler and Hutchins wrote letters, sent telegrams, and made telephone calls to renowned scholars in major universities in the United States and other countries, trying to get commitments from these eminent men to join the "new center." But it was extremely difficult to get such men to leave the projects on which they were already engaged.

While Hutchins and Wheeler engaged in these activities, the remaining former fellows lived in a fog of uncertainty. Wilkinson and others came into my office and expressed their feelings of anxiety. I knew that I would continue as an officer of the Fund, but I was concerned about those who were being forced to leave. I was depressed.

Recalling those three days in a conversation with me later, Wheeler said he had advocated the appointment of scholars so illustrious that he would "feel obliged to resign." He hoped that the acceptance of several brilliant people with international reputations would make it easier for the former Center fellows to bear the pain of being passed over. But the appointments could not be made.

At last Hutchins and Wheeler picked a third man—Rexford Tugwell, who was drafting a proposed new Constitution for the United States. Tugwell had been a fellow at the Center since 1964. He had written twenty books and had won many awards. He was also internationally known and had shown an interest in the world academy that Hutchins had outlined to him in the 1940s.

After the appointment of Tugwell, the selection process again came to a halt for a while. Hutchins, Tugwell, and Wheeler found it hard to agree on the next choices. Finally Hutchins persuaded the other two that Ashmore—as the executive vice president of the Fund—should be added to the group. He also recommended the election of Cogley, saying that he felt that the editor of the *Center Magazine* should be a Senior Fellow. He decided that Ashmore and Cogley should be ex officio members.*

Ashmore and Cogley accepted the Hutchins proposal. The next day, Cogley said he could not serve as an ex officio member. Hutchins, Wheeler, and Tugwell then elected Ashmore as a full fellow, and the four then elected Cogley, removing the ex officio designation.

It became evident that John Seeley, Ferry, Hallock Hoffman, Bishop Pike, and others who had been active fellows under the former organization of the Center were not going to be chosen under the new plan. On May 17 Hutchins sent a letter to Ferry—a letter that struck Ferry with the force of a blow.

After describing the procedure recommended by Cogley, Hutchins said: "The more I thought about it, the more I was convinced that if we were to reorganize we should do so on the best basis we could. The best basis I could think of was the academy, or a real university without students—or without many. Among other things this would relieve us of any obligation to be American or to limit our studies in any way.

"On May 7 I told the staff this was what I wanted to do, that I planned to make this recommendation to the Board on the 9th. Several members expressed approval. Nobody objected except Marin.

"I said I would proceed according to the Cogley plan.

"The Board was enthusiastic and indicated strong financial support.

"I then appointed Wheeler. The 2 of us elected Tugwell. We made no progress. We then agreed that since the magazine and the administration of the Fund for the Republic had to be represented we should elect Ashmore. Cogley ex officio.

"Cogley accepted, but changed his mind the next day. He said I was violating my understanding with the staff because I had not mentioned ex officio members to them.

"Wheeler, Tugwell, and I then elected Ashmore, and the four of us elected Cogley, neither ex officio.

"The five elected Wilkinson, and the six Elisabeth Borgese.

"The seven agreed that Kelly, McDonald, Reed, and Sheinbaum should not be elected fellows but should be asked to continue what they are doing. The same applies to Gilbert, Jensen, and Tagger. It may be that Barr, who was not elected, will be willing to go on supervising the junior fellows.

"Since I am now one of seven, I cannot say with absolute assurance what the next move will be, but I believe it will be to go outside the existing staff to look for new members—no more will be chosen from inside. Hence

---

*The idea of appointing "ex officio" fellows apparently came from Ashmore. In testimony later, Ashmore said the suggestion might have come from him. Hutchins couldn't remember whose suggestion it had been.

I have already told Seeley that in my opinion he will not be elected. He has not obtained a majority in any meeting.

"I am sorry to have to tell you the same thing. In view of our long association and all you have done for the Fund and the Center this is a very unwelcome duty.

"If you want to stay, I'll be glad to take up with the fellows any ideas you have about what you might do. If you want to leave, I'll guarantee financial arrangements satisfactory to you. . . ."

Ferry believed that he could be with the Center as long as he kept his health, as long as he contributed to the dialogues and publications of the Center, as long as the Center itself survived. He thought that a firm, unbreakable understanding existed between Hutchins and himself. Hutchins had often acknowledged his role in the creation of the Fund for the Republic and its offshoot, the Center.

In New York in 1959, after the Fund's board had decided to establish the Center in Santa Barbara, Ferry had shown some reluctance to make the move to California. He had told Hutchins that he thought only the scholars on the Fund's staff should be attached to the Center, and he didn't regard himself as a scholar. But Hutchins had insisted that he wanted Ferry to be a member of the Center's core group and to take part in the dialogues. So Ferry had moved his family and himself to the pacific coast.

Ferry and Hutchins had been friends since the 1950s, when they had met under the rich auspices of the Ford Foundation. As liberal Democrats, they had fought for civil liberties and scorned "fat cats" and complacent citizens. Both appreciated irony and were capable of withering sarcasm. Both had considered going into the Christian ministry and both had the reforming fire of evangelists.

In his fifteen years with the Fund and the Center, Ferry had become a celebrity in his own right. His gift for phrase making and his position as a vice president of the Fund made him what newspaper people called "a quotable source." He took stands and advocated actions that shocked some people, stimulated others, and irritated quite a few. He caused troubles for the Fund and the Center, but he felt that the Fund had been formed to be provocative and that its staff members had an obligation to speak their minds.

He had castigated J. Edgar Hoover, called for the closing of the New York Stock Exchange as a gambling place, advocated unilateral disarmament even at the risk of Russian occupation of the United States, suggested that only older people should be drafted for military service (to put the burden on those who had a smaller number of years to live), recommended the televising of executions, and once chartered a plane with the hope of placing twenty notable Americans in Hanoi as hostages (to get President Johnson to refrain from making air attacks on that city). He produced the motto "Feel Free," which became symbolic of the Fund and the Center.

When he directed the Fund's study of the corporation in modern society—which generated a significant book and several pamphlets widely read and used in colleges and schools—Ferry became alarmed by the growth and strength of corporations. He favored federal charters for corporations, with strict standards of accountability. He thought there should be a corporate bill of rights, covering workers as well as stockholders.

In an article in the *Atlantic Monthly* entitled "The Happy Heretic," Victor Navasky had described Ferry vividly:

> Although he would be the last to admit it, Ferry is a satirist. In America satire usually comes disguised as humor, and so it is difficult at first to recognize what the evangelistic Ferry is up to. But it soon becomes obvious that his central strategy is the deployment of a satire to advance moral imperatives. His charge, for example, that Hoover exaggerates the Communist menace is provocative but not original. . . . But his suggestion that Hoover is inefficient, whether true or false, is 50 percent Mort Sahl. Because he is an intellectual, because he is a committed, serious man, because he has a poker face and a pious delivery (which resembles that of the Episcopalian minister he once thought of becoming), because he is self-righteous, and because he resides in a so-called think-tank, few take him satirically. His ability to pass is what enables so many of his ideas to explode onto the front pages.
>
> Moreover, in contrast to the conventional dissenter, who is traditionally dispossessed, alienated, and disenchanted, Ferry has the credentials and the perspective to operate from within the establishment. He is the son of the former chairman of the board of Packard Motor Company (residence: Grosse Pointe, Michigan), attended a Jesuit high school, inherited the chairmanship of the Dartmouth Fine Arts Club from Nelson Rockefeller, taught John F. Kennedy and his older brother, Joseph, when they were at Choate, and then went on to advise and write speeches for Henry Ford II. Although he is in his fifties, his handsome face has the ruddy, scrubbed, chiseled look of a stern, fledgling scoutmaster. . . .
>
> He is a member in good standing of New York's august Century Club. And he is master of that ultra-establishmentarian trade, public relations. . . . A polemicist, yes; an amateur, no. . . .
>
> Yet it is a mark of his expertise that the last thing one would take him for is a PR man. This is partly because he is affiliated with an organization whose aim is to clarify "the issues involved in maintaining a free and just society. . . . "

When Navasky asked Ferry whether he had a formula for producing his "trouble-making yet issue-raising proposals," Ferry replied: "Go to work for the Center for the Study of Democratic Institutions."

Ferry was more admired by Navasky and others outside the Center than he was by some of his colleagues within the Center itself. When he went off on speechmaking trips, he regarded himself as an ambassador from the Center to the world. Hutchins and Ashmore did not feel that the Center needed such an ambassador, and they told Seeley and others that Ferry spent too much time away from the Center.

When Ferry returned to Santa Barbara after he had received the letter from Hutchins notifying him that he had not been elected as one of the new senior fellows, he met with Hutchins in the president's office. He dictated an *aide-mémoire* a few minutes after the conclusion of this meeting, and later circulated it to members of the Center's board.

"I asked him to tell me about the academy; what was in his mind, how it would work and so on," Ferry said in this memorandum. "It is the same academy that was discussed under Ford Foundation auspices years ago, he replied, and reminded me of the conversations in Europe (of which I was aware but in which I did not take part) with Heisenberg, Huxley, Toynbee, and so on. He said the object was to get similar luminaries to ponder the same questions.

"I inquired how the academy would work. RMH responded by saying that he was not sure whether the kind of people needed were available, or could be enticed, or would be willing to serve full time at the Center. I agreed that these were hard questions that could only be answered by working persistently at invitations. I asked again how the academy would work— whether on the present lines of the Center, or if some other mode had been agreed on. RMH said that nothing had been decided yet or could be decided until the academy was formed, with new members having a part in the decision. But he said he imagined that there would be fewer meetings, and more concentration on single topics; then he checked himself again and said that questions of procedure would of course be decided by the group and not by him. . . .

"I said that, wrongly or rightly, I had a strong proprietary sense about the Center. I said that I felt that I had had something consequential to do with building it up and giving it whatever character it possesses. I said that, at least at the present moment, it was inconceivable to me that I should not be a part of it. I said I had hoped and expected to spend the balance of my working life with the Center, and that this was still my hope and expectation.

"I said I was not in any way asking for a recount. I said that I did not, as a persistent advocate of self-government, intend to challenge its results even though I was deeply hurt by them. I said I had no other comment on the events that took place during my absence. I said that I had never deemed myself a scholar or an intellectual and that I was aware that I did not have a first class mind. I said also that I was aware of my malfeasances and misfeasances from time to time. Despite all this, I said, I felt that I had been useful to the institution and that I could be useful from now on; and that that was the statement of my outlook that he had asked for.

"At first RMH said, 'Very good. Thank you.' I then said that I did after all have one comment to make on what had happened and said that I could understand my non-election to any group whose criterion was scholarship and intellectual excellence. I declared that this was the only discernible criterion of the present group and that he had made it plain that it would be the chief criterion of those invited from outside. In a tone of small surprise, RMH said, 'Does this mean you wish to stay here even though not as a member (of the Fellowship)?' I said that this was exactly what I meant, and that my remarks about usefulness were based on that supposition. I said that I was taking up the first option offered in his letter to me.

"I asked him whether he had any questions and he said, 'No, thanks very much.' Then he said, 'I will take it up with the others. You must remember that I am no longer the dictator or autocrat, but only one of seven.'. . .

"At some point in the conversation, after I had said I had no comment about the recent events, RMH said, 'It did not turn out as I thought it would.'

"At no point in the half hour was the name of any other staff member mentioned, by either of us. The atmosphere was strained, but not unfriendly."

Ferry soon discovered that the senior fellows saw no possibility of his remaining at the Center in any capacity. On June 2, 1969, four days after his conversation with Hutchins, he was asked by John Cogley to talk about his plans. Ferry made extensive notes on his discussion with Cogley.

According to these notes, Cogley indicated that the fellows were eager to know what Ferry intended to do. Ferry declared that he was astonished by the apparent desire of the fellows for swift action. He gave Cogley a copy of the Hutchins letter of May 17 and urged Cogley to consider the paragraph in which Hutchins had written: "If you want to stay, I'll be glad to take up with the Fellows any ideas you have about what you might do. . . ." He also handed Cogley a copy of his summary of his talk with Hutchins on May 28.

"At this point he took up the conversation again and said that Bob had told the group last Thursday that he had 'thought and thought and thought' and could not think of any role for me in the future that would not be humiliating and demeaning," Ferry noted. "It was at this point also, I believe, that RMH said that I had been unwilling to do things for the Center that he and others had asked me to do. John said that the rest of the group (there was one absentee, I don't know who) had agreed that they could not think of anything for me to do that would not be humiliating. I asked John how long this 'effort of imagination' lasted—how long the group gave to consideration or discussion of my possible usefulness. He told me that this discussion lasted perhaps ten minutes. I remarked that it seemed a very short time to devote to the question of a man's future. He agreed. . . .

"Just before our conversaton closed John remarked that he had not realized until last week how seriously my relations with RMH had deteriorated. I told him that I had not realized this either, and was sorry about it. I said that I did not wholly understand the reason for it and felt that it was probably as much a function of distance as anything else. I said that when Harry (Ashmore) had taken over as Executive Vice President, I had regarded it as my duty to work with Bob through Harry; and I had had very little personal contact with RMH from that time to this. There was also the difficulty of a lack of congeniality between Harry and me. There were also episodes like that of the ABM book on which I thought I was standing on perfectly good ground—perhaps quite wrongly—and in which Harry thought I was behaving disgracefully. In this and other cases it was inevitable that RMH should have heard only one side of the situation. But this all falls under the theory of 'distance.' . . ."

Two days after his conversation with Cogley, Ferry received another letter from Hutchins: ". . . The Senior Fellows have asked me to tell you that with all the good will in the world they do not see a place for you in the new academy or university. Various possibilities have been discussed, but none of them seems promising. They have therefore instructed me to ask for your resignation. I do this with the greatest possible regret.

"I suggest that you regard yourself as relieved of your obligations to the Center as of this date; that you resign effective August 31st; that you receive your salary and the financial equivalent of all benefits from the Center for one year from that date; and that for a year thereafter you be entitled to the difference between your salary at the Center and the salary of any other regular position that you accept, if that salary is lower than your Center salary.

"The Senior Fellows are eager to begin reassigning offices and secretaries on July 5th.

"The Senior Fellows are all deeply conscious of everything you have done for the Center and they are all sorry that they do not see a role for you in the new organization. I share these feelings and have some special pangs of my own. I hope our friendship may continue."

Ferry refused to accept the financial settlement offered by Hutchins. In a letter dated June 5, 1969, he demanded payment of 85 days of "accumulated vacation pay"; two years salary, to be paid in equal amounts annually for four years, beginning January 1, 1970; continuation of payments by the Fund into his retirement account; the opportunity to continue in the Fund's medical-dental insurance plan at his own expense, if such an arrangement could be made; with all of these provisions to continue in force in the event of his death, with payments and benefits being made thereafter to his wife. He asked that all such agreements be put into a contract with the Fund.

In this letter, Ferry referred to "my belief, perhaps not well-founded, that I had some form of tenure or some moral claim on the Fund growing out of length of service; and from my position as an Officer, elected in November 1968 to serve until November 1969 or 'at its pleasure.' " He added: "If anything was done by the Board at the May 9 meeting to alter my office I have not been informed of it. I have in fact been signing assignments, transfers, and other legal documents since my return in my vice-presidential capacity." He was not aware that the board had given complete power over him and all other officers and staff members to Hutchins at its executive session on May 9.

Another officer of the Fund and a fellow of the Center who had been an admirer and associate of Hutchins for many years—Hallock Hoffman—was also terminated in the reorganization of 1969. Hoffman was a good-humored, energetic, articulate man without any advanced academic degrees but with a background of experience in business and as a member of the staff of the American Friends Service Committee. From 1954 to 1957 he had been the Assistant to the president of the Fund. When the Center was established, he directed the study of the political process. He had been secretary and treasurer of the Fund from 1957 until 1967, when he had resigned to devote his full time to being the coordinator of studies at the Center, working closely with Dean Seeley in developing the Center's projects and scheduling the dialogue sessions on selected topics.

Hallock Hoffman accepted the new order at the Center with the equanimity characteristic of his attitude toward life. His father, Paul Hoffman, continued to be honorary chairman of the Center's board. He wrote on June 17 to his family and friends: "The New Senior Fellows are a capable and productive group. I hope they will make a great Center in the future. But I am not distressed not to be among them. I have been struggling for some time to import more emotional and psychological qualities into our Center community. I believe I have lost this struggle. I am pleased that the new Fellows are a compatible group. If I had been the only additional one chosen, I would have hesitated to accept the invitation.

"The point I want to make about myself is that I have a rare chance given to few people—to stop in the middle of a working life, and, because of a severance settlement, to take a long time to think through what I will do next. . . . Meanwhile, I am happy about the whole thing."

Hoffman, like Ferry and Seeley, was not really happy about his negotiations with the Center for severance pay. He asked originally for payment of his salary, plus benefits, for three years—and an agreement to cover the benefits and to pay the difference between his salary and whatever he might be earning in the two years after that period. After an exchange of communications with Hutchins and Ashmore—and negotiations between his lawyer and a lawyer for the Center—he finally accepted payment based on the maintenance of his income and benefits for two years.

Hoffman felt that the selection of the new senior fellows had been based on their intellectuality rather than on the "emotional and psychological qualities" he considered important. The announcement released by the Center on June 13, 1969, which I prepared under the guidance of Ashmore and Hutchins, simply stated that "some changes in program and personnel are now under way."

"Ten years ago, in September, 1959, the Fund for the Republic established at Santa Barbara the Center for the Study of Democratic Institutions," Hutchins said in this announcement. "For the past year the Center has been reviewing its programs in the light of its changed situation. Through a bequest from the late Chester Carlson the institution for the first time has sufficient reserve funds to project its operations over a period of years. Also, in the past two years, largely as a result of a new and expanding publications program, more than 100,000 persons have become Center members, contributing $10 or more annually to its upkeep. The *Magazine, Occasional Papers*, and book-length *Center Reports* constitute a sizable and growing publishing enterprise.

"There also have been dramatic changes in the society to which the Center's studies are addressed. Some of the Basic Issues projects to which the Center devoted its attention ten years ago have been discontinued, or incorporated into other studies: those having to do with the corporation, labor unions, church and state, the mass media, and voluntary associations. Others will be discontinued or recast in the course of the current reappraisal. Such program reorganization will require some changes in personnel."

Hutchins indicated that six of the Center's studies would be continued under the direction of members of the reconstituted fellowship: reform of the electoral process, with Harry Ashmore principally responsible; development of world order, directed by Elisabeth Mann Borgese; the constitutionalization of education, with Hutchins as the coordinator; revision of the United States Constitution, directed by Rexford G. Tugwell; the constitutionalization of science, under Harvey Wheeler; and a project on the civilization of the dialogue, with John Wilkinson. The six project directors and John Cogley, editor of the *Center Magazine*, were designated as senior fellows.

The announcement also disclosed that eleven distinguished scholars from the United States and other countries would meet at the Center in July to consider "further revision and expansion of the reconstituted study program." The names of other staff members remaining at the Center were made public. In addition to myself, they included Stanley Sheinbaum, economist; Edward Reed, director of periodical publications; Donald McDonald, managing editor of the magazine; John H. Jensen, director of book publications; Florence Mischel, director of the audiotape program; Richard Gilbert, assistant secretary of the corporation; and Peter Tagger, director of membership services. This announcement was designed to present the Center in the best possible light. It was not regarded as adequate or acceptable by Seeley and other fellows who had been asked to leave. It gave no recognition of the services they had performed. It made no mention of the Center's internal conflicts. I had felt unhappy about the press release myself, but Ashmore and Hutchins had insisted that the statement disclosed as much information as the public needed to have.

Articles in newspapers focused attention on the fellows who had been asked to leave, and speculated on what factors had determined the choice of those who stayed. In the Santa Barbara *New-Press* Robert Sollen wrote on June 13: "It was difficult today to find a policy or ideological split as the basis for the regrouping of Center personnel, although one department fellow said: 'There has been a lot of commotion up here for quite some time.' " The next day, Sollen reported: "A division between the humanists and the intellectuals at the Center was said to be reflected yesterday as the basis for dropping four fellows. . . ."

Reporters for the Los Angeles *Times* and the *New York Times* had different perspectives on the Center's reorganization. Under a headline reading "Hutchins' 'Think Tank' Plotting New Course," Larry Kaggwa and Kenneth Reich wrote, in the June 25 issue of the Los Angeles paper:

> Santa Barbara—Dr. Robert Maynard Hutchins, an educator, turned 70 in January. In September, his Center for the Study of Democratic Institutions will be 10 years old.
>
> "As I told our group," Hutchins said last week, "anniversaries, like the prospect of immediate hanging, tend to powerfully concentrate the mind."
>
> Disclosing plans to resign his administrative functions "at the earliest possible moment," Hutchins said he is first determined to "refound" the Center—bringing it closer to the true, independent community of scholars he has dreamed of most of his life.
>
> This is the background of the recent reorganization of the renowned "think tank" located in a graceful home in the hills overlooking Santa Barbara.
>
> Five of 18 senior fellows were dropped, asked to resign effective August 31 and vacate their offices by July 5. Four others were relegated to administrative duties only. The status of two others remains to be decided.
>
> A large number of part-time "consultants" to the Center also were dropped.
>
> Plans are to add five to seven more fellows in the next year. Ten scholars—mainly from abroad—will come to Santa Barbara

next month to look the Center over for a week and give the remaining senior fellows a chance to look them over.

New financial resources—particularly a $5 million bequest from the estate of the late Xerox millionaire Chester Carlson—and dramatic circulation gains, from 17,000 to 96,000 in 18 months, for the center's magazine provided an opportunity for Hutchins to act.

Now that the years of shoe-string financing are over and the center's continued existence seems assured, he believes he can better attract the scholars he wants.

And, various sources agree, there had been difficulties at the Center, disagreements of approach among the senior fellows, and troubles with the dialogue that formed a focus for the group's activities.

The dialogues—among the fellows themselves and frequently with outside visitors—were edited and then published, frequently in the magazine. Hutchins believes dialogues are one of the most effective means of intellectual inquiry, especially in the sense of clarifying the issues.

But the fellows had been finding there were too many people around the table for true dialogue. The sessions frequently became a series of set speeches, or developed into interviews or sometimes gossip, and not all the fellows were contributing adequately. It was felt the number of those around the table had to be reduced.

Furthermore, some of the fellows—generally paid from $18,000 to $25,000 a year—were more active in Center activities than others. The consultant concept of part-time participation, for its part, had not worked out very well.

So, according to virtually all sources, there were many reasons for a reorganization—but primarily it was Hutchins' desire to act before he got much older.

"Father sat back for 18 months and listened to the quibbling," said one man closely associated with the Center. "Finally, father said, 'This is the way it's going to be.' " . . .

The status of educator Stringfellow Barr and Nobel chemist and peace-prize winner Dr. Linus Pauling was left up in the air. Dr. Pauling has been on leave the last two years to do research. . . . *

With the exception of Ferry and Seeley those dismissed accepted their fate with reserve.

*Barr and Pauling did not continue their connection with the Center. Edward Engberg, another fellow, had resigned in the spring of 1969, informing Hutchins that the dialogue "had become a shambles. . . ." Engberg was also irritated by a barrage of criticisms from Ferry and by Hutchins' apparent inability to get Ferry to change his behavior.

Ferry, who learned of the decision while vacationing in Scotland, said that for a while he was "desolate." He added, "For the first time in my life I spent a sleepless night. After all, I had spent 10 years and had expected to spend the rest of my days here and the intimation that I will not be able to do so was shattering."

Some sources at the Center said Ferry had been critical of Hutchins in many respects over an eight-year period, and there was a reference in Ferry's remarks to personal discord.

Seeley, who had given up a chair at Brandeis for what he regarded as a promise of a permanent fellowship from Hutchins, declined public comment except to say he had placed the matter in the hands of his attorneys.

Dr. Pike—perhaps the best known of those dismissed—accepted it with equanimity. He recently became involved in a new foundation of his own in Santa Barbara, the Foundation of Religious Transition, established to help former priests and nuns.

"I take this on its face," Pike said. "Hutchins had a dream here and saw a chance to fulfill it . . . to bring about more pure thought and science, make it more international.

"Some of us were very active in the anti-Vietnam war movement. I think there will be more of academe, more of a think tank here now, a less activist group."

This interpretation is denied by Hutchins, who said there were "no ideological connotations at any point" in selecting the fellows who remain.

"The only question," he said, "was the kind of people who will contribute most to the kind of institution we're dreaming about."

Hutchins did not deny that he had the most significant role in the "refounding" of the Center. After his first appointment of Harvey Wheeler as a coselector of future fellows, he was the one who saw to it that Rexford Tugwell was the next man chosen. He persuaded Wheeler and Tugwell that Ashmore and Cogley should be elected.

"When we voted on the other names on the staff list, Hutchins had the power to persuade us to appoint anybody he really wanted," Cogley said later. Wheeler confirmed that this was the atmosphere in which the voting took place.

Although Hutchins insisted that he wished to share his power, he continued to be the dominant leader in the new organization as he had been in the old one. When he refused to express his views, the fellows tried to discover what he hoped they would do—and they acted accordingly. He was not strongly opposed on any fundamental issue.

In an article published in the *New York Times* on June 17, Israel

Shenker described the Center as a "scholarly conglomerate" that interminably discussed "reform, revision, adaptation, even preservation" of democratic institutions that were under attack in many other places.

> The Center, currently celebrating its 10th anniversary, is a nonprofit independent body normally composed of about 20 men ("one of whom is a woman," notes Dr. Hutchins) who daily consecrate themselves to the salvific—or at least therapeutic—power of dialogue [Shenker said].
>
> No subject is too vast for their attention, no project too visionary for their concern. They deal daily with concepts as grand as universal law and as remote as the uses of the most distant seabed.
>
> In this echoing think tank, the accent is liberal and the optimism unbounded, as though words could bridge centuries of misunderstanding, and as though no communication were too difficult to establish. One of the fellows—resigned Episcopal Bishop James A. Pike, who is now leaving the Center as well—says that he even communicated with his dead son, an assertion that other fellows pass over in uncharacteristic silence.
>
> The one woman—Elisabeth Mann Borgese—perfected yet another form of communication: She says she taught her dog to type.
>
> Breathing the heady air of transcended frontiers, a daily assembly gathers around a hollow square of green baize, microphones at the ready before each participant in the rite of dialogue. To minimize the incestuous quality of the thinking, scholarly visitors are regularly featured.
>
> But they are not heard regularly enough to satisfy Dr. Hutchins, and he has become increasingly impatient with what he has heard.
>
> Last month Dr. Hutchins told a staff meeting it was time for a change, time to concentrate on "man and the modern world."

Shenker did not mention the effort made to persuade scholars from other countries to join the Center. He did not refer to the contentions of John Seeley that the election process had been seriously flawed. Perhaps he did not know Seeley's views, because Seeley had refused to be interviewed by reporters.

Seeley had, however, told Ferry and others that the selection of the new fellows had not been done in accordance with the procedure discussed in Hutchins' office before the plan had been announced to the whole staff. He thought Hutchins had agreed that the single criterion for selection was to be excellence in the dialogue; that there were to be no "ex officio" appointments; and that no attempt was to be made to persuade any chosen fellow to vote for or against others on the staff. In his view, some of the chosen fellows had not been as active or as valuable in the dialogue sessions as others who were not chosen.

In outlining the proposal for reorganization to the staff on May 7, Hutchins had not cited any of the three points that Seeley considered to be extremely important. Seeley acknowledged later that he had not raised these points in that meeting because there was an "atmosphere of total trust" and he did not think any of the points would be ignored or overlooked.

Hutchins had told Ferry in his letter of May 17 that Cogley had not been willing to take an "ex officio" appointment, and gave Cogley's reason: "He said I was violating my understanding with the staff because I had not mentioned ex officio members to them." Hutchins did not emphasize "excellence in the dialogue" as a factor in his choice of Wheeler or in the agreement of Wheeler and himself to pick Tugwell as the next fellow. He simply described the outcome of the process. He did not tell Ferry that Tugwell had first been chosen "conditionally" and had been finally elected after Hutchins had talked with Tugwell about his ideas for the international academy and had become satisfied that Tugwell enthusiastically supported these ideas.

In any case, Shenker's article in the *New York Times* correctly indicated that Hutchins was the focal point of power in the Center. Shenker reviewed the vast scope of the Center's intellectual exertions, ranging from consideration of a Constitution for the world to a model for a new American Constitution, and then spotlighted the irony of the Center's inability to develop a constitution for its own organization.

Everyone at the Center had been aware that the Center had been reconsidering its program for more than a year. There were arguments within the Center on whether the reorganization had been carried out to launch a new program or whether Hutchins had decided to change the staff and then had decided to stress the significance of the "academy" idea.

Hutchins had said in his letter of May 17 to Ferry: "The more I thought about it, the more I was convinced that if we were to reorganize we should do so on the best basis we could. The best basis I could think of was the academy, or a real university without students—or without many. Among other things this would relieve us of any obligation to be American or to limit our studies in any way." Ashmore apparently preferred to stress the reorganization of the program as the essential factor leading to the "replacement of some personnel."

On June 17 Ashmore sent to the directors and consultants brief biographies of the scholars from Britain, France, Argentina, and American universities who had agreed to come to the Center for a conference on the new program.

One of these scholars was Kenneth Boulding, an economics professor at the University of Michigan, who had participated in Center dialogues in the early 1960s and had written a humorous, irreverent group of verses about "the Hutchins hutch" on Eucalyptus Hill. Born in England, Boulding had received his M.A. at Oxford and had been a Commonwealth fellow at the University of Chicago from 1932 to 1934. Boulding had written many books and had won many awards for his work in economics, conflict resolution, and philosophy. He was a fellow of the American Academy of Arts and Sciences and of the International Institute of Arts and Letters.

Another was Alexander Comfort, a British medical biologist, a self-professed anarchist, and a novelist. Comfort was a sharp, energetic, witty man who had written six novels, several volumes of verse, and books on sexual behavior, authority and delinquency, and the process of aging. Since 1963 he had been director of the Medical Research Council Research Group in Aging at the University College, London.

Bertrand de Jouvenel, another of the notable people invited to the Center for a July planning session, had also been there a number of times before. An economist and a journalist, de Jouvenel was a professor at the Sorbonne in Paris and an active member of a group called the Futuribles, which endeavored to construct possible futures based on studies of economic trends and social factors.

The group also included Mircea Eliade, an internationally known historian of religions, who had been a visiting professor at the University of Chicago and had written many books; Alexander King, a Scotsman who had been a physical chemist and who held advisory positions in European scientific and economic organizations; Sir Arthur Lewis, who was an honorary fellow of the London School of Economics and had been vice chancellor of the University of the West Indies; Raul Prebisch, Argentine economist who had been Executive Secretary of the United Nations Commission for Latin America and had served as Director-General of the Latin American Institute for Economic and Social Planning; Wilfrid Sellars, a noted philosopher from the University of London, who had written books on philosophy, science, and metaphysics; and Jerome Wiesner, of MIT, who had been President Kennedy's assistant for science and technology and chairman of the President's Science Advisory committee.

In a background statement to the conference participants, Hutchins asserted that the new senior fellows and the board of directors of the Center felt that it was "desirable to complete the transformation of the Center into an intellectual community in which the disciplines are forced to come to terms with one another and in which some of the best minds of our time may work together to bring reason to bear on human affairs. This would be a true university."

Hutchins also told them that the directors had indicated that "if the Center can be transformed into the kind of university briefly sketched in the first section of this paper, the members will be autonomous, that is, they will select their own colleagues and determine their own program." He added: "They would also be free to decide whether or not they wanted students. The seven senior fellows now in residence believe that young people should be admitted as assistants or junior partners. . . . The members should regard themselves as professors in a world university, free to study and discuss whatever seemed to them worthy of their attention.''

The invited scholars and the seven senior fellows met for six days in July. They devoted much of their time to the spreading impact of technology in every field of life. They made suggestions for expanding the projects on which the fellows had embarked, and several of them agreed to accept appointments as associates, promising that they would write papers for consideration in dialogue sessions and that they would participate as often as possible in Center meetings.

Two days after this conference at the Center ended, the power of technology was demonstrated in the landing of an American space vehicle on the moon. Pictures transmitted from the lunar surface showed its empty bleakness—and the beauty of the earth, a blue-green ball spinning against the dark void of the vast distances between the planets. The essential unity of the earth—and its fragility—were evident to the eyes of millions of people in many countries.

The vision of the earth hanging in space confirmed what mystics, prophets, and scientists had long proclaimed: the world was one. All problems in a scientific, technological age were world problems. The decision of the Center to try to become a "world university" seemed to be justified.

The Center had been potentially a "world university" from its beginning. People from more than 100 countries had participated in its conferences. All its major projects had international implications.

"The study of democratic institutions, if it is to be anything more than an unhelpful arrangement of irrelevant trivia, must involve some expert knowledge about the state of the world and its probable future," Hutchins had said in *The Center Diary* in April, 1964. " 'The Population Explosion,' 'The New Science,' 'The New Technology,' 'The Revolution of Rising Expectations,' are cliches of our time. They also happen to be descriptive titles of real conditions. They set the context within which democracy exists. They foretell the shape of the world within which democracy will have to find ways to exist tomorrow. What are those conditions and what do they mean for our comprehension of democracy and for the satisfactory operation of our institutions? . . .

"Since institutions evolve and world conditions change, the work of the Center is never completed. If the dialogue is maintained in microcosm at the Center and in macrocosm in the political life of the people, then the final answers—which are never easy—will be written by democrats.''

With the advice and consent of the six other "new" senior fellows, Hutchins announced in August the appointment of twelve associates.

Five of them were scholars who had been in the July sessions—Dr. Comfort; Mircea Eliade; Alexander King; Sir Arthur Lewis; Bertrand de

Jouvenel—and three others were notable in scientific fields the Center wished to explore. These were Richard Bellman, mathematician and physicist, who had produced twenty-three books; Paul Ehrlich, director of graduate studies in biology at Stanford; and Karl Pribram, professor of psychiatry at the Stanford University Medical Center.

The other four appointments were given to people who had been involved in the previous program of the Center—Neil Jacoby, a former member of President Eisenhower's Council of Economic Advisers and former dean of the Graduate School of Business Administration at the University of California in Los Angeles; Fred Warner Neal, professor of international relations and government at Claremont Graduate School; Lord Ritchie-Calder of Balmashannar, professor of international relations, University of Edinburgh; and Stanley Sheinbaum, economist and former faculty member at Stanford and at Michigan State University.

The four former fellows who had been asked to leave—Ferry, Seeley, Hoffman, and Pike—cleared out their offices and left the premises. William Gorman stayed on in a small office, doing work for the Encyclopaedia Britannica. (Gorman's academic abilities were admired by Hutchins and others, and he had come close to being elected a "new" fellow.)

When he announced the names of a group of newly appointed associates, in August 1969, Hutchins said: "As the first ten years of the Center draws to a close, as one era ends and another begins, I look back with some satisfaction at the successful attempt to found a center of independent thought and criticism, to learn how to gain comprehension through dialogue, to clarify the basic issues—and some burning ones—and widen the circles of discussion about them."

Hutchins and the other senior fellows were persuaded by Harvey Wheeler to hold a conference from August 18 to 22 on the implications of discoveries in biology. Declaring that "the biological revolution" might mean the almost indefinite prolongation of human life and the creation of "biological computers," Wheeler said: "The world was not prepared for the immense changes brought about by the release of atomic energy. If what the biologists tell us proves correct, the biological revolution will have even more profound effects. We must develop ideas for public policies to help scientists to put their knowledge at the service of humanity."

Paul Ehrlich and Karl Pribram, two of the new associates, gave advice and assistance to Wheeler in organizing the conference. In addition to Ehrlich, Pribram, and the senior fellows, the participants included Marjorie Grene and Michael Scriven, philosophers from the University of California; Patrick Kelly, from the Georgia Institute of Technology; Robert L. Sinsheimer, California Institute of Technology; Kenneth Tollett, dean of the Texas Southern University law school; Kurt Reinhardt, professor emeritus, Stanford; and Nathan Rotenstreich, former rector of the Hebrew University at Jerusalem.

In September the Center went ahead with a conference on economic development in Latin America, which had been planned before the reorganization occurred. Justice Douglas, Hutchins, Ashmore, Fred Warner Neal, and Neil Jacoby were the Center representatives at this gathering, which was sponsored jointly by the Center and the Parvin Foundation. Fifteen development experts from Argentina, Chile, Mexico, Ecuador, Brazil, and other Latin countries participated.

Senator Frank Church, chairman of the Latin American Subcommittee of the Senate Foreign Relations Committee, warned the participants that a "growing gulf" separated the United States from Latin America. He said that the $9 billion spent under President Kennedy's Alliance for Progress program had not prevented "rising hostility toward the United States." He deplored the fact that the U.S. was aiding many military dictators in Latin America.

Church demanded "a new policy that will end American military assistance [to Latin American governments] and bring home our military missions now located in no less than seventeen Latin American countries." He suggested a plan for "terminating the bilateral economic-aid program and channeling the money we are now putting into that program to the multilateral agencies: to the Inter-American Development Bank, to the World Bank, and to the development agencies of the United Nations."

Soon after Senator Church made these statements at the Mexico City conference, President Nixon indicated that he would abandon the Alliance for Progress program and shift to "a more mature partnership" between the United States and the Latin nations. Nixon said he would begin "untying" American foreign-aid loans to Latin countries so the money could be used to purchase products in Latin America rather than being restricted to purchases in the United States. Senator Church's proposals had received much attention in the press, in the United States Senate, and in the Latin countries.

While Hutchins and others from the Center were in Mexico, the body of one of the most famous scholars once associated with the Center—Bishop James A. Pike—was found in the Judaean wilderness of Israel two miles from the Dead Sea. Hutchins issued a statement expressing his sorrow at the tragic death of a man who had gained the affection of everyone at the Center although he had not been chosen as one of the "new" senior Fellows.

Bishop Pike was a fighter for civil liberties and social justice, a man who had defended the Fund for the Republic against the attacks of the House Un-American Activities Committee, who had taken part in the Selma, Alabama, march with Martin Luther King, who had participated in demonstrations against the Vietnam War, and who had been accused of heresy by some of his fellow bishops in the Episcopal church. He had been married three times, he was a recovered alcoholic, he was a man of action as well as a scholar and a man of faith. He forgave his enemies, he stood by his friends. He charged gallantly from one enterprise to another. He took defeats and frustrations without losing his quick wit or his ready laughter.

His separation from the Center had been a stunning shock to James Pike. He had other interests, he was active in many fields, and yet he had not expected to be removed. He came in to see me after Hutchins had told him that he would have to leave. His face was full of anguish, but he talked vigorously of his ideas for the future. With the graciousness that was typical of him, he said: "I could tell that the whole thing was very painful for Bob. I went over and put my arms around him."

In the autumn of 1969 the Center staff went through a period of mourning for Bishop Pike and for another gifted person whose life had ended—Edward Reed, who had been with the Fund for the Republic since 1954, who had edited most of the pamphlets produced by the Fund, who had produced *The Center Diary*—forerunner of *The Center Magazine*, who had been executive editor of the magazine and director of publications, and had edited several books including *Challenges to Democracy* and *Pacem in Terris: Peace on Earth*. Reed, who had been an editor of *Theatre Arts Monthly* and *The Reporter* before he joined the Fund, was an elegant and perceptive man with high personal and professional standards.

The work of the Center in the last three months of the year was a mixture of elements from the old program and the new one. In October the monthly *Center Newsletter*—a bulletin for members and friends of the Center—was launched with information on Center meetings, forthcoming publications, the availability of audio and videotapes, and questions for discussion based on articles in *The Center Magazine*. Copies were offered to the public without charge.

Topics of Center sessions in October ranged from discussions of the quality of college education in the United States—at a meeting with students and faculty from San Diego State College—to "Multi-National Communities" (with Jovan Djordjevic of the Yugoslav Supreme Court) and "A Reconnaissance of the Future" with William Ewald, development consultant, and the always pressing issues of freedom and authority with Milton Mayer, author of *Man v. The State*, a booklet scheduled for publication by the Center.

On October 23, directors and officers of the National School Boards Association came to the Center for a discussion of what to do about the spreading attacks on public school systems. They shared the alarm expressed by Ashmore over the failure of voters to support bond issues or tax increases necessary to support and improve the schools. "We have in the United States today an anti-education rebellion," Ashmore said.

The fellows recommended that the school board members should make as many innovative changes in the school system as possible, and should resist the growth of bureaucracy. Harvey Wheeler said that "programmed instruction, with each child moving at his own pace, might be the answer to many of the basic problems.'' He advised them to prepare for a "post-industrial society" dominated by scientists and theoreticians.

At the end of October the Center published a book entitled *Asian Dilemma: United States, Japan and China,* based on the conference of American and Japanese leaders in Santa Barbara in January. According to the editor of the book, Elaine H. Burnell, the proceedings revealed "one basic conviction: that the time had come for a fundamental change in American and Japanese foreign policy toward the People's Republic of China."

Senator Edward M. Kennedy, one of the contributors to the book, recommended a "two-Chinas" policy, calling for the seating of both Mao's China and the Chiang Kai-shek government on Taiwan in the UN General Assembly and awarding the Security Council place to the Peking government.

"We should declare ourselves ready and willing to reach agreement on the question of recognition whenever the Peking government is willing to do so," declared Senator Fulbright, another contributor.

Two Republican senators who had participated in the Center conference—Mark Hatfield of Oregon and John Sherman Cooper of Kentucky—strongly advocated new American policies toward China. Senator Cooper said: "Americans are more and more vigorously questioning the policy of containment of China." Senator Hatfield said: "Persistent attempts to exclude China from the community of nations have tended to confirm Peking's view of the United States as a hostile, unyielding enemy."

Publication of this book stimulated more attacks on the Center by right-wing individuals and groups. Representative Charles Teague had already reiterated his demand for another investigation of the Center by the Internal Revenue Service, saying that "the staff is extremely oriented towards the left and is more interested in developing and disseminating extremely liberal propaganda than it is in true education." But the Nixon administration showed no interest in harassing the Center.

On November 9 the Associated Press distributed an article by one of its feature writers, Ralph Dighton, to newspapers and broadcasting stations in the United States and other countries. Dighton said:

> The Center for the Study of Democratic Institutions is about to become a Center for something else. Just what, at this stage, is not clear.
>
> Extremely clear, however, is that this comfortably multi-millioned, confusingly multi-purposed community of intellectuals is at a crossroads.
>
> Its 70-year-old president, Robert M. Hutchins, has announced plans to yield the reins with which he has guided the Center through numerous controversies over the past decade. Its

principal backer, Chester F. Carlson, the inventor, has died, leaving the Center 5 million dollars in stock—"completely without strings," says Hutchins.

Whatever it becomes, it probably will remain what it has been from the start—controversial. It has been accused by anti-communists of leaning too far left; by liberals of being a right-wing mouthpiece; of being pro-Catholic, hyper-Protestant, and ungodly.

Hutchins shrugs. "We live in a paranoid, conspiratorial universe and there are those who believe that you must have a hidden reason for whatever you do." . . .

The Center's current budget is 3 million dollars a year. Its membership has jumped from 17,000 to 100,000, in the last 18 months, and executives are considering a boost in the membership rate to a minimum of $15.

Last June, in preparation for his eventual retirement, Hutchins set up a self-perpetuating rulership for the Center, composed of Senior Fellows. From now on, the surviving scholars will decide what programs the Center will study—a prerogative previously reserved for Hutchins himself—and pick any replacements or additions to the Fellowship.

Harry Ashmore, onetime newspaper editor who is executive vice president of the Center and who may inherit some of Hutchins' administrative duties, says: "We're in the best financial condition in our history. It is the first time any of us could say we feel we're permanent. No matter how unpopular we might become, we can keep the doors open."

Associates say Hutchins probably will remain in an executive capacity until the Center's reorganization is completed, probably in a year or so. Whatever his official role, he still will have a voice in deciding what direction the Center will take.

In November 1969 the largest mobilization against the Vietnam War occurred in Washington. Thousands of young people, members of women's groups, church groups, and other organizations converged on the city. Organizers of the "New Mobe"—as it was named—claimed that 800,000 people participated in the marching, speaking, and shouting that went on for three days. Washington police estimated there were 250,000 protesters in the capital.

At the Center, the cerebral search for understanding led to a discussion on November 12 entitled "Revolution in Mentality," based on a paper prepared by a Visiting Fellow, Mme. Ileana Marculescu, a Romanian philosopher. On November 17 the staff engaged in a dialogue with Victor Paschkis, chairman of a standing committee on technology and society of the American Society of Mechanical Engineers, author of a document entitled *Your Future—Your Fight,* containing his ideas on how to preserve a livable world.

The Center found itself in a fight on November 18, when W. H. Ferry filed suit in the superior court in Santa Barbara County, charging that the Fund for the Republic had breached and terminated his contract of employment through the actions of Robert M. Hutchins and Harry S. Ashmore, its principal officers. Ferry asked for general damage payment of $263,000 and "exemplary damages" of $400,000, accusing Hutchins and Ashmore of acting "with malice" toward him.

Ferry complained that he had not been given a chance to consider "in advance this 'refounding' of the Center or the method suggested . . . for doing it," or to "agree or disagree that there should be such a refounding, or for those purposes, or that the method proposed was fair or legal, or to offer alternatives or participate in whatever discussions occurred in his absence."

Acknowledging that he had no direct personal knowledge of what had happened. Ferry based his suit on information given to him "that the method actually followed differed importantly from the one which had been outlined in advance for the benefit of the Permanent Senior Fellows"—he apparently meant the fellows under the old organization of the Center—and asserted that he had been told that "one person was elected after having been required to agree with those electing him, who his own choices would be, for the next two persons chosen after himself; that he did vote in accordance with that promise; that the persons for whom he was required to vote were in fact elected; and that the person who extracted that promise from him was defendant Robert M. Hutchins."

Ferry expressed the belief that Hutchins and Ashmore had deceived the Fund's board of directors and "all interested outsiders" by representing that "these seven persons (the new Senior Fellows) had in fact been selected in the manner originally proposed, thus effectively and totally destroying any possibility of plaintiff's participation in the work of the Center, while assuring the acquiescence and eventual approval by the board of what had been done by withholding any admissions of how it had been done."

Contending that he had not been informed of his replacement as a vice president of the Fund, Ferry said that he regarded himself at the time of filing of the suit as "an un-salaried vice president . . . and to that extent an officer of the corporation." Describing the "refounding" as a "deliberate realignment of its corporate purposes" away from its original articles of incorporation, Ferry claimed that the Fund could use its accumulated money only for purposes congruent with its original charter.

"The stated purposes of the refounded Center, whether or not praiseworthy apart from the defendant The Fund for the Republic, Inc.'s fiduciary duties, are sufficiently different from its corporate purposes to require their proponents (the board of directors) either to seek a new endowment for them . . . or abandon them," Ferry asserted.

Hutchins sent a copy of Ferry's allegations to J. R. Parten on November 19 with a note saying: "I should think a motion to dismiss the complaint would be enough."

But a motion for dismissal was not granted. Hutchins, Ashmore, Wheeler, Wilkinson, Tugwell, and other senior fellows were subpoenaed and required to give depositions.

Before the taking of these depositions began, the board of directors convened in Santa Barbara. At the meeting on December 5, three new board members were elected: James H. Douglas, Jr., of Chicago, a lawyer who had been Deputy Secretary of Defense under President Eisenhower and who had served on the board in an earlier period; Joseph P. Antonow, also of Chicago, an attorney and a trustee of Roosevelt University; and Frances McAllister of Flagstaff, Arizona, an educator and a trustee of the Blaisdell Institute for Advanced Study in World Religions and Cultures. Edwin Janss, Jr., left the board at this time, requesting that his name not be presented for reelection.

Twenty directors attended the executive session that day, with Justice William O. Douglas presiding as chairman. David B. Lloyd, then a Santa Barbara lawyer representing the Fund, told the board that negotiations with everyone severed from the Center in the May reorganization—except for Ferry—had been completed. John Seeley, who had insisted that he had a moral right to lifetime tenure based on assurances given to him by Hutchins, had recognized the Fund's legal right to dismiss him and had signed an agreement that gave him protection against loss of income for two years.

Lloyd said that Ferry's demands were far beyond the maximum financial settlement under the formula that had been applied to the other cases. He saw no possibility of reaching a "reasonable" agreement with Ferry.

On a motion by Joseph Drown, seconded by J. Howard Marshall, the board adopted a resolution declaring "that the acts of the Fund's directors, officers, employees, and agents in terminating the personnel of the Fund as reported to the board at this, its annual meeting, be and the same hereby are ratified, approved, and confirmed in all respects as the act of this corporation."

Justice Douglas felt that he had served long enough as chairman of the board. The nominating committee recommended the election of Hutchins as chairman; Parten as vice chairman; Paul Hoffman and Elmo Roper as honorary chairmen; Ashmore as president; and myself as vice president. The board approved these recommendations, and elected Justice Douglas as chairman of the executive committee.

Parten, speaking for the nominating committee, said it was understood that Hutchins would continue to be the chief executive officer—as well as chairman of the fellows—and Ashmore would be the chief operating officer. The board was told that this election did not designate Ashmore as the successor to Hutchins: it was an election for one year only, and the reorganization of the Center was still in process.

The board discussed briefly a recommendation for the creation of a Joint Committee on Organization, composed of Fellows and Board members, to develop changes in the by-laws governing the relationships between the Fund and the Center. This proposal had been presented at the urging of Harvey Wheeler, who thought that the Senior Fellows should have more representation on the board.

In a statement released with the announcement of the new officers, Hutchins said: "The changes announced today are designed to bring Mr. Justice Douglas into more intimate contact with the Center, to widen the scope of Mr. Ashmore's responsibilities, and to give me a chance to work more intensively on the Center's academic program.

"Mr. Justice Douglas has lately organized, with Dr. Raul Prebisch of Chile, an important conference conducted by the Center on Latin American development. Further meetings on similar topics in other parts of the world will take place under Mr. Justice Douglas' direction.

"Mr. Ashmore became a director of the Fund for the Republic shortly after its organization in 1952. He has been a fellow of the Center ever since it was established in Santa Barbara a decade ago. He has been Executive Vice-President since December 1, 1967. In this position he has been responsible for developing the publications program, and for the remarkable growth of the Center's membership, which has now reached 100,000."

Hutchins added: "The publications of the Center are built on the contributions to these studies made by the Senior Fellows, Associates, and visiting scholars and experts. These include *The Center Magazine*, edited by John Cogley, and a series of book-length *Occasional Papers*. Through its 100,000 members and its program of continuing education under the direction of Frank K. Kelly the Center maintains a continuing dialogue with concerned citizens throughout the world.

"With the usual reservations about the difference between human aspirations and human accomplishments, it may be said that the Center's program has some chance of demonstrating the utility of a center of independent thought and criticism at what may well turn out to be one of the turning points in history."

Hutchins said that the board of directors had become so "persuaded of the value of the Center's work" that the board had decided "to enter upon a campaign for permanent endowment to guarantee the Center's most precious asset, its independence. Arnold M. Grant of New York City is chairman of the committee that will direct the campaign."

Other directors appointed to the endowment campaign committee were Edward Lamb of Toledo, O., Seniel Ostrow and Harold Willens of Los Angeles, and Howard Stein, head of the Dreyfus Fund in New York.

In an announcement after this meeting, the Center gave the names and backgrounds of all the associates as well as the fellows and listed the names and titles of a distinguished group of consultants, including several who had been among the original consultants to Hutchins when the basic issues program had been started by the Fund in 1957.

In December 1969 Hutchins appeared to be hopeful again about the Center's future. At the board meeting he did not reveal any of the pessimism he had expressed when he had talked with me in the hospital in February. He concealed within him the scars of the reorganization and the suffering it had cost him. Yet he was aware of the charges made against him by Seeley and Ferry, he had received angry letters from their friends, and he knew that their departure might deprive the Center of some support. Still he had the relieved air of a man who had forced himself to make very difficult decisions.

On December 18 Ashmore gave his testimony on what had brought about the refounding and how it had been done. He said he had held many conversations with Hutchins on the long-range organization of the Center, beginning in 1966 or 1967.

Ashmore was asked: "At that time did he discuss the possibility of naming you as president in his stead or to follow after him?"

"I am sure this came up as a possibility, only in terms of a title, certainly not in terms of a function," Ashmore said. "On the contrary, the whole burden of the conversation was how we could reconstitute the place so there would be no successor to Hutchins. . . ."

Until the reorganization, Ashmore acknowledged, Hutchins held all the executive authority: "There was a general discussion of how we might reorganize the place and continue the operation when this one-man rule should end, and one of the things we did, of course, as a result of that was to bring in John Seeley and give him the title of Dean and the responsibility for a great deal of the academic program. . . ."

Ashmore said he knew that Hutchins had informed members of the board of his desire "at some point to be relieved of a good deal of the responsibility that was carried." While all the important decisions were made by Hutchins, Ashmore added, "some, of course, were subject to ratification by the board. All financial matters were certainly referred to the board, if they were of any consequence."

While one-man rule had worked well under Hutchins because "the concept was his, the people had been chosen by him, they all served at his pleasure" and the staff members "felt secure because of their relationship with him," Ashmore said he couldn't imagine such an administration continuing "under anybody else" and that was why he had felt that "the talk of me being president, it seemed to me to be purely academic."

Although he had become president in title, Ashmore indicated that the course of the Center would be charted by the senior fellows as a group, not by a single executive. Hutchins, of course, was chairman of the fellows, and his views certainly carried weight with all the fellows.

After the selection of Tugwell as the third senior fellow, Ashmore said, he had talked with Hutchins about what might happen next. He remembered saying to Hutchins that he thought the administrative officer of the Center—who happened to be himself—and the editor of the magazine (at that time, the editor was John Cogley) should be on the policymaking level in the future organization of the Center. Hutchins had agreed.

Ashmore was asked whether the appointment of ex officio fellows meant that "some standard of academic trade-certified qualifications" that had been used in the selection of Wheeler and Tugwell was not applied "for ex officio members."

"I don't know that that was ever spelled out," Ashmore said. "I think you could probably put that construction on it, if you want to."

When Cogley first accepted appointment on an ex officio basis and then said he couldn't take it on that basis, Ashmore did not share Cogley's views: "He said that he thought to have done so would have departed from the original formulation. This was his argument. I couldn't see the argument myself, nor did I think the others could, but this was the stated reason. Whether that was his actual reason, I don't know. . . . He stated that he felt it was a departure from the procedure, the agreed upon procedure, and I did not understand it to be that, but this was apparently accepted by the others and so we were asked to absent ourselves while they discussed the question of whether or not, since they had made this election, they would reverse themselves."

When Ashmore and Cogley had been called back into Hutchins' office, they were informed that they had been elected full senior fellows. They then participated in going over the list of other Center staff members, to decide whether others should be added to the group.

"I supported Seeley," Ashmore said.

"Anyone else?" Sink asked.

"Well, there was no formal vote taken. . . . I think there were some people who were disposed to support some who were in the end eliminated."

Ashmore said that in his discussions of the performance of Center staff members over a period of years with Hutchins, he had made it clear that it seemed to him "that Mr. Ferry was not an adequate participant in the academic program of the Center—if for no other reason, because he was absent something like a third of the time. Continuity was very important."

"It was my strong impression that Mr. Ferry was not interested in the program of the Center as it was then being developed, that when he was there he objected to practically all of the projects that were adopted," Ashmore said.

Ashmore was questioned about his memorandum of April 15 to Dean

Seeley, in which Ashmore had written: "The Center had provided none of us tenure, and could not have done so, since our hand-to-mouth existence until very recently provided no financial guarantee of continued operations beyond one year—and the present estimate is not better than double that. *However, all, except those who have been invited to Santa Barbara for a specifically limited period, have been assured that they could remain in their present status so long as the Center survived*" [Italics added].

In the memorandum Ashmore had not indicated who had given the assurance of such status. In his deposition on December 18, he said that his memorandum had been written in his capacity as a fellow, not as an officer of the Fund speaking for Hutchins or the board. He did not regard it as a statement of official policy but as a description of what the practice had been at the Center. In his understanding, Hutchins had the legal power to change the practice at any time.

When he had told the staff members on May 7 that he thought "we ought to refound the place," Hutchins had not assured anyone of remaining at the Center. He said he hoped that the reorganization could be done with "a minimum of dislocation," but he gave no specific examples of what he meant. No one asked him to give such details.

Dean Seeley, who asserted in later testimony that he believed he had a guarantee of tenure and who had informed others (according to their testimony) that he was the only one who had such a guarantee, had not brought up the issue of tenure at the May 7 meeting. No one else had raised the issue.

In his December testimony, Ashmore declared that what he had meant to say in his memorandum was that no one at the Center had been subjected to an arbitrary dismissal. He expressed the belief, however, that Hutchins could remove any staff member whenever that seemed necessary—including officers elected by the board. He said that Ferry's status as a vice president had not been discussed at the May 9 meeting of the directors.

"I take it, then, he was a vice president through the December meeting, is that correct?" Sink asked.

"No," Ashmore said. "We considered that he had been relieved. Hutchins had the authority to relieve him, and did so relieve him formally when he asked him to vacate his office, relieved him of all duties."

"Had the board taken any action which authorized that, expressly?"

"Authorized—" Ashmore said.

"Your relieving of an officer of the corporation by Hutchins?"

Ashmore answered: "Well, we consider that the actions authorized under the bylaws, there was no question that the board understood that there would be separations under this procedure. There was no specific action taken in the case of Mr. Ferry."

"At that board meeting on May 9, did the board expressly delegate power, expressly, not inherently, delegate power to anybody to terminate Ferry's status as a vice president?"

"Not by name," Ashmore said. "Not expressly, no."

"I am including a possible delegation to the executive committee in these questions. Was that done?"

"That already existed," Ashmore said.

"Was it done at this meeting?"

"No, it was not."

"Are you saying it had been done at some prior meeting?"

"Yes. I think it is in the bylaws. My understanding is that the power to act between board meetings on the part of the executive committee would include that." Ashmore went on: "I think, actually, this may be arguable. I think the power rests in the president in any case."*

A little later, Ashmore was asked whether he knew of any instance in which Hutchins had "expressly said to any fellow . . . you can remain here at the Center as long as the Center survives."

"No, I don't think so," Ashmore said.

"Do you know whether such an express commitment was made by Hutchins to Seeley when Seeley came?"

"I think I am aware that it was not, because Seeley alleged that he had made such a promise and Hutchins denied it, and I had never heard it until Seeley made the claim."

Ashmore was questioned about the paragraph in his memorandum on April 15 in which he had declared that "all, except those who have been invited to Santa Barbara for a specifically limited period, have been assured that they could remain in their present status so long as the Center survived."

"In the context of the whole memorandum, I think it is quite clear," Ashmore said. "I am referring to the assurance being a personal assurance of Hutchins to each individual that since we all served at his pleasure, that presumably on the record people were not threatened with instant, arbitrary dismissal. There hadn't been any, I didn't think there would be."

He was asked whether Hutchins had questioned the statements he had made in the memorandum.

"I don't recall," Ashmore said.

Ferry had stated in his suit that he had "at all times during his service as vice president, Permanent Senior Fellow and employee of . . . the Fund for the Republic, Inc., duly and properly discharged each and every duty and obligation required to be performed by him in those capacities, excepting only to the extent he has been prevented from doing so by defendant the Fund for the Republic, Inc., in connection with the events beginning in May of 1969."

---

*Actually, the bylaws state: "Any such officer may be removed by the vote of a majority of the whole Board of Directors at any meeting of the Board." There is no mention of a delegation of the power of removal to the Executive Committee or to the president.

Ashmore was asked whether he had made it clear to Ferry that he did not think Ferry was performing his duties properly: "Prior to his termination, had you yourself mentioned to Ferry his shortcomings, such as absences or whatever, had you told him, 'Ferry, you have got to shape up?' "

"Well, Mr. Ferry was not a part of my responsibility," Ashmore said. "Mr. Ferry had no administrative responsibilities, and therefore I had no occasion for that kind of direct dealing with him."

"How long had it been since he had no fixed administrative duties?"

"Certainly not in the last three or four years," Ashmore said.

Ashmore was asked about the general criteria that were applied in the selection of the new senior fellows. He declared that the important factors were "that the person had demonstrated by his performance in our company that he had the kind of academic interest and competence that we felt the program required; that he had willingness to pursue the method of the dialogue, to which we were all committed; that he was willing, certainly, to devote his full time and attention to it, which was a very important consideration, and that he was productive in the sense that we had this commitment to maintain a publishing program." He added: "Our policy was to derive the publications from the material created by the dialogue."

"To what extent was the dialogue a criterion?"

"Well, it was an important factor, because that was a key, the core activity of the institution," Ashmore said.

In his testimony—also given in December 1969—Harvey Wheeler did not stress skill in the dialogue as the most significant criterion for the selection of the new fellows. He declared that Hutchins and he had felt that "the new academy would be more scholarly than the old Center, and the scholarly qualifications of its members would be more paramount in determining choices."

Wheeler wanted people with international renown—"names" so eminent that the Center staff members not chosen as fellows would acknowledge their high qualifications. He said he had also wanted to have the new fellows represented on the Fund's board. He recognized the fact that Ashmore and Hutchins were board members as well as fellows, but he wanted more fellows on the board.

Wheeler denied that he had tried to extract a promise from Tugwell to vote for certain peole as fellows before he gave his approval to the selection of Tugwell. Tugwell, when he testified in the Ferry suit, denied vigorously that anyone had tried to get such a promise from him. So did John Wilkinson and Elisabeth Borgese.

Wilkinson said that Seeley had been obsessed by the idea of "a conspiracy" and that Seeley had claimed that Wheeler had confessed to him that he had obtained promises from Wilkinson and others on how they would vote for future fellows if they were chosen themselves. Wilkinson thought it was most improbable that Wheeler would have said any such thing to Seeley. When he had asked Wheeler about it, Wheeler had answered: "I just talked to him and told him the results, that's all."

Wilkinson testified that Seeley had made statements indicating that Wheeler had "an undue influence on Hutchins," which Wilkinson regarded as "complete trash."

"The conspiracy theory began about the time he was not elected or thought he was not going to be elected," Wilkinson said. "Seeley was in a distraught state after a certain point."

Wilkinson attributed Seeley's removal from the Center to the Dean's frequent absences from the dialogue sessions. Seeley had become passionately dedicated to the youth movement, and spent some of his time in Berkeley and in other places where young people were developing a new style of life.

"We had Seeley on paper but we didn't really have Seeley," Wilkinson said.

Wilkinson testified that Seeley thought there were "other reasons why he hadn't been retained . . . that he was being made a scapegoat . . . he had been told to . . . start a program going . . . it had sagged, so to speak." He felt that he was being blamed "for not doing certain things which, in fact, were not in his power to do."

"He said that to have ex officio members at all betrayed the spirit of the thing," Wilkinson reported.

Asked about Ferry, Wilkinson said: "I didn't hear anyone and I didn't say anything myself in favor of Mr. Ferry. . . . All I remember about Ferry is that he was, as I have described Seeley, looked upon as a more or less of an individual who used the place to work out of rather than to work in."

Elisabeth Borgese testified that she had been strongly in favor of adding Seeley, Hallock Hoffman, and William Gorman to the group of new fellows. She said Hutchins, Wheeler, and Tugwell had talked freely with her about other selections, and she had nominated a Romanian, a Frenchman, a Yugoslav, two Latin Americans, a German physicist, and her brother, Golo Mann. She had also talked about possible appointments with Mrs. Tugwell and Mrs. Wheeler.

"What did Wheeler, for example, have to say about the proceedings?" Ferry's lawyer asked.

"I can't remember the details," she answered. "We—he was at that time really, I mean he as well as Mr. Tugwell—were among my closest friends and we would talk about people very informally and very confidentially. . . . It was not in any way formal, a joke about them, laugh about them, so—as one does with one's friends."

Mrs. Borgese's testimony about her informal discussions with Hutchins, Wheeler, and Tugwell indicated that there was an inner circle at the

Center. Ashmore, who saw Hutchins on weekends at his home as well as in his office, was also close to Hutchins personally.

Five of the first seven senior fellows in the reorganization saw one another fairly often on social occasions. The other two fellows had high standing with this group: Cogley was personally admired and deeply respected for his work as editor of the *Center Magazine*. Wilkinson was admired for his erudition and wit, especially by Wheeler.

Dean Seeley, because of his absences or because Hutchins felt that Seeley had not functioned effectively as a coordinator of the Center's projects, was not in the inner circle. Ferry had lost his close personal relationship with Hutchins, and his acerbic manner had offended a number of the staff members. (Wilkinson had testified: "I don't know if it was Ferry or somebody else who said to Hutchins: 'We can't run this place any longer on your charismatic gas.' This was in my opinion a very impolite thing to be said and a very poor thing to say; it might not have been said by Ferry, but Ferry concurred in it.")

Whatever the outcome of Ferry's suit might be, it was evident at the end of 1969 that the Center's reorganization would continue to go along the lines laid down by Hutchins and the new fellows. Hutchins was extremely careful in the meetings with the other six fellows to refrain from asserting his legal authority, but he still had it. He was the first among equals in the reconstituted fellowship, but he was also chairman of the Fund's board of directors—and the board retained its legal power to determine the Center's future.

While depositions were being taken in the Ferry case, experts in constitutional law from all over the United States came to the Center in mid-December to consider ideas for solving some of the problems arising from the pervasive influence of science.

One of the participants, A.A. Berle, formerly Assistant Secretary of State and lecturer of law at Columbia University, urged that Congress create a new agency to decide what types of research should be federally financed.

Projects of the Center attracted attention in the mass media. William Stringer, national columnist for the *Christian Science Monitor*, devoted much of an article on December 10 to the Center's conference on "today's biological revolution."

"It was noted that genetic experimentation and genetic engineering were moving rapidly ahead," Stringer wrote. "Yes, that people might soon be able to be redesigned, genetically programmed, chemically changed, to produce more stalwart or brainy or otherwise altered individuals. It was noted that this tampering with the race before birth (who would give the orders?) might not always have the best results."

"So it was proposed at this conference that there be an amendment to the Constitution which would guarantee to each citizen the protection of his 'environmental rights.' And these would refer not alone to his rights to pollution-free air and water, but to his right to protection from threats of psycho-surgery, psycho-pharmacology . . . and those aspects of genetic manipulation which would challenge integrity.

"Here is a remarkable concept—that the Constitution, perhaps under its freedoms clause (freedom of religion?), could protect a person's right to individuality and identity. A small beginning—of resistance to the threat of biological manipulation. But an illuminating beam of light!''

While the Center was casting such beams of light on the dangers of genetic programming and the effects upon society of scientific research proceeding without any constitutional limitations, the political and economic situation in the United States deteriorated. Irritated by antiwar demonstrations, new rebellions on college campuses, and the rejection of two of his nominees to the Supreme Court, President Nixon dropped his mask of moderation and assailed his critics with the fury of "the old Nixon."

On television, Nixon informed the nation that the demonstrations against his Vietnam policy were divisive and perilous for the United States. He announced that he had "a plan . . . for the complete withdrawal of all United States ground combat forces and their replacement by South Vietnamese forces." He called this "Vietnamization." He called for support from "the great silent majority of my fellow Americans."

Vice President Agnew called Nixon's new course "the politics of polarization," and received congratulations from the President for describing the critics of the Nixon administration as "an effete corps of impudent snobs who characterize themselves as intellectuals" and referring to those who went along with them as "parasites of passion" and "ideological eunuchs."

This was also the year when hundreds of thousands of young Americans jammed together at "rock festivals" at Woodstock, New York, on a ranch near Tentino, Washington, at Lewisville, Texas (where the Lewisville mayor told journalists that most of the disturbances were created by older Texans who rushed to ogle the young bodies of naked swimmers in the Garza–Little Elm Reservoir), and at Prairieville, Louisiana, where the bands included Country Joe and the Fish, the Grateful Dead, and Canned Heat.

Hutchins and the group around him were aware of the hard-rock culture, the drug culture, the culture of "consciousness raising" which engaged the energies of millions of young people. The new fellows had sensed the tragedy of the Vietnam war long before the demonstrators had taken to the streets. As members of the old Center, they had foreseen the explosions in the black ghettos: Center publications had pointed to the decay of the cities and the desperate wrath of the blacks.

But now the fellows concentrated their attention on other things, with a coolness and detachment that had not been characteristic of those separated from the staff. John Seeley, the paladin of the young, was gone. Ping Ferry, the angry advocate for the blacks, was gone. Jim Pike, the restless seeker for life beyond death, was gone. Hallock Hoffman, the Quaker knight of tender emotions, had been banished.

The seven new fellows cared about the young, about the blacks, about the sufferings inflicted by the Vietnam War. But while they had sympathized with the student rebels (while deploring their tactics), Hutchins and others in the chosen seven had never believed that the students could radically reform the universities. They had not believed that the blacks could be liberated from the ghettos by rescue parties organized at the Center. They had not believed that the so-called counterculture would or could transform the world into a realm of beauty, love, and peace.

Hutchins and the fellows of the emerging academy strove to see every problem in its global implications and ramifications, to examine the forces that had produced the alienated youth in many nations, to analyze the military-industrial-educational policies of a mechanized bureaucratic civilization, to uncover the trends in science and technology that might determine humanity's shifting to a stage in which "freedom" and "dignity" would be meaningless words.

"I say to you in all sadness of conviction that to think great thoughts you must be heroes as well as idealists," Oliver Wendell Holmes once said at Harvard College.

Hutchins did not refer to Holmes in his descriptions of the new Center, but he seemed to be looking for heroes of the mind. Whether he had the right core for such a group or could find the right people for that kind of heroism would be judged by the development of his new community—the "true university" he had been seeking for nearly fifty years.

24

The Center tries to prevent an arms race in the oceans—and unveils a model for a new American constitution

IN THE FIRST SIX MONTHS OF 1970, while Hutchins and his associates pursued their quest for "the very best people in the world," the Center dialogues focused on the peaceful development of ocean resources, preservation of the earth's environment, the multinational corporations and their influence, politics and communication, the consequences of lengthening human life, the ungovernability of giant cities, the failure of the United States policy in bombing North Vietnam, and many other topics. The Center calendar seemed to be almost as crowded as it had been before the reorganization, in spite of the repeated attempts of the new senior fellows to concentrate on a smaller number of major issues.

For three days in January, scholars from several countries investigated ways of preventing an arms race in the oceans. Lord Ritchie-Calder, professor of international relations, University of Edinburgh, a Center associate, presided at these sessions. Those who took part included General Said Uddin Khan, military adviser at the United Nations; Sven Hirdman, assistant director of the International Peace Research Institute, Stockholm; Rei Shiratori, of the Japan Peace Research Group; John Craven, department of naval architecture, Massachusetts Institute of Technology; E. D. Brown, professor in the faculty of laws, University College, London; Commodore Torgil Wulff, of the Ministry of Foreign Affairs of the Swedish govenment, Stockholm; and Elizabeth Young (Lady Kennet), of London, a writer and commentator.

Elisabeth Borgese, organizer of the conference, indicated its themes in her opening statement: "The concept of the ocean floor as an area of potential wealth beyond the limits of national jurisdiction and as part of the common heritage of mankind provides fresh terms of reference for the examination of world security and arms control.'' The conference was one in a series of meetings sponsored by the Center in preparation for the international convocation ''Pacem in Maribus'' to be held in Malta. Mrs. Borgese had assured the Center's board that the funds for that convocation would be available.

A week after the sessions on disarmament in the oceans had ended, ten philosophers came to the Center for three days of spirited arguments about making arguments more rational. A principal speaker was Chaim Perelman of the Free University in Brussels, who had written a book in collaboration with Mme. Olbrechts-Tyteca, another European scholar, entitled *The New Rhetoric: A Treatise on Argumentation*, which had been translated into English by John Wilkinson and Purcell Weaver of the Center.

''The new rhetoric owes its specific character to the relation between speaker and listener, between the man who tries to persuade and those whom he seeks to persuade,'' Perelman said. ''The social aspect of rhetoric makes it easier to understand the attitude of all protesters and contestants who cannot find in the established order adequate means to obtain a hearing, and who seek to attract attention on their grievances by provocative gestures.''

When the rhetoricians departed, the Center turned its attention to a paper by Neil Jacoby, a Center associate who had been appointed chairman of President Nixon's Task Force on Economic Growth in the 1970s. His paper dealt with a question that concerned many nations and their governments: ''The Multinational Corporation—Instrument of Peace or Imperialism?'' He contended that the benefits of such corporations in promoting economic growth and international trade outweighed their defects and dangers.

Other topics taken up during the last week in January 1970 included a statement by Silviu Brucan, a former ambassador from Romania to the United States, entitled ''The Particularities of International Relations'' and one headed ''Progress Means Pollution,'' a statement by Frank Potter, executive director of the Environmental Clearinghouse, Washington, D.C.

On January 20 Robert Hutchins testified about what had caused him to initiate his ''refounding of the Center,'' how the choices of the new Fellows had been made, and what he hoped to accomplish through his international ''academy.''

In a deposition given in response to a subpoena from Ferry's lawyer, Hutchins described the proposal he had presented at the Center staff meeting on May 7, 1969, and his recollection of what had happened at the executive session of the board of directors on May 9.

''I traced the history of the Fund for the Republic and the Center, I traced the interests and the development of an intellectual community at the highest level that I always had and I showed how we had entertained this notion from 1959 and how it had failed to materialize," Hutchins said.

"Would you tell me as well as you can what you did review for the Board at this time along the line of history?" Ferry's lawyer asked.

"The Fund started out with the intention of specializing in civil liberties and civil rights," Hutchins answered. "We found it extremely difficult to do as a foundation and we found that really unprofitable to do because the context never seemed to be understood or appreciated."

"You found it difficult to do?"

"It's difficult," Hutchins insisted. "Just imagine what's involved in giving money to support civil liberties and civil rights without engaging in political activity, without engaging in lobbying, without engaging in advancing the cause of candidates and without engaging in litigation. This is a very difficult thing to do. It's also unprofitable to do. At least, it was, I thought, at that time."

"In what sense unprofitable?"

A Center lawyer intervened. "What time are you referring to?"

"I'm referring to the days of the Fund for the Republic from 1954 to 1959," Hutchins said. "It is unprofitable because you don't get the effects that you anticipate and the reason you don't get the effects that you anticipate, I thought, was that the general understanding of civil liberties and civil rights, the general understanding of democratic institutions and why they were important, was on a very low level in this country so that these isolated activities on the surface of civil liberties and civil rights simply aroused antagonism without advancing the understanding that we were after. So we decided to organize what was called the Basic Issues Program and we worked on the Basic Issues Program in New York for a couple of years. At that point the property in Santa Barbara became available and we decided that Santa Barbara might be a better place to study the basic issues than New York City under the conditions in which we were working."

"Why was that, do you feel?" Ferry's lawyer inquired.

"Well, we were in the top of the Lincoln building opposite the Grand Central Station on the 42nd floor, and they were tearing the whole of New York down all around us," Hutchins replied. "The conditions of life in New York were becoming more and more difficult but one of the principal problems was that since we were so conveniently located for visitors in the City of New York, we were overwhelmed by them and the opportunity to do any serious thinking about anything was very limited."

After describing why the move to Santa Barbara had been made, Hutchins went on to say that he had told the board at the May 9, 1969, meeting: "I believed that you could no longer limit yourself to the United States, you could no longer limit yourself to the study of democratic institutions as such, that now we are living in a world in which everything was so intimately interrelated with everything else that you had to be free of these restrictions either to civil liberties and civil rights or to the United States in order to understand civil liberties and civil rights or democratic institutions. And the board agreed with this.''

He was asked whether he had informed the board that ''in order to follow through and understand the ideas which were to be studied'' he would ''need different and better people'' than some of those on the Center staff.

''That's right,'' Hutchins said.

''The people you needed would not necessarily be attracted by anything that was spelled inherently in terms of the American past?''

''That's right.''

''Or democratic institutions in the American form?''

''That's right,'' Hutchins repeated.

He was asked whether the board had given him ''a reasonably free hand with regard to severance pay.'' He said he did not think he would be free to go beyond the upper limit of two years of such pay.

''Was there any discussion during the meeting of any criteria that might be applied by you in negotiating severance pay with this one or that one?''

''No,'' Hutchins said.

''Did anyone ask or did you tell them whether there would be any ex officio election in this procedure?''

''No.''

''Or whether there would be majority voting, unanimity?''

''No.''

Hutchins said that on the morning of May 12, before he had chosen Wheeler as the second new fellow, John Seeley had come in to see him. ''He dashed into the office without calling or anything and said he wanted to say that neither he nor Mr. Ashmore should be selected as the first person.''

''Did he give a reason?''

''Well, Mr. Seeley didn't sit down, he was simply passing through and I think he muttered something about how it wouldn't be good or something of that sort. And I said, 'Well, you don't need to worry about that because I'm going to select Wheeler.' He said, 'Oh, fine, fine,' and dashed out.''

Seeley's recollection of this conversation, in testimony given later, differed from the statements made by Hutchins. Seeley testified that he had told Hutchins it would be ''unwise'' to appoint Ashmore or himself at the beginning of the selection process ''partly because if he did, there might be a conflict of conscience that he had appointed me in terms of a working relationship before and after; I might have difficulty naming Harry next, and vice versa, but also that it would certainly breach the appearance, if not the reality, of the barring of the ex officio rule.''

Seeley quoted Hutchins as saying: ''I had the same thought in the night; I have been quite worried about it. It is a very honorable and generous suggestion, and in that case I will not appoint either of you first.'' According to Seeley, Hutchins added: "I think I will appoint, then, Harvey Wheeler or Winky Barr," and Seeley asserted that he said: "Well, I think Harvey Wheeler would be fine in terms of competence and Winky Barr in terms of probity."

Asked what he meant by "probity as distinguished from competence," Seeley said: "I meant that Harvey was very competent in the dialogue and in the work of the Center, but that Barr's image and reality was such that no one would suspect him of doing anything except holding the welfare of the Center and the criteria decided upon." (Barr, referred to as "Winky," was Stringfellow Barr, then a fellow of the Center.)

In his testimony Hutchins did not give his reasons for selecting Wheeler, and he did not indicate that he had considered Barr. He told me several months after these events that he had considered Barr but had decided that he should not choose "Winky" at the beginning of the reorganization because Barr was an old friend and he did not want to be accused of favoring anyone because of friendship.

Hutchins testified that he had gone over a list of the Center staff with Wheeler immediately after Wheeler accepted appointment as a new senior fellow.

"Mr. Wheeler was opposed to all of them," Hutchins said. "He proposed that the choice of the existing staff stop at two. That may be unfair in a sense that Mr. Wheeler has always taken a position that he was not qualified to be a member of this group as he conceives it and has always indicated that when the group is completed, he was going to resign and so perhaps he was really saying that he wanted a group of one."

Although Wheeler apparently felt that he would not be qualified to be a member of the illustrious group he considered necessary for the new "academy," he did feel qualified to participate in the search for the members of such a group.

Asked whether Wheeler gave reasons for rejecting the whole staff at the Center, Hutchins answered: "Mr. Wheeler's idea of the Center is the same as mine, it ought to be composed of the very best people in the world. Mr. Wheeler, not being confronted with any practical problems, therefore was at liberty to ask: Are the people we have here the very best in the world? How could you say that in advance of a survey of the world?"

Hutchins recalled that Wheeler and he had discussed "a number of foreigners and some people in the United States," but that he had not taken the discussion very seriously because "I didn't think we had the time to do this."

Mrs. Borgese had been consulted about people to be invited to the Center, Hutchins said. He had talked with her about her brother, Golo Mann, and she gave "an account of his personal situation" that "raised serious doubts" about "whether he would be available." No action had been taken to persuade Golo Mann to join the new fellowship.

"When you were talking to Mrs. Borgese, did you discuss any other possibilities besides her brother?"

"I assume that what we did, since she had very wide connections in Europe, was to talk about various Europeans," Hutchins said. "It seems to me we had a discussion on Von Weizsacker."

"Did you and she discuss people at the Center at this time?"

"No."

"No?" Ferry's lawyer expressed surprise.

"No," Hutchins said.

"I take it you did discuss her views as to who were desirable persons?"

"From Europe."

"But not her views as to who was desirable or undesirable at the Center?"

"Yes," Hutchins said.

"Did you ask anybody else for suggestions at this time, I mean before Tugwell was chosen?"

"I don't recall anybody else."

"So she and Wheeler, then, were the only two people you discussed it with at this stage?"

"That's right," Hutchins answered.

"What happened next?"

"We finally agreed on Mr. Tugwell and proceeded."

"Before you agreed on Mr. Tugwell, did Mr. Wheeler, in effect, say you were right, I can't get anybody from outside?"

"I don't know that Mr. Wheeler went that far."

The lawyer then asked: "Before you elected Mr. Tugwell, did you have any discussions with Mr. Wheeler on the subject of what he called sovereignty?" Hutchins said: "Sovereignty is a word that I don't remember hearing from Mr. Wheeler until long after these discussions were over."

Wheeler had referred several times to his concepts of being a "sovereign" or participating in "sovereignty" after he had been appointed a new senior fellow by Hutchins. He seemed to regard himself as being on an equal level with Hutchins.

Ferry's lawyer asked Hutchins: "Did he indicate he wished to have an equal voice with you, at least, at that stage?"

Hutchins answered: "Mr. Wheeler didn't say he wanted an equal voice with me, no."

Wheeler had wanted to go on trying to bring in new fellows from other countries. Hutchins commented: "We did go on trying in the sense that the whole program in July, bringing in the people from all over the world, was in an effort to appraise these people to determine whether they would be likely candidates for us or not."

The choice of Tugwell as the third fellow had occurred, Hutchins said, when Wheeler "finally became convinced that we had a practical problem we had to solve."

"On the one hand, there was the question of keeping all these people waiting to find out whether they were going to be invited to remain," Hutchins said. "On the other hand, there was the publishing program, projects that were under way. These things had to be handled."

Hutchins had faced the fact that it was impossible to make a complete break with the Center's past. He was willing to build his new "academy" on a step-by-step basis. He could not start off with a group composed entirely of "the very best people in the world." He felt that the nucleus of such a group existed at the Center.

After he had reached a "conditional agreement" with Wheeler on the selection of Tugwell, Hutchins talked with Tugwell and was pleased to find that Tugwell took "substantially the position that Wheeler and I would take as an ideal, namely that we ought to try to get the best people we could, anywhere we could find them."

"Did you have any indication when you said the best people available that that meant the same thing to Tugwell as it meant to you?" Ferry's lawyer asked.

"Mr. Wheeler's standard, Mr. Tugwell's standards [of] what constitutes a first-class person are undoubtedly different from mine, almost everybody's are," Hutchins said. "Mr. Tugwell is a practicing politician and a person who has interests of a certain kind. I am not a practicing politician, I haven't those interests."

Hutchins did not recall whether he had requested Tugwell to give him the names of specific people. He declared: "Our object was not to find out what people Mr. Tugwell would propose but to find out what a seventy-eight-year-old constitutionalist thought about where he was going."

"About the idea of the academy and his possible role in it?"

"That's right," Hutchins said.

"Could you have discussed persons from within the Center who could have been included?"

"I could have but I have no recollection of it."

"Could you have discussed Mr. Ashmore's role in the academy?"

"Seems unlikely."

"Among the people in the Center, might you have discussed Ashmore and Cogley in general with Mr. Tugwell?"

"No," Hutchins said. "I have no recollection of discussing Ashmore or Cogley with Tugwell at any time prior to Tugwell's meeting with Wheeler and myself as Senior Fellows."

In the course of his discussion with Tugwell on the Center's possible development as "a world institution," Hutchins said that Tugwell mentioned that the model for a new American constitution —Tugwell's model—"did have some international application."

"He developed the notion that he expressed later on that what he's really after is not an American constitution but a constitution for a democratic organization of any advanced technological state," Hutchins said.

"Had he expressed that idea to you before this?"

"No."

At the end of this conversation, Hutchins said he had told Tugwell that "he was elected." Hutchins said he had been authorized by Wheeler to make the decision about Tugwell if the conversation proved to be satisfactory.

Ferry's lawyer asked: "In effect, on the basis of what you had previously discussed with Wheeler, you were to determine if Tugwell would be acceptable to Wheeler?"

"That's right," Hutchins said.

When Hutchins, Wheeler, and Tugwell got together, Hutchins was "surprised" by Tugwell's attitude toward members of the Center's staff. He testified that "Mr. Tugwell shared Mr. Wheeler's view in general of the people at the Center."

"Which was what?"

"Which was that he would prefer to look outside before proceeding."

Hutchins continued "I suppose that throughout, I had—I was attaching greater importance to the immediate practical problems of the Center and taking a longer view of the time it will take to get the kind of people that we needed. I don't mean this was a better view, but a longer view than Mr. Tugwell or Mr. Wheeler. . . . Neither of them had any administrative responsibility."

"In other words, Tugwell's idea of best people available was, for practical purposes, higher, more exacting than the one you would prefer to apply at that time for administrative reasons?"

Hutchins replied: "Let me put it this way. I thought that what we would do is guarantee in some way the best we could the preservation of our institution and we would then take whatever many years. . . . Some reporter asked me how long I thought it would take to get a group of the kind I was after, and I said it might take five years. Well, I couldn't, I couldn't wait five years to staff the Center. Therefore, I had to make some kind of interim arrangement."

"Did Tugwell and Wheeler then continue, well, Tugwell especially, with the notion that you should canvass the world . . .?"

"They both felt that we should keep on looking," Hutchins said. "They also, of course, didn't have to worry about, except as individuals, about how the people at the Center felt while they waited."

Hutchins felt a heavy responsibility for all the members of the Center's staff. He had selected them or approved their appointments on the recommendations of Ashmore and others. He did not feel that he could ignore them.

For several days he was blocked by Wheeler and Tugwell. He testified: "I kept saying we can't hold this up, we've got to move. . . . Finally, I don't know who suggested it, a suggestion of electing Cogley and Ashmore as ex officio members was made."

"Both together?"

"Yes."

"In other words, they would be two members that would come in together and not with numerical labels, such as four and five?"

"They were elected together as a practical matter."

Hutchins declared that the doubts of Wheeler and Tugwell "were overcome by the suggestion that these people should be members by virtue of their office, so if they gave up the office, they would presumably cease—or the question would be raised—whether they would cease to be members of the senior fellowship."

He recalled that both Ashmore and Cogley accepted the ex officio appointments. Then Cogley, troubled by the fact that such appointments had not been mentioned to the staff, withdrew his acceptance and indicated that he would resign. After that, Hutchins said: "We decided to elect both of them regular members and get on with it." He added that the idea of ex officio members was "simply abandoned, that's all."

Hutchins testified that he had talked at various times with Ashmore and Seeley while the process of selecting new fellows was under way. When he was asked whether he had obtained Ashmore's views on who should be retained at the refounded Center, Hutchins said: "Mr. Ashmore and I have been engaged in administration of this organization for several years, and Mr. Ashmore and I have discussed everything about the Center."

The testimony of Hutchins on what Seeley had said to him and what he had said to Seeley difered sharply from the statements made by Seeley in a later deposition.

Hutchins said he remembered that Seeley had reported to him that Wheeler had informed Seeley that Wheeler had talked with Wilkinson "in an effort to find out whether or not Mr. Wilkinson would support Mr. Gorman . . . if Mr. Wilkinson were elected a senior fellow."

"Did you take any action as the result of that conversation?" Ferry's lawyer asked.

"I must have talked with Wheeler but I don't recall the conversation," Hutchins answered.

"You did ask Wheeler about conversations with Wilkinson?"

"I must have."

"Did you ask him whether he had inquired of Wilkinson Wilkinson's opinion of Gorman?"

"I don't recall."

Hutchins did recall that Seeley had brought up the question of the ex officio members and "seemed to regard this for some reason as some sort of violation of all understandings."

"Since the statement made to the staff and the board did not exclude this possibility, I didn't see how it was a violation of any prior understandings," Hutchins said. "I couldn't figure out what Mr. Seeley had on his mind, why this was such a dreadful thing."

"Did he tell you anything about Wheeler having said that you had talked to Tugwell about Tugwell's vote?"

"I don't recall that he did."

In his deposition, given two weeks after Hutchins testified, Seeley asserted that Wheeler had telephoned him one night while the election process was going on and had declared that "my whole world has fallen apart, the university has fallen apart."

When he had talked with Wheeler at the Center the next day, Seeley said he had tried to tell Wheeler that the selection procedure was not being done in accordance with the criteria he had accepted.

Seeley quoted Wheeler as saying: "But you don't understand at all, a sovereign is an absolute sovereign, no restraints on him whatever," and then asserting: "Mr. Hutchins and I were absolute sovereigns."

"And puzzlingly the only point that he allowed he was upset about . . . was the point at which he said that Mr. Hutchins appeared not to understand that they were joint sovereigns," Seeley declared. "He was upset and deeply offended by Mr. Hutchins having taken the substance of the agreement of the two of them to Mr. Tugwell instead of their going as joint sovereigns together."

Seeley's testimony indicated that Wheeler had finally realized that he was not on an equal level with Hutchins. Actually, the appointment of new fellows had not altered the legal situation at the Center. Hutchins, as a member of the board and as the highest officer of the corporation, had the responsibility for keeping the Center in operation while the new "academy" was being formed. According to Seeley, Wheeler had been depressed by the appointment of ex officio fellows and felt that the original idea of the new "university" had "fallen apart."

Seeley said he had informed Hutchins about what Wheeler had told him and he had expressed his belief that the ex officio appointments and Wheeler's actions had "clearly tainted" the election. He had urged Hutchins to cancel the whole procedure.

"He said: What other way was there to go?" Seeley recalled. "And I said we could go back to his personal responsibility or forward to what Mr. Ashmore ruled out, a blind ballot between the fellows, but couldn't repeat that kind of election after the trust was dissolved by this kind of proceeding."

Hutchins had then talked to Wheeler. After that, Seeley met Hutchins again in Hutchins' office. According to his recollection, Hutchins acknowledged that "the facts" were "substantially what you state," but Hutchins was not prepared to call off the election.

Seeley quoted himself as saying: "Mr. Hutchins, I think this is very serious, and I think if you take this view, that when you come to the end of the process . . . you are going to be in an indefensible position." He quoted Hutchins as replying: "Well, I can see no practical way out."

According to Seeley, he then asked Hutchins whether it was wise or "unsafe" for him to go to Berkeley to deliver a lecture. Seeley testified: "He said perfectly safe, perfectly in order for me to go on. The electoral process was by no means at an end, and he would keep in touch with me." Apparently Seeley was still willing to be considered for election as a new fellow, even though he regarded the process as "tainted."

Seeley testified that he telephoned Hutchins the next night and asked Hutchins a question: "Is my tenure at the Center affected in any way by anything the Fellows may or may not do?" He quoted Hutchins as answering: "No, it is not."

Two days later, Seeley went on, he had asked Hutchins to amplify the assurance he had been given about his status. According to Seeley, Hutchins said: "It means we would make you comfortable at the Center for life."

Seeley said he asked Hutchins what the situation would be if he refused election as a new senior fellow, since he considered the election "invalid." He said Hutchins told him: "Well, that would be very awkward."

Seeley asserted that he then put another question to Hutchins: "If the fellows should elect me, and holding the election to be invalid and improper, fraudulent, as you know I do, and I should accept, what would you think of me and what would you think of yourself?" As he recalled it, Hutchins replied, "This is a very difficult and delicate question, and I should think it would weigh heavily with us," but added that it would be mostly on Seeley's conscience.

In his testimony, Seeley said that he had asked Hutchins whether Harry Ashmore and Rex Tugwell knew that he had "tenure at the Center." He quoted Hutchins as saying: "No, they do not," and he recalled that he said: "Shouldn't they?" He quoted Hutchins as answering: "Yes, they should." He declared that Hutchins had promised to tell Ashmore and Tugwell that he had such tenure.

The testimony of Tugwell and Ashmore did not show any acceptance on their part of the idea that Seeley had permanent tenure at the Center, or had been guaranteed a lifetime job there.

While his deposition was being given, Hutchins was asked: "Prior to or during or after the refounding process, did you ever promise anyone that if he were not selected as a senior Fellow, he could physically remain at the Center with office, secretary and salary for life?"

"That was obviously beyond the scope of our understanding," Hutchins said. "Our understanding was that those matters would be settled by the senior Fellows."

"For example, you never promised Mr. Seeley that he could remain at the Center with salary for life?"

"No, I said I would take up the question."

At another point, Hutchins was asked: "Prior to your presentation of the Cogley proposal to the staff, did you promise Seeley or anyone else that they could remain at the Center with salary for life?"

"I don't recall any such promise," Hutchins said.

Hutchins made it clear that he had been dissatisfied with Ferry's work for several years, after the study of the corporation in a free society had been terminated. He said that he had asked Ferry to take a reduction in salary and to give up the title of vice president, but Ferry had not been willing to do so.

"Did it seem likely to you in April on the eve of the refounding that the refounded Center would probably be a smaller group than the old one?" Hutchins was asked.

"Certainly at the top," Hutchins said.

"So . . . the presence of the divisive person such as you felt Ferry to be would be more harmful in the refounded Center proportionally than it had been in the old one?"

"Certainly."

"Had you discussed with Ferry in recent years . . . his inability to get along, to function in the group?"

"No."

In response to another question, Hutchins said: "If the Senior Fellows had wanted to elect Ferry, I would have interposed no objection."

Asked about his personal feelings, Hutchins responded: "My feeling was that Mr. Ferry had no administrative duties and since he had no part in the program and since he was not engaged in anything in which the Center had expressed an interest, that it was extremely difficult to justify his continuation, no matter what the organization of the Center was."

Ferry's lawyer quoted Ashmore's statement, made in Ashmore's memorandum of April 15, 1969, that "all except those who have been invited to Santa Barbara for a specifically limited period have been assured that they could remain in their present status so long as the Center survived," and asked Hutchins: "Does that in your opinion accurately reflect the state of governance of the Center on April 15, 1969?"

"No," Hutchins said.

"Did you see this memorandum of Ashmore's before it was circulated?"

"I must have," Hutchins said. Then he added: "I answered too quickly. . . . I have seen the memorandum but I do not recall whether I saw it before it was circulated."

"In the usual course of business, you did attend the next staff meeting after this paper appeared, whatever that was?"

"I think so."

"Did you state then or at any other time that you felt Ashmore had gone overboard or gotten out of line, or however you—"

"I didn't notice it," Hutchins said.

"You didn't notice that language at all?"

"I simply took it that he was saying, in effect, we haven't tenure, can't have it, we all serve at the pleasure of the board, but the president is a nice man." (The president then was Robert Hutchins.)

"Had you assured anyone that they could, any of the fellows, that they could remain there as long as the Center survived?"

"No," Hutchins said.

"Had you ever assured Seeley either before he came or after that he had, in effect, tenure?"

Hutchins answered: "I don't recall it."

"Or that he had a life-long arrangement or some such words?"

"I don't recall it."

"In your opinion is this statement that I read of Ashmore's wholly unsupported by the facts?"

"Correct," Hutchins said.

"Do you feel that you have had the power to discharge any employee at the Center?"

"Yes."

"Including, for example, Ferry in his role as vice president of the corporation?"

"Yes."

"Did that derive from any specific delegation of power from the board?"

"I believe there is a specific delegation, goes way back," Hutchins said. "I think even before I was appointed, there was a resolution to this effect."

"That would be '53?"

"I was appointed in '54 so it would have to be '53."

Hutchins was asked whether "freedom of press, thought, religion, opportunity, problems of racial and religious discrimination" and other civil liberties were among the primary concerns of the refounded Center.

"They remain among our primary interests," Hutchins said.

When Hutchins was asked to describe how the Center in April 1969—before the "refounding"—fell short of what he had in mind, Hutchins replied: "Well, I suppose any actual institution will fall short of the model I have in mind. You never can find the people, you never can find them at the right time, you never can bring them together in the right conjunction, you never get quite the spirit you hope for, you never get quite the quality of work you anticipated."

Hutchins said that the Center had made some progress toward becoming "a true university" in its first ten years and that its "international interests" had constantly broadened, but he had been convinced that a drastic reorganization was needed.

In the testimony he had given in December, Rexford Tugwell said that Hutchins had indicated to him that the criteria for the new group "were that they should be distinguished people, the most distinguished people to be found anywhere in the world."

"Distinguished with reference to what standards?"

"Academic standards," Tugwell said.

"Is that the same as 'famous people'?"

"No, not at all," Tugwell replied. He said that Hutchins, Wheeler, and he were looking for "the most distinguished people in the subject matters we were interested in." Hutchins emphasized that.

"Did he tell you or did you already know what subject areas were the ones that would be critical?"

Tugwell said, "I don't think we had any disagreement about that. They would be distinguished in law, political science or science."

"Natural science and social science?"

"I remember asking him who he thought would be the most qualified person," Tugwell said. Then Tugwell paused, and asked the Center's lawyer: "Am I volunteering too much?"

"You are volunteering," the lawyer said.

"I think two names occurred to him and one was Malraux and the other was Alexander King. Andre Malraux is, of course, the Minister of Culture in France, and Alexander King was the science director of the United Nations in Paris. This was the kind of person that he had in mind (to) associate with the Center."

"Not easy to get."

"No," Tugwell said. "Such people are never easy to get."

Tugwell was asked: "Is it generally true that as far as the Fellows are concerned now, the Center is moving in academic directions which, as Dr. Hutchins put it, would be free of limitation inherent in its American background?"

"I don't think there has been any change to speak of," Tugwell said. "The work that is going on is generally the same as it was before, and before, it was quite wide. It's very difficult to think of any of these things that don't have world repercussions."

"According to what you know of future plans, then, it is still committed to the study of democratic institutions to the same extent that it was?" Ferry's lawyer asked.

"That's right," Tugwell said.

"Do you recall the article in the Center Magazine this summer by Dr. Hutchins in which he said, I think without paraphrasing too much, that the Center would now move into the 70's in directions which would be free of limitations inherent in its American background and its commitment to study democratic institutions?

Tugwell answered: "I don't remember his words. I don't remember if that is exactly what he said."

"But if he said that—"

"I didn't understand that this meant anything more than that we would have other projects and that they might have repercussions of worldwide importance, but then, haven't they always?" Tugwell continued.

The lawyer said, "In the language of the street and the daily press, the Center has not yet found what its thing is—is that right?"

Tugwell replied, "It's always in the process of finding it, it's a continuous process. The Center will never find it, definitely, finally, I hope."

Perhaps because the 1969 reorganization had led to the departure of Center fellows believed to be "activists," some of the Center members wondered whether the lofty dialogues of the new senior fellows would lead to the reforms necessary to preserve civilization. Many of these members were engaged in practical projects or political activities, and they urged the Center to become more of an "action group."

People who supported the Center with financial contributions were strongly concerned about civil rights and civil liberties, stopping the arms race, finding jobs for the unemployed, housing for the poor, schooling for the disadvantaged, equal opportunities for blacks and all other minorities, and the conflicts threatening to tear the world apart. The Center fellows, recognizing all of these issues, still insisted that their principal task was to strive for an "adequate perspective on social action and social change." But the Center did encourage efforts to solve hard practical questions.

Paul Jacobs, a Center consultant, gave a vivid picture of the pains and perplexities he suffered in attempting to arrange a private meeting under Center auspices in Europe between prominent Israelis, Americans, and Palestinian Arabs to find ways of easing tensions in the Middle East. In a book called *Between the Rock and the Hard Place*, Jacobs described the mission he had undertaken. He had been frustrated and heartbroken by "the distorted views of reality held by both sides," and had been unable to get a dialogue going between the Arabs and the Jews. *Publishers Weekly* said: "His chronicle of failure adds up to one of the most revealing documents on the subject thus far published."

While Jacobs' experience showed the torturing difficulties of dealing with immediate problems, the Center took up matters on another plane. Sixteen experts concerned with the process of aging—gerontologists, biologists, psychiatrists, neurologists, and public figures—met at the Center from April 13 to 17 to consider the possible, likely, and desirable consequences of lengthening human life.

The conference "Project Lifespan" was convened at the suggestion of a Center associate, Alexander Comfort, head of the Medical Research Council Group in Aging, University College, London. In a statement circulated as background material, Dr. Comfort predicted that scientists would "know by 1990 of at least one proven way of extending vigorous life by about 20 per cent." He declared that "the direct application of such research will be at about the same rate as that of antibiotics, world-wide" and "all existing medical services and governments will elect to apply it, or be unable to prevent its application."

Biologists, agriculturists, economists, and conservationists from France, Sweden, West Germany, Switzerland, Spain, and the United States arrived at the Center a few days after the neurologists and gerontologists had departed. These experts came together to talk about what was happening to "global ecology," examining "the oceans and land areas of the world as a physical unit."

Many of these experts took part in a day-long meeting attended by 1700 Center members and their friends in Los Angeles. Describing the meeting for the *Christian Science Monitor*, Kimmis Hendrick wrote: "Speakers came from the group of world-renowned ecologists and fellows of the Center who had been in session for a week at its Santa Barbara headquarters. . . .

"It was doubtless, though, the most varied audience the Center had ever attracted. When a show of hands was requested from people who had never attended a Center function previously, probably 1000 were raised.

"Young people came in large numbers. Some were barefoot. The biggest part of the audience looked middle-aged and prosperous. It was largely a white crowd, but not totally."

Hutchins told the audience: "The question is: Can we make the world safe for people? I think the answer must be yes—but the answer has to be accompanied by a qualification that *if* we are going to make the world safe for people we shall have to make fundamental changes in our ways of thought and action."

"It means that we have to adopt a program of rational use rather than reckless appropriation. And then the question becomes: How do you bring about a moral and intellectual revolution? I think that it can't be done by scaring people. It's useful to scare people, in order to get their attention, perhaps—but any long-term program that rests on the notion that people are going to stay frightened fails because they don't."

He cited the history of the reaction to nuclear weapons as an example: "We all believed, at one time, that if we could get out and show what was going to happen to the world by virtue of the atomic and hydrogen bombs that we could in some way bring this insane competition to a close. But we have, in some peculiar way, become adjusted to it.

"And yet we do have the notion—which I think is justified—that we *can* do whatever we make up our minds to do. . . .

"How is it that these great moral and intellectual revolutions occur? Of course, I don't know. But I can pretend to suggest a possible answer. It seems to me that great social changes result because some groups steadily, persistently, press for recognition of the facts of life. Now it is the mission of the Center to make some contribution to the facts of life."

Harvey Wheeler also called for "a profound, moral, ethical reformation." He declared: "I don't think that the individual, unaided, is going to be able to face the needs, the rigors, the requirements of living a sound ecological life. . . . We must help each other to maintain our determination to act sensibly."

"Technology has done what all the preachments of the prophets, the prayers of the saints, the visions of the poets, the principles of the philosophers, and the sanity of the savants have not succeeded in doing through the ages,'' John Cogley said. ''It has made clear, existentially, palpably clear, that the fate of all mankind is linked together.''

Elisabeth Borgese described the plans for the Center's conference on peaceful development of the oceans. By sheer determination and persuasive persistence, she had overcome all the obstacles to this conference, which cost more than the board of directors had expected.

Ten days after the Center's meeting on ''global ecology'' in Los Angeles, Judge John Rickard issued several rulings in the Ferry suit in the superior court in Santa Barbara. Ferry had made Thomas C. Lynch, attorney general of the State of California, a party to the suit, asking the attorney general to intervene on the ground that the Fund was no longer operating in accordance with its original certificate of incorporation. Ferry had declared that the Fund in its ''refounding'' had ''undertaken a deliberate realignment of its corporate purposes and priorities so as to 'remove any limitations found in the American background (of defendant The Fund for the Republic, Inc.). . . .' ''

Judge Rickard sustained a demurrer that had been filed on behalf of the attorney general, removing the attorney general from the case. Carl Boronkay, deputy attorney general, had stated in the demurrer: ''But realignment of corporate purposes and priorities, assuming such is the fact, does not run counter to or exceed the broad purposes set forth in the articles of incorporation which govern the scope of proper activity of the defendant corporation. As quoted in the complaint, said articles provide that the purposes are: 'To receive and administer funds exclusively for scientific, educational and charitable purposes. . . . *Without limiting the generality of the foregoing*, one of the principal purposes of the corporation shall be to foster, encourage and conduct research and study in the field of civil rights and civil liberties, etc.'

''Nowhere in the complaint are facts alleged demonstrating that the defendant corporation has embarked upon or intends to embark upon a course that is not within the broad purposes quoted above.''

Judge Rickard found that the Fund's New York lawyers, in drawing up its basic charter, had provided legal freedom for the Fund to engage in any kind of educational, scientific, or charitable activity authorized by the board of directors.

Objections by Hutchins and Ashmore to Ferry's claims for general damage of $263,000 and exemplary damages of $400,000 were sustained by Judge Rickard on the ground that Ferry had not stated ''facts sufficient to constitute a cause of action against either of said defendants.'' Ferry was given twenty days to amend his complaint and to bring forward facts to convince the judge.

Judge Rickard overruled the Fund's demurrer to Ferry's second cause of action, in which Ferry had contended that the Fund had made ''representations of continued employment'' and had induced ''the Permanent Senior Fellows, including plaintiff'' to place substantial reliance on the idea that ''each of them would continue in their employment, duties and work.'' He gave the Fund twenty days to prepare an answer to his ruling.

The legal battle between Ferry and the Fund extended for many months in 1970 and 1971, with demurrers and counterstatements being filed and argued in Judge Rickard's court by lawyers for both sides. Meanwhile, the Center's activities in many fields went on as energetically as ever, with its conferences and publications drawing much attention in the United States and other countries.

While the Center was fending off Ferry, preparing for a large international gathering on peace in the oceans, and holding dialogues on other topics, the war in Southeast Asia grew increasingly ferocious. American bombers hit hospitals as well as supply bases in North Vietnam. The number of Americans killed in combat rose to 44,000. The South Vietnamese government made insatiable demands for more American arms and more American money.

President Nixon had been secretly bombing Cambodia for fourteen months, but the attacks from the air had been ineffective against the North Vietnamese forces there. In May 1970 President Nixon ordered American troops into Cambodia, telling the American people: ''For five years, neither the United States nor South Vietnam has moved against these sanctuaries because we did not want to violate the territory of a neutral nation.'' He didn't refer to the rain of American bombs that had been dropped there.

Students on campuses across the country exploded with rage. More than 100,000 young people rushed to Washington on May 9 and 10. The White House was surrounded by huge buses, and troops were hidden in the grounds, ready to fire against young Americans demonstrating in the streets. Nixon first described the protesters as ''bums'' and then slipped from the White House one night with Secret Service guards to talk to students who were camped near the Lincoln Memorial. ''I feel just as deeply as you do about this,'' he said in a rambling incoherent discussion.

In that stormy month of May, there were strikes, sit-downs, demonstrations on 415 campuses. A bomb virtually destroyed the Army Mathematics Research Center at the University of Wisconsin. When students and police clashed at Jackson State University in Mississippi, the police dispersed the young people with fire from machine guns, rifles, and armor-piercing shells, wounding nine and killing two of them. National Guardsmen in Ohio, sent to Kent State University after rioting there, shot thirteen students and killed four.

The Senate of the United States, alarmed by signs of a spreading rebellion, adopted a resolution demanding the removal of American troops from Cambodia and a termination of air support for the South Vietnamese there. Nixon's popularity in the opinion polls dropped. He blamed his troubles on "foreign agents", and secretly ordered the formation of a White House intelligence group which engaged in wiretapping, burglaries, and other illegal acts which led eventually to the Watergate scandal.

During that strife-torn month of May, the Center kept calmly on its course. On May 4, the day of the Kent State killings, a Romanian diplomat—Silviu Brucan, a visiting fellow—led a discussion entitled "What Keeps Nations Together." On May 11 Jon Van Dyke, a young lawyer, talked on the subject "The Failure of America's Policy in Bombing North Vietnam." Two days later Kenneth Tollett—a black professor from Howard University, who was also a visiting fellow—spoke on the subject "The Impact of Higher Education on Society." In a dialogue on May 14 Paul Ricoeur, professor of philosophy and dean of the university of Nanterre, France, gave his views in a statement called "Youth in Revolt."

The Center's directors convened on May 15 for a special meeting at its headquarters in Santa Barbara. At the request of David Lloyd, a lawyer for the Center in the Ferry case, the directors clarified their resolution of December 5, 1969, in which they had endorsed the actions taken by Hutchins and Ashmore in terminating Center staff members. On a motion by J. R. Parten, seconded by Joseph Antonow, the directors reaffirmed that policy and declared that it "included without limitation a ratification of whatever refounding process and election procedure was followed, whether or not it deviated from the procedure proposed to the board on May 9, 1969; and that every act of the officers of the corporation in proposing a refounding process and in carrying out the refounding was done by such officers within the course and scope of their employment." The resolution also specifically ratified the termination of W. H. Ferry as vice president of the corporation as of October 1, 1969.

The board approved several recommendations presented by Parten on behalf of the committee. The directors adopted a resolution to amend the corporation's by-laws "to reflect the intention of the board, as expressed at the meeting of May 9, 1969, to delegate authority over academic program and personnel to the Senior Fellows, subject to budgetary and administrative controls to be adopted by the board." The board also resolved that "the Chairman of the Board and Chief Executive Officer should continue to be the Chairman of the Senior Fellows, and that his selection be made by the board in consultation with the Senior Fellows."

On a motion by James Douglas, seconded by Morris Levinson, the directors resolved that "the President and Chief Operating Officer continue to be elected by the board in consultation with the Senior Fellows, and that he continue to be a member of the board and a Senior Fellow." This resolution, coupled with the preceding one, meant that Hutchins and Ashmore would continue to have a special status—and implied that their successors should also have such status.

Accepting a recommendation from Hutchins, the board elected Gary M. Cadenhead, an assistant professor of accounting at the University of California in Los Angeles, as secretary and treasurer. By appointment of the chairman, Cadenhead was also designated to serve as secretary of the senior fellows.

These actions were taken by the board at its executive session on the morning of May 15. At the afternoon session, open to the staff, Hutchins presented his report on the academic program. He announced Cadenhead's election and said that Cadenhead's responsibilities would include the administrative burden of the program and would free the fellows to give full time to their studies.

Responding to questions about the funds available for the projected "Pacem in Maribus" conference in Malta, Ashmore indicated that the money raising had gone rather slowly. He said that about half of the revised conference budget—estimated at $100,000—had been obtained. The Rubin Foundation had expressed its intention to contribute $5000 and might add another $5000. That would bring the total contributions to $62,000. He said that the remaining costs would be absorbed in the Center's budget.

There was a large gap between the Center's income and the Center's expenditures, but Ashmore did not seem to be worried about it. He acknowledged that there had been a decline in the number of special gifts—gifts of $500 or more—but he had not found any convincing evidence that the repercussions of the Center's "refounding" had cut down the flow.

Arnold Grant, chairman of the Endowment Campaign Committee, which had been formed with high hopes in 1969, said that this committee had reluctantly decided to postpone the campaign. Stock market fluctuations had disturbed some donors, and the 1969 revisions in federal tax laws had not yet been clarified. Givers were hesitant to make long-term commitments.

Grant reminded the board that the Center's problem was complicated by the fact that a new chairman had not been chosen to succeed Hutchins. Hutchins had spoken frequently of his age and his desire to retire, but no outstanding candidate to take over the Center's helm had yet appeared. In these circumstances, Grant's committee felt that it was not realistic to talk in terms of endowment. The committee advocated the resumption of fund raising to meet operating costs.

With his usual optimism, Ashmore said he believed that a new money drive would be productive. Ordinary fund raising had been suspended while the endowment campaign had been contemplated, but it could be resumed at once. The Center had been able to raise at least $1 million annually to pay operating costs for several years.

The board accepted the recommendation of Grant's committee and deferred the endowment campaign. In the spring of 1970 most of the board members seemed to share Ashmore's hopefulness. The operating deficit, which was running at a rate of $100,000 a month, did not seem to alarm them. Two members did raise questions: Eulah Laucks challenged Ash-more's financial projections, and Edward Lamb wondered whether cost controls were adequate.* But the board approved the budgets for the 1970–71 fiscal year, and unanimously approved a motion by Justice Doug-las for the appointment of Hutchins as a life fellow upon his relief as chair-man.

Hutchins voiced his willingness to serve as chairman until his successor had been found. After that, he would continue to be at the Center in any ca-pacity sanctioned by the board, with the understanding that this would not put "a dead or dying hand" upon the new chairman.

Ashmore said he would relinquish his office as president if the incom-ing chairman wanted him to step down. He would give the new head of the Center, whenever chosen, his "undated resignation for possible submission to the board."

Hutchins did not go to the Malta convocation on the oceans, which convened on June 28 with several directors of the Center present, including Ashmore and Justice Douglas. Mrs. Borgese had brought together 200 par-ticipants from many of the nations represented in the General Assembly of the United Nations.

Douglas, who presided at the initial session, called for an agreement to halt ocean pollution and to treat the seas as a resource for all countries. Pointing out that the laws governing the oceans and sea beds were "either fragmentary or non-existent," Douglas declared, "At the present rate of deterioration, the oceans will no longer be of any use to man except as a highway by the end of the century."

Lord Ritchie-Calder, another speaker on the first day, said that the scramble for marine wealth would "make the Klondike gold rush look like a Sunday school picnic." He urged the formation of an international regime, backed by the UN, to guide the orderly development of these immense re-sources.

Malta's representative at the United Nations, Arvid Pardo, demanded an international convention to limit the nuclear wastes entering the oceans. Pardo said that the existing international agency for peaceful development of atomic energy had not stringently restricted the stream of poison which threatened life on the planet.

Dr. Roger Revelle of Harvard University took a more hopeful view. He regarded the rigorous controls on radiation pollution established by the United States and Britain as "one of the bright spots of the postwar world." Pardo was afraid that other nations developing nuclear energy would not have such strict controls over atomic power plants and subma-rines.

*After the minutes of this meeting were circulated, in July 1970, Mrs. Laucks asked that the minutes be corrected to show that she had abstained from voting on the 1970–71 budgets and that clarifications of overhead costs were to be provided to the board members.

Douglas had a vigorous role in the Malta conference, ignoring the attacks made upon him in the United States House of Representatives by a group of Congressmen headed by Gerald R. Ford of Michigan. Ford had tried to link Justice Douglas and the Parvin Foundation to Bobby Baker, a former assistant to Lyndon Johnson, who had been involved in a bribery scandal, and to efforts by an organized crime syndicate to penetrate the Dominican Republic. The Washington *Post* and other newspapers had denounced the attacks made by Ford and others as "politically motivated and full of demonstrably false statements and malicious innuendos."

The views of Justice Douglas and others at the Malta meeting were extensively reported by the Associated Press, United Press International, the *New York Times, Time* magazine, and publications in many other countries.

Douglas, Ashmore, Elisabeth Borgese, and others from the Center who participated in the Malta convocation returned to the United States with the hope that the work done by Center scholars and associates would lead to the formation of a new type of international agency. Mrs. Borgese and others at the Center had already drafted a model charter for such an agency.

The July–August issue of the *Center Magazine* gave much of its space to the rebellious activities of young people. All the senior fellows offered their comments on what was happening and what was likely to happen to American society.

"We are in for a long struggle, in which we shall have to absorb much outrageous behavior," Hutchins declared. "The slogan 'Law and Order' cannot be permitted to divert us from revitalizing or revising our institutions and reformulating our ideals. The young are reminding us that we are a long way from achieving peace, justice, freedom, and democracy, and that they will be satisfied with nothing less."

Rexford Tugwell was skeptical of Donald McDonald's statement referring to a "youth-heightened moral vision," contending that "moral visions do not arrive as miracles or occur only to 'the young.' Some people have them; some never will. Those who do will strive to make them materialize; and if they can be heard and their efforts are appreciated they will prevail."

"I do strongly object to the attribution of all good impulses to those under twenty and all bad ones to those over forty," Tugwell added. "If something comes of the present disturbances it will be built on foundations laid a long time ago, not on recent ruins. . . . I refuse to join the breast-beating apologists among the old. We perhaps should have done better; but we did a good deal. More important, we are still trying; and we do bring to the effort something more than demagoguery and destruction.

John Cogley expressed a belief that "there is something special about the new generation, which is not of their own doing. They happen to have come along at a turning period in history. The young were born into a world radically different from the dying one their parents grew up in. More than that, they see the world differently. To their credit, most of them are now trying to make sense of the total picture in order to bring some kind of integrity into their lives.

Harvey Wheeler asserted that "the youth rebellion has converted America into a dual society; a rudimentary new social order is developing inside the old." He warned of the danger that the revolution might grow and become "quite effective, without planning the positive institutions of the future."

"The need for a new utopianism—planning for post-revolutionary institutions well in advance—is shown by history and proved by theory," Wheeler wrote. "The socialist revolution has been betrayed throughout Eastern Europe. Mao's ill-starred permanent revolution was an attempt to forestall the same fate for China. The theoretical point is that once historical materialism is discredited the need for utopianism becomes apparent.

"If history were truly deterministic any good social mechanic could understand history's laws. . . . He could never be wrong, for any ad-hoc arrangements he might devise would necessarily comport with the trend of history; the resulting social order would inevitably be the correct one.

"But determinism has been undermined, even among conservative Marxists. . . . If determinism fails, will, reason, and planning—utopianism —must be resurrected. Today's revolution must plan for the institutions of the future if it is to escape responsibility for awarding power to the likes of Hitler and Stalin."

Harry Ashmore indicated that it was possible that all the manifestations of the youth movement were "the product of trends well advanced in the preceding generation; it was the parents of these agnostics who began to suspect that God was dead, to be repelled by the excesses and inadequacies of the political system, to doubt the relevance of their gray flannel life-style, to find the material rewards of split-level suburbia less than fulfilling, and to abandon the puritan conventions and break up the home with a mounting divorce rate that reflected their own sexual emancipation."

"It is understandable that the young should mistake what is new to them as a kind of revelation, and thus proclaim their world view in theological terms," Ashmore said. "But it seems to me that those who view these matters with the leavening of memory must doubt that the young are experiencing anything unique, except perhaps in degree and in context."

Elisabeth Borgese regarded the youth rebellion as a structural part of social evolution: "I see it as a truly essential, necessary corollary of the end of the age of individualism and the advent of an era of postindividual communitarianism. The spirit of this era is fostered by the population explosion with its changing patterns of density, by technology, by ecology. It permeates all aspects of our lives, from politics (mass society) to the arts (dissolution of form), from philosophy (Gestalt, structuralism) to the sciences (quantum theory and after). Everywhere the emphasis is on *relation, connection*, not on the individual part or actor.

"Now, as Bachofen and other great students of mythology and anthropology have shown, individual-oriented societies tend to venerate old age, as embodied in the patriarch. Group-oriented (pre-individual) societies tend to extol myths of matriarchy and to celebrate youth. . . ."

Voicing a personal feeling, Mrs. Borgese said: "I never wanted to be young, not when I was, and certainly not when I wasn't. Today, for the first time, I would like it. There is a job to be done. Only they can do it, and they are doing it."

John Wilkinson observed that one thing which "appears most striking in the present uproar in every human institution is the way people—circumstances allowing—nowadays tend to carry out in action what they had previously merely asserted in words. Thus, for example, Malcolm X's purely psychic rhetoric of violence turned into physical violence; and the same may be said for the radical students who began with pacifism and appear to be ending with bombs."

Wilkinson agreed with McDonald, however, that the radicalism of the young people was "a long distance from revolution." He did not expect a violent overthrow of the government in the United States or other major countries. He foresaw "a new style of life" but did not think that "our quasi-stable system" would be pushed beyond "the point of no return."

Having delivered these statements to the world on the significance and possible implications of the youth movement in the United States and other nations, the Center sponsored a two-week conference in August on "structuralism," principally focusing on the ideas of Claude Lévi-Strauss, a French social anthropologist. This conference was organized by Wilkinson and Wheeler with the cooperation of Nathan Rotenstreich, philosophy professor from the Hebrew University of Jerusalem.

Lévi-Struass regarded human cultures as systems of communication, and tried to comprehend the patterns of such cultures through the structures of languages, information theories, and cybernetics. He contended that there were structural resemblances underlying all cultures and believed that the analysis of resemblances and relationships among cultural units would ultimately provide insights into an innate and universal human logic—nonrational but understandable. Wilkinson and Wheeler gathered scholars from France, England and the United States to consider these conceptions from various perspectives.

Early in September 1970 the Center released the text of one of the most controversial documents it had ever produced—a model for a new Constitution for the American nation. This model was based on discussions that had been going on at the Center from the time of its establishment, and it could actually be traced back to the conferences of the Fund's consultants in the 1950s.

The model published by the Center in the autumn of 1970—in the September–October issue of the *Center Magazine*—was presented in the polished style of Rexford G. Tugwell, who had been asked by Robert Hutchins to do the drafting and redrafting of the "new Constitution." The text released to the public was Tugwell's thirty-seventh draft, and he was reluctant to have it printed then. He was already engaged in extensive revisions.

The entire issue of the magazine was devoted to the background, the development, and the significance of the constitutional project. The opening article was a review of Tugwell's life and work by Harry Ashmore, who declared that Tugwell had suggested "the directions in which we must move if we are to make our national charter again consonant with the times." Robert Hutchins related the history of the project. Donald McDonald and John Cogley interviewed Tugwell on the whole process of preparing the document and why Tugwell thought it should be continuously revised.

"Those who believe that the United States needs a new constitution will find here a starting point for their own model-making," Cogley said in an editorial preface. "Those who reject the idea out of hand will find a measure against which to weigh the merits of the present long-lived document. A study of the Tugwell model will help all parties to understand the U.S. of the 1970's."

In a memorandum to Center members, Hutchins recalled that the Constitution was "a recurring theme" in the discussions in 1957 and 1958 among the consultants who had helped to formulate the original plans for the Center. Participants in these sessions had included Eric Goldman, Robert Gordis, Clark Kerr, Jacques Maritain, John Courtney Murray, I. I. Rabi, Reinhold Niebuhr, Robert Redfield, Clinton Rossiter, Henry Luce, and many others from many fields.

Hutchins wrote: "Although some consultants thought the Constitution could be interpreted to meet all the new needs it might be expected to serve, others were not prepared to put their full confidence in a court [the Supreme Court] that had often, it seemed to them, failed to find in the Constitution ways of dealing with issues the founding fathers could not have foreseen.

"After all, the Constitution says nothing about the principal concerns of the present day. It does not mention technology, ecology, bureaucracy, education, cities, planning, civil disobedience, political parties, corporations, labor unions, or the organization of the world. It does not contemplate the conquest of the moon. Its references to communications, like its conception of the common defense, are primitive in the extreme. Meanwhile, the subject that necessarily preoccupied the framers, the government of territory, has lost significance because, with modern communication and transportation, geographical considerations no longer amount to much.

"The consultants did not attempt to settle the question whether the United States needs a new constitution. They did agree that the effort to frame one would be a worthwhile undertaking for the Center for the Study of Democratic Institutions: it would bring all the interests of the Center into focus, and it would subject vague ideas to the discipline of drafting. Nobody thought for a moment that a constitution drawn up at the Center would be adopted by the people. But drafting one was regarded as an admirable technique for holding the Center's work together and keeping everybody's feet on the ground."

A series of dialogues entitled "Drafting a New Constitution for the United States and the World" had been held at the Center in January 1964, nine months before Tugwell had been asked to take over this field. Hutchins, Ferry, and Hallock Hoffman had led these discussions, with most of the members of the Center staff participating in them.

Ferry and Hoffman had presented "A Bill of Particular Defects in the Present U.S. Constitution." Ferry found fault with the federal structure of the United States, asserting that "the states are an anachronism and a source of injustice preventing rational use of all resources for all peoples." He regarded the Constitution of 1787 as an obstacle to the achievement of equality and complete citizenship for all. He said it reduced progress in civil rights as a matter of "what part of it can be twisted to cover the sale of a hamburger."

The Constitution as it stood could not deal with the problem of corporate influence and power when "500 corporations set the whole pace and style of our economic life," Ferry declared. He thought that it gave "no purchase for regulating rampant technology." He wanted to see an ombudsman, a protector of the people's right to a fair hearing on their grievances against bureaucracy, placed in the constitutional system. He felt that the ombudsman should be a constitutional officer elected by all the people and responsible to all the people, rather than one appointed by or responsible to, either the legislature or the executive.

Hallock Hoffman had much admiration for the functioning of the ombudsman in the Scandinavian countries, where the idea of such an independent official had originated, but he thought it was "easier to think of an American Ombudsman in state and local governments than in Washington." Hoffman insisted that a new constitution must deal with the problem of communications and the public media, and must recognize that information about government "belongs to all the people and that government has an obligatory role to see that we get it."

Tugwell considered all the ideas that had been offered before he accepted responsibility for the model Constitution, and he drew suggestions from dozens of scholars, judges, senators, journalists, and others who participated in the hundreds of Center meetings that were held between 1964 and 1970. He insisted that he had simply taken on "the job of writing and rewriting what was suggested by the group."

In his conversation with Cogley and McDonald, Tugwell said that the most valuable suggestions he had received over the years had come from Hutchins and the late Scott Buchanan. When he had invited lawyers and teachers to send him comments on earlier drafts, he had found that many of them "didn't think much of the whole enterprise."

"There is a great resistance to doing anything about the Constitution at all," Tugwell said. "That resistance is all but universal among lawyers and almost as general among political scientists."

He felt that the resistance was partly due to "the conviction that any document that has lasted for a hundred and eighty-one years, as our Constitution has, must have permanent virtues," and another reason stemmed from the feeling that "the present Constitution protects essential liberties" which had been greatly endangered in the era of Joseph McCarthy. Lawyers and professors were afraid that "anything done to the Constitution must turn out to be bad—that, for example, our Bill of Rights would probably disappear." He did not share such a fear.

During the reorganization of the Center, Tugwell had indicated to Hutchins that his constitutional model was designed for a modern "technological nation" and could be considered by other countries as well as the United States. But the published model contained only brief references to possible American efforts to contribute positively to a world order, world peace, and world justice.

"We have been guided throughout by two principal considerations," Tugwell said to the editors of the *Center Magazine*.

"The first was to try for an embodiment of essential American beliefs in the suggested basic law—the kind we have in our saner and more reflective moments, the kind we profess when explaining ourselves to others. These are, I think, equality of opportunity; substantial justice; liberty to act and to undertake enterprises provided they do no harm; fair sharing of our affluence; decent respect for the rights and feelings of others, not only at home but in the rest of the world; and affirmation that there are no racial or cultural inferiors, only differences.

"The second consideration has been to acknowledge and contain our expanding technology with all its power for good—and for evil too. At the same time we recognize the necessary scale of modern enterprise and encourage experiment with methods for its management.

"Both of these are sometimes described as pluralism, or more accurately as diversity within unity, justice with order, sharing with the obligation to contribute. However described, they are the essence of democracy."

The *New York Times*, the Washington *Post*, and other major newspapers gave front-page attention to the model for a new constitution. The

Center Magazine contained the text of the Constitution of 1787 as well as the text of the model, so that readers could compare the two. The *New York Times* gave most of a page to a table comparing "key provisions of the present Constitution with provisions proposed by the Center for the Study of Democratic Institutions."*

Fred P. Graham, Washington correspondent for the *Times*, wrote the article that appeared on the first page of the newspaper under a four-column headline: "Study Center Offers New U.S. Constitution." The Center was not offering the model for adoption, but many readers of that headline assumed that it was.

Graham wrote:

> The new constitution would abandon the present theory of a union of small but sovereign states, in favor of a national government with strong central powers. It would be divided into a score or less of regional 'Republics,' with limited powers. . . .
>
> The national government would be composed of six branches rather than the current three—legislative, executive and judicial. In addition to these three, there would be a regulatory branch to house and control all of the present scattered independent agencies; an electoral branch to control political functions that are now supervised by the states or not at all; and a planning branch to prepare six-year and 12-year development programs.

Graham pointed out that the existing Constitution did not provide for much long-range planning, because government programs were usually based on annual appropriations authorized by the Congress.

"The regulatory branch would share its authority with private industry, which could join in multicompany groups to set standards," Graham noted. "This reminder of the Roosevelt Administration's National Recovery Administration runs counter to present anti-trust laws."

Graham reported that some of the other recommended provisions in the Tugwell model seemed to "reflect the frustrations of the Roosevelt years as well as an eye for the future."

> Foremost among these provisions is the elimination of the Supreme Court and its major judicial powers [Graham wrote]. (Mr. Tugwell was Assistant Secretary and Under Secretary of Agriculture in the first four years of the Roosevelt Administration, when New Deal legislation was being bowled over with regularity by the Supreme Court.)

---

*I had written letters to editors of the *Times*, the *Post*, and other major newspapers, enclosing material about the model and urging them to give it front-page attention. I was glad to find that these efforts had been productive. The *Times* was particularly responsive to my suggestions.

In an introductory statement Mr. Tugwell laments that the Supreme Court has achieved "a position of supremacy" through its power to declare un-constitutional actions of other branches, to the point that it can now "tell the other branches what they can and cannot do."

The proposed Constitution would fragment the Supreme Court's powers, leaving the most important—that of interpreting the Constitution—to a high court of the constitution. . . . Under the proposed Constitution, if the high court struck down any law, the Senate could overrule the decision.

In his introduction, Mr. Tugwell also recalls President Roosevelt's difficulties with a cantankerous Congress, even after the President's landslide election of 1936. His constitution would attempt to eliminate the "lame duck" weakness of some Presidents in their second term by having Presidents serve a single term of nine years, unless removed by a 60 per cent vote of the electorate after three years.

It would also make the House of Representatives more responsive to the national vote by having 100 of its 400 members elected at large on a national basis. The 300 others would be elected from districts. Committee chairmen would be picked by the House leadership rather than by the present seniority system, and no chairman could serve more than six years.

The Senate, akin to the British House of Lords, would be composed of officials who would hold their positions for life. They would be former Presidents and other former high officials, plus members chosen by the other branches of government. The Senate could veto all House bills except the annual budget.

The present Bill of rights proved to be the most durable portion of the present Constitution, in the new draftsmen's eyes. Almost all of the safeguards contained in the first eight amendments are carried over into the new document, although they are scattered throughout its provisions.

Mr. Tugwell said in a telephone interview today from his home in Santa Barbara that the major recommendations, made after six years of frequent discussions, represented a virtual consensus of his colleagues at the Center. . . .

Further refinements are contemplated in future drafts, and the Center hopes that it will receive a large "feed-back" from the public as a result of today's publication.

However, Harry S. Ashmore, senior fellow of the Center, said that not everyone connected with the group agreed with Mr. Tugwell.

Newspaper editors, columnists, and scholars subjected the model to searching scrutiny. Some thought it was too radical; others regarded it as "artificial"; still others saw no need for it and felt that the Center had spent too much time on it. Because it happened to appear at a time when the Black Panthers were calling for a new American Constitution, it aroused the wrath of John S. Knight, publisher of the Knight newspapers, who declared in a statement published on September 13, 1970: "Along with the Black Panthers, who have also put together a new Constitution, Dr. Tugwell typifies the fuzzy and radical left who would tear apart our system of government while offering the absolute authority of statism in its place."

In a raging editorial, the New York *Daily News* spewed scorn on the whole project:

> Old New Deal idea man Tugwell has produced an horrendous hodge-podge culled and cribbed from every source of political quackery from Karl Marx to Benito Mussolini. It is a blueprint for destroying the political and economic system that has made Americans the freest and most prosperous people in the world. . . .
>
> Tugwell serves up his hash as something new and forward-looking. That's so much malarkey. Many of the ideas are straight hand-me-downs from the New Deal with far-out alterations aimed at an even greater concentration of power in the hands of a know-it-all, do-it-all central authority run by theorists, technocrats, and self-styled experts like Rex himself.
>
> Thirty-five years of experimenting with such nostrums have convinced even thoughtful liberals that the future of the country lies not in greater centralization of government but in revitalizing the old federal relationship. . . .

"Fascinating though Tugwell's constitution might be, it seemed unlikely to provoke a widespread movement for reform," *Newsweek* observed. "Liberals were certain to take umbrage at his treatment of the Supreme Court and at his elitist proposal for a Senate composed of retired Establishmentarians, while conservatives would hardly welcome his suggestions for beefing up the planning and regulatory powers of the federal governemt.

"Moreover, a sounding of constitutional experts last week elicited little enthusiasm for the whole idea of drastic tinkering with the original. As Professor Alexander Bickel of the Yale law school remarked wryly: 'I would think that the main thing wrong with this country today is not its Constitution.' "

The editors of the St. Louis *Post-Dispatch* understood the educational purposes of the Center: "As great a document as we believe the United States Constitution to be, it should not be considered sacrosanct and therefore simply ignored. . . . In any event, the Tugwell plan offers a considered scale by which to test the existing system. The plan should promote a serious educational exercise in the law we live under."

Editors of the Memphis *Commercial Appeal* expressed similar comments: "It is a useful exercise in the intellectual sense to think about the changes around us, and the necessity of adapting our broad foundation of law to accommodate them. In this, the model is of value—if it is read, disseminated, and discussed."

In a column distributed to many newspapers, David S. Broder, national political correspondent of the Washington *Post*, wrote:

> Constitution-making is a supreme challenge to men's political intelligence and to their capacity to arrange and distribute power to achieve desired objectives and prevent anticipated evils. But it is more than that. The goals that are set forth in a constitution—as well as the dangers against which it guards—offer an insight into the values of its framers and their time.
>
> The founding fathers wrote for the ages, but they wrote from a perspective of their own age. The Constitution they gave us reflected their fear of a powerful executive, their reliance on state government, their preoccupation with commerce—and, of course, their acceptance of slavery.
>
> Similarly, later amendments to the Constitution—covering such assorted topics as prohibition, women's suffrage, and even Presidential disability—reflected the changing concerns and shifting moods of the nation. It could hardly be otherwise, for the actual revision of the Constitution—as distinguished from an academic exercise like that of Tugwell and company—required mobilizing so vast a part of our political machinery that the cause be fundamental.

In Tugwell's view, however, the amendment process was faulty. If the amendment process had worked well, slavery might have been abolished without a civil war. Most of the amendments adopted through the years had not dealt with fundamental problems, because amendments were blocked in the Congress or in state legislatures.

Broder said that the work of Tugwell and his associates had

> its own value, which should not be minimized. By providing an alternative model, they make us more aware of the strengths and deficiencies of the existing Constitution, and some of their suggestions—particularly the provision for constitutional authority and controls for the existing political, planning, and administrative machinery—point us in directions we should go. . . .
>
> But the strongest impression one has of the Tugwell constitu-

tion is its artificiality—which stems, I believe, from its being produced in an isolated, academic laboratory.

Consider, for example, Tugwell's proposal for changing the term of representatives to three years, making the Senate an appointive body with life-time tenure, and granting the President a single nine-year term. What is there in that scheme that would ease the anxieties of those who question the efficacy or responsiveness of the governmental system today? . . .

The great surprise in Tugwell's constitution—and the strongest indication of the abstract process that produced it—is the failure to confront the problem of local government. . . .

Instead of states, Tugwell would provide no more than twenty "republics" that "may charter subsidiary governments, urban or rural, and may delegate to them powers appropriate to their responsibilities; and such governments shall be autonomous in matters exclusive to their citizens, except that they shall conform to the constitutions of the United Republics of America and of their Republics."

That is all he says about local government—at a time when "the quest for community" dominates the national mind, and when the twin desires for participation in decision-making and peaceful acceptance of authority threaten to destroy us, if they are not somehow merged.

While welcoming and supporting "the general spirit" of the Tugwell model, Leslie Lipson of the political science department at the University of California at Berkeley declared that Tugwell's proposals did not deal adequately with the presidency and "the distribution of functions among the various levels of government.

"The Presidency of Lyndon B. Johnson is a tragic example of the ability of a President to take the country into a large-scale, undeclared, colonial-type war which vitiated the excellent domestic program he was simultaneously introducing," Lipson wrote. "Our institutional arrangements did not provide us with adequate safeguards against his errors of omission and commission.

"Nor, as it appears to me, do Mr. Tugwell's proposals. These continue to institutionalize a division of basic functions between the House of Representatives and the President. . . .

"But, in the interest of both unleashing power for good and restraining it from evil, I would prefer that we consider adopting a premiership plus Cabinet and members of the House of Representatives, on the British model. That institutional arrangement, when it is combined with a fairly cohesive party system, does meet the twin needs of using power and controlling its abuse."

While the model was in preparation at the Center, the possibility of adopting the British parliamentary system was considered several times. But Tugwell and others felt that the system would not work in the United States. American political parties were not cohesive bodies, disciplined and responsive to party leadership. In the American tradition, a government with separated powers allocated to the president, the legislative, and the judicial branches had gathered strong support despite its defects.

Under the provisions of the model constitution, Tugwell had tried to prevent a repetition of what had happened in Vietnam. He told interviewers: "In our model, the President cannot declare an emergency and then do as he pleases in foreign affairs. Only the Senate can declare an emergency. Of course, even under the 1787 Constitution, the President had no power to declare emergencies; he just assumed that he could and it was recognized. Our model forbids the deployment of armed forces abroad except with Senate approval. But we are living in an atomic age, and some provision is included for the President to act in the event of an imminent catastrophe."

Publication of the model stirred so many controversies that the Center decided to hold meetings in Philadelphia, New York, Los Angeles, and other cities to give opportunities for debates and criticisms that might be useful in preparing a future draft of a revised model.

The launching of the model constitution was one of the Center's most notable projects judging by the furor it aroused and the attention it received. I took an active part in planning the public meetings and obtaining the media coverage. I had also been invited by the Senior Fellows to return to the dialogue table and participate in the exchange of ideas.

Although lawyers still argued and filed statements and counterstatements in the Ferry case, the painful reorganization of the Center seemed to be receding rapidly into the past. The number of faithful Center members stayed close to 100,000.

But the Center approached the end of its 1970 fiscal year with the largest deficit in its history—a deficit of more than $1.5 million. In October 1970 the effects of a "belt-tightening program" recommended by Gary Cadenhead, the new secretary and treasurer, began to be felt. The academic budget was trimmed, ten people in clerical jobs were terminated, and overhead was reduced. Yet the Center's expenditures were still far above its income.

In the first week in October, the resignation of Stanley Sheinbaum, a well-known Center associate, and the departure of Richard Gilbert, who had been the acting secretary and treasurer, set off rumors that another major shakeup was occurring. On October 7 Harry Ashmore told the Santa Barbara *News-Press* that the Center was tightening its operations but had sufficient funds to carry on its program for at least three more years.

"The recession, the decline in the stock market, and confusing new tax regulations having to do with deductions for contributions to non-profit foundations, have cut into our income," Ashmore explained. "And it is true that we are running a deficit of around a million dollars a year. However, this is par for the course at the Center."

Two weeks later, Ashmore informed the press that the Center had started the publication of a new bimonthly, *Center Report*, which would take over the functions of the *Center Newsletter* and contain excerpts from Center conferences and brief articles. Mary K. Harvey, who had ten years of editorial experience with the *Saturday Review* and with *McCall's* magazine, had been appointed editor.

On November 9 the Center held the first of its public convocations on the model constitution—in Philadelphia, where the Constitution of 1787 had been drafted. The principal debaters at this session were Robert Hutchins, advocating constitutional changes, and Harris Wofford, president of Bryn Mawr College, who insisted that the existing Constitution was as broad as the country's needs. Wofford said that attention should be directed toward a world constitution rather than a new national charter for the United States. The convocation was attended by 600 citizens and received extensive attention by the mass media.

The Center's directors met in New York on November 10, heard the bad news about its deficit—the actual figure was $1,505,442—and received assurances from Ashmore that the next fiscal year would show a marked improvement.

The resignations of Stanley Marcus, Paul G. Hoffman, and Howard Stein were accepted by the board at this meeting with regret. Hoffman did not indicate that his resignation had anything to do with the removal of his son, Hallock, from the Center staff. Hoffman was preoccupied with his duties as director of the United Nations Development Fund, and could not find time to attend Center gatherings. Marcus and Stein had not taken active roles during their relatively short service on the Center's board.

Fagan Dickson of Austin, Texas, a former member of the Texas legislature and a former assistant attorney general of Texas, was elected to the board at the November 10 session. A member of the Central Christian Church in Austin, Dickson was also a cosponsor of the Business Executives Move for Peace in Vietnam, a director of the Texas Bill of Rights Foundation, a member of the Philosophical Society of Texas, and a fellow of the Texas Bar Foundation. In 1968 he had been a candidate for Congress in President Lyndon Johnson's home district in Texas, opposing Johnson's Vietnam War policy and calling on voters to "bring Lyndon home." When Johnson withdrew from the presidential campaign of 1968, Dickson ended his congressional candidacy with a statement that the purpose of his effort had been accomplished.

Most of the Center's directors attended the second public conference sponsored by the Center on whether a new Constitution was necessary. At this assembly, held on November 11 at the New York Hilton hotel, Hutchins and Ramsey Clark took opposite sides.

Describing this event, the *New York Times* reported: "To form an even more perfect union, do we need an even more perfect Constitution?

"In the most forthright but amiable of fashions, two legal authorities—Robert M. Hutchins, chairman of the Center for the Study of Democratic Institutions, and Ramsey Clark, former Attorney General—joined others in debating that question here yesterday.

"Both agreed on the reality of national crisis; but while Dr. Hutchins argued that the nation needed a new fundamental law, Mr. Clark warned that what was needed was not new words but new commitments by the citizens of this nation. . . ."

While the Center tried to get people to think about the resources of the oceans, the possibilities of a new constitution, the potentialities of extending life, and other topics regarded as important by the senior fellows, the scholars based in Santa Barbara paid relatively little attention to a movement that was growing in strength and emotional fire—the women's liberation movement. Few women prepared papers or participated in the Center dialogues. Only one woman—Mrs. Borgese—had been appointed a senior fellow, and no women were being actively considered as additions to the fellowship.

In the November–December issue of the *Center Magazine*, the editors did concentrate attention on three large minorities often afflicted by violence and harsh injustices—Mexican Americans, white middle-class workers on the edge of poverty, and black slum dwellers.

Michael Schneider, a San Francisco electrician, declared in an article entitled "Middle America: Study in Frustration" that "the truth is, the majority of people who work for a living are not part of affluent America."

Schneider pointed out that the tax-reform act of 1969 had not corrected the unequal tax treatment of work-connected expenses of wage earners compared with the treatment given to high-salaried executives: "For example, a worker cannot claim a deduction for driving a car to and from work, even when no public transportation is available to him. The company executive, however, may have the free use of a company limousine and chauffeur without having to pay any taxes for these services. The wages the worker spends for his lunch to fuel up for the afternoon are fully taxable. On the other hand, the executive can take a friend to lunch in an expensive restaurant, deduct this expense, and pay no taxes on it, by merely showing that it is a business-related luncheon."

Millions of middle-classs workers felt abandoned by their government, were frustrated by union bureaucracies, and felt that both major political parties were dominated by rich people, Schneider indicated. Because of their income limitations, they were forced to live in areas where crime was increasing.

In another article in this issue of the magazine, Philip D. Ortego, a teacher at the University of Texas at El Paso, reminded Center members that Mexican Americans were the second largest minority group in the United States, including at least 10 million people, ranking second in numbers only to the blacks among the minorities.

"Just as many black citizens have rejected the description of 'Negro' or 'Negro-Americans,' many Americans of Mexican ancestry reject the hyphenated Mexican-American description by Anglos and instead prefer to be called Chicanos," Ortego said. "What conspicuously characterizes Mexican Americans is that most of them have an inadequate education, a handicap stemming primarily from socio-economic causes rather than from what educators have called the 'language barrier.' . . .

"The long, arduous odyssey of Mexican Americans has been given little public attention. In 1940 George I. Sanchez called them 'forgotten people,' and at the National Education Association meeting in Tucson in 1966 they were described as 'the invisible minority.' But the Chicano renaissance is changing this. . . .

"What is needed—in addition to preparing teachers in linguistic principles—is training in 'lexonomics,' the study of linguistic social relations. As a social creature, man is also a creature of words, and therefore a 'lexistent.' The teacher, as the central figure in the dynamics of social relations in the schools, should comprehend the nature of language and its psychosocial function in human beings, especially children. Failure here is by far the greatest weakness in existing educational programs."

Ortego reported that Spanish-speaking children were frequently assigned to classes for the retarded primarily because teachers identified skill in language uses with intellectual capacity. He said that teachers and school administrators had to be made aware "of the part they play in promoting the myth of Anglo cultural superiority."

The third article in the *Center Magazine* depicting the plight of an American minority was a bleak description of the grim conditions of life on the southern edge of Harlem on New York's West Side, written by Joseph Lyford and originally published in the July–August issue of the *Center Diary* in 1966. The editors decided to reprint it because it was still relevant to the problems of the 1970s.

Lyford was sorrowfully impressed by "the continual waste and loss of human life" in New York City: "I am not talking about the murders or assaults that have terrified most of the people I know. . . . I am talking about the destruction of children. . . .

"Of the enormous number of crimes that take place in the city, the largest amount and the most terrible are committed against children. The ones who suffer the most are the children of the poor. Only a small portion of these crimes have to do with outright physical abuse. From the time tens of thousands of newborn infants are removed from the hospital they become subjected to what I call 'the process.' That is, they are introduced to a style of existence that eventually cripples or destroys huge numbers of them, and occasionally other people with whom they have come in contact.

"I have not been able to discover any good reason why this should be taking place, even an economic reason. It is said over and over that the United States and the City of New York together do not have the public or private money to prevent the destruction of children and see that they are fed and cared for properly, that their illnesses are treated, and their minds and spirits nourished. It is said that the responsibility for such care lies with the parents, which is a *non sequitur* because there are no parents to speak of in this situation.

"Later on, when children born clean, ready and expectant begin to malfunction and cause trouble, hundreds of millions of dollars are appropriated to hire special teachers and policemen and youth workers, build special classrooms and prisons and mental institutions, and finance hospital beds to get these children under control. The children who do survive this tempering process become adults, but in my neighborhood an adult is a dead child. In the end the justification for such procedures is that this is the way things have to be done in a system of free enterprise, but in view of the fact that all the money is wasted, as well as the children, this seems hard to believe. Wasting money is not part of the capitalistic system."

Struggling to understand why the destruction of so many children was permitted in American cities year after year, Lyford concluded: "We are, practically speaking, unconscious of what is going on. We seem to have pushed whatever knowledge we have abut 'the process' into a part of our minds that is not directly connected with our emotions or our motor mechanisms."

Thinking about his experiences in the Harlem ghetto, Lyford decided that most Americans were very much like the "good Germans" who claimed that they had known nothing about Hitler's destruction of millions of lives in concentration camps and furnaces.

Lyford admitted that he had become a "good German" himself: "When I was forced to look over a long period of time at too many objects and acts in my city I felt the German reaction, which was to justify myself by saying that I had been put into a system, that nobody asked by permission for the system, that I hadn't wanted it. I will defend Hannah Arendt when she says that evil is common and most people who commit evil are asleep."

"We are 'good Germans' when we try to explain ourselves," Lyford decided. "We explain by looking for the criminal who involved us in all this. In New York City when we look for a culprit we usually point to the mayor or some other highly visible politician. He is somehow responsible for all this and there are people who would like to hang him for all the things that are going wrong in the city, including the destruction of children. . . This attitude means we are still seeing images of the truth. I think that if we stop looking at the images we would find that executing the mayor would be unsatisfactory, and we might not bother to do anything about him. We would be looking for causes and we would find them everywhere, just as the 'good Germans' turned out to be everywhere. . . .

"What has happened is that we are in the middle of a system that makes the 'process' inevitable: that requires more and more human beings in various parts of the country—Appalachia, Selma, Watts—to grow up to be dead children, or, as some people put it, welfare babies. The system I am talking about is turning more and more of our resources away from the nurture of human life and into the destruction of it. . . ."

Summing up the three poignant articles on the suffering of minorities in American society, John Cogley wrote: "Separately each of the articles is an effective antidote to complacency; together they are devastating."

These articles had been discussed at the Center's table before publication, thus enabling the editor of the *Center Magazine* to publish them. But they were not directly related to the major projects in which the fellows were engrossed. They were not "scholarly" in the academic sense. They might have been published by the "old" Center, under the policy existing before the reorganization of 1969.

In theory, most of the space in the magazine and in the *Center Report* was supposed to be given over to the writings of the senior fellows or products of their projects. In practice, the editors ranged beyond the projects to find material of general interest to the thousands of Center members. There was an intermittent conflict between the interests of the editors and the preoccupations of the scholars. The conflict was never fully resolved.

At the November board meeting, Hutchins told the directors that the Center's program was developing in four areas: civil liberties in the context of demands for "law and order"; what might be done to reform or reduce bureaucracy and rigid structures in education; the effects on the professions—law, medicine, and others—of the spread of licensing and the resulting monopoly power of certain groups; and possible cooperation on joint projects with centers of study in other countries. No new fellows had been added to the group.

Several of the directors had begun to show increasing anxiety about the Center's financial situation. Under pressures from Parten and Marshall, the New York conferences conducted by Crane Haussamen had been shut down. The New York gatherings had been well attended, but the organizational costs were regarded as high.

Hutchins said that the Center's overhead had been trimmed "to a sensible figure without cutting into the efficiency of the staff" and predicted that the new fund-raising actions directed by Ashmore and Tagger would produce enough money to give the Center a surplus rather than a deficit in the 1971 fiscal year. Seniel Ostrow wanted to hold the officers closely to the budgets approved by the board, and Hutchins assured him that expenditures would be carefully checked. At the suggestion of James Douglas, Gary Cadenhead agreed to send quarterly financial statements to all directors.

The December issue of *Center Report* contained excerpts from the reports made by Hutchins and the other senior fellows to the board. In a statement entitled "Income and Outgo," Ashmore said: "Like those of all educational institutions, the Center's expenditures are fated to exceed revenue from income-producing ventures. The proportion is about the same as that for the typical university, which spends at least two dollars for every dollar derived from tuition and fees. The university pattern prevails, too, in salary scale for Fellows and staff."

Ashmore made it plain that the money to cover the Center's deficits must come from generous contributors among the supporting members and large gifts from those he described as "major benefactors." Although he did not refer specifically to the directors, it was obvious that their financial support was essential for the Center's survival.

That issue of the *Report* devoted a page to the ideas of Georgi Arbatov, director of the Soviet Academy of Science's Institute of American Studies, who attacked the notion that the American and Soviet economic systems were converging toward a basic resemblance to one another. Arbatov felt that there was a "kind of intellectual dishonesty" in the convergence theory: "There is a notion in this concept that somehow the problems in the area of world peace will be solved by themselves, that you will get into evolution and eventually—in a distant period—won't have anything to worry about."

"We have had some very serious confrontations—the Cuban missile crisis, Vietnam, the continuing Middle East crisis," Arbatov said at a session with the Senior Fellows. "If we continue to drift in the wave of these trends we can get into a very difficult situation during the 1970's. And to get there you really don't need to do very dangerous things. It's enough *not* to accomplish really positive changes in the nuclear arms race and in the reconstruction of international relations."

The *Report* also presented a highly critical analysis of President Nixon's policy in Vietnam, voiced by George McTurnan Kahin, director of Cornell University's Southeast Asia program. Despite these articles and others on a wide variety of issues in the *Center Magazine*, Fred Warner Neal, a Center associate, expressed dissatisfaction with the Center's course in a letter to Hutchins. Neal told Hutchins bluntly that it was essential to "beef up" the fellowship, and added that he had encountered "a feeling among many people who know about the Center and support it in one way or another (including money) that the Center and its activities are no longer as 'relevant' to them as it was."

"What they seem to be saying is that they believe the issues involving democratic institutions are now more pertinent than ever but that the Center's engagement with them is somehow lacking. . . ."

According to Neal, these people felt involved in foreign policy issues— Vietnam, American intervention in other countries, American economic expansion abroad, U.S.-Soviet relations, nuclear weapons, disarmament, the military, the CIA—and in the revolutionary changes in American life, in the impact of violence and the dangers of reaction, in third-party possibilities, in art and politics on every level; in specific questions like congressional reform, what might be wrong with the State Department, the trends in labor unions, industrial responsibility for pollution. Some of these people had shifted their support from the Center to Common Cause, John Gardner's lobbying group, and to the activities of Ralph Nader.

"Of course, one could argue that the Center should not be concerned with issues of the day in any sense at all," Neal admitted. "There is doubtless always a certain tension in any enterprise of this sort between more immediate and longer term issues, just as there often is a contradiction between concern for fundamental problems and popular interest. Nonetheless, if the Center is to have a meaningful relationship with concerned intellectual (broadly defined) Americans, it is a balance that must be struck."

The senior fellows felt that they were striking the right balances in the Center's projects. Most of Neal's criticisms were rejected, but he had made some points that troubled Hutchins and Ashmore. Hutchins realized again how difficult it was to get many people to see the importance of long-range thinking.

In addition to criticizing the Center's program, Neal had offered the names of several people he considered worthy of consideration as a possible successor to Hutchins—John Kenneth Galbraith, the Harvard economist; David Riesman, the noted sociologist, and Herbert York, acting chancellor of the University of California at San Diego. The fellows talked about these nominations and other names mentioned by Hutchins and by Center consultants, but it was almost unthinkable to envision anyone taking Hutchins' place.

Meanwhile, the Ferry suit went through one stage after another. In August, 1970, in reply to an amended complaint filed by Ferry in which he claimed again that the method of selecting the Fellows was not the one Hutchins had originally proposed, the Center's lawyers said that it didn't matter whether the method had been changed or not. Allan B. Goldman, representing Hutchins and Ashmore, stated: "Nowhere does the plaintiff allege that any of these acts, whichever procedure was in fact used, were against the best interests of the corporation. Nowhere does the plaintiff allege that the board of directors failed to ratify the refounding procedure which was followed."

On September 3, 1970, Judge Rickard had dismissed Ferry's contentions that the "refounding" had substantially changed the corporation's purposes, in violation of its charter. Rickard said that Ferry had not stated facts sufficient to constitute a cause for action. The one major point remaining was the question of whether the Fund had promised "continued employment" to Ferry on which he was justified in placing "substantial reliance." (Legal exchanges on that point went on for another year.)

The difficulties encountered by Hutchins in the refounding process through the year 1970 indicated that Hutchins had probably been right in estimating that it would take five years to complete the process. J. R. Parten and other members of the Committee on Organization doubted whether anyone else could carry the process to a successful conclusion. No candidates eager for the job had appeared, and it did not seem likely that anyone fully acceptable to the fellows and the board would be easily persuaded to take it. The Center had been built around Hutchins, and anyone appointed as a "successor" would face a sea of troubles.

All through the year 1970 the senior fellows groped for ways to develop the "new academy" and to learn how to function as a collective leadership. Hutchins had suggested that the position of chairman might rotate from one fellow to another, but no one seemed able to serve as chairman with quite the authority Hutchins had.

Then Hutchins developed a severe physical problem. Doctors discovered that he had an arterial aneurysm, a dilation of an artery. On December 28, 1970, he underwent the first surgery of his life in the operating room of Michael De Bakey at a hospital in Texas.

Hutchins recovered with astonishing speed, considering his age, but during his recuperation he urged Parten to begin to think very seriously about finding someone who could work creatively with the fellows in carrying on the Center after his retirement or death. Parten was still hesitant to do so, but Hutchins would not permit the matter to be put aside.

Hutchins would not accept the idea that the Center could not go on without him. He believed that the "new academy" was too important to depend on the life of one man. Parten asked Hutchins to recommend people who should be considered, and Hutchins agreed to do so.

The time for thinking about the "unthinkable"—a Center without Hutchins, or with Hutchins in the background—seemed to be approaching.

25

*The Center surveys the
president's powers, atomic
perils, crime control,
corporations, and the
quality of life*

Ａs Nixon began his third year in the White House, with the Vietnam
War still devouring American lives and money, with inflation growing and
the federal budget apparently out of control, the Center released a report on
the powers of the presidency and a statement on what Americans expected
from their chief executive. The report, based on a Center conference, indicated that the president was often a captive of his own staff, veered from
one course to another, often acted on misinformation or misleading advice,
and often tended to think of his opponents as members of a conspiracy
against him.

In the January–February 1971 issue of the *Center Magazine*, Harvey
Wheeler summarized the arguments in the conference in these terms: "One
is that there is overweening strength in the Presidency today. The other is
that at least in domestic affairs the Presidency is not strong enough." The
judgment of the experts at this conference was that the president had perhaps too much power in foreign affairs but was often blocked by pressure
groups and Congress on domestic issues.

"My own proposal is for a weak Presidency combined with a modern-
ized set of limitations," Wheeler said. "I also think there is need for a plural executive. . . . It seems strange to me that we still cling to the cult of personality in our national government."

Another participant—George Reedy, former press secretary to President Lyndon Johnson—asserted that "there must be some way in which one
can have not exactly a plural executive but a peer-group device for making

Presidents accountable.'' Reedy thought the president should be required to submit his policies periodically for review by a joint committee from both branches of Congress.

James Barber, professor of political science at Yale, was disturbed by Nixon's polarizing statements. Barber wrote: "Much as many people want to believe Nixon—almost want to foist some sort of greatness upon him—they have not yet, I think, felt they could drop their emotional guard. . . . Uncertainty about just who Nixon is and where he is going adds to the national anxiety.''

None of the participants in that Center conference had any idea that Richard Nixon would soon install tape recorders in the White House basement to preserve all the conversations that Nixon and his aides wanted to have recorded. No one knew the extent to which Nixon would go in authorizing secret burglaries, wiretapping, and other law-breaking in the name of "national security.'' But all of the conferees were uneasy about the enormous powers which had been claimed for the Presidency by Johnson and Nixon.

Another article in the January-February issue of the magazine revealed the extensive deceptions of the Atomic Energy Commission. Gene Schrader, a Center researcher who wrote the article after months of investigation, declared: "The Atomic Energy Commission has operated for so many years under a system designed to withhold more information than it releases that, although it will not tell a lie, neither can it tell the truth.''

"Secrecy has been the rule for the protection of national security,'' she wrote. "We are now so secure in terms of nuclear weapons that we could wipe out the entire planet if necessary to protect the United States. . . . Secrecy for defense reasons may have been necessary during the early stages of atomic development. To continue to apply secrecy to the development of nuclear power for peaceful purposes is not only absurd, it is dangerous. . . .''

That issue of the magazine also contained the text of an interview with Hutchins by Keith Berwick, a University of California history professor, broadcast by educational television stations in Los Angeles and other cities.

Saying that the Center had been "irreverently called the longest-running talk show in existence,'' Berwick asked Hutchins to describe the discipline involved in productive dialogue.

"Real dialogue is a very difficult thing and requires certain moral qualities,'' Hutchins said. "You cannot participate in the dialogue if you are a show-off; you cannot participate unless you really want to learn.''

"After eleven years there is still a great deal of confusion about what the Center is, and what you are doing there on Eucalyptus Hill,'' Berwick observed.

"That is odd because the name is completely descriptive,'' Hutchins said. "What the Center is doing is studying democratic institutions by taking a multi-disciplinary look at the state of the democratic world—and the un-democratic world as well, because one has to contrast the two and see how they are going to develop. After discovering what is going on, or trying to discover what is going on, the Center offers its observations for such public consideration as the public is willing to give them.''

"There are those who regard the Fellows of the Center as a kind of powerless elite," Berwick responded. "Elite they are. How about power? Or I suppose the real question is how can the influence of the Center be measured?''

"By the same measure that you would apply to any educational institution," Hutchins answered.

"But that opens up a Pandora's box. After twenty-two years at the University of Chicago, you left that institution. . . . Did you give up on the academy?''

Hutchins replied: "No, I simply thought the University of Chicago ought to have another chance, that was all. I haven't given up on the academy. I understand perfectly well, of course, that no educational institution is ever going to realize the ideals of those who originally conceived it. It is simply in the nature of human institutions that they become bureaucratized, diverted, ossified. . . .''

Berwick referred to the "institutional revolution" at the Center and asked Hutchins to depict its course.

"Of course, we used to try this all the time at the University of Chicago," Hutchins mused. "We used to try to keep an argument going which involved the whole population of the university, with the idea that this is what gives an educational institution its vitality. If you can keep this argument going on important subjects, you can avoid the ossification which is the bane of all educational institutions.''

After describing the painful process through which the Center had passed, Hutchins said: "But this, though necessary, perhaps was a little drastic. I think the University of Chicago model was better; that is, it is better to keep the argument about fundamental purposes going in the institution and at as high a level as possible.''

"You seem to imply a kind of fatalism about institutions," Berwick observed at a later point in this conversation. "You say they ossify, become moribund, become bureaucratized. I suppose that applies equally well to institutions based on the dialogue.''

Hutchins nodded. "Yes, I'm sure it does . . . I would think, however, that an institution dedicated to this kind of learning by this method would be less subject to ossification than the usual type of bureaucratic institution.''

Berwick raised a question about the Center's international conferences—its efforts "to project the dialogue onto the international stage in an effort to bring peace. . . . You have been widely accused of being amateur peacemakers. The implication is that matters of peace and war are much better left to professionals.''

Hutchins pointed out that "the Center has never ventured beyond the continental boundaries of the United States without notifying the State Department or the White House or both, so we are not operating without the knowledge of the duly accredited representatives of the American people."

"I am convinced that there is a role for private peacemaking, though if you go into it, you have to be prepared to be disowned by your own government even after it has encouraged you to proceed," Hutchins said. "Time and time again the official accredited representatives of a nation have said to us, 'We cannot get anywhere through governmental channels. All our public positions are frozen. Now, if a private institution like the Center could get together a group of people who can speak as individuals, they could come back to influence the formal positions taken by our government.' "

Hutchins recognized that the Center's "Pacem in Terris" convocations and other peacemaking efforts had taken a great deal of nerve: "Private peacemaking, then, is not an occupation that one should enter if one has a weak heart or is liable to nervous breakdown. . . . Even our own government officers agree that private intervention can sometimes be helpful, whatever they may say before or after. I think the American Friends Service Committee has shown this time and time again."

Berwick asked him about a public statement issued by W. H. Ferry, Irving Laucks, and others associated with the Center "on the Triple Revolution—in cybernation, human rights, weaponry."

"Was that statement, so to speak, an officially sanctioned outgrowth of the Center dialogue?" Berwick inquired.

"No, it was not," Hutchins said. "I think it was affected by the Center dialogue and some Center people were involved in the publication of the Triple Revolution Manifesto, but the Center as such had nothing to do with it."

Berwick went on: "Were you yourself impressed with the concept of the Triple Revolution as a reasonable statement about the nature of our problems?"

"I think the Manifesto provided a reasonable statement about some of the problems, yes," Hutchins answered. "But I would not have signed it. . . . The Center does not take positions, does not recommend action, and, again, does not engage in political activities. This therefore was not a Center action."

"Much of the misunderstanding about the Center has to do with certain ambiguities on that point," Berwick commented.

Hutchins said: "There is, I think, almost every shade of political opinion represented at the Center. . . . For example, Neil Jacoby, who is one of our Associates, is a neoclassical economist. Last week and the week before we invited in other economists who are on the other side in order to make sure, or at least try to make sure, that we understood the economic situation by examining various respectable points of view about it."

The increasingly hard line taken by Nixon and his officials against "crime in the streets" led to violations of civil liberties and aroused much concern at the Center. In the last week of February 1971 Hutchins presided at a conference of lawyers, judges, former police officers, prison authorities, and others to discuss the impacts of the crime control legislation passed by Congress at the urging of Nixon.

Those who took part in this gathering included Ramsey Clark, former attorney general; James V. Bennett, former director of the United States Bureau of Prisons; Gerald Caplan, general counsel to the police department, Washington, D.C.; Troy Duster, associate professor in the department of sociology, University of California at Berkeley; Bruce McManus, director of field services, Department of Corrections, state of Minnesota; Judge Constance B. Motley of the United States district court, New York City; Norval Morris, professor at the University of Chicago law school; Tim Murphy, judge, from the superior court of Washington, D.C.; Herbert Packer, professor at the Stanford University law school; and Carl Rauh, attorney adviser to the deputy attorney general, Washington, D.C.

Most of the arguments revolved around the District of Columbia Court Reform Act, the Organized Crime Control Act, and the Comprehensive Drug Abuse Prevention and Control Act. Carl Rauh defended the major provisions of these acts against a barrage of criticisms from the other speakers.

The Court Reform Act was necessary, Rauh said, because "crime was skyrocketing" and "the court system in the District of Columbia could not handle large volumes of serious criminal cases" under the "inefficient and outmoded court system" that had existed.

"The court reform act creates a new and unified local court system for the District of Columbia including a modern family division," Rauh said. "Judicial manpower is substantially increased at both the trial and appellate levels; and a court executive is established to bring modern management techniques to the court operations. The court executive is given a statutory mandate to bring modern technology, such as the computerization of court operations, to judicial administration. . . .

"The no-knock and pretrial detention sections, which comprise only four pages of the 196-page act, represent but a small part of a vitally needed, comprehensive legislative approach to create a workable court and criminal-justice system for the citizens of the nation's capital."

The "no-knock" section to which Rauh referred was a part of the Act that authorized police officers to enter private premises under certain circumstances to execute a search warrant or to make an arrest without knocking and without disclosing their identity. This was principally designed to keep drug pushers or addicts from disposing of possible evidence against them.

The "preventive detention" section provided that defendants not accused of murder or other capital crimes could be kept in jail for up to sixty days after their arrest and before their trial if they had a record of "past conduct" regarded as dangerous by a judicial officer, even though they had no prior convictions of serious crimes.

To those who were worried about violations of the Bill of Rights, Rauh remarked that there was another "freedom we should be concerned with— the freedom to walk the streets of our major cities without fear of being attacked."

Troy Duster, a black sociology professor, asserted that the "no-knock" and "preventive detention" provisions were "applied very selectively." Such provisions were used in the ghettos, he said, but not in the wealthy sections of cities. He asked why wiretapping and bugging were not employed by the police to catch corporate criminals, officials engaged in price-fixing conspiracies, and pharmaceutical companies producing drugs that damaged people.

Judge Motley said that the police might be greeted with a gun in the poor areas of a city because people in such areas knew they might be treated with brutality. She added: "The corporation executive is not going to be beaten up. He is going to be promptly released on his own recognizance when brought into court. . . So he does not react the same way the man in the ghetto reacts. That may be one of the reasons why you do not need no-knock when you go after a corporation executive, but you do when you go after a man in the ghetto."

Ramsey Clark described "preventive detention" without jail reforms as a way of manufacturing more crime: "It seems to me beyond question that jails and prisons in the United States are, on balance, creating more anti-social conduct than they are controlling."

"Violence in America, the breakdown of individual stability, flows from frustration, anxiety, and psychosis," the former attorney general said. He cited three social factors that contributed to the flourishing of crime syndicates.

"First, there are millions of poor and powerless people who never had much of a chance and are anxious to gamble, use narcotics, and borrow money at any rate of interest," Clark said. "Organized crime provides them with the goods and services they are looking for." The second factor was "over-criminalization," through laws labeling some offenses—such as excessive drinking and gambling—"criminal," when these offenses were usually beyond the legal system's controlling powers. The third important factor, he said, was the corruption of the police: "The police joke with the prostitutes on the corner, watch the numbers-runners, watch the big and little guys in the narcotics traffic. All organized crime does is fit into that general situation."

James Bennett, former director of the United States prison system, estimated that it would cost $18 billion to get rid of the bad prisons and "substitute small, community-based institutions" that might be effective in deterring crime or rehabilitating criminals.

Participants in the Center conference generally agreed that the largest step that could be taken to improve the whole system of dealing with crime in the United States would be to remove many offenses—such as drunkenness, gambling, sexual activities of forbidden types, and the use of marijuana and other drugs—from the criminal statutes. Advocates of "decriminalization" felt that it would unclog the courts, enable the police to concentrate on major crimes, and provide better treatment for people who needed help rather than imprisonment.

Judge Murphy favored such action, but warned that it would not solve all the problems: "There is a danger in believing that if we take the criminal label off certain things and send people to an administrative agency we have automatically solved the problem. . . . You could take everybody out of our prison system and label them something else, but there are still only fourteen psychiatrists in the country who are willing to work with them, no matter how much you pay them."

"Only integrated systems-planning is rational," Professor Morris argued. "That is planning that takes into account the interrelationships between crime legislation, corrections, rehabilitation, courts, police. . . . Until people begin to think of these interrelationships between all parts of the system, we are not going to get rational planning."

After the conferees had explored many ideas and proposals, Hutchins wondered where the money would be obtained to put these suggestions into effect: "Mr. Bennett says he needs at least 18 billion dollars for the penal system alone. If you put on top of that, treatment centers for narcotics addicts, treatment centers for alcoholics, community services of the kind Mr. McManus runs in Minnesota; if you have the state departments of justice Mr. Bennett properly insists on; if you do the job with the police that Ramsey Clark wants; if you rescue the judges and get a new batch, as Judge Murphy suggests; if you fix up the prosecutors; if you really make the public-defender service adequate to the needs of the poor; the amount of public funds that would be required would mean that just to get started you would have to have already achieved a tremendous revolution in the attitude of the public.

"The system of criminal justice really has no clients who are interested in it. The people who are the most affected by it are the people who have the least influence in society. You cannot get anywhere on this issue by seeming to be a do-gooder. You have to recommend that you get in there with a club and a wiretap. The question, then, is how to get the resources needed."

Hutchins spoke with some bitterness. He had been concerned about the failures and the human wreckage caused by the criminal justice system since he had been at Yale. He had tried for almost fifty years to arouse public support for basic reforms that might have provided more justice and might have reduced crime, but crime was steadily rising and injustices existed everywhere.

With the idealism of a comparatively young man, Ramsey Clark saw a possible source of financial support for a better system: "If we took just a fraction of what this country now spends on the military, expenditures that threaten the existence of civilization itself, and poured it into a program of the kind we have been talking about, we could overcome the financial problem."

But the amounts being spent by the federal government on arms were increasing, not declining. No one saw any likelihood that money from the military budget would be diverted into a struggle against the causes of crime and the injustices in the legal and penal system.

The conference on crime control and civil liberties was typical of many conferences on social problems held at the Center. Many exciting ideas were expressed, exchanged, and refined. But Hutchins and his colleagues knew that the ideas were being circulated into a society where the fear of change was rampant and many people had vested interests in old methods and institutional structures. Their awareness of these facts did not keep the fellows from plunging ahead.

Rexford Tugwell had not participated in the conference on crime and punishment. He had been busy in helping to plan the meetings on the possibilities of a new constitution, held in Santa Barbara, Chicago and Los Angeles in the early months of 1971, and in reading and trying to answer some of the 3,000 letters which surged into the Center after the publication of his model Constitution.

"We are now getting more critiques and many of them are embarassing since they point out defects we should have anticipated," Tugwell said frankly in an open letter published in the February, 1971 issue of *Center Report*. "We can only say at this point that we are grateful for the careful attention we have had from so many scholars and commentators, that all suggestions are being considered and that presently we shall try to have a better version."

In the same month a new book by Tugwell—*Off Course: From Truman to Nixon*, published by Praeger—appeared with the thesis that Richard Nixon was the first professional politician elected since Franklin D. Roosevelt who understood that the nation had gone "off course" into the cold war under Truman and had to return a policy of coexistence with the communist countries. This thesis seemed doubtful to some of Tugwell's colleagues at the Center, but he stuck to it staunchly.

Several pages of the February issue of *Center Report* were allocated to excerpts from dialogues in a Center gathering called "The Deinstitutionalization of Education" and the possibilities of a "society without schools." Ivan Illich, head of the Center for Inter-Cultural Documentation in Cuernavaca, Mexico, and Everett Reimer, another educator, led these discussions.

Contending that schools principally existed for the benefit of the professionals who operated them, Illich said: "We must guarantee people their civil rights against the opinion of professional groups who define one's institutional treatment needs. Professionals cannot be trusted with defining human deficiencies.''

Illich cited reports indicating that school systems were breaking down in many countries, with many children unable to read or write and many unable to function in technological societies. He confessed: "I feel very badly about this whole thing frequently. I know that our criticism is destructive of one of the great creations of the last two generations. It pulls the rug out from under the only ritual which at this moment keeps stability. It calls for a radical alternative which we cannot imagine."

"As you universalize, as you extend certain types of education to everybody, you increase costs," Reimer said. "And it's at some level of universalization rather than at some cost level that you begin to have your reading difficulties. As you insist upon applying a certain type of training to everybody, you reach the state where it doesn't work."

"Perhaps schools without walls, museums without walls, console terminals in homes and shopping centers may be what we will get next," Harvey Wheeler offered. "We tend to think of the future as being centrally preoccupied with the educational quest, the cultural quest. We're talking about converting the city into a school, a better school."

Early in March 1971, Hugh Downs of NBC's "Today" program—who had become a Center member—brought a camera crew to Santa Barbara to do a portion of a "Today" program on the Center's work. While there, he participated in a discussion of a paper by a visiting fellow—Donald Harrington, pastor of New York City's Community Church—on religion and culture. He indicated to Hutchins and me that he would like to be a visiting fellow for a month or more.

Praising the "utter freedom" he found at the Center, Downs declared in a newspaper interview: "There are a lot of think-tanks but it seems to me that almost all of them have strings attached that keep them from doing the independent thought that this one has."

The "Today" program reached millions of viewers and aroused interest in the Center in Washington, New York, Boston, and other major cities. When Downs left the program a few months later, he said that he had accepted an invitation from Hutchins to come to the Center for a month.

In the spring of 1971, turmoil over the Vietnam war shook the nation again. South Vietnamese troops, who had invaded Laos in February with Nixon's encouragement, were cut to pieces in March by North Vietnamese tanks, rockets and artillery. The fleeing South Vietnamese were rescued by American helicopters. American bombers began to hammer the North Vietnamese once more. It was obvious that Nixon's policy of turning the war over to the Vietnamese was not working; the corrupt Saigon government demanded more assistance.

American veterans who had returned from Vietnam with revulsion against the situation there had formed the Vietnam Veterans Against the War. Disturbed by the resumption of American air attacks, some of these veterans went to Washington, pitched tents on Capitol Hill, and picketed the Supreme Court. More than 200,000 protesters marched for peace through the streets of Washington on April 24. Some of them were disorderly, littering the streets, lying down in front of automobiles, and abandoning cars at intersections.

The Washington police handled the situation with calm restraint, but Attorney General John Mitchell and President Nixon grew angry at what they regarded as violations of "law and order." Nixon might be willing to deal courteously with communist governments, but he was enraged by American demonstrators.

Memoranda circulated to the senior fellows in preparation for their meetings sometimes reflected the internal conflicts that flared between Elisabeth Borgese and Harry Ashmore, or others who felt that too much emphasis was given to the Center's periodicals and not enough to more scholarly publications. In March 1971 Mrs. Borgese made a strong effort to get the Center to provide an additional $60,000 a year for such publications or to "undertake some reallocation of our available resources."

Mrs. Borgese had tried to persuade Ashmore to authorize a special publication based on a conference on international relations, which had been held at the Center under her direction in January. Ashmore and other fellows had informed her that the papers submitted for the conference would not be "of general interest to our members" and "there is no market for the kind of publication proposed here."

In a stiff memorandum to Ashmore on March 12, Mrs. Borgese wrote: "I am convinced that the re-establishment of an independent publications program should have a priority in our reorganization. As long as we do not have such a program, the investment in our academic program is largely wasted; the most substantial and important part of our material . . . remains unpublished, or, as the very substantial material on the oceans, gets published at the University of Malta, as though the Center did not exist."

The conflict between Mrs. Borgese and Ashmore in this case was partly a conflict over editorial judgment. Mrs. Borgese admitted: "The quality of the papers submitted for the conference is far from exciting. In this I agree with HSA and with the opinion of the Fellows as reported by him. There is *something* in each of the papers, however, that is worth saving. The quality of the dialogue was good, with the emergence of an unusual number of original and concrete proposals, and given the crucial importance of the whole subject, I think that a useful and substantial publication should emerge."

In this instance, she did not prevail. At the meeting of the senior fellows on March 19, Hutchins and Ashmore made it clear that the Center did not "currently have $60,000 to allocate to a new publication." Hutchins and Ashmore were trying to bring the Center's budget under control.

Mrs. Borgese did get a summary of her conference into the April issue of *Center Report*. That issue also had excerpts from a filmed discussion in London based on a *Center Magazine* article by Arnold Toynbee entitled "The Reluctant Death of National Sovereignty." Toynbee had suggested that multinational corporations might be instruments in developing a global unity.

At the London gathering were Aurelio Peccei, vice chairman of Olivetti and chairman of the Committee for Atlantic Economic Cooperation; Eldridge Haines, founder and chairman of Business International, Inc.; Orville Freeman, former Secretary of Agriculture under President Kennedy; and Professor Toynbee. Quotations from their dialogue appeared in the *Report* under the heading: "Will Businessmen Unite the World?"

"The multi-national corporations are against war and for peace," Peccei said. "International tensions go against their interests and their motivations."

Toynbee agreed. "The officers of the great multi-national corporations are world citizens, I believe. So are the civil servants of the United Nations; so are the world's physicists. . . . I think the world's doctors are world citizens, and as for youth—if anything happens on one campus anywhere in the world, within hours the same thing will happen on all the campuses. They have the future."

Freeman endorsed a proposal to give the multinational corporation an international charter: "Why not an island somewhere that could be the *situs* for the multinational corporation?"

"There are some ex-colonial islands that have become independent and don't know what to do about it," Toynbee said. "I think one of them might be persuaded to lend itself as a kind of Vatican City as a seat for the world's multi-national corporations."

"We are faced with strong leaders that have great power in their hands because of national sovereignty, and there is obvious reluctance to relinquish that power," Haines reminded him. "We are faced with millions of people who are religious about sovereignty."

Toynbee said: "I suggest that nationalism is a religion, therefore it's a formidable force; and it can only be replaced by a better religion to get a greater hold on mankind. There is today what I would call a morality gap; scientists and technologists walked right away from our morality. . . . We are like children, armed with atomic weapons—a most dangerous thing.

"This is really a religious question; so it requires a change of heart. I believe fundamentally this is what we have to concentrate on. Unless we can do this we can't do any of the other practical or concrete things we want to do."

In another article in that issue of *Center Report*, Mircea Eliade—a Center associate, described by the editor as "the world's foremost historian of religion"—raised questions on whether modern man could survive without a religious framework for existence.

Describing how men in previous societies had always had an experience of "sacred space," a "center of the world," a relationship to the earth and the universe, which brought stability and order into life, Eliade doubted whether scientific ideas could ever give man such a sense of connection, such a sense of belonging somewhere, of having roots in the past and some importance for the future.

"*If the world is to be lived in*, it must be *founded*," Eliade said. "No world can be born in the chaos of the homogeneity and relativity of profane space."

Meditating on Eliade's statements, John Wilkinson wrote: "If it be true that modern man resolutely rejects the religious axis of his Being, he may be in the condition of being unable to believe what he must believe. One solution to a dilemma of this kind, of course, is to go mad. . . . The view from Eucalyptus Hill convinces me at least that an almost universal crescendo of hysteria and violence is the path through the horns of the dilemma that has actually been adopted in the modern world."

A few weeks later, Wilkinson organized and chaired a week-long meeting of some members of the International Committee for Dialogue on the Fundamental Issues Facing Mankind, which had been established at a gathering of a group of scholars at the Center in 1967. Its members included four other senior fellows of the Center—Hutchins, Ashmore, Mrs. Borgese, and Harvey Wheeler.

The Committee meeting in the spring of 1971 focused on "Priorities for the 1970's in the Developed and Developing Nations." It was held at Ivan Illich's Center in Cuernavaca, and several South American scholars participated in the dialogue with scholars from Western Europe and the United States.

In a summary of these discussions brought together by Arnold Kuenzli, a founder of the Philosophical Society of Basel, the main topics were the misuse of technology, aesthetics and utopian ideas, the variety of revolutions in the Third World, the effects of neo-colonialism, the necessity for a Marxist-Christian dialogue, and the "latent volcano" in Mexico's desperate economic situation. One of the "indisputable priorities of the 70's", Kuenzli concluded, was to prepare for a searching "dialogue with Latin America."

More than 1,000 Center members and their guests attended a six-hour Center symposium in Chicago in April on "Prospects for a Learning Society." Having focused the attention of thousands of people in convocations on the possibilities of a new Constitution, the Center had shifted the main theme of its public gatherings to the future of education.

Speakers at the Chicago meeting were George N. Shuster, former president of Hunter College and former director of the Fund for the Republic; F. Champion Ward, a former dean at the University of Chicago who had become a program advisor to the Ford Foundation; Arthur G. Anderson, vice president for research and development at the International Business Machines corporation, who was spending a year as a Visiting Fellow at the Center; Hutchins, Ashmore, and Donald Harrington, who described the Center's impact on his view of education during his two months as a Visiting Fellow. Harrington declared that his experiences at the Center had convinced him that structural changes had to be made in American society to enable it to survive.

A legal collision between the Nixon administration and major newspapers occurred in June, raising questions about the conduct of American foreign policy and the powers of the presidency—questions that the Center had been bringing before the American public since the beginning of the Vietnam War.

On June 13 the *New York Times* devoted more than six full pages to "secret" documents that had been prepared by thrity-five scholars at the request of Robert McNamara, not long before McNamara had resigned as secretary of defense. McNamara had asked the scholars to pull together a comprehensive record of how the United States had become bogged down in Vietnam.

These documents—called the Pentagon papers, because they had been taken from the Pentagon by Daniel Ellsberg—disclosed the bungling that had gone on behind the scenes in Washington since the days of Harry Truman. The lies and deceptions of Lyndon Johnson were exposed. The expansion of American involvement through covert actions by President Kennedy was revealed.

Angered by the publication of government secrets—and alarmed by the possibility that some of the secrets of his own administration might come to light—President Nixon tried to block the printing of these documents by the *Times*, the Washington *Post*, the Boston *Globe*, and other newspapers. Government lawyers under Assistant Attorney General Robert Mardian—who had persuaded one of J. Edgar Hoover's assistants to remove wiretapping records from Hoover's office to the White House—sought and obtained an injunction to keep the *Times* from continuing to print excerpts from the Pentagon files. The *Times* took the case to the Supreme Court. The Court, by a vote of 6 to 3, held that the government could not "impose a prior restraint on publication of essentially historical data."

While the uproar over the Pentagon papers was at its height—and Nixon was meeting with Charles Colson, John Dean, and other aides to plot the destruction of his "enemies"—the Center's directors met at the Plaza Hotel in New York and elected four new members of the board. One of those elected was Ramsey Clark, former attorney general, who had been a principal target of personal attacks by Nixon and John Mitchell.

There were several vacancies on the Center's board. Elmo Roper, one of the original directors of the Fund for the Republic, who had served as chairman and honorary chairman of the board, had died in May 1971. Crane Haussamen had resigned, and Percy Julian, a Chicago chemist who had not been active, had taken a leave of absence.

In addition to Clark, the new directors were Mrs. Robert Hutchins, Paul Newman, and Bernard Rapoport. Clark and Mrs. Hutchins were in New York, and took their places at the board table as soon as they had been elected. Newman, the film star, and Rapoport, an insurance company president from Waco, Texas, were unable to be present. Rapoport, an ebullient businessman with political and scholarly interests, had been elected on the recommendation of J. R. Parten.

The wife of Robert Hutchins was added to the board with the approval of all the directors. She was well informed about the work of the Center. His health was precarious. If illness forced him to retire, she would be able to represent his views.

At the executive session on the morning of June 24, the officers were authorized to seek a settlement of the Ferry suit by offering to pay him $12,500 a year for eight years—a total of $100,000. Gary Cadenhead, who kept the minutes of this meeting, noted: "This is the amount originally offered to Mr. Ferry as termination pay in 1969; spreading it over an 8-year period enables the Center to earn income on the residue sufficient to recoup the legal costs incurred."

Hutchins began the afternoon session—which was open to the staff— by describing the development of the academic program. He outlined the conference "Medical Malpractice and Tort Liability" to be held at the Center in September with the cooperation of the federal Department of Health, Education, and Welfare. After some discussion of the Center's relationships with government agencies, a resolution was adopted by the board stating that "the Center shall lend assistance to government agencies whenever possible within the framework of the Center's academic program, such assistance to be undertaken on the basis of cooperation and mutual interest and not for financial gain."

At Hutchins' request, John Cogley and Harvey Wheeler then spoke briefly about their current projects. Cogley referred to the meetings he had planned to explore the "revolutions" that were occurring in—or challenging—"the traditional American social and cultural mores." Wheeler said he was forming plans for a symposium of Center fellows and scientists on "the coming crisis in energy sources."

Hutchins said that Mrs. Borgese had two other projects under way in addition to her "Pacem in Maribus" conferences. She had planned an international seminar on the theory of "self-management" and another seminar on economic development, with the results to be supplied to the United Nations Conference on Trade and Development.

Cadenhead reviewed progress on the plans for the meeting "The Corporation and the Quality of Life," and Ashmore described a study that would be launched during the summer by Nathan Rotenstreich of the Hebrew University, Jerusalem, on the influence of Judaic ideas and the Jewish historical experience in the United States and other countries. Some financing for this project would come from the American Jewish Committee, Ashmore indicated.

Hutchins declared that he thought the academic program of the Center was moving forward well. He was pleased by the recognition the Center's projects had received. He told me that he appreciated the work I was doing to keep public attention focused on the Center.

Reporting to the board on his functions as president, Ashmore continued to be hopeful about the Center's financial situation. He said there would be a $30,000 surplus for the fiscal year ending on June 30, 1971—a marked contrast to the deficit of more that $1.5 million that had been incurred in the twelve month fiscal year ending on September 30, 1970.

Ashmore spoke with satisfaction of the reception given by Center members to the two periodicals—the *Magazine* and the *Report*—and said that the five textbooks composed of Center materials, published by James Freel & Company, were off to a good start in the college markets. He announced the resignation of Florence Mischel as editor and director of the audiotape department. She had decided to become a lawyer, and had been accepted as a student at a leading law school.

Under Mrs. Mischel's direction, the scope of the audiotape program had become enormous. Excerpts from hundreds of Center meetings—on dozens of topics—were being used by schools, colleges, and discussion groups. Many of the tapes were in Library of Congress catalogues for use by scholars, members of Congress and Congressional staff persons. The Directors congratulated Mrs. Mischel on her achievements.

Although the Center did have a small surplus for the 1971 fiscal year—and anticipated a larger surplus in the 1972 year, due to a distribution of Xerox stock from the Carlson estate—Peter Tagger expressed concern about the flow of special gifts. The total Center membership remained near the 100,000 level, but the payments by ordinary members would not be sufficient to meet the Center's annual budgets.

"The collection of major gift pledges has been slow and the acquisition of new pledges continues to be difficult," Tagger said. "We do not appear to have found the right fund-raising formula for the Center."

Tagger added that new approaches and techniques would be tried with the aid of Clifford Welch—who had replaced Crane Haussamen as the Center's east coast representative—and William Bidner, who was the west coast representative with an office in Los Angeles. He appealed to the directors for lists of prospective givers and ideas for obtaining substantial contributions.

Cadenhead and Hutchins urged the board to approve an investment of $300,000 for an expansion of the direct mail campaign. In Tagger's opinion, such an investment could bring in more than 20,000 new members. He said the campaign would be developed cautiously, with tests being made of available lists, and the entire $300,000 would not be spent if the tests were not successful. The board authorized the officers "to spend up to $300,000 in acquiring additional members."

On the night before that board meeting—on June 23, at the Alice Tully theater in Lincoln Center—the directors, senators, and representatives, cabinet officials, and leaders in conservation had attended the premiere of a new Stanley Kramer film, *Bless the Beasts and Children*, with the financial proceeds going to the Santa Barbara Center. The proceeds were not large, and the film did not arouse much public or critical enthusiasm.

"The book and the picture deal with some of the 'rejected ones' of our society," Hutchins said. "The Center has associated itself with the film because we feel that it may help to revive in many people the fundamental compassion necessary to make a democratic society truly alive." The film dealt with a group of boys who set out to free a herd of buffalo destined for slaughter. For the Center, it was a fund-raising experiment that faded away without satisfactory results. Few people associated the Center with lonely boys or buffaloes.

It became evident once more that the Center had to pin its financial hopes on its expanded membership rolls, the generosity of its directors, and the possibility of finding another Chester Carlson. While the direct-mail campaign went on and the fund raisers struggled to get wealthy people more excited about the Center, the senior fellows developed their projects and began to worry about what would happen if Hutchins' health collapsed.

Not long after Hutchins recovered from his aneurysm operation, he began to suffer from cancer of the bladder. With Puritan determination, he kept on with his work. But Parten and Fagan Dickson persuaded him in the summer of 1971 to enter the M. D. Anderson Tumor Clinic in Houston. There he underwent another operation, which was drastic and extremely uncomfortable but saved his life.

While Hutchins was away, Ashmore managed the Center. Ashmore did not have the awesome stature or the diplomatic skills of Hutchins, but most of the fellows and the senior staff accepted his leadership on a temporary basis. He consulted Hutchins as frequently as possible and invoked the name of Hutchins when he made difficult decisions.

Norton Ginsburg, a professor of geography at the University of Chicago, who had come to the Center in the middle of March 1971 as a visiting fellow at the suggestion of John Wilkinson, was invited by Hutchins and Ashmore to take over the administrative burdens of the academic program. Ginsburg obtained a leave of absence from the university and agreed to become a full-time dean, with his appointment becoming effective on October 15.

Ginsburg had been associate dean of the college and associate dean of the division of the social sciences at the University of Chicago, and chairman of the board on adult education there. He had been president of the

Association of American Geographers and chairman of the Committee on Environment of the United States National Commission for UNESCO. He had written many articles for scholarly journals and was a contributor to many books. He was an urbane, sensitive, sophisticated man who was able to fit in comfortably with the senior fellows.

On July 14, unaware that Henry Kissinger had made a secret visit to China and that President Nixon was about to make a sudden turn in American foreign policy, Ashmore announced that the Center would sponsor an international conference in Tokyo on relations between the United States, Japan, and China. Ashmore said that Liberal-Democratic members of the Japanese diet were cosponsoring the meeting and had provided the funds for it. He indicated that the American participants at the gathering—to be held from August 19 to 21—would include Supreme Court Justice William O. Douglas; Senator Edward Kennedy; Adlai Stevenson III; Senator Alan Cranston of California, and Senator Daniel K. Inouye of Hawaii.

Three days after Ashmore had released this information to the press, President Nixon delivered a four-minute television speech to tell the world that he had been asked to visit Communist China and had accepted. ''I have taken this action because of my profound conviction that all nations will gain from a reduction of tensions and a better relationship between the United States and the People's Republic of China,'' Nixon said. He asserted that he would seek ''a new relationship'' with Peking, but it would not be ''at the expense'' of Chiang Kai-shek's Nationalist China.

After talking with leaders in Tokyo and Washington by telephone, Ashmore soon declared that the conference scheduled for August had been indefinitely postponed. ''President Nixon's announcement of his coming visit to Peking and Prime Minister Sato's indication that he would accept a similar invitation leave a wide range of imponderables,'' Ashmore said. ''We felt the discussion would be more productive when the emerging lines of policy are clearer.''

Nixon's astonishing shift toward a friendly relationship with Mao's China was welcomed by the fifteen internationally known agriculturalists, economists, soil scientists, food producers, geographers, and conservationists who met at the Center for five days in the middle of August. It was the first conference ever held on earth to consider how the world's needs for food and fiber could be satisfied without damaging the ecological balances on which all life depended.

Views expressed at this assembly ranged from those of Lester R. Brown, formerly administrator of the International Agricultural Development Service of the United States Department of Agriculture—who asserted that ''this conference has been too complacent about environmental stresses in its concern about expanding food problems''—to those of Jonathan Garst, farmer and consultant to the United States, the Soviet Union, Romania, Poland, Iran, Pakistan, and India, who said: "Please, ecologists, don't kill the world with love."

Five of the agricultural experts defended modern methods of food production and declared that the effects of intensive farming on soil and water pollution were very small or virtually insignificant in comparison with the damage done by industrial wastes, sewage, garbage, and chemicals used in cities.

These experts included Charles Hardin, professor of political science at the University of California at Davis, and formerly director of the International Agricultural Institute; W. David Hopper, president of the International Development Research Center in Ottawa, Canada, and a consultant to the World Bank; Charles E. Kellogg, a soil scientist who had received awards for his work in Australia, the Belgian Congo, Canada, New Zealand, Israel, India, the United States, and other countries; Emil Mrak, chairman of the Hazardous Materials Advisory Committee of the Environmental Protection Agency; and Perry R. Stout, vice chairman of the Advisory Committee, Division of Biology and Medicine, Atomic Energy Commission.

"Too often, we see some issues only by themselves," Professor Hardin said. "We see the effect of DDT in the Central Valley of California but fail to understand its significance elsewhere in the world."

All of these participants in the Center conference contended that the environmental consequences of fertilizers and pesticides had been greatly exaggerated.

These agricultural authorities unanimously claimed that food production throughout the world could be increased tremendously without damaging soils or any other part of the environmental ecosystem. Such increases would require more scientific farming and appropriate uses of soils, they said, but the techniques could be learned and applied without excessive difficulties. They also agreed that much new land could be put into production to meet the needs of hungry people, and much of the acreage already producing crops could be farmed far more efficiently if farmers applied the knowledge available to them.

The July–August issue of the *Center Magazine*, which was in circulation while the agricultural experts were meeting there, contained tributes to two men who had done much for the Fund and the Center—Elmo Roper, the former chairman of the Fund's board, and Reinhold Niebuhr, the Protestant theologian who had contributed ideas and criticisms at many of the Center's meetings.

In a statement about Roper, Hutchins said: "His outstanding characteristics were courage and lucidity. He was never afraid to take a position, and he never left any doubt about what it was. The more unpopular the position, the more fearlessly and clearly he stated it. In the darkest days of McCarthyism he did not suggest compromise or retreat." Hutchins had not forgotten that Roper had defended him when he had been under attack in the press and his resignation had been demanded by Dean Erwin Griswold of the Harvard law school.

Niebuhr, one of the Center's original consultants, had died at his home in Massachusetts on June 1, 1971. In the *Magazine*, John Cogley called him "unquestionably the most influential American theologian of the twentieth century." Several of his books—particularly *The Nature and Destiny of Man* and *Moral Man and Immoral Society*—were regarded as masterpieces, with influences on the thinking and policies of leaders in many countries.*

In the last paper he had presented at a Center dialogue—a paper printed in the *Magazine* with Cogley's note about his death—Niebuhr expressed his belief that the religious traditions of the United States had been significant in enabling Americans to maintain a basic consensus. "Only our own nation made freedom of religion one of the foundations of liberty," Niebuhr said, adding that "the secular humanism which arose in the Renaissance" had an impact upon American political institutions.

"We needed the radical emphases of both sectarian Protestantism and secular idealism to challenge the traditional injustices of the old agrarian-monarchial societies," Niebuhr declared. "But we also had to guard against the utopian fanaticism of both these forms of faith, as expressed in both the Cromwellian and French Revolutions. . . .

"In a democratic society, the underlying consensus depends on having confidence that the free play of political forces will make for justice, at least in the long run. . . . "

On September 28, a week-long conference called "The Corporation and the Quality of Life" opened at the Center with representatives of large and small corporations, professors of business administration, and fellows of the Center participating in it. Robert Hutchins had returned to Santa Barbara, well on the road to recovery from his cancer operation in Houston, but he did not take an active part in these sessions.

The discussions focused on the social responsibilities of corporations, the accusations of consumer groups, the impact of corporations on environmental pollution, and their roles in philanthropy. The conflicts between the corporate executives, the environmentalists, and the consumer groups led to lively exchanges at every session. The role of some corporations in corrupting political life was also examined.

Before the conference opened, the close connections between the Nixon administration and large industries had been exposed by newspaper columnists in several cases in 1971. One case involved the leaders of the dairy industry, who told Nixon that they wanted higher federal subsidies for milk

---

*Niebuhr was the second member of the original group of consultants who died in 1971. Adolf A. Berle, Jr., who had contributed to many Center publications and meetings, had died in February. Rexford Tugwell had described him as "one of the movers of his generation, brilliant, penetrating and helpful in all good causes."

products. Nixon gave them what they asked for, and they contributed $527,500 to Republican campaign funds.

Another case was that of the International Telephone and Telegraph Corporation, which wanted to take over the Hartford Fire Insurance Corporation. Lawyers in the antitrust division of the Department of Justice contended that the merger violated antitrust laws. Deputy Attorney General Richard Kleindienst, who backed these lawyers, was ordered to drop the case by Nixon's assistant, John Ehrlichman. When Kleindienst refused, Nixon telephoned him and said: "You son of a bitch, don't you understand the English language?" Kleindienst still resisted, but in the end Nixon prevailed and ITT retained its control of the Hartford insurance company. Harold Geneen, president of the ITT conglomerate, agreed to donate $400,000 to the Republican campaign fund.

A third case revealed the ties between Nixon and Robert Vesco, who had been accused by the federal Securities and Exchange Commission of looting $224 million from the funds of the Investors Overseas Services corporation. According to an indictment brought against him, Vesco gave Edward Nixon, the President's brother, $200,000 for delivery to Maurice Stans, Nixon's Secretary of Commerce, with the understanding that John Mitchell would try to get the SEC to drop the charges against Vesco.

At the Center conference Ray Mulford, chairman of the Owens-Illinois Corporation, conceded that there were dangers in the political activities of some corporations. "I have long advocated that a definite ceiling be put on campaign contributions," Mulford said. "Political candidates should not be dependent on anyone: business, labor unions, or whatever."

Theodore Jacobs, executive director of Ralph Nader's Center for the Study of Responsive Law, asserted: "In the long run corporate power cannot be made accountable by relying only on the law-enforcement efforts of government agencies or the good will of corporate decision-makers.

"Neither the regulator's zeal nor the business executive's conscience is a substitute for continual monitoring and participation by those affected by corporate power, the voluntary and involuntary consumers.

"The consumer and environmental protection advocates who have emerged in the past five years represent the first stirrings of such a movement. They have won some minor corporate concessions and have stiffened the spines of government regulators to carry out statutory responsibilities. But their principal contribution has been educational. By their victories, as in the case of the supersonic transport plane, they have demonstrated that even corporate power bolstered by labor and government is not irresistible. They have proved that organized citizen action can be potent."

Jacobs recommended that the federal criminal laws should be revised to permit courts to disqualify executives from corporate employment "for a period up to five years" after convictions of criminal offenses "committed on corporate business." He said: "The prospect of a forced vacation might encourage executives to be a little less cavalier in deciding to what degree their company will comply with federal statutes.''

Another conference participant, Burke Marshall, a professor at the Yale University law school and a former assistant attorney general, commented: ''Your remedies are almost trivial in a way. You basically accept the function of the corporation. So, all your suggestions are procedural. They are sort of a good-guy, bad-guy kind of approach to the problem.''

''Procedural suggestions are terribly important in specific areas,'' Jacobs responded. ''I think we must talk about structural and procedural changes, not about alternatives to the corporate framework, such as nationalization or socialism. I do not think that those alternatives are preferable to the system we have. I think we have to make our system more democratic. And how do you make a system more democratic? You build into it procedures so that voices may be heard.''

Raymond Bauer, a professor in the Harvard Graduate School of Business Administration and a former president of the American Psychological Association, spoke of ''a broad change of ethos'' in American society ''which encompasses a change in the level of our expectation combined with an increased awareness of a shortage of such resources as money, water, air, and places to dispose of our waste.''

''The corporation's responsibility is to be sensitively responsive to the changes in values occurring in our society,'' Neil Jacoby declared.

John J. Gorson, president of Fry Consultants, a subsidiary of A.R.A. Services, Inc., a conglomerate corporation, described an effort by the A.R.A. to conduct a ''social audit'' to assess how well the corporation was meeting its social responsibilities. The idea of such a ''social audit'' was questioned by Scott Kelso of Kelso and McCollum, Inc., of Houston, and other conference participants.

''A social audit will be like a corporation's annual statement,'' Kelso said. ''The annual statement exercise is one of the biggest game plans going today. I can see it now: next to the profit-and-loss statement a list of your bounty points.''

Richard Parker, a former junior fellow of the Center who had done graduate studies at Oxford and had written a book entitled *The Myth of Middle America*, said it would take a violent revolution to remove the corporations from their domination of American life.

''Our needs cannot be satisfied by the economy getting bigger and bigger, but by society getting better and better and by redistributing what we already have so that people can equitably share in our economy,'' Parker insisted. ''If income were distributed equally, the average American family would get fifteen thousand dollars a year. . . . .

''The kind of alternative society I see requires the dismantling of the big corporations and consequently the disappearance of many of the jobs just mentioned. In that alternative society, businessmen would work in small community-sized enterprises owned by the men and women who work in them. . . . The number of professionals and scientists would decline sharply because the advanced technology they serve could be replaced by simpler, labor-intensive technology. And academics would frequently find themselves unemployed or else teaching in the style Robert Hutchins borrowed from Socrates forty years ago. . . .

"Unhappily, I see America still going the wrong way. Instead of giving greater autonomy and greater human worth to more people, instead of using our technology to maintain a high standard of living, instead of redistributing what we have to let all Americans share in that world, our society is going toward greater and greater control, greater and greater complexity, greater and greater benign supervision by professionals and managers in the name of democracy and efficiency. . . .

"I believe the type of America I would like to see can come about only through violence, only through the long political struggle implied by revolution, because ruling classes do not give up their power voluntarily."

Robert Townsend, former president of the Avis Rent A Car company, contended that drastic changes could be accomplished without a violent revolution.

"Major surgery on our giant organizations is possible," Townsend said. He thought that huge corporations could be reformed by giving non-union employees—those with five years of employment—the right to choose the chief executive officers. Townsend went on:

"Another possibility is to have half the directors elected by the shareholders and half by the employees—provided they give up their union, of course. They can have it either way—a union or half the board—but not both. I think this kind of board would work harder, expect more from the chief executive officer and his management, and identify and fire an incompetent chief executive officer quicker than the usual board of cronies.

Townsend regarded the labor unions and the top managements as the principal obstacles to necessary reforms: "Unions were visited as a plague on the robber barons who abused their corporate power, exploited labor, and seemed to deserve what they got. But the corporations adapted and now we have twin plagues who have given up any real concern with us—the more or less disadvantaged 185 million Americans who are not members of top managements or powerful labor monopolies."

Most of the participants in the Center conference thought it would be extremely difficult to get union leaders or corporation managers to change their ways.

"The real issue today is how management of all institutions—how society as a whole—is going to reconceive the notion of authority," declared Louis Davis, professor of organizational sciences in the U.C.L.A. graduate school of management. "This is a scary question. . .The question is crucial because society's expectations are changing and the nature of work has to be looked at. Work itself will have to be redefined as organizations begin to focus on the question of the role of man in this new situation."

Some of the themes of the corporation conferences were taken up again at the Center in October, when scholars from Britian, Israel, Chile, Norway, Yugoslavia, and the United States joined the senior fellows in a discussion of the "self-management" movement that had developed in Yugoslavia and other countries. Some factories in Yugoslavia were managed entirely by the workers, who participated in all the levels of decisionmaking.

Ichak Adizes, an Israeli economist who spoke at this gathering on the values of this movement, summarized his conclusions: "It has great promise to the world because it has enabled rapid change in the political, social and technological environment."

Two Yugoslavs at the conference—Najdan Pasic, professor of political science, University of Belgrade, and Jose Pacek, labor organizer and secretary to the Slovenian parliament—described the difficulties encountered by workers' councils and committees on self-management.

Fred Blum, a social scientist and president of the New Era Center in London, said that "the basic problem of self-management is two-fold: (1) to give people an opportunity to participate in the operation of economic, social and political institutions according to their knowledge, experience and abilities; and (2) to foster participation in the development of value-power structures which give people the best opportunity for development of their potentiality for self-realization."

Einar Thorsrud, director of the Work Research Institutes in Oslo, declared that "the industrial democracy program in Norway grew out of a wide public discussion of alienation in industry and the desire for a full utilization of human resources."

At the concluding session of the five-day conference Arthur Anderson—vice president of IBM and a Center visiting fellow—offered these observations: "We have asked: 'Is self-management an end in itself?' The answer, of course, is 'no.' Self-management is part of the drive for self-development, a means for achieving the growth of man in a developing society."

The senior fellows of the Center showed a keen interest in the ideas about "self-management" that emerged at this conference. Authority at the Center was still vested almost exclusively in Hutchins, although the fellows were encouraged to speak without inhibitions at their weekly meetings and no decisions were made without the consent of the whole group.

Soon after Norton Ginsburg's installation as dean, the fellows expressed a desire to meet monthly with the visiting fellows and the senior staff to exchange views concerning the program and the personnel of the Center. This step led to a considerable improvement in the flow of communication between the senior fellows and the other people working at the Center.

At the meeting of the board of directors on November 19, the board ratified the settlement of the Ferry suit, which had been reached on September 10 when Ferry's lawyer had requested the superior court in Santa Barbara to dismiss the case "with prejudice as to all defendants." Ferry had accepted an agreement to pay him $100,000, spread over eight years. As Gary Cadenhead had noted in June, this was the amount "originally offered to Mr. Ferry as termination pay in 1969." The suit had, however, enabled Ferry to get Hutchins, Ashmore, and other senior fellows to testify on how the reorganization had been done.

In the November board meeting, the officers tried again to stimulate the directors to raise the large amounts of money necessary to keep the Center going. The amount being received from the Carlson estate was reported to be greater than expected, but the renewed fund-raising efforts of the staff and financial consultants had not generated a satisfactory flow of cash. Peter Tagger's statement at the June meeting—when he said "the right fund-raising formula" had not been found—still remained true.

The new economic policy of the Nixon administration, which had devalued the dollar and had not checked inflation, had frightened some of the wealthy people who might have given money to the Center. The illnesses of Hutchins had caused some donors to wonder whether he would survive very long—and whether the Center would survive if he died or became completely disabled. The ordinary members—those who sent in $15 to $20 a year for the Center publications—continued to renew their contributions at a sustaining rate, but the large donors held off.

Some of the board members who had been asked to give or raise money declared bluntly that they would like to know more about what was going on at the Center. When Hutchins informed the senior fellows that these directors did not feel fully acquainted with the academic program, the fellows agreed to send the board members a monthly report on the progress of their projects and to circulate a condensed version of the minutes of their meetings at the Center.

Hutchins told the fellows at their session on November 23 that four men—Herbert York, Norman Cousins, Dean McHenry, and Louis Pollak—had been mentioned at the board meeting as possible chairmen of the Center. He said that these men would be invited to the Center for discussions with the fellows. He was not sure that any of them wished to be considered as his successor.

Two of the men discussed by the directors had been to the Center fairly often: Herbert York of the University of California at San Diego, who had been a science adviser to Presidents Eisenhower and Kennedy; and Norman Cousins, the internationally famous editor of the *Saturday Review* and

World magazines. The third man, Dean McHenry, the chancellor of the University of California at Santa Cruz, was noted for his interest in new educational ideas and practices. Louis Pollak, the fourth, was dean of the Yale law school and had written a well-received book, *The Constitution and the Supreme Court.*

Recruitment of a fitting chairman for the Center seemed harder to do than to find new senior fellows among "the very best people in the world." And finding Fellows was very difficult, too. By the end of 1971, only one— Norton Ginsburg, the genial geographer from Chicago—had been added to the starting seven.

More than two years had passed since the "refounding," and the process of forming the "new academy" seemed to be blocked. But Hutchins seldom showed discouragement. He continued to tell board members, the fellows, and journalists who descended on him from time to time that he maintained his great expectations for the Center's future.

When his health improved, Elisabeth Borgese and other fellows urged him to defer his withdrawal from the chairmanship. He shrugged off these suggestions, saying that he wanted to be freed from the burdens he had carried for so long.

With Ginsburg coordinating the academic program and Ashmore handling most of the administrative matters, Hutchins told the senior staff that he thought the Center would run smoothly until the new chairman came to take his place. He hoped that 1972 would be the year of decision.

26

*In a year of dirty tricks,
a fight for the White House,
and saturation bombings and a
ceasefire in Vietnam, the
Center ponders human behavior,
cultural change, and a vast
array of other topics*

T HE PACE OF CHANGE in 1972 quickened to such a speed that no persons on earth, whether ordinary citizen, journalist, scholar, senator, judge, cabinet officer, or spy, could understand the full significance of what was depicted in the press or the secret maneuvers that were hidden or partly hidden in many countries. Later it was known to be a year of dirty tricks, but the range and the intricacies of those tricks have not yet been fully discovered—and may never be completely disclosed.

It was a year in which a national election took place in the United States, an election largely invalidated by the trickery that deprived the Democratic front-runner of a presidential nomination he had in sight as the year began, an election stained with the blood of an independent candidate who was shot and crippled for life, an election corrupted by the spending of millions of dollars gathered illegally by agents of the president, an election marred by a bungled burglary at the headquarters of the Democratic National Committee—a burglary that led to the downfall of that president.

It was a year in which the president traveled to China and toasted Chairman Mao, and flew to Moscow and embraced the leaders of the Soviet Union, in what he called a search for peace. It was a year in which the same president authorized the "saturation bombing" of North Vietnam and obtained a "ceasefire" just before the November voting. It was also a year, another year, of huge federal deficits and great inflation, of desperation in the ghettos and decay in American cities, of more crime and more murders and more young people engulfed in drugs and wandering on the roads.

The Center began the year by attempting to deal with two of the painful dilemmas plaguing humanity—the relationships between doctors and patients under treatment, and the relations between human "freedom" and "dignity" and the creation of a "good society" in which human beings might be motivated to behave well.

The first dilemma was tackled in a booklet entitled *Medical Malpractice*, a report on a three-day conference held at the Center in the autumn of 1971 with support from the federal Department of Health, Education, and Welfare. Lawsuits against physicians and surgeons were clogging courts, increasing the costs of medical care, and giving indications of becoming a national crisis. Doctors, lawyers, patients, and insurance companies were getting involved in accusations and recriminations, with blame passed from one to another.

Six lawyers, a hospital administrator, and four physicians—one of whom was also an attorney—gathered at the Center with the senior fellows, visiting fellows, and staff members to look into the effectiveness of the legal system in malpractice cases and the advantages or drawbacks of alternative methods such as no-fault insurance, arbitration, and social security insurance.

Dr. Roger Egeberg, special assistant to the secretary for health policy at HEW, observed that "the whole relationship between physician and patient has changed, partly as a result of advances in medicine, partly because those advances have produced changes in the physician himself. That is a big reason why the patients' attitude has changed. So many see their doctor as a rich businessman and medicine as a business."

Eli Bernzweig, attorney and special assistant to the administrator of the Federal Insurance Administration, Department of Housing and Urban Development, said that the achievements of modern medicine had been "ballyhooed to the point at which patients expect miracles from their physicians. Then when something goes wrong, when there is a maloccurence or a therapeutic misadventure, the public tends to assume negligence is involved and some compensation is due."

Rick Carlson, an attorney and a former visiting scholar at the Center, said that physicians he had interviewed generally were opposed to the fault-and-liability insurance system, which compelled patients to bring civil suits against physicians or hospitals to obtain compensation for medical injuries. "They do not believe it says anything about the way in which medical care is provided," Carlson reported. He said that findings of malpractice were seldom used to revise regulations covering health care.

Mark Blumberg, a physician employed by the Kaiser Foundation health plan, voiced his belief that such litigation "tended to reduce medical misdeeds" and might be to some extent "a definite benefit to society." But he felt that court decisions in such cases were "writing a manual for medical practice," and he did not think such a manual would necessarily produce good medicine. He believed that many doctors were practicing defensively, requiring more x rays and other tests, and sometimes avoiding risky procedures that might be desirable in some circumstances.

Richard Markus, past president of the American Trial Lawyers Association, thought that the many tests ordered by doctors might be beneficial to some patients. "Often what the doctor is really saying is that there is a remote chance, not a totally insignificant chance, that this X-ray or this test may be extremely useful," Markus said.

David Rubsamen, who also had a law degree and edited the *Professional Liability Newsletter* in Berkeley, California, asserted that there had been remarkable improvements in certain parts of medical care in California as a result of malpractice suits or the threat of such suits. "Hospitals are requiring that anesthesia be given by specialists, not general practitioners," Dr. Rubsamen said. "Hospitals have been nailed in the past when there have been anesthetic accidents."

"I also think that the malpractice threat has stimulated the willingness of physicians to obtain consultation, and that is good," Dr. Rubsamen said.

Markus favored the retention of the tort liability system—or private remedy through court action—for major malpractice cases and the arbitration method for smaller, less serious medical injury claims.

"The kind of insurance we should have depends upon the breadth of compensation we want to provide," Markus said. "The inadequate regulation of the insurance industry is a very serious problem. There are almost no available data showing what the insurance companies are doing, how they use their money, what role they play in the overall health care system, what effect they are having on the quality of health care."

Carlson noted: "If we had a no-fault system of some kind, there would be equitable compensation of the victim of a medical injury. And there would also be built into the system regulatory feedback to improve the quality of health care. So why must we keep the private remedy?"

Markus declared: "Really, the norm in almost every country except the United States is to have a broadly based Social Security compensation system for every person who has a disability or an illness; and, alongside that, there is provision for the private remedy. The need for the private remedy is not eliminated by an amelioration of the compensation system."

While expressing his awareness of the deficiencies of malpractice litigation in courtrooms, Dr. Rubsamen said that a no-fault system—if it tried to make distinctions between compensable and noncompensable medical events—would require a huge hearing agency and innumerable hours of medical investigations. He suggested that arbitration could be a step between courtroom cases and a no-fault plan. If arbitration was not satisfactory, the no-fault rule could be put into effect.

Another participant in the conference—J. W. Bush, assistant professor in the school of medicine of the University of California at San Diego—said that many patients signed arbitration agreements without realizing that "they are signing away their constitutional right to a trial by jury."

"I have no inherent opposition to the arbitration model," declared another law school professor at the conference, Richard S. L. Roddis of the University of Washington at Seattle. "We should recognize, though, that it yields results so different from those of the fault-and-liability trial court system that the decision as to which method should be used ought to be made at a public lawmaking level."

Carlson outlined a possible no-fault insurance system that might serve as a "middle ground" between the tort liability system and a social insurance plan. He suggested that compensation should be "paid for the degree of deviation of a patient's outcome from a range of expected outcomes for like procedures."

"A combination of fault and no-fault systems can be worked out in several ways," Professor Keeton said. "One is through staging in which both systems are used to determine what compensation the victim will receive. He receives the first level of compensation on a no-fault, straight insurance basis. Then if he thinks he is entitled to more, he seeks that on the fault basis. . . . There is an infinite variety of combinations you can arrange for the two systems.

Thirty thousand copies of the Center's report on the complexities of the legal and medical issues in malpractice cases were purchased by the Department of Health, Education and Welfare for distribution to physicians, attorneys, and insurers. The booklet was offered to the public for $1 a copy, and thousands of copies were sold to Center members and other citizens concerned about the quality of medical care.

While the booklet on *Medical Malpractice* was reaching people in many communities and stirring up arguments, the Center invited dozens of scholars to comment on the ideas of B. F. Skinner, the Harvard behaviorist who contended that "freedom and dignity" were illusions. Some of these scholars came to Santa Barbara for three days of dialogues with Skinner and the Center fellows, and others sent in written statements, some denouncing Skinner and others hailing him.

Skinner had been involved in the Center's study of the political process in the 1950s, in a group organized by Hallock Hoffman and including Harvey Wheeler. Wheeler had been impressed by Skinner's utopian novel *Walden Two*, which had reached a circulation of more than a million copies in paperback editions and had affected the thinking of thousands of students in the campus rebellions. When Skinner's book *Beyond Freedom and Dignity* aroused new controversies and put Skinner on the cover of *Time* magazine, Wheeler thought it would be valuable to have a thorough discussion of Skinner's proposals for a benevolently planned society aired at the Center.

One of the scholars consulted by Wheeler—Max Black, a professor of philosophy at Cornell university—labeled Skinner's notions "somewhat comic" and asserted that his work had received more attention than it deserved. But Arnold Toynbee rated Skinner's latest volume "an important book," and John R. Platt, a research biophysicist at the University of Michigan, saluted it as "a masterpiece" containing "the design of a new society."

Platt felt that Skinner had submitted convincing evidence that the Skinner system of "positive reinforcements" for changing human behavior really worked. He cited experiments indicating that habits could be changed by giving immediate positive responses when initial shifts in desired directions had been noted. "This makes it easy to 'be good,' or more exactly, to 'behave well,' " Platt said.

He emphasized the fact that Skinner's reinforcement technique did not require electric shocks or brain surgery or implanted electrodes or drugs. The method simply called for a systematic provision of small rewards for each small constructive step, with each reward given quickly enough to enable teachers or managers to manipulate animals or human beings toward satisfactory behavior.

Admitting that many people were disturbed by the use of manipulation, Platt went on: "We are all manipulating each other right now, by positive or negative reinforcement, and always have been. . . . Skinner stresses that what we are always obeying is a reciprocal rule of control and counter-control: no animal or human being can shape the behavior of another by response or reinforcement without the other shaping its behavior in return by the response it gives."

Platt asserted that Skinner's emphasis on positive reinforcement could be seen "as a modern formulation of the principle of Jesus: love your enemies, and do good to those who despitefully use you." He added: "It is the fastest and surest way of changing or converting the behavior of enemies or masters, far more than hostility, which only reinforces their old behavior. . . . We have always known this in a general way, but now we see the mechanisms of the transactions and how they can be improved."

Some of Skinner's critics had called Skinner's planned society with positive reinforcements for everybody a "benevolent fascism," and one opponent had labeled it a "blue print for hell."

"It is true that this is not laissez-faire capitalism, and that it might lead to a very different type of economic system," Platt noted. "But it is surely at the opposite pole from the real fascisms of this century with their goose-stepping and bloodbaths and need of control by continuous expansion and war. . . .

"A society for survival with immediate feedback channels of protest and correction, a society that ends the long reign of punishment and retaliation, a society whose officials are subject to continuous counter-control to insure that they work for the good of everybody, a society that deliberately practices diversity and experimentation with different lifestyles . . . such a society looks to me not like a blueprint of hell but more like a blueprint of heaven from where we stand today.''

Black found Skinner's statements inconsistent and often incoherent. He described the book as a ''mélange of amateurish metaphysics, self-advertising 'technology,' and illiberal social policy,'' and termed it ''a document that is a disservice . . . to all who are seriously trying to improve the human condition.''

''The blunder of humanism, according to him, is to hold men to account for their deeds,'' Black said. ''Skinner claims that purging the 'myth' of responsibility (my description, not his) will be a step forward. . . .

''Would it be a step forward to be in a 'behavioral environment,' arranged by skillful hidden manipulators, in which the very language of responsible action had been expunged by effective conditioning? We might justifiably regard the end product as a dehumanization, in which men were no longer accorded the dignity of being treated as persons.''

Toynbee wondered how Skinner could talk about the shaping of policies by human beings—as Skinner did—when his fundamental thesis was that freedom was a delusion and that ''human beings have no power of taking the initiative; that their behavior is wholly determined by their genetic endowment and by their social setting. . . .

''It is quite credible that a person's behavior, besides being partly determined by his genetic endowment and his social setting, is also partly determined by the person himself,'' Toynbee said.

''Self-determination or self-control (the term used by Skinner) is another name for life. Every living being is a part of the Universe that has tried to separate itself from the rest of the Universe in order to erect itself into a counter-universe. The individual specimen of any species of living beings is striving to keep itself alive by exploiting the rest of the Universe for this purpose.''

Toynbee declared that heredity and environment together could not fully account for the ''great souls'' who broke with the societies in which they had been born and nurtured. He referred to the prophets of Israel and Judah, the Prophet Muhammad, Zarathustra, the Buddha, Socrates, Jesus, and St. Francis of Assisi.

Toynbee shared Skinner's feeling that mankind was living under a threat of annihilation: ''When time is short, people look for shortcuts, and the application of a technology of human behavior would be a providential shortcut to the salvaging of mankind if the methods of technology, which have worked such wonders with inanimate nature, could really be applied effectively to human nature, as Skinner holds that they could be.

''As I see it, this belief is vitiated by an inner contradiction. . . . If human freedom is truly an illusion, no human being would be free to plan and carry out the requisite biological and social 'engineering.' The blind cannot lead the blind, and a camel cannot lead a string of camels. Experience has proved that it needs a donkey to do that.

"I therefore believe that the behaviorists' objective is unattainable."

In his exchanges with the scientists, philosophers, theologians, and humanistic scholars he encountered at the Center, Dr. Skinner kept his temper and yielded little ground. A bright-eyed, energetic, quick-thinking man, courteous and calm, he insisted that his critics often did not understand what he was talking about.

Skinner was not disturbed by the fact that 80 percent of the reviews of his book had been unfavorable. In a conversation at the end of the Center sessions, Skinner said: "Critics think I want to run things, that I want to design the culture my own way. I think one of the worst reviews was published by the Chicago *Tribune*. It had a picture of a rat with my face on it. Two or three publications show me dangling marionette strings. There is a complete misunderstanding."

He said he was consoled by the warm responses he had received from young people all over the country. He said that young people knew that manipulation was inevitable in any culture, that they were being manipulated by the mass media, by the political leaders, by all the institutions in modern society.

"They know that the trick is not to free oneself from control, but to improve control," Skinner said. "That is the whole issue. The literature of freedom has supposed that man could be freed from control. The struggle for freedom has freed man from certain kinds of control, the kinds you resist—religious, governmental, economic despotisms—but it has not freed him from the kinds he cannot resist."

Skinner conceded that the last section of his book—which dealt with the design of a culture that might enable humanity to live in harmony and peace—was the weakest section, "because cultural survival is a very weak value."

"It is the only one by which we will be judged, but it is extremely hard to work with it," Skinner said. "How can you predict the contingencies of survival? No one can do that yet. I think that perhaps behavioral scientists know better than others what kinds of practices will produce behavior which will enable a culture more likely to meet the contingencies of survival. We are just facing that task."

Under the impact of criticisms in the Center dialogues, Skinner said his thinking had changed: "A number of things have emerged in a clearer form. . . . I do not think I quite understood the limitations of control and countercontrol."

Although Skinner had a friendly regard for the Center and its efforts to understand what was happening in modern society through intellectual processes, it was evidently clear from his viewpoint that such processes were largely illusionary. The Center was not attempting to do what he considered necessary—to put forward a design for a "new culture" through which humanity could survive. The Center was appealing to people who believed in "freedom" and "dignity." The fellows did not think that scientific control of human behavior was likely to occur in their time, and they were not ready to convert the Center into an "operant conditioning" laboratory.

No one at the Skinner conference was aware then of Nixon's use of manipulation to control what was happening in the 1972 political campaign. No one knew at that time that Nixon's agents were concocting a series of hidden maneuvers to destroy the candidacy of Senator Edmund Muskie and to advance the candidacy of George McGovern, who had taken the strongest position on ending the Vietnam war and was regarded by Nixon and his aides as a man Nixon could beat. The Fellows of the Center were not aware that Nixon was conducting a campaign that made a mockery of the "freedom" and "dignity" of American voters.

Ramsey Clark had expressed indignation at a Center conference—and to journalists after the conference—about the extent of government surveillance of anti-war leaders and other dissenters in American life. But Clark and others who came to the Center for meetings did not have any conception then of the lengths to which Nixon and his men were prepared to go in their determination to retain their power and to crush their "enemies."

The Center kept nearly all of its attention focused on other things. Following the January meeting with the mass media executives, the Center collaborated in a conference sponsored by the Edison Electric Institute of New York City on "Managing the Environment in the World Ahead"—a gathering arranged by William Ewald, a former Visiting Fellow. Participants included power company executives, government and foundation officials, university scientists and environmentalists.

At the end of January the Center initiated a bulletin on its current and pending activities, a four-page account of its dialogue topics, changes in personnel, development of new projects, and external affairs. It was intended to give directors, associates, and consultants a closer connection with the Center. I was given the responsibility for a section of this bulletin, describing the public impact of the Center's work.

The first bulletin listed topics to be discussed from January 31 to February 18—topics including "The Humanities," in a meeting led by Barnaby Keeney, president of the Claremont graduate school; "Confidentiality vs. People's Right to Know," based on a paper by Ashmore; "Evaluation of the Conference on Behavior Modification," with comments by the fellows and the senior staff; "Decision-Making in the Department of Defense," with David Novick, formerly of the RAND Corporation; and "The Second Development Decade," another international conference with participants from Yugoslavia, Turkey, Mexico, the Soviet Union, and the United Nations.

Other information in this bulletin included a statement that "the Center will move the dialogue to New York during the first week in May for three or four days of meetings devoted to the 'culture' project under the direction of John Cogley" and that "some of the Fellows will be in Europe for the International Dialogue Committee meeting in Vienna, and the *Pacem in Maribus* meeting in Split, Yugoslavia, prior to the New York conference." Because of these gatherings, no dialogue sessions were to be held in Santa Barbara from April 17 through May 5.

Under "Program Notes," the bulletin unveiled other activities: "Alexander Comfort, who was in residence in January, has agreed to undertake planning for a project on the changing role of professions in society. . . . *Prison Inmate Rights*: The Fellows consider the topic suggested by Leonard Opperman, an Indianadpolis attorney, important and will explore the possibilities. . . . *Public Employee Labor Relations*: The Fellows consider the obvious discrepancy between the law and actual practice concerning strikes by public employees a topic worthy of consideration." These items gave glimpses of how the fellows worked and indicated that ideas offered by people outside the Center sometimes led to meetings and projects.

In the "Personnel" section, the bulletin noted that Hugh Downs, the National Broadcasting Company commentator who had left the "Today" program, would be at the Center during February; that Laurence I. Hewes, an agricultural economist, would be a visiting fellow for four months; and that Clifton Fadiman, the editor and critic, had become a general consultant who would "participate frequently in Center dialogues in addition to his advisory role on editorial matters."

While visiting Fellows were arriving and departing, newspapers and wire services gave coverage to the dialogues and the resulting publications. Excerpts from the *Center Magazine* and *Center Report* appeared in January in the Philadelphia *Inquirer*, the Los Angeles *Times*, the St. Louis *Post-Dispatch*, the Chicago *Daily News*, the Oakland *Tribune*, the Arizona *Republic*, the Kansas City *Star*, the New York *Daily News*, and other publications in the United States and other countries.

On February 2 public affairs executives of thirty large American corporations visited the Center for the second of a series of discussions entitled "The Corporation and the Quality of Life," arranged by the Public Affairs Research Council. Three prisoners from the federal penitentiary in Lompoc met with some of the fellows and staff on February 9 to discuss a project for rehabilitation of criminals called "Operation Breakthrough," which had received consideration from members of Congress.

The fellows met on the morning of February 18 with three members of the Institute of Society, Ethics, and the Life Sciences, to discuss new perspectives on ethics and these sciences. On the mornings of February 22 and 23, they met with Harold Rosenberg, art critic for the *New Yorker* magazine, on the American-European art situation. In the afternoon of February 23 they exchanged ideas with six members of the Japanese Economic Planning Agency—a branch of the prime minister's office—who had come to the center to review their proposal to establish an official Japanese economic planning and research institute.

One of my responsibilities during my years as an officer of the Center was to give people from many backgrounds and many areas of the world opportunities to talk informally with the fellows and senior staff. These meetings—held in the afternoons, apart from the morning dialogues—fulfilled the Center's function as a common ground, a sounding board, a resource facility for many individuals and groups.

No fellow or Center staff member was required to attend any of these afternoon sessions, but most of them seemed to welcome a chance to talk easily with corporation executives, students, prisoners, Japanese economists, or any others who appeared at these times. In the months of February and March 1972, students came in busloads, often with teachers and counselors, from many parts of the country. The Center had become fairly well known on campuses, particularly for its booklets on the Vietnam War and the Tugwell model for a new American Constitution. (In later years, I heard from some of these students; many of them said their lives and careers had been affected by the Center.)

The Center's schedule was jammed in March and April. Discussion leaders in March included Charles Cooper of the Center for Regional Environmental Studies, who discussed the ecological consequences of the new technology; Dean McHenry, chancellor of the University of California at Santa Cruz and one of the scholars considered as a possible successor to Hutchins, who presented his views on California's master plan for higher education; and Leo Gabriel, an Austrian scholar and a former lecturer at the Faculty of Sciences of the University of Paris, who spoke on the symbolic significance of Angela Davis, the young black woman revolutionary.

The Center allocated much of its time to meetings on the changes in American foreign policy which Richard Nixon and Henry Kissinger were developing. It was obvious that the balances of power were shifting in the world, and the Center felt a responsibility to understand and portray what the new trends were and what the long-run effects might be.

At a convocation on foreign policy in Los Angeles on February 26, Hutchins brought the 1,500 persons there to their feet with a wave of applause when he described the "impossible" things which had occurred in his lifetime.

"I never expected to see the day when the proportion of blacks and whites in the colleges would be about the same as the proportion in the population, but this is true today," Hutchins said. "Or when discrimination based on race or sex would be outlawed. Or when a state supreme court would hold capital punishment cruel and unusual. Or when a President of the United States would visit Communist China.

"If these 'impossible' things can happen, let us hope that with clarity about our purposes, and firmness and resolution in carrying them out, we may yet help bring about a world of justice and peace."

General James M. Gavin, chairman of Arthur D. Little, Inc., a management planning organization, who had warned repeatedly that the Vietnam War and the economic policies of Johnson and Nixon would be disastrous if not reversed, told the fellows on March 28 that "a very fundamental change in values has taken place in all the societies of this earth."

"The bi-polar Cold War has come to a crashing end," Gavin said. "Five power blocs are emerging quite clearly: the European Common Market, Japan, the U.S.S.R., the U.S. and China. What is the basis of power in this kind of world? Can it be reckoned in terms of weapons? Numbers of divisions? Aircraft carrier task forces? Or is it based on economic well-being?

"In a world in which more and more nations will have weapons adequate to destroy a major portion of the human race, our strength as a people depends upon our ability to demonstrate a capacity for solving the critical problems of our society. Concurrently, we must meet the economic challenges abroad.

"In a world in which new knowledge is outpacing our capacity to understand its meaning, this depends upon maintaining a broad and generously supported technological base. If we handle these problems well, our strategic posture in the global community will be unassailable. We can then look at such problems as maintaining adequate tactical weapons systems in a new and rational perspective.

"The first objective of strategy should be to achieve our national goals without the necessity of employing tactical forces. *The measure of success of a strategy is the degree to which battle becomes unnecessary.*"

Gavin declared that he was sure that the arms race could be brought to a halt: "But on both sides there are generals and admirals who are motivated to insist on more and better arms because they have been brought up to believe that this is what their duty requires. It is up to the President and his opposite number in the Soviet Union to get those priorities straightened out."

"For about a tenth of what we are spending on military operations in Southeast Asia, we could protect the investment of American stockholders involved in Latin America, and give those governments a chance to run their own countries in their own way—the way they're going to try to run them anyway."

Gavin, a trustee of the Council for the Americas, thought that the United States had to steer "a new course in Latin America." He concluded: "John Kennedy wanted to, but his programs have gone by the boards. Now we're back where we started. The rich get richer, the poor get poorer, and that is not a situation that can go on forever."

Gavin was known and admired in many parts of the world for his intelligence and his vision. An airborne infantry general in World War II, he had later become chief of plans and of research and development for the army in the Pentagon. He had resigned in 1958, vehemently disagreeing with the "massive nuclear retaliation" policy of John Foster Dulles, then secretary of state. He had been the American ambassador to France under President Kennedy, and had written two notable books, *Crisis Now* and *War and Peace in the Space Age*.

As chairman of Arthur D. Little, Inc., he met frequently with leaders of African and Latin American countries and was often in contact with cabinet ministers and other leaders in Western Europe. He was a strong advocate of the European Common Market and favored the development of a common market for the Western Hemisphere nations.

When the directors of the Fund and the center assembled for a special meeting on May 2, General Gavin was seated as a board member and his election was warmly welcomed by Chairman Hutchins. Although Hutchins conducted the meeting with vigor, he urged the directors again to intensify the hunt for someone to succeed him as the chief executive officer of the Center. He did not mention it at the meeting, but it became clear later that Gavin was regarded as a man who had excellent qualifications for the post.

Hutchins reviewed the academic program—which had been described in detail in the bulletins sent to the directors—and announced that Lord Ritchie-Calder, professor of international relations at the University of Edinburgh, had accepted a place among the senior fellows, effective August 1. Ritchie-Calder was the ninth fellow chosen in the process of reorganization.

John Wilkinson outlined for the directors the principal themes of a month-long series of meetings he was organizing on "Revolutionary Theory and Western Civilization," to be held at the Center in July. Harvey Wheeler gave a report on the "Behavior Modification" conference with Dr. Skinner, and described the meetings on "Health Care in the Year 2000" which would be held under his direction at the end of May.

At that May meeting in New York, the directors also heard a description by John Cogley of an East-West Conference on Technology, Development and Values he had arranged at the Center in April with the cooperation of the Institute for Religion and Social Change of Honolulu. Cogley extended an invitation to all the directors to attend a symposium on "The Changing Culture" to take place in New York from May 3 to May 5.

Ashmore told the board that the Center had an obligation to hold another large convocation "on the order of *Pacem in Terris I* and *Pacem in Terris II*" to bring together the country's leading academic authorities, foreign policy experts, and government officials to examine the new conditions in the world. Senator Fulbright, Henry Kissinger, and others he had consulted in the weeks before the board meeting had assured him that the Center could make an important contribution to public understanding. He said that the money for the convocation would be raised separately from the funds being sought for the Center's regular operations.

After some discussion, the directors approved a resolution stating that the Center would sponsor a convocation on "New Directions in United States Foreign Policy," with the details to be handled by the officers and staff.

In the absence of Barnard Norris, who had been appointed to head the Center's book and audiotape program, Ashmore gave a report on the sales of textbooks and other volumes generated by the Center. He said the textbooks were doing fairly well and audiotapes were being sold in substantial numbers. He said that he and Norris—who had been the manager of the periodicals department of the University of California Press before joining the Center staff—were hoping to print some of the scholarly papers produced for Center conferences into book form, but it seemed likely a subsidy would be required for each such publication.

Gary Cadenhead, the secretary and treasurer, presented projections of expenditures and income that showed that the Center would incur a deficit of $500,000 in the 1972–73 fiscal year.

Ashmore went over the disappointing history of the Center's previous efforts to obtain an endowment. He suggested that the theme for such a drive in 1972 could be the necessity for funds to give the Center "permanence and stability."

As they had done several times before, the directors endorsed an endowment campaign. This time the amount mentioned as the target was $5 million. Hutchins was authorized to appoint a committee of directors to plan and carry through the campaign.

Fourteen directors were present when this resolution was passed. Among them was Bernard Rapoport, who had been designated (with Arnold Grant) as the cochairman of a previous endowment committee. Rapoport and Grant had found it difficult to get the directors to commit large sums of their own money to the endowment fund.

Morris Levinson expressed the hope that the board members would realize that by approving another authorization for an endowment drive they had made a personal commitment to support the campaign. Cadenhead noted in the minutes of the meeting: "The Board affirmed their acceptance of the obligation."

When Peter Tagger offered his report on membership, promotion, and development, Mrs. Laucks asked what results had been gained from the board's authorization of expenditures up to $300,000 to increase the number of Center members. Tagger assured her that the money invested in the expansion effort would be repaid within the three-year period specified in the resolution adopted by the board in 1971. He said, however, that the tests conducted with this money had led the officers of the Center to decide that it would not be profitable to attempt to increase the membership above the 100,000 level.

Future efforts would be aimed at lifting the income obtainable from the 100,000 members, Tagger said. He also reported that the J. R. Taft Corporation, which had professional staff members in New York and Washington, had been retained to aid the Center's fund raising.

When the May meeting ended, Hutchins and Ashmore tried to get the endowment effort into high gear. But they were no more successful than they had been in previous years. Rapoport, Grant, and other directors were involved in other financial problems. Parten was willing to do what he could, but he found fund raising distasteful. Harold Willens, the director who had raised more money for the Center than any other board members, had not attended the New York meeting. Willens was devoting his enormous energies to the McGovern campaign for the Democratic presidential nomination, feeling that the election of a "peace candidate" to the White House would finally bring the Vietnam War to a halt.

Several of the directors accepted John Cogley's invitation to participate in the symposium on what was occurring in the unprecedented cultural transformations of American life. Some of the statements made in these sessions startled them.

One of the participants—Garry Wills, classicist, political journalist, author of *Nixon Agonistes*—openly scoffed at the idea that the 1972 presidential election was worth the time, money, and energy devoted to it.

"None of the major changes in our society took place because of elections," Wills said. "Nobody 'voted in' the New Deal. Fiscally, Roosevelt's 1932 platform was conservative. He accused Herbert Hoover of spending too much."

Wills contended that changes occurred when a lot of people took stands on issues and compelled the politicians to introduce some of their ideas into legislative action.

"People who start out as 'freaks' generate change," Wills said. "Martin Luther King, starting the bus boycotts; the teachers and students who began the first anti-war teach-ins on Vietnam; the first woman suffragettes. Right now, changes are taking place because of the women's liberation movement. And changes are taking place on such matters as abortion and marijuana and amnesty. The way to change things, even to change the government, is to work outside the government.''

Wills went on: ''We don't have to worry about whether our electoral system can perpetuate itself. It is fed constantly by the tremendous fuels of human ambition and greed and competitiveness.

''What we should worry about is how to make the best use of the energy and ardor that are needed for social and cultural change. If you have bright, imaginative, and sensitive people around, the worst thing you can do is tell them to spend their talents and their time writing speeches for candidates.''

Five of the ten principal speakers at the ''Cultural Change'' conference were women. Cogley had long been disturbed by the small number of women participants in Center meetings. He had noted the letters from women to Mary Harvey, editor of *Center Report*, complaining about the absence of women in Center dialogues. ''How can you ignore women contributors when you look at the mess this male-dominated world is in?'' one letter writer asked. Another commented: ''Your discussants on agriculture are sixteen men, your corporation conference members were twenty-three men, your Center Associates are sixteen men, your participants on education are six men. . . . You are discriminating against women. This discrimination is as important as any of your other conference areas.''

The women who took part in the New York meeting were Mary Calderone, M.D., director of the Sex Information and Education Council of the United States; Sidney Cornelia Callahan, author of *The Illusion of Eve*; Elizabeth Hardwick, essayist, author of *A View of My Own*; Constance Baker Motley, a federal judge who had participated in the Center's conference on crime control; and Mariam Slater, anthropologist, a professor at Queens College.

Dr. Calderone presented a paper in which she insisted that ''society is changing the sexual behavior of people rather than the opposite, as many moralists appear to be professing and bewailing. The major professional groups in education, medicine, religion, nursing, librarianism, and an increasing number of others are effecting this change.''

''Course work in human sexuality is becoming part of the core curricula not only of the majority of medical schools but of teacher-training institutions, theological seminaries, nursing schools, and other professional disciplines,'' Dr. Calderone said.

Dr. Calderone took a hopeful view of humanity's future: ''Unless we fold and disappear entirely, we may be able to call this the century of human liberation, or, perhaps more fairly and realistically, the century of the struggle for human liberation because the struggle is not even close to being resolved. But many signs have pointed the way: laws for protection of workers; elimination of child labor; extension of civil rights to women and more recently to children as persons; internationalism realized by the establishment of the United Nations; ecumenicism in the religions; the race struggle; and so on.''

Michael Harrington, author of *The Other America,* another participant in the conference on cultural change, said that ''one of the great facts about our culture is the breakdown of organized religion and the disappearance of the inhibitions that religion had placed around human relationships, particularly sexual relationships and marriage. . . . I think there should be rules about sexuality. I can't define the limits very well.''

Mariam Slater, the anthropologist, thought that all rules came out of human culture and societal structures: ''I don't see any evidence for a human nature other than a capacity to be pliable in areas where people are programmed.''

''Coming more or less from a Marxist philosophic formation, I happen to believe that there is such a thing as human nature,'' Harrington said. ''I don't take a relativist attitude toward history. You can make an argument, which Friedrich Engels made, that slavery was an advance over cannibalism because putting people to work is better than eating them. But also with Engels, I would say that, objectively—that is, in terms of what man should be-—slavery, however superior to cannibalism it was, was itself wrong.''

John Cogley intervened: ''The issue now seems to be whether the new permissiveness is good or bad for our cultural future. Is it a threat to those abiding values which we would like to keep in our culture? Or does it mark a kind of cultural liberation?''

''I think we can make of it what we will,'' Mrs. Calderone said. ''We can make it good or we can make it bad.''

Sidney Cornelia Callahan remarked: ''What interests me is how do you educate the imagination? How can one form one's imagination so that one can get at the depths of feeling in sexuality, rather than look upon it simply as a matter of healthy hygiene? The question is, how can one be permissive in these matters without becoming or making them shallow?''

''Actually the people who have been most permissive in our society are the older generation,'' Dr. Calderone answered. ''We have been permissive with ourselves—'buy now, pay later.' Our kids are actually retrieving sexuality from shallowness, I think. Sure, there is a lot of trivialization in youthful sexuality, but they are moving away from the kind of trivialization we associated with the Harvard-Yale games in the 1920's, when the object was to get drunk and lay a lot of girls. The kids do not do that any more. They really don't.''

''I have found on campuses a new puritanism, or perhaps a lingering puritanism,'' Mrs. Callahan said. ''Even today, the older values associated with the ideal of chastity can be a positive help to people as they grow up. I think Erik Erikson, too, feels that permissiveness during adolescence might be more damaging to one's sense of identification than a measure of healthy repression. But who is to give the permission or do the repressing? The parents have abdicated. Who will take their place?''

Another participant, Peter Berger, a sociologist and author of *Rumor of Angels* and *Noise of Solemn Assemblies*, pointed out that there were always countermovements and countertrends to all the movements that seemed to be changing human culture. He did not think that "modernity" was an irresistible juggernaut. He recognized that the process of "modernization" had made posible the liberation of humanity from "the narrow confines of tradition, of clan and tribe, and of restrictive collective codes,'' but he added: "There has been a price to pay.''

"Do you think the counterculture is a threat to us?'' Judge Motley asked. "Or is it something good, something we ought to be happy about?''

"I find some elements in it attractive, others repulsive, and still others to which I am rather indifferent,'' Berger replied. "I am more interested in asking to what extent it will influence our society. It is clear to me that it will influence it only to a limited degree.''

Mrs. Callahan said, "I do not know why we cannot design a social situation in which we would not have to choose between individual liberty and a social or communal kind of justice.''

"Your question—what kind of liberation does one want—is crucial,'' Berger responded. "I think modernity has produced loneliness. It has isolated the individual. An important theme of our time is a nostalgia for the kind of solidarity and community that will lift this burden of loneliness from people.

"In political terms, that nostalgia can take either a reactionary or revolutionary form. The reactionary form is to look back to some alleged community of the past. The revolutionary form is to look forward to a community of the future. What the two have in common is the view that the atomized, anomic, alienated, and isolated situation of the individual is evil.

"So, what one must ask people is what do you want to be liberated from and what would you like to be when you have reached the stage of being liberated?''

Mrs. Callahan wasn't satisfied. "Why cannot we get a new form of liberation which will bring both the individual and the communal together? You say that because one does not belong to anything fully or completely, one becomes lonely. A mature person can move about in these different roles without losing his unity or integrity. . . .''

Berger said that many people like Mrs. Callahan—and others like himself—sought "community and solidarity and our real selves in the private sphere with family, friends, lovers. And we take quite a different stance vis-à-vis the public sphere.''

Mrs. Callahan did not think the distinction between private and public life could be made so sharply. She thought that people could achieve a unity between their public and private selves.

"I share your wish for compromise, for synthesis, for higher unity," Berger said. "But I am skeptical about it. I think that in reality one usually must make choices today. The ultimate question is not a scientific one. Often it is: What is more important to you, liberty or security?"

Elisabeth Borgese, who was also at the symposium rejected Berger's statement. "For me, there is no conflict. You cannot have liberty without security. Your conflict is based on a dualistic view of the individual and society which is totally outdated and can no longer be justified."

"I think the most dangerous thing about the nostalgia for solidarity and community—call it a yearning for unity if you will—is that it can move toward totalitarianism," Berger insisted.

Mrs. Callahan said: "That yearning may be a good thing."

Harvey Wheeler suggested that B. F. Skinner's "operant conditioning" might be a possible way to cope with cultural change and develop a better society.

"Operant conditioning differs from the traditional stimulus-response psychology associated with Pavlov," Wheeler said. "The Pavlovian organism was viewed as a physical machine; the Skinnerian organism is regarded as responding to its environment. According to Pavlov, a stimulus was like a force. It produced a response the way a force produces work, or power. In Skinner's analysis, by contrast, behavior is not generated by forces, it is a pattern shaped by consequences."

Wheeler noted that a Skinnerian society might resemble Mao's China in some ways: "Something similar to the group mind-changing practices pioneered in China may appear. That will obviously raise numerous issues, one of them relating to liberty."

"The atmosphere of liberty is not likely to alter as sharply as is described in *Beyond Freedom and Dignity*, but the emphasis is likely to change," Wheeler said. "The role of negative liberty—liberty conceived as freedom from restraint—is certainly not going to disappear, because one of the effects of positive reinforcement is to diminish restraints and hence expand liberty. However, it is likely that the idea of positive liberty as the freedom to do or achieve what one wants is likely to take precedence over the idea of negative liberty. In this restricted sense, the society will have moved to some extent, beyond liberty, if not dignity."

It was sometimes difficult to decide whether Wheeler was speaking seriously when he uttered some of these statements, or whether he was being whimsical or ironic. In the discussion that followed his advocacy of the Skinnerian society, the conference participants tried to see where his arguments might lead. Some of them thought that such a society might require a "new man."

On the day after the conference on cultural change was finished, five of the fellows and six of the directors participated in a one-day public convocation at the Commodore Hotel in New York—"The United States and the

World After the Cold War." More than 1000 Center members and their friends attended. The convocation, which I had organized, was covered by the press and broadcasting networks.

Acting on the assumption that the "cold war" was nearly over, the fellows and other Center speakers took the audience around the world in six hours. Norton Ginsburg, the new dean of the Center, estimated what might happen in Asia, the United States, and the Republic of China. Harvey Wheeler spoke on the Third World and the politics of revolution.

Harry Ashmore exposed the connections he had discovered between the mass media and the politics of prevarication. Fred Warner Neal, a peripatetic Center associate, prophesied on the future relations between Europe, the United States, and the Soviet Union.

General Gavin gave his views on the role of national power, reiterating much of what he had said at a dialogue in Santa Barbara. Elisabeth Borgese took the world communities as her province. Robert Hutchins condensed all the statements of the day in his brief and cogent style.

With the cold war consigned to history and the future of the United States and the world temporarily described, the fellows and staff members returned to Eucalyptus Hill.

On May 16 the topic for discussion was a paper presented by Robert Rosen, a professor of mathematics and biophysical sciences at the State University of New York at Buffalo, who was in Santa Barbara as a visiting fellow. Rosen had entitled his paper "Planning, Management, Policies and Strategies: Four Fuzzy Concepts." After the discussion, some of the staff members who were unable to keep up with Rosen's mathematical mind felt that these concepts were fuzzier than ever.

Sir Roy Harrod, a noted British economist, led a session on money and economics, two baffling subjects whose complexities seemed greater than ever after his statement and a cross-examination of his views by the fellows on May 17.

For three days—from May 22 to 24—the Center was immersed in a conference called "Social Futures Relating to Health Care in the Year 2000." This symposium, financed by the health services and mental health administration of the Department of Health, Education, and Welfare, was put together by Wheeler, who had become known as a "futurologist."

Among those Wheeler had consulted were Edward Engberg, a former fellow of the Center, then a consultant to the Twentieth Century Fund; Edmundo Flores, professor of economics, National University of Mexico; Ray W. Jackson, Science Council of Canada; Otto Kreye, Max Planck Institute, Starnberg, Germany; Raymond Klibansky, McGill University, Montreal; and others in universities, research institutes, and foundations in the United States and Europe.

Those who gathered at the Center to criticize the background papers and advance their own ideas about what American society would be like in the year 2000—and what kind of health care should be provided—included biologists, a psychiatrist, biophysicists, and "futurologists" of other types.

A new direction in the Center's fund raising occurred after consultations with staff members of the Taft Company. Brochures with the smooth touch of these professionals invited contributors to "invest" in four Special Funds, which had been formed with the hope of appealing to givers who had special interests. The Center had not been able to get big contributions for its work as a whole—aside from the bundles of Xerox stock given by Chester Carlson.

The four Special Funds were paraded for public notice in the June issue of *Center Report*. The Early Warning Fund developed the idea that the Center had been far ahead of other organizations in identifying "the emerging threats to the nation and the global ecosystem." Contributors to this Fund were told that they could enable "the Center to expand its singular role which conventional academic institutions cannot and do not carry out."

The turmoil in education was the background for the Robert M. Hutchins Educational Fund, which was to be devoted to "a continuing examination of the multi-faceted parent-teacher-establishment complex," with a search "for solutions which could meet the needs of each of the parts as well as the whole."

The Fund for Transnational Dialogue was expected to use "the Center's experience as an international bridge-builder and peacemaker," with a claim that the Center had "demonstrated the worth of unofficial contacts at a time when ordinary diplomatic channels may be frozen in areas of extreme sensitivity." The Center's "Pacem in Terris" convocations, the "Pacem in Maribus" meetings, and other international activities were cited as examples of what the Center could do.

Contributors to the fourth Fund were invited to aid the Center in three areas: underwriting special publications with a high scholarly value; enabling the Center to produce and distribute videotapes for television and use in educational institutions; and defraying the costs of Center dialogues with Center members in major cities in many parts of the country.

The formation of these four Funds did not have the beneficial results that had been sought. The Center's deficit continued to run at a rate of $60,000 to $70,000 a month, and the financial reserves continued to decline steeply. Nevertheless, the Center went on with a large program of meetings and continued to bring in Visiting Fellows and visiting speakers for dialogues in Santa Barbara.

In the May–June issue of the *Center Magazine*, the women's liberation movement—which had received little recognition at the Center when it first developed in the 1960s—was given an extensive treatment by Donald

McDonald in an 18-page article, in which he looked at the "present condition of women" and tried to measure it by the requirements of a "morality of justice."

McDonald referred to a report from HEW showing that women were discriminated against in "virtually every aspect of American life." He reviewed a vast literature of reports and studies on women's roles and relationships to men and society, and quoted the statements of many women writers, including the leaders of the feminist movement.

He concluded by saying: "The sexual life-style that youth have adopted—androgynous in many important respects, rejecting traditional sex roles and manners, equalizing relations between the sexes—this life-style already is embodying, in however attentuated and unreflective a form, and without any political and social support or enabling legislation, much of what women's liberation has constructed as an ideal. If that is true, then the stream may well become a river in our lifetime."

Responding to an invitation from the editors of the magazine, many people concerned with feminism or in the women's liberation movement commented on McDonald's article in strongly worded letters. Some of them were printed in the next issue of the magazine.

"The article missed the anger, and in doing so missed the gut force of the movement," declared Virginia Carter, president of the Los Angeles chapter of the National Organization for Women. "Feminists are furious and the fury is escalating as public discussion and the media raise women's awareness. . . .

"We need cool, charismatic feminists, thoughtful and sensitive to their sisters' needs, balancing pragmatism and feminist theory, to lead our movement."

Mary Daly, associate professor of theology at Boston College, said she had dropped the *Center Magazine* because she had found nothing in it she considered relevant "to what I consider to be the most fundamental revolution of our time, the women's revolution." Her attitude was not changed by McDonald's article.

"At this point in history we are not looking for men to speak for us," Professor Daly said. "We've had enough of that for thousands of years. . . . Mr. McDonald writes that rage can blur perceptions. We don't need this kind of paternalistic advice. The rage that women are feeling is for many the most authentic expression of self that is making possible a breakthrough to creativity."

Charlotte Klein of New York, a teacher at the New School for Social Research, thought McDonald deserved "a reverberating cheer for what I consider to be a remarkable overview and analysis. . . . It is the most thoughtful, fair, and hopeful view by a male (whose conditioning *almost* prevents objectivity) I have seen to date. . . . "

A negative reaction came from Siew-Haw Beh, coeditor of *Women and*

Film, a magazine published in Santa Monica, California, who declared that the article should have been subtitled "A Man's Way of Leading Women Backward."

"The conclusion of the article is rather loose and ambiguous," Siew-Haw Beh wrote. "Suddenly the question of youth sexual life-styles pops up. Without evidence of analysis these life-styles are seen to incorporate the sexual life-styles posited by the feminists. Yet it is common knowledge that the sexual life-styles and communal living of youth have been thoroughly larded with sexist stereotypes, often regressive, back-to-nature ones that deny women the few benefits technology has won for her."

Mary Lindenstein Walshok, assistant professor of sociology at the California State College, Fullerton, California, felt that several major topics deserved fuller treatment than McDonald had given them. She cited, for example, "the entire question of male domination of women and its historical persistence."

Sister Anita Caspary, president of the Immaculate Heart Community of Los Angeles, said that her "normal interest" in women's liberation had been heightened by her participation in a struggle "for the liberation of a specific group of women dedicated to the service of the church." A majority of the nuns belonging to the order of the Immaculate Heart of Mary had decided to make drastic changes in their community and had encountered much opposition from Cardinal McIntyre and others in the Roman Catholic church, as well as from conservative members of their own order.

"I think the emotional intensity of our struggle was a clear illustration that in the minds of many intelligent and dedicated women there were unbreakable bonds between legitimate authority and the dominant male figure," Sister Anita Said. "Contrariwise, the conflict eventually brought out the hidden potential for liberation and fulfillment in the lives of women whether in the 'religious' state or not. . . .

"I am grateful to live in an experimental community where new life-styles are welcomed for both women and men. For no form of liberation can succeed when it leaves another person more oppressed. No one is really free until all of us are free."

In addition to the space given to critics of McDonald's article on the women's movement, the editors of the *Center Magazine* gave many columns to criticisms of other articles written by senior fellows and other contributors. The allotment of much space to many viewpoints had been a policy of the magazine from its beginning in 1967.

Critical letters from readers of Center publications and listeners to Center tapes were welcomed by the fellows as signs of interest in what the fellows were thinking, but these letters had relatively little impact on the Center's program. That program continued to reflect what the fellows and their appointed associates regarded as important.

In July, while Nixon and his aides were covering up the involvement of the White House staff in the Watergate burglary and George McGovern was gathering enough delegates to capture the Democratic nomination for the presidency, the Center brought together advocates of political and social change for a month of dialogues. The month of discussions, originally focused on the subject "Revolutionary Theory and Western Civilization," explored the differences between "Evolution and Revolution."

Participants came from Israel, Czechoslovakia, Austria, Switzerland, Romania, Poland, France, and various backgrounds in the United States. Some of them were Marxists and a few of them were identified by the Center as "unabashed revolutionary activists."

Roger Garaudy, a French Marxist who had been a leader in the European effort to engage communists and Christians in open conversations, predicted that there would be a "twofold change—in religious conscience and in revolutionary conscience" in "the soul of the new culture."

"The three main pillars of this culture are information theory, aesthetics, and prospection of the future," Garaudy said. "Information theory can liberate culture from the accumulation of knowledge so as to develop in man only that which is specifically human: i.e., asking questions and deciding on the ends to be pursued. . . . The computer, doing away with the repetitive and mechanical tasks of the thought process, permits man to unfold what is specifically human in himself, i.e., creation and choice of purpose.

"Aesthetics is understood as the art and science of living and re-living through works of art specifically human acts, thanks to which, through creative work, man surpasses his past, his constraints, his alienations, even his own definition. . . .

"Prospection of the future will be more important than history, provided it avoids the pitfalls of 'futurology.' For prospection of the future differs from futurology in that the latter is fundamentally positivist. Futurology proceeds by extrapolation; it addresses itself to the question of what will happen if human intervention is disregarded. Prospection of the future, on the contrary, is concerned with the decisions we have to make in order to modify the course of events.

"An enterprise of this kind cannot bring knowledge 'from outside'; it must be a dialogue in which man, far from being treated as the object of teaching, is treated as the subject of it. Not *for* him, but *with* him and *by* him. Pedagogy and politics are one and the same: the matter in hand is a pedagogy of revolution and a revolution of pedagogy. *A socialism not based on this permanent dialogue would necessarily lead to a new dualism between the leader who makes decisions and the masses who carry them out, that is, to a new alienation and subjection.*" [Italics added.]

Wilfried Daim, an Austrian psychiatrist and commentator on religion, politics, and culture, presented a paper describing Moses as a revolutionary leader who directed the reeducation of the Jewish people during their forty years in the wilderness.

"To accomplish the revolution he was prepared to sacrifice an entire generation," Daim said. "Every revolution seems to need a like period of forty years to become established."

Richard Lichtman, a philosopher on the faculty at San Francisco State University and a former fellow of the Center, was severely critical of the contradictions in capitalism between its promises of "material well-being, equality, freedom and human fulfillment" and the actual existence of inequalities and oppression.

"American capitalism attempts domination in Vietnam today through massive brutalization," Lichtman said. "It attempts hegemony in the United States through consumer pacification and political alienation."

Michael J. Brenner, a political scientist at the University of California at San Diego, felt that the Marxists and neo-Marxists had lost touch with the realities of the modern situation. He said that John Kenneth Galbraith's view of industrial organization was more "fruitful."

"Galbraith effectively argues that political authority in the new industrial state is dispersed, fragmented, and characteristically managerial," Brenner observed. "Political officeholders are the managers of interest coalitions, who maintain a balance in representative institutions that in turn permits the managers of the technostructure to pursue the essential tasks upon which the industrial system depends. These managerial brokers do not act on behalf of any self-conscious dominant group or class capable of concerting efforts to achieve selfish ends. The technostructure is qualitatively different from any elite that has preceded it. In fact, the term 'elite' fails to get at its essential formlessness."

Brenner understood the appeal of Marxism to discontented people: "A resurrected Marxism captivates those with an acute sense of personal grievance and keen social conscience. . . . It also offers something approximating an all-encompassing intellectual system. Revolutionary doctrine, for all its distortion, claims to explain everything. Where it cannot, it substitutes moral imperatives."

Ruefully conceding that "the reformer's limited objectives are uninspiring," Brenner contended: "Public action can secure what is needed for physical and psychic survival only through reforms that industrial and technological realities permit. Anything more revolutionary would require changes of an unprecedented order and swiftness. It would require not programmatic reform but a complete transformation of consciousness." He did not think that such a transformation was likely to occur.

While the people at the Center were discussing whether elections had much significance and whether the United States was ready for fundamental reforms or ripe for revolution, the presidential campaign of 1972 revealed the deficiencies of the principal candidates and the two major political parties.

The long struggle in the Democratic party among the major candidates—Muskie, Humphrey, and McGovern—had compelled the wealthy liberals in the country to open their checkbooks again and again. When McGovern finally got the nomination, Harold Willens and others associated with the Center concentrated their fund-raising efforts on appeals for McGovern. The Center's endowment drive was unable to get up any momentum.

At the invitation of the *Los Angeles Times*, Rexford Tugwell commented on reports that McGovern and his advisers were relying on a strategy similar to that developed by Franklin D. Roosevelt in 1932: "Franklin Roosevelt was a radical, they are saying, and in what was a difficult period, 1932, he got himself elected. But to speak of President Roosevelt as a radical is actually to speak of him when he was already firmly fixed in the White House. 'Economic royalists' did not appear in his rhetoric until 1936, and by then he had firmed up the coalition that was to hold together for a generation. . . .

"Roosevelt's campaign—and this is what the McGovern people do not seem to recall—was carefully tailored to the sober advice of the professionals. . . His approach to the depression problem was to blame it all on the bankers and call for reform—weak, perhaps, but reassuring."

Tugwell was skeptical about McGovern's political wisdom: "McGovern is not likely to unseat President Nixon by using tactics which are only appropriate when power has been won. Mr. Nixon has a demonstrated capacity of defeating himself if properly provoked; he almost did it in 1968. But if Democratic Party elders—and their funds—are alienated, McGovern can only win by massive mustering of new voters. It will be a miracle if he manages to do it."

In the autumn and winter months of 1972 the Center continued to give time and attention to a broad range of topics, jumping from one theme to another day after day.

During the period between September 11 and October 6, the topics included "Compatibilities and Contradictions Between United States Interests and Those of the Africa States," with Herschelle Challenor of the Adlai Stevenson Institute; "A Proposed European Security Conference," by Silviu Brucan, former Romanian ambassador to the United States: "Civil Rights in Great Britian," by Piers von Simson of the Warburg Bank, England; and "Retrospective Futurology: A Dialogue of Civilizations," by Richard Bellman, John Wilkinson, and Ann Friedlander, anthropologist.*

On October 4 the fellows and other dialogue participants discussed a

---

*"Retrospective futurology"—as described by Bellman and Wilkinson—was an attempt to describe and discuss "possible futures" by using computers loaded with information about past civilizations and their efforts to solve fundamental problems.

paper entitled "The Necessity and Possibility of Art," by Eduard Gold-stucker, a Marxist philosopher who had been exiled from Czechoslovakia after the Russians had occupied that country in 1968. Goldstucker had been appointed a visiting fellow at the Center for a year beginning in July 1972.

Robert McClintock, associate professor of history and education at Columbia University, led a discussion on October 13 based on his paper "The Perfect Paideia: Study in a Humane Community." Herschelle Challenor, a black woman scholar who had made a favorable impression on the fellows, returned again on October 17, with a discussion entitled "The Influence of Black Americans on United States Foreign Policy Toward Africa." On the next day, Richard Bellman initiated "Large Systems and Human Values."

Two days were given in the third week of October for dialogues on chapters of a book by Dennis Pirages of the Stanford department of biological sciences, entitled *Ark II: Social Institutions and Human Survival*. These sessions were followed by discussions with Bertrand de Jouvenel, the French economist and philosopher, on the subject "Interpretations of Our Times."

Jean Francois Revel, another French philosopher and a journalist who had become internationally known through a book called *Neither Marx nor Jesus*, presented "How Intellectual Fashions Operate" at the morning meeting on November 3. Since the Center itself was susceptible to intellectual fashions, Revel's paper stirred a stormy discussion.

From November 6 to 8, Elisabeth Borgese chaired a conference on the development of world communities, with participants from Italy, Nigeria, the United Nations, and several American universities. One of the speakers at this gathering, Wendell Mordy, a meteorologist and director of the sea grant program at the University of Miami, was asked to become a visiting fellow for the year beginning on January 1, 1973.

Two other visiting fellows had joined in the dialogues in October— Thomas Cronin, a political scientist from the Brookings Institution, who was coauthor and editor of *The Presidential Advisory System*, and Ichak Adizes of Israel, an economist who had been a faculty member at the graduate school of business administration of the University of California at Los Angeles. (Adizes had participated in the Center's conference on self-management.)

Meanwhile, papers presented in earlier Center dialogues and conferences were quoted or reprinted in various publications. A commentary by Robert Hutchins, "The Nixon Court and the Bill of Rights," was syndicated by the Los Angeles *Times* in 350 newspapers in forty-five countries. The Chicago Tribune *Sunday Magazine* published excerpts from an article by Bernard Weissbourd, a Center director, advocating the formation of satellite communities to solve urban problems. An article by Eduard Goldstucker, "Tanks Can't Make Socialism Succeed: Better Conditions Can," was reprinted in the *International Herald Tribune* and in *L'Express* in Paris. John Cogley's article "Ideological Crusades" appeared in the *New York Times*, and *Le Monde Diplomatique* carried an article by George McT. Kahin, a Center visiting fellow, on conditions in Southeast Asia.

UNICEF's information officer asked for 1000 reprints of Donald McDonald's article "The Liberation of Women" for use in a teacher's kit on the women's movement. A feature story on the Center by Jack Fox, a United Press writer, appeared in many newspapers, including the Houston *Post*, the Atlanta *Constitution*, the Arizona *Republic*, and the Chicago *Tribune*. The *Tribune's* headline, describing the Center, was "Man's Warning System."

The Associated Press, United Press International, and a number of broadcasting stations interviewed Harry Ashmore for his comments on the proposed settlement of the Vietnam War outlined by Kissinger and Nixon.

In addition, articles referring to Center-generated ideas or activities were printed in the Hartford *Courant*, Denver *Post*, Seattle *Daily Times*, Salt Lake *Tribune*, San Diego *Union*, Fort Worth *Star-Telegram*, Cleveland *Plain Dealer*, Boston *Globe*, and other newspapers in all parts of the country. The Center was in the news almost as frequently as the Fund for the Republic had been in the days when it was under attack by the House Un-American Activities Committee.

On October 23 the *New York Times* declared in an editorial, "The 'Sick' Foundations," that the most successful programs of the Ford Foundation in its early years had emanated from the Fund for the Republic and the Fund for the Advancement of Education. The *Times* deplored the extreme caution shown by many foundations in the 1960s and 1970s.

The *Times* editorial was based on a Twentieth Century Fund study of the thirty-three largest foundations by Waldemar Nielsen, a former staff member of the Ford Foundation. The *Times* pointed out: "At the very heart of Mr. Nielsen's analysis is the question how foundations can be expected to suggest and support unconventional solutions to controversial social, political and economic problems so long as they remain as close as they currently are to the established power structure. One of the consequences of inbreeding between government, corporate and foundation leadership is that many foundations, instead of being in the vanguard of experimentation and change, rely heavily on a feedback from the essentially conservative 'establishment.' "

Although the *Times* editorial was read with appreciation by directors of the Center—who were supplied with excerpts from it—it did not stimulate the directors into activity on the Center's endowment needs. In the months after the May meeting of the board, one board member had pledged $50,000 for the endowment fund and paid in $25,000. No other pledges or contributions had been made.

Hutchins had spoken or written to many of the board members about getting the endowment campaign into motion in the autumn of 1972 and had received negative responses. The stock market had slumped, the huge expenditures for the Vietnam War had created new economic uncertainties, and prospective donors had been engaged in the effort to defeat Nixon. The directors were not ready to contribute themselves or to try to persuade their wealthy friends to endow the Center.

When the directors assembled in Santa Barbara for their annual meeting on November 17, most of them were depressed by Nixon's electoral triumph but hopeful that the Vietnam struggle might be nearly over. Some of them seemed prepared to help the Center emerge from its financial quagmire.

The predicament of the Center seemed to be as dangerous as it had been in May. The Center's prestige appeared to be high, its publications were in demand, its tapes were being used, its ideas were circulated in the media, but the number of members had leveled off and the flow of contributions had dropped.

The Center severed its connection with the Taft organization. In a report sent to the board before its meeting, Ashmore said: "The effort to step up fund-raising through conventional organizational techniques has attracted no more effective support than did the endowment campaign. We have, therefore, reduced our expenditure for professional fund-raising activities in New York by one-half, and curtailed activity in the East accordingly. . . ."

Despite the reluctance often expressed by the directors and officers about government money and conventional foundation grants, Ashmore informed the board: "In an effort to offset our inability to increase income from contributions, we have launched a new effort to secure foundation or government grants to support specific Center projects. With the active collaboration of Dean Ginsburg and the senior fellows these possibilities are being explored in Washington and elsewhere. While the response is considered encouraging it has not yet produced tangible results."

Gary Cadenhead, the secretary and treasurer, noted that the Center's deficit was running at $70,000 a month in the first four months of the current fiscal year.

Cadenhead indicated that the net income from the membership program had been only $32,000 rather than the $420,000 that had been anticipated. The amount received from membership fees had been $1,176,000 rather than the expected $1,400,000. He noted: "Since the membership expansion drive did not reach the targeted amount, the auditors decided that the costs associated with the expansion campaign should all be written off during the fiscal year. The total written off amounted to $188,000."

The Center had benefited, however, from the receipt of $1,482,976 from the Carlson estate, rather than the $800,000 which had been expected.

This was due primarily to increases in the price of Xerox stock received from the estate. The Carlson bequest constituted most of the Center's cash reserves.

The drop in membership income had been largely due to the fact that the Center had postponed its membership mailings until after the election, Peter Tagger explained in a statement provided to the board. The mails had been clogged with fund-raising appeals sent out by political candidates.

"However, we are experiencing a slight increase in our renewal rate, and in the average contribution from old members, which was $16.75 last year and has gone to $17.58 this year," Tagger said.

Tagger declared that sales of Center books and tapes had increased 50 percent in the first three months of the new fiscal year, compared with a similar period in the previous year. He felt that the publication of the Center's first complete catalogue of printed materials should stimulate "sales of past and present publications."

This catalogue, containing the names of hundreds of leaders who had participated in Center meetings and conferences, and the titles of books and articles ranging from *ABM: Yes or No*? to "Youth Demands the Heroic," covered the thirteen years from the Center's founding in September 1959 to the autumn of 1972. Every major question that had concerned the thinking people of the world in those years appeared in the Center catalogue. The answers to those questions had not been found, but the catalogue was evidence of the Center's determination and ability to involve many significant people from many nations in the quest for clarification and elightenment.

At the November board meeting three new directors were unanimously elected on the recommendation of the nominating committee headed by J. R. Parten. The directors were Blair Clark, a former vice president of the CBS news division and a former associate publisher of the New York *Post*; James C. Downs, Jr., a leader in the real estate field in Chicago; and W. Price Laughlin, chairman of the Saga Corporation and chairman of the board of regents of Gonzaga University.

At the request of Mrs. Laucks, the minutes of the May 2 meeting in New York were amended to show that Mrs. Laucks had made a strong recommendation for the addition of more qualified women to the Center's academic and executive staffs. She had been backed in this recommendation by other board members.

Hutchins asked all members of the board to understand his desire to be relieved of his administrative duties at the earliest possible date. Ashmore assured the board again that the administration of the Center could be reshaped in any way that met the wishes of the board and requirements of a prospective candidate for Hutchins' job as the chief executive officer. He declared that he would cooperate in any such reorganization.

Morris Levinson was appointed chairman of the executive committee. Arnold Grant and Bernard Rapoport were continued as cochairmen of the endowment committee, and Parten agreed to continue as chairman of the committee on organization with responsibility for finding a successor to Hutchins as soon as possible.

Norton Ginsburg presented a description of the Center's far-flung academic program, calling it "The coordinated summation of the interests of the various Senior Fellows," and stimulating a question from Levinson, who wondered whether the program should reflect the interests of the Fellows or whether it more properly should be concerned with the preservation of democratic institutions. Ginsburg said that the Fellows were by definition dedicated to the preservation of such institutions.

Levinson insisted that the intrinsic importance of the issues which had to be studied should be regarded as more important than "the interests" of the Fellows. Ginsburg agreed.

Cadenhead made another plea for an immediate initiation of the endowment drive. He stressed his alarm at the depletion of the Center's reserves. He made it clear that the delay of the directors in providing an endowment could be fatal to the Center and declared that an additional $2.5 million if raised quickly, would give sufficient income to endow the Center's operations at its current rate of spending.

The directors nodded their heads, but no one opened a checkbook at this session. No one announced that a pledge for a large contribution would be forthcoming soon. The meeting ended with the Center still in deep financial trouble.

At a dinner on the closing night of the board meeting—a dinner attended by the directors, the fellows, and the founding members—Ramsey Clark described what had happened in Indochina under Nixon: "Four million tons of explosives dropped while we withdrew the troops. That exceeds the body weight of all the human beings who live in that little corner of the earth. . . . That exceeds the violence unleashed from the air by all of the nations involved in World War II and Korea combined."

Clark had accepted Kissinger's statement just before the national election that "peace is at hand." He had gone on: "The capacity of force and violence to destroy is today so great that other ways have to be tried."

But a few weeks later there was another breakdown in the negotiations with the North Vietnamese. Angered by their recalcitrance, Nixon ordered a punishing bombardment of Hanoi and other North Vietnamese cities, with a hundred B-52 bombers hurling thousands of tons of explosives on power plants, roads, warehouses, bridges, railways, shipyards, factories, and barracks. Schools and hospitals were blown to pieces; many civilians were killed, including hundreds of children.

At the Center in balmy Santa Barbara during that December, the fellows shuddered at the world's condition but went on with their morning meetings. John Wilkinson, who had mournfully noted in the October issue of *Center Report* that many voters and nonvoters had perceived no vital differences between Nixon and McGovern, made no public comments on the bombings.

The topics of December ranged from "The International Economic Order"—a discussion led by James Howe, senior fellow of the Overseas Development Council—to "Responsibilities of Scientists," a paper by Jeremy Stone, director of the Federation of American Scientists.

While the B-52s rained fire and death upon the North Vietnamese, civilized voices went on talking about the future of humanity at the green table in the conference room, with sunlight pouring through the windows and the blue Pacific sparkling below.

The world community, for which Clark and Hutchins and others at the Center yearned, seemed very far away, hidden even from the sight of the wisest people Hutchins had been able to gather on Eucalyptus Hill.

27

*Alex Comfort joins the Center;
the Center sees threats to
freedom of speech, an energy
crisis, monetary chaos, crime
rising, the world in disorder;
and a successor to
Hutchins is chosen at last*

THE GUNS IN VIETNAM stopped firing in January 1973, and Richard Nixon appeared on television to claim the credit, saying that an agreement had been initialed in Paris to bring "peace with honor in Vietnam and Southeast Asia." He announced the pact on January 23, one day after Lyndon Johnson had died in Texas, a bitter and frustrated man. The truce concocted by Henry Kissinger and North Vietnam's chief negotiator, Le Duc Tho, was not the kind of pact Johnson had sent half a million American troops into Vietnam to obtain. But Nixon and Kissinger thought it was the best deal they could get, and they pushed President Thieu of South Vietnam into taking it, although Thieu wasn't sure that it would guarantee a stable peace.

The Vietnam truce did not allay the anxiety in the air, particularly the anxiety about Nixon and his men. That anxiety—and a strong belief that Nixon was still at war with the mass media in the United States—brought leaders of the broadcasting industry to the Center in the last two days of January 1973 to discuss what they regarded as the persistent perils to the First Amendment and the legal protections for free speech and critical comments.

William Benton of the Encyclopaedia Britannica provided the money to bring together executives from the major broadcasting networks, two former chairmen of the FCC, Eric Sevareid, the newly elected chairman of the National News Council, and others concerned. Many of the participants were alarmed by statements made by Kevin Phillips, a columnist close to the Nixon administration.

"The key to the growing feud between the Nixon administration and the news media may lie in legal and economic history," Phillips had asserted. "Quite simply: Is the First Amendment to the United States Constitution obsolescent? My own feeling is yes, the Amendment is obsolescent and therefore cannot cope with Big Media power. This invites—and even obliges—the government to move in."

Antonin Scalia, former general counsel in the White House office of Telecommunications Policy, represented the views of the Nixon regime at the conference. He pointed to a fundamental dilemma in the Federal Communications Act under which broadcasters were regulated.

"It says that the license shall be awarded on the basis of the public interest, convenience, and necessity," Scalia noted. "It also says that nothing in the Act is to confer the power of censorship upon the Federal Communications Commission. Well, there is an inherent contradiction in these provisions. How is one to determine who is the best licensee unless he looks at program content?"

Scalia argued that an adversary relationship had to exist between the government and the communications media. He thought that editors and broadcasters had been too upset by Vice President Spiro Agnew's jabs at the media: "The press, to my mind, is being excessively thin-skinned when it takes the kind of umbrage that it did by Vice President Agnew's comments. I think the press ought to keep whacking at the government whenever it thinks it's wrong. But government officials ought to be able to come back and say so when they think the press is wrong, or is being irresponsible."

Eric Sevareid was troubled by the statements of Clay T. Whitehead, director of President Nixon's Office of Telecommunications Policy, who had asserted that local station owners and managers had to take more responsibility for the contents of news and public affairs programs presented by the networks. Whitehead had asked: "Who else but management can or should correct so-called professionals who confuse sensationalism with sense and who dispense elitist gossip in the guise of news analysis?"

"I think that in simple, practical terms the local stations would be encouraged to break up network programs as such, and make us over into an A.P. or U.P.I. news service," Sevareid said. "So the local station can throw out me or some other fellow, put in somebody of its own choice, put its own thing together, sell it, maybe make more money that way. Well, it would be different. I am sure we couldn't afford to do a lot of tough, expensive investigating reporting if acceptance by the local stations was very, very speculative. I think that is really what the Nixon administration would like to see happen."

The conference on broadcasting and the First Amendment received considerable coverage in the news media, with some attention being given to Harry Ashmore's statement that President Nixon was able to "exploit an evident backlash of public opinion against a decade of radical rhetoric and confrontation politics."

"The polarization produced by the unrestrained polemics of the young, the racial minorities, and the assorted 'liberation' movements predictably has produced a political division that leaves a substantial majority not only committed against sudden and drastic change, but deeply resentful of the minority's strident attack upon its morality—and of the media which have borne it home," Ashmore said. He did not raise the question of whether Nixon sought to intimidate the media to prevent deeper investigations of the Watergate burglary and other scandals.

After the communications conference ended, the Center reverted to its pattern of shifting rapidly from one topic to another. In February, Eduard Goldstucker presented a paper, "The Young in the 30's and 60's," John Wilkinson and Lafti Zadeh, a mathematician, talked about "The Structure of Language," Laurence Hewes spoke on "Agricultural Development and the Environment," and Elisabeth Borgese discussed the agenda for a conference on "Energy Policies and the International System," which she wanted to hold in India.

The Center's schedule did not often reflect the economic storms that were hitting the world and the United States. Nixon had relaxed the wage and price controls he had installed in 1971, and wholesale prices of all goods began to soar at an annual rate of more than 20 percent. The stock market, after reaching a peak in January, sank steeply and steadily. The rise in inflation and unemployment in many countries led one economist—Irving Friedman of the World Bank—to refer to the imminence of "a world-wide disaster."

When the Fund's directors arrived in Houston for a special meeting on March 2, they had before them a report from Dean Ginsburg expressing general satisfaction with the Center's academic program. They had also received reports from Harry Ashmore and Gary Cadenhead indicating that the Center's financial status had continued "to erode."

Ginsburg took note of what he called the "heterogeneity" of the speakers and papers presented in the Center's dialogues, and he soothed the board by saying in his report that the "heterogeneity" was "more apparent than real."

"Most of the topics presented can be related to the major thematic interests of the Center as reflected in the activities of the Senior Fellows and to some extent in the Visiting Fellows," Ginsburg insisted. "Apart from these thematic considerations, a number of the individuals invited to the Center for short visits are candidates for longer-term association with the Center. . . . The topics to which they address themselves may not fit the broad themes that characterize the Center's program as closely as in other cases, but this may be regarded as a healthy attempt to add a variety to the program on the one hand and on the other to assist in the continuing evaluation of the relevance and significance of the established programmatic interests at the Center.''

The compulsions of the Center's perpetual search for money were evident in Ginsburg's statements. He reminded the board that financing was being sought or had been promised for most of the projects and conferences he had described. The Center had operated for a long time without federal money, but now it was eager to get grants from the National Science Foundation and other federally supported agencies.

With evident satisfaction, Ginsburg informed the directors that the science foundation had made "a preliminary commitment to partial financing of the energy project" and had shown an encouraging interest in the education study under Hutchins and Schwab, and in Harvey Wheeler's proposal for an analysis of "operant-conditioning as a social technology."

"Whether or not funds are made available through these applications or others, it seems clear that the current Center policy of attempting to seek outside support for individual conferences and projects is wise," Ginsburg concluded. "But it also means problems. One of the difficulties with seeking financial support from foundations and even individuals is the need for a considerable lead-time in order to prepare proposals, submit them, obtain reactions to them, and frequently resubmit them."

He was candid about the negative effects of such requirements: "Not only does this mean constraints on spontaneity, but also the time involved frequently takes the edge off the immediacy with which the Center can act and lessens the comparative advantage the Center has over other institutions in anticipating important problems and issues. It also diverts the energies of the fellows from what they do best to entrepreneurial and managerial activities that they are bound to do less well."

Ginsburg made it plain that no acceptable alternative was in sight, as long as the Center suffered from recurrent shortages of funds. He did not say so, but it was fairly obvious that he hoped the Center's directors would stir themselves to provide the Center with the substantial endowment it needed for full independence.

The Dean's report did not seem to have any galvanizing effect on the directors. Most of them regarded the Center's academic program with respect, but they were not in any hurry to support it with their own bank accounts. Few of them felt any personal responsibility for the Center's survival. J. R. Parten, James Douglas, Frances McAllister, Morris Levinson and Bernard Weissbourd were among the exceptional staunch supporters.

"Our efforts to increase the Center's income during the first half of the fiscal year have been unsuccessful," Harry Ashmore admitted sadly. "Our financial position has continued to erode. . . .

"Although it is impossible at this stage of the mailing cycle to accurately project the result of this year's membership (direct mail) effort, it appears that the net return will be below projections. For the first time since we initiated the membership program we have been unable to increase or maintain the membership by direct mail solicitation."

A membership total of around 90,000 to 100,000 people seemed to be the ceiling for the Center. Ashmore said that the possibilities of finding new mailing lists that would return new memberships "at a rate sufficient to offset costs of solicitation and conversion" had been exhausted.

Ashmore did not offer any explanations for the blockage encountered by the membership program. It seemed likely to John Cogley and other Center fellows, however, that there was a definite limit on the number of persons interested in the articles and excerpts from dialogues on complicated subjects that appeared in the *Center Magazine* and *Center Report*. The Center could not compete with the Common Cause organization headed by John Gardner: Common Cause was a lobbying group that stimulated hundreds of thousands of "activist" citizens who sought to reform Congress and reach other specific goals.

"The area of greatest concern is development," Ashmore said. "Our total income from gifts in excess of $500 is now projected at only $247,000, a reduction of $46,000 over actual income in the last fiscal year." He called the board's attention to the fact that "this decline corresponds almost exactly to the decline in total gifts from the Board of Directors from calendar 1971 to calendar 1972."

The most generous donors on the board in 1971 had been Jubal Parten, Paul Newman, Morris Levinson, and Frances McAllister, with Parten's gifts considerably larger than those made by the others. Altogether, however, these four directors accounted for more than half of the substantial gifts received by the Fund in that year from board members. Mrs. McAllister, Joseph Drown, Parten, and Bernard Weissbourd were the principal givers in 1972. Paul Newman, who had given $30,000 in 1971, gave nothing in 1972.

At the Houston board meeting in March of 1973—it was held in Houston because the Texas directors were then the most enthusiastic supporters of the Fund—Hutchins stressed two themes: the necessity for a new chairman and the necessity of bringing in more money to keep the Center alive. He reiterated his satisfaction with the academic program and the other activities of the Center, and regretfully said that there was "no tangible progress" toward finding his successor.

The idea of the endowment fund appeared once more. Arnold Grant, cochairman of the Endowment Committee, proposed that the board establish the Robert M. Hutchins Endowment Fund, with the directors to contribute $2.5 million and to raise an additional $2.5 million from other donors.

Grant's proposal—a variation on a proposal that had been offered before—was endorsed by the directors present at the Sheraton-Lincoln Hotel in Houston. Those who were there included Harry Ashmore, Fagan Dickson, James Douglas, Grant, Mr. and Mrs. Hutchins, Eulah Laucks, J. Howard Marshall, Parten, and Bernard Rapoport. It was agreed that Grant and Rapoport would meet with all members of the board before the May meeting in Santa Barbara and would give "the results of their canvass" at that gathering.

After that action had been taken in the executive session—and had been duly recorded in the minutes—Norton Ginsburg, Peter Tagger, and I were invited to join the directors in an open session.

Ginsburg reviewed the report he had previously submitted to the board, declared that the Center had an outstanding group of senior fellows, expressed happiness that Gunnar and Alva Myrdal had consented to become visiting fellows, and voiced delight in the apparent willingness of Alexander Comfort to accept an appointment as the tenth senior fellow.

Ginsburg had given a rhapsodic description of Comfort in his memorandum to the board: "Alex Comfort is an Honorary Research Associate, the Department of Zoology, and Director of Research in Gerontology at University College, London. He is probably the world's most distinguished gerontologist. He is a medical doctor as well as a biologist. Moreover, he is a distinguished poet, playwright, and novelist. . . . His presence at the Center should substantially strengthen the science element among the Senior Fellows; and his humanistic inclinations and talents will help provide that kind of interdisciplinary bridge which is so characteristic of the Senior Fellows already in residence."

The Center's dean made no mention of the fact that Comfort had written (or put together) a vividly illustrated, enormously popular book called *The Joy of Sex*. He said nothing about the possibility that the Center would receive a percentage of the royalties from this sex book—royalties that would cover Comfort's proposed salary of $28,000 a year and provide additional thousands of dollars annually to the Center.

Eulah Laucks was a little uneasy about the appointment of Comfort. Gary Cadenhead noted in the minutes of this meeting: "Some questions were raised about the suitability of Alex Comfort's appointment. . . . But Board members raised the question as to whether the Board should approve appointments of Senior Fellows, or whether this should be left to the judgment of the Fellows." After some discussion the directors decided unanimously that the "function of the Board was not to approve or disapprove the selection of individual Senior Fellows. Also, the Board agreed that the Center could not come to a halt, but should maintain its present program in general outline."

Cadenhead then advised the directors that appointing another senior fellow would increase the fixed costs of the Center by "at least $50,000 per year, and must therefore be considered in terms of increasing fixed costs in the face of the prospective deficit." Ginsburg and Ashmore swiftly assured the directors that costs "in other areas could be reduced" and declared that "adding Mr. Comfort as a Senior Fellow would not necessarily increase the overall cost of the academic program."

Hutchins strongly endorsed the appointment of Comfort—without mentioning the employment agreement to be offered to Comfort—and said that he would report the board's concern to the whole group of senior fellows.

On March 3, the day after the board meeting, several of the directors and six of the senior fellows participated in a Center convocation in Houston, "Changing Social Values and Priorities: Where Are We Heading?" Many of the participants wondered where the world's monetary system was heading. Foreign exchange markets in London, Tokyo, and other cities had closed down on March 2, and currencies fluctuated from day to day. When the markets reopened, all of the currencies of Western European nations were permitted to "float" by their governments, with the dollar drifting downward.

Ronald Segal, a visiting fellow who happened to be writing a book about the world's monetary chaos, led a dialogue at the Center on March 7, based on his paper entitled "A Matter of Money and Inflation." He did not think the dollar would regain its old strength unless the American government took drastic steps to curb inflation and check federal spending, but he did not believe Nixon's government would take such steps.

The Center did not allow the monetary crisis to interfere with its schedule. On March 19 and 20, professors from the University of Chicago, Stanford, and the University of California—as well as a teacher from a Chicago public school and F. Champion Ward, program adviser to the Ford Foundation—met with Hutchins, Joseph Schwab, and other fellows to consider a question Hutchins regarded as more important than money: the future of public education in America.

For Hutchins, education was always a painful subject. He had been trying for nearly fifty years to get his fellow citizens to build an educational system that would teach people to think. He felt that many citizens did not know why the public schools existed.

"The political community should be required to justify the prolonged detention of its citizens in an educational system," Hutchins said, when he announced that the Center would launch "a major enquiry" into education. "We need to answer the question whether public education is any longer useful. If so, on what terms? If not, what is the alternative?"

He asked the participants to consider whether the primary concern of education should "be the creation of a political community" or whether the public school should "concern itself as well with the development of a wide range of human potentialities." He also urged them to dig into the educational responsibilities of other organizations: the church, the family, the professions, industry, and new institutions that might be created.

The deficiencies of American political leaders in confronting economic and political problems—made evident by Nixon's floundering and the resignations of his principal lieutenants—gave some citizens a deeper appreciation of the Center's attempts at long-range thinking. William Matson Roth, addressing a thousand persons at a Center convocation on "Changing Social Values" in San Francisco on April 21, said he regretted that he had resigned from the Center's board.

"I resigned, with some impatience, because I thought that the continuing dialogue enjoyed by its Fellows could not justify the expense," Roth confessed. "Of course, I was entirely wrong. How poor and thin a society of such wealth would be if it could not affort quiet pockets of contemplation! . . . In this era of massive simplifications, dialogue that refuses to compress the actual into the isolated categories of political rhetoric is to be cherished."

Roth did not, however, rescue the Center from its financial difficulties.

When the directors assembled in Santa Barbara on May 4 for another special session, the reports presented to them indicated that the budget had been reduced, but there remained a projected deficit of $548,000 for the 1973–74 fiscal year.

Ashmore did not think that budget reductions could be carried further "without raising questions of program policy." He declared: "We are making no new appointment of Senior or Visiting Fellows beyond our present commitments. . . . We have re-examined all costs in the Membership-Publication program, and made reductions wherever possible. Our projections for direct mail expenditure have been cut back to the point where testing indicates that any further reduction would result in an actual dollar loss."

The Center had planned to hold a third "Pacem in Terris" convocation from May 7 to 9 in Washington, but difficulties in completing the arrangements had caused its postponement to October 8 to 11. Ashmore told the board that the plans had been carried forward, and introduced Sander Vanocur, a television correspondent with wide experience, who had been hired to serve as a consultant. Ashmore asked for suggestions and assistance in finding donors for the "Pacem in Terris III" expenses.

Gary Cadenhead brought up the endowment fund that had been approved at the Houston meeting, and said that the $5 million projected for such a fund would eliminate the Center's deficit and provide sufficient income to maintain its current level of operations. There were no indications that any progress had been made in obtaining this fund.

Chairman Hutchins announced to the directors that Harold Willens, at his urging, had consented to be the chairman of the "Pacem in Terris" convocation and would take charge of raising the money for it. Hutchins said that the money would be "sought from sources not considered available for the endowment drive to be undertaken by Arnold Grant and Bernard Rapoport."

Rapoport then looked around at the board members who were present in the Center's conference room—Ashmore, Blair Clark, Patrick Crowley, Grant, Mr. and Mrs. Hutchins, Eulah Laucks, Morris Levinson, Frances McAllister, Seniel Ostrow, Parten, Rapoport, and Willens—and called for pledges to the endowment fund. When it was evident that no one seemed prepared to make a pledge at that moment, it was agreed that possible pledges would be discussed privately with the directors.

After the May board meeting, the fellows resumed their dialogues. On May 14, a professor from Sweden, Jorgen Westerstahl, presented a paper entitled "Representative Democracy—Conceptual Problems Encountered in a Study of Local Swedish Government"; on May 15, Leo Mates, professor of international relations at the Wharton School, gave a statement called "Non-Alignment in a Multi-Nodal World"; and on May 17 Clark Kerr, chairman of the Carnegie Commission on Higher Education, summarized the commission's report in "The Purposes and Performance of Higher Education in the United States."

Robert Rosen, a Center Associate and professor at the State University of New York, led a discussion of his paper, "The Identification of User-Groups for Socio-Ecological Control Strategies," on May 23. From May 24 to 26 the fellows were absorbed in discussions of a new book by Jonas Salk entitled *The Survival of the Wisest*. Participants included Dr. Salk; Richard Bellman, Center associate and professor at USC; James Danielli, professor of theoretical biology at the State University of New York; Martin Grotjahn, psychoanalyst, and Professor Rosen.

While the fellows were considering "The Survival of the Wisest" and other topics, Nixon was trying to bolster confidence in his regime, and governments in many countries were striving to beat back the flood of inflation. Nixon announced a major reorganization of his administration on May 10, naming a former CIA director, James Schlesinger, as secretary of defense, and John Connally, former secretary of the treasury, as a special adviser to the president. On the same day, however, his former attorney general, John Mitchell, and his former secretary of commerce, Maurice Stans, were indicted by a grand jury in New York on charges growing out of financier Robert Vesco's secret contribution to Nixon's 1972 campaign. Vesco fled to Costa Rica.

United States Senate select committee headed by Senator Sam Ervin opened public hearings on the Watergate affair on May 17, and the next day one of the Watergate conspirators—James McCord—testified that a former White House aide had tendered him executive clemency for his silence on the possible involvement of high officials in the case. Four days later Nixon released another statement, admitting that he had tried to limit the federal investigation into the Watergate matter because of "national security," but adding that his assistants had gone into a "cover-up" exceeding his instructions. Nixon's statement raised new questions and did not satisfy his critics.

Nixon's attempts to halt inflation were no more successful than his attempts to convince his fellow citizens that he hadn't done anything very wrong in connection with the Watergate burglary. Prices kept climbing, the dollar sank on world markets, and the American stock market plunged lower. Although the anti-inflationary policies of other Western countries were not more effective than Nixon's, he was blamed in Europe and Japan for veering erratically from "controls" to "no controls" and back to "limited controls" again. His preoccupation with the Watergate scandal tarnished his leadership efforts in every field.

It seemed to some of the Center fellows that the United States was sinking into a political and economic crisis that might be worse than the economic collapse in 1932—and there were no leaders on the horizon with the abilities of Franklin Roosevelt and his advisers. The fellows kept on with their projects, seeing nothing else that could be done. They hoped that ideas generated at the Center would be helpful to future leaders, but they did not think it was their responsibility to solve the crises of 1973.

On June 7 the Fellows exchanged ideas with Russell Peterson, former Dupont Company executive, former governor of Delaware, an advocate of environmental protection and head of the Third Century Commission, a group of prominent citizens interested in what the United States should become in its third century of independence. Peterson, who was under consideration as a possible successor to Hutchins, demonstrated that he had a broad range of knowledge.

In the third week of June, several of the Fellows attended the fourth *Pacem in Maribus* convocation organized by Elisabeth Borgese and convened on the island of Malta. From June 24 to June 26, Hutchins and Harvey Wheeler were in Chicago for meetings with Rick Carlson, a Center Visiting Fellow, and with Norval Morris and other staff members of the Center for Studies in Criminal Justice at the University of Chicago.

At the Chicago conference Carlson made a statement which received widespread attention when it was published later in the *Center Magazine*: "If everyone imprisoned in the United States were released tomorrow, the impact on the rate of crime would be negligible. The simple reason for this is that our correctional system has very little to do with the control of criminal behavior. A solution to the problem of corrections, then, will not solve the problem of crime."

"Most crimes go undetected," Carlson observed. "For many people, crime is the easiest way to make a living, and a jail sentence is looked upon as an occupational risk. . . In such cases, criminal conduct can become routinized and perhaps as stultifying as an assembly-line job. . .

Carlson said that many methods designed to "rehabilitate" or "correct" criminals had been tried, but the rate of relapse into crime—rearrest and conviction—remained at roughly fifty per cent. Although law enforcement systems were not efficient or effective, he noted that the number of people employed in these systems continued to grow: "*In economic terms alone, then, the country cannot afford to eliminate crime.* Perhaps it is not just whimsical to suggest that there is a supply demand function at work in criminal justice."

Carlson estimated that only twelve per cent of the crimes committed in the United States were "processed" by law enforcement units and added: "For such crimes as rape and burglary, the rate of clearance is even lower, somewhere around two or three per cent." Carlson did not refer directly to the Watergate burglary, in which an official of the Committee to Re-Elect the President had been caught, but he did cite a survey which depicted "an alarming number of instances in which the government itself has broken the law."

"Can a society expect to deal effectively with crime or expect its citizens to be law-abiding when the government ignores the law?" Carlson asked.

One of the citizens troubled by this question was John Dean, formerly a special counsellor to President Nixon. On June 25, millions of Americans watched and listened while Dean read a 245-page statement to the Senate Watergate committee, directly implicating the President and his top assistants in a conspiracy to obstruct justice. Dean had realized that he was a criminal, and had decided to tell what he knew.

At the Center on June 27 the fellows engaged in a dialogue with Harlan Cleveland, president of the University of Hawaii, on what had happened to "public ethics." Cleveland, a scholar who had held high positions in the Department of State, was also on the list of possible successors to Robert Hutchins. He was an articulate, sensitive, keenly alert man who made a favorable impression on the fellows.

The Center released an attack on the Carnegie Commission's study of higher education in the United States early in September. Donald McDonald, executive editor of the *Center Magazine*, described the commission's activities—which cost $6 million—as "a six million dollar misunderstanding." He was critical of Clark Kerr, a Center Associate, who had served as chairman of the commission during the six and a half years of its existence.

After examining the group's twenty volumes of reports and surveys, McDonald concluded: "It is not going to lead to any reform or revitalization of higher education in America. It is not going to persuade professors or administrators to ask themselves any hard, self-critical questions about what they are doing or the way they are doing it."

A former faculty member and dean of the journalism school at Marquette University, McDonald ascribed some of the commission's deficiencies to Clark Kerr's fundamental acceptance of the way "most colleges and universities now operate," Kerr's confusion about "the nature and purpose of higher education," and "partly because Kerr and the Commission decided to do a strictly social science job on higher education—they climbed all over it, counting, measuring, describing, gauging, and projecting enrollment trends, demographic patterns, financing practices, student and alumni attitudes, governance procedures, and community relations. . . . The Carnegie authors, for their part, are largely concerned with the contours of the educational process and how that process can be better financed, made more accessible, and more surely adjusted and accommodated to the demands of the American society."

In his analysis, contained in an article published in the September–October issue of the *Center Magazine*, McDonald quoted comments offered by Hutchins: "The Commission ought to strengthen and clarify its discussion of certain issues. If this is not done, the confusion that has plagued American education for at least fifty years will continue, and may even deepen. . . ."

Hutchins did not feel that the commission had placed much emphasis on the "critical function" of the university, or had indicated what could be done "to repair the ravages of specialization," or had supported "the confrontation of the disciplines." He was disturbed by the willingness of the commission to abandon the idea of community "as a lost cause."

With the statements by Hutchins and McDonald, the Center released counterarguments made by Kerr, who acknowledged immediately that there would always be "some fundamental disagreement" between the Hutchins lines of thought and his own.

"I agree that general education has been greatly slighted because of the emphasis on more technical training," Kerr said. "Our Commission has very much hoped that there could be a renaissance of general education. But I think that, with the exception of a few places, we must be reconciled to the fact that occupational training and general education are going to go along together and that we cannot just throw occupational training out of higher education. . . . I also argue that at least in some occupational training there is a fair amount of intellectual content or that at least there can be."

Although he took responsibility for having "helped to coin the word 'multiversity,' " Kerr asserted that he had never intended to suggest that any educational institution should do everything: "There should be differentiation of functions, beyond the specialization from one institution to another. Not all fields have to be covered within particular functions at any institution. Our Commission has also recommended that universities get rid of all secret research and get rid of all 'company-town' aspects such as housekeeping, housing, police, food service."

"We do call for the critical function," Kerr said. "We are very much concerned that it be carried out in a constructive way and not, as it sometimes has been, in a destructive way. Political action carried on in the wrong way can impair the exercise of this very important function, a function which is probably as important now as never before, given all the problems of modern society and the need for the application of scholarship to solve them."

The commission's investigations had convinced Kerr that "the idea of community, at least in the current situation, cannot be revived." This was a finding he had been extremely reluctant to accept.

"Our Commission has met at a great many places around the country and we have been told this universally," Kerr declared. "Even Swarthmore, with its traditions and its small size, has broken down into a series of sub-communities or 'families,' little friendship groups. In fact, students generally are limiting their contacts to a small number of very compatible people. I think that is very unfortunate. They are losing the broader intellectual and personal contacts, even on the small campuses. . . . Under these circumstances, we do not know how you can regain a sense of community. The very people who have talked about wanting the campus to be a community are the ones who then have hived off into their own sets of people."

Kerr noted that Hutchins had spent much of his life in trying "to force the confrontation of the disciplines" and in attempting to get "the great dialogue to continue."

"I have spent some of my life in that, too," Kerr said. "But I must admit a sense of almost complete defeat."

Kerr's statements accentuated the sense of loneliness that often seemed evident in Hutchins. He knew why it was so difficult to raise the money to keep the Center going. The Center was operating against the "academic system," against the pressures for specialization and "practical results" that characterized a society obsessed with technology and dedicated to the production of quantitative goods rather than a high quality of life.

Hutchins would not yield to the idea that the concept of the community could not be revived. He would not abandon hope for the spread of "the great dialogue." He continued to cling to his belief—shared with his old friend Justice Douglas and others connected with the Center—that there should be Centers for dialogue in all the cities of the United States and in many other countries.

In September, 1973, a few weeks before the outbreak of another armed conflict between Israel and the Arab countries, the Center brought some of the most brilliant Jewish scholars in the world to Santa Barbara for a three-day conference on "The Jewish Tradition and its Relevance to Modern Life." The dialogue at this gathering, in which some of the participants were survivors of the Nazi holocaust, reached an intensity seldom experienced even at the Center.

The atmosphere in Washington was thick with tension when the directors of the Fund and the Center convened in the Madison Room of the Sheraton-Park hotel on the morning of October 8. News broadcasts indicated that the Soviet Union was supplying planes and weapons to the Arabs, and the United States was flying military supplies to Israel. The danger of a clash between Russian and American forces in the Middle East seemed to be growing hour by hour.

Twenty-three of the Fund's twenty-eight directors were present at the executive session, which began at 10:30 A.M. Hutchins presided and Ashmore kept the minutes. Hutchins began the meeting by announcing that the Committee on Organization—headed by J. R. Parten and composed of five members, including Parten, Hutchins, Arnold Grant, James Douglas, and Harold Willens—was ready to make its recommendation for the election of his successor.

All five members of the committee were in the room when Parten reported its action. Parten said the committee had considered three active candidates—Malcolm Moos, president of the University of Minnesota; Harlan Cleveland, president of the University of Hawaii, and Russell Peterson, former governor of Delaware. While the Committee had found all three highly qualified, Moos was the committee's first choice.

Parten said that an agreement had been reached with Moos on his salary requirement. Moos, who had been furnished a house by the University of Minnesota, would need financial aid to buy an appropriate home in Santa Barbara. Parten said he would try to develop a satisfactory arrangement to meet the housing problem if the board felt that Moos should be elected.

Ashmore's minutes recorded: "There was general discussion of the three candidates, with strong support for Mr. Moos offered by several Board members who had had previous personal associations with him. The consensus was that Mr. Parten should resume negotiations with Mr. Moos by telephone, with the view of announcing his appointment and presenting him to the audience then assembling in Washington for the Center's Pacem in Terris III convocation."

Parten went to a telephone outside the Madison Room. When he came back, he said that Moos had accepted his offer of private aid in purchasing a house and had accepted the board's appointment without any additional condition. Parten said Moos would be available to begin work at the Center on July 1, 1974, and would come to Washington in time to be presented by Hutchins to the audience at the "Pacem in Terris" convocation.

Parten then made a motion that the directors should elect Malcolm Moos a director, chairman of the board, and chief executive officer of the Fund, as well as chairman of the senior fellows of the Center. It was passed without a dissenting vote. However, it did not appear in the minutes.* Ashmore's minutes simply noted that Parten had reported that Moos was willing to accept the board's appointment, indicated that he would "undertake his duties July 1, 1974," and would be in Washington to be presented publicly.

"There followed a discussion of the possible reorganization of the administration of the Center," Ashmore recorded. "Mr. Hutchins insisted that the appointment of Mr. Moos must carry with it all the responsibility and authority presently vested in him. Mr. Hutchins would function as chief executive officer until June 30, 1974, and thereafter would be available for any services the Board might call upon him to perform. But, after his retirement as chief executive officer, he would not participate actively in the administration, or in the formulation of policy for the academic program.

"He hoped to continue and enlarge upon the studies and projects in which he has been engaged as a Fellow of the Center, but he would insist that he not be called upon to function in a fashion that would 'lay the dead hand of the past upon the new Chairman.' The Board reluctantly accepted this dispensation, but voted unanimously to reaffirm the title of Life Fellow conferred upon Mr. Hutchins at the time of the reorganization of the Center."

Ashmore then reported that Gary Cadenhead, the secretary and treasurer, would be leaving the Center staff by June 30, 1974, to take a job with a new institute that was being created at the University of California at Los Angeles.

There would be no need to replace Cadenhead, Ashmore said, because some of his functions as secretary had been taken over by Dean Ginsburg and others could be handled by Peter Tagger, the director of development and membership services.

Ashmore made these statements about Cadenhead's projected departure despite the fact that Cadenhead had given him a note saying that Malcolm Moos had asked Cadenhead not to make any commitments about leaving the Center. Parten had talked with Moos about the desirability of retaining Cadenhead. Parten felt that Cadenhead had proved to be an efficient and trustworthy Secretary and Treasurer, and Parten was sure that Moos would need such a financial officer to bring the Center's budget under control.

After indicating to the board that Cadenhead was ready to leave—and should leave, because his services were no longer needed—Ashmore said

---

*Parten was disturbed when he received a copy of the minutes and noticed that the passage of his motion had not been recorded. Ashmore apparently thought it was sufficient to note that Moos had accepted the board's action.

that the path was clear "for any appropriate reallocation of administrative functions." He offered to continue in any capacity assigned to him by the board and the new chairman. Parten and other directors gained the impression that Ashmore wanted to be retained in a high executive position.

Ashmore was disturbed by Cadenhead's unwillingness to accept the departure date that had been announced. Ashmore did not think it was appropriate for Moos to intervene in such matters until Moos was actually installed as chairman. The clash between Ashmore and Moos over Cadenhead's role was the first of a series of clashes between the two men that had repercussions in the board and among the senior fellows.

From the time when Hutchins had asked him to be chairman of the committee to search for Hutchins' successor, Parten had been concerned about the likelihood of opposition by Ashmore to any successor. He was sure that Ashmore enjoyed being the president of the Fund. During the times when Hutchins had been ill, Hutchins had transferred much of his power to Ashmore. Parten had accepted that as a temporary arrangement.

As a trustee of the University of Texas, Parten had observed the behavior of an interim president of the university when a new president had been finally elected by the trustees. The interim president had not wanted to relinquish his executive power and had made trouble for the incoming president. Parten thought that a similar situation might arise at the Center. He was prepared to stand by Moos.

In the board meeting, after Ashmore's statements about Cadenhead and the "reallocation of administrative functions," Hutchins raised the question of undertaking another effort to consider how the Center could "best be established on a permanent basis." He urged the committee on organization to work on "constitutionalizing" the Center "in consultation with the new Chairman."

Endorsing the idea, Parten said he would like to have detailed descriptions of the functions of the fellows and staff from Hutchins and Ashmore, along with their recommendations on what needed to be done.

Ashmore then informed the board that funds had been obtained to cover all the costs of the impending "Pacem in Terris III" convocation "from special sources outside the regular budget, with enough left over to assure wide dissemination of the printed, audio and video materials to be derived from the proceedings."

Encouraged by the flow of money for this convocation and by an indication from William Laughlin that the Saga Foundation might donate $50,000 for another effort on this scale, Ashmore said he had recommended—and Hutchins had approved—a plan to hold another convocation in Washington in the autumn of 1974.

According to the minutes, Ashmore said: "This activity also affords an opportunity to sustain the interest of the Center's supporting membership and perhaps extend it." He said that Sander Vanocur, who had been active in organizing and promoting "Pacem in Terris III," had been appointed "as a consultant for another year beginning January 1, 1974."

Vanocur would continue to work out of Washington, where the Center now maintained an office, Ashmore went on. Vanocur would also collaborate with him in developing "possibilities for regular television programming by the Center." Ashmore asserted that the costs of the Washington operation had been covered by funds raised for "Pacem in Terris III," and that it was expected that "this will be the case in 1974."

Ashmore did not ask for formal approval by the board of the continuance of Vanocur as a consultant or the maintenance of the Washington office. But no one at the meeting raised any objection. Ashmore took the silence of the board members for tacit consent. Parten did not voice an objection in the meeting, but he supposed that any arrangements with Vanocur would have to be approved by Moos, the newly elected head of the organization.

The board then discussed a statement by Hutchins that the Center planned to assemble a group of "constitutional experts representing the spectrum of conservative to liberal opinion for a dialogue on the basic issues raised by current conflicts over division of powers in the federal government." Hutchins said that the conference had been scheduled in response to a request from Arthur Miller, special counsel to the Senate Watergate Committee.

Hutchins declared that the dialogue to be held at the Center—along with a number of papers "solicited by Mr. Miller"—was designed "to provide a broad philosophical background for the deliberations of the Watergate Committee legal staff in preparing its final report." Hutchins said that the Center had decided to hold the conference only after the meeting had been "certified as non-partisan by both Chairman Sam Ervin and the Republican Vice-Chairman, Howard Baker."

None of the senators on the committee was expected to take part, Hutchins indicated, but four members of the legal staff were to participate: Sam Dash, the majority counsel; Fred Thompson, counsel to the Republican minority; Rufus Edmisten, deputy to Dash, and Miller himself, a professor at the George Washington University law school who was a "constitutional advisor" to the committee.

Ashmore noted in the minutes: "Mr. Douglas expressed reservations about the Center's entering into such a relationship with an official body involved in extreme partisan controversy. Mr. Hutchins said that he believed all due safeguards had been taken to guarantee against partisanship, and to remove the deliberations at the Center from involvement in any of the specific matters that would be dealt with in the Committee report. He regarded the conference as an exercise in 'practical philosophy,' and he thought it fell within the charter of a body devoted to the study of democratic institutions.

The Board agreed that the conference should go ahead as scheduled in early December under the stipulations set forth by the Chairman."

Several members of the board made it clear that they felt the conference should not be "promoted" or "heavily publicized." Ashmore and Hutchins agreed. Ashmore said: "Ultimate publication of material derived from the conference would provide an opportunity for dissemination in proper context." The board adjourned for lunch.

At the afternoon session—which was open to the senior fellows and the senior staff—no mention was made of the election of Malcolm Moos. Hutchins was reelected chairman of the board; Ashmore, president; I was reelected vice president; and Cadenhead, secretary and treasurer.

Dean Ginsburg once more gave a cheerful report on the academic program, declaring that the fellows had been "highly productive" and the schedule had been fuller than ever, in spite of budgetary reductions. He referred again to the coming of the tenth senior fellow, Alexander Comfort, and to the arrival in the autumn of Gunnar Myrdal, Alva Myrdal, and Paul T. K. Lin as visiting fellows. To hold down expenditures, he said, the number of visiting fellows would be gradually dropped from seven or eight each year to six or fewer.

Ashmore said that Secretary of State Kissinger and Senator J. William Fulbright, the two principal speakers at the opening session of the "Pacem in Terris III" convocation, were expected to appear that night despite the fact that both men were deeply involved in efforts to stop the Arab-Israeli war. More than 3000 people had bought tickets to attend that session and another 400 hundred would watch the proceeding on television in a nearby hall.

Ashmore said it would be the first such activity sponsored by the Center "to be completely pre-funded." Tickets had been sold separately for each of the sessions. Through contributions or the buying of tickets, more than 6000 people would participate in the conference. (Harold Willens and other members of the Businessmen's Educational Fund had produced some of the money for the convocation.)

"This is the most remarkable response the Center has ever enjoyed," Ashmore said. He felt that it confirmed the staff's conviction that Center members considered themselves actual sharers in the Center's work, not simply subscribers to a magazine.

The reports of Gary Cadenhead and Peter Tagger brought the board's attention back to the Center's recurrent problem—the gulf between its income and its spending. Although expenditures had been cut below the budget authorized by the board, the prospective deficit for the 1974 fiscal year was larger than the one for 1973.

"With our present reduced rate of expenditures, the Center has a life expectancy of a little over two years," Cadenhead said.

Tagger told the directors that tests of an increased membership fee had been run but had not produced good results "either in numbers or in dollars." When asked to increase their basic membership payments voluntarily, Center members had responded. The average membership payment had risen from $16.68 to $18.32 during the first month of the test.

Tagger stated that fund raising was "our weakest area." While substantial amounts had been raised for the "Pacem in Terris" convocation, the convocation also had substantial expenses. He estimated that the Center would gain a net profit of $90,000 from the conference, but that "it will probably be used for post-convocation activities."

"This leads us back to the Center's need for an endowment," Tagger concluded.

Bernard Rapoport, cochairman of the Committee on the Permanent Endowment Campaign, said that the committee had been waiting for the results of the board meeting before beginning its efforts on a sustained scale. He thought that the committee was "ready to move ahead."

Mrs. Stevenson, noting the important role of Hutchins in creating the Center, proposed that the name be changed from the Center for the Study of Democratic Institutions to "The Robert M. Hutchins Center" or "The Hutchins Center." Although all the directors admired Hutchins, her proposal did not generate immediate support. It was referred to the executive committee and the committee on organization for study.

Hutchins had told several of the directors that he did not want the Center to be identified with one particular person. He wanted it to have an institutional identity that might help it to survive for generations. He was grateful for Mrs. Stevenson's warm friendship, but he did not endorse her suggestion.

William Laughlin, stirred by the response of Center members to the "Pacem in Terris" convocation and encouraged by the election of Malcolm Moos, urged the directors to aid Rapoport in raising money during the four days of the convocation. He pledged a contribution of $50,000 toward the cost of a fourth "Pacem in Terris" conference.

The board meeting closed on a note of enthusiasm, with the members promising to attend a fund-raising luncheon Rapoport planned to hold on the third day of the convocation. Since Moos had been elected unanimously—and several directors had voiced their support for him—Rapoport was hopeful that the endowment campaign would soon develop some momentum.

That night, at the opening session of the convocation, Senator Fulbright called for a ceasefire in the Arab-Israeli war with American military support for Israel if it seemed in danger of being overwhelmed. His proposal was received with applause by some of the 3000 people in the Sheraton-Park ballroom and with shouts of disagreement by others.

Henry Kissinger came to the Center convocation directly from a crisis meeting at the State Department. Demonstrators interrupted his speech with noisemakers and battery-powered laughing boxes. Two men scattered leaflets headed "Bellum in Terris—War on Earth" in the crowd, and shouted that Kissinger was one of "the warmakers" and his choice as a speaker made the Center conference on peace "a charade." Security officers removed the demonstrators from the room.

"The need for a dialogue about national purposes has never been more urgent, and no assembly is better suited for such a discussion than this Pacem in Terris convocation," Kissinger said.

Kissinger seemed certain that the Middle East crisis would be surmounted and that the American-Soviet "détente" would be maintained. He was confident that both sides would act responsibly to avoid a collision between the United States and the Soviet Union.

"Detente cannot survive irresponsibility in any area, including the Middle East," the secretary of state said. He added: "However well we contain this crisis, as we have contained others, we must still ask ourselves what we seek beyond the management of conflict."

The fact that Kissinger spoke at the Center conference at a time of international crisis drew dozens of correspondents from broadcasting organizations and reporters from many newspapers and magazines in the United States and many other countries. The speeches of Kissinger and Fulbright were telecast in full by many of the educational television stations. Excerpts were carried to American audiences and to people around the world by the commercial broadcasting networks.

Kermit Lansner, a columnist for *Newsweek*, indicated that the convocation had made a significant impression upon him and upon other journalists who were there. After noting that "this vast and ambitious talkfest" opened shortly after the outbreak of a "terrible war" in the Middle East, Lansner wrote: "Somehow, the occasion 'to consider new opportunities for United States foreign policy' was taken with a high seriousness that was underlined—not undercut—by both the savagery of the Mideast war and the political disarray at home."

In referring to "political disarray," Lansner cited the resignation of Vice President Spiro T. Agnew, which occurred while the convocation was in its third day. Agnew had resigned with an admission that he had evaded payment of some of his federal income taxes. Through an agreement with the Attorney General, he escaped a prison sentence.

Dismissing Agnew, Lansner said: "What was most impressive about the conference was the way in which the speakers—politicians, journalists, bureaucrats and scholars—questioned foreign policy. They were not strident, or picayune, or pragmatic. . . The politics of humility was the order of the day and it somehow seemed to reflect the national mood."

The improved relations between the United States and the Soviet Union—and the contacts with China—were lauded by speakers at the convocation, but the foreign policy of the Nixon administration was depicted as riddled with contradictions by Clark Clifford, former secretary of defense, and others who voiced their views.

"Is it not clear that we simply do not need all the military forces which we now maintain?" Clifford asked. In spite of the reduced tensions between the major nations, Clifford said, the United States had "practically as large a force as we did in 1964, when the global confrontation seemed to be much sharper and America's goals more ambitious."

Another speaker, Richard Barnet, codirector of the Institute for Policy Studies, said that "national security" was a "slippery concept" that was manipulated by policymakers.

"Most of the changes in U.S.-Soviet relations took place in Washington, not Moscow," Barnet declared. "The 'mellowing process' which was supposed to be the result of surrounding the mightiest land masses in the world with nuclear rockets has, much like 'peace with honor' in Vietnam, simply been stipulated. The military might of the Soviet Union has never been greater. What has happened is that the foreign military threats have been redefined to a manageable level."

Professor Stanley Hoffman of Harvard University said that "the great art of the administration" under Nixon had been to make "many believe that we had transformed, or were transforming, the 'U.S. world system' into a pluralistic, multipolar 'stable structure of peace.' " In reality, Hoffman asserted, "we have only changed the method of operation and control of that system" through a "policy of indirect primacy."

While the proceedings of the conference were going on in front of the television cameras, Hutchins and Ashmore were striving to make sure—as far as they could—that the election of Malcolm Moos as the Center's chairman would not mean an accession to power by Harvey Wheeler. They were afraid that Wheeler would try to rule the Center through Moos. They wanted Moos to become chairman on their terms, not Wheeler's.

Although Hutchins had indicated to Parten that he considered Moos to be the best of the available candidates, Hutchins had developed misgivings about Moos because of Wheeler's active role in the final phase of the negotiations. Parten had also been irritated by Wheeler's statements to Hutchins about what Moos required as "conditions" for his election, but Parten felt confident that Moos could control Wheeler.

While Hutchins respected Wheeler's productive capacity, he did not think that Wheeler should be given power to shape the Center's future. He had picked Wheeler as the second new senior fellow (after himself) in the reorganization of 1969 and then had found him difficult to handle. Wheeler had alienated some of the other fellows and staff members and had attempted to step into administrative territory that Hutchins considered to be

Ashmore's domain. Ashmore repeatedly reinforced Hutchins' feeling that Wheeler was "trying to take over the Center."

Hutchins had favored the election of Moos with the belief that Moos would consult him on all major decisions, at least in the first phase of the new administration. He knew that Moos and Wheeler were close, but he had not fully anticipated that Moos would place so much reliance on Wheeler. Moos and Wheeler had been friends ever since they had been faculty members at Johns Hopkins University in the 1940s, and Moos apparently felt that Wheeler had been largely instrumental in getting him elected by the Fund's board.

Actually Moos had been on a list of possible successors to Hutchins since 1970, when his name first appeared on a list sent by Hutchins to Parten and other members of the committee on organization. In the spring of 1973, when Wheeler had decided that Hutchins really did intend to retire, Wheeler had asked whether Hutchins would consider Moos as a leading possibility. Hutchins said he would. Wheeler had then telephoned Moos and asked whether Moos was interested. After thinking about it overnight, Moos called Wheeler and said that he was. (Hutchins had previously offered the chairmanship to Kingman Brewster of Yale and John Kenneth Galbraith of Harvard and had been turned down. James Gavin had also indicated that he did not want the position.)

The selection of Moos had occurred because Parten who had reluctantly served as chairman of the committee, which had spent years searching for a successor satisfactory to Hutchins and the board, had been completely convinced that Hutchins preferred Moos to any of the others who had been interviewed. James Douglas, who had participated with Parten in reviewing the candidates, also had been willing to support anyone Hutchins preferred. Harold Willens and Arnold Grant, the other two members of the committee, had not been active in the search but had been prepared to vote for anyone considered suitable by Hutchins.

Before Parten's committee had decided to back Moos, Bernard Rapoport had gone to Minneapolis at Parten's request to talk with Moos and to ask several Minnesota leaders what they thought of the man. He had found that these leaders admired Moos as a person, as a warm human being with intelligence and sensitivity, but they had reservations about his administrative abilities. He had relayed these comments to Parten.

Parten had already received other criticisms of Moos—originating among doctors in Minneapolis, who were critical of Moos's action in establishing a medical branch of the University of Minnesota with the Mayo Clinic at Rochester—but he discounted them. During his six years as a trustee of the University of Texas, Parten had discovered how much backbiting occurred at a university.

Parten had discussed the critical information he had received about Moos with Hutchins. Hutchins, who had suffered from faculty sniping at the University of Chicago, shared Parten's views that these criticisms were not weighty enough to damage Moos severely. Parten told Rapoport that he knew Hutchins wanted Moos, and his committee then supported the man Hutchins had endorsed.

In October, in Washington, while the "Pacem in Terris" conference brought a parade of celebrities to the conference platform, Rapoport met with Moos and Wheeler at the Jefferson Hotel. He told Moos that if Moos insisted on the provision of a "whole house" in Santa Barbara instead of the financial assistance Parten had offered—and if Moos was determined to make Wheeler the officer in charge of the academic program—Moos's election was in jeopardy. Moos finally accepted the financial arrangements Rapoport suggested, and he withdrew his requirement for Wheeler's designation as the academic officer.

The next morning Rapoport went to the hotel where Robert and Vesta Hutchins were staying. Moos was secheduled to have breakfast there. Rapoport told the Hutchinses what had happened the night before.

"Bob acted as though he was very unhappy with the whole process," Rapoport told me later. "Before Moos arrived, Hutchins said to me, 'I wish it would fall through.' I said: 'Bob, I really think he accepts the conditions. We've gone this far. I don't see how we can pull out at this time.' And I still feel I was right about it—you know, you just can't lead people on, you know, that far."

Moos arrived a few minutes afterward. "He'd calmed down," Rapoport recalled. "He just took my advice and was very amiable and compliant. There was no real discussion. It was just like everything was falling in place."

Without knowing about the conversations between Rapoport, Moos, Wheeler, and Hutchins, I had prepared a press release announcing the election of Moos. When it was presented to Parten, he approved it immediately and urged that it be given to the press and broadcasting correspondents at the conference as soon as possible. When I presented it to Hutchins, he scowled and said: "Don't send this out to anybody until I've told you to do it. This thing may still fall through." A few hours later, Hutchins approved it and wrote in a paragraph about Moos: "Malcolm Moos seems to me the ideal man to continue and develop that unique institution, the Center for the Study of Democratic Institutions. The future of the organization is bright. . . ."

Hutchins had apparently decided, after his conversations with Rapoport and Moos, that Moos understood what his role was to be. Hutchins evidently reassured Ashmore. That same day, Ashmore said to me: "Moos is coming in on *our* terms."

On the concluding day of the "Pacem in Terris" convocation, Hutchins presented Moos to an audience of 3000 people and to the millions who would see the videotapes later. He described briefly Moos's background as a political scientist, as a journalist, as an assistant to Dwight D. Eisenhower, as a Ford Foundation official and as a university president, and declared that Moos was "uniquely qualified" to become the chairman of the Center.

Judging by his background, Moos had many of the qualifications the Center needed at the time of his election. He was favorably known to the directors of large foundations. He was a director or trustee of many national organizations, including the American Council on Education, the National Public Affairs Center for Television, the Governmental Affairs Institute, and the Carnegie Foundation for the Advancement of Teaching.

Moos had been an associate editor of the Baltimore *Evening Sun* and a consultant to the CBS news division, in addition to his service as a professor at the University of Wyoming and at Johns Hopkins. He had degrees from six major universities.

From 1957 to 1961, Moos had been a special assistant to President Eisenhower. He had worked on many of Eisenhower's speeches, and had drafted Eisenhower's farewell address to the nation, in which the retiring president had warned the people against the dangers of the "military-industrial complex." That speech had been quoted around the world.

After the Eisenhower administration ended, Moos became an adviser to the Rockefeller brothers. In 1964 he had been appointed director of policy planning for the Ford Foundation and later he had moved over to head the foundation's office on government and law, where he stayed until 1967, when he was chosen as president of the University of Minnesota.

The range of his experience was wide. He was not known as a reformer or innovator, as Hutchins had been, but he had served for almost seven years as the head of one of the notable state universities in the United States. During his administration the university had suffered from some disruptions by student demonstrators but not on the scale of the riots at other large institutions. He was generally liked and respected by many of the students and had a reputation for dealing fairly and calmly with his opponents.

During his stay in Minnesota, the fund-raising department of the university had been successful. He had encountered attacks from the faculty, from some of the trustees and some of the students, as all university administrators did. He had friends in all of these groups, but his resignation at Minnesota had apparently been due to pressure from trustees who felt that he had not been a forceful executive. According to Frank Wright of the Minneapolis *Tribune*, Moos had resigned after eleven of the twelve regents had asked him to leave "because of continuing defections of high-ranking faculty and university administration officials, and growing complaints that Moos was allowing problems to fester."

A staff writer for the St. Paul *Pioneer Press*, reporting on the selection of Moos by the Fund's board, noted that Moos had been "under fire from some faculty members and regents for an alleged lack of leadership." The writer added: "In recent months, he met the challenge of some of his critics by shoring up his central administration with key appointments, largely from among the faculty corps."

Yet nothing in the experience of Moos at a large university really prepared him for what he had to face at the Center. At a big university, one group of faculty members might balance off another group. With agility and support from the trustees, a university president could keep a distance between the warring factions and maintain a position above the battle.

That was not possible at the Center. There were only ten fellows, and each had been scarred in one way or another by clashes between them or in jockeying for places close to Hutchins. In such a small organization, every action—or hint of possible action—triggered the defense mechanisms of the fellows and the senior staff.

The difficulties that would face any successor to Hutchins had been anticipated by Parten. That was why Parten had refused for years to engage in a vigorous search for a successor. Through those years, in letters and phone calls, Hutchins had pleaded for relief from his burdens, saying, "I am not getting any younger." When Moos had been tapped as the man for the job, Parten had telephoned Hutchins to get his approval. "That's fine," Hutchins had said. "I'm satisfied."

While Hutchins stood on the platform in Washington and hailed Moos as "uniquely qualified" to head the Center, Parten was watching. He was glad that Hutchins had made such a strong statement to the press and the public. Hutchins had promised him that he would give solid support to Moos, and Parten had relayed that promise to Moos. Parten had pledged his own word to stand by Moos in the storms that he expected to come.

Parten was sure that trouble would occur. He knew that Elisabeth Mann Borgese had not wanted Hutchins to retire. He was positive that Harry Ashmore did not relish the prospect of yielding executive authority to a new man. Hutchins had sent him a copy of a memorandum from Lord Ritchie-Calder, in which Ritchie-Calder had said that no one in sight had all the necessary qualities to succeed Hutchins. He knew that other fellows did not believe that any man could take Hutchins' place.

In spite of these danger signals, Parten believed that Moos could meet the demands of the situation. Moos was the man Hutchins had approved, and the fellows would have to accept that. The directors had ratified the choice. As long as Hutchins stood behind Moos—and Hutchins had always fulfilled his commitments during the years Parten had known him—Moos could ride through the turbulence he would encounter.

To clear the road for Moos, Parten had tried to provide a graceful way for Hutchins to withdraw completely from the administrative load that had become so irksome to him. At the board session on October 8, Parten had taken Hutchins aside and had suggested that he should have a year's vacation with pay. Hutchins had not given any immediate response but had seemed willing to consider the idea.

Parten did not know that Hutchins had already expressed doubts about Moos to Rapoport. He would have been shocked to learn that Hutchins had voiced a hope that "the whole thing" would "fall through." Like Rapoport, he felt that a commitment had been made to Moos—and the commitment could not be withdrawn. Hutchins could not have persuaded him to change it.

The public ceremonies on October 11 were carried through with an apparent atmosphere of pleasure and courtesy. In the presence of the celebrities who had graced the "Pacem in Terris" convocation—Senator Hubert Humphrey, Governor Nelson Rockefeller, Senator Sam Ervin of the Watergate Committee, Senator George McGovern and others—Moos said that he was "proud" to be succeeding Robert Maynard Hutchins as the chairman of the Center.

Applause thundered through the ballroom of the Sheraton-Park Hotel in Washington when Moos paid his tribute to Hutchins. The thousands of Center members who were gathered there left the convocation with a feeling of assurance that Moos and Hutchins would certainly work together to make the Center's future "brighter than ever."

Moos returned to Minnesota and plunged into meetings with the regents and faculty members there, to develop arrangements for an easy transition for the man who was to follow him as president of the university. Hutchins, Ashmore, and the other fellows who had participated in the Washington conference returned to Santa Barbara. Hutchins told friends that he was glad that he would soon be relieved of the responsibilities he had shouldered for so many years.

On November 11, 1973, Hutchins wrote to Parten, accepting the offer of a year's leave with pay. "You took me by surprise by your kind suggestion," Hutchins said, declaring that Parten's proposal had been so generous that he was "too embarrassed to reply." He went on: "I suppose the answer is that a year's vacation would be a fine thing for me. I would like to feel free to get out of town and do anything I wanted to for a year. The question is whether it would be good for the Center."

After reflection on that point, Hutchins continued: "Perhaps it would be best for the Center if I were officially on vacation during Moos's first year. He will certainly want to propose some changes. It might be painful to him to have the feeling that I was looking over his shoulder. . . . The last thing I want to do is to get in the way. . . .

"So I'd be glad to accept your suggestion of a year's vacation if you still think it appropriate and not too expensive for the Center. During the year I would be on call from Moos and would try to get ahead with the writing on education and the 14th Amendment I mentioned."

At that point, Hutchins evidently felt there would be ample time for him to give Moos any necessary advice in the eight months between Moos's election and his entry into the administration of the Center. He had apparently overcome the qualms he had felt about Harvey Wheeler's possible role. He recognized the fact that his continuing presence at the Center might make it particularly painful for Moos to make changes.

In any case, Hutchins knew that Parten felt strongly that Moos had to have a free hand to deal with the Center's pressing problems. And Hutchins had told the board in Washington that "the appointment of Mr. Moos must carry with it all the responsibility and authority presently vested in him." That was in the minutes of the executive session, recorded by Ashmore.

Moos, however, was disturbed when he learned that those minutes did not contain any specific reference to his election, by a vote of all the directors present, as the chairman, chief executive officer, chairman of the senior fellows, and director. He called this to Parten's attention.

Parten sent a letter to Hutchins, stating what the board had done. Hutchins replied quickly, saying that Parten's letter would be appended to the minutes. The minutes themselves did not contain any record of a formal vote by the directors for Moos.

Ashmore and Moos had met in Washington on October 23, and Ashmore had reviewed the principal decisions taken by the board, as he understood them. Ashmore assumed that Moos would have no objection to the projected plan for organizing a fourth "Pacem in Terris" convocation to be held in Washington in the autumn of 1974.

But Moos did object. On November 23 Moos sent a handwritten letter to Ashmore—a letter that surprised both Ashmore and Hutchins.

"I want to review with you several conclusions relative to my election as Chairman of the Center," Moos said. "During my discussions with Robert Hutchins at the Hay-Adams at the time of the *Pacem in Terris* conference we agreed that no long-range commitments concerning either staff or programs would be made pending my arrival without my approval.

"The resources of the Center, contrary to my original perception of being adequate to fund us through the next three years, are at the moment hardly likely to carry us beyond the next two years. The compelling need, therefore, is a careful, selective retrenchment and reallocation of programs as we catch our breath and move ahead with new intellectual directions and a muscular, long-range funding program.

"This leads me to say that I do not want any commitment to a fourth *Pacem in Terris* program or supporting consultants made at this time. It is my intention to present my own plans to the full Board meeting in January."

Ashmore realized that Moos wanted to terminate the services of Sander Vanocur, to whom he had made a commitment for another year's work as a consultant with Hutchins' approval. He did not think that Moos understood that the board of directors—by not objecting to the proposal he had outlined with Hutchins' support—had tacitly approved a fourth "Pacem in Terris" convocation. Ashmore was not willing to accept Moos's authority to cancel the project.

On December 4 Ashmore dispatched a long letter to Moos, saying that he had talked to Hutchins: "He and I are in complete accord with the understanding reached in your Hay-Adams conversation that no long-range commitments . . . would be made pending your arrival without your approval.

"However, Bob points out that in the case of the Washington convocation scheduled for the fall of 1974 there is no long-range commitment, since the obligation to continue Sander Vanocur as a consultant is specifically limited to the calendar year 1974; that the proposal for continuing the successful convocation series was presented to the Board of Directors and approved prior to Bob's conversation with you at the Hay-Adams; and that no allocation or diversion of funds otherwise available to the Center is contemplated."

Ashmore presented a summary of the financial results of the third "Pacem in Terris" convocation, indicating that there would be a "net return" of almost $50,000 "as the nucleus of the 1974 convocation fund." He referred to the pledge of a $50,000 contribution made by W. Price Laughlin at the board meeting, and informed Moos that he and Peter Tagger were "willing, in effect, to guarantee that the 1974 convocation would be self-sustaining, or better."

"There is a proper question, of course, as to whether some of the funds raised for this special purpose could not have been brought in for the general purposes of the Center," Ashmore acknowledged. "It is our conclusion that this would apply only to a minor percentage. . . . Tagger's quite detailed analysis indicates that the funds collected for *Pacem in Terris III* essentially represent 'new money,' or were derived from fees that could be charged only in relation to a public event."

Ashmore contended that the large conferences were valuable in galvanizing financial support from Center members "in a way that more general solicitations of the past have failed to do." He said the 1974 convocation could be "the focus for all the organized activities involved in our direct communication with our supporters."

Hutchins then sent a short note to Moos—dated December 5, 1973—completely backing Ashmore. "You may not have had a chance to look at the minutes of the Board meeting held before you and I met in Washington," Hutchins said. "Plans were outlined, commitments were authorized, and a large pledge was made for a convocation in Washington next year. I want to make sure you know how the record stands."

Hutchins concluded with words of approval for Moos's meetings with directors: "I'm glad the Chicago meeting went well and that you are seeing Board members as you get around the country. Let me know if I can help in this activity—or anything else."

The conflict between Moos and Hutchins and Ashmore over the desirability of a 1974 convocation indicated that there would be immediate differences between them. Moos, busy with tasks at the University of Minnesota, did not make a written reply to their letters, so the question of whether plans could be developed for the 1974 conference remained unsettled for several weeks.

In an 18-page memorandum addressed to Hutchins and Moos on December 21, Ashmore bombarded Moos with arguments designed to persuade him that such convocations were essential. In describing the background of the 1973 convocation, Ashmore referred to the trip Hutchins had taken around the country in 1972, when he had tried to arouse the board members to participate vigorously in giving or raising money for the Center's projects and for an endowment fund. Hutchins had hit a row of stone walls.

Except for Parten, James Douglas, Mrs. McAllister, and a few others, the directors did not show much enthusiasm for supporting the Center. Hutchins had decided that another "Pacem in Terris" convocation might arouse new interest in its work, by showing how many people were stirred by its efforts for peace, and might open up new sources of money. So the 1973 conference had been assembled with a galaxy of famous speakers, and new enthusiasm for the Center had evidently been produced.

The question that bothered Parten, Howard Marshall, and other directors was whether the enthusiasm demonstrated for a peace conference could be converted into a steady flow of income to meet the large deficits that had eaten away the Center's financial reserves. Parten and Marshall—both successful businessmen, with experience in running organizations efficiently—felt that some of the Center's money was being wasted. They had made their views known to Malcolm Moos.

The 1973 convocation had cost several hundred thousand dollars. Ashmore's figures indicated that it had brought in enough money to cover these expenditures and to give the Center a "net return" of almost $50,000, which Ashmore wanted to use as "the nucleus of the 1974 convocation fund." But the "net return" of $50,000 looked small to Parten and Moos, compared with the Center's estimated 1973–74 deficit of $925,000.

Although Ashmore did not mention it in this memorandum, the Center's first convocation on "Pacem in Terris" in 1965 had deeply impressed Chester Carlson, who later became the Center's principal benefactor, who donated more than $4 million in annual installments and left the Center a bequest of nearly $5 million in his will. But it was obvious to Moos and Parten that Hutchins and Ashmore hoped that a series of "Pacem in Terris" conferences might attract other philanthropic millionaires who would donate enough to keep the Center going on a large scale.

In his long memorandum, Ashmore told Moos that the Center had tried to use the Carlson bequest of $5 million to set off an endowment drive. He ascribed the failure of this effort to "the erratic stock market," the "uncertainties engendered by changes in income tax laws governing deductible contributions," and "uncertainty about the succession to Robert Hutchins among the members of the board, upon whom the primary burden for making or raising major gifts necessarily rested.''

When Parten had committed himself—after years of urging by Hutchins—to finding a satisfactory successor to Hutchins, he felt deeply committed to help that successor in confronting the almost desperate financial situation of the Center. It became a weight on his conscience. He lived by a definite code of responsibility. His code demanded that he had to urge Moos to take rapid action to end the Center's budgetary bleeding—even it it meant a confrontation with Hutchins and Ashmore.

Parten knew the history of the Fund for the Republic better than any of the other directors. He knew that the original grant from the Ford Foundation had been given to a group of directors, including himself, because those directors were known to be financially responsible people. He remembered the early years of the Fund, when its first chairman, Paul Hoffman, had exercised some control over the Fund's spending, and every substantial expenditure had been discussed and reviewed by the directors.

Parten realized that deficits did not seem to bother Hutchins. Hutchins did not think that educational institutions could be or should be run on tight budgets. Hutchins had said frequently, "I ran the University of Chicago for twenty-two years on a deficit." To Hutchins, a deficit in an educational nonprofit institution simply indicated how much money had to be raised by the president and the trustees. In the depression of the 1930s, he had sharply reduced some of the expenditures of the University of Chicago, but he had refused to cut faculty salaries. He felt that excellent scholars had to be well compensated.

The Center's academic expenses, which largely accounted for its deficits, were due to the good salaries paid to the senior fellows and their supporting staff. To live within its income—the membership generated by the membership program and from gifts by board members and others—the Center would have been forced to cut salaries drastically or to fire some of the fellows and staff members. Hutchins had not wanted to do that. He did not think that the Center was perfectly efficient, but efficiency was not its aim: its aim was to provide a place for independent thinking, thinking for the benefit of mankind. He did not think much money had been wasted in striving to attain that goal.

Parten believed that the Center had done important work and had the capacity to do more under new leadership. But he feared that the deficits would soon make its survival impossible. He was not prepared to donate a million dollars a year to enable the Center to continue its existing projects, and he did not know of anyone else who was convinced enough of their value to subsidize them on such a level.

In his lengthy memorandum, Ashmore had declared that Arnold Grant and other directors had asserted that it would not be possible to approach individual donors or foundations for major endowment gifts "unless they had some clear-cut indication of what the future program of the Center would be—and in practical terms this meant they would have to know and be exposed to the man who would be in charge after Hutchins stepped down.''

By implication, Ashmore had conceded that it had been virtually impossible to raise large amounts of money for the academic enterprises of the Center, although he did refer to special purpose grants from foundations, government agencies, and individuals for specific projects. He said: ''This has been significantly increased under the leadership of Norton Ginsburg, but is not yet a major factor in Center financing.''

Ashmore repeated his contention that another national convocation—focused on ''general questions of public policy-making raised by the crisis in Presidential leadership''—would provide ''a complementary base for whatever special gifts efforts could be mounted under the leadership of Moos while his responsibilities were still divided between the University of Minnesota and the Center.''

Knowing of Harvey Wheeler's critical attitude toward the convocations, Ashmore informed Moos that the conflicts between those who regarded the Center as primarily an educational enterprise and those who emphasized its involvement in contemporary problems had existed from its earliest days. He attributed some of these conflicts to the fluctuating descriptions of the Center presented in statements by Hutchins: ''The Founder has described the institution variously as an intellectual community, a university without students, a center of practical philosophy, an early-warning system, and a bridge between the world of scholarship and the world of men.''

''It obviously cannot be all these things without offending the sensibilities and challenging the perceptions of some, or, on occasion, perhaps all its Fellows,'' Ashmore admitted.

Warning Moos that the communications program had ''never had anything better than passive support from the Fellows,'' he added: ''I suspect this situation is compounded of the primal antagonism between academics and administrators and scholars and journalists; the understandable feeling of scholars that the effort to widen the circles of discussion may impose a form of the publish-or-perish syndrome; resentment of the fact that the self-sustaining publishing policy precludes our issuing the kind of scholarly and specialist works that require subsidy: and human jealousy based on the fact that by its nature the communications program at any given moment is likely to accord more prominence to some Fellows than to others.''

He refused to entertain the idea that the communications program constituted a ''diversion of time and energy from scholarly pursuits'' that was excessive or damaging: ''The active participation by individual Fellows in 'external affairs' does not average more than three or four appearances a year, and these rarely require extensive special preparation since they typically are asked to deal with their work in progress.''

Wheeler was one of the fellows who felt that the large convocations, the *Center Magazine*, and other phases of the external affairs operations under Ashmore took too much time, money, and attention away from the Center's scholarly pursuits. Wheeler thought that the money spent on a Washington office and a salary plus expenses for Sander Vanocur could have been better spent on scholarly publications. He felt that the wide publicity generated by the convocations diverted public attention from the significant projects going forward quietly at the Center.

During the months immediately following his election, Moos talked almost daily on the telephone with Wheeler. Moos had not been able to get Wheeler appointed as his executive vice president, but Wheeler's advice was sought and often heeded. Wheeler's critical attitude toward the proposal for a 1974 convocation and the continuation of Vanocur had a lasting impact on Moos.

In the period after the Washington convocation, the principal projects of the fellows continued to unfold. Six major conferences were held in November and December 1973. There were meetings with many participants on the topics "Global Science Policy," "Energy Policies and the International System," "Legal, Political, Social, and Economic Aspects of Climate and Weather Modifications," "The Criminal Justice System: Barriers to Reform," "The Public Interest in Education," and "The Constitutional Implications of Watergate."

The topics of the conferences did overlap to some extent but it was sometimes hard to see why so much attention was given to particular subjects, except on the theory that each fellow was being active and trying to demonstrate his productivity to Hutchins. It was also difficult to find a coherent program for the Center emerging from these varied projects, except on the principle often voiced by Hutchins that everything was related to everything else.

The conference on criminal justice—a field that fascinated Hutchins—involved judges, sociologists, lawyers, police officials, correctional officers, and people concerned with juvenile delinquency, the impact of poverty, and substandard education. Scientists from Sweden, the Soviet Union, France, Britain, the United States, and the United Nations talked for five days at the global science conclave under the chairmanship of Lord Ritchie-Calder, trying to discover whether it was possible to shape useful guidelines for science and technology on a global scale.

At the assembly on climate and weather modification, Wendell Mordy presented a proposal for the formation of a World Atmospheric Management Community. Like Elisabeth Borgese, Ritchie-Calder, and other fellows at the Center, he assumed that world government was bound to develop if humanity survived in a nuclear age. "A new view of the importance of the atmosphere as a resource is emerging," Mordy said. "As an exploitable resource, the atmosphere will ultimately, and perhaps soon, yield to large-scale manipulation and control. . . . Great caution and effective political control will be needed."

The conference on possible manipulation of the atmosphere and climate did not get much coverage in the press. Neither did the sessions of Mrs. Borgese's gathering "Energy Policies and the International System," although an energy crisis had hit the United States in November and December as a result of the embargo enforced against the United States and other nations by the Arab oil-producing countries. The shutdown of the flow of Arab oil threatened to disrupt the economic life of the United States and had severe repercussions throughout the world.

The Center conference "The Constitutional Implications of Watergate" received more attention by the press than any of the other gatherings at the Center in November and December. Harvey Wheeler and Arthur S. Miller, chief consultant to Senator Sam Ervin, brought together some of the leading scholars on constitutional issues and some of the staff members of the Watergate Committee.

One of the participants—Professor Sam Beer of the department of government at Harvard—pointed out that "as the pressures of scale and complexity force more powers on the executive, the foundations on which purposive social control of that power might be erected are weakened and torn away."

Beer did not think that the Watergate revelations indicated that Nixon and his lieutenants would be able to foist a dictatorship on the country. He saw them as confused, frightened men, trapped in a rightwing ideology, crippled by their paranoia, drawn into acts of folly by their feeling of being surrounded by enemies and plotters.

"I sense a real hatred and fear of the 'counter-culture' in the rhetoric of Ehrlichman and Haldeman," Beer said. "It is an irony of Watergate that some of its authors shared this paranoid ideological view of politics with the very radical extremists they were trying to combat."

Beer felt that the exposure of Nixon and his associates would help to prevent abuses in the future. He thought that the condemnation of Nixon was due in part to the Biblical heritage of the United States: "In its moralism, its self-reproach, and especially in its lack of cynicism, the mood that pervades the public discussion of these matters is uniquely American. It could never happen in France. I have never been quite so impressed by the unacknowledged power of the Old Testament over American life."

Christopher Lasch, a professor of history at the University of Rochester, another participant in this conference, declared that Nixon had only carried to greater lengths the policies of his presidential predecessors "until he has arrived at a kind of parody of those practices—sowing ignorance and confusion through the executive departments in order to obscure the responsibility for decisions, withholding information from all but a handful of subordinates, deliberately destroying the 'pertinent facts.' "

Another speaker—Theodore Lowi, a professor of government at Cornell University—also asserted that Nixon was carrying on patterns that had been established under Kennedy and Johnson.

Lowi declared that the form of government created under Kennedy and Johnson—and ratified under Nixon—could be "accurately entitled 'a state of permanent receivership.' " He said: "When a business is in receivership, it is in the hands of a receiver, an official appointed by a court to administer the properties of a bankrupt. . . Permanent receivership involves maintaining the assets and never disposing of them at all. However inequitable the permanent arrangement might be, it is nevertheless a possible way for government to provide for an orderly process for the indefinite future."

In Lowi's view, the federal government had taken "a steadfast position that any institution large enough to be a significant factor in the community shall have its existence underwritten." He added: "It is a system of policies that sets a general floor under risk and then sets a series of specific guarantees against instability for any organization of any significant size. The stress is on organizational, not personal or elite, stabilization."

"This is what national planning has come to mean in the United States," Lowi said. "It is tremendously significant because this kind of planning is extremely authoritative and effective. It is also ironic because it is planning that grew without recognition and is being carried out systematically even though it is not even conceptualized as planning."

With the repeated assertions of "executive privilege"—made by Kennedy, Johnson, and Nixon—Lowi declared that "there is almost no notion of constitutionality or real legality any longer."

Lowi urged the courts to exercise their power to prevent Congress from delegating its powers to the President and the executive branch of government: "This is the most orderly and legitimate way to restore constitutional government, and it has the very special virtue of working through denial or abnegation of power rather than the expansion of it."

At the initiative of Federal Judge John J. Sirica in Washington, the judiciary had already begun the process of bringing the Presidency back to constitutional principles. Judge Sirica had ordered the President to produce the White House tapes related to the Watergate case for his examination. After the judges of the U.S. Circuit Court of Appeals had upheld Sirica's ruling, the President had bowed to the power of the judiciary and surrendered the tapes.

After the Center's conference on "the constitutional implications of Watergate" ended, Wheeler and Hutchins had a dialogue on the principal proposals that had emerged from the discussion.

Noting that in Europe issues always seemed to be articulated "in terms of class-consciousness and class-interest: the aristocracy, the middle classes, the laboring classes," Wheeler commented: "Here in America, where we have not yet had that history of class conflict, we tend to convert all our differences into constitutional issues. That is what happened during the Civil War. It happened with Watergate. It happened during our conference here. . . . Perhaps if we are to restructure and revitalize democracy, we will have to find some way to bring the constitutional issues into the public forum and make this an epic drama."

The Center had, of course, brought constitutional questions into "the public forum" when it published a model for a new Constitution in 1970, long before the Watergate scandal. But the interest in the new model had died down, and Wheeler thought that what was needed in 1973 was "an epic drama." He felt that it was extremely important to keep the people's attention focused on constitutional ussues.

"I don't see why that cannot be done," Hutchins said. "The Lincoln-Douglas debates were over constitutional issues. They were held before a relatively small audience of Illinois farmers. But those debates had a tremendous influence. . . .

"The Constitution of the United States is an attempt to say, in a highly abbreviated form, what kind of country this is going to be, what we can do about it within our constitutional framework and what changes we can make in that constitutional framework. This has all the elements needed for the kind of epic presentation you have suggested."

That December conversation showed that Hutchins and Wheeler shared many ideas. Their minds leaped quickly over a broad array of topics, from the pervasive influence of the mass media to the functions of the CIA, the accountability of the president, the reform of Congress, the need for a "Council of State," the use of computers in government, the control of the economy, the energy crisis, and a dozen other complicated subjects. Few men could have dealt with these topics as audaciously as these two did. Hutchins seemed to encourage Wheeler to develop his thoughts as far as he could carry them.

That dialogue was one of the last scholarly conversations between Hutchins and Wheeler. In the conflicts that erupted at the Center in the following months, the two men separated, and a chasm opened between them that dialogue could not bridge. Wheeler's role in advising and guiding Malcolm Moos disturbed and angered Hutchins.

When Moos came to Santa Barbara for a visit of several days in the last week of December 1973, he spent much of his time with Wheeler. He was in a euphoric mood, and so was Wheeler. Parten had told him that Hutchins had accepted Parten's offer of a year's vacation with pay. To Moos, that meant he would have a year in which he could show what he could do.

Confident that Hutchins would stay out of his way, Moos spoke decisively in his talks with Ashmore. He made it evident that he could not be persuaded to approve the project for another Washington convocation in

1974. Ashmore reluctantly gave ground, agreeing to shift his planning to a series of regional conferences. Moos said he would unveil his own ideas for the Center's future at the board meeting scheduled to be held in January 1974.

Moos knew that the Center's financial reserves were dwindling at a shocking rate, but he believed that he could turn the situation around. He was hopeful that some large donors—who would not give money to a Center headed by Hutchins—would be generous to a Center with a different program, headed by Malcolm Moos. He saw the Center on the verge of bankruptcy, as Parten and others did, but he thought he could save it.

It was clear that fund raising by Moos or anybody else was going to be extremely difficult. The Dow-Jones average for industrial stocks had dropped almost 170 points in 1973. Wealthy stockholders were feeling poor. The value of stocks owned by the major foundations had plunged, and all of them were reducing their expenditures.

But Moos knew that there would be money available for some projects. He resolved to cut the Center's spending, even at the risk of a rebellion among the fellows, and to point the Center in a new direction that might bring in some substantial gifts.

He saw no alternative. So he prepared a plan to place before the board, believing that a majority of the directors would see the necessity for revitalizing the Center along new lines. With Parten's staunch support, Moos thought that the board would back him.

28

A crisis of leadership shakes the nations; a new encyclopedia, influenced by Center dialogues, brings a great compendium to the world; the Center is racked by conflicts; the dialogue breaks down

I N 1974 THE UNITED STATES reeled from one shock to another. Millions of people lost their jobs in the worst recession since the 1930s. Rising prices devoured the money of people who had work or incomes. The stock market fell like a broken rocket. The bastions of the supposedly impregnable fortress called "the presidency" tumbled down under blows from the courts and the Congress. Nixon resigned and fled from Washington after the House Judiciary Committee voted to impeach him. Gerald Ford, a little-known congressman with a mediocre record, moved into the White House.

While the clouds of distrust and confusion darkened the nation, the Center was riddled by dissension and shadowed by fear. The ordinary jealousies and rivalries usually plaguing academic institutions were magnified and multiplied. The fellows, preoccupied with internal struggles, rejoiced only briefly in the acclaim given to a new edition of the Encyclopaedia Britannica, which had been deeply influenced by dialogues conducted at the Center in 1960 and 1961, when scholars had pondered and argued about what a completely new encyclopedia should contain.

The response to the new Britannica was greater than Hutchins had hoped for when he had assembled the scholars at the Center in the 1960s. Mortimer Adler, Warren Preece, and other editors who had brought the huge project into being after a decade of thinking and organizing had gone far beyond the points developed in the Center meetings. But the Center dialogues had played a vital part, and Hutchins was exhilarated by the critics who described it as "an intellectual event," "an enterprise so daring it has not been attempted for centuries," "a game plan for learning everything there is to know about anything."

His exhilaration over the encyclopedia did not last long. He was depressed by the fact that Moos had quickly accepted Norton Ginsburg's offer to resign as the Center's dean when Moos became chairman. In accepting Ginsburg's proposal to submit a resignation, Moos had made it clear again that he intended to give Harvey Wheeler a powerful role in his administration.

On January 14 Norton Ginsburg had written to Moos, enclosing a memorandum he had prepared on the structure of the Center. Pointing out that there was no written constitution for the Center, Ginsburg said "there is virtually nothing in writing about who does what, to whom, for whom, and why."

"With this as preamble, I would like to suggest that in our next conversation we talk about organizational matters and particularly the office of the Dean," Ginsburg continued. "In this connection, it may ease your entry into the system and in general 'clear the air,' if I submit my resignation as Dean, effective the first of July, 1974.

"We must also talk about my own rather unusual situation. As you may not know, I remain on leave from the University of Chicago, even though I am a Senior Fellow at the Center, with all that implies about continuity, as well as Dean. My decision about staying, and under what circumstances, will depend upon how you view the Center's operations and what your plans might be for them. Thus, the sooner we can get to these matters, the better it will be for me.

". . . I would only urge you in addition, and this is not intended to be a *pro forma* suggestion, that you consult also with each of the Senior Fellows of the Center about these matters. . . . Sincerely, Norton. (Copies to Robert M. Hutchins, Harry S. Ashmore)."

Moos had discussed the letter with Wheeler, and had dispatched a prompt reply on January 18: ". . . In my plans for the academic program I contemplate some departures from the immediate past, while building for the future upon the Center's traditions. The administrative arrangements, therefore, will not require a Dean. I expect to orchestrate the academic program myself and take the reins in my own hands as Chairman of the Senior Fellows. Your recognition that your resignation would ease my entry into this responsibility is appreciated, and the terminal date you have indicated is acceptable to me.

"To strengthen the Center's creative and productive work and personnel, I believe it essential that some substantial appointments be made, especially in the areas of the social sciences not now represented at the Center.

In projecting new directions for the future, I am asking Harvey Wheeler to assist me."

Moos went on: "Clearly, transitions always involve patches of unsettlement and uncertainty, but I trust that the change-over will be accomplished with a minimum of friction and a tankful of good will. I realize that you have a splendid post at Chicago, and I know that the expectation of some of your colleagues there is that you will return. . . . The actual date of departure can be at your convenience, and if for any reason you wish to leave before the University of Chicago picks up your income, the Center will certainly carry your salary during the interim."

Ginsburg was startled by the speed with which Moos had replied and dismayed by Moos's statement that he would rely on Wheeler to aid him in "projecting new directions." There had been friction between Ginsburg and Wheeler, and Ginsburg believed that Moos knew about it. He had not intended his letter to convey the idea that he had decided to resign as a senior fellow as well as dean. He had wanted to discuss that possibility with Moos before he reached a decision.

Hutchins was unhappy. He said to John Cogley: "Moos has fired my dean." Ritchie-Calder, Elisabeth Borgese, Cogley, and other senior fellows thought that Ginsburg should have consulted them before submitting a resignation. They decided to draft a statement informing Moos that the fellows had expected to be consulted before any drastic changes were made.

Harry Ashmore, who was on the telephone from time to time with Mrs. McAllister, Blair Clark, Morris Levinson, and other board members, communicated his own negative reaction—and that of Hutchins—to these directors. Ashmore had telephoned Moos and had found it difficult to get through to him. Then Moos invited Ashmore and Wheeler to come to St. Paul to discuss his plans for the future.

Meanwhile, Wheeler had begun to speak as though he had administrative authority. He told me that Moos wanted all the officers to submit their resignations as soon as possible, as "a necessary formality." It seemed to me that this request should have come directly from Moos.

In a telephone conversation, Parten assured me that Wheeler had not been authorized to make such a statement. "Don't resign," Parten said. He told me that he knew Moos wanted me to stay on. Ashmore and Clark also urged me to ignore what Wheeler had said. Clark telephoned me and said: "We're going to put Moos on a short leash." Parten chided Moos for permitting Wheeler to claim such authority, and Moos telephoned me and told me that he was not under Wheeler's domination and he hadn't intended to have Wheeler bring up the question of resignations.

Ashmore and Wheeler met with Moos at his St. Paul home a few days later. During their conversations, Ashmore felt that he was offered "a deal," with Moos indicating that he could stay on as the vice president for external affairs if he consented to a reorganization plan Moos and Wheeler had outlined. Under this plan, Ashmore said later, several of the senior fellows were supposed "to go," including Tugwell, Ritchie-Calder, and Mrs. Borgese.

To Wheeler, this meeting was "a rather intensive week-end encounter session." Moos had expressed a hope to him that the "encounter" would lead to a cooperative relationship between Ashmore and himself. He had been asked by Moos "to help him on the academic side of the Center's affairs." Ashmore was not willing to accept his role.

Recalling the St. Paul session later, Wheeler said: "I know that Moos discussed the need to reduce the budget and that would mean the departure of some of the Fellows, and reduction of some expenditures. I know that he had discussed this with various board members and that they had insisted that it be done. . . . So, whether or not he discussed the names, I'm sure that he discussed something like reducing the number of Fellows to four or five. Cutting it in half, let's say: Cutting the entire budget as nearly in half as possible."

When Ashmore returned from Minnesota, he told Hutchins and others that he had rejected a proposed deal and he felt it was "outrageous" that Moos had allowed Wheeler to take part in a conversation about releasing some of the fellows. Rumors circulated through the Center that Moos planned to fire four or five of the fellows. The fellows feared that Wheeler, not Moos, would attempt to choose the ones who would be asked to leave.

Ashmore sent an eight-page letter to Moos on January 21, saying that he felt it was "essential that the administration of the Center should be reorganized," and asserting that it was his purpose "to clear the way for you to do so with as little disruption as possible." Then he warned Moos that any effort to appoint Wheeler to succeed Ginsburg "necessarily re-opens a set of fundamental policy questions still pending before the board of directors."

"Wheeler and I clearly are in disagreement in our basic approach to the role of the Fellows as it may extend beyond the clear boundaries of the academic program," Ashmore said. "Ideally Wheeler would like to establish the Center as 'a self-governing intellectual community' in which administrators and Board members would serve the scholars. . . . Conceding that the ideal is probably unattainable, he proposes a 'compromise' that would leave the Board with significant but greatly reduced powers: 'The Board should have final authority over financial matters; the Senior Fellows should have final authority over programs and goals.' Any degree of autonomy for the administration as presently constituted under the Chairman and the President would thus be eliminated."

Hutchins and Ashmore had possessed a wide area of autonomy since the reorganization of 1969. Before that, Hutchins had been able to make many decisions on his own, informing the board later. Hutchins and Ashmore had opened and closed New York offices, had launched plans for large projects with the expectation that the board would approve, and had set the salaries of the senior fellows and the senior staff, including their own salaries. The senior fellows and the staff members were not expected to question the administrative decisions of the chairman and the president.

Wheeler clearly represented a threat to the type of administration Ashmore sought to preserve. In his letter of January 21 Ashmore told Moos that the board had rejected Wheeler's proposals for reorganization of the Center in 1970 and had reaffirmed its own legal control over the Center, with such control being exercised by the chairman and the president under rules laid down by the board.

The board meeting scheduled for January had been postponed to February 15. Moos, who had spent some strenuous weeks in Minnesota in sessions with university regents and faculty members, flew off to the Caribbean for a vacation without replying to Ashmore's letter. At the Center, Ashmore indicated to the fellows and staff that he was baffled by Moos's unwillingness to engage in an exchange of letters and memoranda.

During the last days of January, Ashmore participated in the drafting of a statement to Chairman Hutchins—eventually signed by six of the fellows—which was to be transmitted to Moos. The fellows who signed it were Ritchie-Calder, Elisabeth Borgese, Rexford Tugwell, John Cogley, Ginsburg, and Ashmore.

This statement, finally dated February 4, 1974, took a stern line:

"Without presuming to discuss legal/constitutional relationships, the Senior Fellows are and have been in fact a self-governing community of scholars which determines collectively the academic program of the Center. . . . They have had an important voice in the appointment of any officer in charge of, or in any way connected with, the substance of the academic program. . . .

"The Senior Fellows have adopted a policy of not making, during this stage of transition, any changes on the academic staff without prior consultation with the Chairman-Designate whose term of office begins on July 1. In return, the Senior Fellows have assumed that no changes would be effected by the Chairman-Designate prior to his taking office. We have also assumed that no serious changes in either academic personnel or procedures will be made without the previous advice of, and consultation with, the Senior Fellows.

"We should like some reassurances on this point."

Wheeler and John Wilkinson sent a separate statement to Hutchins, asserting that the declaration signed by the six fellows was drafted with "too much haste and too little reflection."

"The document may (possibly) unduly limit the freedom of the Chairman-Elect," Wheeler and Wilkinson said. "It is appropriate that a new leader have evolving plans of his own; and he should have the capability of implementing them."

Wheeler and Wilkinson hoped that the matter would not be submitted to the board of directors "for it carries to them an *internal* dispute which could be worked out *amicably* by the Senior Fellows in deliberation with Mr. Moos." They asked that Moos and Ginsburg resolve any differences of interpretation on what Ginsburg had intended in his letter to Moos, and they reminded the other fellows that Ginsburg had offered "his resignation of the deanship to Mr. Moos rather than to the Senior Fellows."

Alex Comfort, who had been in residence as a senior fellow for just a few weeks when the dispute occurred, typed a brief letter to Hutchins expressing his annoyance at the whole squabble:

"My Dear Bob— As the new boy here I simply do not feel strong enough to sign any of the alternative documents which are being so zealously canvassed. . . .

"If I wrote one myself it would probably say:

"(1) Norton [Ginsburg] appears for some reason to have written a letter he both did and didn't mean to someone he both did and didn't recognize as competent to act on it.

"(2) Any problems arising from this fact would surely be better settled by conversation, rather than by manifesto, when all of us including Mac (Moos) are here at one time.

"(3) Colleagues occupationally distrust each other and engage in backbiting—this is part of the university life. It would be a damn sight less divisive if they would bitch to each others' faces rather than by cabal, behind each others' backs.

"(4) This place studies Democratic Institutions. It's a little disconcerting to find it being run like a cross between a Committee to De-Elect Someone and the court of Byzantium. I think, in an English phrase, everyone should take their finger out and stop plotting and squabbling so that we can all get on with some work."

The tension at the Center was heightened by the circulation of these documents. The plotting and squabbling did not stop. Ritchie-Calder, Tugwell, Ginsburg, Cogley, and Ashmore felt that important principles were at stake. Elisabeth Borgese, who had not wanted Hutchins to retire at all, had deep apprehension about Moos and Wheeler. She had once been close to Wheeler, but personal differences between them had broken their friendship.

Hutchins maintained a formal position of aloofness above all factions, though he was known to be wary of Wheeler and sympathetic with Ashmore. Cogley told me that he knew Ashmore wanted to continue to be a dominant figure at the Center, and Hutchins had indicated to everybody that he wanted Ashmore to have a place of power.

As a member of the board—as well as being the president and chief operating officer—Ashmore had frequent telephone conversations with Morris Levinson, then the chairman of the board's executive committee, and with Frances McAllister, Blair Clark, and other directors. These directors soon learned of the disturbances among the senior fellows.

On January 24, Mrs. McAllister wrote to Parten: "Several distressing rumors have come to my attention regarding acts of the newly named Chairman of the Board and of the Fellows. This period of transition while Dr. Moos is still at the University of Minnesota is at best difficult. I fear that further problems may arise from some procedures—and decisions—which appear to have been initiated.

"It was my understanding that no substantial changes in structure of program were to have been made during the first year under the new administration. However, these items have been called to my attention:

"1. Mr. Cadenhead was re-installed as Secretary of the Board and of the Fellows.

"2. Mr. Ginsburg has been told summarily that he is to leave as of September 1 at the latest.

"3. An intention has been expressed to initiate a college student program.

"4. Mr. Wheeler is being moved toward increased administrative responsibility.

"5. The follow-up to the PIT III (Pacem in Terris convocation) was ordered stopped.

"As Board member my only communication with Dr. Moos has been at a hurried lunch in December. At that time I told him that when he feels he has a more satisfactory trustee to replace me he should let me know.

"The signs are bad if the reports cited above are accurate. It is unfortunate for a new Chairman to make changes before he is actually on the job. Furthermore, I believe that in the absence of specific directives from the Board, methods of making decisions would better stand for a period adequate to provide perspective on internal relations and performance.

"There have for several years been problems of internal relations at the Center. I had hoped that selection of a new chairman would reduce the plays for power. I hope that the matter of a more *Democratic Institution* will be considered before it is too late. If the method of making and communicating decisions is what it appears, I would consider it useless to serve after June 30. If I could be of any service I would expect an open discussion in the February 15 Board meeting of projected staff assignments and any new orientation of program."

Agitated by Mrs. McAllister's letter, Parten tried to reach Moos by telephone. Finding that Moos had left Minnesota, Parten wrote to him on January 30:

"I have this date received from Frances McAllister the enclosed communication which disturbs me greatly. Failing to reach you on the telephone today and finding that you were on vacation, I decided to write.

"No doubt there is considerable confusion at the Center. Mr. Wheeler poses as your representative and seems to be causing a good deal of unnecessary disturbance. In our last meeting in Houston, I counseled you to go slow on changes until you had gotten on the ground and studied the problems personally, taking the necessary time to get all points of view.

"The changes that are made before you take over naturally are going to create disturbance. For example, it was quite understandable that you would want to relieve Dr. Ginsburg of his duties as Dean as you wished personally to take over the program guidance yourself, as did Hutchins in the early days. With this, I was sympathetic, but it did not occur to me that you would discharge Dr. Ginsburg as a Senior Fellow without more investigation than the advice of Mr. Wheeler.

"Harvey Wheeler is a brilliant man without a doubt. He is a real scholar; however, he has shown a monumental deficiency in administration and in working with people. Harvey has a reputation at the Center as a pusher for power which is a fact that should concern you.

"My own personal view is that you will make a great mistake by dealing with the Senior Fellows through Harvey. My belief is that you will find direct dealing with the Senior Fellows much more effective.

"It seems to me that it would be appropriate and helpful for you to invite full Board participation in discussion of the problems of transition at our meeting on February 15. This, I assume, would be best done in executive session."

If Moos had heeded Parten's counsel "to go slow on changes" until he had been installed at the Center, some of his troubles might have been avoided. If he had consulted each of the fellows—and a number of the directors—as frequently as he consulted Wheeler, he might have consolidated his position and might have survived the internal attacks which eventually brought him down. But he thought he had to act rapidly, and he believed he could persuade the board that big changes had to be made at a swift pace. He underestimated the power of his opponents.

Parten was reluctant to give Moos day-to-day advice. As a trustee of the University of Texas—and as a director of the Fund—he felt there were specific limits to his responsibilities. It was not the function of a trustee or a director to run an educational institution. That was the job of the president or the chief executive, whatever the title might be. In Parten's view, trustees were responsible for selecting a good president—and ought to give their views on important issues—but the president had to have freedom to make administrative decisions.

In the months between the selection of Moos as the head of the Center and his arrival in Santa Barbara, Parten defended him against the sniping that came from the fellows and some members of the board. Parten admired the courage Moos had shown in taking on such an enormously difficult job. Parten did not think that the mistakes Moos made—in dealing with Ginsburg or in permitting Wheeler to claim too much authority—were grievous enough to justify the attacks launched by Blair Clark, Frances McAllister and others. He did not wish to see Moos placed "on a short leash." He felt that Moos had to be given a fair chance.

When Parten arrived at Hutchins' office at the Center on the morning of February 15, he began to talk with Hutchins about the situation. Just as he began to speak, Levinson entered the room. Levinson was angry. "Moos has got to go," Levinson said. "He won't fit in here." Parten was shocked. "What do you mean he has to go? He hasn't taken over yet." At that point Arnold Grant came into Hutchins' office and denounced Moos for his handling of the Ginsburg matter.

Parten insisted that Moos had made a proper interpretation of Ginsburg's letter. Parten said that members of the board should not attempt to dictate decisions to Moos. The board had wanted new leadership for the Center, and his committee had spent years in searching for a new chairman. Moos had been elected by a unanimous vote, and Parten felt the board had an obligation to support him.

While Parten was arguing with Levinson and Grant, Hutchins did not speak. Parten, who was certain that Hutchins had favored Moos as his successor, was surprised by Hutchins' silence. But he continued to stand up for Moos, and at last Levinson and Grant agreed to give Moos an opportunity to show what he could do.

When the board convened in an executive session at 11 o'clock that morning, Moos read to the directors a statement describing his plans for the development of the Center.

"I have followed the Center's work for over fifteen years," Moos said. "Throughout the years I have been a constant admirer of and an intermittent participant in the work of the Center. Here is my vision of the way we can drive an ever widening wedge of influence into the future. . . .

"I would like to recall to your minds Mr. Hutchins's perennial quest to develop a genuine academy. The University has failed. The tradition of the Academy, properly understood, must be preserved at the Center.

"My proposal for developing this, as well as the aims already described, is through an emphasis on the proper idea of a true University; a university devoted to independent thought and criticism and to the widening of the circles of discussion about the basic issues of our time. Hence, it would be something like a Rockefeller University for the humanities, interpreted broadly, but also more modestly. I shall say more about this later.

"The opening move, it seems to me, can well begin with a drive to endow a few high-prestige named chairs. Ideally, it would be good to have four to six endowed chairs, but the actual number must depend upon our fund raising capacity."

Moos had been thinking about such a university—"an academy of practical and political philosophy"—for more than thirty years. He told the board: "I first thought about it when I was a very young instructor at Johns Hopkins University and discussed the problems besetting American higher education with several of my colleagues there. One was Abba Lerner, a very bright young man. We discussed the fact that nothing comparable to the London School of Economics existed in the United States.

"I felt it would be a great idea to form an instituion with a small group of students—eight, ten, or a dozen, and a very distinguished faculty, perhaps eight or ten people. I went so far as to look into buying a small Quaker college which had gone bankrupt in Western Maryland. It had a beautiful setting, although not so lovely as that in Santa Barbara.

"I sought foundation support and I think, except for the onrushing war, there would have been real interest to start such a university. I remained convinced that the idea had merit; if one could develop a reputation for getting some of the most talented people in the social sciences, the humanities, and possibly the bio-medical area—we didn't want to spread too thin in the beginning—it would be a creative and innovative experiment in higher education, a real partnership of the learners and the learned. It did not work out because of the war, but I never forgot it."

Years later, in a conversation with Robert Oppenheimer, the atomic physicist, Moos was stirred again by the possibilities of this idea: "Oppenheimer told me about life at the Institute for Advanced Studies at Princeton. He said, 'You know, Malcolm, it's a great place to be, a kind of academy of the exalted brood—distinguished scholars, internationals, and some of the best minds in the United States. But after the first two years you really miss students and the collision of minds and the stimulation you get from students.' I never forgot that. . . .

"Later I became quite familiar with the Rockefeller University. . . . It is a remarkable place. There are some fifty students and 350 scholars. I suspect that no place in the world has ever had this kind of plentitude of teachers to students. I have no such thought in mind for the Center; but it does strike me that a much more modest effort would be desirable."

The directors listened to him thoughtfully. Parten felt that the Center had to move into a new phase, and he was impressed by the sweep of the Moos proposal. Moos sought to create what he called a "communiversity."*

"Our new Center must be a university of the highest possible quality," Moos said. "This is what the nation, and indeed the world, truly needs: not more conference centers; not more behavioral science institutes; not more opinion survey research centers. And this, I can assure you, is a need the

---

*Moos used the term "communiversity" to describe what he had in mind.

major foundations recognize. Some institution inevitably will try to serve that need if we do not, but the Center is the only one that can. It is the one that has earned the right to truly serve it. This, I repeat, is a goal that not only builds upon our established traditions, but also serves a need that must be performed. . . .

"The learning society of the future must be realized through learning communities: communities built around their educational institutions just as the manufacturing communities of the past were built around their industrial facilities. . . .

"Our problem at the Center is to figure out what ought to be the educational experiences of the citizens of the learning society: those who will live and learn in the 'communiversities' of the future. Some elements of the educational experience they will need are already apparent.

"Our future citizens must learn the lessons of citizenship, as a life-long profession; the higher learning, the public law, the political processes, world order, communications, the scientific revolution, and so on. In short, this is the unifying theme that not only incorporates the Center's established interests but at the same time focuses them creatively on the needs of the future: the learning society facilitated by the 'communiversity' and informed by the appropriate objects of study. This, it seems to me, is the challenge the Center must accept. It is the challenge no other institution can understand, much less accept, and it is the single most important task that will face our society in the near future."

Moos linked his own proposal for a "communiversity" of the humanities and social sciences with Hutchins' call for the creation of "the learning society" in a book Hutchins had written under that title: "My view is that these conceptions, compatible in any case by their essential natures, can now be married."

Hutchins did not speak up to welcome the proposed marriage. Blair Clark said he thought that such an academy would mean a drastic change from the existing Center program. Moos answered that the plan would require long-range refining—he had stated in his speech to the board that its full realization might take five years—but he believed it could be accomplished without any major departure from the program that had been created under Hutchins. He assured the board again that he was dedicated to the continuance of Hutchins' ideas, and said his program would be shaped with the advice of the Fellows and the directors.

Moos did not ask for any resolution by the directors approving his proposal—and none was offered—but the minutes kept by Ashmore and Moos noted: "The statement . . . met with general approval."

After a brief discussion of Moos's statement, expressions of concern over "unrest" among the fellows and staff members of the Center were voiced by several directors. Moos said he had learned that there had been "unfortunate incidents" due to a misunderstanding of the role Harvey

Wheeler would have under his management. He said he did not intend to have Wheeler acting as an administrator; he would run the academic program himself and he did not wish to have a "dean."

At the afternoon session of that meeting on February 15, the directors wrangled over whether Moos had been correct in believing that Ginsburg had really wanted to resign as a senior fellow as well as "dean." Moos said he would talk with Ginsburg and he was sure that the matter could be "worked out." Mrs. McAllister asked whether he took the view that Ginsburg had a right to keep on being a senior fellow. Moos said he would consider that idea when he talked with Ginsburg.

Bernard Weissbourd suggested that there was a chance that Ginsburg might retain his faculty position at the University of Chicago and continue as a senior fellow. Moos answered that he regarded "a joint appointment" as a shift in the Center's policy. He said he would consider appointing Ginsburg as an associate, but he was not willing to make an unprecedented appointment of a fellow, involving a university.

Parten intervened, saying that he did not think the board should tell Moos what to do on administrative matters. Weissbourd agreed that the directors should not do so, and said he had not intended to compel Moos to take any particular action. Weissbourd then left the conference room.

Levinson urged Moos to accept Ginsburg's interpretation of what Ginsburg had meant to say in his letter and to reach an agreement on that basis. Mrs. McAllister and Bernard Rapoport also thought that was a good idea. Parten spoke again, declaring that he thought Moos had already made "a reasonable interpretation" of the Ginsburg letter, and Fagan Dickson supported Parten.

Moos offered to send copies of the correspondence between Ginsburg and himself to all members of the board. Levinson recommended that the statements of the senior fellows should also be made available, and Moos accepted that suggestion.

While saying that he did not want to get into "internal administrative affairs," Levinson referred to the activities of Harvey Wheeler and advised Moos "to get together with the Fellows and get all matters at issue out on the table and see if the alleged damage could be repaired." Rapoport favored Levinson's proposal.

Harold Willens, who spoke warmly of Wheeler, regarded such "a confrontation" as "extreme" and felt that the difficulty could be settled in a more subtle manner. Mrs. Laucks said she didn't know what Wheeler was supposed to have done or hadn't done, but she considered Wheeler "one of the most valuable members of the Senior Fellows."

Moos indicated that he would take all the suggestions made by the directors under consideration. Then he put forward two proposals that were received warmly by the board. One was that the position of chairman of the board—which had been conferred upon him, effective July 1—should be offered to Parten. Moos's title, if the board agreed, would be president of the Fund, chief executive officer of the Center, and chairman of the Fellows. Parten was willing to serve as chairman of the Fund's board, and all the directors liked that idea.

The second recommendation Moos proposed at this point was that Harry Ashmore be elected executive vice president when Moos became president. This idea had been suggested to him at lunch by James Douglas, and undoubtedly had the backing of Hutchins. Moos had been reluctant to agree to it—as Parten had sensed—but Moos had recognized the fact that Ashmore had powerful friends on the board. Douglas, Levinson, Mrs. McAllister, and others felt that Ashmore had earned the right to continue as an executive of the Center.

Moos had not wished to have Ashmore as an officer of the Fund and as an administrator of the Center. He felt that it was inevitable that a president and an executive vice president in a small organization would collide with each other. But he also knew he had to placate Hutchins and the other directors who admired Ashmore.

Blair Clark pressed Moos to specify that Ashmore had special status. The minutes of the executive session on February 15, 1974, show that Clark asked whether Ashmore was to be "*the* executive vice president, or merely one of several bearing that title." Moos answered that Ashmore was "the only executive vice president he contemplated." Ashmore then declared that he would be willing "to continue to serve in any capacity the board might deem useful."

With Ashmore retained in the top administrative structure of the Center, Moos realized that he was actually "on a short leash." He had to try to convince the fellows and the directors to accept his new program under the skeptical eyes of Clark, Ashmore, and others who felt that drastic changes might destroy the Center Hutchins had built. At the same time he would be expected to convince foundation executives and other donors that the Center was changing—that it was not simply going around and around in the old grooves.

After his concessions in the executive session of the board, it was clear that Moos would have to spend a great deal of time with individual directors, explaining his program, if he hoped to get anywhere. He did not have any time to spare. The financial records presented by Gary Cadenhead at the open session of the board that afternoon indicated that the Center had a life expectancy of about eighteen months unless the budget could be drastically reduced and new sources of money could be found.

Hutchins and Ashmore thought that a possible fountain of money existed in Randolph Compton, chairman of the Fund for Peace, who was seeking an affiliation with the Center. Hutchins reported to the directors that he had met with Compton in New York for preliminary talks, and Ashmore and Tagger had held conversations with staff members of various projects financed by the Fund for Peace.

Compton had a considerable amount of money in a family foundation, and Hutchins indicated that it could be assumed that this cash was "intended for a reconstituted institution that commends itself to him." He said that several representatives of the Fund for Peace would be in Santa Barbara that weekend to carry on the discussions that he and Compton had begun.

Hutchins was authorized by the board to appoint a committee to look into the feasibility of a close relationship between the Compton organization and the Center. That action did not stir enthusiasm in Moos, who knew that the Fund for Peace was principally concerned with international convocations, public interest broadcasts over radio stations, and a university consortium for world studies. An affiliation with the Fund for Peace might carry the Center toward greater emphasis on public convocations and communications—and might diminish the board's interest in his own plans for the Center's development.

Moos vexed Ashmore and Hutchins by the coolness he showed toward the negotiations with the Compton representatives. Moos did not openly oppose these conversations, but it was evident that he did not wish to get deeply involved in them.

Many of the directors, the fellows, and the staff members of the Center were not happy about the results of that February 1974 board meeting. Wounds had been opened that proved to be impossible to heal. The hostilities that had almost led to a demand for the removal of Moos before his installation as the Center's chief officer still smoldered.

Ashmore and Moos found it hard to understand each other. Ashmore wanted a clear picture of what his duties and responsibilities were to be, and Moos was reluctant to put powers into Ashmore's hands. He wanted Ashmore to be on his team, or "on the bridge of the ship"—a term Moos used frequently—but he didn't want Ashmore to be regarded as the second in command. In spite of the anger shown by some board members and fellows toward Wheeler, Moos continued to rely on Wheeler as a confidant and adviser. He had known Wheeler for a long time, and he did not feel at ease with anyone else at the Center.

When Hutchins had not spoken out for him in the executive session, when Hutchins had not reiterated that he wanted Moos to have the authority and scope that the board had given to him, Moos was sadly disappointed. He felt that he had very few friends at the Center; he did not believe that Hutchins was staunchly with him. He felt sure that he could count on Wheeler—and Wheeler's close associate, John Wilkinson.

Although they were on different wavelengths and differed on many points, Ashmore and Moos—and Wheeler, too—agreed on one significant point. The fellows weren't working together very well. The "intellectual community" that was the high objective of the Hutchins program had not been achieved. The quality of the dialogue had gone down. The Center had been losing its sense of what its mission was.

Ashmore scolded the senior fellows in a memorandum he sent to them on April 4—with a copy to Moos: "It is not the external demands of communications, but the centrifugal effect of the specialized interests of the Fellows that has increasingly debilitated the dialogue." He said the fellows were depending too much on conferences with visiting experts. He did not call for the abolition of conferences altogether, saying that occasional gatherings could be "regarded as adjuncts which might, upon certification by a responsible Senior Fellow, be expected to illuminate some aspects of his ongoing project."

Recognizing that his propositions were "easy to state and difficult to put into practice," Ashmore acknowledged the fact that some fellows considered it impossible to separate the dialogue from "the variety of activities that more or less flow from it." But he felt that "the dialogue is perishing as we seem to be moving steadily in the direction of a conference center which serves as a kind of administrative hub for a variety of unrelated projects."

Although Ashmore believed that the dialogue was "perishing," he was not eager to embrace the Moos proposal for a model university somewhat similar to the Rockefeller University. He said: "It would seem to me the old concept of the dialogue also would be profoundly affected by Malcolm Moos' proposal that we look toward the ultimate establishment of a degree-granting graduate school in the social sciences."

Wheeler, who had been frustrated by the outcome of the 1969 reorganization, felt that the Moos plan opened a way for the Center to emerge from "an intellectual and a moral crisis" that had existed since 1969. He told Moos that he thought the Center had become "a kind of archaic, in some ways nostalgic, liberal organization that was not sufficiently attuned to the needs of society."

Moos did not reply in writing to Ashmore's memorandum of April 4, but he apparently felt that his plan for changing the Center into a university of the humanities and social sciences, with much emphasis on community relations, might give the Center the new "mission" that he and Wheeler felt it needed.

In the spring of 1974, in the weeks following the uproar at the February board meeting, Moos tried to end the controversy over Ginsburg by offering Ginsburg an appointment as an associate with a guaranteed relationship with the Center over a period of years. He talked with Ashmore, Ginsburg, and other fellows about this. Ashmore and other fellows insisted that Moos had no right to terminate Ginsburg's appointment as a senior fellow, but Ginsburg seemed willing to accept an appointment as a special associate.

On April 12 Ashmore sent Moos another memorandum, stating what he thought Moos could do about academic appointments: "As I understood our conversation yesterday, you are prepared to work out a special Associate status for Norton Ginsburg as a possible alternative to his continuing as a full-time Senior Fellow. If this proved acceptable, and Norton chose to resign as a Senior Fellow *on his own motion*, this would, of course, resolve the issue raised in the letter sent to you by a majority of the Fellows protesting that they had not been consulted in the course of your earlier action in regard to the deanship. I'm sure this would be taken as affirmation of the fact that, upon taking over as President and Chairman of the Fellows, you intend to continue the constitutional relationship that existed under Robert Hutchins.

"What I understood that to mean in practice is that the Fellows, functioning collegially under the leadership of the Chairman of the Fellows, would continue to have the right to name academic personnel and determine the content of the academic program."

Ashmore reminded Moos that such a delegation of authority had been approved by the board of directors on March 4, 1970, "subject to budgetary and administrative controls to be adopted by the board." So far, he said, these controls had consisted "only of annual approval of the academic budget."

Responding to a statement by Moos that the question of tenure for the fellows had never been settled, Ashmore said: "While the board did not act on a recommendation from its own committee on organization formally endorsing tenure, it has confirmed that the post of Senior Fellow is regarded as permanent. In the absence of any prescribed retirement age, this must mean that removal (presumably by the Senior Fellows, since the right of removal would seem to be embodied in the right of appointment) could only be for cause. The principal difference between this and the usual university tenure arrangement is that neither cause, nor any formal means of establishing it, is specified.

"There are no employment contracts with Senior Fellows or Senior Staff, although there are letters of understanding in the case of the last two appointees—Lord Ritchie-Calder and Alexander Comfort—and there is doubtless relevant correspondence with others. It is my judgment that these would constitute legally binding commitments of continued employment under the terms set forth. Nothing less could be expected to prompt a man to permanently transfer his residence from one continent to another. . . .

"As you will see from the attached file, the issue of a formal contract has now been raised by our accountants and legal counsel in the case of Elisabeth Borgese, who has been compensated and is taxed on a different basis from the other Senior Fellows as a result of her joining the Center while domiciled in Italy. I have taken the position that I do not have the authority to negotiate the kind of contract the lawyers recommend until we have established some clear policy as to conditions of employment, which on the Center's side would necessarily include expectations of performance. . . .

"I hope that none of this will be construed as an intervention from the administrative side in your right to make the ultimate determination in these matters in consultation with the board," Ashmore said.

Having sent this communication to Moos, Ashmore subsided for a while. But the atmosphere of the Center was still uneasy. The fellows were divided and critical of one another. Their status had not been clarified under Hutchins, and they were not sure of what their functions would be if Moos persuaded the board to go ahead with his plan to convert the Center into a "communiversity."

Parten tried to improve relations between Hutchins and Moos. He talked by telephone from Houston with each of them and was assured that each wanted to do everything possible to make the shift from a Hutchins administration to a Moos regime as harmonious as possible.

In April, Parten was told by Moos that Moos wished to nominate three new directors to serve on the Fund's board. Moos wanted to add directors who were sympathetic to his ideas and who might counteract the skepticism or opposition of Clark, McAllister, and Ashmore. Parten thought the request was reasonable: all the current directors had been placed on the board by Hutchins, and it seemed sensible to add new directors to serve with a new administration.

The first two suggested by Moos were Bernard H. Ridder, Jr., publisher of the St. Paul *Pioneer Press* and other newspapers, and Arthur A. Burck of Palm Beach, Florida, a management consultant and merger expert, who had graduated from the University of Minnesota. Parten sent these names to Hutchins and received a note of approval from Hutchins on April 29: "I am happy to approve the nomination of B. H. Ridder, Jr., and Arthur A. Burck to the board of the Fund."

Then Moos recommended L. Emmerson Ward, chairman of the board of governors of the Mayo Foundation, Rochester, Minnesota. Parten and Hutchins approved that nomination quickly. Dr. Ward had an eminent position in the medical world, and Parten felt that he also would make a constructive contribution to the Fund's board.

Early in May, Parten heard from Gary Cadenhead that Ashmore was reported to be gathering proxies from directors who might be opposed to expansion of the board. Parten took the precaution of obtaining proxies for the addition of new directors from four board members who had indicated that they probably could not attend the meeting scheduled for May 17 in St. Paul. He received telegrams granting their votes from Paul Newman, J. Howard Marshall, Seniel Ostrow, and Harold Willens.

On the plane trip from Santa Barbara to St. Paul for that meeting, I rode in a seat next to Hutchins. "I want you to tell Parten that Ashmore is not plotting against Moos,'' Hutchins said. "Somebody has put that idea into his head. Harry has tried to work with Moos. I don't think Wheeler and Moos want him in the picture. If there is a split in the board, it isn't Harry's fault.''

At the hotel in St. Paul, on the night before the board session, I conveyed the message from Hutchins to Parten. Parten gave me a quizzical glance. "I know what Ashmore and Blair Clark are doing," Parten said. "They don't want these new men on the board. I'm prepared for them.''

Eighteen directors attended the board gathering on May 17: Joseph Antonow, Ashmore, Blair Clark, Patrick Crowley, Fagan Dickson, James Douglas, Arnold Grant, Hutchins, Monsignor Francis Lally, Eulah Laucks, W. Price Laughlin, Morris Levinson, Moos, Stewart Mott, Frances McAllister, Parten, Bernard Rapoport, and Bernard Weissbourd. Many of the directors had talked to one another the night before, and there was a tense feeling in the room.

Hutchins, who presided as chairman, announced that Moos would be ready to take over his responsibilities as chief executive officer of the Fund and the Center on June 1, instead of July 1, 1974, the original date set by the directors at their Washington meeting. Hutchins said he would like to retire on the earlier date, and a motion making the appointment of Moos effective on June 1 was unanimously passed. Considering the tension at that time, the unanimous vote for an earlier installation of Moos was astonishing.

Speaking as chairman of the nominating committee, Parten presented the names of the three nominees Moos had recommended. There was a technical problem. The board was already at its authorized strength of twenty-nine members. To add three more directors would require a vote to expand the board to thirty-two.

James Douglas advocated that the membership be immediately increased by three members and that the nominees presented by Parten be elected. Grant said that an increase in the size of the board would call for an amendment of the bylaws, and to authorize an amendment would take a majority of the whole board—that is, fifteen votes—rather than a majority of the members present, which would ordinarily be enough to elect new members.

Blair Clark then opposed the election of the nominees, saying that there had not been enough time for directors not on the nominating committee to consider the qualifications of the men Parten had presented. This was the first occasion in the history of the Fund when directors offered by the nominating committee had been questioned. Clark suggested that consideration of the election of the nominees should be delayed until the next board meeting.

Clark was supported in this proposal by Mrs. McAllister and Stewart Mott. Hutchins and Ashmore sat in silence. Moos was rather pale. He had invited the three nominees to attend a dinner for the board at his home that night, assuming that they would be elected.

When a motion was made to amend the bylaws and elect the nominees, the motion received thirteen votes. That was not sufficient, according to Arnold Grant. There was some discussion of what could be done next.

Rapoport vehemently urged the board to demonstrate its backing for the new chairman by electing the nominees. Then Joseph Antonow, to Parten's relief, proposed to separate the issues—voting first on the basic question of enlarging the board and then having the votes on each of the candidates.

The motion to expand the board received the necessary fifteen votes —a majority of the entire board. Clark voted against it, and Mrs. McAllister and Mott asked to be recorded as "abstaining."

Burck, Ridder, and Ward were then elected to the board on separate votes, and the directors unanimously approved the election of Parten as chairman of the board effective on June 1, with Moos as president and Ashmore as executive vice president. The board reaffirmed my election as vice president and that of Gary Cadenhead as secretary and treasurer.

Parten had taken an active part in the St. Paul sessions without mentioning to the other directors that his home in Madisonville, Texas, had been destroyed by a fire on the night of May 15, two days before the board meeting. His wife had been injured in the fire, and he might have been excused from attendance at the Minnesota gathering. But he had given his word to Moos that he would help him. He had made a commitment, and he fulfilled it.

After the battle over the new directors, Hutchins informed the directors that conversations with Randolph Compton and other officers of the Fund for Peace were still in progress. The board approved a continuation of discussions with the Compton organization by the committee appointed by Hutchins, with the addition of Moos and any other directors Moos might wish to add to the group.

Morris Levinson then asked the board to place in its record a statement on the future of the center, which had been provided to the directors by Clark. Levinson thought it was appropriate "upon the occasion of the retirement of Robert M. Hutchins, its founder."

The Clark statement, a two-page document, was a general description of the Center's history and purposes: "The Center for the Study of Democratic Institutions is, and will remain, a community of intellectuals concerned with, and thinking and acting in relation to man and the ways in which he organizes the life of his society. Its basic assumption is that a democratic society, with all its problems, is the ideal. Its focus is on the American society and its institutions but, recognizing a growing interdependence of all mankind, its reach extends beyond our shores.

"At the heart of the Center's life is a continuing dialogue among the Fellows who, for varying lengths of time, constitute its intellectual community. The dialogue contributes to the general purposes of the Center through exchange of information and ideas among a group of scholars and persons experienced in public affairs, with different perspectives and knowledge but with a common concern for the central human and social problems of the age.

"The Center propagates the knowledge and ideas of its Fellows, and of the wide range of able thinkers it brings to Santa Barbara, through public meetings and convocations which it organizes around the country and, occasionally, abroad.

"Its contact with a broad public is enhanced by a membership of more than 70,000 which receives the *Center Magazine* and the *Center Report*.

"This is the way the Center works and there is nothing immutable about it. The Board believes that it has worked remarkably well for 15 years in this fashion and that the forms that have evolved have proven their value. Therefore any substantial changes in the aims and methods described here will be the subject of full consideration by the Board, upon recommendation of such committees as it may establish to consider, in full consultation with the officers and Fellows, new forms of organization and activity for the Center."

Although Clark said in his statement that "there is nothing immutable" about the working of the Center, it was evident that the statement was designed to endorse the programs and structures developed by Hutchins and Ashmore—and to make any changes a matter of step-by-step development largely under the control of board committees, all of the officers (including, of course, the executive Vice President), and the fellows. It meant that Moos would be hedged in by many requirements.

No director voiced an objection to the Clark statement. In the brief discussion of it at that meeting, Clark agreed that his document did not necessarily cover all aspects of the Center's activities, and he said it "was not intended to be exclusive." Parten asked that the record include his own affirmation that the Fund had been—and should continue to be—deeply concerned with constitutional liberties, and dedicated to freedom and justice.

Moos declared that he did not interpret the document to conflict with his own statement of the Center's goals, which was distributed to the board members. The Moos statement, headed "The Center Program," and the Clark document were attached to the board's minutes.

The Minnesota meeting ended with apparent harmony among the directors. The three new directors nominated by Moos had finally been accepted, giving Moos some confidence that he would have more solid supporters on the board, and the Clark statement—backed by Levinson, Ashmore, and others closely associated with Hutchins—had been accepted without any arguments.

But the harmony was very fragile. Mrs. McAllister was angry at Moos, feeling that he had pushed through the election of the three new board members and had not shown enough respect for Hutchins. She did not appear at the dinner Moos gave for all the directors that night and consequently did not hear the graceful speech Moos gave, expressing his admiration and affection for the retiring chairman of the Center.

On the trip back to Santa Barbara, I remarked to Ashmore and Hutchins, "Gary Cadenhead stayed in Minneapolis. He seems to be quite close to Moos." "Yes," Ashmore said, nodding grimly. "He's with the winning faction this time."

Moos and Hutchins appeared together at the Center's regional convocation "The State of the Democratic Process" at the Beverly Hilton hotel in Los Angeles on June 1 before an audience of 2000. The theme of the conference was "The Crisis of the Contemporary Presidency," and the principal speakers were Senator Walter F. Mondale, Democratic Senator from Minnesota, and Robert Packwood, a Republican Senator from Oregon.* The proceedings were broadcast by KCET, the public television station in Los Angeles, and videotapes were prepared for the national Public Broadcasting Service network.

A report prepared by Peter Tagger showed that the expenses of the convocation were $37,073 and the income (including a $15,000 pledged contribution) totaled $46,353. Once again, Ashmore was enthusiastic about the results and wrote to Moos, telling him that the other regional convocations could also bring important benefits to the Center.

But Moos was absorbed in thinking about the possibilities of the educational program he had proposed in his statement to the board in February. He had returned to Minnesota for a few days to prepare his files for shipment to California. On June 7 he wrote a letter to Harvey Wheeler from his office at the university and sent copies to Parten and other directors.

"As you know, my involvement with and interest in higher education in this country long pre-dates my seven years' tenure as President of the University of Minnesota," Moos said to Wheeler. "The future of the university was uppermost in my mind already as a beginning teacher at Johns Hopkins, and this was referred to briefly in my statement to the board. . . .

"These concerns intensified during my stint at the Ford Foundation and with the Rockefeller Brothers," Moos continued. "Moreover, the long years spent with the Carnegie Commission, helping to shepherd the massive Clark Kerr study (as well as its sequel, which we have just funded) convinced me that a very significant departure from accepted educational practices must be undertaken. Indeed, I think this is one of, if not *the*, most serious problems facing our nation today. Accordingly, I want to move with all deliberate speed to prepare an educational program at the Center to be developed along the lines of the Rockefeller-type university for the social sciences and humanities that is described in my address to the Board.

"I am asking you to accept appointment as Coordinator of this pro-

---

*This conference grew out of a proposal I had made for a continuing search for potential Presidents—a continuing examination of new candidates and new ideas for the Presidency.

gram. I hope you will take it on, for I am convinced that your guidance in seeing the program through its initial stages to maturity is essential to its success. It will be a hard job, but we will be able to work together in developing it into what I am convinced can be the most important innovation in American higher education since the development of the graduate schools in the mid-nineteenth century.

"In preparing our proposals for submission to various foundations and grant-giving sources, we shall want to give thought to various distinguished scholars who can help us make this into the important endeavor it deserves to be. I think of Clark Kerr, Jacques Barzun, David Riesman, among others, for I know from personal conversation that they will be receptive to the project.

"As Coordinator you will have responsibility for developing the materials describing the program and preparing them in such fashion that I can use them in the solicitation of support. In doing this, you should give thought to those persons, both inside and outside the Center, who might be able to help in the preparatory stages as well as later. We should be in a position to make our first requests for the support of feasibility studies within three months after my arrival as President and Chairman of the Center. Our major solicitation of endowment funds should commence not later than October. . . ."

In his letter to Wheeler, Moos did not mention Hutchins as a possible participant in the creation of the innovative program in higher education. Parten had sent him a copy of a note Hutchins had sent to Parten on May 3, in which Hutchins had said he would like to have six months of vacation rather than the year's leave of absence Parten had suggested. Hutchins had decided that he should not be away from the Center for a full year. But he would be absent during the first six months of the Moos administration—a period in which Moos wanted to get his program going. In any case, Moos did not indicate that he sought Hutchins' advice.

A few days after Hutchins turned over his office at the Center to Moos, Israel Shenker of the *New York Times* arrived in Santa Barbara to do an article on what was happening there. Shenker interviewed fellows and staff members who spoke candidly. When Shenker's article appeared in the *Times* on June 5, the caustic comments made by some of them increased the friction between the fellows. John Cogley, who was especially disturbed by what Shenker had written, suffered a stroke on June 11 and was taken to the Cottage Hospital.

Under a headline saying "Center for Study of Democratic Institutions Has New Chief and a Fiscal Crisis," Shenker wrote:

> Its philosophy is liberal and its substance patrician: a 42-acre sylvan retreat whose central building, known as El Parthenon, houses a jamboree of full-time scholars, sometime authors, one-time journalists, occasional iconoclasts and perennial academics.

Their mission is to think deeply and speak loudly, scorning no human problem as too difficult, evading no issue as too divisive.

But the issue of the Center's survival now is overriding trifles of routine concern such as global law and peaceful order. While seeking immortality, the Center is running out of money, and intimations of mortality contend with the hope that something may turn up.

"Institutional micawberism," Harvey Wheeler, a senior Fellow, called it, and Harry S. Ashmore, another senior Fellow, scored it as "a constant tambourine-shaking operation."

For the last several years Dr. Hutchins has been suffering from ill health and he has had several operations. John Wilkinson, a senior Fellow, complained that the Center "has meanwhile marked time."

"We've been drifting," he said. "Everybody made an itinerary taking him away for long periods, and found a focus and locus outside the Center. How could people think when they were above a cloud? They thought about meeting, they didn't think about thinking."

Dr. Moos would like the Center to be "something like a Rockefeller University for the Humanities"—with some post-doctoral students and "a few high-prestige name chairs." He plans to launch a fund drive and prove that the Center is not merely the lengthened shadow of its founder.

"It's Hutchins' Center," said Mr. Wheeler. "It's a bureaucratization of Hutchins, an extension of his personality—and he's a strong and compelling person, with a piercing mind and an alarming ability to see behind social facades. He's a master of shaft and foe of sham."

The long and short of it is that Dr. Hutchins—6 feet 3 inches, white-haired, more handsome than egalitarian Democrats would think just—has enormous presence and staggering charisma, and Dr. Moos will simply have to shake the tambourine harder. "Moos might get charisma if he gets money," suggested Dr. Wilkinson.

The statements of some of the senior fellows and visiting fellows to Shenker were not laudatory of the Center. Alva Myrdal, former Swedish minister for disarmament, and Gunnar Myrdal, the noted Swedish economist, made negative remarks that were quoted by Shenker.

"I've heard what the Center was supposed to be, but I think the Center is in a period of transition, seeking its true role," Mrs. Myrdal said. "The atmosphere is very congenial, but the subjects of conversation are spread quite thinly, so there's a diffusion of energies."

Gunnar Myrdal shrugged his shoulders at the dialogue conferences he had attended at the Center. "It's not my method," Myrdal said. "I've always learned more from individual talks, not from conferences."

Alexander King, a Center associate who had been a director of the Organization for Economic Cooperation and Development in Paris, told Shenker: "I'm very disappointed with the dialogue. It's too inbred . . . incestuous." Norton Ginsburg said: "When a meeting is good you can call it dialogue; when it's bad you can call it lousy." Alex Comfort, the newest senior fellow, said: "Some of the papers are abysmal, some are excellent. It's impossible to have the number of dialogues we have without a certain number of lemons. We try to squeeze each lemon, but some have very little in them but pits."

"The group is pretty polarized," Mrs. Borgese admitted. "There are those who are trying to do something—not just be intelligent—and those who feel they have to be cynical and revel in destructiveness and pessimism and get a kick out of it."

Moos was quoted by Shenker as saying that the Center had to "find some way to achieve an infusion of youth." Moos declared, "The average of our Senior Fellows is older than I am [58]. We flirt dangerously with the vicissitudes of fate."

Shenker concluded his article with quotations from Wendell Mordy, a visiting fellow, who called the Center "the best academic institution I know in terms of size and input and excellence of ideas and the quality of people they have in touch," and the irrepressible John Wilkinson, who said: "My only hope is that as a university president, Moos is used to having cuckoos in the woodwork."

The parade of negative statements in Shenker's story increased the difficulties Malcolm Moos encountered when he tried to raise money for the Center. Executives of the large foundations—and many individual donors —read the *New York Times*. The statements by the Myrdals, Alexander King, Mrs. Borgese, and Wilkinson presented a picture of the Center as "incestuous," "polarized," "spread quite thinly," with "cuckoos in the woodwork" and a shortage of money.

In that summer of 1974, Moos endeavored to get the Fellows to work together, to make peace with the directors who had been angered by his treatment of Ginsburg, to reduce expenditures as rapidly as he could, and to encourage Mordy and Wheeler to draft proposals for presentations to foundations with requests for substantial grants. He ran into one obstacle after another, but he maintained an optimistic attitude. He tried to improve his relationship with Hutchins.

"I believe that Moos and the Center will make it," Hutchins wrote to Parten on June 24. "It will not be the first time this organization has owed its survival to you."

But there was one director Moos could not win over to his side. That was Frances McAllister, who sent critical letters to Parten, Douglas, and other directors. She was disturbed when Moos formed a staff advisory committee that included Wheeler, Cadenhead, and Wendell Mordy. She felt that Ashmore's status as the executive vice president of the Center was diminished by the formation of this committee.

On August 14 she informed Parten that Moos had agreed to have lunch with several of the directors in Chicago "after several weeks of effort to communicate with Malcolm at a serious and sustained level." He had invited her to attend a meeting in Houston to develop plans to overcome the Center's continuing financial crisis.

"It is still possible to salvage the Center, but sober and profound dedication must be applied," Mrs. McAllister admonished Parten, who had been dedicated to the Center since its establishment. "After the ordeals of this republic in the past two years, and the plight of the whole globe, we need a center where qualified scholars, diplomats and judges can focus on moral and political solutions. When I know that the money will be used for these purposes, I will expand my giving."

Parten replied to her patiently and calmly, thanking her for her concern and for the memoranda she poured upon him. He knew she cared about the Center and she had supported it generously in the past.

James Douglas, the host of a luncheon for Moos on August 16, wrote to Parten a few days later: "Just a brief note to say that Frances McAllister, Malcolm Moos, Jim Downs and Joe Antonow lunched with me at the University Club last Friday. Pat Crowley joined us for a half hour at the end of the luncheon. I thought we had a very satisfactory discussion, without criticism or controversy.

"Malcolm outlined the areas of activity that he regarded as most important in the near future. We talked about the need for foundation support. I asked if I was right in thinking that the principal foundations are not much interested in overall support but in special projects, and Malcolm said that this was the case. . . .

"Joe (Antonow) and I talked to Frances afterwards. We had both read her three memoranda addressed to your committees. These were not referred to at the luncheon, but after luncheon Frances told Joe and me that she thought she would write a note saying she felt much better about the situation than when she had written the memoranda. All of us were very glad to be brought up to date by Malcolm on program."

But Mrs. McAllister was not pacified for long. She had expected Moos to stop over and visit her at her home in Flagstaff, Arizona, on his way to Chicago, and he had not done so. He had not discussed her memoranda at the Chicago luncheon.

So she wrote again to Parten, expressing her dissatisfaction: "Less than two hours spent with Malcolm and four other Board members in Chicago Friday leaves several critical and urgent questions to be answered. He is making substantial changes in the kind of program and in the way it is administered. Unfortunately he did not take advantage of serious discussions with his predecessor nor with members of the Board including Harry Ashmore. . . .

"The time was given over to superficial remarks about possible sources of funds, primarily to fund new *projects*. We questioned the availability of *institutional* grants and he indicated that foundations can be relied on for this. I doubt if the core of the Center would have substantial (and prompt) gifts during this period of transition."

She was still upset about Norton Ginsburg, although Moos had told the directors at Chicago that he had reached an agreement with Ginsburg. She was worried about Mrs. Borgese, and she warned Parten: "As you know it is probable that Mrs. Borgese will be dropped. He did not reveal how he will either replace her or Norton Ginsburg. (I consider the loss of Ginsburg is unfortunate)."

She referred to the advisory committee Moos had formed. She called it "an administrative council," and complained: "What the real function of this is I could not find out. I gathered that Ashmore is not serving as chief administrative officer as the Board named him, but is consulted on some external affairs."

Describing Moos as "a brilliant, imaginative, high-strung man," Mrs. McAllister concluded: "He needs a supporting structure to provide continuity and internal order at the Center. We are in a critical state, not because of the cash balance as much as the changes which may be under way. I hope that something good comes out of the September meeting in Houston!"

She sent a copy of this letter to Douglas. Douglas wrote to Parten on August 22, saying: "Her letter seems to me just as critical as her memoranda to the Finance Committee, the Organization Committee and the Executive Committee. I am disappointed."

"I will make a few brief observations on what she has written to you," Douglas said. "The discussion, I think, was rather better than her characterization which puts it down as 'superficial remarks,' etc. . . . I heard nothing that makes me think that Elisabeth Borgese 'will be dropped.' Malcolm did refer to the arrangement arrived at with Norton Ginsburg which anticipates his being at Center three months in the next year as a Visiting Fellow, and perhaps on other occasions.

"My memory may be faulty but I don't think we discussed the 'administrative council.' I am quite sure Harvey Wheeler was not mentioned. There was mention of Mordy, who Frances had told me is on the administrative council. I must say that I, too, am troubled that Malcolm seems unable to give Harry the opportunity to perform as Executive Vice President.

"I thought that Malcolm handled himself well at the luncheon. I hope he will have quite definite recommendations as to program for the months ahead and as to how the activities of the Senior Fellows will fit in when he meets with you and other Board members on September 10."

Douglas did not mention the fact that it was he, not Moos, who said that the foundations would not be much interested in "overall support" for the Center but might be persuaded to give money for special projects.

But Mrs. McAllister had gotten across one point to Douglas—a point that evidently had been called to his attention by Hutchins or Ashmore, too. That was the apparent unwillingness of Moos to share his executive authority with Ashmore. Moos wanted to make more changes than Ashmore was willing to accept: Moos felt that he had to go ahead with his program without permitting Ashmore to block him. Ashmore indicated to Douglas that he felt an obligation to keep Moos within the policy lines originally laid down by Hutchins and the board.

Douglas forwarded to Parten a letter from Mrs. McAllister dated August 19, which revealed that her objections to Moos were deep-seated. She was sure that he sought financial aid from "big business" and she was alarmed by that. She said to Douglas: "It is still not clear how he will build a support from big business without altering the aims of the program."

She was not pleased by the statements Moos had made to her and other directors that he was "his own man" and did not intend to be subservient to Hutchins. She commented to Douglas: "It is unfortunate that he continues to find it necessary to downgrade or belittle Robert Hutchins. The fact that he does this on every occasion that he talks to me suggests either that he is insecure or that he does not accept the significance of Hutchins' criticism of some aspects of society. . . ."

Douglas, who was a close friend of Hutchins', had not interpreted any of Moos's statements to mean that Moos intended "to downgrade or belittle Robert Hutchins." Douglas indicated to Parten that he thought it was natural for Moos to advocate a new program and for Moos to insist that he had to stand on his own feet. Douglas was willing to help Moos with financial support as well as advice. But he wanted Ashmore's role to be clearly defined.

On August 30 Moos sent a memorandum to Ashmore—with copies to Parten and other directors—outlining "the pre-eminent responsibilities I would like you to have in this administration."

"First, as we have discussed a number of times, I am hopeful that you will continue to conduct the various convocations and public symposia which so effectively supplement our periodicals in achieving wide visibility for the Center and which help to solidify the membership program," Moos said. "In this effort I will see that you have the assistance of all members of the staff in their respective functions.

"Second, I am counting very heavily on you for exploring and conceiving our efforts to develop both radio and television exploitation of the Center's work, whether in connection with the excellent programming that has come out of the Convocation activities, or any alternative avenues that you may be able to discover. In that connection, the Center will need your energies and experience in funding these new activities. I also hope that you will coordinate the various radio opportunities that have surfaced for us. . . .

"Third, I want to be able to count on your continued advice on the various phases of publishing that are under discussion and that require the most thorough examination if they are to contribute to the Center both substantively and financially.

"Fourth, in connection with your various communications functions, I would like you to take a major responsibility for working with Frank Kelly in improving our media relations. I feel very strongly that we must accelerate our coverage in the print media."

Moos said he was sure that Ashmore would concur in his judgment that few functions were more essential to the Center than the ones he had assigned to Ashmore. He added: "And I am convinced that no one else can perform them so well."

This conciliatory memorandum, while it was full of praise for Ashmore's past work, relegated Ashmore to a lower status than the level he had reached under Hutchins. Previously, the heads of the continuing education program, the development program, the membership program, and the book and audiotape programs had reported to Ashmore and had been under his general supervision. Ashmore also had functioned as the publisher of the *Center Magazine* and the *Center Report*, although the editors of these publications had claimed and maintained editorial independence in their judgments of articles to be printed.

In the Moos administration, all these department heads reported their activities directly to Moos. The Moos memorandum gave Ashmore primary responsibilities for two areas—the development of public convocations and "exploring and conceiving" possibilities in radio and television—and secondary responsibilities in publishing and media relations. But in all these areas, Moos emphasized the fact that he would really be the man in charge. Perhaps anticipating that Ashmore would not consider these assignments to have sufficient scope for an executive vice president, Moos also had reminded him that he had often said to the senior fellows that he would like to drop administrative burdens and serve purely as a fellow.

Feeling that he had done what he could to clarify the situation for Ashmore, Moos turned his attention to other matters. Ashmore did not consider the situation satisfactory. His unhappiness continued to be evident to the other fellows and to the staff.

To prepare for his meeting with Parten and other directors in Houston in September 1974, Moos asked Mordy and Wheeler to draft a long statement on the Center's program, its personnel, its organization, and possible procedures in seeking financial support.

This memorandum, which Moos gave to Parten and the others present at the session on September 10, began with a warning preface: "The purpose of this memorandum is to make clear the hard truth that, taken together, present reserves and the present talent pool—one or the other, or both of which are essential to a 'bootstrap operation'—are both entirely inadequate for this purpose. This situation is different in kind from past crises; this is the first time that reserves have been so low that to draw upon them to meet the crisis would mean possible termination of the operations of the institution.

"The institution is too valuable to be allowed to die, both in terms of what it stands for and what it has done and is doing, and also in terms of its future potential. . . . On the assumption that the Board will recognize this, serious planning is already underway for development and furtherance of the Center program by the new administration and dedicated academic staff."*

The memorandum contained highly critical statements about the handling of money by the Hutchins-Ashmore administration: "Depending on how 'administration' is defined, the overhead for the Center core program at the maximum can be estimated to be 125% and at the minimum perhaps 80%. Even the minimum figure is very large by the standard of most organizations and the maximum figure might be considered by some as exorbitant. At least, it would seem that for these sums there should be some unusual and uniquely effective administrative procedures and achievements for growth.

"Instead, it would now seem that the Center has long been steering an impossible course. Over the history of its existence, the Center has been steadily diminishing its resources until at the present time it has only sufficient funds to insure one more year of operation. It appears that Center policies must be re-evaluated. Deficit financing has been a way of life, and perhaps realistically so for periods when the economy is healthy and growing, making gifts more probable. But now, serious thought must be given to the perpetuation of the organization in present conditions."

In this memorandum, "overhead" was defined to include the expenditures on communications, development, the membership program, the continuing education program—all of which Hutchins, Ashmore and I had considered essential to promote public understanding of the Center and to create a good atmosphere for fund raising. In a statement to Moos on July 10 Ashmore had said: "Aside from the income received on contract from Encyclopaedia Britannica, the Center has received $24,000,000 in donations over these 15 years. The bulk of this must be attributed to these interrelated promotional activities. . . . Our greatest single benefactor, Chester Carlson, designated his gifts and bequest to support and expand such popular outreach."

---

*Moos was apparently not aware that the Center had been close to financial collapse in 1962. Hutchins and I had felt then that donors could be found to keep it going—and donors were found.

The Mordy-Wheeler memorandum Moos gave to Parten and other directors lamented the fact that the Carlson money had not been placed in an investment program: "The membership now provides about a million dollars of the Center's budget. In addition, were it in hand now, the nine million dollar Carlson bequest and gifts invested in the Center's current arbitrage investment program would produce a sufficient sum of money to more than cover, on a *continuing* basis, the total annual budget of the Center as it is now constituted. However, because of earlier expenditures, the Center is now running a $900,000 per annum deficit with a $700,000 reserve!*

"In part, the unfortunate financial circumstances we face are due to optimistic estimates of the Center's fund raising potential, which were based on market conditions prior to 1969. Since then, of course, there has been a general decline in the market, and it is now in a crisis stage. The present economic circumstances are certainly not favorable for fund raising or for deficit financing."

The memorandum noted: "Another part of the current predicament can be traced to the fact that, due to the imminent resignation of Mr. Hutchins, the future of the Center was considered uncertain for an extended time by many potential donors. Confidence in the Center's program could not be re-established until the Chairman's replacement had been named and the program thus reinforced.

"In addition, a few feel that an important part of the problem has been at least some lack of long range prudence and thrift in the management of the large and generous support that the Center has enjoyed in the past. Present administrative policy of the Center might be described in general as the simple exercise of good judgment on a day-to-day basis. Specific problems are dealt with as they arise, and decisions are often made without careful regard to the total context. Up to a point, and for a small organization, such administrative practices may be adequate, and even more efficient than systematic and planned approaches. But with time, they can lead to an accumulation of problems, and can also invite rationalizations and abuses."

The directors who met with Moos at Parten's request in Houston agreed that the budget deficit had to be reduced by contributions from the board members and their friends, and by stringent economies and temporary curtailment of some of the Center's activities. Moos asked the directors to try to raise $400,000 for "short-range funding."

Moos said that the Center's Fellows and other staff members were being encouraged to submit proposals to federal and private agencies in efforts to obtain what he called "intermediate funding" to pay some salaries and overhead expenses. He took a hopeful view: "Assuming success with

*Some of the Carlson money had been spent to build up the Center's membership—members who provided a million dollars a year to help meet the Center's needs.

project funding, the Center would be able to limp along for some time, while a major fund-raising campaign was mounted.''

While these efforts were in full swing, Moos promised that "a detailed plan for long-range financing will be completed and instituted.'' He said that Wheeler, Tagger, Mordy, and he were working on such a plan.

"The prospects are frightening to me and doubtless terrifying to many of the long-term staff of the Center whose financial security as well as idealism is wrapped up in the work of the Center,'' Moos said. "The situation is far more difficult than I anticipated when I accepted the presidency.''

The directors at the Houston gathering were willing to give Moos the "cost reduction authority'' he sought, and declared they would do what they could to raise money immediately. But they indicated that the primary responsibility for dealing with the financial emergency rested on Moos.

In spite of the dire straits in which he found himself, Moos hesitated to ask any of the senior fellows or senior staff members to retire or to accept a severance agreement. He decided to make the whole board aware of the crisis he had presented to the group of directors in Houston, thinking that some of the directors might be moved to send the Center some substantial contributions.

On September 20, copies of the comprehensive memorandum on "Funding the Center'' were sent to board members with a letter by Parten, who asked the directors to join him in making a large donation to the Center. In addition to the long memorandum, the mailing to the board included three documents on "severance pay policies,'' and copies of Moos's statement to Ashmore, Moos's letter to Mary Harvey appointing her "Assistant to the President for Periodicals'' and asking her to aid him in preparing articles and speeches, Moos's letter to Wheeler appointing him coordinator of the university project, and memoranda to Peter Tagger, Mordy, Gary Cadenhead, and all the senior fellows and visiting fellows.

In transmitting the material from Moos to the directors, Parten had urged those who had the means to do so to match him in making a commitment to give or raise $100,000 per year to the Fund for three years. Few of the directors responded. Those who did were not willing to commit themselves. Mrs. McAllister continued to be critical, and she made her views known to other members of the board.

Mrs. Laucks, who was friendly to Moos and wanted him to succeed, wrote to Parten on October 16: "Malcolm Moos's *Review* of September 20 is, I think, more than 'illuminating.' . . . I think the whole document is very sobering, indeed.

"I have some report of the deliberations of the meeting of the partial board in Houston, and of the alternatives suggested there to fend off the impending crisis. . . .

"One can hardly see drastically cutting the fellowship and senior staff without facing greatly adverse repercussions both in and out of the Center.

(And who would do this—the Board or Malcolm Moos—and according to what documented authority can any of the Fellows be let go?) . . .

"One thing is certain, and must be weighed by the board: *whatever* is done at this time will be sure to gain national notoriety. Rumors are already afloat outside the fold. Also, with a divided Board and a divided Fellowship, it is spitting in the wind to expect financial help from anybody. The impossible task is to get our house in order.

"I am very discouraged. I hope to have a chance to talk to Bob one of these days soon. I would dearly hope he might want to suggest some answers in this extremity."

Hutchins had no answers to the dilemma faced by Parten and Moos. Hutchins had traveled around the country in 1972, seeking financial support from the directors, and he had received encouragement from very few of them. Arnold Grant and others had told him that it would not be possible to stir the board until a new man had taken over as chairman of the Center. The new man had been installed—and most of the directors remained as lethargic as ever. .

On October 18 Ashmore came forward with a proposal that sent a quiver of alarm and rage through the senior fellows. In a memorandum to Moos, he suggested that "economies of scale" might be obtained by merging some or all of the membership-communications-development functions of the Fund for the Republic with the Fund for Peace, leaving the academic program and related costs to be financed by gifts from board members or other sources. He produced figures indicating that this might reduce the annual deficit of the Center from $900,000 to approximately $531,000.

Moos supplied all the fellows with copies of this proposal and brought it before them at their meeting on October 25. The indignation of John Cogley, Alex Comfort, Harvey Wheeler, and John Wilkinson was quickly evident in the questions they fired at Ashmore.

Ashmore shrugged. "I realize that there are people who feel that in some fashion this represents a kind of a rip-off of the viable part of the financial operation here, leaving behind the academic program, which, of course, has no visible means of support and never has had. I don't see it that way. I can understand that argument. I don't myself have any particular interest, any personal interest in doing it."

According to Ashmore, Compton was definitely eager to get the *Center Magazine, Center Report,* and the membership of the Center (then numbering about 75,000) included in any merger with the Fund for Peace. The senior fellows would have to shift for themselves. Ashmore indicated that his salary and that of his secretary would be transferred into the merged organization.

Referring to the accounting figures that showed a profit of $200,000 annually for the Center from the membership fees, Harvey Wheeler said: "As I understand it . . . that $200,000 would go with the operation."

"Well, I think we could get some cash back and that would be a part of the heart of the negotiations," Ashmore said.

Ashmore made it clear that he regarded the membership operation as his own achievement: "I created it and set it up and got it going."

"If you take the communications operation out of the Center you are taking $200,000 out of the Center's support program," Wheeler said.

Ashmore answered, "Well, that's one way to look at it. But on the other hand if you are taking out $400,000 off the deficit—"

"That doesn't work because you are not taking $400,000 off the deficit," Wheeler interrupted.

Moos intervened: "I guess that the major question seems to be that the academic caucus would be left standing without any visible means of support."

"Well, it doesn't have any now," Ashmore said.

Ashmore insisted that the plan would help the Center because it would remove the cost of his own salary, his secretary's salary, and other overhead costs from the Center's budget, thus reducing the deficit chargeable to the Center.

"Gentlemen, I think we have not been fair to Harry with such a little time for this," Moos said.

Cogley, Wheeler, Wilkinson, and Comfort felt that Moos had been more than fair to Ashmore. They did not think that Ashmore was entitled to the full credit for the success of the membership program, which had been based on the *Center Magazine*—edited by Cogley—and other publications and activities of the Center.

In his memorandum of October 18 Ashmore had asserted that "the immediate effect of the joint venture with the Fund for Peace would be to remove from the current budget of the Fund for the Republic all expenditures directly related to membership-communications-development. . . . This would represent a total annual expenditure of $1,260,268 at current rates, to be covered by income from membership, sale of tapes and printed materials, and additional operating funds and capital investment from the Fund for Peace and other sources not available for general support of the academic program of the Center." He said "the residual budget of the Fund for the Republic could then be stripped down to cover $408,000 for the academic program, $282,090 for administration, and $63,000 for continuing education." He estimated current income for this "residual budget" from "major gifts and applicable special purpose grants" would total $222,000, with a projected deficit of $531,349.

"I assume that in any case a holding operation for the Center involves the continuation of some core activities built around a continuing dialogue," Ashmore said. He thought that "special project financing" might "offset all or part of the payment of the Fellows by the Center." He did not indicate where he thought such financing could be found.

Ashmore added that it was "obvious" that his proposals would "have the effect of further fragmenting the operations of the Center for the Study of Democratic Institutions, and in sum might move the direction of its further development away from the concept of central, continuing dialogue upon which it was founded by Robert Hutchins." He said he offered his suggestions with regret: "I recommend their consideration only in the absence of any alternative source of general purpose financial support."

When Parten was informed by Moos of Ashmore's proposals and the angry reaction of the fellows, he shared the views of Cogley and others. He thought the suggestions would take care of Ashmore and Tagger and staff members closely associated with them, and leave the fellows—including Moos—out on a shaky limb. He urged Moos to appoint a new group of directors to conduct the negotiations with the Fund for Peace, with Ashmore removed from the conversations.

Parten called a special meeting of the board to be held November 4 at the O'Hare Inn in Chicago. When the directors gathered there, he voiced his disappointment at the board's failure to join him in his efforts to save the Center from financial disaster. The absence of substantial support from other directors meant that severe reductions in the Center's staff would have to be made. He knew the pain that would cause, and he had hoped to avoid it.

Moos presented a budget for the coming fiscal year totaling $1,450,000. His budget provided $350,000 for the academic program and continuing education and $200,000 for administrative costs. The expenses of the membership, publishing, and development program were estimated at $900,000. With a net income of $200,000 generated by the membership program, $220,000 in gifts from the board, and $30,000 in royalties from Alex Comfort's book *The Joy of Sex*, Moos believed that the budget would be balanced.

It was clear to Parten, Moos, and all the directors that some of the senior fellows and senior staff members would have to be retired or discharged under such a budget. The academic programs had been costing between $800,000 and $900,000 a year, and the Moos plan provided for $350,000—a drop of approximately half a million dollars.

Cadenhead, the secretary and treasurer, reminded the board that the Center would have to make plans to meet a severance pay obligation of $600,000 or more under the policy laid down by Hutchins and Ashmore. Ashmore insisted that it had been understood for a long time that the Eucalyptus Hill property—estimated to be worth $1 million or more—was to be considered as a surety for the severance payments.

Bernard Weissbourd proposed that the Center in Santa Barbara be closed down, with operations moved to Chicago, where steady financial support for a limited group would be available. He said that fifteen members of the University of Chicago faculty could be induced to participate in dialogues on a part-time basis with annual retainers of $5000 for each professor. He declared that Moos, Ashmore, and other self-sustaining fellows could move to Chicago. The other members of the staff in Santa Barbara would be terminated. He estimated that the total cost of a Chicago program would not exceed $250,000 annually.

Hutchins was quiet during the meeting. Edward Lamb asked him to comment on Weissbourd's proposal. Hutchins said that the important thing was the continuation of the dialogue—and the dialogue could be maintained at Santa Barbara, in Chicago, or elsewhere. He indicated that the responsibility for the Center's future rested on the board.

Stewart Mott suggested that only those fellows who were able to get their own funding should be retained and the Center should be open to other scholars who could raise enough money to support themselves. Mrs. Laucks, Mrs. McAllister, and others said that the Mott proposal would not be well received in the academic world. Blair Clark declared that the Center would be the laughingstock of the intellectual community if its fellows were dependent on sex books and the shah of Iran. (Mrs. Borgese had said that she could get money from the shah for her energy project.)

Finally Bernard Rapoport moved that the president—Malcolm Moos— be instructed to take whatever actions were necessary to reduce expenditures to an annual rate of $1,450,000. Arthur Burck seconded the motion. Eight of the directors then present voted for the Rapoport motion; four were recorded against it. Mrs. Laucks and several others abstained.

Mott, a director of the Fund for Peace as well as a director of the Center, asked the board to renew its interest in possible ventures with the Fund for Peace. Moos presented a statement that he had previously discussed with Randolph Compton. This statement declared that the Center and the Fund for Peace would establish "a joint committee of trustees to plan and coordinate mutually advantageous cooperative activities of the two organizations." This statement was approved by the Center's directors, and Moos appointed Parten, Burck, Lally, and himself to serve on the joint committee.

At that emergency meeting on November 4 the Center board also authorized the formation of a committee on alternative sites for the Center. This committee was asked to explore two basic questions: "Can the Center survive at its present location in Santa Barbara? If not, can the Center survive elsewhere in Santa Barbara, Chicago, San Diego, Palm Beach, or any other location?" The directors appointed to this group were Parten, Mrs. Laucks, Moos, Burck, and Weissbourd.

In the weeks after the November 4 meeting, Moos slashed the Center's budget. Secretaries, file clerks, and mail room employees were terminated with severance pay. He ordered the closing of the Washington office and the Los Angeles office. He asked the senior fellows to hold down their expenditures and to refrain from organizing conferences.

Angered by the statements made by some of the fellows at their meeting on October 25, Ashmore withdrew his proposal for a merger of the membership-communications-development activities of the Center with the Fund for Peace. He chided the fellows at their session on November 14, saying that his suggestions had not received serious consideration.

He took a gloomy view of the actions taken by the board in Chicago: "It was made evident that the new budget will provide no funds for any promotional or communications activities outside of Santa Barbara, and none here that are not immediately self-sustaining." He felt that the three regional convocations held in 1974 on the subject "The State of the Democratic Process"—in Los Angeles, New York, and Chicago—had proved again that large numbers of Center members wanted to take part in such public assemblies.

Ashmore declared that "the curtailed academic program will not provide adequate content for the Center publications, nor provide the kind of activity at the Center that our members have come to expect. It is the judgment of all of us who have had responsibility for building the membership program that elimination of the public affairs activities we have conducted away from Santa Barbara will result in accelerated erosion of the total membership."

In a conversation with a Los Angeles *Times* reporter after the Chicago board meeting, Moos had appeared to be optimistic. He had said that the directors had approved a "reduced budget" for the 1975 fiscal year, but the directors had also given assurances of adequate financial support. "It was a very successful meeting," Moos was quoted as saying to the *Times* correspondent. "We're determined to keep the Center going onward and upward."

In his statement to the Fellows on November 14 Ashmore differed strongly with Moos. He reiterated his belief that the only possibility of avoiding the bad consequences of the truncated budget would be "through joint ventures with the Fund for Peace which would provide without cost some of the essential services that are being eliminated, and might bring in additional money."

"If we are to proceed in that direction, however, there will have to be a manifestation of genuine interest and good faith on the part of the administration, the Fellows, and the board," Ashmore said. "More is involved here than the possible relationship with the Fund for Peace. These negotiations have become the focus of factional differences on the board, as well as internally at the Center."

While Ashmore was asking for a sign of the "good faith" of the Moos administration, the fellows, and the board, Mrs. McAllister continued her stream of letters to Moos and Parten. She had made periodic visits to the Center and had found little to be happy about.

On November 12 she sent two memoranda to Moos for his consideration and possible guidance, one entitled "Toward Fund Raising Policies" and one entitled "Toward a Viable Relationship Between Board and Staff." In the letter accompanying these documents, she wrote: "As you know, I remain troubled about certain projects, both as to their quality and as to their relevance to the commitment of the Fund for the Republic. If you could resolve the difficulty I could possibly be of immediate assistance."

She supplied Parten with a copy of this letter and its attachments. In a handwritten note to "J.R.," referring to a clipping of the Los Angeles *Times* story quoting Moos, she commented: "Several people have sent me copies of the enclosed clipping. It is embarrassing to have such glib statements made!" Evidently some of the Fellows supplied her with information about Moos that might be regarded as "embarrassing."

In this letter to Moos she also referred to "the turmoil preliminary to 'constitutionalizing the Center' " and suggested that "speedy deliberateness may be crucial to wise Board Action." Moos was apparently baffled by some of her comments and asked her for explanations in his reply to her on November 21.

When she made another visit to the Center in November, Moos was away on a fund-raising expedition. After her return to her ranch in Arizona, Mrs. McAllister wrote again to Moos. In this communication, dated November 26, she showed irritation.

"Your letter dated November 21 (signed by your secretary) was handed to me by Gary Cadenhead," she said. "I was sorry that you were not there to handle questions in person.

" 'Constitutionalizing the Center' refers back to our first brief conversation in December, 1973. Recognition of this need has been cited by various members of the Board in your presence and mine several times. One criticism of Robert Hutchins' tenure which you made to me was that his strong personal leadership puts you at disadvantage in the absence of a structure from which to build.

"My experience confirms that Mr. Hutchins' role as chairman, administrator and teacher made for a 'loose' organization on which Board and Staff relied, probably too much. What we need is to move in the direction of defining tasks and internal relationships, lines of authority and communication, and with this hopefully more clarity as to what end the Fund for the Republic exists.

"Meanwhile, last week I found increasing confusion at the Center. Rather oddly, Gary Cadenhead was under the illusion that the Board's intent in electing Harry Ashmore Executive Vice President was to give him honorary status to compensate for his removal as President! The matter came up as I was studying the budget and current finance reports and noted that Mr. Ashmore's salary is fully attributed to academic and communications programs. Later I asked Mr. Ashmore about his duties as Executive Vice President. He indicated that you have not assigned him any, but have conferred with him casually.

"I learned that you have formed an 'Administrative Council' chaired by a Visiting Fellow, Mr. Mordy, and that Mr. Wheeler is an active member and that Mr. Ashmore has a minor role in that body. It would be useful to have 1) your précis of the duties of the 'Administrative Council' and 2) copies of minutes of the 'Administrative Council.' "

Mrs. McAllister concluded by urging Moos to call for "a Board retreat"—that is, a gathering of the board for several days of intensive meetings in Santa Barbara. She thought that such a "retreat" should not be "hastily scheduled" but should have "adequate preparation, with material on your plan for program, with full availability of books and records."

Mrs. McAllister had been particularly alarmed by the assumptions she thought she had detected in a paper prepared by Harvey Wheeler for a discussion at the Center on October 25. She had written to Parten about the Wheeler paper: "It presumes that there are to be changes and expansions in staff and program. I do not accept the implication that staff members can do this without considerable review by the Board." Mrs. Laucks had also been disturbed by the Wheeler paper, and she had told Moos that she could not support the transformation of the Center into a "communiversity" along the lines indicated by Wheeler.

Wheeler and Moos were more interested in the university project than in any other development. With encouragement from Moos, Wheeler had written a memorandum to him in September 1974, proposing the formation of a special $10 million trust fund "to receive and invest endowment funds for the establishment and maintenance of a Center academy." Wheeler had said that donors should be assured that "funds given would not be used merely to support the operating deficit for the Center."

Wheeler had recommended that a group of trustees for the $10 million special fund should be appointed, and stipulated that "these would be persons of considerable national esteem." His memorandum—dated September 6, 1974, and not circulated widely to the Center's staff or directors—did not say whether the Center's board members would be invited to become trustees of the academy fund.

Parten was not disturbed by the scope of Wheeler's proposals or the evident interest of Moos in developing a Center academy. He was sure that any such plan would be thoroughly discussed by the board for months before any action could be taken. Moos had made it clear to him that the academy was a long-range proposal.

But Parten was upset by the unending barrage of criticisms Mrs. McAllister poured upon Moos. He was especially annoyed by a letter she sent to Paul Newman on December 4, in response to an indication from Newman that he was ready to give a substantial sum to the Center if other directors gave, too. (She sent copies of this letter to Parten and Morris Levinson.)

"In the month since I received your letter I have pondered the question of committing any large sum to the Center before I know for what the money is to be used," Mrs. McAllister said. "All of us feel somewhat removed from the activities there. Malcolm Moos' communications are very much adman style and conceal more than they reveal of facts. The calendar for events at the Center is, to say the least, thin. The conduct of the program in Santa Barbara is casual and sporadic and ill-prepared as the two special Board meetings in May and November have been.

"Because of my concern for the Center I have gone to Santa Barbara to try to learn the facts. The staff there seems to be despondent, several junior staff members having been dismissed and a budget proposed which would also require that several senior staff members go. Malcolm was not present during the three days I was in Santa Barbara. He has since returned for a few days but is now back in New York.

"In his absence I felt it my duty to inquire of the treasurer regarding the financial predicament. I found his reports very slick but I am not sure of the sources of his projections and I am sure that he does not have an adequate basis for understanding the priorities in various categories of prime obligations.

"Fortunately while I was in Santa Barbara there was an excellent analysis and evaluation of recent Supreme Court decisions which had prompted Robert Hutchins to present the seminar on the 18th of November. This was a very important opinion, concisely written and discussed with very few people present. I am considering making some contribution toward the cost of printing this paper and its discussion.

"I do not know of other positive actions which would encourage support by serious members of the Center and its board."

His patience almost exhausted, Parten wrote to Mrs. McAllister on December 11: "I would be less than honest if I did not tell you that, in my opinion, your continued criticism of President Moos, in this time of struggle for survival, is surely destructive of the Fund for the Republic. Surely this is not your intention. The several memos you have sent to me and to others support this conclusion."

Parten reviewed in his letter the selection and election of Moos as the successor to Hutchins and reminded her that Ashmore had declared that he would "gladly step aside" and support that successor.

"Unfortunately, Dr. Moos, although elected in October of 1973, could not take office until after he finished his duties as President of the University of Minnesota terminating July, 1974. So this eight months of interregnum afforded time for some of the Fellows and some of the Board members to rethink the wisdom of the October election," Parten said. "This erupted in the February, 1974 meeting of the Board. But the vast majority of the Board voted to stand fast in continued support of the new President."

Parten then went over the fight that had occurred in St. Paul when his nominating committee had presented the names of three men with distinguished records as nominees for board membership. He wrote: "For the first time in its history, the Board was confronted with a well-organized opposition to the recommendation of a Board committee. After a miserable debate, the Board voted to accept the recommendation of the nominating committee.''

Parten reminded her of the hostility she had shown toward Moos at that meeting. Parten wrote: "At the end of this Board meeting you arose and made to me a most hateful and irrational declaration directed at President Moos for which you later, in a letter to me, apologized. In this letter you assured me you were wrong and that you were going to change your conduct and support the President. In several letters later, you have continued to criticize, criticize, and criticize. It seems the President can do nothing right in your opinion. Frances, I am still hopefully looking forward to the cooperation you promised.

"At the peril of making this long letter too long, I feel I must mention a few specific examples as follows:

"(1) In your letter of November 26, you were upset about the idea of calling the Center a university. Let us be reminded that 20 years ago some of the staff and some of the Directors referred to the Fund as a 'mini-university.' It did not disturb anyone. Later, under the leadership of Dr. Hutchins in the reorganization, he styled the Center an 'academy.' It seemed to disturb no one. Now, if calling the Center a university will help finance it, I see no objection. . . .

"(2) Further in your letter to Dr. Moos on November 26, you say: 'My experience confirms that Mr. Hutchins' role as Chairman, administrator, and teacher made for a loose organization on which Board and staff relied, probably too much.' I say that you may be right; but, on the other hand, you may be wrong because ideal organization is very difficult in an institution as small as the Fund. We cannot have the elaborate organization both desirable and justified for a much larger entity. It seems to me that we may have to get along with a thin organization for some time yet.

"(3) In the same letter to Dr. Moos, you complain about his use of the expertise of Mary Harvey in the writing of a speech. Since the president must of necessity make a great many speeches in the interest of the welfare of the Fund for the Republic, I can see nothing wrong with him calling upon any member of the staff for assistance.''

Parten continued: "(4) In your memorandum to the Directors on November 14, you conclude and I quote: 'Within the past year, I addressed to Robert Hutchins my first effort at describing the roles which seemed to me appropriate to the Board. . . . At that time, I stated that except in unusual circumstances or crisis, Board members should not assume direct oversight. To me, it appears that the present situation requires a much more active role for the Board.' My response is 'Yes.' The board should be active in the making of policy and the raising of money, but let us not tinker with administrative detail. As Board members, we should support the administration that we have elected in the regular order.

"(5) In your letter of November 12, you complain about a press release the President gave to the Los Angeles *Times* for its issue on November 6, 1974, a clip of which you have enclosed and which I have read. Personally, I can see no reasonable foundation for your concern. It is basically factual.

"(6) In your letter under date of December 4, 1974, to our fellow Director, Paul Newman, of which you were kind enough to send me a copy, you say among other things and I quote: 'In the month since I received your letter I have pondered the question of committing any large sum to the Center before I know for what the money is to be used. All of us feel somewhat removed from the activities there. Malcolm Moos' communications are very much adman style and conceal more than they reveal of facts.' And in conclusion, you say, 'I do not know of other positive actions which would encourage support by serious members of the Center and its board.' Naturally, I am at a loss to know who you mean by 'All of us.' Certainly, you cannot mean the members of the Board or the staff. For I'm sure a vast majority would not agree with you. Frances, it seems to me, a Director has an absolute right to elect to give or not give to the institution, but one has neither the right nor the license to dissuade others from giving."

Parten concluded with an attempt to calm Mrs. McAllister's fear that Moos was engaged in changing the whole program of the Center: "Our program, as I see it, will continue to be consistent with our basic charter to protect the constitutional freedoms of the individual and the principles of the Declaration of Independence, to promote freedom and justice, and, as amended, to identify the basic issues of our times pertaining to our basic charter and promote discussion thereof and publish in the interest of a free society."

Making another plea for her cooperation, Parten said: "It's my earnest hope that all of the Directors can join on this common objective. Let us forget personal likes and dislikes and bear down to support this administration and continue the Fund for the Republic in its chief endeavor, The Center for the Study of Democratic Institutions, the continuation of which, in my opinion, is even more necessary now than when it was created."

After consulting with Parten, Moos also wrote a lengthy letter to Mrs. McAllister. On December 6, responding to her chilly letter of November 26, Moos said he was sorry that he had not been in Santa Barbara during her visit. He thought he might have been able to clarify some matters for her.

"But as you know, there are few problems the Center now has that will not be eased substantially by new financial support," Moos said. "My first priority must be, for the time being at least, an all out effort to secure new funding. I wish to respond to each of the points in your letter because, quite clearly and understandably in such a short visit, you left here with some misunderstanding and misinformation.

"Each administrator has his own style and methods. I am accustomed to working in a well defined structure for policy determinations. This led me to remark that it would take some time to arrange things in a way that seems proper to me. This process, of course, has been under way for several months now; some of the actions which have been taken were included in the report I sent to the Board of Directors on September 20. . . .

"You will recall that I have stated from the beginning that an institution of such modest scope as ours does not require a large administrative structure. I felt there was no need for a Dean to oversee a program conducted by ten Senior Fellows and indicated my decision to serve as my own Dean. In fact, this was the way the Center had worked under Bob until his period of serious illnesses. Similarly, an institution of our small size does not need two executive officers. This, coupled with Mr. Ashmore's repeated declarations that his only desire was to be a Senior Fellow, prompted me to outline specifically his new duties."

Moos described the advisory committee he had formed to obtain counsel on internal administrative matters and to improve communications among staff members who had administrative or special functions. Before he formed this committee, the only regular meetings concerning the operations of the Center were meetings of the senior fellows. The officers and senior staff members had reported individually on their activities to Hutchins and Ashmore.

Informing Mrs. McAllister that Wendell Mordy was not a member of the advisory committee and had not chaired any committee meetings, Moos wrote: "I am sure you are aware that my business and fund raising trips away from the Center require that I have competent personal assistance. . . . In view of the fact that Mr. Mordy had extensive administrative experience as director of a large research institute, as a university Vice President and as Vice Chancellor of a state-wide university system, I decided that this fortuitous situation would allow me, without adding to the staff, to utilize him for a number of administrative tasks during the present period of our financial stress. He graciously, though reluctantly, agreed to do this because of his sincere belief in the Center's programs and purposes."

Moos then took up Mrs. McAllister's question about the use of fellows for administrative activity and whether the cost of their time was properly allocated: "Except for Mr. Ashmore, and Mr. Cogley who recently resigned as editor of the *Center Magazine* and as Senior Fellow, none of the Fellows has an assigned administrative role. In this time of crisis at the Center, however, there is a great willingness on the part of several of the Senior Fellows to help in any way possible. . . .

"In this regard, Mr. Ashmore, Mr. Mordy, Mr. Wheeler and Mr. Wilkinson have all been assisting me in various ways to expedite projects, programs and policies, as have others. In view of our limited numbers and resources at the moment, no attempt has been made to ascribe portions of the salaries or expenses to the administrative budget. . . .

"In regard to Mrs. Harvey, my memorandum to her of August 6, included in the document sent you dated September 20, shows that in addition to her publication duties, I asked her to help me from time to time 'with the preparation of articles and speeches. . . .' I think you will find this understandable, since in the six months I have been at the Center I have been asked to deliver more than twelve public addresses, to a number of rather important organizations, and thus a considerable demand has been placed on my time to produce the requisite quality of work.''

Responding to Mrs. McAllister's criticisms of the university project, Moos asked her to remember that the documents she had read thus far had been "working papers," with ideas "put forward bluntly or in a preliminary manner, for the purpose of provoking discussion which will assist in their development and refinement." He said: "To read in an intent to 'alter the program and purpose of the Fund for the Republic' involves, I believe, a serious misapprehension about the work of many of those here at the Center who are trying sincerely and devotedly to work for what they believe to be the highest goals and objectives of the Center."

Moos welcomed her suggestion for a "Board retreat," saying that he stood ready to attend any meeting "in whatever format we decide would be practical and useful, and which is concerned with any matters which are deemed appropriate for Board consideration."

Mrs. McAllister wrote back rapidly to both Moos and Parten, indicating that she was not fully satisfied by their replies to her previous letters. She relied on her own impressions of what was going on at the Center and reports she received from friends there.

"My concerns remain," she told Moos in a letter dated December 10. "Is the Center abandoning goals which the Board established? Is the broad human-social-political-economic field to be dealt with in dialog and then disseminated to the membership and the public as approved by the Board?

"Harvey Wheeler's Communiversity has been around for a while. It recurs through the years. If his draft presented in September were prefaced with, 'This is entirely hypothetical. The Board of Trustees have not adopted a policy to re-orient this institution; my presentation intends to test implications of such a change in the character of CSDI,' that would have been a legitimate dialog. As presented, and distributed in the academic community, his paper presumes to reflect suggested changes of design as if already under way. You enclosed copies of nine responses addressed to Mr. Wheeler with comments of wide range, some raising questions which I share:

"Is this paper a preliminary statement of program proposed to the Center? or is the Center committed to such a new emphasis?

"Is it an academic project, or is it a proposed solution of problems of universities?

"Does Mr. Wheeler know that the Board rather than the Fellows would decide changes in the policies of the institution?"

Mrs. McAllister said she had read many papers during her association with the Center and she knew that papers are frequently revised. But she declared that Wheeler's papers on the university project did not provide clear answers to the questions she had raised.

She asserted that she recognized the right of the chief executive officer "to re-order business and re-assign personnel," but she had noticed a "general malaise" at the Center. She said: "The decline in visitors and even in visibility of the regular staff must be depressing in itself. Only once in the week I was in Santa Barbara was there dialog presentation, the excellent one by Robert Hutchins: 'The Public Interest in Education.' "

Mrs. McAllister showed plainly that she wanted more responsibility given to Ashmore and none to Wheeler: "The Board elected Mr. Ashmore Executive Vice President after discussing it with you. At that time you clearly indicated you recognize Mr. Wheeler is not suited to administrative responsibility and that you require only one executive vice president. A different course is to an extent your prerogative as Chief Executive Officer. The trust vested in you, nevertheless, implies that you shall be responsive to the Board.

"I am glad to hear—for the first time—that you are accustomed to work in a well-defined structure. However, policy making is the responsibility of the Board and we await with understanding changes in format, administration, program; but do not undertake changes in institutional policies except with full Board approval. The Fund for the Republic is a public trust. The Board is obligated to a large constituency to use funds in accordance with policies defined by the Board."

After this admonition, she concluded: "Exchange of letters may yet bring about a mutual trust, essential between Executive Officers and Board members. I should prefer open-ended discussions among the whole Board but your schedule seems to prohibit extended conversations or regular Board meetings. Meanwhile I shall be glad to learn what steps are being taken to bring a productive order to the program itself."

On December 16 she sent a brief letter to Parten, with copies to Moos, James Douglas, and Morris Levinson: "I accept with substantial reservations your criticism of my effort to get you to look at the situation of the Center.

"The Chief Executive Officer is answerable to the Board. He is not licensed to move to change the character of the institution without examination and deliberation by the Board. In this regard I refer you to Malcolm Moos's statement to the Board in its meeting February 15, 1974 and his letter to me dated December 6, 1974.

"I refer you to minutes of the Board meetings of the past thirteen months with their attached resolutions, statements of purpose and proposed amendments to the minutes.

"You are wrong in suggesting that Board members have no right to exchange among one another their observations of the quality of leadership of the institution. In the absence of adequate Board meetings and prompt and full reports from appointed committees we can do no other.

"Let the Board have disclosure of progress and let us find resolution of difference by carrying out the public trust vested in us."

Parten felt that his record as a trustee of the University of Texas, his services to other educational and charitable organizations, and his years as a director of the Fund for the Republic demonstrated that he understood the meaning of a "public trust" as well as Mrs. McAllister did. He hoped that he would eventually persuade her that Moos had to have some freedom of action in order to function effectively as the Center's chief executive.

While he was carrying on his exchange of letters with Mrs. McAllister, Parten was shocked by reports he received from Cadenhead, Moos, and Arthur Burck concerning a New York meeting between Harry Ashmore and Randolph Compton. Ashmore had gone to the east coast for meetings with Fund for Peace officials on the possible establishment of an institute for policy analysis, which was under consideration as a project of that Fund with or without the cooperation of the Center.

On December 6 Peter Tagger received a telephone call from Nick Nyary, president of the Fund for Peace, in which Nyary said he understood from Compton that Ashmore had declared that a meeting between Moos and Compton should be called off because Moos had lost the support of the Center's board and did not have the authority to negotiate with the Fund for Peace. Tagger also talked with Lynn Mattison, a Fund for Peace staff member in Washington, who said that Ashmore had told him that the Compton-Moos meeting had been canceled by Compton.

Tagger told Gary Cadenhead about these telephone conversations, and Cadenhead passed the information to Harvey Wheeler, who relayed it that night by phone to Moos, who was then in Palm Beach, Florida, discussing the Center's financial future with Burck. Moos had stopped in Florida on his way to a New York meeting with the Fund for Peace officials, which had been scheduled for December 10.

Moos went on to New York and met with Nyary and Mattison at the Century Club there. Nyary and Mattison informed him that Compton had been told by Ashmore that Moos did not have the backing of the Center's board and advised them to cancel the scheduled meeting with Moos. At the urging of Nyary and Mattison, the meeting between Moos and Compton was held, although it produced no conclusive results. The two men discussed generally the possibilities of cooperation between the Center and the Fund for Peace.

At the suggestion of Burck, Moos placed in his hands the responsibility of deciding how the matter should be investigated. Burck talked with Bernard Rapoport and Parten, and decided to ask David W. Louisell of the

University of California law school in Berkeley to look into it. Louisell was a renowned legal scholar, the author of a legal textbook that had become a standard work on pretrial procedures and the author or coauthor of seven other legal books. He was a graduate of the University of Minnesota and a member of the New York, Minnesota, District of Columbia, and U.S. Supreme Court bars.

Parten as chairman of the Center's board, approved the appointment of Louisell to consider the matter because he regarded the charges against Ashmore as extremely serious. He felt that Ashmore had a right as a director to speak to anyone about Moos's standing with the board, but he believed that Ashmore as an officer had an obligation to be loyal to the president who had been elected by the board.

Arthur Burck's letter of December 26, 1974, to Louisell asked the professor to conduct a full and fair investigation and to provide Parten with an opinion letter on two questions: "1. Do the facts provide basis for the Center to terminate for cause the employment of any person or persons? 2. If the answer is in the affirmative, is there legal basis for the Center to decline to authorize termination pay for any such person or persons?" Burck wrote: "You should of course give any employee and/or his legal counsel, if he elects to have counsel, full opportunity to explain any actions or activities that may be in question."

Burck sent copies of his letter to Parten, all other members of the board's executive committee, and to Ashmore. Ashmore felt that the letter carried an implied threat to remove him from his office and to deny him any severance pay. He asked for legal advice from Morris Levinson, then the chairman of the executive committee, and from Hutchins.

On December 30 Ashmore informed Moos in a long letter that he had decided that he could not continue as an officer of the Fund for the Republic. He insisted that his discussions with Compton had been perfectly proper and that he had simply informed Compton that any proposal for a merger between the Fund for Peace and the Center would require action by the boards of directors. He said he had told Compton that he had "no authority to negotiate" but that he would relay Compton's suggestions to Moos and other directors on the committee originally established to discuss joint projects with Compton's group.

Moos sent Parten a copy of Ashmore's communication. Parten did not find it convincing. Parten thought that the statements made by Nyary and Mattison about Ashmore's declarations required a thorough investigation.

At Parten's suggestion, Moos referred Ashmore's letter of December 30 to the executive committee of the board. After a conversation between Parten and Levinson, it was agreed that a meeting of that committee would be held in New York early in February 1975. Parten sought to have a thorough discussion of the negotiations between the Center and the Fund for Peace, as well as a report by Moos on his fund-raising efforts.

In the last week of December, Parten sent a contribution of $100,000 to the Center from his family's foundation. He reaffirmed his support for Moos, and asked Hutchins to make an effort to get other directors to make substantial gifts to the Center. On December 30 Hutchins wrote to Parten, saying that he had been in touch with a dozen directors, "urging them to follow your example." (Hutchins was technically on a leave of absence, but he had not left Santa Barbara.)

The directors did not respond to Hutchins' plea with a shower of money. Parten's gift was not matched. Yet he refused to be discouraged. He told Moos to increase his efforts. He was sure that the Center could be saved.

Dialogues were not flourishing at the Center. The senior fellows—except for Wheeler, Wilkinson, and Comfort—had not fully accepted Moos as their leader. Most of the dialogue sessions in November and December were conducted by Wilkinson, Wheeler, Comfort, and Mordy. Tugwell, Borgese, Ritchie-Calder, and Ashmore were not on the academic calendar very often. Hutchins had interrupted his leave to lead one discussion in the autumn. Cogley had retired.

No one was sure of what the deepening conflicts between Moos and Ashmore would lead to. The number of supporting staff members had been drastically reduced, and the pulse of the Center was slower than it had been. Moos was away for days at a time, hunting for money.

Still, Parten and Moos were not men who gave up easily. Moos continued to present a brave face. Parten was positive that the Center would get a new burst of life when the internal conflicts among the fellows and the directors were overcome.

PART FIVE

The Final Years: Hutchins Returns and Departs

29

The depression deepens;
the Vietnam War ends;
the Center is torn apart and
Hutchins returns to power

$\mathbf{F}$AITH IN GOVERNMENTS, in the wisdom of experts, in all institutions, went down in the deep economic depression in 1975. The victory of the Communist forces in Vietnam, after enormous expenditures of American money and the sacrifice of thousands of American lives, produced rage and disgust in the nation. While Nixon enjoyed a peaceful exile in San Clemente, his assistants in the Watergate conspiracy received prison terms. Cynics felt justified in scoffing at American justice.

The Center, the court of reason, came near to dissolution. While Moos struggled to get financial transfusions for the Fund from foundation executives and other donors, his standing with the board was steadily eroded.

The investigation of Ashmore was interpreted by Hutchins as an attack on an officer and director who had served the Center and Hutchins faithfully for many years. The incessant barrage by Mrs. McAllister against Moos made it necessary for Moos to spend some of his time in defending himself.

Eulah Laucks, who had defended Moos through the grueling months of 1974 despite her reservations about his project for a "model university," became alarmed by what she regarded as the dangerous implications of this project. In a letter to Parten on January 9, Mrs. Laucks said she thought that "the intention may still persist—in spite of protestations to the contrary—to transform the Center into a prototype university." She told Parten she was "grieved also that such a basic project as 'The University'—which is so pre-eminently the domain of Bob Hutchins—goes on without his close involvement and advice. Why? Bob Hutchins is the Center's most valuable resource."

Mrs. Laucks sent Parten a copy of a memorandum she had given to Harvey Wheeler and Joseph Schwab, who had led a discussion of the university proposal at the Center on January 8. In this statement, she said that "the scope of the proposal as set forth in the January 8 paper" would "require a commitment of resources and an orientation of activities that would radically change the character of the Center." She concluded: "In fact, since many details in the working out of the proposal look toward prescriptive results, I would think it could change the Center from an institution concerned with effective ideas to one more interested in the invention of functional structures."

Replying, Parten assured Mrs. Laucks that Hutchins was freely engaged in the fields he had selected as a senior fellow—"law and education"—and added: "I know he can write his own ticket and work in any field he wishes." Parten felt that Mrs. Laucks had been overly disturbed by the Wheeler-Schwab paper, which had been presented to evoke reactions and critical comments. "You should not worry about us going astray," Parten said. "I assure you that I will do everything in my power to avoid this. Personally, I am satisfied that, if we all get behind Malcolm Moos and support him, we will achieve great ends."

Hutchins felt that Moos had made a blunder in sanctioning Arthur Burck's inquiry into Ashmore's activities at the Fund for Peace. On January 6, Hutchins wrote to Parten, saying that he interpreted Burck's letter to Professor Louisell as "an effort to 'get' Ashmore" and asserting: "I could have no part in such a project. Ashmore has been a board member for twenty years. He has been an officer as well since 1964. . . . Mr. Burck is off on a wild goose chase."

"I have been hoping we could hold the board together so that they could come to know Mac Moos and he might have time to develop his program and make it clear to them," Hutchins said. "Mr. Burck's activities will not advance the realization of this hope. On the contrary it will split the board still further.

"When I have spoken to you about Ashmore in the past, you have said he couldn't raise money and was a big spender. I don't agree, but I'm sure you will agree that neither or both of these criticisms, if correct, would sustain a charge of 'treason.' In fact I am not sure that in an institution devoted to argument, disagreement, discussion and dissent we have a place either for blind loyalty or 'treason.' "

Parten answered Hutchins on January 16: "I accept your advice, but I cannot accept your reasoning. At any rate, I persuaded Arthur Burck to suspend this investigation, but I want you to know that I intend to obtain personally the facts in this situation both from Mr. Compton and from Mr. Ashmore. In the meantime, you may rest assured that no investigation by an outsider is proceeding." Parten felt that Ashmore, as an officer subordinate to Moos, did have an obligation to be loyal to the chief executive of the Center. He felt that it was his duty to gather the facts.

Ashmore tried to convince Parten that Moos was responsible for the divisions within the Center. In a letter to Parten on January 15, he said that the allegation that he had told Compton and others that Moos had no authority to negotiate on behalf of the Center was "not only without substance, but represents a total reversal of the facts."

"I went to see Compton at Moos' suggestion to discuss specifics of a possible joint foreign policy project," Ashmore said. "When we met, however, Compton immediately reverted to his original proposal for a corporate merger of the two Funds. . . . I told Compton, as I had in all our previous conversations, that I had no authority to negotiate any such agreement, but that if he were prepared to discuss terms that I could be persuaded were of financial benefit to the Center, I would relay them to Moos, and to the board committee of which I am a member. This is precisely what I have done.

"The allegation that I attempted to persuade Compton to cancel a meeting with Moos is equally false, but could result from an honest misunderstanding. Confusion very well could have arisen from Compton's consistent failure to make any distinction between the proposal for a corporate merger, which continues to be his primary personal objective, and the much more limited arrangement for cooperation in publishing and public affairs programming which has been under negotiation at the staff level."

Ashmore said he did not see how he could be accused of "treason" except in "the context of prior suspicion of my motives." He attributed such suspicion to Cadenhead, who had indicated that the Fund for Peace proposal could be viewed "as an effort on my part to initiate an 'end run' to serve my own interest by undercutting Moos' authority."

"However, Moos has never said anything to me to indicate that he lends any weight to Cadenhead's imputation of bad faith," Ashmore said.

In a lengthy memorandum accompanying this letter to Parten, Ashmore insisted that he had tried to cooperate with Moos, but concluded that he "had been unable to establish a tenable working relationship." He said he had assumed that Moos would consult with Hutchins and himself in making any changes, but "no effective consultation with Hutchins and the other principals ever took place." He told Parten that Moos "appeared to act on the assumption that he faced a deteriorating internal situation that required drastic action, and that he had the authority to immediately initiate reconstitution of the administration, the Senior Fellows, and even the Board of directors, without reference to the fact that Hutchins remained in office as Board Chairman and chief executive officer."

Ashmore said he had informed Hutchins in February 1974 that he intended to resign as president of the Fund. "Hutchins asked me to withhold my decision until he could consult with key members of the board," Ashmore noted in his memorandum to Parten. "On the eve of the board meeting I was informed by Hutchins and James Douglas that an acceptable compromise on the Ginsburg matter had been worked out, that Moos had assured them that Wheeler would be given no responsibility for administering the academic program, and that Moos had agreed to recommend to the

Board my election as Executive Vice President. . . . You then asked me privately if I were willing to accept the executive vice presidency, and I replied that I would serve in any capacity that you, as incoming chairman of the board, believed would serve the best interests of the Center."

"The fact is that I have not functioned as executive vice president since my election to that office by the Board," Ashmore said. "The authority previously located in the office was redistributed under a series of directives issued by Moos to staff members previously answerable to me. I was not consulted on any of these changes."

Ashmore declared that his reduction in authority had "inevitably" disturbed board members who had accepted his election as the executive vice president "as an affirmation by Moos that there would be no radical departure from the Hutchins program without full consideration by the Board."

As Ashmore depicted the situation in his memo to Parten, Moos and Wheeler were developing a "grand design" to convert the Center from the Hutchins model into a university of the social sciences. Not mentioning the fact that the minutes of the board session in Santa Barbara in February 1974 —prepared by Ashmore—had reported "general approval" of the program outlined then by Moos to the directors, Ashmore contended that the activities of Moos and Wheeler had eliminated or reduced "the support of most of those board members who were attracted to the Center because of the intellectual dialogue presided over by Hutchins, and by those whose interest mainly lay in the public affairs programming typified by the *Pacem in Terris* convocations."

Ashmore asserted that the Center received a total of $166,775 from board members in 1973, and indicated to Parten that "in the same tax period last year (1974), aside from the $100,000 you gave for general purposes and the additional $25,000 you made available in connection with Moos' relocation, the total is down to $63,499. . . . Twenty of the members of the Board who served during the calendar year, including those elected since Moos' accession, gave nothing at all."

"I do not believe the present state of affairs at the Center can be explained by any conflict of personalities or presumed factional differences among Fellows and Board members who might be sentimentally attached to Hutchins and therefore resistant to change," Ashmore said. He claimed that the divisions among the fellows and the directors could be traced to "what has been done, and not done, from the beginning of this transition period fourteen months ago."

Saying that he had tried to "prevent a breach between the new administration and key members of the Board," Ashmore said he had decided that he no longer had "any useful role to play in that regard," and he asked "to be relieved of the responsibilities conferred upon me by election as executive vice president." He said he had told Moos that he was willing to take his severance pay or to continue as a senior fellow, and he felt that Moos had indicated "that he desired my continuation as a Senior Fellow."

In a letter to Parten on January 24, Moos replied sharply to Ashmore's statements. He did not write to Ashmore directly. He described Ashmore's memorandum as an "intemperate attack," which he regarded as "directly related to Mr. Ashmore's effort at self defense."

"I did not initiate the investigation of Mr. Ashmore's acts in New York," Moos reminded Parten. "Indeed, I might never have heard about his undercutting had it not been for Peter Tagger. I was in Palm Beach visiting a Board member, Arthur Burck, when these matters first came to my attention. Mr. Tagger, who was in Santa Barbara, was queried by Fund for Peace staff members who were perplexed by Mr. Ashmore's behavior and wanted to know what was going on.

"Mr. Tagger concluded that this was a matter deserving my attention and informed Gary Cadenhead of the facts so they could be relayed to me. Mr. Tagger's prompt action brought the story to light in time for Arthur Burck to make an independent personal verification.

"As you know, Mr. Burck, following his personal verification of the first report, reported to you on this matter and advised that competent legal counsel be commissioned to make an investigation to be certain that no unjust or overly hasty conclusions be drawn. Following your approval of this course of action, Mr. Burck informed me that the matter was completely out of my hands. I have not received the report from legal counsel on this matter but nothing I have been told since contradicts Mr. Tagger's report."

Moos had agreed to put the investigation completely into the hands of Burck and Parten because he did not wish to be accused of persecuting Ashmore. While Burck had been elected to the board on his recommendation, he knew that Burck had no personal animosity toward Ashmore. He was sure that Parten, as the chairman of the board and the director who had served the Fund for twenty-two years, had the full confidence of all members of the board.

By this time, Moos had felt reasonably sure that Ashmore had no intention of working with him on the terms he had offered. Because Ashmore was so close to Hutchins, Moos knew that he had to move carefully. He had felt that Hutchins, as a legal scholar, would respect a report prepared by a nationally recognized law school professor. He had not been prepared for Hutchins' demand that Professor Louisell be removed from the inquiry into Ashmore's activities.

In his letter of January 24 to Parten, Moos said: "Mr. Ashmore's defense pleads a misunderstanding. He does not actually deny having told Randolph Compton that I had no authority to negotiate but implied that this statement related to the issue of a full corporate merger of the two institutions. Beyond this, Mr. Ashmore says nothing about conversations he held with other Fund for Peace personnel besides Mr. Compton.

"Next Mr. Ashmore claims the charge that he tried to persuade Compton to cancel his meeting with me could have resulted from an honest confusion. This, he again suggests, might have derived from Mr. Compton's failure to distinguish between a full corporate merger and the more limited cooperation discussed by our own board. While he does not actually deny having urged cancellation of the meeting with me, his line of argument is difficult to follow. It appears to rest upon the charge that Mr. Compton was confused. All I can say is that the state of confusion he attributes to Mr. Compton was never apparent to me in my conversations with him. I have found Mr. Compton to be a very determined and singularly *un*-confused negotiator.''

Moos said it was ''uncalled for'' on Ashmore's part to attribute all the suspicions of Ashmore to Gary Cadenhead: ''Most of the Senior Fellows and Senior Staff at the Center voiced the so-called 'end run' sentiment quite openly. At two meetings of the Senior Fellows, Mr. Ashmore's own draft proposal for a partial merger (with the Fund for Peace) was greeted with quite uninhibited criticism.''

Referring to Ashmore's statement that he had offered to resign with severance pay but had understood that Moos wanted him to continue as a senior fellow, Moos told Parten: ''Deliberately I neither encouraged nor discouraged him to continue as a Senior Fellow. The best way to clarify the situation is to quote from a recent letter by Mr. Ashmore: 'This seems to be an appropriate time to implement our understanding that I would ultimately be relieved of the administrative responsibilities I have carried in addition to my role as a Senior Fellow. . . . I am prepared to accept a reduction in compensation to the level of that of other Senior Fellows of comparable service, with the understanding that I retain my present right to severance pay based on the highest rate paid during the 15½ years I have been associated with the Center.''

Moos said he was transmitting this letter to Parten and asked Parten to bring it to the attention of the executive committee. He said he had notified Ashmore of this action.

Reminding Parten that he had sought ''the assurance that I was in fact being offered the authority necessary to direct the business and academic affairs of the Center,'' Moos said he had perceived that ''considerable financial retrenchment and reallocation would be necessary if the Center were to survive.'' He felt that he had consulted Hutchins sufficiently on these matters; he had informed Hutchins at the beginning of their conversations in Washington that he saw no necessity for keeping a dean, and he had indicated to Hutchins and Ashmore that he intended to close down the Washington office and to curtail expenditures.

(Moos told me later that Hutchins had asked him to come to the Center as soon as possible after his election, in October 1973. He said he had finally offered to leave Minnesota and take over the Center in February or March 1974, but Hutchins had then asked him to delay his arrival until June 1—the twentieth anniversary of Hutchins' taking office as president of the Fund for the Republic. He had deferred to Hutchins on that point.)

In his letter to Parten in January 1975, Moos was bluntly critical of the board. He wrote: "The financial support of our board members is distorted in Mr. Ashmore's memorandum. His reference to board support might leave the impression that ours has been a generous board. With a few notable exceptions that has not been the case. Over the past five years only six members have consistently given $5,000 a year or more. Major support of $25,000 a year has come from only one member consistently, yourself."

Declaring that "the enclosed schedule of the five year history of contributions by board members shows that the board gave *more* in 1974 than in any of the previous four years," Moos added: "Without the continuous personal vilification and efforts to sabotage my program plans for the Center's future, I dare say the level of giving by the board during the past year would have been substantially higher."

Indicating that he regarded Ashmore's memorandum as representing "Mr. Ashmore's personal disapproval of and obstructionist activities concerning my programs for the Center's future," Moos declared that Ashmore "seems to be saying that he will support only a figurehead chairman who will hew strictly to the ways of the past and do nothing to give the Center new life and new leadership."

"This was not my understanding of the job when it was offered to me," Moos said. "I can say with conviction that to hold the Center to a straight-jacketed program patterned on the past would mean its rapid demise. I intend to see that the Center moves forward creatively and vigorously."

The executive committee of the Center's board of directors met in Parten's suite at the Barclay Hotel in New York on February 4. Those present that day included Morris Levinson, chairman of the committee; Moos; Arthur Burck; and Parten. After hearing a report from Moos on conversations with Compton and other Fund for Peace directors, the committee concluded that the Fund for Peace would not supply a solution to the Center's financial problems.

Gary Cadenhead distributed a financial statement showing that the Center's deficit for the six months ending on June 30, 1975, would be approximately $350,000. Cadenhead said that major gifts were required to keep the Center going.

Moos expressed a hope that the Hill Foundation would make a $108,000 grant to the Center's study of public education, and he reported that the McKnight Foundation had shown an interest in funding the study of aging, a project directed by Alex Comfort. He said that the Joint Economic Committee of the House and Senate, headed by Hubert Humphrey, had agreed to provide money for a Center conference on the possible need for a national economic planning system.

The committee approved an annual salary of $30,000—plus life and health insurance coverage—for Robert Hutchins. Hutchins had been receiving $68,000 a year as the Center's chief executive officer and had recommended that his salary be reduced to the $30,000 level on January 1, 1975, when he had returned to active service as a life fellow after the expiration of the leave of absence granted him during the last half of 1974. The committee left to Hutchins the question of whether he wished to retain rights to severance pay in the event of the Center's dissolution.

The possibility of a new policy on severance pay was discussed by the executive committee in the light of a legal opinion submitted to the members by Cadenhead. Parten, believing that the amount of accumulated severance pay under the Hutchins-Ashmore policy had become a heavy burden on the Center, said he would propose that a ceiling of $25,000 in severance pay for an individual staff member be established by the board at its next meeting. Levinson said he would seek another legal opinion on whether it would be possible for the board to change the policy created under Chairman Hutchins and President Ashmore.

The committee accepted Ashmore's offer of resignation of his administrative responsibilities, indicated in his letter of December 30, 1974, to Moos. With the understanding that Ashmore would continue as a senior fellow, the committee set his salary at $39,500 a year, effective on February 15, 1975. (This salary amount was the same as the salary being paid to Harvey Wheeler. Wheeler's compensation had been increased by Moos when Moos took office in June, from $34,500 to $39,500, the highest salary paid to any senior fellow.)

The committee did not agree to Ashmore's request that his severance pay should be available to him if he decided to resign, and the committee did not solve the question of whether his severance pay would be based on his former salary of $57,000 a year or his new salary, if he was asked to resign at the convenience of the Center.

Parten informed the committee that he, Monsignor Lally, and Arthur Burck had met with Randolph Compton, Nick Nyary, and Lindsay Mattison and discussed Mr. Ashmore's alleged statements in his conversations with Fund for Peace officials in December. Parten said he intended to discuss these statements—and the statements made to him and to Lally and Burck—with Ashmore as soon as possible. After that, Parten said, he would make a report to the whole board.

At the luncheon session with Compton, Nyary, and Mattison—which occurred before the members of the Center's executive committee gathered in his hotel suite—Parten had been told by Compton that he did not recall Ashmore's saying that Moos had lost the support of the Center's board. Compton's memory was apparently vague on what he and Ashmore had talked about. But Compton was positive that several members of the Center's board, who had visited him, had declared to him that Moos did not have the support of the board.

Nyary told Parten, Lally, and Burck that several of the Center's directors had conveyed to him a clear impression that Moos did not have the backing of the Center's board any longer. Mattison said that Ashmore had visited him in Washington on December 6 and had informed him that Moos's scheduled meeting with Compton had been canceled because Moos had lost the board's support. Under questioning by Parten and the other two directors, Mattison repeated his summary of his conversation with Ashmore several times, insisting that his memory of what Ashmore had said was clear and accurate.

On February 11, 1975, after his return to his office in Houston, Parten received a letter from Professor Louisell, enclosing copies of statements sent to Louisell by Wheeler, Cadenhead, and Moos, containing their reports on the conversations Ashmore had held with Compton and other Fund for Peace officials. Moos said he had talked with Nyary and Mattison in New York, and both men had told him that Ashmore had said Moos no longer had the backing of the Center's board.

"On January 10, 1975, I had a telephone conversation with Nicholas Nyary of the Fund for Peace," Louisell said in his letter to Parten. "Nyary said that a meeting in December, 1974 had been arranged between Malcolm Moos and Randolph Compton of the Fund for Peace, and that Compton came to Nyary and asked Nyary to call off that meeting because Harry Ashmore had told Compton that Moos had lost the support of the directors of the Center. Nyary further said that he thereupon told Compton that arrangements for the meeting should go ahead, and that Compton then said that in view of the fact that final arrangements had been made the meeting should go ahead, which it did.

"On January 10 I also had a telephone conversation with Lynn Mattison of the Fund for Peace who said that Ashmore had told him that the proposed December, 1974 meeting of Moos and Compton had been cancelled.

"On your direction I have desisted from pursuing this investigation and have not been in touch with Ashmore."

Ashmore talked with Morris Levinson soon after the meeting of the executive committee and learned that Parten was going ahead with his investigation. On February 10 Ashmore wrote to Levinson, addressing him as chairman of the executive committee. He sent Levinson a 21-page memorandum entitled "Severance Pay Policy," saying that he sent it in response to Levinson's request.

"As I understand it, three related matters were presented at the meeting of the executive committee," Ashmore said. "(1) The charge of a breach of ethics brought against me by Burck as the basis of dismissal for cause, which, if it could be made to stand up, would have the effect of relieving the Fund of a substantial sum in severance pay obligation. (2) The proposal that I be relieved of administrative duties as Executive Vice President effective at the annual meeting of the board on February 22, and continued as a Senior Fellow with an appropriate salary adjustment—which also involves a severance pay consideration. (3) A proposal that the Fund adopt a new policy that would have the effect of abrogating the present general commitment of severance pay at the rate of one month's salary for each year of service in case of dissolution or relocation of the Center, or separation of any employee for the convenience of the Fund.

"I understand that no action was taken by the executive committee. This memorandum is in response to your request that I forward information relevant to these matters, which presumably are still pending and may now go forward for consideration by the board at the annual meeting February 22, 1975."

Taking up the charges against him, Ashmore said: "To the extent that these allegations may be the product of honest misunderstanding, I assume that this arises from my statement to Compton that his reiterated proposal for a corporate merger of the Fund for Peace and the Fund for the Republic could not be dealt with at the level of the staff negotiations scheduled for the following week, but would have to be considered by our board of directors, where it faced considerable opposition. That is simply a statement of fact, and it hardly could have been news to Compton, since it is the position taken by Steward Mott, a director of both Funds, at conferences attended by Moos and Burck, along with Compton and members of the Fund for Peace staff.

"My statement could not have been construed by Compton as a challenge to Moos' status, since I had from the outset of our discussions taken the position that a merger could not possibly be considered, much less approved, by our board without the support of Moos. I left Compton with a promise to present the latest version of his merger proposal to Moos at the first opportunity, which I did."

Ashmore asserted that he had reported all his conversations with Compton and other Fund for Peace officers to Moos, and said that "after Moos assumed his duties as chief executive officer of the Fund for the Republic, I urged him to take over the negotiations personally so as to avoid any possible misunderstanding with Compton, and removed myself. I met with Compton again on December 5 at Moos' request to discuss a specific proposal for a joint foreign policy project. When Compton reintroduced the corporate merger proposal I transmitted its substance to Moos. I have had no further conversations with Compton, or with any staff personnel connected with the Fund for Peace.

"In a letter to me of January 28, 1975, Arthur Burck wrote in reference to his move to retain an attorney to investigate his allegations: 'I would think that anyone suspected would himself plead for the fullest, most complete investigation of all pertinent facts so that the matter can be properly assessed before improper conclusions are reached. Remember that at least four Center people, plus at least three outsiders, were talking about the incident. Rumors are bound to spread if the matter is not put to rest by independent investigation.'

"The seven purported witnesses apparently were talking about a conversation at which only Randolph Compton and I were present. Messrs.

Parten, Burck and Moos now have had full opportunity to explore these allegations with Compton, and I am informed that he confirmed my account of our conversation and denied any suggestion of impropriety, as did Nicholas Nyary. In the case of Lindsay Mattison, I am informed that he was interrogated several weeks ago by Gary Cadenhead and David Louisell, and informed them that he had no information that could be said to confirm the Burck charges. If my information is correct it would seem that the charge of unethical conduct might apply in reverse."

Ashmore went into the question of how much severance pay he had coming to him under the policy that Hutchins and he had established: "I felt it necessary to stipulate that in the event of future separation I would expect severance pay to be computed at the rate of income I received as chief operating officer, rather than at the lower compensation for a Senior Fellow, and that I also would expect payment in the event of resignation on my own motion. Both these conditions are special, and I understood that they would have to be agreed to on an individual basis."

As a former president of the Center, Ashmore felt that he was entitled to special treatment. He noted that if he waived his right to be paid severance at his highest level of salary, he might lose $27,155. He said: "I wish I could afford to make such a contribution to the Center, but my personal circumstances do not permit it."

"Reserving the right to resign without waiving severance pay claims is justified, I think, by the campaign to force my removal," Ashmore told Levinson. "For the first time in more than 20 years of association with the Fund for the Republic, I cannot assume that I am being dealt with in good faith."

Once more, Ashmore reviewed the history of the severance pay policy put into effect by Hutchins and himself, and he concluded: "Whatever the legal situation may be, it seems quite clear that the Board has repeatedly recognized a moral obligation to compensate employees whose service to the Center is terminated through no fault of their own."

Ashmore quoted from the minutes of the senior fellows' meeting of November 14, 1974, in which Moos had told the fellows that he had received a "mandate" from the Center's board to reduce the Center's staff and its budget drastically and immediately. When Moos had been asked about severance pay, he had said that there was a "moral feeling on the part of the majority of the board" that severance pay should be available.

Ashmore criticized Moos for giving increases in salary to Harvey Wheeler, Gary Cadenhead, Peter Tagger, Donald McDonald, and Mary Harvey on his own initiative. "Unless there has been some supporting action by the executive committee, these salary increases would appear to represent a departure from standing board policy. While the board has never exercised its prerogative to pass on individual salaries paid to Center Fellows and staff, it has received regular reports on pay schedules at all levels, and has required the officers to justify any significant changes."

Ashmore renewed his attack on the budget approved by the board at its special meeting on November 4 in Chicago: "It is already evident that the dialogue program as conceived by Hutchins cannot be maintained under the new budget, which will require reduction of academic and support personnel below the minimum required to maintain the kind of intellectual activity that has always characterized the Center."

He raised the question of whether such budget reductions were unfair to the Center's members, who expected the "dialogue program" to be maintained at a high level: "Board members who are aware of the implications of these budget cuts have suggested that there is a moral obligation to the Center's members on the order of that recognized for employees under the severance policy. This implies that some arrangement should be made to guarantee that funds contributed to support the Center's basic issues program not be employed to maintain an organization so altered as to be unable, or unwilling, to carry out the general purposes of the founder."

In this memorandum to Levinson, Ashmore tried to move from a defensive position into a full confrontation with Moos. It was obvious that he regarded Levinson as an ally and that he had abandoned any hope of persuading Parten to withdraw support from Moos.

On February 13 Parten wrote to Ashmore, acknowledging the letter and memorandum Ashmore had dispatched to him in the middle of January. After assuring Ashmore that he had read and studied these materials carefully, Parten said: "For your information, I have interviewed Randolph Compton, Nick Nyary, and Lindsay Mattison. I would like very much to have a meeting with you at some convenient time after lunch on Friday, February 20, in Santa Barbara. I will call your office on arrival."

A day earlier, Parten had sent all members of the board a brief summary of his conversations—and those of Monsignor Lally and Arthur Burck—with the Fund for Peace officers in New York. This summary was signed by Lally and Burck as well as by Parten. Parten wanted the board to consider this statement at its meeting on February 22.

On February 21 Parten, Lally, and Burck talked with Ashmore at the San Ysidro ranch in Santa Barbara. Ashmore said he had no recollection of saying the things "attributed to him by Messrs. Nyary and Mattison," and reiterated that such statements "did not in fact represent his sentiments then or now."

Parten was most concerned about the statements made by Compton, Nyary, and Mattison that several of the directors of the Fund for the Republic had told them that Moos had lost the board's backing. Ashmore said he could not name any director who might have made such a statement.

Blair Clark, Steward Mott, and Frances McAllister had been on the original committee appointed by Hutchins to meet with Fund for Peace officials. Parten felt that Clark and Mrs. McAllister might have made such statements to Compton, Nyary, and Mattison. But the Fund for Peace officials would not give any names.

On the evening of February 21 Bernard Rapoport came to Parten's cottage at the San Ysidro ranch and told Parten that Hutchins was extremely disturbed by the investigation of Ashmore. Rapoport said that Hutchins had indicated that he would resign from the Center's board if Parten insisted on presenting a report on the Ashmore matter to the whole board when it assembled on February 22.

"I have to present that report," Parten said. "It's my obligation to do it. The board is entitled to it. And Hutchins won't resign."

When the directors gathered at the Center on the morning of February 22, all of them realized that they faced a day of battles. With Parten's support, Moos had decided to have a showdown with his implacable opponent, Frances McAllister. Parten and Moos also felt that the board had to face what they regarded as strong evidence that Ashmore and other directors had attempted to undermine and damage Moos in his conversations with the Fund for Peace officials.

The directors assembled at 10:30 A.M. in their capacity as trustees of the Fund for the Republic. Hutchins was present; he had dropped any idea of resigning. Under the bylaws of the Fund, the directors had regularly elected themselves as trustees. The trustees were supposed to meet annually.

After obtaining ratification of the minutes of the last meeting of the trustees, held in Washington on October 8, 1973, Parten asked for formal approval of the amendment to the bylaws passed by the directors on May 17, 1974, at their special meeting in St. Paul. That amendment had expanded the number of directors from twenty-nine to thirty-two and had permitted the seating of the three new directors recommended by Moos.

Joseph Antonow objected to the amendment's being considered, saying that it had not been mentioned in the notice of the annual meeting of the trustees, as required by the by-laws. No action was taken on the proposed amendment after Antonow's objection.

Moos then reported that the board had lost six trustee-directors through the death of Patrick Crowley and the resignations of Ralph Ablon, James C. Downs, Jr., Joseph W. Drown, Arnold Grant, and Eleanor Stevenson. He noted that there had been four additions: Burck, Ridder, Ward, and himself. The number of trustee-directors, after these changes, was twenty-six.

The crucial moment came when Moos moved the reelection of five trustee-directors, to serve as members of the class of 1977. He called the names of Ramsey Clark, Vesta Hutchins, W. Price Laughlin, Seniel Ostrow, and L. Emmerson Ward but conspicuously omitted Frances McAllister, who had been scheduled to be among this group. Moos did not want her to stay on the board. She had attacked him in letters and phone calls to board members. She had brought an auditor to the Center to go over the account books. She had sent him scornful notes about some of his correspondence.

Howard Marshall promptly seconded the motion by Moos. Morris Levinson then moved that the motion be amended to include the reelection of Mrs. McAllister, and his motion was immediately seconded. After some discussion, in which Robert Hutchins and Mrs. Hutchins made it clear that they supported Mrs. McAllister, the Levinson amendment was approved by a vote of 12 to 10. Moos had lost.

Until the vote was taken, Moos had hoped that James Douglas, who had joined with Parten in October 1973 in recommending his election as chief executive officer of the Center, would stand by him. He was sure that Douglas knew of the attacks made on him by Mrs. McAllister, and Douglas had shown his sympathy to Moos on several occasions. But Douglas had been convinced, apparently by Hutchins, that if Mrs. McAllister was not reelected to the board, Moos intended to call for the removal of Ashmore.

Moos had also hoped that Eulah Laucks, who had been friendly to him and who had defended Harvey Wheeler against his critics, would vote with him. But Mrs. Laucks abstained. She liked Moos and she knew the difficulties he faced, but she could not bring herself to vote against Mrs. McAllister. And she had become critical of his university project.

The vote had been extremely close. If Douglas had voted with Moos, there would have been a tie—and Parten (who had not voted because of his position as chairman) had intended to cast a tie-breaking vote against Mrs. McAllister. Since Parten was still a firm supporter of Moos, it was evident that he actually had 11 votes on the board. The directors were divided almost evenly between those who backed Moos and those who were against him on the issue of Mrs. McAllister.

The executive session of the trustees lasted only 15 minutes. When it was over, the survival of Moos as the president of the Center seemed to be very much in doubt. But Moos was not ready to surrender, and neither was Parten. Moos believed that some of the directors who had voted against him on the McAllister question might still be persuaded to support his program for the Center's future.

Immediately after they ended their session as trustees, the directors convened in the same conference room as a board of directors. The tensions between the Parten-Moos group and the Ashmore-Hutchins group became quickly evident again.

Parten described the investigation he had initiated into Ashmore's activities with the assistance of Monsignor Francis Lally and Arthur Burck. He explained how the allegations against Ashmore had been received at the Center, and cited Burck's request for an inquiry. He said that he had responded to Burck's request as he would have responded to any request from a board member.

Cadenhead distributed copies of the February 12 memorandum Parten had sent to the board, and a copy of the supplemental statement summarizing what Ashmore, Tagger, and Cadenhead had reportedly said to Parten and the other members of his committee.

After reading these reports, Ashmore told the directors that he had never said at any time to Randolph Compton or to anyone else that Compton or anyone else should not negotiate with Moos because Moos had lost the board's support. He declared that he had said just the reverse of that. Ashmore said that the charges had not been brought to him directly, and he asserted that he had not been given a chance to respond to the allegations until the day before the board meeting. He added that he had spoken with both Nyary and Mattison by telephone, and that they had denied having quoted him as ever having said anything that could be construed as supporting the charges made against him.

Parten said that he had acted in the light of his conception of the duties and responsibilities of the chairman of the board. Since Ashmore had denied all the allegations against him, Parten said he was personally willing to let the matter rest. (Monsignor Lally stated that the committee's report on what Nyary and Mattison had said to them was accurate. In a letter to me later, Lally said he had spoken to Nyary personally and Nyary confirmed the first report given by Tagger to Cadenhead—that Compton had received an impression from Ashmore that Moos had lost the board's backing.)

Steward Mott, who was a director of the Fund for Peace as well as a director of the Center, said he believed that some confusion and misunderstanding had occurred among the Fund for Peace officers. Other directors, who had been involved in the negotiations, shared Mott's view of the situation. No one commented directly on the statement Compton had made to Parten, Lally, and Burck—a statement confirmed by Nyary and Mattison—that several of the Fund for the Republic's directors had told him Moos did not have the backing of his board.

Urging the board to drop the entire matter, Mott said he thought the board should not investigate officers or directors without approval by the executive committee or the full board. The board approved a resolution to drop "charges of misconduct" against Ashmore, and they adopted Mott's proposal to require endorsement by the executive committee or the whole board of any future investigations of officers or directors.

Levinson did not vote on the Mott resolution and asked that the record show that he considered the charges against Ashmore "ridiculous" and "unsubstantiated." (Parten learned later that Levinson had served as Ashmore's legal counsel.)

Parten then asked the directors to consider the question of establishing a formal policy on severance pay. Cadenhead distributed an opinion by the Center's law firm, Hatch & Parent, indicating that the board had the authority to revise or eliminate the severance pay arrangements instituted by Ashmore and Hutchins. Parten felt that it was important for the board to establish a definite policy.

Cadenhead said that the severance pay obligation, under the Ashmore-Hutchins plan, amounted to more than $600,000. Parten asked why a fund to amortize this contingent liability had not been set up in the Center's financial statements. Ashmore repeated what he had said on other occasions: it had been his understanding that the valuable real estate owned by the Center in Santa Barbara represented a financial reserve large enough to cover the severance pay. Price Laughlin declared that the trustee-directors had to assume the responsibility ethically and morally for the commitment that had already been made to the employees.

Monsignor Lally said he shared Ashmore's recollection that the Center's real estate had been regarded as insurance for the payment of severance obligations to employees if the Center had to be dissolved. Laughlin moved that the board should honor all financial commitments for severance pay through February 22, 1975, and that no further accumulation of such obligations be permitted until a committee of directors reviewed the situation.

Some of the directors were alarmed by the possibility that they might have to dig into their own resources to meet the severance pay obligations if the real estate did not cover them. Seniel Ostrow objected to recognizing the liability, since the Center apparently did not have funds to meet it. Howard Marshall questioned whether the Laughlin resolution would make the individual directors personally responsible and asked whether the board was then legally obligated for the pay. Cadenhead said he thought the board was obligated under the current policy.

At Parten's suggestion, the board finally decided to instruct the executive committee to resolve any questions about the severance pay arrangements and "to negotiate with employees concerning severance pay." An amendment offered by Joseph Antonow, stating that any agreements would have be approved by the full board, was accepted.

There seemed to be no doubt in the minds of the directors—whether they supported Moos or not—that some senior fellows and some senior staff members of the Center with many years of service would have to be terminated. The directors showed no willingness to make sudden contributions to continue the work of the Center on the scale it had reached under Hutchins and Ashmore.

When Parten called for a report by the committee on alternative sites, Weissbourd read a statement that had been approved by Moos, Mrs. Laucks, Burck, and other directors who had participated in a meeting of the committee on February 21. There was a general consensus among the committee members that a reorganization of the Center with a transfer of its headquarters to Chicago could be workable, but there was no agreement that such a plan was the best possibility.

James Douglas asked whether the Center could survive in its location on Eucalyptus Hill. Moos said the answer depended on how generous the board members were willing to be in the next few months. Antonow said his study of the Center's financial statements indicated that the Center would be on the edge of dissolution before June 30. He wanted the board to act quickly.

Antonow promised that Bernard Weissbourd and he would guarantee that the Center's reduced budget under the Chicago plan would be met for two years. Weissbourd said the plan assumed that the Center would no longer have permanent senior fellows, and would use University of Chicago professors on a temporary basis to keep the dialogue going.

Bernard Rapoport and Paul Newman voiced their misgivings about the Center as it existed. "Nobody is really excited about the Center," Rapoport said. "The reason that directors are not giving money is that *they* are not excited about the Center." He thought that the Center had to become more coherent and then redefine its purpose. He did not mention Moos's proposal for changing the Center gradually into a new type of university. He said that a new policy had to be developed to bring in new people at the senior fellow level. After that, he felt it would be possible to raise money for the Center.

After saying that he didn't glimpse any lasting benefit in shifting the Center to Chicago, Newman said the Center had to get "higher visibility." He urged the directors to consider transferring it to Washington, D.C., where it might be able to make more of an impact on Congress. Apparently overlooking the fact that the Center was barred from politics under its charter as a tax-exempt institution, Newman declared that the Center had "to take a much more activist position." He felt that funds could be obtained to support its work under such conditions.

At this stage in the meeting, James Douglas recommended that Hutchins be asked to make a study of what could be done in the Chicago area. (Douglas had served as a trustee of the University of Chicago when Hutchins had been president of that university.) Without hesitation, Hutchins said he would be willing to survey the Chicago situation if the board wanted him to do it.

Laughlin put forward a proposal that the board might close down the Center for a year and that the directors might give fifteen days to brainstorming sessions that might generate "a new plan, new concepts and ideas which could really influence people." After that, Laughlin said, the directors could decide it would be worthwhile to move the Center to Washington or Chicago or to take another alternative. Weissbourd answered that "this was, essentially, the Chicago plan."

Mott said that the Chicago plan might be used at the Eucalyptus Hill location, with part-time scholars drawn from people available in California. Weissbourd thought that could be done, but he expressed a belief that it would cost more to operate in that manner in Santa Barbara than it would in Chicago.

Moos sat in silence while the directors tossed ideas into the air and knocked them down again. The directors seemed to have forgotten that he had submitted a budget in Chicago on November 4—a budget that would permit the Center to operate with five fellows instead of ten, a budget that had been approved by the board. No one referred to what had happened at the Chicago meeting.

Then Parten, undaunted by the evident opposition to Moos and the signs of confusion in the board, asked how many of the directors at the table in the Center's conference room would match him in either giving or raising $100,000 "for the remainder of this year's operations." The directors looked at one another. Six or seven of them—Paul Newman, Stewart Mott, Price Laughlin, Morris Levinson, Bernard Ridder, Bernard Weissbourd, Seniel Ostrow—were capable of matching Parten's offer.

Only Rapoport spoke up, saying that he was willing to donate or obtain contributions totaling $100,000. Rapoport had a deep admiration for many of his fellow directors. He particularly admired Parten and Hutchins, and he hated to see the growing division between them. He was not excited by the Center as it stood, but he wanted to stand by Parten—and he knew that Parten believed that Moos should be given a chance to keep the Center going under his leadership for the remaining months of 1975. Moos had been in office for only a few months, and those had been months of economic depression, when fund raising was hard, months marred by dissension and backbiting at the Center. Parten did not want to see Moos toppled before Moos had been given enough time to show what he could do. So Rappoport stood by Parten.

Parten was disappointed by the silence of James Douglas, who had shared the responsibility of choosing Moos as Hutchins' successor. He was saddened by the readiness of Douglas and Hutchins to consider a plan offered by two Chicago directors who had not helped Moos to raise any money or shown any interest in Moos's program for the Center's future. But he still hoped that Douglas and Hutchins would not join the group of directors who seemed eager to bring Moos down. In that group, he included Blair Clark, Mrs. McAllister, Stewart Mott, Morris Levinson, and Harry Ashmore.

When it was evident that Rapoport was the only director then willing to join Parten in making a major gift or raising a substantial sum for the Center headed by Moos, Antonow moved that the board should meet within thirty days to decide whether to dissolve the Center, to reorganize and relocate in Chicago, or to approve a reorganization at some other site. He recommended that Moos should produce facts and figures on plans other than the Chicago proposal and that Hutchins should be authorized to look into the kind of academic program that could be carried on in Chicago.

Fagan Dickson, a director supporting Parten and Moos, knew that Moos needed more than thirty days to develop possible support for maintaining the Center in Santa Barbara or in San Diego, where Moos had explored a possible affiliation with the University of California at the campus there. Dickson moved to set the date for the next meeting of the board on April 19—rather than on March 22, the date proposed by Antonow.

Seniel Ostrow and another director had left the meeting. There were twenty-one directors remaining in the conference room. When a vote was taken on the Dickson amendment, there were 10 votes in favor of it and 10 opposed. Chairman Parten cast the deciding vote for the Dickson proposal, setting the date of the next meeting on April 19.

The close vote on Dickson's proposal showed again that the board was split into two halves, with one group backing Moos and Parten and the other group pressing for early action on a drastic reorganization evidently designed to take the leadership of the Center from Moos.

Antonow asked the directors to indicate by raising their hands whether they wanted the Chicago directors to continue "to develop the Chicago alternative." Enough hands went up to indicate that the board was willing to have a study of the Chicago plan continued.

The intentions of the Chicago directors were made very clear when Monsignor Lally proposed that the officers recommended by the nominating committee—Parten as chairman of the board, Moos as president, me as vice president, and Cadenhead as secretary and treasurer—be elected for one year. Weissbourd moved to hold off the election until the April 19 meeting, saying that it would not be fair to elect officers for a year when they might be terminated in 60 days "because of the Center's dissolution or relocation."

The Weissbourd amendment to postpone the election of officers was defeated by a vote of 13 to 5, and the officers headed by Parten and Moos were then elected. The directors then unanimously approved a statement of appreciation for the work of John Cogley, who had retired because of illness, especially for what he had done to make the *Center Magazine* an excellent publication. At 4:30 in the afternoon, after that day of arguments, they adjourned.

Moos was disheartened but not quite ready to abandon hope. The three directors he had placed on the board had not come forward with financial aid. These directors were shocked by the treatment he had received from his opponents and did not wish to commit themselves to donations until there seemed to be likelihood that Moos could move forward with his program. They were not willing to put money into a Center that seemed to be on the verge of internal destruction. But they were ready to help him.

Parten, an indomitable fighter, exhorted Moos and Cadenhead to bring pressure to bear on directors who made pledges to pay those pledges before the next board meeting. He also urged Moos to send out fund-raising letters to Center members, and to redouble the efforts being made to persuade people in Santa Barbara to support the Center.

I had organized a Santa Barbara committee for the Center and I had publicly acknowledged that the Center was in dire straits—and might be forced to move its headquarters. The financial response from Santa Barbara citizens was not very substantial. Ashmore and Tagger were angered by my efforts. They thought I had damaged the Center by making a frank appeal for immediate help.

My attempts to aid Moos enraged Blair Clark, who came up to me after the board meeting and called me "a traitor." I had felt legally bound to support Moos, who had been chosen by Parten's committee and had been unanimously elected by the board. I had always supported Hutchins and Ashmore during their years of authority.

After that February meeting, the families and friends of the fellows and staff members of the Center were deeply disturbed. My wife wrote to Hutchins and Moos on March 20, proposing an analysis of what was happening at the Center in a series of dialogues led by members of the faculty of St. John's College. In both letters, she pointed out that "the Center has been deeply venerated by many more persons than we have as members, and these will all consider themselves to have been traduced by impending April events (no matter what various image makers produce for explanation)."

"If the Center breaks up in wrangling, vituperation, skulduggery and violence against reason and spirit, then the rest of our world has not long to wait for the same acts on an increased and horrible scale," Barbara Kelly said. She hoped that the dialogues led by the St. John's College teachers could examine painful questions: "What, basically and objectively, has been happening amongst us? Is this part of a necessary throe in the progress of the good? Is it an avoidable evil? Why? What do our experiences have to offer other groups?"

She emphasized that she was not suggesting "an encounter group," or "a psychotherapy clinic," but a review by "scholars, examining in scholarly fashion the big forces at work, the meaning of details, the relative values of history." She urged Hutchins and Moos to remember that "all our friends and supporters, most of whom have invested their life's savings of ideals and altruism in the Center, have a right to understand why our solid method is crashing before their eyes." She reminded them: "Our own people began with a sacrificial commitment to nobility, honor, truth and concern for others, and they also deserve the opportunity for insight as to why there is no point to their best efforts and dreams."

Moos wrote her that he was willing to have such dialogues conducted by St. John's scholars at any time. Hutchins replied negatively in a letter dated March 26: "Your idea would have been timely if it had been taken up before we began or at any point in history up to the present. If carried out now it might serve as instruction to others—like an autopsy. But the Board meeting is April 19 and something is going to have to be decided then. Whatever it is, it will not be pleasant. I'm afraid that our experience shows that the achievement of an intellectual community can be thwarted by all kinds of apparently trivial factors and that it is possible only if luck is added to the basic requirements of character, commitment, and intelligence."

Hutchins had never been very sanguine about the Center's long-range future. He often quoted words he attributed to William the Silent or Charles the Bold: "It is not necessary to hope in order to undertake, nor to succeed in order to persevere."

In March, Moos persevered in his attempts to get commitments of financial grants from foundations. He did not have much luck. He did receive a promise from a cousin—a man who had become wealthy through oil production—of a contribution of $100,000, with a much larger donation as a possibility if he continued as the chief executive of the Center. He made telephone calls and sent letters to wealthy citizens of Santa Barbara. He did not obtain the large gifts he sought.

Hutchins went to Chicago in March and had meetings there with University of Chicago professors and Center supporters, who assured him that a Center program in Chicago would be welcome. Hutchins prepared a report for Parten and other board members, describing the evident interest of people in the Chicago area. But Hutchins did not commit himself to the idea of moving the Center's headquarters to Chicago.

On April 9, 1975, Parten wrote to Moos in his capacity as president of the Parten Foundation, saying that the directors of his foundation had decided to give $100,000 to the Fund for the Republic in 1975, provided that the officers of the Fund were able to raise $200,000 in gifts or "legally enforceable pledges" from other sources. Parten said that another $100,000 commitment would be available to the Fund in 1976, if "the operation continues successfully at Santa Barbara with the aid of this first grant."

A week later, while Parten was preparing to leave Houston for Santa Barbara for a meeting with Moos before the board assembled there, Mrs. Parten died in her sleep in the Parten residence in Madisonville. The funeral services for Mrs. Parten were set for April 19, the day on which the Center's board had been supposed to meet.

Moos telephoned and telegraphed the directors, saying that he had decided to cancel the board meeting. With Gary Cadenhead and me, he made arrangements to attend the funeral services. Hutchins and Ashmore stayed in Santa Barbara, and met informally with Levinson, Douglas, Antonow, Weissbourd, and other directors who had flown into Santa Barbara for the board session.

Hutchins and Parten had been friends for forty years, but Hutchins was not with his friend on the day of Mrs. Parten's burial. When I asked him, a few months later, why he had not gone to Texas to be with Parten on that day, Hutchins answered: "Some of the other directors had already arrived in Santa Barbara. I felt an obligation to be with them. The Center was in the worst crisis in its history."

After the funeral service in Madisonville, I telephoned Hutchins at the suggestion of Cadenhead. Cadenhead had heard a report from Santa Barbara that Hutchins had definitely decided to join the Chicago directors in recommending a plan that would eliminate Moos. When I reached Hutchins on the phone, I said, "We've heard here that you've come out for the so-called Chicago plan."

"Come out?" Hutchins said, his voice tense. "What do you mean, 'come out'? That sounds as though I've been hiding somewhere."

"How would you like to put it?"

"I've joined the consensus," Hutchins said slowly. His voice was weary and sad. "That's the right way to put it."

His sadness was understandable to me. He had joined a "consensus" that would mean the end of the senior fellows program he had established with such high hopes in the reorganization of 1969. The first phase of the Center's existence had lasted for ten years. The second had endured for only six.

During these six years he had insisted that it was essential for the Center to maintain a permanent group of fellows—"the best people in the world"—to carry on a continuing dialogue to generate the ideas the world needed. Now he had apparently accepted a reorganization plan that would terminate all the fellows except for himself and Dr. Comfort.

Cadenhead urged me to ask him whether he would support Moos under any circumstances. I said, "Is it a matter of money? Would you support an operation headed by Moos in Santa Barbara or San Diego if he raised the money?"

"No," Hutchins said flatly. "I would not."

He had decided that the time had come to remove Moos. Moos had not proved to be the kind of successor he had wanted. Moos had not consulted him enough. Moos wanted to change the Center drastically. To remove Moos, Hutchins was willing to take part in drastic changes along a different line.

When Cadenhead and I returned to Parten's house, I told Parten what Hutchins had said. It wasn't an easy thing to do. As I spoke, I remembered the years Parten had spent in searching for Hutchins' successor—at the urging of Hutchins. I could see the pain in Parten's face.

"Why didn't Hutchins call me and tell me that?" Parten said. "If Hutchins has turned against Moos, it's over. We'll get the best severance arrangement we can for Moos. That's all we can do."

The reluctance of Hutchins to call Parten was consistent with his character. Hutchins had always found it extremely difficult to tell his colleagues negative or unpleasant things. He had avoided Ping Ferry after he had decided that Ferry had to leave the Center. He had not wanted to tell his old friend Parten that he had withdrawn his support for the man he had favored as his successor, the man Parten and Douglas had recommended to the board with his backing.

At a meeting of the board's executive committee on May 9 in Santa Barbara, the committee agreed to recommend the adoption of the so-called "Chicago plan." There was apparently no discussion of the proposals that had been advocated by Moos. After a conversation with Douglas, Moos felt that the committee expected him to resign. He indicated that he was ready to do so.

In the course of the committee's discussions, Hutchins said at one point, "Moos has been here for nearly a year and he hasn't raised any money." Parten answered sharply, "He hasn't had a chance. He was attacked and undermined before he got here."

At Parten's request, Howard Marshall met with Joseph Antonow to develop the terms for an agreement between the Fund for the Republic and Moos. Marshall said later that Antonow insisted that the agreement had to carry a statement binding Moos not to say or do anything "detrimental to the Center." "I don't think he thought that Dr. Moos would lie about anything," Marshall said. "I think he feared that Dr. Moos would think he had been let down, and after all he is a prominent educator, and he—Antonow —was afraid that Moos might say something in explaining why he resigned that might be in some way detrimental to the Center."

The agreement, which Moos signed the next day, declared that it was necessary to terminate his employment along with that of other officers and employees "to facilitate the orderly relocation of the corporation's offices and activities." The Fund agreed to pay Moos a total of $75,000 over a period of three years, with stipulations in the contract severely limiting his freedom of speech and his freedom to act.

"During the period commencing on the date of the execution of this Agreement and continuing until May 15, 1978, Malcolm Moos agrees that he will commit no act or acts seriously detrimental to the interests of the Corporation," the contract said. "The parties hereto agree that any and all documents, papers, writings or other works written, produced, made or authored by Malcolm Moos while an employee of the Corporation and in his capacity as an employee, shall be and shall remain the sole and exclusive property of the Corporation and shall not be used by Malcolm Moos in any form or for any purpose nor shall they be removed by Malcolm Moos from the premises of the Corporation."

Howard Marshall felt that this contract provided a settlement of differences between Moos and the Fund "on a happy basis." He said later that "Bob Hutchins came over and thanked me for getting it done." It did not make Moos happy—as Moos indicated later—but he accepted it as the best settlement he could get at the time.

Eighteen directors gathered in the Center's conference room on the morning of May 10 to discuss the recommendations presented to them by the executive committee. Moos was present, at the urging of Parten, but the three new directors who had been elected on his recommendation in Minneapolis in May 1974—Arthur Burck, Bernard Ritter, and Dr. Ward—were not able to be there.

Representatives of several newspapers entered the conference room with Dr. Comfort, who told the directors that he thought the meeting should be open to the press. Antonow requested that the meeting be held in a closed session. After some discussion, Parten called for a vote on Antonow's request. A majority of the directors indicated that they wanted the session to be closed to observers.

Two lawyers for the Center—Stanley Hatch and John Berryhill, both of Santa Barbara—were present in the room. Dr. Comfort asked that the lawyers get in touch with his attorneys, as he had requested in a letter to Chairman Parten on April 25. In this letter he had referred to his contract with the Center as a senior fellow.

Accompanied by several of the other fellows who had entered the room with the reporters, Dr. Comfort withdrew from the meeting. Berryhill was asked by Parten to record the minutes of the board's executive session.

Before the directors turned to the main topics of the meeting, they had to perform a legal ritual. Joseph Antonow had challenged the legality of the election of Moos in Washington and the three directors elected in Minnesota, declaring that a trustee's meeting necessary under the Fund's bylaws had not been held. Upon investigation, Hatch & Parent—the Center's law firm—had found that a number of other directors had questionable status because the legal formalities of trustees' meetings had not been performed.

Hatch read a resolution to the board, saying that the adoption of the resolution would give all twenty-six members of the board legal standing as member-trustees of the Fund for the Republic. The resolution—which simply stated that "the persons whose names are hereinafter set forth are hereby confirmed, individually, as elected members (Trustees) of the Fund for the Republic, Inc."—was immediately adopted. The directors' meeting was then recessed, while the directors convened themselves as trustee-members. As trustee-members, they elected themselves as directors.

This ritual was necessary because the New York law under which the Fund had originally been established in 1952 had required trustees to elect and classify directors, and directors to elect future trustees. The directors had been given the power to formulate the policy of the corporation. Over the years, the two groups had become identical, but the legal ceremony of trustee meetings to elect directors had continued to be required. Parten later referred to the process which occurred at the meeting on May 10, 1975, as a legal "rebaptism."

When the directors reconvened as the board of directors—after electing themselves in their capacity as trustees—they adopted a resolution ratifying previous actions of the board, with a stipulation by Antonow that such action did not constitute a contract "or undertaking by the corporation with respect to the election of any officer of the corporation."

The directors then considered the minutes of the stormy meeting of February 22. Antonow suggested that the reports submitted by Parten on Ashmore's meetings with Fund for Peace officials be detached from the minutes and put into the corporation's records, since the matter involving Ashmore had been dropped. Knowing that Hutchins and other directors wanted such a step to be taken, Parten did not object.

Ashmore had heard a rumor that Cadenhead might sue the Center for a year's salary, based on the wording of the February 22 minutes referring to the election of officers for "one year terms." Antonow recommended that the minutes be reworded to say simply that certain officers had been elected, without any mention of the length of their terms. His proposal was accepted.

With these amendments, the minutes of the February 22 meeting were at last approved. All references to the investigation of Ashmore were expunged. (In a deposition given later, in a suit filed by Dr. Comfort against the Center, Parten said: "That report speaks for itself. Father Lally signed it. Burck signed it and I signed it, and the board had a vote, and decided not to do anything about it. . . . I thought it was foolish to try and cover it up because all they did was expunge it from the minutes." Parten added: "My committee never recommended anything. It reported the facts of what happened to the board and we didn't recommend any action. It never was our purpose to recommend any action.")

After disposing of the Ashmore matter, the directors confronted the problem of what to do about Dr. Comfort. Comfort's attorneys had sent a telegram to Parten on April 18, citing the existence of a legal agreement between Comfort and the Fund involving the royalties from Comfort's book *The Joy of Sex,* and Dr. Comfort had written a letter to Parten on April 25, stating that he expected the Center to abide by his agreement with the corporation.

Because the Center's law firm, Hatch & Parent, had been involved in the drafting of the agreement, Parten had asked the firm of Price, Postel, and Parma to provide a written opinion to the board on the legal issues that might arise. The directors approved Parten's action and authorized the retention of this firm as "special counsel" in dealing with Dr. Comfort. At this point, Malcolm Moos left the meeting.

The board was uneasy about a possible suit by Dr. Comfort if the board authorized the removal of all of the Center's activities to Chicago, one of the directors recalled later. This director—Howard Marshall—declared that Comfort's attitude was "one of the reasons" for modifying the original "Chicago plan" to place more emphasis on activities that were to be conducted in Santa Barbara.

When Morris Levinson, the chairman of the executive committee, presented the recommendations of that committee to the board on May 10, he said that the plan approved by the committee provided "for the expansion to Chicago of the academic program" and for "the retention of the Center's Santa Barbara academic and publication activities." He indicated, however, that this "expansion" and "retention" of academic and other activities would still require the resignation of "all present officers of the corporation except the chairman of the board of directors, and of all employees except those connected with publication and membership activities and with the exception of Dr. Hutchins and Dr. Comfort who would be retained as Life Fellow and Senior Fellow, respectively."

Levinson presented what he called a settlement of "the issue of Mr. Moos' contract rights," and recommended that the settlement endorsed by the executive committee be adopted. He also said that the committee had recommended that the Fund's real estate on Eucalyptus Hill be placed in trust to secure the payment of severance pay to the officers, fellows, and other employees who were being terminated, and to protect the severance rights of employees who might be terminated later.

Indicating that he was disturbed by reports in newspapers that he had helped to develop the "Chicago plan" to secure a position for himself, Ashmore said that he would not consider a permanent appointment with the corporation in Chicago or elsewhere. He said he had resigned as an officer in February, hoping that his resignation "would serve to alleviate dissension in the organization." Several weeks later, he had resigned as a senior fellow "at reduced severance pay." His resignation had been accepted on April 15.

Declaring that his only remaining function was to serve as a director of the Fund, Ashmore indicated that he expected his severance pay to be supplied to him as it would be to other employees terminated in the Center's reorganization. He said he would be willing to aid in putting the "Chicago plan" into effect "without compensation" and asserted that he had "no ambitions" to become an executive or an administrator again.

Chairman Parten then asked Hutchins to describe the activities that would occur in Santa Barbara and Chicago under the plan recommended by the executive committee.

In a calm, controlled voice Hutchins referred to "the enormous intellectual resources" located in the Chicago area. He said he thought the Center could make connections with faculty members from most of the twenty-one institutions of higher learning in Chicago. He did not think it would be necessary to employ any full-time staff members in the initial phase. In response to a question from Antonow, Hutchins said he had talked with Ralph W. Tyler, a social scientist and well-known educator, and Tyler had indicated that he was willing to take an administrative position.

Hutchins said that the dialogue in Chicago would be carried on by part-time participants, with a sliding scale of compensation ranging up to $5000 a year. He indicated that "an intensive academic program similar to that heretofore carried on in Santa Barbara" could be developed in that way in Chicago.

Hutchins went on to say that the Center's Santa Barbara academic activities "would be vigorously continued," with the use of part-time participants—except for Dr. Comfort and himself, of course—and would draw scholars "from San Francisco southward." He added that he hoped "small resident staffs" could be employed eventually in Santa Barbara and Chicago—if the Center could raise the necessary funds.

Although he later indicated that he felt sorrow for the departure of senior staff members and fellows who had long been associated with him, Hutchins expressed no regret about the scrapping of the senior fellows program in the meeting of the directors. He had often said, "When you have a lemon, try to make a lemonade out of it," and he acted on that principle. For him, the drastic reorganization of the Center was an opportunity for a new beginning.

After Hutchins had finished his statement, Parten asked Antonow and Weissbourd to explain their plans for financing the Chicago and Santa Barbara activities. Antonow indicated that the executive committee had found that severance pay obligations were larger than had been expected, and he said it would be necessary to use the Eucalyptus Hill property "as a source of additional funds, either through its mortgage or sale."

Antonow said that the severance payments could be spread over an extended period, thus reducing the amount of cash needed to meet the Center's obligations during the coming fiscal year. He indicated that he and Weissbourd would guarantee $100,000 a year for two years, if the other members of the board agreed to produce the same amount. He said the board should not adopt the "Chicago plan" if the board did not think that it had adequate financial backing.

Hatch and Berryhill, legal counselors for the Fund, said that Antonow's proposal differed from the original guarantee of Antonow and Weissbourd "to meet any deficit resulting from the implementation of the 'Chicago plan' for a two year period." The lawyers declared that the board then appeared to have two alternative proposals, and urged that the directors decide clearly which one they preferred. Weissbourd then said that he and Antonow would be willing to carry out their original commitment.

Trying to stave off a legal challenge by Dr. Comfort, Antonow said that contributors of money to the Center for its future operations could designate their donations for "the Santa Barbara academic program" if they wished to do so. He announced that royalties received by the Center under the agreement with Dr. Comfort on the *Joy of Sex* book "would be directed toward maintaining and improving the Santa Barbara academic program and would not be diverted to support Chicago activities."

When several directors said they were confused about the financial projections, Antonow agreed to present the basic information on a blackboard. After a short recess for lunch, the directors assembled again. Antonow detailed his suggestions for financing the Chicago operations and the Santa Barbara activities, using the blackboard to show each step.

Antonow made no references to the comparative analysis of the costs of the three plans—the Santa Barbara, San Diego, and Chicago proposals—

which had been prepared by Gary Cadenhead in April and submitted to the board. The directors no long wished to give attention to alternative possibilities.

"Each plan involves substantially reducing the staff," Cadenhead had pointed out. "The Chicago plan is the most drastic. . . . Twenty-five employees would be terminated, resulting in an obligation including severance pay and accumulated vacation of $560,000."

The Santa Barbara plan, which Moos had regarded as the best possibility, would have provided for a continuation of the Center's work on Eucalyptus Hill with a rigorously reduced budget. The plan would have permitted the retention of four resident fellows plus six visiting fellows to be funded from outside sources. With a pledge from Parten of a $100,000 gift, Moos had tried to obtain an additional $200,000 to make the plan workable. On May 5 he had written to Parten, releasing the Parten Foundation from its $100,000 commitment. Expressing his appreciation, he had said regretfully, "I am unable to comply with the conditions."

Cadenhead's analysis had indicated that the Santa Barbara plan offered by Moos would have produced a possible deficit $100,000 higher than the Chicago plan, but he had reminded the board that the Center's right to $150,000 as its share of the royalties from Dr. Comfort's sex book was "not in question under the Santa Barbara plan." Cadenhead had warned the directors that "some question exists as to whether the Chicago plan would nullify the agreement between the Center and Alex Comfort."

But Antonow and the other directors supporting the Chicago plan thought that Comfort would go along with the plan, since it provided for Dr. Comfort's continuation as a senior fellow and the specific allocation of royalties from *The Joy of Sex* to Santa Barbara activities.

The outline Antonow put on the blackboard in the afternoon of May 10 indicated that the first year's deficit under the Chicago plan would be $342,000—assuming that the Center paid 40 percent of the severance obligations in that year. He estimated that this would require the payment of $220,000 to former staff members during the year, and other necessary expenditures would be $410,000. He said that $288,000 would be available in that fiscal period, including $180,000 from the Center's remaining reserves and $108,000 from contributions and membership fees.

Antonow declared that the other $342,000 would possibly come from $100,000 in gifts by board members, $100,000 in contributions guaranteed by Weissbourd and himself, and $142,000 "from the sale or mortgage of the real property." If the Chicago plan were approved, he indicated that Weissbourd and he would guarantee the availability of additional mortgage funds of $600,000.

Impressed by Antonow's figures and aware of the support given by Hutchins, the directors voted to approve the plan with one exception. Fagan Dickson asked to have the record show that he had dissented.

Parten was silent. He was not happy about what the board had done, but he felt that he had to accept the will of the majority. And it was evident that a majority of the board wanted to endorse the plan that had the blessing of Hutchins.

Howard Marshall then presented to the directors the proposed agreement between the Fund and Malcolm Moos. He went over its clauses, and told the board that it was designed to settle any dispute with Moos as to the corporation's contract liability. He said it was not an agreement providing for severance payments.

Although the agreement obviously limited Moos's freedom to speak and write about the Center from May 1975 to May 1978, no member of the board questioned the fact the Fund for the Republic—once called "the most resplendent champion of civil liberties"—was entering a contract that effectively silenced a former president of the Fund. The directors were disturbed by newspaper stories that had presented the Center in a bad light, and some of them were afraid that Moos might denounce the Center's treatment of him.

Harry Ashmore, who had won a Pulitzer prize for his courageous work as an editor in Arkansas and who had spoken eloquently in defense of freedom on many occasions, did not ask that the clauses restricting Moos be removed from the contract. Robert Hutchins, who had reminded Jubal Parten in a crisp letter in January 1975 that the Center was "an institution devoted to argument, disagreement, discussion and dissent," said nothing when Marshall finished.

These limitations on Moos, which had been insisted upon by Antonow, had been reluctantly accepted by Marshall and Parten. They knew that Moos had to have a source of income while he looked for another job, and Parten and Marshall had done their best to assure him of such an income. If they had not accepted the clauses stubbornly advocated by Antonow, they knew it was possible that the board might not provide any financial payments for Moos. They did not want the whole matter to become bogged down in a lawsuit.

After a brief discussion—with no objections expressed to the limitations on Moos—the directors adopted a resolution authorizing the chairman of the board and the secretary of the corporation "to execute the agreement between the corporation and Mr. Moos."

After making sure that the directors understood that payments to Moos under the agreement were to be secured by the Fund's real estate, Marshall left the meeting. He felt that Moos had been roughly treated by some of the directors, but he had done what he could to help Moos. He did not want to participate in the session any longer.

Parten continued to preside. He had been asked by Levinson and other directors to continue as the chairman of the board, and he had agreed to do so, on condition that Robert Hutchins agreed to return to the responsibilities of the presidency. Hutchins had recommended the election of Ralph Tyler as acting president, but Parten had felt that it was fitting for Hutchins to take over the responsibilities that Hutchins had removed from Moos. Hutchins had finally agreed to become president again.

Parten had consented to remain as an officer of the Fund with the hope that he could help the Fund—and help Moos and all the other employees who would be forced to leave their jobs under the drastic provisions of the "Chicago plan." The future of the Center seemed doubtful to him, but he was not willing to abandon his interest in it or in the people who had worked for it for so many years.

One of Parten's principal objectives at the May meeting was to get the directors to approve a clear policy on severance pay. The directors did adopt a resolution that embodied the recommendations of the executive committee. The resolution provided for payment of severance benefits up to a maximum of two years.

One clause in the resolution seemed threatening: "If, subsequent to an employee's termination for the convenience of the corporation, facts are discovered which would have resulted in the employee's termination for cause had such facts been know, such employee will be deemed to have been terminated for cause and no further severance pay shall be paid to the employee; in such event the corporation may, at its option, sue to recover all severance payments previously paid to such employee. 'For cause' for purpose of this Resolution, shall mean a breach of ethics, which shall include misconduct such as fraudulent or dishonest acts or gross abuse of authority or discretion with reference to the corporation, or failure or inability to competently perform the duties of employment."

On a recommendation from the lawyers for the Fund, the directors unanimously approved a resolution to put the corporation's real estate into a trust, and authorized the officers to mortgage or sell it if that seemed to be necessary "in the best interests of the corporation." On a motion offered by Antonow and seconded by another director, all employees and officers except those in the membership and publication departments and "with the exception of Mr. Hutchins, Dr. Comfort, Ms. Donnelly, Ms. Green, Mr. Ibarra and Ms. Rylander" were terminated "for the convenience of the corporation."*

After that, Antonow moved that Parten be elected chairman of the board again, with Hutchins as president, Ralph Tyler as vice president, Eulah Laucks as secretary, and James Douglas as treasurer. Mrs. Laucks and Douglas would not accept the nominations. After some discussion, Antonow nominated Peter Tagger to serve as secretary and treasurer. Tagger was willing to serve in these capacities.

*That meant my elimination as an officer of the Fund. I had served 19 years—longer than any other officer except Hutchins. I had expected this to happen after Moos had been defeated. I had made plans to devote my time to writing and lecturing.

All the officers nominated by Antonow were then elected. Hutchins said he would work with Ralph Tyler to aid Mr. Tyler in becoming his successor, and declared that he and Tyler would try to find a younger man to become the chief executive officer of the Center when Tyler became "unable to carry out the duties of that position." (Tyler was seventy at the time of the board meeting.)

As the meeting came toward its conclusion, Parten sent a message to Moos, asking him to come into the conference room and make a statement. Moos entered quietly. Looking at the directors who regarded him with impassive faces, Moos said that he believed in the Center and would continue to believe in it because he felt that the Center was needed in modern society. He regretted that the board had not really given him an opportunity "for some new directions that I suggested."

A tall, thin, graceful man, Moos showed no bitterness or anger. He concealed his pain with a mask of humor. He told a story about a heckler at a baseball game in Minnesota, who had jeered at the third baseman until the player went over and gave the heckler his glove, telling the heckler to get on the field and play his position. The heckler got into the game, made several errors, and angrily threw the glove to the third baseman, saying, "You go back in there. You goofed up that position so badly nobody can possibly play it."

Many of the directors smiled or chuckled at this tale, but no one spoke. They knew that Moos had been wounded; some of them shared his anguish, but in that moment it was difficult for any of them to find any words. Moos walked over to Hutchins and said, "God bless you. Any way I can help, I will do so for the Center." Hutchins did not rise to his feet to thank him.

Parten alone at that moment expressed his appreciation to Moos. Parten knew what Moos was going through. Parten, too, had been wounded in the battles that had erupted in the board meetings. But Parten, like Moos, did not show any outward signs of his suffering.

Hutchins usually kept his emotions under strict control. He did not show any feeling. Those who knew him well realized that he rarely expressed his emotions in a group of people. He stayed within the citadel of his calm reserve.

Some of the other directors were embarrassed and didn't voice their compassion. Fagan Dickson, Monsignor Lally, and others in the room felt a strong sympathy for Moos, but found it impossible to speak. It was a sad and depressing moment.

After Moos had gone, the doors of the conference room were opened to admit reporters. Before the journalists began to fire questions at Hutchins and Parten, Ashmore came over to Hutchins and said softly, "Well, Bob, you're back in the saddle."

In a sense, Hutchins had never left the saddle. As the Founder of the Center, he had held a controlling power over it from the beginning.

At the press conference Hutchins tried to stress the positive side of the Center's reorganization. He referred to the "expansion" of the Center's academic program to include dialogues with university professors in Chicago. Parten also took a hopeful view, saying that he thought the board would support Hutchins in the future development of the Center.

But the reporters who were there that day wrote articles emphasizing the elimination of nearly all the senior fellows, the deep reduction in the Center's staff, and the removal of Moos. Some of the articles, referring to the plans for the Chicago operations, gave readers the idea that the Center was moving to Chicago and closing down its Santa Barbara headquarters.

> Perhaps the Center for the Study of Democratic Institutions always has been too good to be true [William Trombley said mournfully in the Los Angeles *Times*]. A band of scholars gathering daily in a sun-splashed mansion in the Santa Barbara hills to talk and write about the fundamental problems of democracy—such a notion is probably too ideal to survive.
>
> At present, the Center is in something of a shambles, after months of intramural strife and a relentless series of financial problems. . . . The budget has been slashed to the bone. The staff has been cut to 17 or 18, from 64 a year ago. There are no plans for any more of the national or international conferences the Center once sponsored.
>
> These budget cuts and dismissals have been accompanied by bursts of acrimony of the sort only very articulate, very angry people can unleash.
>
> Dr. Alexander Comfort, the eminent gerontologist and author of "The Joy of Sex," has called some of his colleagues "a pack of truffle-digging academic hounds" who "savaged" Moos and forced his resignation. One of the targets of this attack, former Senior Fellow Harry S. Ashmore, fired back that Comfort "spent too much time doing field work on his book" and "it had addled his brain." This prompted another ex-fellow, John Wilkinson, to reply: "Ashmore may be a Pulitzer Prize winner but he's no great brain."

Trombley spent several days in Santa Barbara, interviewing people connected with the Center, and talked on the telephone with Arthur Burck, who made some scathing criticisms of the Center's management under Hutchins and Ashmore.

"There were many years of ignoring huge losses," Burck said. "When I got on the board and looked at the fiscal statements, I gasped." Burck added, "Moos found himself with his hands tied because of intramural bickering." He said that many of the directors would not support Moos's efforts to cut expenses, to get rid of aging senior fellows, or to start new programs.

Burck went on. "I reasoned that this would pass in time. I've spent a lifetime reorganizing businesses and the lesson I've learned is that when you're in extremis is frequently a good time to break with the past because there's no other choice.

"So I felt some of the bitterness would disappear and the Center would move on, but I was wrong. The world of academe, I discovered, does not operate like any other world. There are some who would rather sink than swim."

"It was clear from the time Malcolm arrived that there were a number of people out to get him," Harvey Wheeler said. "There were people who called him 'Malcolm Mouse' and 'The Mouse That Roared' and said, 'We'll get him out within a year.' "

Dr. Comfort, who thought Moos was a fine person and felt that Moos had been badly treated, told Trombley that he believed Moos should have fought harder: "One problem was that Moos was a rather timid man who would make a speech of thanks if you kicked him in the behind."

Trombley reported that Moos had accused Hutchins of actively organizing opposition to his presidency. He quoted Moos as saying: "He did— he got enormously mad at Arthur Burck and other people who were supporting me."

Donald McDonald who had succeeded John Cogley as the editor of the *Center Magazine*, retorted: "Bob didn't go after him, either directly or through his deputies. Moos let it get away through his own weakness."

Trombley commented: "There seems to be little doubt, however, that when Hutchins endorsed the Chicago plan, it had an important impact on the board of directors and helped to mold the decision on May 10. Now the fight is over, but much bad feeling remains."

Dr. Comfort told Trombley and other reporters that he would have nothing more to do with the Center, and said he was seeking the return of $93,000 in royalties on *The Joy of Sex* which he claimed that the Center owed him. When asked why he had not resigned as a Senior Fellow, Dr. Comfort snapped: "How can I resign from something which no longer exists? What they've done is prop the corpse into a sitting position but that's no good. It's a zombie organization."

Trombley asserted in his Los Angeles *Times* article: "Wheeler and Wilkinson are afraid to speak out against Hutchins or the Center because they fear they will lose their substantial severance payments. However, Wheeler, Wilkinson and Comfort are talking about starting a new center, to carry on their work.

"So it is possible that an entire flock of Phoenixes may arise from these ashes—the Center for the Study of Democratic Institutions in Santa Barbara, in Chicago, perhaps in Boston, and the Wheeler-Wilkinson-Comfort endeavor."

Hutchins had already begun to plan a new program, Trombley discovered. He was aided by a committee of twelve including Ashmore, Cogley, and Rexford Tugwell. Cogley had made a remarkable recovery from his stroke. Knowing that Hutchins had suffered several major illnesses, Trombley was surprised to find him "chipper and vigorous."

Hutchins voiced a belief that the Center's new academic program—using part-time scholars in Santa Barbara, Chicago, and possibly Boston—might be more productive than the old one with the senior fellows.

"I believe we can make this work," Hutchins said blithely. "We may have found a way to operate on a high intellectual level at minimal cost. If that can be done, it's probably more needed now than it ever has been in the past."

Hutchins did not call attention to the fact that the "new" program bore a strong resemblance to the Santa Barbara and San Diego plans Moos had presented to the Center's board on April 19. In both of these plans, Moos had proposed to reduce the number of resident fellows to a small core group and rely for additional academic work on visiting fellows drawn from universities. Under either of these plans, the Center could have operated "on a high intellectual level at minimal cost."

In an ironic way, the drastic actions of the board on May 10 had cleared the path for Hutchins to carry forward programs very similar to those advocated by Moos—but without the presence of Moos.

If Moos had realized that Hutchins had not really wanted to retire from participation in shaping the Center's projects, Moos might have retained Hutchins' support. If he had installed Hutchins in an office next to his and presented his recommendations to the board as Moos-Hutchins recommendations, he might have survived. But Moos had taken seriously the idea Hutchins had often expressed—that the Center had to be more than Hutchins' place, that the Center had to grow as an institution with a life of its own.

Parten, too, had initially believed that Hutchins actually did want to retire completely from administrative duties. Parten had refused to believe that for years, but Hutchins had at last persuaded him. And Parten had assured Moos that it was so. Perhaps Hutchins had intended it to be so—and then had changed his mind when he became convinced that Moos was "all at sea" and might wreck the institution he had tried to build.

In any case, Parten was a man who thought that when a man made a decision to retire that decision should be regarded as irrevocable. As a trustee of the University of Texas, he had made that clear to a football coach who had retired and then had tried to withdraw the decision. Parten had asked the coach to think carefully before he announced his retirement. After the announcement, Parten told the coach that the decision could not be changed.

Despite the attempts of Ashmore, Levinson, and other directors to convince him that Moos had not proved to be the right man for the Center, Parten was unshakable in his support for the Minnesota educator. Parten had bowed to the will of the majority of the Fund's directors—that was part of his creed as a democrat, to acknowledge the rule of the majority—but he had never turned his back on Moos. He had asked Hutchins to take the helm again because he thought Hutchins had to take responsibility for the situation created by the removal of Moos.

The bitter conflict within the Center during the short, unhappy tenure of Malcolm Moos had been deeply affected by two factors: the economic depression in the United States and the personal relationships between Hutchins, Parten, and Moos. Although Hutchins had at last decided that he would not back Moos even if Moos had the money in hand for his program, Hutchins had told Moos at one point that he would support him if Moos could balance the Center's budget. If Moos had raised large sums of money in 1974 and in the first three months of 1975, it would have been extremely difficult to remove him.

Although the board of directors was loaded with millionaires, the Center was repeatedly on the verge of a financial collapse. How could that be? That was a painful mystery to Hutchins, and an equally painful mystery to Moos. Why were so few of the directors excited about the Center, despite the impact of its national and international conferences and the respectful attention it received in the press?

Newsweek magazine, commenting on the reorganization of the Center in its issue of June 30, 1975, tried to explain what had happened in these terms: "In the activist 1960's, America was bullish on brains. It was an era when think tanks flourished on the assumption—shared by government and the private sector alike—that the proper mix of time, money and highly educated manpower could solve most problems.

"Today, however, many think tanks are struggling for funds and identity, victims not only of the recession but also of a growing suspicion that the brightest are not necessarily the best—or even the most discerning—beacons of society.

"Hardest hit of all the think tanks is the Center for the Study of Democratic Institutions, founded sixteen years ago by Robert M. Hutchins as a humanistic retreat where intellectuals could ponder the fundamentals of society. . . ."

The *Newsweek* analysis touched upon some of the factors that made existence hard for many "think tanks" in the 1970s. But such factors did not really account for the behavior of the Center's board. Nearly all of the board members had been personally chosen by Hutchins. All of them professed to believe that it was important to keep the Center going. Yet they expected Hutchins—and later, Moos—to bring in most of the money.

In many cases, their devotion to Hutchins seemed to be based on his personal radiance, his reputation as an educator and as a wit, his ability to jab the Establishment and yet remain on good terms with the people of power in New York and Washington. Even then, their devotion had not caused many of them to open their checkbooks very often. Their actions in the crisis of 1975 indicated that they were willing to contribute enough to sustain Hutchins as a life fellow and to try an experiment in Chicago, but they weren't going to support a group of ten or twelve independent senior fellows.

If Moos had been able to bring the directors to a high pitch of enthusiasm for his vision of a "communiversity," of the Center as a teaching institution sending forth brilliant young scholars capable of changing the world, they might have financed the Center adequately even in the depression years of 1974 and 1975. They had the resources to do it. But before Moos had a chance to arouse enthusiasm for his program, his leadership was questioned and he was smothered in a blanket of suspicion. Few of the directors took the trouble to study his proposals, and several of those who did read the discussion papers on the university project suspected him of trying to swing the Center away from the course Hutchins had set.

After Moos had been ousted and the senior fellows had been removed from the payroll, several of the directors conceded that Moos hadn't been given a full and fair opportunity to show what he could do. Howard Marshall commented, "We didn't think we had done completely right by Malcolm." "The situation proved to be worse than Moos had thought it could be," Parten said. Monsignor Lally said: "I always felt he started with too many enemies to succeed. . . . Only Bob (Hutchins) could have saved him and he was being influenced in other directions."

In a letter to me two years after the bitter events of 1975, James Douglas said that Malcolm Moos "may have had an almost impossible task, but I think his failure has to be attributed to his losing the confidence of a majority of the board of directors." Douglas declared that Moos had made damaging mistakes in his handling of Norton Ginsburg, and "incurred opposition when he and Harvey Wheeler indicated their plans for the future of the Center, and he incurred serious resentment from various board members with his seeming inability to discuss problems with Bob Hutchins and to call on Bob's knowledge and experience."

Douglas stated that he regarded the investigation of Harry Ashmore "by outside counsel" as a serious blunder. He acknowledged that Moos's troubles were compounded by "the worsening financial situation and the discouraging response Malcolm got from the foundations that were approached."

Parten, who had fought harder for Moos than anyone else, felt that Hutchins could have made it possible for Moos to stay in office long enough to demonstrate his capacities. He thought that Hutchins had allowed himself to be swayed unduly by Ashmore, Clark, and Mrs. McAllister. But he bore no rancor toward Hutchins or any of the other directors. When the fight was over, he wanted the board to unite in an effort to keep the Center alive.

When Hutchins took the reins again in May 1975, he confronted difficulties that might have daunted a much younger man. He had to face the fury of Dr. Comfort, who was heading toward a lawsuit. He was expected to make sure that the huge severance obligations were met, while the Center's cash reserves were dropping to a low level. And he had to get some meetings held on Eucalyptus Hill to show skeptical observers that reports of the Center's death had been exaggerated.

His return to executive power seemed to renew his energy. His health improved. He gathered his chosen remnant around him on the hill in Santa Barbara, and dialogues began anew, with visiting scholars coming in. He flew to Chicago and New York on fund-raising missions. Although he talked of transferring the presidency to Tyler, he seemed to be prepared to go on for a long time.

30

The last years of Robert Hutchins: many dialogues on many topics; another peace convocation; legal battles; departure, with a chorus of praise

IN THE ISSUE OF *Center Report* that appeared a few weeks after the removal of Malcolm Moos, there was no reference to Moos or to me or to the other officers of the Moos administration. The names of Moos, these officers, and the fellows most closely associated with Moos—Wheeler and Wilkinson—had vanished. The category of senior fellows had disappeared, but nearly all of them were listed again as associates and consultants. And there was a new academic group called the Chicago Program Advisory Committee.

In his first message to the Center's subscribing members after the May 1975 meeting of the directors, Hutchins referred to what he called the expansion of the Center's program to Chicago and assured the members that the Center had a bright future. He gave no explanation of what had happened to Moos and other colleagues. He told me later that he had not mentioned Moos and the others who had lost their jobs because he did not wish to embarrass them. He wanted to put the internal conflicts of the Center behind him.

Hutchins was a master of the arts of advertising. Soon after he returned to the president's office at the Center, he urged the directors to approve another "Pacem in Terris" convocation to be held in Washington. Parten thought it would be costly and questioned its value, but Hutchins was eager to get the Center favorably depicted in the press.

"I think we need *Pacem in Terris IV* to show that we are alive and well," Hutchins insisted in a letter to Parten on June 11, 1975. He tossed in a few big names, as he often did: "Kissinger has already endorsed the idea and agreed to participate. The President's lawyer has promised to try to persuade him to take part. Since the Chicago group cannot get started until fall, we need to do something, like announcing *Pacem in Terris IV*, as soon as we can."

Hutchins prevailed over Parten's objections. The convocation was announced, with an array of well-known speakers with reputations big enough to impress the newspapers and broadcasting stations. In a blaze of publicity, the Center seemed to be vigorously alive again.

While the Chicago group was getting organized under Ralph Tyler, Hutchins brought in Otis Graham, a professor of history at the University of California in Santa Barbara, to help him in planning and developing a series of dialogues on Eucalyptus Hill. Joseph Lyford, a Center Associate at the University of California in Berkeley, was also helpful in lining up scholars to take part in Center meetings.

In July, Hutchins released a list of topics and the names of participants in meetings and conferences to be held during the summer and autumn of 1975 at the Center. The topics included "The Proposed Criminal Justice Code" and its possible conflicts with the First Amendment; "The Individual and the Community," focusing on a five-year study of the Berkeley community by Professor Lyford; "Long-Range Federal Planning," with participants led by Rexford Tugwell and Otis Graham; "Electoral Reform," a conference directed by Harry Ashmore; "Alternatives to Litigation," based on a study by Frank Gibney of the Encyclopaedia Britannica; and "The Character and Extent of Equality in America," with dialogues led by William Gorman and Mortimer Adler.

Hutchins also disclosed that the Center would hold sessions on "The Limits of 'Implied Powers,' " examining court rulings and constitutional interpretations; "The Possibilities and Limitations of Public Education," using studies by Hutchins and Joseph Schwab; "The Mass Media," with participants including Ashmore, John Cogley, former editor of the *Center Magazine*, Clifton Fadiman, and others; and on "Exclusionary Zoning," considering the rights of minorities and the poor to attack local ordinances excluding them from the community.

At the same time, Hutchins announced that a conference to be called "The Fourth World" would be held in Racine, Wisconsin, in cooperation with the Johnson Foundation, with scholars from Santa Barbara and Chicago—including Elisabeth Borgese, Norton Ginsburg, and Lord Ritchie-Calder—presenting papers. It was evident that Hutchins was striving to show that the Center was flourishing, although it was running on a very limited budget.

On July 24, 1975, Dr. Comfort filed a suit in a United States District Court in Los Angeles, challenging the very existence of the Center. He contended that the action taken by the directors and trustees on May 10, 1975, constituted "a dissolution of the Center; the incorporation of the Center into another organization which will not or cannot meet the obligations of the Center; and a declaration of the insolvency of the Center; or any one or more of these."

Dr. Comfort claimed that he was entitled to the immediate payment of royalties totaling $93,320 from *The Joy of Sex* book that had been transmitted to the Center under his 1973 agreement with the corporation. He declared that he was also entitled to $63,000 in severance pay, and he sought "exemplary or punitive damages" of $250,000, charging that the Center "by way of its authorized agents and representations . . . acted . . . with malice" and "was guilty of a wanton disregard of Dr. Comfort's rights."

In a countersuit filed on September 5, the Fund for the Republic accused Dr. Comfort of "breach of contract," "interference with advantageous contractual relationship," and "defamation." On the same day, the Fund made a reply to Comfort's suit, denying all his allegations.

The Fund claimed in its countersuit that Dr. Comfort—"without the written consent" of the Fund—wrote and marketed a literary work entitled *More Joy* on the same subject as *The Joy of Sex* which "competes with and injuriously affects the sale of 'The Joy of Sex.' " The Fund alleged that Comfort wrote *More Joy* while employed as a senior fellow of the Center, and that he used the Fund's facilities and staff "to accomplish said work." The Fund estimated its loss as a result of *More Joy* as in excess of $250,000.

Asserting that Comfort had acted aggressively "and with malice and with the intent to injure" the Fund in writing and marketing *More Joy*, the Fund claimed that it was entitled to "punitive or exemplary damages" totaling $2 million. The Fund also asserted that Comfort had damaged the reputation of the Center to the extent of $780,000 and said it was entitled to "exemplary or punitive" damages amounting to another $2 million.

While these legal skirmishes were occurring, the Center's immediate financial needs were met by a contribution of $100,000 from Seniel Ostrow. Hutchins asked other members of the board to make gifts to match Ostrow's donation. Parten had contributed $12,000 soon after the May board meeting, and other directors had made substantial contributions. With such evidence of renewed support, Hutchins was confident that the Center would weather its 1975 crisis.

But Parten became increasingly disturbed by the delay of the Fund's officers in the matter of placing the corporation's real property in a trust. He felt that action should have been taken within a month after the May meeting. In July, Howard Marshall voiced concern about the lack of progress, and in August Arthur Burck wrote to Parten, saying: "Ever since the last board meeting I have been disturbed by the difficulty in getting a Trust agreement that protects the Center's obligations to the severed employees. In view of past history it seems to me that if there are any loopholes, the money is going to be spent, and these former employees may be left out on a limb."

On September 5, Parten sent a letter of inquiry to Hutchins: "Several have inquired of me, the Board Chairman, as to the status of this matter and I have been embarrassed to have to say I didn't know. Please bring me down to date on what has been done pursuant to this resolution." (He referred to the board's resolution on May 10, authorizing and directing the officers to put the property into a Trust.) He went on: "If action to comply with this resolution has already been taken, please favor me with a copy of the document. If no action has been taken, then it seems to me that action should be taken without further delay."

Three days later, Hutchins replied with a short note, which Parten found to be a very unsatisfactory statement. "We are waiting for the appraisal, which is due any day, and for some way of reconciling the conflicting views of the board," Hutchins said. "Morrie Levinson has suggested a meeting of the executive committee, to which all members of the board would be invited, in Chicago on October 21, beginning at lunch. If he calls that meeting, I hope you can attend."

Parten felt that he should have been asked, as chairman of the board, to call a special meeting of the board if there were conflicts among the directors on what should be done. Instead of consulting him, Hutchins was acting in close consultation with Levinson, the chairman of the executive committee.

A previous letter from Hutchins, in which Hutchins had stated that Randolph Compton was willing to take a mortgage on the property, had made Parten wonder whether Hutchins and other directors were planning to have a mortgage placed on the real estate before it was put into a Trust. Parten showed Howard Marshall the note dated September 8 from Hutchins and asked for Marshall's comments.

On September 15 Marshall wrote to Parten: "Of course, Bob Hutchins' letter of September 8 to you is not responsive in any sense to your letter of September 5. The appraisal value of Eucalyptus Hill has nothing to do with establishing a Trust secured by the property to pay the severance allowances for which the board obligated itself some months ago. Moreover, unless there are those on the board who contemplate going back on the obligation which the board voluntarily assumed . . . there is nothing to reconcile with respect to so-called conflicting views of the board."

With Marshall's comments reinforcing his own judgment, Parten sent a three-page letter to Hutchins on September 25, outlining the situation as he saw it.

"Your letter of September 8, 1975, in response to mine of September 5, raises more questions than it answers," Parten said. "You propose an executive committee meeting for October 21 at Chicago for the purpose of deciding whether we will burden the Eucalyptus Hill real estate with debt before we act in accordance with a resolution of the board on May 10 to place this property in trust. I respectfully suggest that such action should more appropriately be directed to a special meeting of the Board of Directors for the specific purpose of altering a former action taken on May 10. In other words, I doubt this is a proper action for the executive committee.

"The board of directors on May 10, 1975, did not have to endorse severance pay though Mr. Harry Ashmore, a former president, informed the board that in his administration he and you had promised it to employees on a certain basis, and he further represented that you and he had promised employees that they could consider the Eucalyptus Hill property as security for severance payments.

"These representations caused the board to vote the pledge of severance pay on a basis more generous than some directors thought wise. These representations also caused the board to vote favorably on a resolution authorizing and directing the officers of the Fund to place this property in trust to secure obligations that day ratified and accepted. Moreover, this action was announced to the employees promptly.

"It is true that the board also resolved that the officers of the Fund were empowered to sell or mortgage the real estate provided the officers could agree that it was in the best interest of the Fund to do so. This accord has not been established."

Parten then referred to a letter dated June 11, in which Hutchins had reported that Randolph Compton would lend the Fund 60 percent of the appraised value of the Eucalyptus Hill property. Parten reminded Hutchins that he answered on July 9, saying that he thought "it would be a big mistake to mortgage this property for 60 percent of its appraised worth with the high interest rates that now prevail. If we should do this, I feel that we would never be able to repay the loan to lift the mortgage and the property would probably go at a distressed sale and for a much lower figure than we could now realize." He had urged Hutchins and other officers to sell the property and to invest the proceeds where they could earn 8 per cent or more.

"I might add why I think it would be imprudent to mortgage this property," Parten said in his letter of September 15. "I think it is costing too much money to occupy. It seems to me that the cost of occupancy is approximately $100,000 per year. This is arrived at by adding the $52,000 now in the budget for taxes and maintenance to the possible receivable interest on the probable sale value of $600,000, which interest income would approximate $50,000. . . . I feel sure that we could get suitable quarters in downtown Santa Barbara for a small fraction of this cost."

Parten was sure that Hutchins did not want to move the Center from its beautiful location on Eucalyptus Hill. He concluded: "It now seems clear to me that you and a majority of the members of the executive committee favor the mortgage loan before the property is placed in trust as the board of directors directed on May 10. With this I cannot agree because I consider such an action would amount to a breach of trust. In the circumstances, I find myself with only one option and that is to step aside and yield to majority opinion.

"To this end, on this date I am forwarding my resignation as an officer, director and trustee to the Secretary of the corporation.

"I want you to know that as the only member remaining of the original board of directors of the Fund for the Republic selected by the Ford Foundation board in 1952, I have thought long and hard over this decision to step aside. I will continue to wish you well and that you may have ultimate success in getting solved the financial problems of the Fund."

Parten made this decision with deep regret. He had given twenty-five years of devoted service to the Fund. He had stood staunchly beside Hutchins in many battles, resisting congressmen, senators, newspaper columnists, broadcasters, leaders of the American Legion and others who had tried to destroy it. Hutchins had given him the credit for saving the Fund on several occasions—and he had earned it.

But Parten had been profoundly shocked by the suggestion that the Fund's property could be mortgaged before a trust had been established to protect the severance payments. He hated to use the words "breach of trust" in writing to his old friend, but he felt that no other words were appropriate to describe what he thought the executive committee was prepared to do.

Parten's letter wounded Hutchins. He was not totally surprised by the resignation, because he knew that Parten had been grieved by the removal of Moos. But he thought he had been behaving honorably, and he did not think he deserved to be accused of being willing to commit "a breach of trust."

Four days after Parten had sent his letter, Hutchins replied: "I was very sorry to get your letter of September 25, particularly because it seems to be based on a misunderstanding."

"You appear to believe that I want to mortgage the property in order to pay the operating expenses of the Center," Hutchins said. "Nothing could be further from the truth.

"We don't *need* mortgage money to pay current expenses. We are in the black. We have raised $45,000 new money from outside the board in our effort to match Seniel Ostrow's gift; the effort continues.

"You seem to think a mortgage would in some way deplete the trust now being formed to protect ex-employees on severance pay. On the contrary, they will be better protected by money, derived from a mortgage and placed in trust, than they are by land, which may take some time to sell. On an appraisal of $685,000 we should be able to get a mortgage of $400,000. The cash severance obligation to ex-employees is now $339,273.

"Interest on the mortgage could be kept low, because we would draw down only what we needed from time to time. Severance pay runs more or less around $16,000 a month."

Hutchins insisted: "We all want to sell the property. There have been numerous inquiries, the last one from Brussels, but no firm offers. . . .

"You have served so long and with such distinction that I hate to have you resign on the basis of actions that I think you have misinterpreted. . . . If you want a board meeting rather than an executive committee meeting, I'll be glad to try to arrange one."

Parten did not change his position. On October 8, he wrote again to Hutchins, declaring: "Frankly, I can see no misunderstanding. To the contrary, it seems that we are in disagreement as to whether we as officers of the Fund were obligated to carry out the mandate of the board of directors on May 10 when, by resolution of the board, we were 'authorized and directed' to place the Eucalyptus Hill property in trust to secure the severance pay of all employees, those remaining as well as those dismissed.

"An announcement of this action was made to the employees promptly after that meeting, and, of course, it was of more concern to those employees dismissed than to those who were retained. I considered then, and I consider now that we, as senior officers, had the responsibility of putting the property in trust to secure the severance pay of the employees. Four months later I wrote you on September 5 disclosing my serious discomfort because some of the dismissed employees were asking me why the trust had not been created. Your reply of September 8 informed me that no action had been taken and that some of the directors were objecting, which would require another meeting. This led me to feel that by our failure to place this property in trust, as promised on May 10, we were doing an injustice particularly to the dismissed employees to whom we had made a commitment.

"I certainly do not want to belabor the point. Bob, you and I have been friends for 40 years, since we worked out that famous joint venture between Chicago University and Texas University in 1935 that resulted in the McDonald Observatory at Mount Locke, Texas. Our mutual respect has never flagged. It is my earnest hope that we can and will conclude that this disagreement on financial policy should not adversely affect this longstanding relationship.

"I want you to know that I aspire to and do remain your friend."

Parten was astonished by Hutchins' apparent failure to recognize the gravity of proceeding with a mortgage before the property had been placed in trust. Hutchins saw nothing wrong with the procedure, and held to his position as firmly as Parten held to his. This gap between the two old friends was never closed.

After the meeting of the Fund's executive committee in Chicago on October 21, Joseph Antonow announced that the committee had approved a plan to establish a trust. (The trust actually came into existence in 1976, after several more months of discussion among lawyers and board members.)

On November 19, 1975, when Hutchins gave the first part of a deposition in the legal conflict between Dr. Comfort and the Center, he described the Center as simply the program of the Fund and declared it had no legal standing in its own right.

"We went from a period in which I decided everything, really, to a period in which I thought it was important to see if we could establish a more oligarchical as distinguished from an autocratic system," Hutchins said.

"Are there any officers of the Center?" Ira Lurvey, Comfort's lawyer, asked him.

"Well, there may be in sort of a colloquial sense but there are no legal officers in the Center," Hutchins answered.

"And the Center does not exist?"

"The Center exists, certainly."

"In what form does it exist, sir?"

"I think that you can have things existing that are not legal entities," Hutchins said. "You can have activities going on, and you have a program going on, and you can call it the Center. That is not a legal entity."

"And the sole leader or director as an individual of the Center then is yourself as chairman or president of the Fund for the Republic?"

"That's right," Hutchins said.

"And there is no other source of authority insofar as the Center is concerned?"

"Except the Board of Directors."

"But the Board then delegates to you all authority for the operation of the Center?"

"Well, it defines what it's willing to have me do and what it's not willing to have me do."

". . . Has the board of the Fund ever defined in writing what it was willing for you to do with the Center and what it was not willing for you to do?"

"No," Hutchins said. "There have been actions of the Board over the years describing what they are willing to approve and what they are not willing to approve, and there have been discussions of the constitution of the Fund for the Republic and of the constituent elements of its program, and there was never any action taken, at least recorded in the minutes."

"Well, is there a constitution for the Center?"

"No," Hutchins said.

Hutchins was then asked about the status of Moos, and Hutchins declared that Moos was receiving severance pay from the Center.

"And there is no act that he can do that would terminate the severance pay in that it has already been agreed—" Lurvey said.

"I'm not positive on that," Hutchins replied. "I can conceive that Mr. Moos might do certain things that might imperil the severance pay but I simply don't know."

"Is there a written agreement between the Center and Mr. Moos pertaining to his severance pay?"

"I'm sure there is," Hutchins said. "I have never seen it myself. I was not an officer during that period."

In response to questions from Lurvey, Hutchins said that Ashmore had been reemployed by the Fund to do "a special job in connection with *Pacem in Terris IV*," a conference scheduled to be held in Washington in December.

"His severance pay is suspended during this period," Hutchins explained.

"So he is receiving additional compensation and his severance pay is suspended as long as it takes him to operate *Pacem in Terris IV*; is that correct?"

"Yes, that's correct," Hutchins agreed.

Lurvey then went into the events leading up to the resignation of Parten from the Fund's board. Hutchins said that he had "some correspondence" with Parten, but had not talked with him personally.

"And you had no occasion to have any conversation with this gentleman as to why he was leaving?" Lurvey inquired.

"Well, he made it pretty clear."

Hutchins declared that there had been "discussions for a considerable period between Mr. Parten and me" and he "saw no reason to pursue the matter orally."

When Lurvey asked him what were the topics on which he had engaged in discussions with Parten, Hutchins paused for several minutes. Then he said he had had "important differences with Mr. Parten" over "the failure to renominate a director" and "an investigation of Mr. Ashmore."

Hutchins said that Arthur Burck, a member of the Fund's board, had proposed to hire a lawyer to investigate derogatory remarks Ashmore had allegedly made about Moos, and Parten had agreed to Burck's recommendation.

"I objected," Hutchins said.

Hutchins declared that he believed the purpose of the investigation was "to discredit Mr. Ashmore."

"Did you inquire of Mr. Burck as to the reason for his proceeding?" Lurvey asked.

"I have forgotten what the exact content of any communication I had with Mr. Burck was," Hutchinson answered. "The only one that I recall was to Mr. Parten."

"Did you inquire of Mr. Parten why he had approved such an investigation?"

"Certainly, but Mr. Parten proceeded to call off the investigation. . . ."

"At the time that you then inquired of Mr. Parten, sir, as to why he approved the investigation, what did Mr. Parten respond to you?"

"He responded that he would call it off," Hutchins said. Hutchins did not mention the fact that Parten had persuaded Burck to suspend the law-yer's investigation, but Parten had added: "I want you to know that I in-tend to obtain personally the facts in this situation."

When the lawyer asked again whether Hutchins had inquired of Mr. Parten why he had initially approved the investigation, Hutchins gave a dif-ferent answer: "Well, I didn't inquire why he had approved it. I told him that I was opposed to the way it was being done, and suggested that—I thought that it would produce unnecessary difficulty."

"Did you state what unnecessary difficulties you thought that it would produce?"

"No," Hutchins said. "I think it was obvious that to take a man who was a member of the board, who had been associated with the Center for well onto twenty years, and *whom we all knew intimately*, and handle him in this fashion seemed to me cavalier, was not appropriate."

"Did you make any personal inquiry into the matters alleged by Mr. Burck or Mr. Parten . . . ?"

"Well, I went over the matter with Mr. Ashmore."

". . . in sum and substance, what did he say to you?"

". . . I asked him what conceivable basis there was for this, and he said there was none."

"Did you ask Mr. Ashmore if he had made any derogatory remarks about Mr. Moos?"

"I did," Hutchins said.

"And he flatly denied it?"

"Yes," Hutchins said.

"Did you relate this denial to Mr. Parten?"

"I'm not sure what the order of events was, but I certainly indicated to Mr. Parten that I didn't believe the charges."

Hutchins declared that Ashmore had said in the board meeting on Feb-ruary 22, 1975, that "the charges were without foundation."

"Did Mr. Parten say anything?"

"My recollection is that all that Mr. Parten did was to say that he had done for Mr. Burck only what he would do for any member of the board; that if any member of the board asked him to do something, he would do it, and I believe it was Mr. Parten himself that suggested that nothing further be said or done about this matter."

After Hutchins had indicated that his opposition to the Ashmore inves-tigation was one of the factors leading to Parten's resignation, he added that he had also clashed with Parten over the renomination of Mrs. McAl-lister to the board. Parten had not favored her renomination, and Hutchins had supported her.

Lurvey asked: "And it was your understanding that because of the dif-ferent position that you took with Mr. Parten on those two issues that Mr.

Parten ultimately proceeded to resign from the board, and you felt it not necessary to inquire of him why he resigned?''

"I was explaining my psychological condition and my attitude, not what Mr. Parten said,'' Hutchins answered. "Mr. Parten gave other reasons for resigning in his correspondence.''

"Dr. Hutchins, have you now stated to us every reason why you made no effort to orally communicate with Mr. Parten about his resignation?''

Hutchins looked at the lawyer. "Well, that is a very broad question. I would have to think about it. I was indicating that there had been differences between Mr. Parten and me, and I'm not sure that there were other differences that I could dredge up out of my memory.''

"Well, what was the reason that Mr. Parten actually gave for his resignation?'' Lurvey asked.

". . . I think he principally referred to the question of the mortgage and sale of the real estate and the trust that had been agreed to be set up to protect the people on severance pay.''

". . . How did he refer, sir—I mean, what did he say?''

Hutchins replied: "Well, he said that since the trust hadn't been set up, and since there was talk about a mortgage which might make things difficult, that he felt that he should resign from the board, and I explained to him that the trust was in the process of being set up, and it was only because of legal delays and differences among members of the executive committee as to the precise form of the trust that this had not been done, and is now being done . . . and so on.''

After some questions on other subjects, Lurvey returned to the controversy over the renomination of Mrs. McAllister to the board at the February 22 meeting.

"Do you recall who nominated her from the floor?''

"I remember, yes,'' Hutchins said. "I did.'' (According to the minutes of the meeting, Morris Levinson nominated Mrs. McAllister and his motion for her nomination was immediately seconded. Parten recalled later that Hutchins did speak for Mrs. McAllister.)

"So Mrs. McAllister now sits on the board?'' Lurvey said.

"That's right,'' Hutchins answered.

"And Mr. Moos no longer sits as president of the Fund?''

"That's right.''

In response to questions, Hutchins said he knew that Mrs. McAllister had sent an accountant to inspect the financial records of the Fund while Moos was president.

". . . During the period you were president of the Fund did any director of the Fund ever have an accountant do the same thing, inspect the books of the Center?''

"No,'' Hutchins said.

"Well, when it came to Mr. Ashmore you were cognizant of what you felt was an impropriety in the investigation," Lurvey noted. "Did you feel any such impropriety when Mr. Moos was somewhat the subject of an accountant's investigation?"

"No," Hutchins said.

Hutchins was then asked about the gathering of a group of directors in April 1975 at the Center in Santa Barbara while Mrs. Parten's funeral was being held in Madisonville, Texas. This was the meeting in which he decided to "join the consensus" in favor of the reorganization plan advocated by two Chicago directors, Antonow and Weissbourd.

"It was a meeting of the directors who were in town," Hutchins said. "It had no legal status as a board meeting."

"That conclusion was reached after Mr. Hatch, who was present and serving as counsel to the board, so advised it; is that correct?"

"I don't recall," Hutchins said.

"Well, wasn't the fact, Dr. Hutchins, that there was an attempt to hold a meeting of the board in the absence of Mr. Parten on the occasion of quashing the investigation against Mr. Ashmore?"

"That is not my impression," Hutchins answered.

Lurvey then examined Hutchins on the relationships between the senior fellows and the board of directors during the period from 1969 to 1975, when the senior fellows were described as being in charge of the Center's academic program.

"Sir, did you ever tell any Senior Fellow that their vote as to whether to accept a new Senior Fellow or their consensus, if you will, was simply advisory in concept, and that the actual decision could only be made by the board of the Fund for the Republic?"

"I'm sure I did," Hutchins said.

"Do you specifically recall ever so stating to anyone?"

"No," Hutchins said. "Well, I suppose I would have to say that it seems obvious to any educational administrator . . . the final word has to be said by somebody who was in control of the money."

"With respect to an authority, the Senior Fellows were authorized simply to carry forward whatever program they were entrusted with at any given point?"

Hutchins assented: "That's right."

"So the existence of the Senior Fellow program was dependent upon the state of the financial affairs of the Center?"

"Absolutely."

"And there was no fixed term for any Senior Fellow?"

"No," Hutchins said.

"Now, in 1972 and 1973 was there any writing or policy statement ever existing, to your knowledge, pertaining to the duties and terms and compensation for Senior Fellows . . . ?"

Hutchins answered: "Not to my knowledge."

Lurvey reviewed the testimony Hutchins had given concerning the reorganization of the Center in 1969: "Essentially, you put into being the Senior Fellows residence program, and the idea of from time to time inviting thinkers from nations other than the United States to come and join and participate in the Center . . . would that be correct?"

Hutchins said: "We removed—the Board removed all limitations that seemed to confine us to problems in the United States or that seemed to limit us even to the study of democratic institutions."

". . . and incident thereto, and together therewith, there was the adoption of the Senior Fellows residence program?"

"Yes. They were not really connected."

"But they both occurred in 1969?"

"They occurred but not connected."

Hutchins discussed the letter he had sent to Dr. Comfort on May 2, 1973, offering him an appointment as a senior fellow and saying that the "dourest predictions" indicated that the Center would continue for "at least three full years," or until May of 1976.

In one paragraph in this letter, Hutchins wrote: "Should the Center cease to exist you would be entitled to severance pay of at least one full year." Asked to explain what he meant by the Center's ceasing to exist, Hutchins testified: "All I had in mind was that we might be wiped out. . . . You have an organization with a payroll. If you can't meet your payroll, you can't meet your other expenses, then you are wiped out."

Lurvey asked him about his statement in the letter that Dr. Comfort would be expected to participate in the planning and implementation of the Center's academic program.

"But the Senior Fellows had no authority for hiring or firing anyone, did they?"

"No," Hutchins said.

"Or expending any money for any academic program?"

"No."

"Where does it say . . . that in truth and in fact Dr. Comfort would really have no authority for any planning and implementation?"

"There is no reference to authority in the letter," Hutchins said.

In response to other questions, Hutchins said he could not recall whether he asked the board to approve Dr. Comfort's appointment before he sent his letter of May 2, 1973, or after Dr. Comfort had accepted his offer.

"So you made the offer to Dr. Comfort and he accepted it, and then you brought it to the board for its approval?"

"That is my recollection."

"Well, Dr. Hutchins, when you made the offer to Dr. Comfort did you tell him that the offer was conditioned upon the board's approving it?"

Hutchins answered, "I don't see any reference to the board there. . . . I have no recollection of that."

After the letter had been sent to Dr. Comfort, Hutchins said he recalled that Norton Ginsburg or Harvey Wheeler told him that Comfort might not be able to accept the appointment because of "his tax situation," arising out of his book *The Joy of Sex.*

"I said we should do whatever we could within the law to assist Dr. Comfort," Hutchins declared. "And that, therefore, the matter should be turned over to counsel. . . . Our counsel was Hatch and Parent."

"So the full extent of your participation, involvement and knowledge . . . was limited to advising either Ginsburg or Wheeler that the matter should be turned over to the Center's attorneys . . . ?"

"That is correct," Hutchins said.

"What is your recollection of the next communication of any kind pertaining to Dr. Comfort . . . ?"

"All I remember is a report from somebody, I don't know who it was, that it looked as though the matter could be straightened out."

Lurvey demanded: "Is it the fact that you never spoke or communicated with anyone about this 'tax situation' . . . or how 'the matter could be straightened out' except as you have now testified . . . ?"

"That is right," Hutchins said.

"Then you never discussed this tax situation of Dr. Comfort or how the matter, whatever it was, could be straightened out with Dr. Comfort; you never discussed either subject with the board?"

Hutchins answered: "I have no recollection of a discussion with the board. . . . At any time."

Lurvey presented to Hutchins a copy of the agreement made between Dr. Comfort and the Center on July 31, 1973, which provided that a share of Dr. Comfort's royalties from *The Joy of Sex* would go to the Center. He referred to this document as "Exhibit 7."

"Have you ever seen Exhibit 7 before this afternoon, Dr. Hutchins?"

"I assume that I have," Hutchins said. "I don't remember seeing it."

A little later, Hutchins testified that he could not recall whether or not he had ever seen the argreement, but he had been told about its terms.

"I believe that Wheeler, Ashmore and Ginsburg, among them, recited to me the terms of Exhibit 7," Hutchins said.

"What did all three of these gentlemen say to you about what were the main terms in this item or contract?"

Hutchins replied: "They had to do with a readjusting of Dr. Comfort's tax problems, solving his tax problems in England, and in providing the Center with a percentage of the income on the book."

Under questioning, Hutchins said he could not recall the precise terms of the agreement or the exact words that had been spoken to him about the contract by Ashmore, Ginsburg, and Wheeler.

In response to several questions from Lurvey, Hutchins said that the minutes of the board's meeting on May 10, 1975, reflected the board's decision to continue the program in Santa Barbara and to develop a program in

Chicago. He refused to accept any contention that the Center had been dissolved or had ceased to exist as a result of the board's discharge of nearly all the senior fellows and the curtailment of the Center's activities.

Hutchins gave his testimony in the Comfort suit in two parts—the first part on November 19, 1975, and the second half on December 9, after he had returned from the "Pacem in Terris IV" convocation held by the Center in Washington. He felt that the conference had been effective in gaining more attention for the Center in the press and in stimulating statements by national leaders on the foreign policy issues that would be most important in the 1976 presidential election.

Two thousand people attended the Washington sessions, to see and hear a group of notable speakers. The Fund for Peace, which cosponsored the convocation, paid for half the costs. The Center was able to raise enough money to meet its share of the expenses. Hutchins told the Fund's directors at their next meeting, "We broke even."

The legal struggle between Dr. Comfort and the Center continued without a truce. When Comfort testified on December 16 and 17 he argued vehemently that the Center had been dissolved or had become insolvent. He declared that Hutchins had led him to think that the Center was on a sound financial basis when he accepted his appointment as a senior fellow and when he entered an agreement with the Center to have royalties from *The Joy of Sex* given to the Center.

Comfort said that the book agreement had been suggested to him by Harvey Wheeler and that he had discussed the possible benefits of such an agreement in a conversation with Wheeler while they were both guests at an international conference in Zurich. With Comfort's permission, Wheeler had recorded the conversation.

Gary Ricks, attorney for the Center, showed Comfort a typed transcript made from Wheeler's recording and asked, "Insofar as you can determine, was this an accurate transcription of what was said . . . ?"

"I cannot entirely recollect the exact course the conversation took, but this would seem to be in general the correct transcript, shall we say," Dr. Comfort responded.

Ricks went on: "Referring to Page 2, seven lines up from the bottom, you were quoted as saying: 'The point is, what I now propose to you is this: I would propose that I assign the rights to the Center. In so doing, I require a clause that says that the book was written by me while an Associate or employee or whatever of the Center, and in the United States.' Now, my question, Dr. Comfort, is: Were you requiring such a clause because this was the truth of what had, in fact, happened?"

"I was—" Dr. Comfort began to answer, when his lawyer intervened: "I'll advise the witness not to answer."

"Dr. Comfort, is your statement true and correct that the book was written by you while an Associate or employee of the Center, while you were in the United States?" Ricks asked.

Lurvey, Comfort's attorney, said: "What statement?"

"I've made no such statement," Comfort replied.

Ricks went on: "Dr. Comfort, I'm referring to the statement I've just read to you from Exhibit VV [the Wheeler transcript]."

"There's no statement there that I was either an Associate or an employee at the time of writing or that it was written in the United States," Comfort said.

"Were you asking that a clause be put into the agreement which was an incorrect statement?" Ricks inquired.

Lurvey intervened again: "Mr. Ricks, I'll use the same type of innuendo, inflection, that you are using in your question. The question is blatantly argumentative, and I advise the witness not to answer."

Ricks continued: "Dr. Comfort, the sentence of what I quoted to you says, 'Those points are absolutely essential to make it the proceeds of offices performed outside the United Kingdom.' Did you make that statement?"

Comfort replied, "I presume I made the statement which Mr. Wheeler recorded, if this is a true transcript of his recording."

"All right," Ricks said. "I ask you once again, was the statement that you made, that 'I require a clause that says that the book was written by me while an Associate or employee or whatever of the Center, and in the United States,' was in addition to whatever purpose was given a true, factual statement by you?"

"I don't understand the question," Comfort said.

Ricks rephrased his question: "You were asking that such clause be put in the agreement between you and the Center; isn't that correct?"

"I was exploring the possibility that such a clause be put in it," Comfort said.

"Did you, in fact, write the book 'The Joy of Sex' while you were an Associate or employee of the Center?"

"While I was an Associate of the Center, yes."

"Did you write it while you were in the United States?"

Comfort answered, "I did not, no."

"Dr. Comfort, when you became an Associate with the Center did you agree that the Center would have a lien on your rights to 'The Joy of Sex' from the time you joined them?"

"No way," Comfort said.

"Why were you asking the Center to make such a statement then?"

Comfort declared: "I was asking them because it was going to facilitate the creation of the legal structure which we required for purposes of the contract which we were then envisioning."

"And such a statement then would have been an incorrect factual statement; is that correct?"

Objections were raised by Lurvey. The question was finally repeated by Ricks.

"No, sir," Comfort said. "It would have been a true statement that we were agreeing to act as if that had been the case."

Ricks noted that. "I see. Did you, in fact, agree that the Center had a lien on your rights?"

"We were discussing whether I should so agree."

"My question is: Did you so agree?"

"I agreed subsequently to the extent set forth in Exhibit TT," Comfort said. (Exhibit TT was a copy of the agreement between Comfort and the Center on *The Joy of Sex*, signed July 31, 1973.)

Ricks asked, a little later: "And you wanted to create a legal structure that agreed that something existed prior that had not, in fact, ever existed; is that correct?"

"I wanted to do that upon the basis of the advice given me at the time by Mr. Hatch."

"Mr. Hatch so advised you to create such a structure by June 11, 1973?" Ricks asked.

Lurvey objected, saying that Ricks was intruding into the confidentiality of the lawyer-client relationship.

Comfort answered, however: "I believe he had done so at the time. If he had not at that time, he did soon afterwards."

Ricks inquired: "Well, did anyone at the Center or its counsel, Hatch and Parent, express opposition or a position against the Center entering into the agreement as you had proposed in your original draft agreement which we have introduced here as an exhibit?"

Lurvey again objected to the tenor of the question.

Comfort said: "Mr. Hatch discussed the pros and cons with me in correspondence."

"Did anyone write or talk to you, prior to your meeting with Hatch, that the Center or its counsel was taking a position contrary to your proposed draft agreement?"

"I don't recall it," Comfort said. "I was asked for further elucidation when they discussed with me the problems that might arise."

Ricks then referred to a letter sent by Harvey Wheeler to Comfort, dated July 5, 1973, which had been entered as Exhibit CCC. Ricks pointed out: "The second paragraph of Mr. Wheeler's letter states: 'The Center lawyer turns out to have a restricted view of the law and made a few objections in his first reaction to your original proposal.' Did you understand what lawyer Mr. Wheeler was referring to . . . ?"

"The lawyer he was referring to was Mr. Hatch."

Ricks asserted that he found it difficult to reconcile "this statement about the Center lawyer having a restricted view and objections to the proposal and squaring that with your statement that Mr. Hatch was acting as your lawyer drafting an agreement during the same period of time, namely around July 5, 1973." Ricks asked, "Can you explain that to me?"

Comfort responded: "Mr. Hatch was, in fact, the lawyer for the Center, of which I was a member; and he was acting to resolve the problem which concerned all of us. We were partners in this enterprise. There was no adversary proceeding in progress."

(Hatch testified later that he believed what he was told by Dr. Comfort, and drew up the agreement between Comfort and the Center in accordance with that understanding.)

In his deposition, Comfort contended that the Center as he understood it had been "dissolved" by the action of the directors in firing a group of the senior fellows and in removing Malcolm Moos from his position.

"Did you feel that the Board of the Fund had sole responsibility for determining policies of the institution?" Ricks asked him.

Comfort answered: "Certainly not. . . . I was not aware that the board of the Fund had a right to hire or fire anybody." He said he thought the senior fellows had the right to decide who should be connected with the Center's program.

"When Mr. Moos was kicked out by a conspiracy, I regarded it as one of the factors which would compromise the reality of the organization which I had joined," Comfort said. "I did not regard his appointment as compromising it."

Ricks asked: "If his appointment to replace Robert Hutchins as chief executive officer did not compromise it, as you put it, why did the change from Mr. Moos back to Mr. Hutchins compromise it?"

Comfort said: "Because the second decision was not taken by the Fellows. It was taken over their heads, and it was accompanied by a great deal of what I can only term Watergate business, which seemed to me quite incompatible with the form of the organization I had believed myself to be joining."

Comfort declared that he believed "conspirators" were "ready and waiting" for Moos before Moos was actually installed at the Center.

"What conspirators were ready and waiting for him?" Ricks asked.

Comfort asserted: "The gentlemen notably, I believe, Mr. Ashmore, Mrs. Borgese, possibly Mr. Ginsburg and certainly Mr. Tagger, who were later instrumental in organizing his downfall. An ambush had been prepared."*

"What facts do you have to prove their conspiracy?"

Comfort said: "The fact that they were circulating petitions in which they were trying to induce me to join even at this early stage with the object of embarrassing Dr. Moos."

---

*In a letter to me dated September 18, 1978, Ginsburg said: "Comfort was completely off the mark in alleging the existence of a 'conspiracy' against Mac [Moos]. There simply wasn't any. There might have been increasing lack of confidence in him, and I sensed all this early on and decided to return to Chicago. . . . Whenever the question of the organization of the Center came up at Senior Fellow meetings during the period between Mac's appointment and January of 1974, Comfort did not participate. . . . Therefore, he had no basis for judging what the temper of the Senior Fellows might have been."

"You say 'they.' Did all four of them circulate the petition?''

"Those were Fellows who circulated," Comfort replied. "Mr. Tagger I think was hovering in the rear."

"So Ashmore, Borgese and Ginsburg circulated the petition?''

"Ashmore and Borgese circulated the petition," Comfort said. "Ginsburg, who appeared to be the hit man of the operation, first tendered his resignation to Mr. Moos and then, when it was accepted, contended that Mr. Moos had never had—which was true—the power to accept the resignation in the first place. And a very unpleasant atmosphere was generated in the collegium of Senior Fellows by the circulation of petitions and the formation of cabals."

Ricks asked: "At any time prior to Mr. Moos coming as chief executive officer of the Center, were you aware of any disputes between the Senior Fellows?''

"The Senior Fellows must have squabbled before I got there, and they continued to squabble on occasions after I got there, but until the time of the Ginsburg episode the minimal decencies had always been preserved. There had not been the atmosphere at any time of personal bitterness and conspired divisiveness which arose at that time. Nobody up to then had been trying to break up the Center."

Michael Cooney, a lawyer for the Center, later said to Dr. Comfort: "You are quoted as saying, 'We've had spying, back-knifing, paper stealing and Watergating.' Do you recall making that statement?''

"Yes," Comfort said.

"To what were you referring specifically?''

Comfort answered: "Senior Fellows and others certainly listened at each other's doors and interfered with each other's correspondence. Mr. Ashmore's going around behind Mr. Moos sabotaging his fund-raising efforts is what I would describe as back-knifing. Papers were stolen from Mr. Moos's desk and were returned to him with impertinent remarks by Mrs. McAllister. . . .''

"You indicated that Mr. Ashmore was sabotaging Mr. Moos's fund-raising activities. Can you give me any specific details?''

Comfort said: "In particular, Mr. Moos told me that Mr. Ashmore had been interfering with contacts which he had made, I think it was, with the Fund for Peace, and I think with other organizations with whom he was trying to elicit contributions."

Moos did not testify in the Comfort suit. Ashmore gave a deposition in which he supported the statements made by Hutchins. Under questioning by Lurvey, he denied that he had attempted to sabotage any of Moos's fund-raising efforts. (In a conversation with me, he also denied that there had been any "conspiracy" by Mrs. Borgese, Ginsburg, Tagger and himself against Moos. Tagger also said that no conspiracy had existed.)

At one point Lurvey asked: "Did you ever state to anyone at the Fund for Peace that there was no purpose for them to pursue the subject of a merger between the Fund for Peace and the Fund for the Republic because Mr. Moos was on his way out as president of the Fund?''

"No, sir," Ashmore said.

Ashmore, like Hutchins, insisted that the Center had no legal status as an independent entity: it existed solely as the program of the Fund for the Republic.

Lurvey inquired: "And can you explain to me, then, why in signing Exhibit 2 (the contract between Comfort and the Center) there was reference only to the Center?"

". . . we use the term The Center and The Fund interchangeably, and also on our letterheads," Ashmore said. "So when this agreement was presented for signature, the name The Center—never occurred to me that there was anything exclusive about that. . . ."

When Parten testified in the Comfort case, he said that he had not been aware of the existence of a large severance obligation when he was searching for a successor to Hutchins. There had been some discussions in the board about severance payments, but he had not realized that Hutchins and Ashmore had made definite commitments for large payments. He said he had told Moos that the Center was "financially weak," but he had not mentioned the size of the severance debt because he had not known about it himself.

After he and Moos became aware of the severance obligation hanging over the Center, Parten said that he and Moos felt that it was necessary to reduce the budget as far as possible.

"The trouble commenced when Dr. Moos started to cut expenses," Parten said. "The first act he took to cut expenses was to suggest to the Dean that he return to his post in Chicago. . . . This act created a great disturbance among the Senior Fellows and among some members of the board."

Parten reviewed the conflicts that had occurred, and summarized his investigation of Ashmore's activities and conversations with the Fund for Peace officials.

"There is no doubt in my mind that Ashmore did, in New York, exactly what the vice-president of the Fund for Peace said he did," Parten said. "He told Mr. Randolph Compton, the chairman of the Fund for Peace, that he needn't waste his time negotiating with Moos because Moos had lost the support of his board, which at that time he hadn't lost. It was later that Moos lost the support of his board. . . .

"A lot of my colleagues on the board attempted to claim that I was out of line in conducting the investigation because Ashmore was a director, but Ashmore was also a paid vice-president and I was investigating him because he was a vice-president, not because he was a director. I thought a director would have been doing badly to make such a statement but it was even worse for a vice president to make such a statement."

Parten said he thought that the primary difficulty for Moos as chief executive officer arose from "the fact that it is hard to succeed an interim president. Harry Ashmore had been an interim president." Recalling the difficulties that had occurred at the University of Texas when an interim president wanted to stay in power, Parten said, "That's been historically true with a lot of educational institutions."

When Parten was asked about the delays in getting the Fund's real estate put into a trust for the employees, Parten said he had been astonished when "Dr. Hutchins told me that one of the directors had suggested that the directors of the Fund be their own trustee. I couldn't visualize how we could do that." He thought it should be handled by a professional trustee, such as a title company.

"I regarded the vote by the board on May 10th, 1975, as instructions to Hutchins and to me and to the secretary-treasurer to get this thing done," Parten said. (Later he pointed out to me that the board resolution had "authorized and directed" the officers to take action.)

Lurvey inquired: "So despite differing views of directors, you felt the charge was to do it regardless of whatever the differing views were; is that right?"

"I didn't think it was appropriate for us to hesitate doing it because the trust deed might cost us $2,000," Parten said. "That indicated to me that somebody didn't want to do it. . . . That's the reason I was very uncomfortable about it."

"Did Dr. Hutchins ever express to you a personal opinion that he didn't think it should be put into trust?"

"No, it was the other directors who expressed that." (Parten did not say who they were.)

Asked about the way Hutchins administered the Center, Parten said: ". . . He operated with very broad authority as chief executive officer. . . . Historically, it just went that way . . . and a lot of times things were done that should have required board approval, when they were simply done with the idea of getting the board to ratify it later."

"I never knew of the Comfort contract coming before the board and I have failed to find it in the minutes," Parten declared.

Gary Ricks, a lawyer for the Fund, then asked, "By May 10, 1975 the board knew of the contract?"

"It had been informed of the contract before that meeting, that's true."

"Upon learning of the contract, did the board at any time, at May 10, 1975 or thereafter, take action to disapprove . . . the contract?"

"Not of which I am aware," Parten said.

Dr. Comfort had charged that the Center was conducted for the "personal aggrandizement and benefit" of Robert Hutchins. In response to a question from Ricks about this accusation, Parten said, "I never thought so." He declared that he would not have participated as a member of the board if he had believed that the institution was functioning principally for the benefit of Hutchins.

In his testimony in the Comfort case, Harvey Wheeler expressed the opinion that Hutchins had a "dominant" influence in both the Fund for the Republic and "in the institution known as the Center" until the reorganization in May of 1969.

"But after 1969 the Center and its academic activities were directed by the Senior Fellows collectively," Wheeler said. "Mr. Hutchins continued to have a very strong personal influence."

Wheeler asserted that he believed the Center "ceased to exist on May 10, 1975."

Ricks asked, "Upon what facts do you base that statement?"

Wheeler answered: "The Center had been a residential research institution conducting its activities on the basis of academic members, with an understanding of continuing employment and operating under conditions appropriate for a university or legitimate academic enterprise guaranteeing academic freedom; and when the board of the Center stepped into the position of determining academic affairs and conditions of employment or discharge of specific academic personnel, they so seriously violated the conditions under which a proper, legitimate, and traditionally understood academic enterprise can take place as to effectively cease its pretensions to that status. . . ."

"Do you personally dispute the right—authority of the Fund to have made the decision it made on May 10, 1975?" Ricks demanded. "Do you dispute the authority of the board of directors of the Fund to adopt the Chicago plan . . .?"

John Sink, attorney for Wheeler, advised him not to attempt to answer the question.

"I believe I am qualified to make statements about the validity, nature, purpose, and propriety of the conduct of academic institutions, not from a legal standpoint but from an academic standpoint," Wheeler said. "And my previous statement spoke to my calculations as an academician."

"Did you understand, prior to 1975, that the board of the Fund had the authority to reduce the budget for the operation of the Center?"

Wheeler replied: "The responsibility for the budget lay with the budget officers of the Center, and the responsibility that they exercised was to prepare the budget and submit it to the board for approval."

"What was your understanding as to the position of the Fund as a corporate entity if the budget for the Center's programs exceeded the income that came in?"

"My understanding was that board members, as individuals or as committee members, would undertake to meet the deficit," Wheeler said.

Ricks asked, "Did you understand that the Center was capable of being financially insolvent?"

"I don't know what the meaning of 'insolvent' is here," Wheeler replied. "In a sense, the Center was insolvent during its entire history."

"What I'm getting at, Dr. Wheeler—I'm sure you know—is the distinction between what the Center was and what the Fund was with respect to financial responsibility and authority, whether the Center was capable of operating without regard to the financial capability of the Fund to finance it."

Wheeler answered, "My answer to the question is that the Center, unfortunately, found it necessary to assume responsibility for financing itself without being able to look forward to such assistance from board members."

Wheeler had been disappointed by the inability or reluctance of most of the Fund's directors to supply financial support for the Center. That was why he had encouraged Dr. Comfort to enter an agreement to make available some of the royalties from *The Joy of Sex* to the Center.

"I wanted to see if we couldn't have an arrangement with all of the Senior Fellows whereby they would contribute as much as possible of their net proceeds from commercial publications in the future to the Center," Wheeler said. "I thought we had sufficient writing talent there that we might make a substantial solution to the Center's financial problems that way."

Wheeler was asked whether he had suggested to Dr. Comfort any strategy or theory on which Comfort might base a lawsuit against the Fund.

"I may have, but I don't recall anything specifically," Wheeler said. "Well, the reason that I hesitated a little bit is because I have an interest in constitutional theory that is quite obscure, and at one time I may have mentioned that interest, and that refers to the development now occurring in what is called group constitutionalism and the rights of individuals in organizations being extended along the lines of rights contained in the federal constitution."

"Did you articulate any basis for that theory in applying it to Dr. Comfort's situation with the Fund or the Center?"

"No, not particularly. I have written about this in an academic fashion previously."

"Did you ever discuss with Dr. Comfort's attorneys any strategy or theory for his case?"

Wheeler said, "No, I don't think so."

Charles Daly, one of Dr. Comfort's lawyers, spoke up: "I hope, counsel, that is not intended as a reflection on our ability to think up our own theories. We do the best we can."

Wheeler endorsed Dr. Comfort's contention that there had been a "conspiracy" to undermine Malcolm Moos when he had become president of the Fund and head of the Center.

"What facts do you have about that?" Ricks asked him.

Wheeler said: "There were two separate instances that were of a concrete nature, one of them involving representations made about Mr. Moos by Mr. Ashmore at the Fund for Peace offices in Washington and New York, which actions and representations later became the subject of an investigation by members of the board, and there was activity on the part of a board member named Frances McAllister.

"What activity are you referring to by her?"

"She conceived an unmitigated dislike for Mr. Moos."

"Did she tell you she disliked Dr. Moos?"

"Not directly," Wheeler said. "I observed her demeanor and overheard her disparaging remarks and read correspondence about her activities and statements to other people."

Ricks asked him, "You have no personal observations or statements by Mrs. McAllister that would confirm or deny that she was working in conjunction with someone else?"

"I think not," Wheeler said.

A little later, Ricks put another question to him: "As you sit here today, do you have any information that Mr. Ashmore was working in conjunction with anyone else at the Fund or the Center to undermine Mr. Moos, separate and apart from the alleged statements to the Fund for Peace. . . ?"

"I have no concrete information," Wheeler said.

Charles Daly then asked, "Dr. Wheeler, did Malcolm Moos ever tell you that his desk at the Center had been broken into and documents taken therefrom?"

"Yes," Wheeler said. "I don't recall the document, but the way in which he found this out was that a letter came across his desk that contained a Xerox copy of a private communication that he had kept in his desk. . . . I have forgotten what the subject matter of the communication was."

"Who was the author of the letter to which the private communication was attached?"

Wheeler replied, "I believe that that was Mrs. McAllister, but I cannot be absolutely certain."

Howard Marshall, who gave a deposition in the Comfort case after Wheeler had finished giving his statement, did not support Wheeler's view that the directors of the Fund should have produced whatever amounts of money the Center needed.

"The Center always incurred deficits," Marshall said. "I think they spent money like the Russians were coming up the river. . . . You didn't have to do anything but look at the balance sheet, if you had any business experience at all, to make a good guess as to what was going to happen."

"What was that, sir?" a lawyer asked.

"Insolvency."

Marshall said he had voiced his feelings about the financial condition of the Center in 1972 and 1973. "Harry Ashmore always disagreed. He said everything was going to be all right. Why worry about it? . . . We could go out and raise the money."

"Well, sir, was it your personal opinion that the Center, as you understood it, terminated its existence and essentially dissolved by virtue of the action taken on May 10, 1975 . . . ?"

"That was my opinion at the time," Marshall said. "And I expressed it. . . . That is still my opinion, even though I hope I am wrong."

When Marshall was asked about the work of the Center during the years between 1959 and 1973, Marshall said: "Bob Hutchins pretty much ran it." He could not remember any action ever taken by the board to restrict Hutchins' power: "All of us not only admired him but thought he was doing a good job. I still do."

In a report prepared for the Fund's board, for the meeting of the directors in Chicago on April 13, 1976, Hutchins made an ebullient statement. Undaunted by the Comfort suit and the declarations of Marshall and others that the Center had ceased to exist, Hutchins asserted: "Since the board meeting on May 10, 1975, the Center has maintained its program in Santa Barbara, started a new one in Chicago, covered its severance obligations, reduced its expenditures by approximately two-thirds and begun to rebuild the board of directors."

Hutchins expressed his gratitude to all the directors who had "participated to some extent in these developments." He gave special thanks to Seniel Ostrow, saying that "Ostrow's gift of $100,000, which was matched by other contributions, enabled the Center to survive the year."

"Bernard Rapoport provided the mortgage that underwrote severance payments," Hutchins said. "In addition to putting up $15,000 to help meet those payments on March 1, Jim Douglas has allowed himself to be imposed on almost daily in connection with the complicated transactions of the year. The Executive Committee has been called on to study and approve these transactions, on which Fred Nicholas also helped. Barney Weissbourd and Joe Antonow have accepted responsibility for the Chicago program up to $100,000 a year for two years; $56,000 for 1975–76 has already been paid."

Hutchins told the directors that Peter Tagger had "admirably handled the affairs of the Center during a difficult period. He has continued to manage the membership program and in addition has been busy day and night with legal, accounting, real estate, and housekeeping matters. He has also found time to work on money raising and public relations. We could not have got through the last eleven months without him."

Ralph Tyler, the vice president in charge of the Chicago program, had established "close working relations with the educational institutions that are represented on his advisory committee," Hutchins said. He added, "Meanwhile, the Center has held meetings large and small in Chicago for the purpose of trying out people and techniques. It is clear that there is a good deal of interest in the academic community."

The expenses of the Chicago program had been kept low, Hutchins indicated. He added, "The Santa Barbara program has been managed on the same parsimonious lines. Very important dialogue sessions and conferences have been held at minimal cost. The most that is paid for a paper is $250. Participants who do not write papers receive only their expenses. Few of them come from any distance."

Hutchins admitted that there were problems and difficulties: "When we get better organized or can add more staff, we can do better planning and can hope to get meetings and conferences financed from outside sources. Such efforts as we have made have not been notably successful because they have come too late to fit the deliberative machinery of foundations."

Commending the work done by Otis Graham, professor of history at the University of California, who had been given the responsibility for organizing the academic projects in Santa Barbara, Hutchins said: "In spite of the financial limitations under which he has labored, he has done an excellent job. The subjects have been important and the participants of high quality. The *Magazine* and the *Report* display the vitality of the Center today."

"We of course have to face the possibility that we cannot indefinitely beg, borrow, or steal our program and hope to maintain its quality," Hutchins warned the board. "Of the eleven regular participants in the dialogue resident in Santa Barbara, four receive no compensation at all. Four get nominal sums. The three who are on salary have full-time administrative or editorial jobs.

"Nevertheless, as the *Magazine* and the *Report* show, the Center has been able to carry out its mission of identifying and clarifying the basic issues and widening the circles of discussion about them. The constitutional questions raised by the Campaign Practices Act and the revision of the federal criminal code; the moral and legal problems inherent in the effort to provide decent housing for all our people and at the same time preserve the environment; the necessity of innovation in world organization to meet threats to survival . . . new issues concerning the freedom and responsibility of the press; the possibilities of liberal education in the United States; full employment; planning; equality—these are among the topics being debated in Santa Barbara."

With his usual insistence on the value of the Center, Hutchins concluded: "I think there will not be any argument about the desirability, even the necessity, of the work the Center is doing. That the Center has been able to withstand the trials of the last two years is a tribute to the power of the ideas on which it is founded and a reflection of the dedication of the board.''

The Center continued its dialogues along the lines Hutchins had indicated in Santa Barbara and Chicago during the summer and autumn of 1976. On November 22 of that year, a stinging opinion on the Comfort case was issued by Judge David W. Williams of the United States District Court in Los Angeles, who had received the case for a judicial ruling after the Center had rejected an effort by Comfort's lawyers to negotiate a settlement.

Judge Williams was highly critical of Dr. Comfort and of the officers of the Fund. He confined his opinion to the legal issues involved in the contract, which had provided a share in the royalties of *The Joy of Sex* to the Center. He did not refer to Comfort's charges that there had been a "conspiracy" against Malcolm Moos.

"The Center must be held to have effectively breached its agreement with Comfort respecting the book royalties when on May 10, 1975, it brought about the collapse of one of the principal considerations which led Comfort to agree upon the defendant as the nonprofit group with which he would share his royalties,'' Judge Williams said.

"Implicit in both parties' understanding of what led to the unholy contract was knowledge that Comfort wanted Eucalyptus Hill as a change of scene from the many years he had spent on the faculty at University College, London, where he had tenure; that he cherished a fuller participation in the Center's dialogues; that he wanted to do the type of research that Eucalyptus Hill encouraged; that he wanted to contribute to the prestigious *Center Magazine*. . . . In this respect the Center must be held to have dissolved itself on May 10, 1975 within the meaning that term is used in paragraph 1(e) of the book contract.''

Judge Williams ordered the Center to return to Comfort all royalties it had received since May 10, 1975, with 7 percent interest on the money the Center had been holding, and with a reassignment of copyrights to Dr. Comfort.

Reviewing the background of the suit, Judge Williams said: "In his spare time from his duties as a professor in a London college, Dr. Alexander Comfort wrote what proved to be a popular book which he titled 'The Joy of Sex.' . . . After signing the publishing contract Comfort realized that his gathering wealth from royalties was going to be substantially taken from him in English taxes and he contrived a scheme to salvage those funds. He would find an American nonprofit organization that would claim that it had contractual rights to the copyright of *Joy* and together they would direct the flow of the money to American dollars rather than English pounds to the American organization. It would then share these royalties with Comfort, who planned to become a resident of this country. Then only the lower American taxes would be due on the author's portion.''

Noting that Dr. Comfort had come to the Center in Santa Barbara on several occasions to participate in conferences, Judge Williams continued: "Dr. Hutchins was impressed by him and wanted him to join the organization as a Senior Fellow. Comfort resisted these invitations until he became enmeshed in tax problems surrounding his book, and then he realized that the Center might be exactly the type of nonprofit American organization that his English tax counsel had told him could be used as a conduit to funnel *Joy's* royalties to America and away from the British tax collector. Moreover, Comfort wanted to escape to America and get away from a distressing marriage and the boring tedium his long years at the London college had brought. He solicited a formal invitation from Hutchins to join the Center staff and was given a letter employment contract at $28,000 per year plus unspecified severance pay upon termination.

"Comfort then proposed the book contract to his new colleagues, mailing them from London several drafts of the agreement he wanted to negotiate with them. He proposed to assign the copyright of *Joy* to the Center so it could collect the royalties from Modsets [the publishers]; then the Center would remit 80% of the money to plaintiff [Comfort] and retain 20% to itself. The men on Eucalyptus Hill were uncomfortable with Comfort's scheme but the thought of adding him to the staff, plus having him effectively pay his own salary, was tempting. The shabby pact was one in which Comfort untruthfully represented that he had written *Joy* in the United States and under the auspices of the Center while using its facilities; the Center winked at the fraud."

Judge Williams went on: "At the trial, by the use of evasive testimony and feigned legal ignorance, Comfort would have the Court believe that he joined the Senior Fellows only because he felt they were a self-perpetuating, independent, intellectual group who could not be fired; that the book contract was one between himself on the one hand, and himself and the other Senior Fellows on the other; that he, Comfort, was the victim of unethical conduct on the part of the Center's lawyer in the negotiations which led to the book contract, because he thought the lawyer was also representing him. I conclude from the evidence that plaintiff [Comfort] knew exactly what the status of the Senior Fellows was when he joined them; that he was told of the risks attendant to membership including that there was no tenure; that he was aware that Stanley Hatch was exclusively the Center's lawyer; and that he was acting as his own lawyer (with the help of a book called 'Be Your Own Lawyer') and with some occasional advice from his British lawyer, Mr. Appelby."

"I further conclude that there is no merit to plaintiff's allegations of fraud and he is entitled to no punitive damages," Judge Williams declared.

Because Dr. Comfort had rejected the Center's offer to continue him as a senior fellow and he had voluntarily ended his work at the Center, Judge Williams ruled that the Center had no obligation to provide severance pay or other benefits. But he also ruled that Comfort was "deemed to be" the "prevailing party" on the contract issue, as that term was used in the book agreement—and so Comfort was entitled to recover "reasonable attorneys' fees" from the Fund.

The rulings of Judge Williams were not received happily by Dr. Comfort or by the directors of the Fund. Hutchins made no public statement. He had testified that he had left the details of the contract with Comfort to Ashmore, Cadenhead, and Wheeler, and he had no direct knowledge of the provisions which the judge had labeled "shabby" and "unholy." Ashmore, Cadenhead, and Wheeler relied on the judgment of the Center's lawyer, Stanley Hatch, who testified that he accepted what he was told by Dr. Comfort.

Neither the Center nor Comfort filed an appeal from Judge Williams' rulings. The appeal process would have taken two years, and neither side wanted to carry the legal battle any farther.

With the end of the Comfort case, all the litigation that arose after the Center's reorganization in 1975 was finished. Harvey Wheeler's suit against the Center—which he had filed after his severance pay had been withheld for almost a year—had been settled in May 1976. This dispute had focused on certain papers that Wheeler believed he had a right to use and the Center regarded as its property. When the suit was settled, Wheeler received his severance payments.

The news stories about the sharply critical opinion rendered by Judge Williams in the Comfort controversy did not cause a drastic decline in the Center's membership. The number of members had been dropping since the Center's widely publicized reorganization, and the Center had not had the money in 1975 and 1976 to seek new members through a large direct-mail campaign. But the members who stayed on the subscription rolls remained loyal to the Center through all the uproar over the Comfort case and the Wheeler suit. These members, in many instances, actually increased the size of their contributions.

In October 1976, Hutchins announced a change in the name and the scope of one of the Center's publications. *Center Report* was retitled *World Issues*. Hutchins informed the members: "We now believe that world issues require more intensive examination than the Center has given them hitherto. It is expected that *World Issues* will help to focus attention on a set of problems that must be solved if civilization is to survive."

The retitled periodical, put together by Mary K. Harvey from a broad variety of sources, contained some familiar names and articles on topics the Center had explored through the years. There were excerpts from a speech delivered by Gunnar Myrdal when he received the Nobel Prize in economics; a "Report from the Kremlin," by Fred Warner Neal, based on Neal's talks with Soviet leaders in Moscow; an article entitled "The New Pentagon Strategy: 'Limited' Nuclear War," developed by the Center for Defense Information, a project of the Fund for Peace; a summary of a book describing "the economic legacy of the Vietnam war"; quotations from a discussion on "Man's Threat to His Atmosphere"; and other articles on international questions.

The Center had covered many of the "world issues" in its dialogues and convocations since its founding in 1959, but Hutchins and his associates felt that the problems had to be confronted again and again. Hutchins had not abandoned hope that solutions to these extremely difficult problems might be found—or new avenues toward understanding them might be discovered.

In the early months of 1977, the ebbing vitality of Robert Hutchins became noticeable to members of the staff and visitors to the Center. His handsome face showed deep lines of pain and fatigue. He walked slowly, he spoke softly. When I encountered him one day and inquired about his health, Hutchins answered wearily, "Don't ask me. There's no point in talking about it."

As his life drew toward a close, he continued to write and speak about the ideas that had dominated his thoughts for fifty years. He knew that he would not live to see the realization of his visions of a learning society in which human beings would act rationally and morally. He was fully aware that all men and women were touched by corruption as they moved through life.

With a passionate intensity he had desired and pursued "the whole," the complete understanding that he knew that no one had ever captured. He knew that he had fallen short of his own standards. He considered himself a failure. He did not think that he had come close to doing what he had set out to do.

He was poignantly aware of the deterioration that afflicted the human body in severe illness and old age. When he was in a Santa Barbara hospital in 1969—suffering from the pain of an illness that may have been made worse by the pain he knew he had inflicted on staff members who had been forced to leave the Center—Hutchins replied to a friend who had comforted him, "Do you remember what the Earl of Rochester said about the end of the Philosopher? 'Huddled in dirt the reasoning engine lies, who was so proud, so witty and so wise.' "

In the spring of 1977 he entered a Santa Barbara hospital again for another long siege of illness. From time to time he seemed to be recovering, but finally he lapsed into a coma and died there during the night of Saturday, May 14. He had suffered from a high fever and delirium before he gave up the struggle to hold on to life.

In his last statements, written for Center publications a few weeks before his final illness, Hutchins voiced another condemnation of American foreign policy and pleaded again for the formation of "intellectual communities." His missionary spirit gleamed in his last words.

Hutchins wrote: "I have lived long enough and read enough books to know that every generation tends to think that its age is at the crossroads, that the survival of mankind is at stake. Ours may indeed be such an age. The techno-culture may threaten to sweep all before it. But if that is true, all the more reason to rally human resources, summon the best in man, and try to create those intellectual communities which will subordinate technology to higher purposes.''

Hutchins never lost sight of "higher purposes"—the growth of the mind and the spirit—although he was in many ways a worldly man, a man who appreciated the refinements of luxury, a man who had grown fairly wealthy in the world's goods as well as wise in the world's expectations. He was a dedicated democrat, but he placed his faith in those who were bold, those who were bright, those who were free from conventional blinkers—"the very best people" who might bring technology under control and might get the people of the United States to return to their professed ideals. He was an intellectual paladin, but never a Don Quixote.

He thought of himself as a philosopher—proud, witty, and wise. And he was. And yet he was also a son and a grandson of Presbyterian ministers. He knew how to persuade the members of a board of directors to give him virtually anything he wanted; he was admired, he was loved, he had a beautiful wife and a beautiful home, he owned a silver Jaguar, he had all the outward signs of success—and yet his Puritan sternness would not let him rest. He was a Puritan in Babylon, and he found no place of peace there.

He had been around a long, long time—and thousands of successful people in America had been his students. His wit had flashed in many speeches. He was what he called a "perpendicular man," who felt confident enough of his own integrity to pour scorn on congressmen, presidents, and judges of the Supreme Court. He had questioned the morality of using atom bombs on Japan. He had attacked the legal standing of the trials of German leaders conducted in Nuremberg, Germany, by the victorious Allies after World War II. He had fiercely defended freedom for dissenters of all kinds, including people whose views he detested.

Like many other men with many gifts and the ability to manipulate other people, he was susceptible to flattery. He liked to have men around him who let their admiration for him be known in subtle ways. He declared repeatedly that he wanted to make the Center an "intellectual community" run by scholars who were equals—but the men he picked for the Center were not always men who matched him.

After the death of Scott Buchanan in 1968 and the departure of Stringfellow Barr in 1969, Hutchins had no one at the Center who could change his perspectives as Buchanan and Barr had occasionally been able to do. Buchanan and Barr had loved him, as nearly all his associates did, and they had the intellectual strength and solid standing to give him the philosophical advice he often needed and seldom received. Among the other fellows, Ashmore and Cogley were close to him. He admired Ginsburg and Mrs. Borgese. He showed some personal affection for me and often listened to my suggestions. He was frequently receptive to the ideas of Harvey Wheeler and John Seeley at one stage of the Center's development. But the losses of Buchanan and Barr were irreparable, and the Center after 1969 suffered deeply from their absence.

Hutchins was known and admired by many journalists. Despite his scathing criticisms of the press and his references to journalism as a less-than-respectable profession, Hutchins was partly a journalist himself, and he liked to have fugitives from journalism around him—notably Ashmore, Cogley, Ferry, McDonald, Edward Reed, and myself. He wrote a weekly column for the Los Angeles *Times* for several years, and it was syndicated to other newspapers across the country.

His death evoked an outpouring of comments from columnists and commentators in many publications. Some of them had been students at the University of Chicago or had known him at Yale.

David Broder of the Washington *Post*, commenting on Hutchins' impact, wrote:

> University of Chicago alumni of the Hutchins era found it difficult, when reminiscing about the man who died Sunday at 78, to explain—even to each other—why a man who worked so hard to humiliate them had so endeared himself to them. . . . He regarded students in general as a nuisance, or so he said, and managed to ignore most of them. Student editors felt his wrath only because they were, at inconvenient moments, impossible to ignore. . . .
>
> But there was an excitement of intellectual discovery, a sense of shared adventure there, that even now, 30 years later, remains tingling in the memory. In a time of rampant specialization and vocationalism, Hutchins insisted that an educated person was one who could read critically, think independently and engage good-naturedly in the controversies of his time.
>
> Arrogant in all things petty, he was immoderately tolerant of dissent, and practiced it himself—often wrong-headedly. . . .

Max Lerner, writing in the New York *Post* and other papers, depicted Hutchins from another vantage point: "He was a man who didn't like to run anything, yet found himself administering law schools, universities, foundations, study centers, and he was always happy to have someone else do the running—provided he did it in the Hutchins way.

"A stormy man of iron will, despite his urbane surface, he was determined not to follow any road that seemed well traveled. He believed in the creativeness of intellectual exchange, yet he got skittish at any sign that his highly dogmatic doctrines were being accepted. Like Groucho Marx, he wouldn't belong to any club that would have him.

"Nor could you place him on any liberal-conservative scale. He was a liberal in his libertarian convictions, a radical crusader in temperament, and yet deeply a traditionalist and conservative in his educational thinking."

To Colman McCarthy, another commentator, Hutchins was both the Thomist who relished the contemplative beauty of reasoned thinking and the American pragmatist who asked 'How can we use that idea?' "

"Despite his achievements and despite his restless intellect, Mr. Hutchins remained modest and almost self-deprecating about his own ideas," McCarthy said. "At the same time, he was passionately curious about the views of others. No one who visited him at Santa Barbara in recent years failed to realize that the intellectual life, as personified by Robert Hutchins, could be both interiorly stimulating and socially beneficial."

Hutchins had a gift for being modest and lofty at the same time. He described the Center for the Study of Democratic Institutions as "not a very good Center" and then added a line that emphasized the Center's unique quality. "But it is the only one there is."

Norman Cousins in the *Saturday Review* called attention to the paradoxes of Hutchins:

> He was a professional educator who sought to rescue the theory and practice of education from the professionals. . . . He was a classicist in literature and philosophy who constantly charted the future. He seemed, to many of his friends, to embody the Platonic ideal of the philosopher-king, but he couldn't be persuaded to accept the Socratic concept that anyone who is manifestly equipped to lead politically has the obligation to do so.
>
> But these are creative and growth-making paradoxes. They lent color and substance to a life in which enormously complicated and troublesome challenges led to ever higher plateaus of achievement. . . .
>
> Apart from the University of Chicago and the Encyclopaedia Britannica, the undertaking for which Hutchins is best known is the Center which he founded. National attention has repeatedly been called to disaffection and turmoil at the Center. The absence of a collective tranquillity, however, has never prevented the Center's scholars and public figures from exercising their main responsibility—defining significant challenges for one another and for society in the pursuit of essential knowledge. In that sense, the Center has made, and is continuing to make, its mark. . . .

The Center had made its mark on me, as it had on hundreds of people who had entered the sunlit conference room on Eucalyptus Hill to wrestle with the agonies of the world. The beauty of the place aroused guilt in some of the scholars who were there, and jealousy in some of the visitors who thought it had too much splendor. A visitor asked me once, "What did you ever do to deserve this?" No answer seemed possible.

Hutchins had made a thousand impressions in my mind. He had the mobile, expressive face of an actor. He sat at the head of the conference table, listening to everybody, hoping to hear something new. His eyebrows climbed in ironic disbelief when someone soared on a flight of rhetoric. He blew columns of smoke from his pipe when he was pondering over the course of the dialogue.

Sometimes while he sat there, dignified and alert, memories came to me of what he had told me about his early days as a stern teacher in a school for boys who had been fired out of other schools. When the boys didn't pay attention, he hit them with erasers. He had lined the delinquent ones against a wall and banged their heads with books. He hadn't wanted to be a teacher; he had wanted to study law after he had got his bachelor's degree at Yale, but he didn't have the money to go to law school. So he had gone into teaching to earn money.

While he engaged in learned conversation with the fellows he had chosen for the Center, other memories flowed through my mind—often of his ironic humor. He claimed that he had become the secretary of Yale because the president of Yale believed he was the only Yale man of his generation "who had gone into education" and because the treasurer of Yale was deeply impressed by his willingness to take a train to meet the treasurer in Utica at 3:41 in the morning.

He told me that he was probably chosen president of the University of Chicago at thirty because his father had forced him to get out of bed at 5:30 in the morning. His early rising had convinced Harold Swift, chairman of the university's board of trustees, that he was the right man to run the university. In Chicago, he had thought of himself as "a great evangelist." He was shocked by what happened at the university when he left it after twenty-two years.

"I had been in Chicago for years preaching the gospel, and I assumed that because there wasn't an open revolt that everybody was convinced," Hutchins said to me once. "I discovered that instead of being the great evangelist I was just the stopper in the bathtub. Take the stopper out, the water runs out. So that naturally the University of Chicago had a tendency to revert to type when the president was not there to prevent it. . . . The University of Chicago has tended to become more and more like Harvard. We were trying to establish the proposition that it was not only different from Harvard, it was better."

He once gave me a little book of his father's sermons, entitled *Never Lose Heart*. When it seemed to me that the world's problems were getting worse and worse—and the Center wasn't solving them—Hutchins exhorted me to remember what his father had said.

"Have you ever lost heart?" That question was important to me.

"I never had one," Hutchins said. "I just kept on working away because that was what I was supposed to do and I didn't know anything else to do."

Was he speaking ironically then? Perhaps he was. Yet he said a little later, "I've always been depressed and infuriated. At all times. There's never been any change."

My response at that time was, "You seem to get a lot of joy out of life in a very ironic manner."

Hutchins shrugged. "That's public relations. . . . The only overwhelming feeling that I have is a feeling of pressure."

He denied that he had a feeling of loneliness. "I feel busy, but I never have felt lonely. I've always wanted to. I would like to be, but I never have had the chance."

He found it almost impossible to deny other people some of his time, some of his attention. He had often been compassionate and generous to me and to many others. He had never wounded me with his rage, although he had wounded other people.

Friends of mine had urged me in 1959 to try to get Hutchins nominated for President on the Democratic ticket in 1960. He was willing to have me try—but he wasn't surprised when I didn't get very far. He frightened the politicians with his ironic wit. He might have made a fine President if he could have been nominated.

He may not have been lonely, but he often quoted a line from Walt Whitman: "Solitary, singing in the West, I strike up for a new world." He was certainly not satisfied with this world. That line from Whitman was quoted in a leaflet presented to people who attended a memorial service for Hutchins at the Center a few days after his departure from this life.

There was a deep sadness in him. He told me once that he thought "Some Natural Tears" would be an appropriate title for his biography. The words came from the last lines of Milton's *Paradise Lost*:

> Some natural tears they drop'd, but wip'd them soon;
> The World was all before them, where to choose
> Their place of rest, and Providence their guide. . . .

The death of Hutchins was another survival test for the Center. He had been so intimately identified with it that the Center's capacity to exist seemed doubtful without him. But the directors of the Fund knew that Hutchins had hoped that it would go on. They made new efforts to keep it operating.

Harry Ashmore was appointed acting president in May 1977 while the directors searched for another chief executive. There were some discussions of a merger with the Aspen Institute for Humanistic Studies, but the board decided that the Center should continue to be an independent organization.

Although Ashmore had once been Hutchins' choice to be his successor, Ashmore again disclaimed any desire to take over. The board looked elsewhere.

In November a new president was selected—Maurice B. Mitchell, chancellor of the University of Denver. Mitchell had been closely associated with

Hutchins at the Encyclopaedia Britannica. He had been in charge of Britannica's educational films, and later had become president of the Britannica's parent company.

Like Hutchins and like Malcolm Moos, whose tenure had been short and stormy, Mitchell was a professional communicator. He had been a newspaperman and a radio broadcaster before he had emerged as a producer of educational films. In 1967 he had become chancellor of the University of Denver.

Mitchell had served as chairman of the Denver branch of the Federal Reserve Board, as a member of the United States Civil Rights Commission, as a trustee of the Committee on Economic Development, and as a director of the Foreign Policy Association. He was witty, likable, and dedicated to the Jeffersonian ideals that had inspired Robert Hutchins.

In announcing Mitchell's appointment, Morris Levinson—who had succeeded Parten as chairman of the Fund's board—stressed the connection with Hutchins. He described Mitchell as "the practical philosopher" Hutchins had in mind when he developed the Center. "The board has sought a successor who will carry on in the Hutchins tradition as he builds for the future," Levinson said.

Mitchell got along well with the board of directors, but he was not able to raise the money to keep the Center going as an independent entity. In the spring of 1979, he talked with Robert Huttenback, chancellor of the University of California at Santa Barbara, about a possible affiliation with the university. In June, Mitchell resigned—and the university took over the Center.

Huttenback became chairman of a new board consisting principally of the executive committee of the university's own foundation. In a letter to Center members, Huttenback said that the new Center, located in a building on the campus, would "link the institution's brilliant future to its glorious past." He appointed Brian Fagan, an archaeologist and anthropologist, as director of the Center and placed Walter Capps, a highly respected professor in the department of religious studies, in charge of its program.

After a few months, Fagan resigned. Capps became the top executive at the Center. Under Capps's direction in 1980 the Center sponsored more than fifty conferences, lectures, and dialogues. Topics included the crisis in literacy, governmental policies, economic problems, social changes, international relations and economic issues. A leaflet sent to Center members and prospective donors contained this description of the Center: "In an age of fragmentation, one-issue politics, and increasingly narrow fields of expertise, the Center fights to maintain a common language and a broad perspective in the public dialogue. . . ."

In 1981, the Fund for the Republic was dissolved. The corporate name of the Center became The Robert Maynard Hutchins Center for the Study of Democratic Institutions, Inc. Dr. James Grier Miller, former president of the University of Louisville, was chosen as the new head of the Center.

Capps was informed by Chancellor Huttenback that Miller would take over his duties.

Capps released a public statement saying that he saw "a danger that the Center will abandon its permanent agenda and refocus its attention on topics more benign or on issues easily translated into academics. . . ." Miller told a reporter for the Santa Barbara *News-Press* that he felt the Center might have become too closely identified with political liberalism. He declared that it would be "expanding its scope" to bring in "a broader range of viewpoints."

The fact that Dr. Miller was being paid to serve as a member of the U.S. Army Science Board was cited by Capps. Saying that he did not regard Miller's connection with the army as "a moral wrong," Capps said that nevertheless "it was totally predictable that both the academic community and the Center's constituency of some 20,000 members would find this association problematic, given their sensitivities to the reintensification of cold-war rhetoric, fears about dramatic current increases in military spending, and worries about shipments of U.S. arms to El Salvador."

Dr. Miller told me that the issues regarded by Capps as important would continue to receive attention in his regime. He said he had no desire to shift the Center to the right but "there will be an expansion of participants." He said he would invite conservative speakers and spokesmen for radical positions, "including the Russian ambassador and other communist leaders if they are willing to come."

Miller referred to the breadth of his own background as one reason for confidence in the Center's future. A physician and psychiatrist, he had been a pioneer in the behavioral sciences. He received his M.D. and his Ph.D. from Harvard and has served on the faculties of Harvard, the University of Chicago, the University of Michigan, and Johns Hopkins University. He said that his membership in the Army Science Board was only one of his many activities in the public service. Miller has been connected, as a consultant and in other capacities, with the Commission on the Crisis in Welfare established by Mayor Stokes of Cleveland, the Arms Control and Disarmament Agency, the National Institute of Mental Health, the National Research Council, the American Psychological Association, the American College of Psychiatrists, the Executive Office of the President, and many other organizations.

31

The Fund and the Center:
What was accomplished? Were
the achievements worth the
cost? Could anybody tell?
What could the future hold?

IN THE VAST COMPLEXITY OF MODERN SOCIETY, with hundreds of organizations striving to exert an influence on the course of events, with change in every field occurring at an enormously rapid rate, it is extremely difficult to estimate the importance and value of an educational foundation. Showered with money by the Ford Foundation, the Fund for the Republic was ushered into the world with a flourish of trumpets—proclaimed to be a champion of civil liberties and civil rights, with a board of directors composed of famous and powerful people. The Fund set out to preserve the American Constitution and to defend the Bill of Rights against demagogues and hysteria.

During the first five years of the Fund's existence, the directors spent or appropriated more than $11 million from the $15 million provided by the Ford Foundation. In the process of making grants to dozens of groups seeking to maintain the vitality of the rights and liberties of the American people, the Fund enraged the chairman of the House Un-American Activities Committee and others who felt they had a monopoly on what was patriotic and what wasn't.

In those highly active years—from 1952 to 1957—the Fund generated support for peaceful desegregation of American schools, exposed the influence of communism in American life in a series of books written by experts, financed an analysis of American attitudes on conformity and dissent, aided a study of wiretapping and secret surveillance methods used against citizens, fostered an epoch-making report on racial integration in housing, established a Commission on the Rights and Liberties of American Indians, analyzed the government's security system and the pressures against academic freedom in colleges and universities, took a hard look at censorship movements, and financed an explosive report on blacklisting in the entertainment industry—a report that shook Hollywood and the broadcasting systems.

The 1950s were years in which people generally kept their heads down and avoided controversies. The Fund plunged head-on into one controvesy after another.

The reports and recommendations of the studies financed by the Fund in its first five years produced more tangible results than the publications later generated by the "basic issues" projects and the Center for the Study of Democratic Institutions, which grew out of these projects. The assault to which the Fund was subjected by the House Un-American Activities Committee was so outrageous that Sam Rayburn, Speaker of the House of Representatives, set in motion a movement among Democratic congressmen to abolish the committee—and that movement finally succeeded. The Fund's exposure of blacklisting was used by John Henry Faulk, a CBS commentator who had lost his job, to win the largest libel suit in history—and led to the breakup of the blacklisters.

The Fund's aid to interracial groups in the South was a factor in the gradual acceptance of desegregation in that region. The Fund's reports on communism dispelled much of the hysteria about the extent of communist influence in America.

It was virtually impossible to measure the success or failure of the Center, which Hutchins and his colleagues founded in 1959. What are the measurements of "success" in a series of endless dialogues? Who could tell what effects were being evoked in the minds of the hundreds of people from many fields who took part in Center conferences and international convocations? Or how far the repercussions spread?

When Supreme Court Justice William O. Douglas was chairman of the Center's board, he repeatedly advocated the establishment of Centers in all the major cities of the United States and in other countries. He called for an enormous continuing education program to stimulate the flow of new ideas and the presenting of such ideas in terms that would awaken millions of people to the need for reforms to meet the requirements of human survival. But the money necessary for the Douglas proposals could not be obtained.

In the 1960s, the concerns of most citizens were focused on the cold war with communist antagonists, the maintenance of economic growth, the technological competition with the Russians, "containing" the Chinese Maoists, and preventing the spread of communism in Asia and Europe. The arms race grew more horrifying year by year, but no one seemed to know how to slow it down or stop it. The power of the Pentagon expanded, and so did the industrial complex related to the gigantic military forces considered necessary for national security.

From its inception, the Center gave much attention to the impact of the arms race and the cold war on Ameican society. Two Center pamphlets by the noted military historian Walter Millis—*Individual Freedom and the Common Defense* and *The Constitution and the Common Defense*—were widely circulated. Millis described what he called "the war system" and declared that it would have to be dismantled if humanity wished to survive. He predicted that the devastating power of nuclear weapons would force the great nations to avoid a nuclear war. Thus far, his predictions have proved to be accurate.

Nuclear war was avoided, but the United States plunged into a disaster in Vietnam under Presidents Kennedy and Johnson. The Vietnam War disrupted the world's economy and contributed to the raging inflation that brought poverty and hardship to millions in many nations. President Nixon took four years to sanction American withdrawal and continued the huge budgetary deficits that slashed the value of the dollar and brought the United States to the verge of economic collapse.

The scholars at the Center did not ignore these developments or retreat into an ivory tower. The Center published a series of warnings, urging the American people to get their leaders to consider more constructive policies.

In 1965 the Center issued a booklet entitled *How the U.S. Got Involved in Vietnam*, outlining the dictatorial nature of the Saigon government and the corruption that infected the whole regime in South Vietnam. In 1967, two directors of the Center—Harry Ashmore and William Baggs—went to Vietnam and returned with proposals that could have ended the war in that year, saving many thousands of American lives and preventing the expenditure of many billions of dollars.

While the Vietnam tragedy went on, the Center brought together groups of experienced people who suggested alternative policies for American relations with Asian nations and released a series of taped discussions that revealed the misconceptions, misinformation, and miscalculations of American officials. George Kahin of Cornell University, a visiting fellow at the Center, widely recognized as a leading specialist on Indochina, insisted that Vietnam was only a small part of far thornier problems confronting the United States in Asia. He also pointed out the mistakes and misunderstandings of the Soviet Union in that area of the world.

The publication of the so-called Pentagon Papers later confirmed the accuracy of the criticisms made by Kahin and others at Center meetings. The warnings from the Center were heeded by some senators and endorsed by many citizens but were brushed aside by Presidents Johnson and Nixon.

The Center tried in many ways to build foundations for peace through realistic exchanges of ideas and proposals by leaders from many countries who participated in the convocations based on Pope John's statement "Pacem in Terris" (Peace on Earth). No other educational institution brought together so many leaders to examine the requirements for international order. The Center convocations helped to pave the way for better relationships between the United States and the Soviet Union and helped to create an atmosphere in which new relationships were established with Mao's China.

But the Center was active in many other fields at the same time. Scholars at the Center issued warnings on the decay and disarray of democratic institutions long before the Watergate scandal appeared in the headlines. Other Center publications warned of the creeping pollution of the planet, long before millions of people realized that the web of life might be destroyed by such pollution.

Far in advance of actual developments, people at the Center revealed the thinking of radical students, the changing attitudes of the young toward the whole society, the implications of the changes in race relations, and the demands of ethnic minorities. The Center showed the defects and the power of the mass media at a time when many people were not aware of the pervasive impact of the press and broadcasting industries on every aspect of modern life.

Six years of discussions, involving dozens of meetings and the thoughts of 200 consultants (including historians, judges, political scientists, economists, and many others), went into the Center's model for a new American Constitution, published in 1970. The principal drafter was Rexford G. Tugwell, a former member of President Roosevelt's "brains trust." But the man who pushed the project along was Robert Hutchins, who had repeatedly cited the fact that the Constitution of 1787 made no mention of political parties, labor unions, corporations, ecology, education, technology, or other areas with which modern government had to deal.

The model Constitution was not conceived as a document to be presented to the people for ratification and implementation, but as an instrument for thinking about the issues of the 1970s. At a time when American institutions did not seem to be functioning effectively, the Center scholars hoped that the model might awaken hope in millions of apathetic citizens and bring new vitality to a sagging democracy.

But the development of that model Constitution turned out to be one of the most controversial projects in which the Center had ever engaged. It was regarded as foolish, futile, and possibly dangerous to the American system. It stirred some discussions for a couple of years but it did not produce the long-range effects Hutchins had tried to evoke.

When internal strife occurred at the Center in 1969 and in 1975, it became evident to people outside the Center that the scholars on Eucalyptus Hill were not able to solve their own constitutional problems. From 1959 to 1969 the Center did have some of the characteristics of a community. While there were many disagreements among the staff members, there was a feeling that everyone had an assured position under the benevolent reign of Hutchins. The expulsion of Ferry, Hoffman, Seeley, Bishop Pike, and others in the spring of 1969 destroyed that feeling of security for those who remained as well as those who were evicted.

The fierce factional fighting, which damaged and eventually destroyed the administration of Malcolm Moos, showed again that the struggle for power overrode the devotion to dialogue. Hutchins, who had been largely responsible for the installation of Moos, finally decided that Moos had to be removed and that determined the outcome.

Personal attacks made by members of the opposing camps upon one another revealed the passionate feelings of those involved in the civil war. These explosions of anger saddened me and disturbed many people who regarded the Center as a citadel of reason. But people with keen intellects have engaged in angry disputes all through history. The people at the Center were as vulnerable to their emotions as other people in other places and other times.

In spite of its own internal failures, in spite of the defects and limitations of its own projects, in spite of the distortions in purposes and programs forced upon it by the necessity for a perpetual fund-raising campaign, the Center has undoubtedly had an impact on scholars, editors, broadcasters, political leaders, lawyers, economists, and others in many fields in many countries. As the principal program of the Fund for the Republic, it was an important factor in the survival of the principles of freedom and justice in a technological, bureaucratic, fast-changing society.

Were the projects of the Fund and the Center worth what they cost? It is difficult to make a final judgment. In the years between 1952 and 1977, the Fund obtained and spent about $42 million. Over a twenty-five-year period, this means an average annual expenditure of about $1,680,000. Most of this money went for salaries, consultants' fees, payments to people. Hutchins believed in living well himself and in paying his associates good salaries. Some of them earned what they got, and others didn't. Hutchins was not deeply concerned about administrative details or deficits.

Undoubtedly some of the money received and spent by the Fund might have been put to better uses. But Admiral Hyman Rickover, who took part in several Center conferences and once donated $1000 to help keep the Center going, told me that he thought the Center's budget was very small for an institution performing such a significant service. He referred to the billions he could easily get for nuclear submarines, and he said he thought that the Center's work was more vital for the future of humanity than submarines or other weapons.

Paul Dickson, in his authoritative book on American research organizations, entitled *Think Tanks*, described the Center in these terms: "The Center's particular form of megalomania is an accompaniment of its own style: fierce independence, chronic optimism, and iconoclasm. Its singular dedication to clarification of existing issues and to the attempt to give early warning to those issues that will crop up in the future is a task of ever-increasing difficulty. If dialogue—rather than war or revolution—ever becomes the vehicle by which the nation and the world cope with present issues and face future ones, then the Center will have made an impact.''

There have been some signs in the 1970's and 1980's that the idea of the dialogue—often neglected, often praised, and often abandoned—still appeals to some of the leaders and many of the people in the world. As long as people have minds and voices, they will attempt to communicate with one another. Whether the Center—without Robert Hutchins—will be able to make major contributions to the thinking and planning of humanity in the coming years remains to be discovered.

The Center's new president, James Miller, declared in the July–August issue of the *Center Magazine* that he hoped "to add something to the Center's tradition—a greater emphasis on science." He said that the Center will "continue to conduct an unbiased forum, one committed to no cause except—as Robert Hutchins often said—the causes of justice and democracy."

The terrible problems of the nuclear era still loom over us. The death of humanity may be imminent. The darkness is immense around us. Whatever light the Center can shed in the future will be needed, as it was in the past.

NOTES

Chapter One

1. Information on the meeting between Griswold, Parten, and Joyce, directors of the Fund, with the trustees of the Ford Foundation in February 1953 came from several sources: an interview with J. R. Parten on January 26, 1976; notes made by Thomas C. Reeves in his book *Freedom and the Foundation*, drawn from a "Trustees Meeting—February 1953" folder in the Ford Foundation files; and a confirmatory conversation with Erwin Griswold in Washington on May 25, 1977.

2. A copy of "The Fund for the Republic: A Prospectus" is in the papers of Paul G. Hoffman. This is the prospectus to which Griswold referred in his talk to the Ford trustees.

3. The two-page memorandum by Robert Hutchins, prepared in August 1951, outlining a "Fund for Democratic Freedoms," is in the Ford Foundation files.

4. The list of Fund for the Republic directors appeared in a press release issued by the Fund on December 13, 1952. The names appeared in the *New York Times* on December 14.

5. The application for a certificate of tax exemption was made in a letter sent by Bethuel M. Webster, general counsel to the Fund, to the Commissioner of Internal Revenue, March 20, 1953.

6. The grant to the American Bar Association's Special Committee on Individual Rights as Affected by National Security, which stirred the wrath of some right-wing groups, was made at the first meeting of the Fund's board on December 10-11, 1952.

7. When the search for a Fund president began, William H. Joyce of Pasadena approached Earl Warren. Other directors sounded out Justice Jackson and Erwin Canham. A reference to Joyce's approach to Warren is in a letter he sent to David Freeman, March 25, 1953; a copy is in the William H. Joyce folder, Fund for the Republic files.

8. The action taken by the directors on the recommendations of Elmo Roper's committee—on the best methods for conducting the study of domestic communism—is recorded in the minutes of the board, April 9, 1953.

9. The Committee on the Legacy of American Liberty, headed by Huntington Cairns, was authorized to spend $25,000 on studies, according to the minutes of the board meeting on May 18, 1953.

10. The candidacy of Clifford Case for the presidency of the Fund was supported by Paul Hoffman and by David Freeman, a lawyer who served as acting president while the search for a nationally known person to head the Fund was con-

ducted. Information on this is in the general folder on Clifford Case in the Fund's personnel file.

11. Actions by the directors at the May 18, 1953 meeting—at which Case was elected—and at the June 16 session were recorded in the minutes of the board, in the Fund files.

Chapter Two

1. The statement by Clifford Case in the House of Representatives, announcing his acceptance of the Fund presidency, is contained in a press release issued by Case on August 1, 1953.

2. The vote in the House for an inquiry into tax-exempt foundations was recorded in the *New York Times* on July 28, 1953.

3. The attack on the Fund, the Ford Foundation, Hutchins, Eric Sevareid, and others by Representative B. Carroll Reece appeared in the *Congressional Record*, with some excerpts in the *New York Times* article on July 28.

4. The Hoffman letter to the Iowa editor is in the papers of Paul G. Hoffman (P. G. Hoffman, writing to Earl Hall, Sept. 2, 1953).

5. The actions of the Fund's directors on August 4 and September 10 were recorded in the minutes (Fund files).

6. The statement accusing the Ford Motor Company and the American Bar Association of aiding "the Communist conspiracy" was written by Joseph P. Kamp and appeared in *Headlines*, a pamphlet issued by the Committee for McCarthyism, November 1, 1953.

7. The impatient letter from Robert Hutchins on November 3, 1953, is in the Parten folder (Fund files).

8. Actions of the Fund's directors at their November 18, 1953, meeting are in the recorded minutes of the board (Fund files).

9. The charges made by Representative Velde against Eleanor Roosevelt and other controversial people were reported in the *New York Times* and other papers. So were the charges made against former President Truman, and Truman's angry reply.

10. Case's memorandum of January 22, 1954, on the granting of tax exemption is in the Board of Directors' Work Papers file (Fund files). This memorandum mentions Case's appointment of three program advisers.

11. The correspondence by Case with staff members of the Reece Committee on Tax-Exempt Foundations is in the same file.

12. The acceptance of Case's resignation as the Fund's president and the appointment of a special committee to find a successor is in the March 16, 1954, minutes of the Fund's executive committee.

13. The fact that Griswold and Joyce were the directors who first recommended Robert Hutchins was recorded by Thomas Reeves in his book *Freedom and the Foundation* (New York: Knopf, 1969) and confirmed by me in a conversation with Griswold in Washington in May 1977.

Chapter Three

1. The brief biography of Robert Hutchins was based on my interviews with Hutchins. His lack of preparedness for the attacks made on him and on the Fund was indicated in his statement in *Freedom, Education, and the Fund*, a collection of his speeches published by Meridian Books, New York, in 1956. Hutchins said: "Nothing in my experience had prepared me for the public effects of the campaign of misrepresentation that began as soon as the program of the Fund became known."

2. The text of the speech given by Hutchins in January 1941 on the NBC radio network was supplied to me by Esther Donnelly, Hutchins' secretary, from his speech files.

3. The statement by Hutchins on "the tradition of the West" was drawn from *The Great Conversation*, the first volume of *Great Books of the Western World*, published by Encyclopaedia Britannica, 1952.

4. The biographical information about W. H. Ferry came from an interview I had with him. The statement by Ferry on his reluctance to become vice president of the Fund because of his "fear of boredom" was made to Thomas C. Reeves and appears as a note in Reeves' book *Freedom and the Foundation*.

5. The actions taken by the Fund's board in its meetings on June 30 and September 14, 1954, appear in the board's minutes (Fund files).

6. The statement outlining the scope of the Fund's legal activities was made in a memorandum to the board dated October 1, 1954, by Thomas W. Chrystie of Webster, Sheffield & Chrystie, the Fund's legal counsel.

7. The Reece Committee issued its report charging that the large foundations were engaged in a "diabolical conspiracy" on December 20, 1954 (Report of the Special Committee to Investigate Tax-Exempt Foundations and Comparable Organization, 83d Congress, 1954).

8. Actions taken by the Fund's board in its meeting on November 18, 1954, appear in the board's minutes (Fund files).

9. Information on the hundreds of millions of dollars in assets possessed by tax-exempt foundations was drawn from a report issued by Representative Wright Patman in 1962 (*Tax-Exempt Foundations and Charitable Trusts: Their Impact on Our Economy*, House of Representatives, 87th Congress).

Chapter Four

1. An account of the speech by Robert Hutchins at the National Press Club appeared in the Washington *Post and Times-Herald*, January 27, 1955.

2. The quotations from the address by Reece, replying to Hutchins on February 23, 1955, were taken from a press release issued by Reece's office.

3. The comments by Wayne Hays appeared in a letter written to Thomas C. Reeves in 1965 and quoted with permission from Professor Reeves.

4. Information on the Fund's projects described on pages 49–51 came from the Fund's files and press releases.

5. The grant to the Plymouth Quaker Meeting for its defense of Mary Knowles was described in the minutes of the Fund's board on May 19, 1955, and announced to the press by Hutchins on June 23, 1955.

6. The proposals made by Hutchins for projects requiring expenditures of $1,412,200 were contained in the "Recommendations to the Board," which he sent to the directors on September 1, 1955 (Fund files).

7. The remarks of J. Edgar Hoover about "pseudo liberals" appeared in the text of his speech at the meeting of the International Association of Chiefs of Police in Philadelphia, October 3, 1955.

8. The attacks by Fulton Lewis, Jr., were made in his radio broadcasts and newspaper columns intermittently for several months in 1955. He called Hutchins "an ultra-liberal," Clifford Case "a darling of the ADA" (Americans for Democratic Action), and Paul Hoffman a "Fair Dealing Internationalist." (In 1956 he published a book, *The Fulton Lewis Jr. Report on the Fund for the Republic*, containing the texts of his broadcasts from August 22 through October 27, 1955.)

9. The Fund obtained copies of the favorable remarks of Chet Huntley, Edward P. Morgan, and Cecil Brown from *Radio Reports*, a broadcasting service (Fund files).

10. The salute given to the Fund by President Pusey of Harvard was contained in the text of his address at the John Marshall Bicentennial Dinner, released by Harvard University (Fund files).

11. The Washington *Post* editorial supporting the Fund appeared on September 25, 1955.

12. A copy of the statement by the trustees of the Ford Foundation in October 1955, backing the Fund, is in the files of J. R. Parten, a Fund director.

13. The quotations from the Hutchins memorandum of October 19, 1955, defending actions of the Fund's officers, came from a copy of this memorandum (Parten files).

14. An account of Hutchins' controversial press conference of November 7 appeared in the *New York Times*, November 8, 1955, under the headline: "Hutchins Condemns Red Party but Would Give Job to Member."

15. The actions of the board at the November 17, 1955, meeting, restricting the powers of Hutchins and other officers, were recorded in the board's minutes, along with the proposed letter to Arthur Dean drafted by Bethuel Webster (Parten files).

Chapter Five

1. The number of tax-exempt foundations—estimated at 18,000 in 1955, with assets of $10 billion to $15 billion—was drawn from Internal Revenue Service reports and from a House of Representatives report, *Tax-Exempt Foundations and Charitable Trusts*, issued in 1962. The fact that only 107 foundations released reports to the public appeared in *Philanthropic Foundations*, a study published by F. Emerson Andrews in 1956.

2. I examined hundreds of the letters written to Henry Ford II about the Fund—and others were read by Joseph P. Lyford of the Fund Staff—in Mr. Ford's offices in New York City in 1956.

3. The remarks of Roy Cohn attacking the Fund and accusing Ford of "keeping silence" appeared in the New York *Mirror*, November 18, 1955.

4. Buckley's letter to Ford, asking for a comment on the Fund, was dated November 29, 1955. It appeared in the *National Review* a few days later.

5. Clippings of favorable articles about the Fund in the period from 1952 to 1955 were in the Fund files. Articles appeared in the Boston *Herald*, Atlanta *Constitution*, Chicago *Sun-Times*, New York *Times*, *Christian Science Monitor*, and other publications

6. The Hutchins exchange with Fred Woltman appeared in an article by Irwin Ross in the New York *Post* on February 20, 1956.

7. A copy of the letter by Erwin Griswold, asking Hutchins "to step aside," is in Parten's files.

8. A copy of Paul Hoffman's letter to Mrs. Roger Lapham, deploring Hutchins' statement about hiring a communist, is in the papers of Paul G. Hoffman.

9. Roper's statement about the defense of Hutchins made by Parten, Mrs. Stevenson, and himself was made in an interview with Thomas C. Reeves, and later confirmed by me in an interview with J. R. Parten.

10. The editorial in the Denver *Post*, headed "American Legion and American Rights," defending the Fund, appeared on September 14, 1955.

11. The long discussion by the board on January 6, 1956, and the actions taken on January 7, 1956, are recorded in the board's minutes for those meetings (Parten files).

12. The board's discussion of the Cogley *Report on Blacklisting* and other actions on March 22, 1956, are in the board's minutes (Parten files).

13. Actions taken at the Board sessions on May 15 and May 16, 1956, are in the board's minutes (Parten files).

Chapter Six

1. Truman's speech calling for aid to Greece and Turkey appeared in the *New York Times* on March 13, 1947, and in many other newspapers. The *Times* also reported the warnings of General Wedemeyer and Senator Taft on the dangers of Truman's "containment" policy, and many papers carried Walter Lippmann's column expressing alarm at the "Truman doctrine."

2. The 1947 hearings on "communism in Hollywood" by the House Un-American Activities Committee and the reactions of Hollywood stars, film producers, and others are vividly described in *Report on Blacklisting*, by John Cogley (New York: Fund for the Republic, 1956, 2 volumes).

  Another source of information on this period is *The Judges and the Judged*, by Merle Miller (New York: Doubleday, 1952), and a vivid picture of how blacklisting developed in the broadcasting industry was given by Erik Barnouw in *The Golden Web*, volume 2 of his history of broadcasting in the United States (New York: Oxford University Press, 1968).

3. The column by George Sokolsky on the impairment of civil liberties by congressional committees appeared in the New York *Journal American* on March 25, 1940.

4. The statement by Justice Douglas on the case of "the Hollywood Ten" appeared in *Go East, Young Man*, by William O. Douglas (New York: Random House, 1974).

5. The reference to the notorious Appendix IX compiled by the Un-American Activities Committee in 1944 was drawn from an authoritative study of the committee from 1945 to 1950—Robert Carr's book, *The House Committee on Un-American Activities* (Ithaca, N.Y.: Cornell University Press, 1952).

6. John Henry Faulk—referred to in Chapter 6 of the present book—described his own struggle against the blacklisters in *Fear on Trial* (New York: Simon & Schuster, 1964).

Chapter Seven

1. The three-year report of the Fund, summarizing all the grants made from the time it began to function in the spring of 1953 to May 1956, was largely prepared by John Cogley.

2. Congressman Walter's statement of his intention to examine the Fund appeared in the *New York Times* on June 11, 1956. The wild questions about the Fund's being "a friend or a foe in our national death struggle against the Communist conspiracy" appeared in a press release issued by the Un-American Activities Committee on June 7, 1956.

3. Parten's action in bringing Walter's plan to the attention of Speaker Rayburn was described in an interview Parten gave to Thomas C. Reeves in 1966 and in subsequent conversations I had with Parten.

4. A copy of the letter sent by Hutchins to Walter is in the Board of Directors' Work Papers file.

5. Walter's announcement of the postponement of the hearings appeared in the *New York Times*, June 21, 1956.

6. The Fund's 88-page report on its work in the 1953–56 period told how it had spent $5,414,201 of the Ford Foundation's grant. The report was divided under five headings: "To Study Communism in the United States," "Equality Before the Law and Equality of Opportunity," "To Make the Bill of Rights a Living Document," "To Maintain Due Process and the Principles that Underlie It," and "To Maintain Freedom of Speech and Belief." The report was released on June 21, 1956.

7. Frederick Woltman's attack on the *Report on Blacklisting* appeared in the New York *World Telegram and Sun* on June 25, 1956.

8. Senator Mundt's onslaught on the Fund appeared in the *Congressional Record*, 84th Congress, 2d Session, 1956, and in the *New York Times*, June 26, 1956.

9. J. Addington Wagner's criticism of the Cogley report, Hutchins, and the Fund was printed in the *New York Times* on July 2, 1956.

10. The statements by Hutchins and Cogley appeared in a press release issued by the Fund on June 28, 1956.

11. Radio Reports, Inc., supplied the Fund with copies of remarks made by Fulton Lewis, Jr., on July 6, when Lewis disclosed that the hearings on the Cogley report would be open to the press and the public.

12. Quotations from questions asked by Arens and replies by Cogley are taken from transcripts of the committee hearings obtained by me.

13. The Hutchins statement that the subpoenaing of Cogley "to justify his study" was "an unprecedented invasion of freedom of thought and expression" and his demand for a statement by the Committee certifying the Fund's patriotic purposes or "a full and impartial hearing" were in a Fund press release issued July 11, 1956.

14. The exchange between Walter and Arnold Forster was taken from the transcript of the committee hearings. So were the comments by Fred Woltman, James F. O'Neil, Vincent Hartnett, Roy Brewer, and Paul Milton.

15. Hutchins' letter to Walter, asking for cross-examination of witnesses, was dated July 13, 1956. Walter replied on July 20, 1956 (Fund files).

16. The nomination of Paul Hoffman to be a member of the U.S. delgation to the United Nations appeared in the *Congressional Record* July 13, 1956. McCarthy attacked Hoffman in a speech in the Senate. The Senate vote confirming Hoffman to the United Nations post was taken on July 20, 1956.

17. The editorial in the *New York Times* excoriating the House Un-American Activities Committee was printed on July 13, 1956, and placed in the *Congressional Record* by Senator Herbert Lehman.

18. The Washington *Post and Times-Herald* carried an editorial on July 13, 1956, denouncing the conduct of Richard Arens, staff director of the Un-American Activities Committee.

19. *Commonweal*'s defense of John Cogley appeared in its July 13, 1956, issue. Patrick O'Donovan, the London observer who found the behavior of the Un-American Activities Committee uncivilized, wrote an article about it that was printed in the Toronto *Globe and Mail* on July 18, 1956.

20. The *Christian Century* editorial supporting Cogley appeared July 25, 1956.

21. A report on Walter's hearings in Philadelphia, involving Gale Sondergaard and Jack Gilford, appeared in the New York *Herald Tribune* on July 18, 1956.

22. The stinging statement by the Library Committee of the Plymouth Monthly Meeting of the Quakers appeared in the Conshohocken (Pennsylvania) *Recorder*, July 26, 1956.

23. The quotations from the FACTS leaflets distributed by the Fund in July 1956 were taken from copies of these leaflets in my files. On August 4, 1956, acting on the basis of information supplied by this writer, the *New York Times* carried an editorial describing Walter's attacks on the Fund as "sorry sniping expeditions" marked by "hit-and-run tactics."

24. The Fulton Lewis broadcast of August 6, 1956, in which he quoted from documents subpoenaed by Walter, was recorded by Radio Reports, Inc., on August 6, 1956.

25. A copy of the telegram sent by Bethuel Webster to Walter on August 7, 1956, is in the Fund files.

26. A copy of the letter sent by Hutchins to Rayburn and to all members of the Un-American Activities Committee is in the Fund files.

27. Rayburn's anger at the treatment given by Walter to the Fund was reported to this writer in an interview with Parten in January 1976.

28. The articles in *Facts Forum* by Karl Baarslag, which J. R. Parten gave to Rayburn, were called to my attention by a friend who was an assistant to a Democratic senator. These articles disturbed Rayburn greatly and helped to convince him that the assault on the Fund came from right-wing fanatics who had also tried to remove Rayburn from Congress.

29. The quotations from Reeves were taken from pages 235 and 236 of his book *Freedom and the Foundation: The Fund for the Republic in the Era of McCarthyism* (New York: Knopf, 1969). Reeves made available to this writer the notes, clippings, and other documents he had used in writing his book, which covers the period from 1952 to the founding of the Center for the Study of Democratic Institutions in 1959.

30. The Hartford *Courant* editorial, calling upon Congress to remove Walter if he did not treat the Fund fairly, was published on August 31, 1956.

31. Walter's statement describing the Fund as a "multi-million dollar propaganda machine" and saying that he would continue his investigation appeared in the *New York Times* on August 30, 1956.

32. The negative attitude of W. R. Hearst, Jr., toward the Fund was expressed in a letter Hearst sent to Paul Hoffman September 12, 1956, the day after Hoffman and Lapham had tried to explain the Fund's work at a luncheon with Hearst. Hearst complained that neither he nor J. Edgar Hoover, the director of the FBI, had been consulted by the Fund in its researches on communism. He insinuated that Hutchins had deceived Hoffman and Lapham about the Fund's purposes.

33. The excerpts from Catton's speech at the Fund's dinner in Washington on February 21, 1957, were taken from a booklet published by the Fund, entitled "The American Tradition" (a copy is in this writer's files). Excerpts were published in the *Christian Science Monitor*, and the text was placed in the *Congressional Record* on February 22, 1957, by Representative Udall.

34. Moulder's statement that he was not in agreement with Walter's attempts to cast doubt on the loyalty of the Fund's officers and directors appeared in the New York *Herald Tribune*, March 10, 1957.

35. A copy of Walter's letter of March 29, 1957, to Bethuel Webster, demanding many documents from the Fund, is in the Fund's files, along with a copy of the reply Webster sent to Walter on April 12, 1957.

36. In response to a subpoena he received early in May, 1957, Cogley wrote to Walter on May 3, saying that he would not supply Walter with the material Walter had demanded. Walter renewed his demands in a letter to Cogley on May 7, 1957 (Fund files).

37. In his book, *A Canterbury Tale: Experiences and Reflections: 1916–1976*, published by the Seabury Press in 1976, Cogley wrote: "I put myself beyond temptation forever by burning the coveted files. [The material sought by Representative Walter.] I almost set the neighborhood on fire while I was at it, but I felt

better for having performed the irrevocable deed. The next day I phoned to tell the staff man what I had done, and a few hours later a new subpoena-server appeared." Cogley added that he consulted this writer about what to do next, and went on: "At Kelly's suggestion, I wrote an article for *Commonweal*. He sent the article, after it was rushed into print, to a number of newspaper editors he knew personally, and to politicians he had encountered during his service as a congressional aide in Washington. The result was a rash of editorials in papers from coast to coast, castigating the committee. . . . After this publicity, a second telegram came from Washington which postponed the threatened hearing. Then a week later a third wire postponed it further. Finally, as the scheduled hearing came close, Congressman Walter put off the hearings indefinitely. Kelly's strategy had worked" (pp. 69–70).

38. The *Wall Street Journal* editorial, depicting the harassment of Cogley as a threat to freedom of the press, appeared on June 11, 1957. The *Editor & Publisher* statement, also strongly endorsing Cogley's position, was printed in that publication on June 1, 1957. (Copies in the Fund files.)

39. The article based on copies of documents handed to reporters by Representative Walter appeared under the byline of Jack Steele, a Washington correspondent for the Scripps-Howard newspapers, in the Washington *News* on February 3, 1958.

40. A column by Fulton Lewis, Jr., also obviously based on "the staff report" passed to him by Walter, declared that the report had verified "everything that has ever been charged against the Fund for the Republic." The Lewis column appeared in the New York *Mirror* on February 26, 1958.

41. J. R. Parten's statements about the meeting with Robert Anderson, secretary of the treasury, were made to me in several interviews in 1976 and 1977. Actually Anderson's respect for Parten, whom he had known for more than twenty years, was a major factor in his refusal to accept the charges made in the so-called "staff report." In one interview with me, Parten said that Anderson had gone to see Speaker Rayburn and Lyndon Johnson, then the majority leader of the Senate, and had told these congressional leaders that Walter was behaving irresponsibly. Anderson told Parten that Rayburn said: "I'll see what I can do about it." Rayburn evidently persuaded Walter to drop his campaign against the Fund.

Chapter Eight

1. The memorandum by Hutchins suggesting the formation of an Institute for the Study of the Theory and Practice of Freedom was first drafted in April 1956 and finally sent to the board of directors on May 4, 1956 (Parten files; Fund files).

2. Although Hutchins later credited the idea for a "basic issues" program to George Shuster and Monsignor Francis Lally, the first mention of such a program appears in a statement by Meyer Kestnbaum in a board meeting in September 1954. (The minutes of the September 14, 1954, board session, which are in Parten's files and the Fund files, record Kestnbaum as saying: "The basic

problems, the two or three central issues, should be defined, within which broad areas the Fund could work." Kestnbaum had been an enthusiastic supporter of the Great Books program at the University of Chicago and had been convinced by Hutchins and Mortimer Adler that deep discussions of fundamental issues were vital to human development.)

3. Hutchins' long-standing interest in a World Academy was evident in his participation in the London conference, May 4–8, 1953, sponsored by the Fund for the Advancement of Education (documented in the Ford Foundation's files, London Conference folder).

4. The action of the board in establishing an advisory committee to study the Hutchins' proposal was taken at the directors' meeting on May 15, 1956 (copies of the minutes in Parten files and the Fund files).

5. The reports Hutchins gave on the progress of the advisory committee are noted in the minutes of the board meetings on June 22 and September 12, 1956 (Parten files; Fund files). The memorandum Hutchins sent to the board on September 6, calling for the formation of "a group of men of the highest distinction" to examine the basic issues, is in Parten's files and the Fund records.

6. On October 15, 1956, Hutchins sent a 44-page memorandum to the directors, urging the board to shift the program of the Fund toward "the study and discussion of basic issues in civil liberties" (copies in Parten's files and the Fund files).

7. In an analysis of this crucial memorandum, Thomas Reeves wrote in *Freedom and the Foundation*: "No longer was the Fund for the Republic to be a short-lived grant-making body; it was now planned to be self-sustaining and permanent. . . .

"Hutchins knew his board members well and framed this memorandum carefully. He used the word 'practical' eighteen times in the first fourteen pages; his style became charitably repetitive. The directors were promised less controversy ('The first effect of this plan would be to take the Fund off the defensive'), while at the same time they were assured that the Fund could not be thought to be retreating from the line of fire."

8. Roger Lapham's letter of October 26, 1956, telling Paul Hoffman his misgivings about Hutchins' proposal for an institute to study the theory and practice of freedom, is in the papers of Paul G. Hoffman.

9. The 17-page memorandum by David Freeman and Adam Yarmolinsky, opposing the Hutchins proposal and recommending termination of the Fund's functions by 1961, was dated October 31, 1956 (Parten files; Fund files).

10. Hutchins' boredom with the idea of continuing the Fund as a grant-making foundation was expressed in conversations with me in the spring and summer of 1956. John Cogley told Thomas Reeves later: "Foundation life just wasn't cut out for me—reading long requests for money and so on. I went to Hutchins to resign. Hutchins said: 'If you're bored there must be a reason. I'm bored too. If we're both bored we must do something about it. Facts are boresome.' "

11. Yarmolinsky's statement that he and Freeman felt an obligation to the directors to express their disagreements with the Hutchins proposal was made in an interview with Reeves on August 31, 1967.

12. The actions of the board of directors at the November 14–15, 1956, sessions are recorded in the minutes (Parten files; Fund files).

13. The authorization given to Hutchins by the board at the meeting on February 20, 1957, to retain consultants to try "to work out and clarify the meaning and significance of civil liberties in the United States today" was recorded in the minutes of that meeting (Parten files; Fund files).

14. The approval given by the board for a one-year trial run of the basic issues program was noted in the minutes of the directors' meeting held on May 15, 1957 (Parten files; Fund files).

15. At the May 15 meeting Hutchins was authorized to go ahead with studies known as "The Individual and the Corporation," "The Individual and the Union," and "The Individual and the Common Defense," but a proposed project on "Religion in a Democratic Society" drew criticisms from five directors—Herbert Lehman, Albert Linton, Roger Lapham, Erwin Griswold, and Alicia Patterson. The project was modified and retitled "The Individual and Religious Institutions in a Democratic Society" and finally approved by the board, although Lehman, Linton, Lapham, Griswold, and Patterson voted against it.

Chapter Nine

1. The names and backgrounds of the Consultants on the basic issues were contained in a press release (drafted by this writer) issued in July 1957. In an editorial on July 19, 1957, the *New York Times* commented: "The Fund has been spending its money by and large in some exceedingly useful directions despite ill-informed and often irresponsible criticism directed against it. In so doing, the Fund has helped to strengthen American democracy, and the new study . . . gives every indication of being a major contribution to this end." Copies of this editorial were sent to all members of the board and reinforced the feeling of many directors that they had made a wise decision.

2. Berle made his statement about holding "the pen that wrote the Atlantic Charter" at the meeting of the Consultants at the Greenbrier hotel in September 1957. This writer was present at all of the sessions of the Consultants.

3. The projects on the mass media and the study of the political process in the United States were approved by the board at its meetings on November 21, 1957 (minutes in Parten files and Fund files).

4. The highly critical memorandum sent by Mortimer Adler on the early meetings of the Consultants was dated October 9, 1957 (Fund files).

5. Scott Buchanan expressed his view that there was "no meeting of minds" in a memorandum to Hutchins dated January 2, 1958 (Fund files). The unhappiness of John Courtney Murray, Eric Goldman, and other Consultants appeared in conversations with me, John Cogley, and other staff members.

6. Quotations from the Millis pamphlet *Individual Freedom and the Common Defense* are taken from a copy of this pamphlet in my files.

7. The comments in *Editor & Publisher*, the St. Paul *Pioneer Press*, the Tucson *Star*, and the New York *Mirror* on the Millis pamphlet appeared in September and October 1957 (my files).

8. Quotations from the Berle pamphlet, *Economic Power and the Free Society*; the Kerr pamphlet, *Unions and Union Leaders*; Buchanan's pamphlet, *The Corporation and the Republic*; Mitgang's paper, *Freedom to See*; and other publications resulting from the basic issues program were taken from copies of these publications in my files.

9. The information about the range of the Fund's public information program and the responses of newspaper and magazine editors was drawn from reports I prepared for the Fund's board of directors in 1957 and 1958 (my files; Parten files; Fund files).

Chapter Ten

1. Quotations from the Mike Wallace interviews on ABC-TV with Reinhold Niebuhr, Cyrus Eaton, William O. Douglas, Aldous Huxley, Adlai Stevenson, Erich Fromm, Henry Kissinger, Sylvester L. Weaver, Jr., Francis J. Lally, Henry Wriston, and Hutchins are taken from the published transcripts (my files; Parten files; Fund files).

2. Wallace's interview with Cyrus Eaton made news on the front page of the *New York Times*. The statements made by Drew Pearson, Hubert Humphrey, Paul Douglas, and others supporting Eaton against the Un-American Activities Committee appeared in many newspapers.

3. The Washington *Post* editorial entitled "The Law and the FBI" appeared on May 24, 1958, two weeks after the Eaton broadcast. Clippings of statements about Eaton's right to free speech, made in the New York *World-Telegram*, the New York *Post*, and other papers, are in my files.

4. A copy of the memorandum sent by Hutchins to the Fund's board on May 6, 1958, on "the public interest in the basic issues program," is in Parten's files and the Fund files.

Chapter Eleven

1. The statements on what happened at the directors' meetings on May 21 and May 22, 1958, are based on the minutes of these meetings (Parten files; Fund files).

2. The quotations from Hutchins' letter to the consultants, inviting them to a Santa Barbara conference from July 30 through August 3, are taken from a copy of the letter in files made available to me by Thomas Reeves. I was present at the Santa Barbara sessions, July 30–August 3, 1958.

3. Quotations from the booklet *Foreign Policy and the Free Society* are taken from a copy of this booklet in my files.

4. The statement by Hutchins announcing that the Fund had appropriated $4 million for an extension of the basic issues program for three years appeared in a press release issued in July 1958.

5. Excerpts from the booklet *Religion in a Free Society*, published by the Fund in July 1958, are taken from a copy of the booklet in my files.

6. Quotations from the report issued by the Fund's Commission on Race and Housing in November 1958 are taken from a press release based on this report issued by the Fund (Parten files; my files).

7. The educational television series "The Press and the People" was announced in a Fund press release that I prepared and issued in the middle of November 1958 (Parten files; Fund files).

8. Harry Ashmore described the impact of the Mike Wallace series in a memorandum to the board on November 17, 1958 (Parten files; Fund files).

9. The figures on the number of broadcasting stations carrying "The Press and the People" series are taken from a report I prepared for the board of directors.

10. Actions taken by the Fund's board at the meeting on November 19, 1958, were recorded in the minutes (Parten files; Fund files).

11. Copies of the Hutchins memorandum to the board on May 7, 1959, referring to the wide circulation of the Wallace programs and stating that "the basic issues are becoming burning issues," are in Parten's files and the Fund files.

 In this memorandum Hutchins recommended the establishment of a Center for the Study of Democratic Institutions.

12. The details of the meeting Hutchins and I had with Cyrus Eaton in May 1959 were recalled from notes I made after Hutchins and I returned to the Fund's office in Manhattan.

13. The interview with Hutchins on his sixtieth birthday was conducted by Hal Boyle of the Associated Press on January 17, 1959, in Hutchins' office in the Lincoln building in New York. I was present.

14. Hutchins made the announcement of the formation of the Center in a press release dated June 4, 1959 (Parten files; Fund files; my files).

Chapter Twelve

1. The verses by Kenneth Boulding about "the Hutchins Hutch" on Eucalyptus Hill were written after a meeting in 1962. He gave me a copy of the verses, now in my files.

2. Quotations from the Fund booklet *The Corporation and the Economy* are taken from a published copy of the booklet (Parten files; Fund files).

3. Excerpts from *The Art of Government*, by James Reichley, are taken from a press release based on Reichley's booklet, issued by the Fund on November 23, 1959.

4. Information about the founding of the Center and the names of the directors, consultants, and staff members appeared in a *Bulletin* issued by the Fund in November 1959 (Parten files; Fund files).

5. Quotations from the Fund pamphlet *Broadcasting and Government Regulation in a Free Society* are taken from a copy published by the Fund in December 1959 (Parten files; Fund files).

6. Excerpts from the pamphlet *To Pay or Not to Pay* and the booklet *The Relation of the Writer to Television* are from published copies of these publications, issued by the Fund in March and July 1960.

7. The study conducted by Patrick McGrady, Jr., of television critics received extensive coverage in *Variety* and other publications dealing with the mass media (copy of McGrady's study in the Fund files).

8. The visit of two of President Eisenhower's assistants to the Center in November 1959—Karl Harr and Malcolm Moos—was reported in the Santa Barbara *News-Press*. So was Hutchins' address to the United World Federalists. (Clippings of these reports are in the files of the *News-Press* and were made available to me).

9. Copies of my report to the FCC, entitled "Who Owns the Air?," are in Parten's files, the Fund files, and my files.

10. A report on the award given to the Fund by the Anti-Defamation League appeared in the Santa Barbara *News-Press* on January 21, 1960.

11. The announcement of the appointment of Rabbi Robert Gordis as a special consultant to the Center was printed in the Santa Barbara *News-Press* in April 1960. The presence of Reinhold Niebuhr at the Center from July to October 1960 was noted in the *News-Press*, which also carried stories about the participation of John Courtney Murray and the other consultants in the meetings held in August 1960.

12. The *News-Press* printed a report on the Center's seminar "The Crisis in Collective Bargaining Practices" in the last week of July 1960.

13. A report on the session held by the Center staff and some consultants with leaders of the National Conference of Christians and Jews appeared in the *News-Press* on September 26, 1960.

14. Bertrand de Jouvenel was interviewed by a reporter for the *News-Press* when he came to Santa Barbara for a Center meeting on October 8, 1960.

Chapter Thirteen

1. The fire at the Center's headquarters was reported in the Santa Barbara *News-Press* on October 9, 1960. The statement by Fire Marshal May about the fire's origin was quoted in that newspaper, along with the declaration by Hutchins that the Center's meetings would proceed.

2. Hutchins had reached an agreement with the editors of the Encyclopaedia Britannica and William Benton, the publisher, for the Center to review "the fields of the Center's interests from the standpoint of the Britannica." This agreement, reached in September 1960, provided a flow of income to the Center at a crucial moment in its history.

3. Copies of the memorandum sent to the Fund's board about the Britannica

agreement by Hutchins on November 7, 1960, are in the Fund files and Parten's files.

4. The directors approved the Britannica agreement without objection at the November 19, 1960, meeting of the board, according to the minutes of that meeting (Parten files; Fund files).

5. The statements of Paul Jacobs, John Cogley, Walter Millis, Harry Ashmore, W. H. Ferry, Hallock Hoffman, and me on the progress of the basic issues projects were contained in reports and recommendations submitted to the board prior to the November 19, 1960, meeting (Parten's files; Fund files). Edward Reed's report on the circulation of the Center's publications also was prepared for this board meeting.

6. The formation of a Continuation Committee—a group of directors designated to prepare a request to the Ford Foundation for more money—was approved at the November 19, 1960, meeting (minutes in Parten files).

7. The hasty decision of the Santa Barbara library trustees not to cosponsor a series of talks by Center staff members and consultants at the Lobero Theater was reported in the *News-Press*, December 16, 1960.

8. The speeches that Ferry and I gave on the advantages and disadvantages of unilateral disarmament were reported in the *News-Press* in December 1960.

Chapter Fourteen

1. Hutchins' statements about the American character are taken from an announcement to the press made in April 1961 (Parten files; Fund files).

2. Excerpts from the Hutchins speech to the Modern Forum in Beverly Hills came from a Fund press release on the speech (Parten files; Fund files).

3. The quotation from Gertrude Stein came from *Everybody Who Was Anybody: A Biography of Gertrude Stein*, by Janet Hobhouse (New York: G. P. Putnam's, 1975).

4. The Center's conference on the American character, held in Washington from May 29 through June 1, 1961, was described fully in a Fund *Bulletin* issued in October 1961. Martin E. Marty, editor of the *Christian Century*, commented on the conference: "Meetings of this type, while decisive and influential, do not 'make news' immediately. . . . Beyond the performance, the inter-disciplinary squabbles—behavioral vs. social sciences, the quest for a common language (religious or non-religious)—there seemed to be a salutary consequence. Awareness arose that no single, facile attempt to define national purpose will grow from a single definition of American character. . . . We thought we knew the nature of the American character until we were asked."

5. The press releases issued by the Center on September 21, 24, 25, and 27 on a variety of topics—the scheduled conference in Greece, the discussions on Pope John's encyclical, the visit of American and Soviet scientists, and the pamphlet *Government and Business in International Trade*—are in Parten's files and my files.

6. William Shannon's arrival as a visiting fellow at the Center in October 1961 was reported in the Santa Barbara *News-Press*.

7. The publication of Fred Warner Neal's pamphlet *United States Foreign Policy and the Soviet Union* was accompanied by the issuance of a Fund press release on October 30, 1961 (Parten files; Fund files).

8. The trips Ashmore and I made to Ecuador were reported by Hutchins to the Fund's board of directors at the board's meeting on November 18, 1961 (reports prepared for this meeting are in Parten's files and the Fund files).

9. The relationship between the Center and the Parvin Foundation was announced in a Fund press release dated November 13, 1961 (Parten files; Fund files).

10. The decision of the board to seek another grant from the Ford Foundation was made at the November 18, 1961, meeting, according to the minutes in Parten's files. Parten's views on the effort to get money from the Ford trustees were expressed to me in an interview in January 1976.

11. Two other booklets were also published by the Center in November 1961—the statements *Religion and American Society* and *The Decline of the Labor Movement* (Parten files).

12. The interviews by Donald McDonald on the state of television with Jack Gould of the *New York Times* and with A. Whitney Griswold on the university (accompanied by comments from Hutchins) received wide coverage in the press in December 1961. The statements by Griswold and Hutchins were quoted on the front page of the *New York Times*.

13. The figures on the Center's fund raising in 1961 were drawn from a report submitted to the board for its November 1961 meeting (Parten files).

14. The quotations from Hutchins' proposed memorandum requesting $16 million from the Ford Foundation are taken from a copy of this memorandum in Parten's files. The request for this substantial grant was finally sent to Henry T. Heald, president of the Ford Foundation, and to John J. McCloy, chairman of the foundation's board of trustees, on December 12, 1961.

Chapter Fifteen

1. A copy of the letter from Henry Heald, president of the Ford Foundation, rejecting the Fund's application for a grant of $16 million, is in the collected papers of Elmo Roper, at the Roper Public Opinion Research Center, Williams College. This writer was given permission to examine Roper's papers.

2. Excerpts from Roper's letter of March 28, 1962, and Hutchins' reply on April 5, 1962, are taken from copies of these letters in the Roper papers.

3. The statements by Hutchins and Sheinbaum at the opening of the Center's conference "Democracy in the New Nations" are taken from a Center press release dated January 8, 1962 (Parten files).

4. Quotations from Donald Michael's pamphlet *Cybernation: The Silent Conquest* are drawn from a copy of the pamphlet in Parten's files. Information on the number of requests for the pamphlet was given to this writer in February 1962 by Edward Reed, the Center's director of publications.

5. Excerpts from David Horowitz's pamphlet *The Haves and the Have Nots* are taken from a Center press release issued in February 1962.

6. The statements by Gallup and Roper are taken from a pamphlet published by the Center in March 1962, entitled *Opinion Polls* (Parten files; Fund files).

7. Quotations from the Center pamphlets *Science* and *Stage and Screen* are taken from published copies of these pamphlets (Parten files; Fund files).

8. The statements about the meeting Hutchins held with the officers of the Fund in May 1962, to decide whether to launch a national fund-raising campaign, are based on my recollections. In an interview with Hallock Hoffman, Hoffman confirmed the fact that he and Ferry had misgivings about the possible effects of fund raising on the Center's program.

9. The Hutchins report on the first three years of the Center's work, released to the press on June 6, 1962, is in Parten's files and the Fund files.

10. A copy of the memorandum sent by Harold Oram to Hutchins on June 1, 1962, is in Parten's files.

11. The action taken by the Fund's board at the New York meeting on June 7, 1962, is recorded in the minutes of that meeting (Parten files; Fund files).

12. A copy of Oram's six-page program for a fund-raising campaign, sent to Hutchins on July 16, 1962, is in Parten's files.

13. Information about the meetings and dialogues at the Center in the spring and summer of 1962 is taken from press releases issued by the Center and from articles in the Santa Barbara *News-Press*.

14. Information about the Center's study of the news coverage given to Latin America was drawn from a Center press release.

15. Quotations from the pamphlet on the American character, the booklet on the "great debates," and the Buchanan pamphlet on civil disobedience were taken from published copies (Parten files; Fund files).

16. The departures of Yosal Rogat, Carl Stover, and James Brady were noted in the *News-Press*.

17. The election of Justice William O. Douglas as a director and as cochairman of the board at the September 6, 1962, board meeting was recorded in the minutes of this meeting, as were the other actions of the board (Parten files; Fund files).

18. Information about John Cogley's role in suggesting to President Kennedy that a statement by Pope John XXIII might help to avert war in the Cuban missile crisis of 1962, are taken from Cogley's book *A Canterbury Tale: Experiences and Reflections 1916–1976* (New York: Seabury Press, 1976).

19. The meeting of the Council for International Progress in Management members with the Center staff on October 25 was reported in the Santa Barbara *News-Press* on October 26, 1962.

20. A story on the publication of the Burdick-Wheeler novel *Fail-Safe* appeared in the *News-Press* on October 17, 1962.

21. Articles on the Reich pamphlet *Bureaucracy and the Forests* and the Naftalin-Temko pamphlet also appeared in the *News-Press* in October 1962.

22. The actions taken at the board meeting of November 9, 1962, are recorded in the board's minutes for that date (Parten files and the Fund files).

23. The Center's symposium "Prospects for Democracy" was given front-page coverage in the *News-Press* on December 3 and 4, 1962.

Chapter Sixteen

1. The list of speakers at the Fund's tenth anniversary convocation in January 1963 was taken from a press release issued by the Fund. So were the quotations from Hutchins (copies in Parten's files).

2. The quotations from the statements by Gunnar Myrdal, Lewis Mumford, Harrison Brown, Senator Fulbright, Senator Clark, Charles Frankel, Walter Reuther, A. A. Berle, Arthur Burns, Willard Wirtz, Robert Heilbroner, Newton Minow, Lord Francis-Williams, Sylvester L. Weaver, Lord James of Rusholme, Admiral Hyman Rickover, Robert Hutchins, Rosemary Park, and Adlai Stevenson were taken from texts distributed to the press (copies in my files). Excerpts from these statements appeared in a book published in November 1963 entitled *Challenges to Democracy: The Next Ten Years*, edited by Edward Reed (New York and London: Frederick A. Praeger).

3. The tabulation of gifts and pledges made at the New York convocation in January 1963 was taken from a report made by Harold Oram to Robert Hutchins.

4. Information about the extensive news coverage of the New York conference was sent by me to the board of directors (Parten files; Fund files).

5. Quotations from the fund-raising pamphlet issued by the Center on April 11, 1963, are taken from a Fund press release based on this pamphlet (Parten files; Fund files).

6. Actions taken at the Fund's board meeting on May 15, 1963, were recorded in the board's minutes (Parten files; Fund files).

7. The Chicago convocation celebrating the Fund's tenth anniversary was held from June 14 to June 16, 1963.

8. The threatening phone calls received at the Center and the appearance of 150 friendly citizens at the airport to meet the thirty United Nations delegates on June 22 were reported in the Santa Barbara *News-Press* on June 23, 1963. I was at the airport.

9. The picketing of Governor Edmund G. Brown, Sr., at the entrance of the Center on July 10, 1963, I witnessed when I met Governor Brown at the Santa Barbara airport and escorted him to the Center.

10. A report on the picketing appeared in the *News-Press* on July 11, 1963, along with a report on Governor Brown's speech at the Center dinner at the Biltmore and the remarks of Robert Hutchins.

11. My report of my conversation with Hutchins on the idea of sponsoring a convocation based on Pope John's *Pacem in Terris* is based on recollections and notes. Hutchins later told Joseph Bagnall, a faculty member of Santa Barbara City College, that I had persuaded him to go ahead with a "Pacem in Terris" convocation. Ostrow's enthusiasm was a major factor in his decision, however.

12. The quotations from my memorandum to Hutchins about my conversations with Monsignor Pietro Pavan are taken from a copy of this memorandum in my files, dated July 9, 1963. I also have a copy of Ferry's note of July 10, 1963.

13. Monsignor Pavan, who came to Santa Barbara at my invitation, led a discussion of *Pacem in Terris*—which he had helped Pope John to write—at the Center on August 28, 1963.

14. My report on my conversation with Robert Hutchins about Linus Pauling is based on recollections and notes. (A few days after the Los Angeles *Times* editorial criticizing Pauling had appeared, I met Frank McCulloch, then the managing editor of the *Times*, at a dinner in Los Angeles. McCulloch told me he was sorry the editorial had appeared. He said it had been written by Kirby Ramsdell, an editorial writer who disliked Pauling. When McCulloch saw the editorial in the first edition of the *Times*, he had gone to the composing room with the intention of having it removed from subsequent editions. He encountered Ramsdell, who told him that he was retiring that day from the paper's staff and that the Pauling editorial was his swan song. "I'd wanted to yank it out," McCulloch said to me. "But I didn't have the heart to do it when Ramsdell told me that." So the editorial appeared in the edition that reached Santa Barbara; I called it to Hutchins' attention; Hutchins wrote to Pauling—and Pauling joined the Center staff with financial support from a millionaire whose money made it possible for the Center to survive in subsequent years.)

15. Clippings of the articles about the pamphlets *Labor Looks at Labor, Science, Scientists, and Politics*, and *The Negro as an American* are in the Fund's files. The *Center Diary*, in its first issue, published in October 1963, also contains references to these articles (copies of the *Center Diary* are in Parten's files and the Fund files).

16. The suggestion for the Hutchins newspaper column was made by Richard Buffum through me, and I urged Hutchins to try it. Hutchins welcomed the idea.

17. I was present at the Center dialogue on November 22, 1963, when the message concerning the shooting of President Kennedy was brought to Hutchins, and Hutchins insisted on going on with the meeting.

18. The statements about the recruitment of Harold Willens by Hutchins as chairman of the Center's Founding Member Committee were based on an interview given by Willens to me on August 16, 1976, at the Beverly Hills tennis club. Willens said that Hutchins encouraged him in his first fund-raising efforts, and he soon learned that he could get businessmen to support the Center by persuading them that donations to the Center were "investments" in democracy.

19. The actions taken by the Fund's board at its meeting on December 6, 1963, were recorded in the board's minutes (Parten files; Fund files).

20. Information about the speakers at the Fund's convocation on December 7 and 8, 1963, was taken from the *Center Diary* (vol. 1, no. 2), January 1964. The *Diary* also contained the quotations from Admiral Rickover's speech urging the audience to support the Center.

Chapter Seventeen

1. Lyndon Johnson was aware of the Center's work and had been happy to have his statements on the topic "The Negro as an American" included in a Center pamphlet, but he was preoccupied with the legislative process and the manage-

ment of foreign policy. He was not as open to the Center's ideas as Kennedy had been.

2. The quotations from the Center pamphlet *Race and Housing* are taken from a Fund press release on this pamphlet (Parten files; Fund files).

3. The information about Hutchins' statements to Willens on fund raising as "a fishing trip" came from an interview given by Willens to me on August 16, 1976.

4. Quotations from the Center pamphlets *The Flexible Work-Year, Jobs, Machines and People, The Mazes of Modern Government,* and *First Things First* were taken from press releases on these pamphlets (Parten files; Fund files).

5. The announcement on Irving Laucks' association with the Center as a consultant was made in a Fund press release on April 2, 1964.

6. The appointment of Michael Harrington to the Center staff under the Laucks Fund and the announcement of the study of the civil rights movement in San Francisco were contained in press releases issued by the Fund for the Republic in May 1964 (Parten files; the Fund files).

7. Actions taken by the directors of the Fund for the Republic at their meeting on May 16, 1964, at the Wingspread Conference House in Racine, Wisconsin, are in the board minutes for that date (Parten files; Fund files).

8. The atmosphere at the Johnson Foundation headquarters at the May 1964 meeting attended by the directors of the Fund and the planners preparing for the *Pacem in Terris* convocation was noted by this writer, who attended these sessions.

9. The statement about the subjects of the *Pacem in Terris* conference was taken from an announcement given to the press on May 19, 1964. The list of leaders participating in the Wingspread gathering was also taken from this announcement (Parten files; Fund files).

10. Excerpts from the note sent by Harold Willens to all founding members were taken from a copy of this note in Parten's files. The election of Willens and the other new directors at the May 1964 meeting of the Fund's board was recorded in the minutes of this meeting (Parten files; the Fund files). An extensive report on the Wingspread gathering appeared in the *Center Diary* (vol. 1, no. 4), July 1964.

11. The appointments of Marjory Collins and Eleanor Garst to the Center's staff were announced in a press release in May 1964 (Parten files; Fund files).

12. Tom Shearer's appointment as director of development for the Center was announced in a press release from the Center on June 8, 1964 (Parten files; Fund files).

13. The participation of Hutchins, Wheeler, and William Gorman in a Berlin conference was reported by the Santa Barbara *News-Press* on June 26, 1964 (noted by this writer in the *News-Press* files).

14. Appointment of Mayor John Houlihan of Oakland, California, to direct a study of the problems of American cities in a technological age was announced in a Center press release at the end of June 1964 (Parten files; Fund files). Houlihan's appointment was also reported in the *Center Diary*, July 1964.

15. Quotations from John Wilkinson's booklet *The Quantitative Society* are taken from a copy of this booklet issued on June 27, 1964 (Parten files; Fund files).

16. Information on the fifteen dialogues at the Center on the First Amendment in July 1964 was taken from the *Center Diary* (vol. 1, no. 5), October 1964 (my files; Parten files).

17. The dinner for Seniel Ostrow was described in the *Center Diary* listed above.

18. The quotations from Justice Douglas on why the world needed the Center were taken from a leaflet containing his speech distributed by the Center (Parten files; Fund files).

19. The headlines on President Johnson's order to the U.S. Air Force to attack North Vietnamese bases appeared on the front page of the *New York Times*, August 5, 1964. The quotations from Johnson's statement to the world were taken from the *Times*, August 5, 1964. See *Page One*, a volume containing front pages of the *Times* on major events, 1920–1975. (New York: Arno Press, A New York Times Company, 1975).

20. The references to Johnson's varying explanations of why he authorized air raids on North Vietnam are based on a description of Johnson's actions and statements in *The Glory and the Dream: A Narrative History of America, 1932–1972*, by William Manchester (Boston: Little, Brown, 1973, 2 vols.).

21. The statements of Senator Fulbright, Senator Morse, Walter Lippmann, the Washington *Post*, and the *New York Times* and the results of the Harris Poll on public approval of Johnson's action are also drawn from *The Glory and the Dream*, vol. 2.

22. Descriptions of the topics and participants in the Center's dialogues in August and September 1964 were drawn from the *Center Diary*, (vol. 1, no. 5), October 1964.

23. The fact that Justice Douglas had invited President Kennedy to speak at the first *Pacem in Terris* convocation was reported to me and other Center staff members in September 1963. Douglas told Hutchins of his conversations with Kennedy and later with Johnson, and Hutchins gave the information to the Center staff.

24. The Romero Canyon fire, which destroyed more than 100 houses in Santa Barbara, including houses owned by Hutchins and Hallock Hoffman, was reported in the Santa Barbara *News-Press*, September 22–25, 1964.

25. Quotations from the Millis pamphlet *The Demilitarized World* were taken from a press release issued by the Center on this pamphlet September 8, 1964 (Parten files; Fund files).

26. Excerpts from William Lloyd's *Peace Requires Peacemakers* were taken from a press release on Lloyd's pamphlet issued by the Center in October 1964 (Parten files; Fund files).

27. The quotations from Harold Willens came from *The Quest for 1,000 Americans*, a four-page leaflet distributed by the Center in November 1964 (Parten files; Fund files).

28. The pledges and contributions obtained by the Fund from July to November 1964 were reported in a memorandum prepared for the meeting of the board of directors on November 11, 1964 (Parten files; Fund files).

29. The actions taken in the Fund's board meeting of November 11, 1964, were recorded in the minutes (Parten files; Fund files).

30. Quotations from the Center pamphlet *Segregation, Subsidies, and Megalopolis*

were drawn from a Center press relase on this pamphlet (Parten files; Fund files).

31. The list of speakers scheduled to address the *Pacem in Terris* convocation appeared in a press release issued by the Center and the Johnson Foundation on December 31, 1964. The quotations from Johnson's statement came from this release (Parten files; Fund files).

32. Humphrey's eagerness to speak at the Center convocation was mentioned to me by Hutchins after a telephone conversation Hutchins had with him in December 1964.

Chapter Eighteen

1. In his memoirs, *The Vantage Point* (New York: Holt, Rinehart and Winston, 1974), Johnson wrote: "The idea of attacking North Vietnam with air power had been a feature of several planning exercises and position papers in 1964. One such plan, developed at Pacific Command Headquarters, suggested air action against the enemy in three phases, the third of which would be a sustained aerial offensive." He said the proposal had been considered and rejected in August, September, and December 1964, principally because of strong objections by McNamara and Rusk. He put it into effect in February 1965, saying in his memoirs: "The North Vietnamese had deliberately and flagrantly struck at our men and installations, and we felt it necessary to respond." (p. 128.)

2. The texts of the messages from Pope Paul VI to Hutchins and Cardinal Spellman in February 1965 are reproduced in *Pacem in Terris: Peace on Earth* edited by Edward Reed, published by Pocket Books in a paperback volume in August 1965. This book contains the texts of the principal statements made by participants in the Center's first *Pacem in Terris* convocation in New York, in February 1965.

3. The excerpts from the statements by Hutchins, Humphrey, H. Stuart Hughes, Stanley Sheinbaum, Stevenson, Paul Tillich, Linus Pauling, N. N. Inozemtsev, Yevgenyi Zhukov, Adam Schaff, George F. Kennan, Henry Luce, Claiborne Pell, George N. Shuster, Eugene McCarthy, Grenville Clark, Carl Stover, Eugene Burdick, Jerome Frank, Gerard Piel, George McGovern, Fred Warner Neal, and U Thant were drawn from the *Pacem in Terris* volume issued by Pocket Books.

4. The distribution of audiotapes, videotapes, and films of the proceedings of the 1965 *Pacem in Terris* convocation is described in the *Pacem in Terris* volume and in reports to the Fund's board of directors by Edward Reed (Parten files; Fund files).

5. Excerpts from John K. Jessup's commentary on the *Pacem in Terris* convocation appeared in the March 5, 1965, issue of *Life* (Parten files; Fund files)

6. Clippings received from hundreds of magazines on the *Pacem in Terris* convocation in New York in February 1965 are in the Fund files. (Copies of many of the articles on the convocation, including those in Catholic publications, are in Parten's files and the Fund files.)

7. The gradual involvement of American forces on land in Vietnam began with Johnson's approval of the landing of two marine battalions in March 1965. In *The Vantage Point*, Johnson wrote: "In March I agreed to General Westmoreland's request that we land two Marine battalions to provide security for the Danang air base. This released for offensive action against the Viet Cong some of the Vietnamese troops who had been protecting the base." (p. 138).

8. The pledges and contributions made at the Hutchins dinner were reported to the board of directors at their meeting in May 1965. The statement of Chester Carlson to Harold Willens—"If you raise a million, I'll give $200,000 more"— was quoted to me in an interview with Willens August 16, 1976.

9. The meeting on "money in politics" was reported in the Santa Barbara *News-Press* on February 26, 1965.

10. The visit of Chester Carlson to the Center, the conference with the California Commission on Manpower, the appointment of John Cogley as religion editor of the *New York Times*, the announcement of the "Forces of Change" program, the appointment of Donald McDonald to the Center staff, and the telephone attacks on the Center were reported in articles in the *News-Press* in March, April, and May 1965.

11. Excerpts from Robert Scheer's pamphlet entitled *How the United States Got Involved in Vietnam* were taken from a copy of this pamphlet (Parten files; Fund files).

12. The vandalism at the Center on the night of September 14 was reported in the *News-Press* on September 15, 1965.

13. Chester Carlson's pledge to match all contributions received by the Center through September 30, 1966, was made in a letter to Hutchins in November 1965 (Parten files; Fund files).

Chapter Nineteen

1. The quotations from Rexford Tugwell on the reasons for the Center's exploration of "the emerging Constitution" were taken from the *Center Diary*, (no. 11), April 1966. The dialogues on the subject "Presidential Disability" and on other aspects of the Constitution are described in that issue of the *Diary*. (Parten files; Fund files).

2. The speech by Johnson on the dangers of a dictatorial president was printed in the *Congressional Record*, March 9, 1949 (81st Congress, 1st session).

3. A copy of Chester Carlson's letter in February 1966 announcing that he was giving the Fund 7000 shares of Xerox stock, is in Parten's files.

4. The appointment of John L. Perry as director of development was announced in a Center press release on March 12, 1966.

5. The quotations from Hutchins' statement "The University in America" were taken from a Center press release dated March 13, 1966. This also contained the Hutchins' statement on the need for "a distillation of the best thought on the condition of higher education," quoted earlier.

6. Quotations from the statements made by Senator Fulbright at the conference "The University in America" were taken from a report of this conference printed in the *Center Diary* (no. 12), May–June 1966.

7. The Los Angeles *Times* printed a column summarizing the conference on May 15, 1966. Art Seidenbaum's salute to the Center appeared in the *Times* on the same day. (Copies in Parten's files.)

8. The description of the Center conference in Geneva in June 1966 was based on statements in *Mission to Hanoi*, by Harry S. Ashmore and William C. Baggs, published by G. P. Putnam's–Berkley Books, 1968. The quotations from Ashmore are taken from page 4 of the prologue, "The Uses of Demi-Diplomacy.

9. The statement about Luis Quintanilla's role in endeavoring to get representatives from Mao's China and North Vietnam to participate in "Pacem in Terris II" is taken from the Ashmore-Baggs book referred to above.

10. The meetings with Jerome Frank entitled "Survival and Sanity" were noted in the *Center Diary* (no. 14), September–October 1966.

11. The appointments of Bishop Pike, John Seeley, and Stringfellow Barr, as well as that of Dr. Frank on a temporary basis, were announced in a Center press release July 16, 1966 (Parten files; Fund files).

12. The dialogues at the Center in July, August, and September 1966, with the names of topics and speakers, were published in the *Center Diary* (no. 14), September–October 1966 (Parten files; Fund files).

13. The dinner in honor of Paul Hoffman, which demonstrated the Center's connections with powerful people in many fields, was originally announced in a Center press release on May 15, 1966, and scheduled to be held on May 26. It was postponed to September 29 at Hoffman's request. Hutchins' statement about Hoffman was taken from a Center press release.

14. The information about the Center's financial condition at the end of September 1966 was drawn from a report submitted by Hutchins to the board of directors (Parten files; Fund files).

15. The description of the Center pamphlet *Looking Forward: The Abundant Society* was based on a Center press release, December 12, 1966.

Chapter Twenty

1. The conversations Ashmore and Baggs had with Ho Chi Minh are described in their book, *Mission to Hanoi*, previously cited.

2. Senator Fulbright's statements to Harriman, Bundy, and Katzenbach in the Department of State were reported in the Ashmore-Baggs book.

3. The Ashmore-Baggs trips to Hanoi and their efforts to aid in bringing peace to Vietnam are noted in Johnson's book, *The Vantage Point*, previously cited. Johnson makes no mention, however, of the feeling of Ashmore and Baggs that they were victims of "duplicity" in the State Department and the White House.

4. The difficulties created for the Center in organizing the "Pacem in Terris II" convocation, which was held in Geneva from May 28 to May 31, 1967, were de-

scribed in the Ashmore-Baggs book and in a long article by Ashmore entitled "The Public Relations of Peace," published in the first issue of the *Center Magazine*, October–November 1967.

5. Quotations from the statements made by many speakers at the Geneva convocation were drawn from *Pacem in Terris*, a book based on this conference (Bahamas: Frontiers, 1968). The book is dedicated to Martin Luther King, who was one of the speakers at the convocation. It was financed by Investors Overseas Services, of which James Roosevelt was president. The I.O.S. was founded by Bernard Cornfeld.

6. The quotations from the New York *Daily News*, the Chicago *Tribune*, William Buckley, and the Indianapolis *Star* came from the Ashmore-Baggs book, *Mission to Hanoi*. So did the quotation from Robert Lasch of the St. Louis *Post-Dispatch*.

7. The article entitled "Hutchins Center Examines the Nature of Democracy" appeared in the Santa Barbara *News-Press* on June 19, 1967.

8. The *News-Press* carried a story on July 8, 1967, describing the plans for the launching of the *Center Magazine*.

9. The appointment of Harry Ashmore as executive vice president of the Fund, the election of John Perry as secretary and treasurer, and the appointments of John Seeley as the dean of the academic program, and of Richard Gilbert and Peter Tagger to the Center staff were announced in the *News-Press* on July 14, 1967.

10. The appointment of Crane Haussamen to manage the Center's New York office was also disclosed in the *News-Press* story, July 14, 1967.

Chapter Twenty-one

1. The quotations from the article by Tom O'Brien in the *News-Press* on August 24, 1967, describing the goal of the conference of radical students at the Center, were taken from a copy of O'Brien's article in the *News-Press* files, with permission from the *News-Press*.

2. My conversation with Tom Storke on the reactions of Santa Barbara citizens to the conference of radical students occurred at Storke's home on the evening of August 25, 1967. Mrs. Storke was present.

3. The quotations from the newspaper articles on the students' meeting on August 25 and 26, 1967, are taken from copies in the files of the *News-Press*.

4. Excerpts from the statements by Frederick Richman, Robert Hutchins, Michael Lerner, Deveraux Kennedy, Jeffrey Elman, Daniel Sisson, Mary Quinn, Peter Lyman, John Blood, Frank Bardacke, Robert Pardun, David Seeley, Rexford Tugwell, Michael Lerner, Stringfellow Barr, W. H. Ferry, Stanley Wise, John Seeley, Sheila Langdon, and Scott Buchanan are taken from a copy of *Students and Society*, a Center pamphlet based on the student gathering, published in December 1967.

5. Quotations from Ashmore's letter to the *News-Press* are taken from a copy of a clipping in the files of the *News-Press*, dated August 30, 1967.

6. The *News-Press* editorial on Ashmore's letter appeared on September 1, 1967. A copy is in the files of the *News-Press*, examined by this writer.

7. Excerpts from the *News-Press* editorial of September 8, 1967, are taken from a copy of this editorial in the files of the *News-Press*.

8. Quotations from Representative Teague's speech to the Thousand Oaks Republican Women's Club, attacking the Center, are taken from a clipping of a *News-Press* article dated September 8, 1967.

9. The actions of the California Republican Assembly criticizing the Center were reported in the *News-Press* on September 11, 1967.

10. Quotations from the chilly editorial that appeared in the *News-Press* on September 11, 1967, are taken from a copy in the newspaper's files, with permission.

Chapter Twenty-two

1. Quotations from Ashmore's criticisms of Johnson, Rusk, and the Washington *Post* were drawn from his long letter printed in the January 1968 issue of the *Center Magazine*. The statement by Frank Sieverts of the Department of State, denying Ashmore's previous charges against him, also appeared in that issue of the magazine, with Ashmore's comment.

2. Information about the second journey made by Ashmore and Baggs to Hanoi, and their second round of difficulties with the State Department and other journalists, was drawn from the Ashmore-Baggs book, *Mission to Hanoi*.

3. The statements by Lyndon Johnson are drawn from his book, *The Vantage Point*, previously cited.

4. Quotations from Hutchins' statements on the Center's work, its staff, and its problems are drawn from a booklet entitled *Center for the Study of Democratic Institutions: Report of the President*, published by the Center in April 1968 (Parten files; Fund files).

5. Stanley Sheinbaum's congressional campaign was covered by the Santa Barbara *News-Press*. The *News-Press* also carried reports on the antiwar statements by John Seeley, Bishop Crowther, and Bishop Pike.

6. The murder of Martin Luther King in Memphis on April 4, 1968, set off a wave of riots and violence in American cities. National Guard troops were sent into action in Chicago, Detroit, and Boston. Regular army troops were mobilized to protect the White House and the Congress in Washington. (See the *New York Times*, April 5 and 6, 1968.)

7. Senator Robert Kennedy was shot a few hours after his victory over Senator Eugene McCarthy in the Democratic presidential primary in California, on June 5, 1968, and died the next day (see the *New York Times*, June 6, 1968).

8. Information about the series of lectures sponsored by the Center with the University of California in April and May 1968 was drawn from a pamphlet published by the university (Parten files; Fund files).

9. Descriptions of the actions by students and the demonstrations in Chicago's Lincoln Park in August 1968 were drawn from articles in the *New York Times*,

the Los Angeles *Times*, and other newspapers, as well as from the radio and television broadcasts.

10. Quotations from Harrop Freeman, Rexford Tugwell, John Cogley, Harry Ashmore, Robert Hutchins, Judge Warren E. Burger (later Chief Justice of the United States), Judge Walter Schaefer, Sam Dash, Gerald Gottlieb, Gresham Sykes, Robert F. Kennedy, Neil V. Sullivan, and Kenneth B. Clark were excerpted from the November 1968 issue of the *Center Magazine* (Parten files; Fund files).

11. Statements by John Seeley as Dean of the Center's academic program were quoted from a report he transmitted to the Fund's board for the meeting of the directors on November 22, 1968 (Parten files; Fund files).

12. The reports made by Hutchins and John Perry at the board meeting on November 22, 1968, were noted in the minutes of the meeting (Parten files; Fund files). So was the statement by William Baggs, asking board members to contribute substantially to the Center, and the establishment of a Committee on Funding.

13. The minutes also noted the election of Stewart Mott and Howard Stein as directors of the Fund. (Parten files; Fund files).

14. The question raised by Morris Levinson on whether the Center had a "frozen" staff—and Hutchins' reply, saying that there was a policy against "permanent appointments"—appeared in the minutes of the meeting on November 22, 1968.

15. I was one of those who saw Hutchins almost daily in the last weeks of 1968. He indicated to me and to John Cogley that he was not satisfied with the performance of some of the staff members who were listed in Center publications as "Fellows." He made it plain that a reorganization had to be carried out, but he kept putting it off, knowing that it would be extremely painful for the ones who had to leave.

Chapter Twenty-three

1. The quotations from Richard Nixon's inaugural address on January 20, 1969, were drawn from a report in the *New York Times* on January 21, 1969.

2. A report on the Center conference with Japanese and American leaders appeared in the *News-Press* on January 24, 1969.

3. Hutchins' reluctance to go on a trip to India because of the suffering he would encounter there was mentioned to me by Hallock Hoffman in an interview. Hallock told me that his father, Paul Hoffman, had reported this to him.

4. A copy of the handwritten note sent by Hutchins to Seeley at the staff meeting at the Center on April 30, 1969, is in the collection of the papers of W. H. Ferry at Dartmouth College. With permission from Ferry I examined the Ferry papers at the Dartmouth library in December 1976.

5. The information about Hutchins' meeting with Ashmore, Cogley, Seeley, Wheeler, and Neil Jacoby on April 30 to discuss a reorganization was given to me in June 1969 by John Cogley in a conversation about what had preceded the Center's drastic reorganization.

6. Quotations from the statements of Hutchins and others at the staff meeting on May 7, 1969, are based on notes I made after listening to a tape recording of what occurred at the meeting. The staff meetings were recorded with the approval of all those who participated in them.

7. Hutchins' statements to the members of the Fund's board are taken from the minutes of the executive session of the board, held on May 9 at the Santa Barbara Biltmore hotel. The fact that the directors spent about one hour in listening to Hutchins and approving the reorganization plan was recorded in these minutes (Parten files; Fund files.)

8. Quotations from the afternoon meeting of the board on May 9, 1969, are drawn from the minutes of that meeting (Parten files; Fund files).

9. The financial report on the Center's situation, given by Richard Gilbert, was recorded in the minutes (Parten files; Fund files).

10. The description of the relationship between Hutchins and Harvey Wheeler is based on my own observations, conversations with both men, and conversations with John Cogley, who knew both of them very well.

11. What Hutchins and Wheeler did in the interlude between Wheeler's appointment and the appointment of other new senior fellows was described by Hutchins and Wheeler later in their testimony in the suit filed by W. H. Ferry against the Center.

12. Wheeler's statement about his advocacy of the appointment of scholars with international reputations was made to me in an interview with him in June 1969 and later reiterated in his testimony in the Ferry case.

13. In an interview with me on July 6, 1977, Wheeler said that the appointment of the ex officio fellows "did change the entire character of the rest of the procedure" and was also "a violation of the agreement that we all had had." Wheeler declared: "I was upset, but I did not, I did not firmly oppose it, and that's the thing that I blame myself for."

14. Quotations from the letter Hutchins sent to Ferry on May 17, 1969, are drawn from a copy of Hutchins' letter in Parten's files. (Ferry sent copies of his correspondence and his conversations with Hutchins, noted in memoranda, to Parten.)

15. Ferry's feeling that only the scholars on the Fund's staff should be attached to the Center had been expressed to John Cogley and others at the time, in 1959, when the board decided to establish the Center in Santa Barbara.

16. The article about Ferry by Victor Navasky entitled "The Happy Heretic" appeared in the July 1966 issue of the *Atlantic Monthly*. A copy is in my files.

17. Quotations from Ferry's *aide mémoire*, dictated shortly after his meeting with Hutchins at the end of May 1969, are taken from a copy of this memorandum in Parten's files, dated May 28, 1969.

18. Excerpts from Ferry's memorandum of June 2, 1969, about his conversation with Cogley, are drawn from a copy of this memorandum in Parten's files.

19. Quotations from Hutchins' letter to Ferry dated June 4, 1969, are excerpted from a copy of this letter in Parten's files.

20. Excerpts from Ferry's letter of June 5, 1969, to Hutchins are drawn from a copy of this letter in Parten's files.

21. Quotations from Hallock Hoffman's letter to his friends about the reorganization of the Center, dated June 17, 1969, are drawn from a copy of this letter given to me. Hoffman also made available to me copies of the correspondence he had with Hutchins and Ashmore, and information on the terms of the settlement that was finally reached between the Center and himself.

22. Excerpts from the Center's announcement of its reorganization—made in a press release that I prepared—are drawn from a copy of this statement in my files.

23. Quotations from Robert Sollen's articles in the Santa Barbara *News-Press* on June 13 and 14, 1969, are drawn from copies of these articles in the *News-Press* files.

24. Excerpts from the article in the June 25, 1969, issue of the Los Angeles *Times* and the June 17, 1969, issue of the *New York Times* were drawn from copies of these articles in my files.

25. The quotation from Cogley was based on a conversation I had with him in June 1969 in my office at the Center. In an interview I had with Wheeler on July 6, 1977, Wheeler said: "I think that Cogley was the first one to point out, at least in my awareness . . . that the reorganization had achieved nothing and that it was the same as before only with a different kind of charade being carried forward, and that the Senior Fellows actually didn't have any authority after all."

26. Quotations from Ashmore's memorandum of June 17, 1969, are drawn from a copy of this memorandum in Parten's files.

27. Information from the background statement sent to the Center's consultants before their meeting in July 1969 was drawn from a copy of this statement by Robert Hutchins in Parten's files.

28. Quotations from Hutchins' statement in the April 1964 issue of the *Center Diary* are taken from a copy of this issue of the *Diary* in my files.

29. Appointment of the twelve associates of the Center was announced by Hutchins in a Center press release in August 1969 (Parten files; Fund files).

30. Information about the Center's conference in August 1969 on "the biological revolution" also was drawn from a Center press release.

31. Senator Church's speech at the Center seminar on Latin America was printed in the November 1969 issue of the *Center Magazine*, which carried a brief report on this conference in Mexico City.

32. Nixon's change in American policy toward the Latin countries was reported in the *New York Times* in October 1969.

33. The death of Bishop James A. Pike in Israel in September 1969 was reported in the *New York Times* and many other newspapers.

34. My conversation with Bishop Pike occurred in my office on May 10, 1969, soon after Hutchins told him he would not be one of the new senior fellows.

35. Information on the launching of the *Center Newsletter* was drawn from a Center press release that I issued on October 5, 1969.

36. The topics of the Center dialogues in October 1969 were taken from the first is-
    sue of the *Center Newsletter*, as were the quotations from Ashmore and
    Wheeler.

37. Quotations from *Asian Dilemma*, a Center book published in October 1969,
    were drawn from a copy of this book in my files.

38. Representative Teague renewed his demand for an investigation of the Center
    in a letter sent to Randolph Thrower, Commissioner of Internal Revenue. Ex-
    cerpts from Teague's letter were published in the Santa Barbara *News-Press* on
    May 9, 1969.

39. Excerpts from Ralph Dighton's article about the Center were drawn from a
    copy of this article that appeared in the *News-Press* on November 9, 1969.

40. Description of the anti–Vietnam War demonstrations in Washington was based
    on articles in the *New York Times* and the Los Angeles *Times* in November
    1969.

41. The topics of the Center dialogues on November 12 and 17, 1969, were drawn
    from a copy of the *Center Newsletter* in my files.

42. A report on the damage suits filed by W. H. Ferry against the Fund, Robert
    Hutchins, and Harry Ashmore appeared in the Santa Barbara *News-Press* on
    November 19, 1969 (*News-Press* files; Parten files).

43. Quotations from Ferry's legal complaints are taken from a copy of these com-
    plaints sent by Hutchins to Parten (Parten files; Fund files).

44. The actions and statements made at the directors' meeting on December 5,
    1969, were noted in the minutes of that meeting (Parten files; Fund files).

45. Quotations from Hutchins' statements on the election of new officers of the
    Fund were drawn from a press release dated December 9, 1969. A report based
    on this release appeared in the *News-Press* on that date.

46. The names and backgrounds of all the associates, fellows, and consultants of
    the Center were contained in this press release of December 9, 1969.

47. Quotations from Ashmore are taken from a sworn deposition given by Ash-
    more in a lawyer's office in Santa Barbara on December 18, 1969. John Sink,
    attorney for Ferry, questioned Ashmore.

48. The quotation from the bylaws of the Fund was taken from a copy of these by-
    laws in my files.

49. Access to a copy of Ashmore's deposition in the Fund files was given to me by
    Ashmore and by Peter Tagger.

50. Quotations from Wheeler and Wilkinson were drawn from copies of their dep-
    ositions in the Fund files. Permission to examine these depositions was given to
    me in 1976 by Peter Tagger, then secretary-treasurer of the Fund.

51. Quotations from Mrs. Borgese's testimony were drawn from a copy of her dep-
    osition in the Fund files. Permission to examine her deposition was given by Pe-
    ter Tagger.

52. A report on the Center's conference on constitutional problems in December
    1969 appeared in the December 18, 1969, issue of the Santa Barbara *News-
    Press* (*News-Press* files).

53. William Stringer's article on the Center's conference on "the biological revolution" appeared in the *Christian Science Monitor*, December 10, 1969 (Parten files).

54. Attacks by Nixon and Agnew on critics of the Vietnam War was reported on television and in the *New York Times* and other newspapers in December 1969.

55. Reports on the rock festivals at Woodstock and other places appeared in newspapers and magazines in many cities in 1969.

Chapter Twenty-four

1. A report on the Center conference on the arms race in the oceans and use of sea bed resources for mankind appeared in the *News-Press*, January 10, 1970.

2. The *News-Press* also carried an article on the Center conference on "the new rhetoric," January 25, 1970, and a report on the conference on "the legal development of ocean resources" held at the University of Rhode Island.

3. Hutchins testified in the Ferry suit on January 20, 1970, in a lawyer's office in Santa Barbara. His deposition was made available to me by the Center.

4. Quotations from John Seeley's statements in his deposition in the Ferry case—made in February 1970—were drawn from a copy of Seeley's deposition in Ferry's papers in the Dartmouth College library.

5. Excerpts from Tugwell's statements were taken from a copy of Tugwell's deposition in the Center's files. I was given access to this deposition by the Center.

6. A report on the Center's conference, "Project Lifespan" appeared in the Santa Barbara *News-Press* on April 14, 1970 (Parten files; Fund files).

7. Kimmis Hendrick's article on the Center conference on "global ecology" appeared in the *Christian Science Monitor* in April 1970.

8. The quotations from statements by Hutchins, Wheeler, Cogley, and Elisabeth Borgese at the conference in Los Angeles were drawn from a report on this conference in the *Center Newsletter*, May 1970 (May–June issue).

9. Quotations from Judge Rickard's rulings in the Ferry case are taken from a copy of his rulings in the Santa Barbara County Court House files.

10. Nixon's statement on his reasons for invading Cambodia appeared in the *New York Times* and many other newspapers.

11. The student demonstrations in Washington on May 9 and 10, 1970, and the uprisings on 415 campuses are described vividly by William Manchester in *The Glory and the Dream* (Boston: Little, Brown, 1974), vol. 2, p. 1484.

12. The Senate resolution in May 1970 demanding the removal of American troops from Cambodia was reported in the *New York Times* and other papers.

13. Topics of the Center dialogues in May were reported in the June 1970 issue of the *Center Newsletter*.

14. The actions and statements at the Center's board meeting on May 15, 1970, were noted in the board's minutes (Parten files; Fund files).

15. The opening of the Malta conference on peaceful uses of the oceans was reported in the *New York Times* and many other papers on June 29, 1970. Articles on statements made at this conference appeared in the Kansas City *Star*, St. Louis *Post-Dispatch*, and dozens of other publications (copies of many of these articles are in Parten's files and the Fund files).

16. Marjorie Hunter's report on the investigation of Justice Douglas on charges brought against Douglas by Gerald Ford and others appeared in the *New York Times* on December 16, 1970. .

17. The Washington *Post* editorial excoriating Ford and other representatives for their attacks on Justice Douglas appeared in the *Post* on December 18, 1970.

18. Quotations from the statements on the activities of young people by Donald McDonald, Hutchins, Tugwell, Cogley, Wheeler, Ashmore, Elisabeth Borgese, and John Wilkinson were drawn from the July–August 1970 issue of the *Center Magazine*.

19. A report on the Center conference on "structuralism" organized by John Wilkinson and Harvey Wheeler, with cooperation by Nathan Rotenstreich, appeared in the Santa Barbara *News-Press* on August 13, 1970.

20. Excerpts from the statements made by Ashmore, Tugwell, Cogley, and Hutchins about the genesis and development of the "model for a new Constitution" are drawn from a copy of the September–October 1970 issue of the *Center Magazine* (copies in my files, Parten's files, and the Fund files).

21. The ideas offered by Hallock Hoffman and W. H. Ferry on the defects and possibilities for revision of the U.S. Constitution were noted in the *Center Diary* (no. 3), April 1964. Quotations from Hoffman and Ferry were drawn from this issue of the *Diary*, which also contained statements by Robert Heilbroner, Hutchins, Stanley Sheinbaum, George McGovern, and Michael Harrington.

22. Fred Graham's article about the Center's "model for a new Constitution" appeared on the front page of the *New York Times* on September 8, 1970. The table of comparisons between the Center's model and the Constitution of 1787 was suggested to the editors of the *Times* by this writer. (Copies in Parten's files, the Fund files, and my files.)

23. The attack on Tugwell appeared in the New York *Daily News* a few days after the publication of the model constitution on September 7, 1970.

24. The editorials from *Newsweek*, the St. Louis *Post-Dispatch*, and the Memphis *Commercial Appeal* and the article by David Broder in the Washington *Post* were reproduced in the November–December issue of the *Center Magazine*. Quotations from these statements are drawn from that issue. (Copies in Parten's files and the Fund files.)

25. Quotations from the statements by William Havard, Leslie Lipson, and others who wrote to the Center about the model constitution are drawn from letters printed in the November–December 1970 issue of the *Center Magazine*.

26. The total paid circulation of the *Center Magazine* on September 16, 1970, was reported by Peter Tagger, business manager, as 98,514. This figure appeared in the "Statement of Ownership, Management and Circulation" published in the November–December 1970 issue of the magazine.

27. A report on Sheinbaum's resignation and Ashmore's statement about the reduction of the Center's income appeared in the October 8, 1970, Santa Barbara *News-Press*. The departure of Richard Gilbert was also reported in that issue of the *News-Press*.

28. The launching of *The Center Report*, with Mary K. Harvey as editor, was described in an article in the Santa Barbara *News-Press* on October 26, 1970.

29. The Center's conference on "the model for a new Constitution" received extensive coverage in the Philadelphia *Inquirer* and the Philadelphia *Bulletin* on November 10 and 11, 1970 (copies of the *Inquirer* and *Bulletin* articles are in Parten's files and Fund files).

30. The actions taken by the Fund's board at its meeting in New York on November 10, 1970, were noted in the board's minutes (Parten files; Fund files).

31. The quotations from the *New York Times* article on the Center's convocation in New York on "the model Constitution" were taken from a copy of this article that appeared in the *Times* of November 12, 1970.

32. I suggested the idea of a series of public debates by Hutchins and Justice Douglas on the desirability of a new constitution. Hutchins told me that Douglas had accepted and a week later said that Douglas had changed his mind.

33. Excerpts from Michael Schneider's article and the statement by Philip Ortego and Joseph Lyford were drawn from the November–December 1970 issue of the *Center Magazine*.

34. The problems raised by the conflicts between the journalistic needs of the Center publications and the interests of the scholars at the Center was frequently discussed with me through the years by John Cogley and Mary Harvey, who were on the journalistic side, and by Harvey Wheeler and John Wilkinson, who felt that the Center should devote more of its resources to scholarly publications.

35. Quotations from the first issue of the *Center Report*, in October 1970, are drawn from a copy of this issue of the *Report* in my files (copies are also in Parten's files and the Fund files).

36. The statement by Hutchins about trimming the Center's overhead "without cutting into the efficiency of the staff" was noted in the minutes of the November 10, 1970, board meeting (Parten files; Fund files).

37. The statement by Ashmore is drawn from the December issue of the *Center Report*, from a published copy in my files.

38. Quotations from Georgi Arbatov and George Kahin are also excerpted from the December 1970 issue of the *Center Report*.

39. Fred Warner Neal's criticisms of the Center's policies were contained in a long letter he sent to Hutchins in November 1970 (a copy of this letter is in the Fund files).

40. The quotation from Allan B. Goldman, a lawyer representing Hutchins and Ashmore, indicating that it didn't matter whether the selection procedure for the choice of senior fellows had been changed in May of 1969 or not, was drawn from a copy of Goldman's statement in the files of the Santa Barbara County Courthouse.

41. Judge Rickard's ruling on September 3, 1970, dismissing Ferry's contention that the "refounding" of the Center had substantially changed the organization's purposes, is on file in the Santa Barbara County Courthouse.

42. Information on the date of Hutchins' operation in December 1970 was given to me by Esther Donnelly, Hutchins' secretary.

43. Hutchins had sent a list of possible "successors" to himself with a letter to Parten and other members of the Fund's Committee on Organization on October 14, 1970. He had indicated no preference for any of the people on the list. Malcolm Moos, president of the University of Minnesota, who was elected to succeed Hutchins by the Fund's board in October 1973, was one of the educators on Hutchins' list in 1970. (Copies of the Hutchins letter and list are in Parten's files.)

Chapter Twenty-five

1 Quotations from the statements by Wheeler, George Reedy, and James Barber on the presidency were drawn from the January–February 1971 issue of the *Center Magazine* (copies of this issue in Parten files and the Fund files).

2. Excerpts from Gene Schrader's article on the deceptiveness of the AEC are drawn from a copy of the January–February 1971 issue of the *Center Magazine* in my files.

3. Keith Berwick had been interested in the Center for a long time, and had attended meetings in Santa Barbara. His interview with Hutchins appeared in the January–February 1971 issue of the *Center Magazine*, previously cited.

4. An article on the Center's conference on crime control appeared in the Santa Barbara *News-Press* on February 22, 1971.

5. Quotations from Carl Ruah, Norval Morris, Herbert Packer, Troy Duster, Judge Constance Motley, Ramsey Clark, Judge Tim Murphy, James Bennett, and Robert Hutchins, who participated in the crime control conference, are drawn from statements printed in the May–June 1971 issue of the *Center Magazine*.

6. Tugwell's letter acknowledging the many criticisms of the "model Constitution" was published inside the front cover of the February 1971 issue of *Center Report* under the heading "Constitutional Critics."

7. Tugwell's statements about Richard Nixon were written in his book *Off Course: From Truman to Nixon*, published by Frederick Praeger, Inc., in February 1971.

8. Quotations from Ivan Illich, Everett Reimer, Harvey Wheeler, and Grant Masland were drawn from the February 1971 issue of *Center Report* (Parten files; Fund files).

9. The interview with Hugh Downs, in which he praised the "utter freedom" at the Center, was published in the March 3, 1971, issue of the Santa Barbara *News-Press*.

10. The crushing defeat of South Vietnamese troops in Laos in March 1971 and the march of 200,000 protesters against the Vietnamese War in Washington in

April 1971—and the violent reactions of Attorney General Mitchell and President Nixon—were described by William Manchester in *The Glory and the Dream*, vol. 2 (pp. 1503–6).

11. Excerpts from Mrs. Borgese's memorandum to Harry Ashmore on March 12, 1971, came from a copy of this memorandum in the Center's files, made available to me.

12. The decision of the fellows to refuse a recommendation for the allocation of $60,000 to a new publication was recorded in the senior fellows' minutes, made available to me.

13. Quotations from Arnold Toynbee, Aurelio Peccei, Eldridge Haines, and Orville Freeman are taken from an article on the London discussion in the April 1971 issue of *Center Report* (copy in my files).

14. Excerpts from Mircea Eliade's statement on the religious framework for existence are also taken from the April 1971 issue of the *Report*, along with John Wilkinson's comments.

15. The meeting of the International Committee for Dialogue in the spring of 1971 in Cuernavaca was described in the June 1971 issue of *Center Report* (copy in my files).

16. The Chicago *Daily News*, April 3, 1971, and the Chicago *Sun-Times*, April 4, 1971, carried reports on the Center's symposium in Chicago on "Prospects for a Learning Society." The Chicago *Tribune* and Chicago *Today* also had articles on the meeting, which was also covered by the Associated Press and United Press International. (Copies of many of these articles are in Parten's files.)

17. The references to the Pentagon Papers, Nixon's reaction, and the Supreme Court's ruling denying the government's right to prevent their publication were based on articles in the *New York Times* in June and July 1971.

18. Actions of the Fund's board at its meeting in New York on June 24, 1971, were noted in the board's minutes (Parten files; Fund files).

19. Information on the Center's sponsorship of the premiere of Stanley Kramer's film *Bless the Beasts and Children* was drawn from the June 1971 issue of *Center Report*.

20. In interviews with me, Parten and Fagan Dickson told me of their successful efforts to persuade Hutchins to undergo a cancer operation at the Anderson Clinic in Houston.

21. Ashmore notified Parten and other members of the board in September 1971 that Norton Ginsburg had agreed to become the Center's Dean, effective on October 15, 1971 (a copy of Ashmore's letter to Parten is in Parten's files).

22. Ashmore's announcement of the Center's plans for an international conference in Tokyo was reported in the Santa Barbara *News-Press* July 14, 1971.

23. Nixon's statement on July 17, 1971, that he had accepted an invitation to visit Communist China appeared in the *New York Times* and other papers.

24. Ashmore's announcement of the postponement of the Center's proposed meeting in Japan was published in the Santa Barbara *News-Press* on July 27, 1971.

25. The *News-Press* carried articles on the Center's conference with agricultural experts on August 11 and August 16, 1971.

26. Hutchins' statements about Elmo Roper, John Cogley's tribute to Reinhold Niebuhr, and the quotations from Niebuhr's article in the *Center Magazine* are taken from a published copy of the July–August issue of the magazine (Parten files; my files).

27. The Santa Barbara *News-Press* carried an article on the Center's conference "The Corporation and the Quality of Life" on September 28, 1971.

28. Quotations from statements made at the conference on "The Corporation" were drawn from the January–February 1972 issue of the *Center Magazine* (Parten files; my files; Fund's files).

29. The Center's conference on "self-management" was described in the Santa Barbara *News-Press*, October 24, 1971.

30. Excerpts from the statements made by Ichak Adizes, Najdan Pasic, Jose Pacek, Fred Blum, and others at the conference on "self-management" were taken from the December 1971 issue of *Center Report*.

31. Actions and statements at the Fund's board meeting on November 19, 1971, were recorded in the board's minutes (Parten's files; Fund files).

32. Hutchins' references to Herbert York, Norman Cousins, Dean McHenry, and Louis Pollak as possible successors to himself were noted in the minutes of the November 23 meeting of the senior fellows (Fund files).

Chapter Twenty-six

1. The report on the Center's conference "Medical Malpractice" was released to the press on January 2, 1972. An article based on this report appeared in the Santa Barbara *News-Press* on that date. The article noted that copies of the report were offered to the public for $1 per copy.

2. Quotations from Roger Egeberg, Eli Bernzweig, Rick Carlson, Mark Blumberg, Richard Markus, David Rubsamen, J. W. Bush, and Robert E. Keeton were taken from a published copy of this Center pamphlet, entitled *Medical Malpractice* (Parten files; my files).

3. Quotations from statements made at the conference with B. F. Skinner on "behavior modification," held at the Center in January 1972, are drawn from the statements published in the March–April 1972 issue of the *Center Magazine* (Parten files; my files).

4. The news media executives who came to the Center for this conference included Charles Riley, president of the Radio-TV News Association of Southern California; John Lowry, manager of the Los Angeles bureau of United Press International; and Art Kevin, public affairs director for KHJ, Los Angeles.

5. The "battle plan" presented by Gordon Liddy of the Committee to Re-Elect the President (CREEP) on January 27, 1972, to Attorney General Mitchell, Jeb Megruder, and John Dean was described in William Manchester's book *The Glory and the Dream* (pp. 1561–63) and later in the testimony of Mitchell, Magruder, and Dean before the Senate Committee headed by Senator Ervin of North Carolina.

6. A report on the conference with power company executives, officials of the Edison Electric Institute, government and foundation officials, and environmen-

talists at the Center appeared in the Santa Barbara *News-Press* January 28, 1972.

7. The bulletin "Current and Pending Activities" was initiated by Harry Ashmore at the end of January 1972, in response to indications from directors and major contributors that they felt remote from the Center and did not know enough about its work.

8. The topics of the dialogues and other statements about Center activities in the period from January 31 to February 18, 1972, were described in the first issue of "Current and Pending Activities," mailed to directors, associates, and consultants on January 28, 1972.

9. The visit by executives of IBM, Borg-Warner, Chase Manhattan Bank, Quaker Oats, Procter & Gamble, Minnesota Mining and Manufacturing, General Motors, and other large corporations on February 2, 1972, was noted in *Center Report* in its April 1972 issue.

10. I was present at the Los Angeles convocation on foreign policy at the Beverly Hilton hotel, where Hutchins received a standing ovation after his statement on the "impossible" things that had happened in his lifetime.

11. Quotations from General Gavin's statement at the Center on March 28, 1972, are drawn from an article in the June 1972 issue of *Center Report*.

12. Actions and statements at the Fund's board meeting on May 2, 1972, were noted in the board's minutes (Parten files; Fund files).

13. Quotations from Garry Wills and other participants in the Center's conference on "Cultural Change," held in New York from May 3 to May 5, 1972, were drawn from statements printed in the July–August 1972 issue of the *Center Magazine*.

14. A summary of the Center's convocation on "new directions in American foreign policy," held in New York on May 6, 1972, appeared in the June 1972 issue of *Center Report*.

15. The meetings at the Center from May 16 through May 24, 1972, were noted in the "Current and Pending Activities" bulletin covering the period from May 15 to June 3, 1972 (Parten files; Fund files).

16. The conference on "Social Futures" was described by Mary Harvey in the June 1972 issue of *Center Report* (Parten files; Fund files).

17. Descriptions of the "Special Funds" recommended by the Taft Company appeared in the June 1972 *Center Report*, previously cited.

18. The financial problems of the Center continued to be described in specific terms in reports rendered regularly to the board of directors.

19. Quotations from Donald McDonald are taken from his article on "the present condition of women" in the May–June issue of the *Center Magazine*.

20. The comments from *Center Magazine* readers, criticizing and commending McDonald, appeared in the July–August issue of the magazine (copies of these issues are in Parten's files and the Fund files).

21. Quotations from Roger Garaudy, Wilfried Daim, Richard Lichtman, and Michael Brenner were taken from statements by these writers in the September–October 1972 issue of the *Center Magazine* (Parten files; Fund files).

22. Tugwell's statement about the "McGovern-Roosevelt Analogy" appeared in

the Los Angeles *Times* in September 1972 and also in the October 1972 issue of *Center Report*.

23. Topics of the Center dialogues and discussion leaders between September 11 and October 6, 1972, were noted in the Center's "Current and Pending Activities" bulletin covering that period (Parten files; Fund files).

24. The names of speakers and dialogue topics from October 4 to November 8, 1972, were noted in the "Current and Pending Activities" bulletins covering the periods between October 2 and 27, and October 23 to November 17. (These bulletins were issued at irregular intervals, and often covered overlapping dates or repeated information that had appeared in previous bulletins.) (Copies in Parten's files and the Fund files.)

25. Information on the use of Center materials by newspapers, magazines, news agencies, and broadcasting stations was sent to the Fund's board periodically by this writer. (Copies of my reports are in Parten's files and the Fund files, with copies of many of the clippings from various publications.)

26. The *New York Times* editorial on "The 'Sick' Foundations" appeared in the *Times* on October 23, 1972.

27. Ashmore's statements about the endless difficulties of fund raising appeared in a "docket" containing "Reports and Recommendations to the Board" sent to the directors in advance of the November 17, 1972, board meeting. These dockets were prepared by the officers and principal staff members for each board meeting. (Copies in Parten's files and the Fund files.)

28. Cadenhead's statements about the Center's deficit and the drop in net income from the membership program were reported in the materials included in the board "docket" for the November 1972 meeting (Parten files; the Fund files).

29. Peter Tagger's explanation of the decline in membership income, and his statements about the sales of Center books and tapes and the publication of a Center catalog, were also in the board "docket" referred to above.

30. Actions and statements at the Fund's board meeting on November 17, 1972, were noted in the board's minutes (Parten files; Fund files).

31. The statements of Ramsey Clark at the board's dinner on November 17, 1972, were quoted several months later in the February 1973 issue of *Center Report*. The excerpts used by this writer were drawn from that issue. (Copy in my files, Parten's files, the Fund files.)

32. The bombardment of Hanoi and other North Vietnamese cities under Nixon's order was reported in the *New York Times* and other publications in December 1972. William Manchester, in *The Glory and the Dream*, described the negative reactions of European newspapers and American senators (vol. 2, pp. 158–86).

33. The topics of Center dialogues in December 1972 were noted in the Center's "Current and Pending Activities" bulletins (Parten files; Fund files).

Chapter Twenty-seven

1. Nixon's announcement of the Vietnam pact in January 1973 appeared on the front page of the *New York Times* on January 24, 1973.

2. Quotations from the statements made by Kevin Phillips, Antonin Scalia, Richard Salant, Paul Porter, Newton Minow, Reuven Frank, Eric Sevareid, Blair Clark, Ronald Segal, and other participants in the Center's conference on "Broadcasting and the First Amendment" were taken from statements printed in the May–June 1973 issue of the *Center Magazine* (Parten files; my files; Fund files).

3. The topics discussed at the Center in February 1973 by Eduard Goldstucker, John Wilkinson, Lafti Zadeh, and others were noted in the Center's "Current and Pending Activities" bulletin.

4. Ginsburg's statements about the Center's academic program were contained in his report distributed to the Fund's board before their meeting in Houston on March 2, 1973 (Parten files; Fund files).

5. Ashmore's statement about the "unsuccessful" efforts to increase the Center's income appeared in a report he included in the "docket" sent to the directors in advance of the March 2 meeting (Parten files; Fund files).

6. Actions and statements at the Fund's board meeting on March 2, 1973, were noted in the board's minutes (Parten files; Fund files).

7. The Center's convocation in Houston on March 3, 1973, received coverage in the Houston *Post* and the Houston *Chronicle*.

8. Articles on the monetary crisis in March 1973 appeared in the *New York Times* and other publications.

9. The topics of the dialogue at the Center in March and April 1973 were taken from information in the Center's "Current and Pending Activities" bulletins.

10. The statement made by William Matson Roth about the Center at the convocation in San Francisco on April 21, 1973, was noted at the time by this writer, who was present when Roth said it.

11. Quotations from statements by Ashmore about the Center's budget and income problems were taken from reports prepared for the Fund's board meeting on May 4, 1973.

12. Actions and statements at the May 4, 1973, board meeting were recorded in the board's minutes (Parten files; Fund files).

13. Topics and speakers at the Center dialogues from May 14 to May 29, 1973, were noted in the Center's "Current and Pending Activities" bulletins (Parten files).

14. The meeting with former Governor Russell Peterson on June 7, 1973, the participation of several fellows in the "Pacem in Maribus" fourth convocation, and the meetings attended by Hutchins and Wheeler in Chicago were also noted in the "Current and Pending Activities" bulletins.

15. Excerpts from Rick Carlson's statement about the failures of the American correctional system appeared in the July–August 1973 issue of the *Center Magazine* and were quoted from that issue (Parten files; Fund files).

16. The meeting with Harlan Cleveland on June 27, 1973, was noted in the Center's "Current and Pending Activities" bulletins.

17. Donald McDonald's comments on the Carnegie Commission's study of higher education were published in the September–October issue of the *Center Magazine*, along with statements by Hutchins and Clark Kerr.

18. The actions and statements at the Fund's board meeting in Washington on October 8, 1973, were noted in the minutes of the meeting, except for the action of the board in electing Malcolm Moos chairman and a director of the Fund. J. R. Parten corrected this omission in a letter he sent to Hutchins several weeks later. Parten's letter was appended to the minutes.

19. The demonstrations against Henry Kissinger, which interrupted his speech at the "Pacem in Terris" convocation were reported in the Washington *Post* on October 9, 1973, with excerpts from his speech.

20. The quotations from Kissinger's speech came from the text of Kissinger's statement printed in the *Center Magazine* in its January–February 1974 issue.

21. Kermit Lansner's column about the *Pacem in Terris* convocation appeared in *Newsweek* on October 22, 1973. Quotations are taken from a copy in Parten's files.

22. Quotations from Clark Clifford's address at the "Pacem in Terris" conference are drawn from an article by Linda Charlton in the *New York Times*, October 10, 1973.

23. The statements by Richard Barnet and Stanley Hoffman appeared in the Washington *Post* on October 10, 1973 (Parten files; Fund files).

24. The desire of Ashmore and Hutchins to have Moos become chairman on "our terms" was expressed in a statement to me in Washington in October 1973 and reaffirmed later in a statement by Bernard Rapoport to me in July 1977.

25. The statements about Hutchins' misgivings about Wheeler and his desire to be consulted by Moos were based on comments made to me on October 8 and 9 in Washington, D.C.

26. Parten's reluctance to engage in an active search for a successor to Hutchins was well known to Hutchins. Through letters and phone calls, Hutchins had prodded Parten year after year, saying, "I am not getting younger" and "I think we ought to try to make some progress in finding a successor." In a letter dated April 18, 1972, Hutchins had reminded Parten: "You will remember that you are the chairman of the Committee on Organization, whose principal duty is to try to find a new chief executive officer for the Center."

27. Rapoport's statements about his discussions with Moos and Wheeler at the Jefferson Hotel in Washington were made to me in an interview on July 8, 1977.

28. I was present when Hutchins presented Moos to the audience at the "Pacem in Terris" convocation, and noted his words.

29. The description of Malcolm Moos's background is based on information supplied to me by the University of Minnesota.

30. Frank Wright, correspondent for the Minneapolis *Tribune*, wrote an article about the presentation of Moos by Hutchins to the Washington convocation. It appeared in the Minneapolis *Tribune* on October 12, 1973. (Copies in Parten's files and the Fund files.)

31. The article in the St. Paul *Pioneer Press*, reporting that Moos had "met the challenge of some of his critics," appeared in the *Pioneer Press* October 11, 1973.

32. The statements about Parten's awareness of the difficulties Moos would face at

the Center were based on several interviews I had with Parten in 1976 and 1977 and on Parten's statements in his deposition in the Comfort case.

33. A copy of the memorandum from Lord Ritchie-Calder, stating that no one in sight had all the necessary qualities to succeed Hutchins, is in Parten's files.

34. The fact that Parten offered Hutchins a year's leave with pay was mentioned to me by Parten in an interview.

35. The letter from Hutchins to Parten, dated November 11, 1973, confirmed the fact that Parten had made the suggestion, and indicated that Hutchins was willing to accept (Parten files).

36. A copy of the letter Parten sent to Hutchins in December 1973, asking that the election of Moos as chairman and a director be duly noted in the board's records, is in Parten's files.

37. A copy of the letter dated November 23, 1973, by Moos to Ashmore is in Parten's files.

38. A copy of the long letter dispatched by Ashmore to Moos on December 4, 1973, is also in Parten's files.

39. A copy of Hutchins' note to Moos, backing Ashmore, dated December 5, 1973, is in Parten's files.

40. Parten's files also contain a copy of Ashmore's 18-page memorandum of December 21, 1973, addressed to Hutchins and Moos.

41. The views of Parten and Marshall on the Center's spending under Ashmore and Hutchins were expressed to me in interviews in 1976, and in their depositions in the Comfort case.

42. Hutchins often had remarked to me when I expressed concern about the Center's deficits: "I ran the University of Chicago for 22 years on a deficit." When Hutchins left his office at the Center on June 1, 1974, the date of his formal retirement as chairman of the Fund and the Center, he strolled into my office and said, "Frank, I'm leaving you the Robert Hutchins Memorial Deficit." "Why do I get that honor?" I asked him. He smiled. "Because you worried about it so much."

43. In interviews and in public statements I witnessed, Hutchins gave varying descriptions of what the Center was.

44. Wheeler made known to me and other staff members his feeling that too much money had been spent on the Washington office and the external affairs operations under Ashmore.

45. The fact that Moos and Wheeler were in frequent communication was communicated to me in statements by Wheeler and mentioned to me by John Cogley and other senior fellows.

46. Summaries of the six major conferences held at the Center in November and December 1973 were printed in the February 1974 issue of *Center Report* (Parten files; Fund files).

47. Quotations from statements by Sam Beer, Christopher Lasch, Theodore Lowi, Harvey Wheeler, and Robert Hutchins at the Center's conference on "The Constitutional Implications of the Watergate Scandal" in December 1973 are drawn from statements printed in the March–April 1974 issue of the *Center Magazine* (Parten files; Fund files).

48. The fact that Moos did not want to have another Washington convocation in 1974 and his determination to disclose his own plans to the board were made known to this writer in statements by Hutchins and Ashmore.

49. Moos's hopeful attitude about the Center's future was communicated in conversations with me and with other staff members.

Chapter Twenty-eight

1. The economic recession of 1974 was described in the *Encyclopaedia Britannica Yearbook: 1975* as the worst since the depression of the 1930s.

2. The collapse of the stock market, the resignation of Nixon, and the accession to the presidency by Gerald Ford were reported by the *New York Times* and all the mass media in 1974.

3. The *New York Times* gave front-page coverage to the new edition of the *Encyclopaedia Britannica* in January 1974. Critics on many newspapers hailed it.

4. A copy of Norton Ginsburg's letter of January 14, 1974, to Moos is in Parten's files.

5. Parten's files also contain a copy of the reply sent by Moos to Ginsburg on January 18. Moos said later to me and others that he had discussed Ginsburg's letter with Wheeler before drafting his answer.

6. Cogley told me in January 1974 that Hutchins had been very upset by Moos's letter to Ginsburg and had interpreted it to mean that Moos wanted to get rid of the man Hutchins had appointed as dean.

7. Wheeler's statement to me that Moos wanted all the officers to submit their resignations as soon as possible was made in Wheeler's office at the Center in January 1974.

8. Wheeler described the Minneapolis meeting at Moos's house in January 1974 as "a rather intensive weekend encounter session" in an interview with me on June 29, 1977.

9. John Cogley told me in January 1974 that Ashmore had been angry when he returned from the Minneapolis meeting and had told Hutchins that Wheeler and Moos planned "to get rid of" some of the fellows.

10. A copy of Ashmore's letter to Moos dated January 21, 1974, is in Parten's files.

11. Quotations from the statement sent to Hutchins for transmission to Moos signed by Ritchie-Calder, Elisabeth Borgese, Rexford Tugwell, John Cogley, Norton Ginsburg, and Ashmore, are taken from a copy of this statement—dated February 4, 1974—in Parten's files.

12. The quotations from Alex Comfort's letter to Hutchins expressing his annoyance at the squabble were taken from a copy of Comfort's letter in Parten's files.

13. Quotations from a statement signed by Wheeler and Wilkinson are taken from a copy of this statement in Parten's files.

14. Excerpts from Mrs. McAllister's letter to Parten on January 24, 1974, were drawn from a copy of this letter in Parten's files.

15. Quotations from Parten's letter to Moos on January 30, 1974, are taken from a copy of this letter in Parten's files.

16. The description of Parten's meeting with Levinson, Grant, and Hutchins before the February 15, 1974, board meeting is based on statements made to this writer in a conversation that evening and on statements reiterated by Parten in later interviews.

17. Excerpts from the statement made by Malcolm Moos to the Fund's board on February 15, 1974, are taken from a copy of this statement in Parten's files.

18. The statement by Blair Clark that the Moos proposal would mean a drastic change from the existing Center program was noted in the minutes of the February 15, 1974 board meeting (Parten files; Fund files).

19. The statements of Moos, Mrs. McAllister, Weissbourd, Parten, Levinson, Willens, Rapoport, and Mrs. Laucks were noted in the minutes (Parten files; Fund files).

20. Moos had made it clear to me, to Gary Cadenhead, and others at the Center that he wanted to have Ashmore involved in the Center's external affairs program and did not want him to continue as an officer of the Fund.

21. The fact that Blair Clark pressed Moos to say specifically that Ashmore was to be "*the* executive vice president" showed that Clark and other directors were insistent that Moos had to share his executive authority with Ashmore.

22. The actions and statements in the afternoon session of the February 15, 1974, board meeting were noted in the minutes. My report of what happened is based on the minutes. (Parten files; Fund files.)

23. Moos's feeling of disappointment about Hutchins' lack of support for him—and Moos's feeling that some of the fellows were hostile to him—were communicated to me in several conversations in February, 1974, after the board meeting.

24. Excerpts from Ashmore's memorandum to the senior fellows dated April 4, 1974, were drawn from a copy of this memorandum in Parten's files.

25. Wheeler's statements about the Center having become "a kind of archaic, in some ways nostalgic liberal organization" were made to me in an interview on July 6, 1977.

26. Excerpts from Ashmore's memorandum of April 12, 1974, concerning the status of Ginsburg, were drawn from a copy of this memorandum in Parten's files.

27. A copy of Hutchins' note approving the nominations of B. H. Ridder, Jr., and Arthur Burck to the Fund's board is in Parten's files. It is dated April 29, 1974.

28. Copies of the telegrams to Parten from Paul Newman, J. Howard Marshall, Seniel Ostrow, and Harold Willens, granting him their proxies for the May 17, 1974, meeting of the Fund's board, are in Parten's files.

29. The statements by Hutchins to me about Ashmore's noninvolvement in a plot against Moos were made on May 16, 1974, while Hutchins and I were sitting together in a plane going to the Minneapolis-St. Paul airport. I gave the message to Parten at his hotel that night.

30. The actions and statements at the board meeting on May 17, 1974, were noted in the board's minutes. My report of what occurred is based on the minutes. (Parten files; Fund files.)

31. Quotations from Blair Clark's statement "The Future of the Center" are drawn from a copy of this statement in Parten's files.

32. I was present at the dinner given by Mr. and Mrs. Moos for the Fund's directors on the night of May 17, 1974. Mrs. McAllister was conspicuously absent.

33. Ashmore's statement that Cadenhead was "with the winning faction this time" was made at the Los Angeles airport on May 18, 1974, while Hutchins, Ashmore, and I were waiting for a plane to Santa Barbara. Hutchins did not comment on Ashmore's statement.

34. The Center's convocation on "The State of the Democratic Process" on June 1, 1974, received coverage in the Los Angeles *Times*, Santa Barbara *News-Press*, and other publications.

35. The report prepared by Peter Tagger on the expenses and income of the Los Angeles convocation on June 1, 1974, was prepared for Ashmore and sent by Ashmore with a letter to Moos (Parten files).

36. Parten's files contain a copy of the letter written by Moos to Harvey Wheeler on June 7, 1974, in which he asked Wheeler to accept appointment as "Coordinator" of "an educational program at the Center to be developed along the lines of the Rockefeller-type university."

37. Parten's files also contain a copy of the letter Hutchins sent to Parten on May 3, 1974, indicating that Hutchins would like to have six months of vacation rather than the year's leave of absence Parten had suggested.

38. Professor Walter Capps of the University of California (who was visiting the Center on the day when John Cogley became very ill) and I took Cogley to the Cottage Hospital on the afternoon of June 11, 1974.

39. Quotations from Israel Shenker's article in the *New York Times* on June 5, 1974, are drawn from a copy of this article in Parten's files.

40. Parten's files also contain a copy of a letter sent by Hutchins to Parten on June 24, 1974, stating: "I believe that Moos and the Center will make it. . . . It will not be the first time this organization has owed its survival to you."

41. Quotations from Mrs. McAllister's letter dated August 14, 1974, to Parten are taken from a copy of this letter in Parten's files.

42. Excerpts from James Douglas' letter of August 19, 1974, to Parten are drawn from a copy of this letter in Parten's files.

43. Quotations from Mrs. McAllister's letter of August 20, 1974, are taken from a copy of this letter in Parten's files.

44. Parten's files also contain a copy of Douglas' letter of August 22, 1974, expressing disappointment at Mrs. McAllister's interpretation of a luncheon meeting with Moos.

45. Excerpts from Mrs. McAllister's letter of August 19, 1974, to Douglas—a copy of this letter was sent by Douglas to Parten—are drawn from a copy of her letter in Parten's files.

46. Quotations from a memorandum by Malcolm Moos dated Auguest 30, 1974, to Ashmore are taken from a copy of this memorandum in Parten's files.

47. Quotations from the long memorandum sent by Moos to Parten and other directors in September, 1974, are drawn from a copy of this memo in Parten's files.

48. Copies of Parten's letter to members of the board, dated September 20, 1974, are in Parten's files.

49. Excerpts from the letter from Mrs. Laucks to Parten, dated October 16, 1974, are taken from a copy of this letter in Parten's files.

50. The suggestions in Ashmore's memorandum of October 18, 1974, to Moos are drawn from a copy of this memorandum in Parten's files.

51. Quotations from statements made by Ashmore, Wheeler, and Moos at the senior fellows' meeting on October 25, 1974, are drawn from a transcript of recorded remarks made at this meeting—a transcript in Parten's files.

52. Parten's critical reactions to the proposals made by Ashmore in his memorandum of October 18 were expressed to Moos and made known to this writer in interviews with Parten in 1975 and 1976.

53. Parten's statements at the special board meeting in Chicago in November, 1974, were noted in the minutes of this meeting—minutes that were made available to me (Parten files; Fund files).

54. Ashmore's negative reactions to the actions taken at the November 4, 1974, board meeting were expressed in his memorandum to the fellows dated November 14, 1974 (Parten files; Fund files).

55. Moos's optimistic statement to a reporter for the Los Angeles *Times* appeared in the *Times* on November 6, 1974.

56. Parten's files contain copies of the two memoranda sent by Mrs. McAllister to Moos on November 12, with her handwritten note saying that she was embarrassed by "glib statements" made by Moos.

57. A copy of Moos's letter to Mrs. McAllister dated November 21, 1974, is in Parten's files.

58. Excerpts from Mrs. McAllister's letter of November 26, 1974, are taken from a copy of this letter in Parten's files.

59. The quotations from Harvey Wheeler's memorandum on the possible formation of a special trust fund of $10 million, were taken from a copy of this memorandum in Parten's files.

60. Excerpts from Mrs. McAllister's letter to Paul Newman, dated December 4, 1974, are taken from a copy of this letter in Parten's files.

61. Quotations from Parten's letter of December 11, 1974, to Mrs. McAllister are drawn from a copy of this letter in Parten's files.

62. Excerpts from Moos's letter of December 6, 1974, to Mrs. McAllister are taken from a copy of Moos's letter in Parten's files.

63. Parten's files contain a copy of Mrs. McAllister's letter of December 10, 1974, replying to Moos, and her letter of December 16 to Parten. Quotations from these letters are taken from these copies.

64. Statements made about the purported comments of Ashmore to Fund for Peace officials concerning Moos are based on letters written to David Louisell by Moos, Wheeler, and Cadenhead, while Louisell was engaged in looking into the matter.

65. Quotations from Arthur Burck's letter of December 26, 1974, to Professor Louisell are taken from a copy of this letter in Parten's files.

66. My summary of Ashmore's letter of December 30, 1974, to Moos is based on a copy of this letter in Parten's files.

67. Parten's files also contain copies of the letter he sent to Moos in the last week of December, 1974, with a contribution of $100,000 to the Center.

68. The quotation from Hutchins' letter of December 30, 1974, to Parten is taken from a copy of this letter in Parten's files.

69. Copies of the academic calendar of the Center for November and December 1974 are in Parten's files. According to this record, most of the dialogues in this period were led by Wheeler, Wilkinson, Comfort, and Mordy.

Chapter Twenty-nine

1. Quotations from Mrs. Laucks's letter to Parten dated January 9, 1975, are taken from a copy of this letter in Parten's files. The files also contain a copy of her memorandum on the Wheeler-Schwab paper.

2. A copy of Parten's reply to Mrs. Laucks is in Parten's files.

3. Parten's files contain a copy of Hutchins' letter of January 6, 1975, defending Ashmore. Excerpts in my narrative were taken from this letter.

4. Excerpts from Parten's reply to Hutchins are drawn from a copy of Parten's letter of January 16, 1975, to Hutchins (Parten files).

5. Quotations from Ashmore's long letter to Parten on January 15, 1975, are drawn from a copy of Ashmore's letter in Parten's files. A copy of his attached memorandum is also in the files.

6. Excerpts from Malcolm Moos's letter of January 24, replying to Ashmore's statements of January 15, are taken from a copy of this letter in Parten's files.

7. In conversations with me during this period, Moos said he was trying to defend himself against Ashmore without antagonizing Hutchins.

8. My report on the actions of the Fund's executive committee on February 4, 1975, is based on a copy of the minutes of the executive committee meeting, in Parten's files.

9. The statements made to Parten by Compton and other officials of the Fund for Peace were later incorporated into a report given to the Fund's board by Parten, Lally, and Burck (Parten files).

10. Excerpts from Professor Louisell's letter to Parten dated February 14, 1975, are taken from a copy of this letter in Parten's files.

11. A copy of Ashmore's 21-page memorandum and his letter to Levinson dated February 10, 1975, is in Parten's files. Quotations are taken from this copy.

12. The quotations from Parten's letter to Ashmore dated February 13, 1975, acknowledging the letter and memorandum Ashmore had sent to him previously, are taken from a copy of Parten's letter in Parten's files.

13. A copy of the report by Parten, Lally, and Burck dated February 12, 1975, is in Parten's files.

14. The results of the conversation held by Parten, Lally, and Burck with Ashmore on February 21 were included in the "supplemental report" signed by these three directors and dated February 22, 1975 (Parten files).

15. The statement about Rapoport's telling Parten that Hutchins would resign if Parten presented the report of the three directors at the board meeting is based on a statement by Parten to this writer in an interview in 1976.

16. My report on the meeting of the Fund's directors on February 22, 1975, is based on a copy of the minutes of this meeting, in Parten's files.

17. Monsignor Lally sent this writer a statement with a letter dated September 14, 1977; he declared in this statement: "In this connection, Cadenhead's recollection of what N. Nyary said is precisely the same as my own. Nyary is an old friend and he personally told me that he had understood Ashmore as Cadenhead indicated. Compton first agreed, then found his memory less certain. I also share Parten's recollection that Ashmore did not recall in any detail his conversation with Compton—he was sure, however, he couldn't have said what was charged because he 'did not at the time believe it.' My strong impression was, and is, that Ashmore discouraged a meeting between Moos and Compton."

18. Excerpts of Parten's letter dated March 13, 1975, to Moos are taken from a copy of this letter in Parten's files.

19. Hutchins wrote to Parten in the middle of March 1975, saying that he was going to Chicago simply to explore the possibilities there. A copy of this letter is in Parten's files.

20. A copy of Parten's letter of April 9, 1975, saying that the Parten Foundation would give $100,000 to the Fund if the officers were able to raise another $200,000 in gifts or pledges, is in Parten's files.

21. Parten's secretary in Houston telephoned Moos's office in Santa Barbara and notified Moos of the death of Mrs. Parten on April 16, 1975.

22. Hutchins made the statement about why he had not gone to Texas for Mrs. Parten's funeral in a conversation with me after I returned to Santa Barbara on April 25, 1975.

23. Cadenhead was in the room at the Village Inn in Madisonville, Texas, when I telephoned Hutchins and asked whether he had "come out for the Chicago plan." Cadenhead suggested that I ask Hutchins whether he would support Moos if Moos could raise enough money to keep the Center going in Santa Barbara or San Diego. I made notes on Hutchins' answer and showed them to Cadenhead.

24. My report on what happened at the Fund's executive committee meeting on May 9, 1975, is based on statements made to me by Parten in interviews in 1976 and confirmed by testimony given by Parten and Marshall in their depositions in the Comfort case.

25. Excerpts from statements by Howard Marshall are drawn from his deposition in the Comfort suit.

26. Quotations from the text of the agreement signed by Moos, promising that he would "commit no act seriously detrimental to the interests of the Corporation," were taken from a copy of this agreement in Parten's files.

27. Marshall's statement that he regarded the contract with Moos as a settlement on "a happy basis" was made in his deposition in the Comfort case.

28. Moos indicated to me in conversation after this board meeting that he was grateful to Parten and Marshall for negotiating a settlement for him but he was not happy about the provisions limiting his freedom to speak and act.

29. My report on what happened at the sessions of the Fund's board meeting on May 10, 1975, is based on copies of the minutes of this meeting in Parten's files.

30. Quotations from Parten on the expunging from the minutes of references to the investigation of Ashmore were taken from his deposition in the Comfort case.

31. A copy of Parten's letter to Price, Postel & Parma, asking that firm to provide legal counsel in the dispute with Dr. Comfort, is in Parten's files.

32. Howard Marshall's statement that Dr. Comfort's attitude was "one of the reasons" for modifying the original Chicago plan was made in his deposition in the Comfort case.

33. Hutchins' statements were noted in the minutes of the May 10, 1975, meeting —minutes taken by John Berryhill, a lawyer for the Center, at Parten's request (Parten files; Fund files).

34. Cadenhead's analysis of the three proposed plans—Santa Barbara, San Diego, and Chicago—had been circulated to the directors in April 1975. Copies are in Parten's files.

35. The fact that Parten was responsible for the return of Hutchins to the Fund's presidency was told to me in an interview with Parten in 1975, a few weeks after the board meeting. Parten also mentioned this to me on May 10, 1975, after the meeting ended.

36. The severance pay provisions approved by the Fund's directors were recorded in the minutes of the May 10, 1975, meeting (Parten files; Fund files).

37. The description of Moos's return to the conference room and his statements to the directors were given to this writer in interviews with Parten, Lally, and other directors.

38. I was in the conference room when the reporters entered, and heard Ashmore say to Hutchins, "Well, Bob, you're back in the saddle."

39. The quotations from William Trombley's article in the Los Angeles *Times* on May 16, 1975, were taken from a copy of this article in my files.

40. In a conversation with me on June 29, 1977, Harvey Wheeler said: "What was actually adopted was Moos's No. 2 plan. He did all of the ground work, preparation, and his plan was what was adopted—without him."

41. Parten's statement about his reaction to the resignation of a football coach at the University of Texas—and his belief that a man who said he was going to resign had to stand by that decision—were expressed to this writer in an interview with Parten in September 1977.

42. Quotations from the *Newsweek* article on the Center in its June 30, 1975, issue are taken from a copy of this article in this writer's files.

43. Howard Marshall made his statement about the treatment of Moos in his deposition in the Comfort case. Parten expressed his views also in a deposition in

that case. James Douglas told me that he thought Moos had faced "a virtually impossible situation" in a letter to me in 1977. Monsignor Lally expressed his views in a letter to me in September 1977.

44. Parten's attitude after the reorganization of May 1975 was expressed to me in an interview a few weeks after the board meeting. He also expressed his willingness to continue to help the Center, in letters he sent to other board members (Parten files).

45. The energetic activity of Hutchins in the months after he returned to the Fund's presidency was noted by Parten, Ashmore, and other directors.

Chapter Thirty

1. In the April 1975 issue of *Center Report*, Malcolm Moos had signed an appeal to Center members: "As many of you know, the Center faces its most serious financial crisis ever—one that has been developing for years and one that now threatens its very existence.

    In the June 1975 issue of *Center Report*, Moos seemed to have disappeared from existence. That issue contained a statement signed by Hutchins:

    "When Justice William O. Douglas was chairman of our board, he used to say that every major city in America ought to have a Center for the Study of Democratic Institutions.

    "On May 10th the Board followed this advice by establishing a program in Chicago involving scholars from the twenty-one educational isntitutions in the area. The program in Santa Barbara will continue, also involving scholars in the area. The *Center Magazine, Center Report*, and other publishing activities of the Center will be conducted from Santa Barbara.

    "The Board took this action because it believes that the kind of work the Center has been doing is more necessary now than ever. The record of the past sixteen years shows that the Center has been able to identify and clarify many of the basic issues with which the contemporary world must deal. Through its communication network and its public meetings it has been able to widen the discussion of these issues, here and abroad. The new program now to be developed should broaden and deepen the influence of the Center in these critical times.

    "New officers elected at the Board meeting were: Robert M. Hutchins, President; Ralph W. Tyler, Vice President; and Peter Tagger, Secretary and Treasurer.

    "Mr. Tyler, one of the leading educators of the country, will direct activities in Chicago."

2. At a luncheon meeting on December 11, 1975, Hutchins told me that he had not mentioned Moos and the other Center staff members who had lost their jobs because he did not wish to embarrass them.

3. Quotations from Hutchins' letter to Parten dated June 11, 1975, are taken from a copy of this letter in Parten's files.

4. The October 1975 issue of *Center Report* contained announcements of Otis Graham's appointment as a Center associate and Peter Tagger's biographical background.

5. Information about the topics and speakers at meetings at the Center during the summer and autumn of 1975 is taken from a Center press release issued in July 1975.

6. Quotations from Dr. Comfort's claim that the Center had been dissolved, made in his complaint filed in a United States District Court in Los Angeles on July 24, 1975, are taken from a copy of Dr. Comfort's complaint in the files of Price, Postel & Parma. With the permission of Harry Ashmore and Peter Tagger, I was given access to Comfort's complaint, the document filed by the Fund in its countersuit, and the depositions given by Hutchins, Ashmore, Comfort, Wheeler, Parten, and others.

7. Howard Marshall's concern about the delay of the Fund in establishing a trust for the separated employees was expressed in a letter to Parten in July 1975, and Arthur Burck's feeling that these former employees might be "left out on a limb" was mentioned in a letter to Parten in August, 1975. Copies of these letters are in Parten's files.

8. Quotations from Parten's letter of September 5, 1975, to Hutchins are taken from a copy of this letter in Parten's files.

9. Excerpts from Hutchins' reply, dated September 8, 1975, are drawn from a copy of Hutchins' answer in Parten's files.

10. Quotations from Marshall's letter of September 15, 1975, are taken from a copy of Marshall's letter in Parten's files.

11. Excerpts from Parten's letter to Hutchins dated September 25, 1975, are drawn from a copy of this letter in Parten's files.

12. Hutchins' hurt at Parten's reference to "a breach of trust" was made evident to me at a luncheon I had with Hutchins at the Santa Barbara Biltmore hotel in December 1975. Hutchins said to me at the end of the lunch, "Nobody's going to get gypped. Remember that."

13. A copy of Hutchins' letter of September 29, 1975, replying to Parten's letter of September 25, is in Parten's files. Excerpts have been taken from a copy of that letter made available to me by Parten.

14. Excerpts from Parten's letter of October 8, 1975, to Hutchins are taken from a copy of this letter in Parten's files.

15. Quotations from James Douglas' letter of October 8, 1975, to Parten are drawn from a copy of this letter in Parten's files.

16. Quotations from the *News-Press* story of October 19, 1975, on Parten's resignation were taken from a copy of this story in my files.

17. Joseph Antonow's statement that the Fund's executive committee had approved a plan to establish a trust for the severance obligations of the Fund appeared in the *News-Press* on October 21, 1975. A copy of this article is in my files.

18. The first check I received—as part of my severance pay from the Fund—bearing the designation "The Fund for the Republic Trust," was dated in January 1976.

19. Quotations from Hutchins' statements in the first part of his deposition in the Comfort case are drawn from a copy of the deposition made available to me by Price, Postel & Parma. It was dated November 19, 1975.

20. Hutchins' statement that the Fund "broke even" in connection with the expenses of the fourth Pacem in Terris convocation was made in a report he submitted to the board of directors for their meeting in April 1976. A copy of this report was made available to this writer by Monsignor Lally, who had continued to serve on the board.

21. Quotations from Dr. Comfort's statements in answers to questions are drawn from a transcript of his depositon in the files of Price, Postel & Parma. The deposition was made available to me.

22. Excerpts from Ashmore's statements in the Comfort case are drawn from a transcript of his deposition in the files of Price, Postel & Parma, made available to me.

23. Excerpts from Parten's testimony in the Comfort case are drawn from a copy of his deposition, which was given in April 1976 in his office in Houston. A transcript of this deposition was made available to me by Price, Postel & Parma. A copy of it is also in Parten's files.

24. Wheeler's statements are drawn from a transcript of his deposition in the Comfort case, also made available to me by Price, Postel & Parma with permission from Ashmore and Tagger.

25. Quotations from J. Howard Marshall's deposition in the Comfort case are drawn from a transcript of the deposition in the files of Price, Postel & Parma, made available to me.

26. Quotations from Hutchins' report prepared for the meeting of the Fund's directors on April 13, 1976, are drawn from a copy of this report made available to me by Monsignor Lally.

27. Quotations from the opinion in the Comfort case issued on November 22, 1976, by Judge David W. Williams were drawn from a copy of Judge Williams' opinion that I obtained.

28. In an interview with me on July 6, 1977, Wheeler said that the agreement he finally reached with the Center stipulated that he had "full rights to all my writings, all my files, everything." Wheeler added: "We both released any claim against either party for anything." Peter Tagger, in an interview with me in September 1977, said the settlement was achieved after Wheeler returned some documents to the Center.

29. Quotations from Hutchins' statement about the change of name of *Center Report* to *World Issues* were drawn from the October 1976 issue of that publication.

30. The topics and authors in the October 1976 issue of *World Issues* were listed in a copy of this publication in my files.

32. I saw Hutchins on several occasions in the early months of 1977 and noted the deterioration in his physical condition.

33. In many conversations with me over the years between 1956 and 1975, Hutchins said he had not done what he had hoped to do. He had expressed these feelings of frustration and failure to Milton Mayer and other friends.

34. In the July 1977 issue of the *Progressive* magazine, Milton Mayer wrote: "He thought he had been a failure. He didn't know that it is better to fail trying to do what he was trying to do than to succeed at anything else."

35. His note about the Earl of Rochester was written to my wife, in response to a note of affection and encouragement she had sent him during his illness.

36. Hutchins' statement about American foreign policy appeared in the April 1977 issue of *Center Report* (my files).

37. Hutchins' statement about the necessity for "intellectual communities" was printed in the January–February 1977 issue of the *Center Magazine* (my files).

38. David Broder's comments on Hutchins appeared in the Washington *Post*, the Los Angeles *Times*, and other newspapers on May 18, 1977. I have taken excerpts from the column as it appeared in the Los Angeles *Times*.

39. Max Lerner's comments appeared in the New York *Post* and other newspapers a few days after Hutchins' death.

40. Colman McCarthy's statements about Hutchins appeared in the Washington *Post* and other papers.

41. The editorial about Hutchins by Norman Cousins was printed in the *Saturday Review* dated June 11, 1977. A copy is in my files.

42. My statements about Hutchins are based on many observations of him through the years and an audiotaped interview I did with him about his life for a series of radio broadcasts entitled "Slightly Autobiographical," issued by the Center. I have a transcript of this interview in my files. Parts of it appeared in the *Center Magazine* in its November–December 1968 issue under the title "Trees Grew in Brooklyn."

43. Information about Maurice Mitchell is drawn from an article about him that appeared in the Santa Barbara *News-Press* in November 1977.

44. The quotation from Morris Levinson about Mitchell was drawn from the *News-Press* article.

45. The statements by Walter Capps and James Miller appeared in an article by Jerry Rankin in the Santa Barbara *News-Press*, May 3, 1981. I also interviewed Miller on May 7, 1981.

Chapter Thirty-one

1. Statements made about the Fund's activities from 1952 to 1957 are documented in earlier chapters of my book.

2. The information about Sam Rayburn's action in setting in motion a movement to abolish the House Un-American Activities Committee was obtained in an interview with Parten in 1976. It was confirmed in a conversation in May 1977 with John Holton, former assistant to Speaker Rayburn.

3. Admiral Rickover's statements about the value of the Center were made in conversations I had with him after he participated in the Center's convocation "The University in America" in 1966. He made similar statements in public at that convocation.

INDEX